ADOLESCENCE IN AMERICA

An Encyclopedia

THE AMERICAN FAMILY

The six titles that make up **The American Family** offer a revitalizing new take on U.S. history, surveying current culture from the perspective of the family and incorporating insights from psychology, sociology, and medicine. Each two-volume, A-to-Z encyclopedia features its own advisory board, editorial slant, and apparatus, including illustrations, bibliography, and index.

Adolescence in America

EDITED BY Jacqueline V. Lerner, Boston College,
and Richard M. Lerner, Tufts University;
Jordan W. Finkelstein, Pennsylvania State University,
Advisory Editor

Boyhood in America

EDITED BY Priscilla Ferguson Clement, Pennsylvania State
University, Delaware County, and Jacqueline S. Reinier,
California State University, Sacramento

The Family in America

EDITED BY Joseph M. Hawes, University of Memphis,
and Elizabeth F. Shores, Little Rock, Arkansas

Girlhood in America

EDITED BY Miriam Forman-Brunell,
University of Missouri, Kansas City

Infancy in America

EDITED BY Alice Sterling Honig, Emerita, Syracuse University;
Hiram E. Fitzgerald, Michigan State University;
and Holly Brophy-Herb, Michigan State University

Parenthood in America

EDITED BY Lawrence Balter, New York University

ADOLESCENCE IN AMERICA

An Encyclopedia

Volume 1
A–M

Jacqueline V. Lerner, EDITOR
Boston College

Richard M. Lerner, EDITOR
Tufts University

Jordan Finkelstein, ADVISORY EDITOR
Pennsylvania State University

FOREWORD BY **Mark L. Rosenberg**
Center for Child Well-Being
Atlanta, Georgia

A B C ⬛ C L I O

Santa Barbara, California
Denver, Colorado
Oxford, England

Copyright © 2001 by Jacqueline V. Lerner and Richard M. Lerner

Library of Congress Cataloging-in-Publication Data
Adolescence in America: an encyclopedia / Jacqueline V. Lerner and Richard M. Lerner, editors; Jordan Finkelstein, advisory editor.
        p. cm.—(The American family)
Includes bibliographical references (p. 827) and index.
        ISBN 1-57607-205-3 (hardcover)—ISBN 1-57607-571-0 (e-book)
        1. Adolescence—United States—Encyclopedia. I. Lerner, Jacqueline
        V. II. Lerner, Richard M. III. Finkelstein, Jordan. IV. American family
        (Santa Barbara, Calif.)
    HQ796.A33244 2001
    305.235′0973′03–dc21
                                                    2001002276

07 06 05 04 03 02 01   10 9 8 7 6 5 4 3 2 1 (cloth)

ABC-CLIO, Inc.
130 Cremona Drive, P.O. Box 1911
Santa Barbara, California 93116-1911

This book is also available on the World Wide Web as an e-book. Visit www.abc-clio.com for details.

This book is printed on acid-free paper ∞
Manufactured in the United States of America

ABOUT THE EDITORS

Jacqueline V. Lerner is professor of psychology and chair of the Counseling and Developmental Psychology program at Boston College.

Richard M. Lerner holds the Bergstrom Chair in Applied and Developmental Science in the Eliot-Pearson Department of Child Development, Tufts University.

Jordan Finkelstein, advisory editor, is professor of behavioral health, human development, and pediatrics at Pennsylvania State University.

Contents

A-to-Z List of Entries   *ix*
Contributors and Their Entries   *xiii*
Foreword   *xxvii*
Preface   *xxxi*
Introduction   *xxxiii*

Volume 1: Entries A to M   *1*
Volume 2: Entries N to Y   *465*

Bibliography   *827*
Index   *903*

A-to-Z List of Entries

VOLUME 1, A–M

A

Abortion
Abstinence
Academic Achievement
Academic Self-Evaluation
Accidents
Acne
Adoption: Exploration and Search
Adoption: Issues and Concerns
African American Adolescents,
  Identity in
African American Adolescents,
  Research on
African American Male Adolescents
Aggression
Alcohol Use, Risk Factors in
Alcohol Use, Trends in
Allowance
Anemia
Anxiety
Appearance, Cultural Factors in
Appearance Management
Apprenticeships
The Arts
Asian American Adolescents:
  Comparisons and Contrasts
Asian American Adolescents: Issues
  Influencing Identity
Attention-Deficit/Hyperactivity
  Disorder (ADHD)
Attractiveness, Physical

Autonomy

B

Body Build
Body Fat, Changes in
Body Hair
Body Image
Bullying
Bumps in the Road to Adulthood

C

Cancer in Childhood and Adolescence
Career Development
Cheating, Academic
Chicana/o Adolescents
Child-Rearing Styles
Children of Alcoholics
Chores
Chronic Illnesses in Adolescence
Cigarette Smoking
Cliques
Cognitive Development
College
Computer Hacking
Computers
Conduct Problems
Conflict and Stress
Conflict Resolution
Conformity
Contraception
Coping
Counseling
Cults

D

Dating
Dating Infidelity
Decision Making
Delinquency, Mental Health, and
    Substance Abuse Problems
Delinquency, Trends in
Dental Health
Depression
Developmental Assets
Developmental Challenges
Diabetes
Discipline
Disorders, Psychological and Social
Divorce
Down Syndrome
Drug Abuse Prevention
Dyslexia

E

Eating Problems
Emancipated Minors
Emotional Abuse
Emotions
Empathy
Employment: Positive and Negative
    Consequences
Environmental Health Issues
Ethnic Identity
Ethnocentrism

F

Family Composition: Realities and
    Myths
Family Relations
Family-School Involvement
Fathers and Adolescents
Fears
Female Athlete Triad
Foster Care: Risks and Protective
    Factors

Freedom

G

Gay, Lesbian, Bisexual, and Sexual-
    Minority Youth
Gender Differences
Gender Differences and Intellectual and
    Moral Development
Gifted and Talented Youth
Gonorrhea
Grandparents: Intergenerational
    Relationships

H

Health Promotion
Health Services for Adolescents
High School Equivalency Degree
Higher Education
HIV/AIDS
Homeless Youth
Homework

I

Identity
Inhalants
Intelligence
Intelligence Tests
Intervention Programs for Adolescents

J

Juvenile Crime
Juvenile Justice System

L

Latina/o Adolescents
Learning Disabilities
Learning Styles and Accommodations

Loneliness
Lore
Love

M

Maternal Employment: Historical
    Changes
Maternal Employment: Influences on
    Adolescents
Media
Memory
Menarche
Menstrual Cycle
Menstrual Dysfunction
Menstruation
Mental Retardation, Siblings with
Mentoring and Youth Development
Middle Schools
Miscarriage
Moral Development
Mothers and Adolescents
Motivation, Intrinsic

VOLUME 2: N–Y

N

Native American Adolescents
Neglect
Nutrition

P

Parent-Adolescent Relations
Parental Monitoring
Parenting Styles
Peer Groups
Peer Pressure
Peer Status
Peer Victimization in School

Personal Fable
Personality
Physical Abuse
Political Development
Poverty
Pregnancy, Interventions to Prevent
Private Schools
Programs for Adolescents
Proms
Prostitution
Psychosomatic Disorders
Psychotherapy
Puberty: Hormone Changes
Puberty: Physical Changes
Puberty: Psychological and Social
    Changes
Puberty, Timing of

R

Racial Discrimination
Rape
Rebellion
Religion, Spirituality, and Belief
    Systems
Responsibility for Developmental Tasks
Rights of Adolescents
Rights of Adolescents in Research
Risk Behaviors
Risk Perception
Rites of Passage
Runaways

S

Sadness
School Dropouts
School Engagement
School, Functions of
School Transitions
Schools, Full-Service
Schools, Single-Sex
Self
Self-Consciousness

Self-Esteem
Self-Injury
Services for Adolescents
Sex Differences
Sex Education
Sex Roles
Sexual Abuse
Sexual Behavior
Sexual Behavior Problems
Sexuality, Emotional Aspects of
Sexually Transmitted Diseases
Shyness
Sibling Conflict
Sibling Differences
Sibling Relationships
Single Parenthood and Low
    Achievement
Social Development
Spina Bifida
Sports and Adolescents
Sports, Exercise, and Weight Control
Standardized Tests
Steroids
Storm and Stress
Substance Use and Abuse
Suicide

T

Teachers
Teasing

Teenage Parenting: Childbearing
Teenage Parenting: Consequences
Television
Television, Effects of
Temperament
Thinking
Tracking in American High Schools
Transition to Young Adulthood
Transitions of Adolescence
Twins

V

Violence and Aggression
Vocational Development
Volunteerism

W

Welfare
White and American: A Matter of
    Privilege?
Why Is There an Adolescence?
Work in Adolescence

Y

Youth Culture
Youth Gangs
Youth Outlook

Contributors and Their Entries

Michelle Abdala
Independent Scholar
Niles, Illinois
　Spina Bifida

Gerald R. Adams
University of Guelph
Guelph, Ontario
　Family-School Involvement
　Identity
　Runaways

Sandra Alcala
Loyola University
Chicago, Illinois
　Spina Bifida

David Almeida
University of Arizona
Tucscon, Arizona
　Fathers and Adolescents

Billie V. Andersson
St. Martin's Episcopal School
Metairie, Louisiana
University of New Orleans
New Orleans, Louisiana
　Learning Styles and Accommodations

Dita G. Andersson
Independent Scholar
Brighton, Massachusetts
　Moral Development

Sally Archer
The College of New Jersey
Ewing, New Jersey
　Sexuality, Emotional Aspects of

Andrea Bastiani Archibald
Teachers College, Columbia University
New York, New York
　Body Fat

Jeffrey Jensen Arnett
University of Missouri–Columbia
Columbia, Missouri
　Media

Pamela Aronson
Indiana University
Bloomington, Indiana
　Allowance

Christopher Ashford
University of Pennsylvania
Philadelphia, Pennsylvania
　Career Development

Susan Averna
University of Connecticut
Farmington, Connecticut
　Anxiety
　Attention Deficit/Hyperactivity
　　Disorder (ADHD)
　Conduct Problems
　Personal Fable

Catherine E. Barton
Boston College
Chestnut Hill, Massachussetts
　　Cancer in Childhood and Adolescence
　　Learning Disabilities

Jessica Beckwith
Teachers College, Columbia University
New York, New York
　　Conflict Resolution

Peter L. Benson
Search Institute
Minneapolis, Minnesota
　　Assets

Aida Bilalbegović
Tufts University
Medford, Massachusetts
　　Puberty: Psychological and Social
　　　Changes

Deborah L. Bobek
Tufts University
Medford, Massachusetts
　　Cults
　　Prostitution

Lynne M. Borden
Michigan State University
East Lansing, Michigan
　　Programs for Adolescents
　　Volunteerism

Shireen Boulos
Tufts University
Medford, Massachusetts
　　Emancipated Minors
　　Welfare

Mary M. Brabeck
Boston College
Chestnut Hill, Massachussetts
　　Gender Differences and Intellectual
　　　and Moral Development

Emily Branscum
Florida International University
Miami, Florida
　　Delinquency, Mental Health, and
　　　Substance Abuse Problems

Jeanne Brooks-Gunn
Teachers College, Columbia University
New York, New York
　　Body Fat, Changes in
　　Body Image

Jennifer S. Brown
Tufts University
Medford, Massachusetts
　　The Arts

Jean-Marie Bruzzese
College of Physicians and Surgeons,
*　Columbia University*
New York, New York
　　Rights of Adolescents in Research

Christy M. Buchanan
Wake Forest University
Winston-Salem, North Carolina
　　Divorce

Phame Camarena
Central Michigan University
Mount Pleasant, Michigan
　　Self

Maya Carlson
Harvard University
Cambridge, Massachussetts
　　Rights of Adolescents

Danielle Carrigo
Texas Tech University
Lubbock, Texas
　　Chicana/o Adolescents
　　Latina/o Adolescents

Domini R. Castellino
Duke University
Durham, North Carolina
Maternal Employment: Influences on
Adolescents
Mothers and Adolescents
Parent-Adolescent Relations

Stephen J. Ceci
Cornell University
Ithaca, New York
Single Parenthood and Low
Achievement

Heather Cecil
University of Alabama at Birmingham
Birmingham, Alabama
HIV/AIDS

Laurie Chassin
Arizona State University
Tempe, Arizona
Cigarette Smoking

Jana H. Chaudhuri
Tufts University
Medford, Massachusetts
Freedom

Anna Chaves
Boston College
Chestnut Hill, Massachussetts
Eating Problems

George P. Chrousos
National Institute of Child Health and
Human Development, National
Institutes of Health
Bethesda, Maryland
Georgetown University Medical School
Washington, D.C.
Puberty

Kenneth M. Cohen
Counseling and Psychological Services,
Cornell University
Ithaca, New York
Counseling

Teresa M. Cooney
University of Missouri–Columbia
Columbia, Missouri
Chores

Deborah Corbitt-Shindler
University of Houston
Houston, Texas
Sibling Conflict
Sibling Differences

Michael Cunningham
Tulane University
New Orleans, Louisiana
African American Male Adolescents

William Damon
Stanford University
Stanford, California
Youth Outlook

Nancy Darling
Penn State University Park
University Park, Pennsylvania
Discipline

Patrick Davies
University of Rochester
Rochester, New York
Dating

Imma De Stefanis
Boston College
Chestnut Hill, Massachussetts
  Cheating, Academic
  Ethnic Identity
  Middle Schools
  Private Schools
  School Transitions
  Schools, Single-Sex
  Transitions of Adolescence

Joseph Solomon Dillard
University of Michigan
Ann Arbor, Michigan
  Adoption: Issues and Concerns

Lorah D. Dorn
University of Pittsburgh
Pittsburgh, Pennsylvania
  Female Athlete Triad
  Puberty, Timing of

Sanford M. Dornbusch
Stanford University
Stanford, California
  Homeless Youth
  Tracking in American High Schools

Jennifer Douglas
University of Massachusetts–Boston
Boston, Massachusetts
  Welfare

Elizabeth Dowling
Tufts University
Medford, Massachusetts
  Love

Candice Dreves
Independent Scholar
Eagan, Minnesota
  Academic Self-Evaluation
  Gender Differences

Jerome B. Dusek
Syracuse University
Syracuse, New York
  Bumps on the Road to Adulthood
  Dating Infidelity
  Sex Roles
  Why Is There an Adolescence?

Felton Earls
Harvard University Medical School
Boston, Massachussetts
  Rights of Adolescents

Patricia L. East
University of California–San Diego
  Medical Center
San Diego, California
  Sibling Relationships

John Eckenrode
Cornell University
Ithaca, New York
  Neglect

David Elkind
Tufts University
Medford, Massachusetts
  Cognitive Development

Douglas W. Elliott
Cornell University
Ithaca, New York
  Peer Pressure

David Engberg
Boston College
Chestnut Hill, Massachussetts
American Council on Education
Washington, D.C.
  Higher Education

Elizabeth N. Fielding
Boston College
Chestnut Hill, Massachussetts
The Meadowbrook School of Weston
Weston, Massachussetts
    Homework

Jordan Finkelstein
Penn State University Park
University Park, Pennsylvania
    Abortion
    Accidents
    Acne
    Aggression
    Anemia
    Birth Control
    Body Build
    Body Hair
    Gonorrhea
    Health Services for Adolescents
    Menarche
    Menstrual Cycle
    Menstrual Dysfunction
    Menstruation
    Miscarriage
    Puberty: Physical Changes
    Sex Education
    Steroids

Lisa B. Fiore
Boston College
Chestnut Hill, Massachussetts
Lesley College
Cambridge, Massachussetts
    Fears
    Proms

Sean N. Fischer
Loyola University Chicago
Chicago, Illinois
    Parenting Styles

Celia B. Fisher
Fordham University
Bronx, New York
    Racial Discrimination
    Rights of Adolescents in Research

Constance Flanagan
Penn State University Park
University Park, Pennsylvania
    Political Development

Rosalind D. Folman
University of Michigan
Ann Arbor, Michigan
    Foster Care

Kristine Freeark
University of Michigan
Ann Arbor, Michigan
    Adoption: Exploration and Search

Sara Gable
University of Missouri–Columbia
Columbia, Missouri
    Chores

Laura A. Gallagher
Boston College
Chestnut Hill, Massachussetts
    Self-Injury
    Suicide

Jessica Goldberg
Tufts University
Medford, Massachusetts
    Emancipated Minors
    Welfare

Adele Eskeles Gottfried
California State University–Northridge
Northridge, California
    Motivation, Intrinsic

Julia A. Graber
Teachers College, Columbia University
New York, New York
   Body Image

Sandra Graham
University of California–Los Angeles
Los Angeles, California
   Peer Victimization in School

John W. Hagen
University of Michigan
Ann Arbor, Michigan
   Adoption: Issues and Concerns
   Chronic Illnesses in Adolescence
   Foster Care

Monica J. Hanson
Boston College
Chestnut Hill, Massachussetts
   Contraception

Vinay Harpalani
University of Pennsylvania
Philadelphia, Pennsylvania
   African American Adolescents,
      Identity in
   African American Adolescents,
      Research on

Penny Hauser-Cram
Boston College
Chestnut Hill, Massachussetts
   Down Syndrome

James Henry
Western Michigan University
Kalamazoo, Michigan
   Emotional Abuse
   Physical Abuse
   Sexual Abuse

Donald J. Hernandez
State University of New York at Albany
Albany, New York
   Family Composition: Myths and
      Realities
   Maternal Employment: Historical
      Changes
   Poverty

Laura Hess Olson
Purdue University
West Lafayette, Indiana
   Bullying

Grayson N. Holmbeck
Loyola University
Chicago, Illinois
   Family Relations
   Parenting Styles
   Spina Bifida
   Storm and Stress

Angela Howell
Boston College
Chestnut Hill, Massachussetts
   Down Syndrome
   Sadness

Wendy Hubenthal
Boston College
Chestnut Hill, Massachussetts
   High School Equivalency Degree

Lisa R. Jackson
GEAR UP, Boston Higher Education
   Partnership
Chestnut Hill, Massachussetts
   School Engagement

Lauren P. Jacobson
Penn State Altoona
Altoona, Pennsylvania
   Sports and Adolescents

Leanne J. Jacobson
University of California–San Diego
San Diego, California
  Juvenile Crime
  Sibling Relationships

Matthew Jans
University of Massachusetts–Boston
Boston, Massachusetts
  Sex Differences

Janna Jilnina
Independent Scholar
Cambridge, Massachusetts
  Attractiveness, Physical
  Conformity
  Empathy
  Intelligence
  Memory
  Personality

Sara Johnston
Penn State University Park
University Park, Pennsylvania
  Sports, Exercise, and Weight Control

Jasna Jovanovic
University of Illinois–Urbana-
  Champaign
Urbana, Illinois
  Academic Self-Evaluation
  Gender Differences

Linda P. Juang
California State University–San
Francisco
San Francisco, California
  Asian American Adolescents: Comparisons and Contrasts

Tami Katzir-Cohen
Tufts University
Medford, Massachusetts
  Dyslexia

Sean Kennedy
Boston College
Chestnut Hill, Massachussetts
  Computers

Maureen E. Kenny
Boston College
Chestnut Hill, Massachussetts
  Depression
  Intelligence Tests
  Psychotherapy
  Self-Esteem

Marty Wyngaarden Krauss
Brandeis University
Waltham, Massachussetts
  Mental Retardation, Siblings with

Deanna Kuhn
Teachers College, Columbia University
New York, New York
  Thinking

George T. Ladd
University of Connecticut Health
  Center
Farmington, Connecticut
  Rebellion
  Substance Use and Abuse

Susanna M. Lara Roth
Tufts University
Medford, Massachusetts
  Psychosomatic Disorders

Reed Larson
University of Illinois–Urbana-
  Champaign
Urbana, Illinois
  Emotions

Christine M. Lee
University of Arizona
Tucson, Arizona
  Teenage Parenting: Consequences

Jacqueline V. Lerner
Boston College
Chestnut Hill, Massachusetts
  Academic Achievement
  Employment: Positive and Negative
    Consequences
  Gender Differences
  School, Functions of
  Transition to Young Adulthood

Richard M. Lerner
Tufts University
Medford, Massachusetts
  Academic Achievement
  Cliques
  Developmental Challenges
  Employment: Positive and Negative
    Consequences
  Gender Differences
  Intervention Programs for
    Adolescents
  Lore
  Mentoring and Youth Development
  Peer Status
  Risk Behaviors
  School, Functions of
  Schools, Full-Service
  Sexual Behavior Problems
  Television
  Transition to Young Adulthood

Benjamin D. Locke
Boston College
Chestnut Hill, Massachussetts
  Rites of Passage

Barbara J. Long
University of California–San Francisco
San Francisco, California
  Female Athlete Triad

Alexandra Loukas
University of Texas–Austin
Austin, Texas
  Inhalants

Christine M. Low
Penn State University Park
University Park, Pennsylvania
  Temperament

Tom Luster
Michigan State University
East Lansing, Michigan
  Emotional Abuse
  Physical Abuse
  Sexual Abuse

Maureen Sweeney MacGillivray
Central Michigan University
Rockford, Michigan
  Appearance Management

Jennifer Maggs
University of Arizona
Tucson, Arizona
  Teenage Parenting: Consequences

Kerry Maguire
Tufts University School of Dental
  Medicine
Belmont, Massachusetts
  Dental Health

Beth Manke
University of Houston
Houston, Texas
  Sibling Conflict
  Sibling Differences

Lyscha A. Marcynyszyn
Cornell University
Ithaca, New York
  Neglect

Deborah N. Margolis
Boston College
Chestnut Hill, Massachussetts
Catholic Memorial Middle/High School
Gloucester, Massachussetts
  Disorders, Psychological and Social
  Self-Consciousness
  Teasing

W. Alex Mason
University of Alabama–Birmingham
Birmingham, Alabama
  Delinquency, Trends in

Cami K. McBride
University of Illinois–Chicago
Chicago, Illinois
  Sexual Behavior

Daniel A. McDonald
University of Arizona
Tucson, Arizona
  Fathers and Adolescents

Shirley McGuire
University of San Francisco
San Francisco, California
  Computer Hacking
  Loneliness

Jeanne S. Merchant
University of Alabama–Birmingham
Birmingham, Alabama
  Sexually Transmitted Diseases

Rachael B. Millstein
Loyola University
Chicago, Illinois
  Parenting Styles

Susan Millstein
University of California–San Francisco
San Francisco, California
  Decision Making
  Risk Perception

Maya Misra
Tufts University
Medford, Massachusetts
  Social Development

Raymond Montemayor
The Ohio State University
Columbus, Ohio
  Parental Monitoring

Jodi E. Morris
Boston College
Chestnut Hill, Massachussetts
  Juvenile Justice System

Jeylan T. Mortimer
University of Minnesota
Minneapolis, Minnesota
  Allowance
  Work in Adolescence

Jennifer A. Murphy
Boston College
Chestnut Hill, Massachussetts
  Juvenile Justice System

Jennifer T. Myers
University of Michigan
Ann Arbor, Michigan
  Chronic Illnesses in Adolescence

Katherine Nitz
Independent Scholar
Olney, Maryland
  Pregnancy, Interventions to Prevent

E. Ree Noh
Boston College
Chestnut Hill, Massachussetts
  Asian American Adolescents: Issues
    Influencing Identity

Anne E. Norris
Boston College School of Nursing
Chestnut Hill, Massachussetts
  Abstinence
  Contraception

Patrick M. O'Malley
University of Michigan
Ann Arbor, Michigan
  Alcohol Use, Trends in

Alyssa Goldberg O'Rourke
Tufts University
Medford, Massachusetts
  Standardized Tests

M. Kim Oh
University of Alabama–Birmingham
Birmingham, Alabama
  Sexually Transmitted Diseases

Christine McCauley Ohannessian
Independent Scholar
Storrs, Connecticut
  Children of Alcoholics
  Twins

Roberta L. Paikoff
University of Illinois–Chicago
Chicago, Illinois
  Sexual Behavior

Paul B. Papierno
Cornell University
Ithaca, New York
  Single Parenthood and Low
    Achievement

Daniel F. Perkins
Penn State–University Park
University Park, Pennsylvania
  Programs for Adolescents
  Risk Behaviors in Adolescence
  Volunteerism

Erik J. Porfeli
Penn State–University Park
University Park, Pennsylvania
  Apprenticeships
  Vocational Development

Clark C. Presson
Arizona State University
Tempe, Arizona
  Cigarette Smoking

Nora Presson
Independent Scholar
Tempe, Arizona
  Cigarette Smoking

Kevin Rathunde
University of Utah
Salt Lake City, Uta
  Gifted and Talented Youth

Geoffrey L. Ream
Cornell University
Ithaca, New York
  Religion, Spirituality, and Belief
    Systems

Melinda M. Roberts
Youth Substance Abuse Program, Bay
    Area Community Resources
San Francisco, California
  Drug Abuse Prevention

Judith E. Robinson
Boston College
Chestnut Hill, Massachussetts
  Violence and Aggression

Lauren Rogers-Sirin
Boston College
Chestnut Hill, Massachussetts
  Appearance, Cultural Factors in
  Rape

Jennifer Rose
Indiana University
Bloomington, Indiana
　Cigarette Smoking

Pamela A. Sarigiani
Central Michigan University
Mount Pleasant, Michigan
　Shyness

Ritch C. Savin-Williams
Cornell University
Ithaca, New York
　Gay, Lesbian, Bisexual, and Sexual-
　　Minority Youth

Lawrence B. Schiamberg
Michigan State University
East Lansing, Michigan
　Environmental Health Issues
　Grandparents: Intergenerational
　　Relationships

Barbara Schneider
University of Chicago
Chicago, Illinois
　College

John Schulenberg
University of Michigan
Ann Arbor, Michigan
　Alcohol Use, Trends in

Diane Scott-Jones
Boston College
Chestnut Hill, Massachusetts
　Teenage Parenting: Childbearing

Inge Seiffge-Krenke
University of Mainz
Mainz, Germany
　Conflict and Stress
　Coping
　Diabetes

Marsha Mailick Seltzer
University of Wisconsin–Madison
Madison, Wisconsin
　Mental Retardation, Siblings with

Wendy E. Shapera
Loyola University
Chicago, Illinois
　Family Relations
　Parenting Styles

Francine T. Sherman
Boston College Law School
Newton, Massachussetts
　Juvenile Justice System

Steven J. Sherman
Indiana University
Bloomington, Indiana
　Cigarette Smoking

Lonnie R. Sherrod
Fordham University
Bronx, New York
　Youth Culture

Erika Shore
Grady Memorial Hospital
Atlanta, Georgia
Boston College
Chestnut Hill, Massachussetts
　Gender Differences and Intellectual
　　and Moral Development

Jason Sidman
Tufts University
Medford, Massachusetts
　Television

Le Anne E. Silvey
Michigan State University
East Lansing, Michigan
　Native American Adolescents

Selcuk Sirin
Boston College
Chestnut Hill, Massachussetts
    Child-Rearing Styles
    School Dropouts

Margaret Beale Spencer
University of Pennsylvania
Philadelphia, Pennsylvania
    African American Adolescents, Identity in
    African American Adolescents, Research on

Arlene Rubin Stiffman
Washington University
St. Louis, Missouri
    Services for Adolescents

Jill C. Stoltzfus
University of Pennsylvania
Philadelphia, Pennsylvania
    White and American: A Matter of Privilege?

Elizabeth J. Susman
Penn State–University Park
University Park, Pennsylvania
    Puberty: Hormone Changes

Dena Phillips Swanson
Penn State University Park
University Park, Pennsylvania
    Ethnocentrism

Carl S. Taylor
Michigan State University
East Lansing, Michigan
    Youth Gangs

Deborah M. Trosten-Martinez
Independent Scholar
Gainesville, Florida
    Responsibility for Developmental Tasks

Jonathan G. Tubman
Florida International University
Miami, Florida
    Delinquency, Mental Health, and Substance Abuse Problems

Wadiya Udell
Teachers College, Columbia University
New York, New York
    Thinking

Marcia Vandenbelt
Michigan State University
East Lansing, Michigan
    Nutrition

Susan Verducci
California State University–San Bernardino
San Bernardino, California
    Youth Outlook

Fred W. Vondracek
Penn State–University Park
University Park, Pennsylvania
    Apprenticeships
    Vocational Development

Scyatta A. Wallace
New York University
New York, New York
    Racial Discrimination

Kathryn R. Wentzel
University of Maryland–College Park
College Park, Maryland
    Peer Groups
    Teachers

Venette C. Westhoven
Loyola University
Chicago, Illinois
    Spina Bifida

Wilma Novalés Wibert
Michigan State University
East Lansing, Michigan
  Youth Gangs

Christine Wienke
University of South Florida
Tampa, Florida
  Storm and Stress

Michael Windle
University of Alabama–Birmingham
Birmingham, Alabama
  Alcohol Use, Risk Factors in
  Delinquency, Trends in

Rebecca C. Windle
University of Alabama–Birmingham
Birmingham, Alabama
  Alcohol Use, Risk Factors in

Melanie J. Zimmer-Gembeck
University of Minnesota
Minneapolis, Minnesota
  Autonomy

FOREWORD

"Something's happening here
What it is ain't exactly clear...."
—Stephen Stills, *For What It's Worth,*
as sung by Buffalo Springfield

Adolescence: A Movement to Help Us Know It For the First Time

This is much more than a book. This is part of a movement to make the world a better place. A former governor of Georgia was once approached by a group of reporters after a large-scale prison riot had just broken out and asked, "What are you going to do, Governor, to fix the prison system and make sure that deadly riots like this don't happen again?" "Gentlemen," the governor replied, "what we need here is really perfectly clear: we need a higher quality of prisoners!" This book is an attempt to make the world a better place, one that will help to generate a higher quality of people who populate it. But the quality of the world isn't the responsibility of adolescents any more than improving prison conditions is the responsibility of the prisoners. The world at large has an important responsibility and this encyclopedia is part of the effort to help all interested parties do their part. It is an effort to improve the experience of adolescence in America. In that sense, this book is part of a movement.

This movement shares much in common with the field of public health. Public health is grounded on four principles. These principles apply equally well to the transformational challenge facing the authors of *Adolescence in America.*

First, *this is a cause and effect world.* If we can understand the causes, we can use that understanding to change the effects. Stephen Hawking has written that the whole history of science has been the realization that events do not happen in an arbitrary manner. This concept rests on the premise that there are rational answers that can be determined by rational, common sense approaches. Using a simple set of questions, public health researchers have learned that they can understand what happens in the world and change the outcomes. If we can understand the causes, we can change the outcomes. This leads to an activist stance with optimism as a value: we can change things and we can change them for the better. For public health practitioners, this means that understanding is the key to preventing disease, disability, and death. For those raising or working with adolescents, working in the field of youth development, or working with children who will become adolescents, this understanding means that we can improve the physical health and safety of adolescents, their cognitive development, and their socio-emotional development.

Public health practitioners ask four types of questions to understand what happens in the world relevant to public health problems. First they ask, "What is the problem? How many people are affected? Who are they? Where does it happen? When does it happen?" The next question they might ask is "What are the causes? What are those factors that seem to lead to this problem and what are the factors that might prevent it?" Next, they would ask the question: "What works to prevent this problem? Do we have evidence to show that interventions designed to prevent this problem from occurring are effective?" And the final question would be: "Once you know what kind of interventions are effective, how do you get them to be carried out? How do you get resources to pay for them, how do you muster the political will to support these programs?" While it is important to equip adolescents, parents, and teachers to help adolescents avoid problems, *Adolescence in America* goes well beyond a concern with these problems that adolescents face. It also seeks to deliver information about how adolescents can acquire those strengths that will help them to overcome the challenges and problems they will encounter. The same four type of questions asked in the public health sphere can be reformulated to help acquire the type of information needed to understand and build strengths in adolescents. In this framework, the focus of the questions would shift: First, what are the strengths that can help adolescents to live rich and satisfying lives? What are these strengths that promote physical health and safety? Who has these strengths? Are there places or groups where they seem to be concentrated? Second, what are the antecedents of these strengths, and how do they change over the life course of an individual? Third, what works to promote these strengths? How do you use the many possible influences in an individual's life to promote these strengths, from the relationship with parents, to the physical environment in which a child lives, to the various individuals outside the immediate family, to the characteristics of the community, and the media, as well as macroeconomic factors? Finally, once you know what works to promote these strengths, how do you get individuals or communities to adopt these practices and programs? For many of these questions, there are answers and the big challenge is to deliver information to those who need it, an important way to accelerate support for adolescent programs.

The second principle that grounds public health: *Public health problems are constantly re-emerging in new forms.* Public health practitioners know that they live in a constantly changing environment, where microorganisms and manmade hazards are constantly changing. When scientists thought most infectious diseases had been conquered, new ones emerged; just when we solved the problem of injuries to railroad passengers, automobile travel replaced trains as the most common form of transportation. Continuous surveillance and continuous improvement of our interventions is required to hold onto our health and safety. The same is true for the world in which adolescents live today. A look at the list of entries in these volumes suggests that many of the issues discussed in this book were not even considered to be significant issues for adolescents 10 years ago.

The third principle: *Public health takes responsibility for people in the aggregate.* Public health is everybody's health. This drives public health to study people in relationships, in families, in communities, in nations, and globally. It provides efficiencies in interventions, when intervention programs are mounted at the community level, as with seatbelts or immunizations. Even more than that, it imposes a responsibility on those who enter public health. If you go into medicine you expect to use that knowledge for the benefit of your patient. But if you go into public health you have the obligation to use that knowledge for the benefit of everyone. Therefore, the philosophy behind public health is social justice. This is the secular version of "We are our brothers' keeper." Because public health takes responsibility for people in the aggregate, it works across national boundaries and without time boundaries. The vast majority of the public that public health serves has not yet even been born. In this same way, the movement to improve the well-being of adolescents looks to affect more than a single adolescent at a time. It thinks about involving schools, businesses, youth-serving organizations, and community-wide efforts.

The fourth principle: *Public health takes responsibility for the future health of people living now and for the health of the people of the future.* Public health addresses the future health for everybody. Traditionally, the Good Samaritan story encourages us to think about helping our neighbors, people we don't know, and even people we don't know living in places we have never seen. Public health goes further and asks us to help people we don't know because they will live in the future. This is a new dimension to the Good Samaritan story. The movement to improve the well-being of adolescents also looks to the future, paying attention not only to those who are adolescents now, but to the parents they will become, and their own infants and children who will become adolescents in the future.

There are noteworthy aspects of this encyclopedia that underlie its organization. First, this is a *collaborative* effort. Realizing that no one group or discipline alone possesses all the knowledge necessary to inform the users of this encyclopedia, the editors have assembled contributors who collectively possess knowledge of children and parents, national and local groups, both public and private, and knowledge that crosses many areas, such as education, early childhood development, health, psychology, social services, faith communities, civic groups, and many others.

Second, this volume is structured around a *strength-based* model for adolescent health and development. While it recognizes the need to provide information about the prevention of risks or even on the treatment of problems that face adolescents, the editors have made a strong effort to go beyond prevention models and look at the development of positive strengths such as the development of self-worth, trust, and attachment to positive role models, creativity, and habits to promote physical health. The idea is that promoting the health and well-being of children and adolescents can buffer risks and prevent problems.

Third, this volume provides *evidence-based* information that results from scientific research and from practice. Knowledge about what works to foster the well-being of children and adolescents comes from many disciplines. This evidence-based information is the most valuable way to help support families and others who support children to make sound decisions.

Fourth, a *developmental* approach recognizes that different positive characteristics are more or less prominent throughout different developmental periods across the lifespan. A developmental approach also implies a focus on developing strengths as early as conception, building a strong foundation in the early years.

Fifth, the book's approach is *ecological,* in that the authors and editors recognize the interaction among parents, children, caregivers, community, and the environment that shape an adolescent's well being.

Finally, the approach is *universal.* The authors and editors have made a special effort to make sure that the information applies to all adolescents, regardless of their socioeconomic status, their race, or their ethnicity.

This book fills a very important niche in adolescent well-being: It provides valuable information that is stunningly clear and easily accessible to both adoles-cents and the adults in their world. These adults include parents, teachers, mentors, family, and counselors. The information is concise, accurate, and written in a helpful and nonjudgmental way. And it is comprehensive in whole while succinct in each part. It covers all of the major issues that affect the lives of adolescents. What difference does this make? All the difference in the world. As I read the chapters in this magnificent work, I wished that I had known then what I know now. This is truly a work to enrich our lives.

"And the end of all our travels
Shall be to return to the place
From which we started
And to know it
For the first time."
　　　　　—T. S. Eliot, *Little Gedding*

—*Mark L. Rosenberg*
Center for Child Well-Being
The Task Force for Child
Survival and Development
Atlanta, Georgia

PREFACE

The purpose of *Adolescents in America: An Encyclopedia* is to present the best information currently available about the physical, psychological, behavioral, social, and cultural characteristics of the adolescent period. The contributions found in the volumes of this encyclopedia demonstrate that adolescence is a dynamic, developmental period, one marked by diverse sorts of changes for different youth. These changes are brought about because—for all characteristics of adolescents—development involves changing *relations* among the developing person and his or her social world.

The fact that these changes derive from the relations between adolescents and their contexts constitutes an optimistic and powerful approach to applications (for instance community-based programs, school curricula innovations, professional practices, and public policies) aimed at promoting positive adolescent development. By changing the character of the relations youth have with their social world, we may be able to enhance their chances for healthy development.

Accordingly, the contributions to the encyclopedia illustrate the diversity of adolescent life found across different physical, behavioral, racial, ethnic, religious, national, and cultural characteristics. In turn, the encyclopedia presents the key social relationships (e.g., involving peer groups, siblings, parents, extended family members, teachers, or mentors) and institutional contexts (e.g., schools, community organizations, faith institutions, and the work place) that influence the development of today's youth.

Both normal development and problems of development (medical/physical, psychological, and social) are discussed in the encyclopedia. Policies and programs useful for alleviating problems, for preventing problems, and for promoting positive and healthy development are included.

Our main audience is youth, parents, professionals, and researchers. We hope to reach these audiences through their use of middle school, high school, college, and public libraries, and by the dissemination of the information in this encyclopedia through the innovative electronic means used by our publisher, ABC-CLIO.

The contributors to this encyclopedia are experts in either the study of adolescence or in the use of knowledge about adolescent development in programs designed to promote their positive development. All contributors have provided authoritative but nontechnical entries based on their scholarship but at a level accessible to our audience. The authors (e.g., psychologists, sociologists, educators, social workers, lawyers, pediatricians, psychiatrists, and nurses) have drawn on their empirical research and professional practice in compiling the information pertinent to their entries. We believe that their contributions will inform our audience about the character of adolescence and, as well, will enhance the capacity of our readers to understand how current information about America's youth may be used to promote positive adolescent development.

There are numerous colleagues to whom we are indebted for helping us develop this encyclopedia. Most important, we are grateful to the authors who contributed their expertise to the encyclopedia and whose passion for helping young people lead better lives is clearly evident in their essays. We are especially appreciative to Mark Rosenberg, Director of Programs at the Center for Child Well-Being, for his kindness in writing such a generous and useful foreword to the encyclopedia.

Our doctoral student, Imma De Stefanis, was an invaluable colleague throughout the development of this volume, providing knowledge, wisdom, organizational efficiency, and a never-flagging positive attitude. We are grateful as well to the two editorial assistants who assisted us in the organization of the encyclopedia, Sophia T. Romero and Lisa Marie DiFonzo. Their professionalism and dedication to the project were extraordinary. We deeply appreciate as well the advice and support of our insightful and able editor at ABC-CLIO, Marie Ellen Larcada. Her guidance was critical in the creation, direction, and completion of this project. Over the course of the development of this project, two other editors at ABC-CLIO—Jennifer Loehr and Karna Hughes—have been ideal colleagues and efficient and productive collaborators. We greatly appreciate all the special efforts on our behalf.

Finally, our own three adolescents—Justin, Blair, and Jarrett—have taught us more than perhaps we want to recognize about adolescence. When they were all children, we used to describe ourselves as "experts" in the field of adolescent development. Now, having seen the completion of Justin's adolescence, its imminent completion by Blair and, at this writing, being immersed in the middle of Jarrett's adolescence, we currently describe ourselves as people who study adolescence. For all they have taught us and all that we anticipate they will continue to teach us, we dedicate this encyclopedia to them.

—*J. V. L., Chestnut Hill, Massachusetts*
—*R.M.L., Medford, Massachusetts*

Introduction

The word *adolescence* can be traced to the Latin word *adolescere,* which means "to grow into maturity" (Muuss, 1996). Growing into maturity involves change and, even today, adolescence is regarded (perhaps with the exception of infancy) as the most change-filled period of life (Lerner and Galambos, 1998; Petersen, 1988) It is a period of change from being childlike to being adult. Most people who study adolescence define the second ten years of life (from the ages of ten to twnety years) as the adolescent period. All people who study adolescence—or who experience it, as either parents or as young people themselves—agree that the period is one not only of numerous, major changes but, as well, of dramatic ones that often can be remembered for all the years of life succeeding this period.

Adolescence has been described as a phase of life beginning in biology and ending in society. One way of understanding this observation is to recognize that the external and internal bodily changes of puberty may be the most visible and universal features of adolescence, but the social and cultural words within which young people develop in large measure texture this phase of life.

Accordingly, adolescence may be *defined* as the period within the life span when most of a person's biological characteristics (for example, his or her primary and secondary sexual characteristics), psychological processes (involving thoughts, emotions, and personality), and social relationships (e.g., with parents, peers, and key institutions such as schools) change from what is typically considered childlike to what is considered adultlike. In other words, adolescence is a period of transition, one wherein the biological, psychological, and social characteristics that are typical of children become the biological, psychological, and social characteristics that are typical of adults. When most of one's characteristics are in this state of change, one is an adolescent.

The Challenges of Adolescence

Given, then, the multiple changes a teen experiences, it is clear why adolescence is regarded as a challenging phase of life. Of course, not all people experience adolescence as stressful and not all youth undergo these changes in the same way, with the same speed, or with the same results. As we emphasize below, there are differences in their paths through life. There is *diversity in development* among adolescents.

A major cause of these differences in development is the particular biological characteristics of the adolescent *and* the specific family, peer group, neighborhood, community, society, culture, and even period of history within which an adolescent lives. For example, in modern American society, adolescents experience important changes in their school setting, typically involving moving from elementary school to either junior high school or middle school; and in late adolescence, there is a transition from high school to the worlds of work, university, or child-rearing. In short, one must consider *the context* of adolescents in order to understand them adequately.

The hopes, challenges, fears, and successes of adolescence have been romanticized or dramatized in novels, short stories, and news articles. It is commonplace to survey a newsstand and to find a magazine article describing the "stormy years" of adolescence, the new crazes or fads of youth, or the "explosion" of problems with teenagers (e.g., involving crime or sexuality).

However, until the past thirty to thirty-five years, when medical, biological, and social scientists began to study intensively the adolescent period, there was relatively little sound scientific information available to verify or refute the literary characterizations of adolescence. Today, however, such information does exist. It affords several generalizations about the character of adolescent development.

Key Features of Adolescent Development
The results of research on adolescence indicates that, to understand young people, we need to combine knowledge from biology, medicine, and nursing; the social and behavioral sciences; social work; law; education; and the humanities (Lerner and Galambos, 1998; Petersen, 1988). This range of knowledge is represented in this encyclopedia. This multidisciplinary knowledge allows several generalizations to be made about the life of young people and provides information about how best to intervene when adolescents are experiencing difficulties.

By the beginning of the second decade of life, numerous types of changes begin to occur. Both internal and external bodily changes, cognitive and emotional changes, and social relationship changes all occur. Adolescence is, then, a period of life involving biological, psychological, and social change.

In regard to biology, the adolescent must cope with changing physical (bodily appearance) characteristics and physiological functions (e.g., the beginning of the menstrual cycle or the first ejaculation). The adolescent looks in the mirror and sees himself or herself differently: hair is growing in places where it has not grown before; his or her complexion is changing; and his or her body is taking on a different shape. Moreover, new feelings, new "stirrings," are emanating from the body, and the person begins to wonder about what this all means and what he or she will become.

These biological changes must be understood and accepted as part of the self if the adolescent is not to become separated from, alienated by, or simply frightened and confused by what is happening in her and to her. The adolescent must come to accept these changes as part of who he or she now is and what he or she may become. For example, "I am a person who has breasts, who can become pregnant, who can be a mother." Thus, these biological changes must be coped with—understood—if an adaptive sense of self is to exist. As such, these biological changes constitute a developmental task with which the person must deal.

The sorts of reactions engendered in the adolescent by his or her biological changes pertain to a second set of changes, that is, psychological ones of cognition and emotion. New characteristics of thought and emotions arise: Cognition becomes abstract and hypothetical and emotions involve feelings of genital sexuality. The adolescent's new psychological characteristics must themselves be coped with; the adolescent must become able to recognize abstractions and hypotheses as different from reality if he or she is to interact adaptively in the world; means must be found to deal in socially acceptable ways with his or her sexuality if he or she is to avoid problems of health and adjustment.

These tasks clearly involve the adolescent in his or her social world and thus, in this way again, illustrate the interwoven nature of the tasks of this period. But, the psychological changes of adolescence also interrelate with the biological alterations the person is undergoing. It is, most centrally, the adolescents' new cognitive abilities that allow them to understand their current physical and physiological characteristics and to prospect (guess, if you will) what these characteristics are likely to mean for them as individuals. For example, "My breasts probably won't grow much more, but I'm sure my complexion will clear up. I will be pretty. I think I'll be able to attract a nice-looking guy someday."

Thus, adolescents' thought capabilities allow them to know who they are, given their changing characteristics of individuality; allow them to guess who they might become; and allow them to plan what they may do with their new feelings—"I'll be someone who can and will attract an attractive mate."

The demand imposed by the psychological changes of adolescence is for the person to deal with her changed biology by forming a revised sense of self—a new self-definition. It is this self-definition that, in recognition of who the adolescent understands herself to now be and plans to become, will allow the adolescent to choose where he or she wants to end up in life. It is one's self-definition that fosters the selection of the niche one picks to occupy in life, i.e., the role (or roles) one will plan to play in society: "I'm too skinny and small to play in team sports. Besides, I think I like reading and writing more than athletics. If I work hard in school, I think I can become a teacher."

The psychological nature of adolescence blends inextricably, then, into the third type of challenge of the period. Adolescence is also a matter of society and culture; it is a matter of learning the range of activities and roles available in your social world and coming to understand their value. Then, the developmental task becomes one of putting together who one is physically and who one is psychologically to find the right role, the correct place, a niche, in one's society. But, one must understand who one is as a biological and psychological individual in order to fit into a social role optimally suited for one's own specific characteristics, one's particular sense of self.

It is one's self-definition, therefore, that will allow one to meet the social role tasks of one's social world. Meeting the developmental task—finding a social role—is crucial to *adaptive* (that is, healthy, positive, and successful) functioning. It is such a role that gives meaning to one's life and it is one's responsible and successful performance of such a role which will elicit from society those protections, rights, and privileges that will safeguard one as a person and allow for continued healthy functioning.

In short, finding a social role that allows one to contribute to society in a way that is both best suited to the individual and helpful to society will be adaptive for both individual and the greater social world. Thus, there is—ideally—a convergence among the three developmental tasks of adolescence, one that will allow the person to best integrate his/her changing self with his/her particular social world. Indeed, this linkage between the adolescent and his/her social world constitutes another significant feature of adolescent development.

Multiple Levels of Context Are Influential During Adolescence. We have noted that individual differences are an important part of adolescent development. All differences arise from connections among biological, psychological, and societal factors—and not from one of these influences (e.g., biology) acting either alone or as the "prime mover" of change.

Adolescence is a period of extremely rapid transitions in such characteristics as height, weight, and body proportions. Indeed, except for infancy, no other period of the life cycle involves such rapid changes. Hormonal changes are part of the development of early adolescence. Nevertheless, hormones are not primarily responsible for the psychological or social developments during this period. In fact, the quality and timing of hormonal or other biological changes influence and are influenced by psychological, social, cultural, and historical factors.

Good examples of the complex changes in adolescence arise in regard to cognitive development during this period. Global and pervasive effects of puberty on cognitive development do not seem to exist. When biological effects are found they interact with contextual and experiential factors (e.g., the transition to junior high school) to influence academic achievement. Accordingly, there is no evidence for general cognitive disruption over adolescence.

The period of adolescence is, then, one of continual change and transition between individuals and their contexts. These changing relations constitute the basic process of development in adolescence and underlie both positive and negative outcomes that occur.

When the multiple biological, psychological, cognitive, and social changes of adolescence occur simultaneously (e.g., when menarche occurs at the same time as a school transition), there is a greater risk of problems occurring in a youth's development. In adolescence, poor decisions (e.g., involving school, sex, drugs) have more negative consequences than in childhood, and the adolescent is more responsible for those decisions and their consequences than in childhood; that is, the adolescent is more often involved than are younger individuals in making the behavioral and contextual choices (e.g., engaging in drug use with a particular peer group) associated with involvement in problem behaviors.

Nevertheless, most developmental trajectories across this period involve positive adjustment on the part of the adolescent. Furthermore, for most youth there is a continuation of warm and accepting relations with parents. Accordingly, adolescence is an opportune time in which to intervene into family processes when necessary.

Individual Differences—Diversity—Characterize Adolescence. We have noted that there are multiple pathways through adolescence (e.g., Offer, 1969). It is important to recognize that normal adolescent development involves such variability. There is diversity among and within all ethnic, racial, or cultural minority groups. Because adolescents are so different from each other, one cannot expect any single policy or intervention to reach all of a given target population or to influence everyone in the same way.

Furthermore, normal adolescent development involves also variability within the person as well as between people. There are differences among adolescents in such characteristics as personality, attitudes, values, and social relationships. In addition, a given adolescent may change over the course of his or her life in all of these characteristics.

Conclusions about the Features of Adolescent Development. The scientific information available about development in adolescence underscores the diversity and dynamics of this period of life. Adolescence, in short, is a period of life marked by diversity, both among different youth and, as well, within any given young person—he or she will change across the adolescent years and do so in a manner unique to him or her. Such diversity indicates that any generalized statement about what is true for "all adolescents" is apt to be inaccurate. Therefore, a stereotype that indicated that there was only one type of pathway across the adolescent years—for instance, one characterized by inevitable "storm and stress"—would not stand up in the face of current knowledge about diversity in adolescence.

Such diversity in development is stressed across the entries in this encyclopedia. Yet, at the same time such diversity exists, it is possible to make generalizations about adolescence, such as those noted above. Thus, both general and specific features of development mark the lives of American youth. In fact, one key generalization that may be made about adolescents is that, for most young people in America, adolescence is a period wherein health and positive growth are predominant. Indeed, by the end of the second decade most youth seem to be in a time of constant commitment—to partners, family, and work.

The Goal of This Encyclopedia
How, in the span of ten years, does the individual bridge the gap between coping with the several challenges of early adolescence and the launching of a now young adult life at the end of this period? Answering this question engages the fascination and energies of scientists, practitioners, parents, teachers, and young people themselves. Providing the key information pertinent to understanding this issue is the goal of this encyclopedia.

The aim of *Adolescents in America: An Encyclopedia* is to present the best information currently available about the adolescent period and the ways in which scientists and practitioners understand the period and, as well, take actions to successfully promote positive development among youth. That is, the information in this encyclopedia will illustrate that, by understanding the relations that diverse adolescents have with their contexts, one may formulate *appli-*

cations that may be useful in improving these relations. These applications may involve community-based programs, professional practices, education curricula, and public policies. All applications, however, have the intent of serving either to resolve or ameliorate challenges to healthy adolescent development, to prevent problems of adolescent behavior from developing, or to promote positive development among youth.

Accordingly, the encyclopedia will emphasize that adolescence is a dynamic, developmental period marked by diverse changes for different youth, changes brought about because development involves changing *relations* among biological, psychological, and social/ecological processes. Together, these diverse developmental changes involve the relations adolescents have with their biological, social, and cultural contexts, and provide the basis for innovations, in the above-noted types of applications, aimed at increasing societal ability to improve the lives of America's adolescents. If the basis of the development of young people lies in their particular relationships with their social world—with their specific family, peer group, schools, and neighborhoods—then by taking steps to improve these relations one may be enacting the key steps needed to promote positive development.

Accordingly, across this encyclopedia readers will find that four themes are interwoven: Development, diversity, context, and application. Together these themes will enable readers to understand how scholars and practitioners may contribute to identifying knowledge that "matters" in respect to enhancing the lives of the diverse young people of our nation (Lerner, in press).

The Contributions of the Entries in This Encyclopedia

The themes of developmental diversity, adolescent-context relations, and the links among theory, research, and applications to programs aimed at enhancing the life chances of young people are key foci in contemporary scholarship about, and practice pertinent to, adolescence. As such, these themes will frame the entries in this encyclopedia. Across the entries in this encyclopedia, readers will find that several types of information are emphasized:

The stress on adolescent development in the encyclopedia involves both the antecedents in earlier life periods of changes in adolescence and the consequences of changes in adolescence for later, adult development and aging. The treatment of development in this text will include a discussion of the intertwining of the development of a youth with the development of parents and other relatives, with peers, and with other individuals important in the life of an adolescent (for instance, teachers, mentors, and coaches).

The focus on diversity in the encyclopedia provides understanding of the variation among adolescents that is associated with race, ethnicity, gender, sexual orientation, and physical characteristics.

The emphasis on the context of adolescence involves discussing: (1) the role of culture and history in shaping the processes and products of adolescent development; (2) the role of the social, interpersonal, familial, and physical context in influencing youth development; (3) institutional contributions to adolescent development, including educational, political, economic, and social policy influences; and (4) community needs and assets, including programs promoting positive youth and family development. In addition, several disciplines and several professions that are involved in understanding the contexts that influence human development will be discussed.

The stress on application involves indicating current foci of policies and programs pertinent to youth intervention programs, education, re-training, and services.

Conclusions

Certainly, it is a daunting task to raise healthy and successful children eventually capable of leading themselves, their families, their communities, and our nation productively, responsibly, and morally into the new century (Benson, 1997; Damon, 1997; Lerner, 1995). Nevertheless, all of America must rise to this challenge if our nation is to not only survive but to prosper.

Simply, the young people of today represent 100 percent of the human capital on which the future health and success of America rests. To enhance the lives of American adolescents requires that we continuously educate all citizens—young and old—about the best means available to promote enhanced healthy lives among *all* youth and the families, schools, and communities involved in their lives. It is our hope that *Adolescence in America: An Encyclopedia* will contribute to an educational and community-collaborative effort to help insure, for the new millenium, a socially just and civil society populated by healthy and productive children and adolescents.

References

Adelson, J., ed. 1980. *Handbook of Adolescent Psychology*. New York: Wiley.

Benson, Peter. 1997. *All Kids Are Our Kids: What Communities Must Do to Raise Caring and Responsible Children and Adolescents*. San Francisco: Jossey-Bass.

Damon, William. 1997. *The Youth Charter: How Communities Can Work together to Raise Standards for All Our Children*. New York: The Free Press.

Grotevant, Harold D. 1998. "Adolescent Development in Family Contexts." Pp. 1097–1149 in *Social, Emotional, and Personality Development*. Edited by Nancy Eisenberg. (Volume 3 of the *Handbook of Child Psychology* 5th ed.. Editor-in-chief: William Damon.) New York: Wiley.

Lerner, Richard M. 1993. "Investment in Youth: The Role of Home Economics in Enhancing the Life Chances of America's Children." *AHEA Monograph Series* 1: 5–34.

Lerner, Richard M. 1993. "Early Adolescence: Toward an Agenda for the Integration of Research, Policy, and Intervention." Pp. 1–13 in *Early Adolescence: Perspectives on Research, Policy, and Intervention*. Edited by Richard M. Lerner. Hillsdale, NJ: Erlbaum.

Lerner, Richard M. 1995. *America's Youth in Crisis: Challenges and Options for Programs and Policies*. Thousand Oaks, CA: Sage.

Lerner, Richard M., and Nancy L. Galambos. 1998. "Adolescent Development: Challenges and Opportunities for Research, Programs, and Policies." *Annual Review of Psychology* 49: 413–446.

Muuss, Rolff E. 1996. *Theories of Adolescence*, 6th ed. New York: McGraw-Hill.

Offer, Daniel. 1996. *The Psychological World of the Teen-Ager*. New York: Basic Books.

Petersen, Anne C. 1988. "Adolescent Development." *Annual Review of Psychology* 39: 583–607.

Abortion

There are two types of abortion. The first is a spontaneous loss of a fetus from natural causes before the twentieth week of gestation (normally forty weeks in length). The second is a medical termination of pregnancy, sometimes called an induced abortion. Information only about induced abortion is presented here.

Induced abortion is legal in the United States. The largest age group of women who have abortions is adolescents, probably because adolescents are much more likely than young adult women to use contraceptives improperly, or not to use them at all. Many states do have laws that restrict access of minors to abortion services, requiring them to obtain parental consent or the permission of a court.

Abortion methods depend to some extent on the duration of the pregnancy. The earliest method involves use of the morning-after pill, which can be used within seventy-two hours of unprotected intercourse. Women using this method take very high doses of oral contraceptives for several days. Nausea and vomiting are common side effects of this method. Surgical emptying of the uterus is used for about 95 percent of abortions; it is almost always used for pregnancies shorter than twelve weeks. In this method a health-care provider will open the woman's

vagina using a speculum (an instrument used during a routine pelvic examination) so that she can see the opening of the cervix (the part of the uterus that is at the top of the vagina). Another instrument is then used to stretch the opening of the cervix so that a slender tube can be inserted up into the main part of the uterus. The contents of the uterus are then suctioned out, removing the fetus and the placenta (the organ allowing exchange of nutrients between mother and fetus). In the very early weeks of pregnancy, this method sometimes does not work well, since the fetus is so tiny that the suction tube may miss it. This procedure is essentially painless. The woman is usually given some medication to prevent excessive bleeding after the procedure.

For pregnancies between seven and twelve weeks, the cervix opening needs to be stretched more; sometimes a slowly expanding plug is placed in the cervical opening overnight, and the abortion is performed the next morning. The fetus and placenta are then removed by suction. Antibleeding medication is always given after this kind of abortion.

For pregnancies of more than twelve weeks the procedure is the same as for seven to twelve weeks, except that in addition to suctioning, the inside of the uterus will be scraped gently to ensure removal of all contents. Again, antibleeding medication is always given after the abortion.

There are now some drugs, such as mifepristone, that can be used along with other medications to help the uterus contract and expel the fetus. These are commonly used for pregnancies greater than sixteen weeks, although they can be used also in pregnancies earlier than seven weeks. Unwanted side effects include nausea, vomiting, diarrhea, flushing of the face, and fainting. An asthma attack can be brought on in some women.

The longer a woman waits after she knows she is pregnant, the more complicated will be the abortion. Some possible complications include puncturing of the uterus or the intestines by the instruments used, prolonged or uncontrollable bleeding, infections of the uterus, and scarring of the lining of the uterus (resulting in sterility). The most important complication, however, is the psychological turmoil that most women experience after an abortion, no matter when it is performed. This turmoil is apt to be especially severe among adolescents. Indeed, teens are likely to be frightened both before and after the abortion. They will keep the abortion secret if they can and may have none of their usual support system—parents, friends, siblings, religious leaders—with whom to consult. Health-care providers should use support staff to help decrease this problem.

Jordan W. Finkelstein

See also Abstinence; Adoption: Exploration and Search; Adoption: Issues and Concerns; Contraception; Decision Making; Foster Care: Risks and Protective Factors; Pregnancy, Interventions to Prevent; Sexual Behavior; Single Parenthood and Low Achievement; Teenage Parenting: Childbearing

References and further reading
Berkow, Robert B., ed. 1997. *The Merck Manual of Medical Information: Home Edition.* Whitehouse Station, NJ: Merck Research Laboratories, pp. 1128–1129.
Pojman, Louis P., and Francis J. Beckwith, comps. 1998. *The Abortion Controversy.* Belmont, CA: Wadsworth.
Poppema, Suzanne P., with Mike Henderson. 1996. *Why I Am an Abortion Doctor.* Amherst, NY: Prometheus Books.
Sachdev, Paul, ed. 1985. *Perspectives on Abortion.* Metuchen, NJ: Scarecrow Press.

Abstinence

The term *abstinence* can mean different things to different people. Some adolescents believe abstinence is the same thing as engaging in protected or "safe" sex. Some researchers define abstinence as not having experienced vaginal intercourse. The rhythm method of contraception uses abstinence to refer to avoiding vaginal intercourse during the point in a woman's cycle when she is most likely to become pregnant.

There are problems with all these different meanings for abstinence. First, abstinence is not the same thing as using condoms during vaginal intercourse. Second, some people experience vaginal intercourse and then decide they want to wait to have it again until they get married. Third, avoiding vaginal intercourse for a short time to avoid conceiving a child is different from postponing intercourse until one decides it is the right time to experience it.

For the purposes of this discussion, abstinence is defined as a commitment to postpone engaging in vaginal intercourse. This commitment is made by unmarried people who may or may not have experienced vaginal intercourse in the past. In other words, someone does not have to be a virgin to be abstinent. Note that this definition does not cover abstinence within a homosexual context: The nature of abstinence as advocated by the Catholic Church for gays and lesbians is qualitatively different from the type of abstinence discussed here.

Abstinence is defined as a commitment because it involves more than just saying "no." It is a lifestyle choice. Many people fail at practicing abstinence because they do not realize this. In addition, practicing abstinence requires different skills than using a condom or other method of contraception.

Practicing Abstinence
Like using contraception, abstinence takes planning and commitment. The goal is to avoid being in situations where it would be difficult to maintain a commitment to sexual abstinence. First, this means choosing a lifestyle where one does not drink alcohol. Research has shown that even small amounts of alcohol limit the ability to think about long-term consequences and can make individuals more susceptible to social pressure (Steele and Josephs, 1990). Second, one needs to choose friends who support a commitment to wait to have sex. Research on conformity has shown that when someone has at least one person who agrees with him, it is easier to stand up to social pressure (Allen and Wilder, 1979). Adolescents who are successful at practicing abstinence report that it is good to have a friend who is committed to abstinence. Third, one needs to avoid parties and being alone with someone to whom she is attracted

in a home where the adult supervision is poor or unavailable. In short, it means living a life where it would be hard to have sex, should one feel tempted. A benefit of this lifestyle is that it protects people from having sex forced upon them, as in a date rape situation. Finally, one needs to choose a lifestyle that incorporates playing a sport or musical instrument, doing volunteer work, or engaging in some regularly occurring activity that gives a sense of accomplishment and importance. This kind of activity feeds one's self-esteem and self-worth. When these are strong and someone says, "If you loved me, you'd do it," it is easier to confidently say back, "If you loved me, you wouldn't ask!"

In addition to the right lifestyle choices, practicing abstinence involves cognitive and interpersonal skills. The cognitive skill required is that of remaining committed to one's choice when it is challenged by events and people, rather than allowing these challenges to stimulate self-doubt. For example, if a close friend decides to have sex, someone who is committed to abstinence needs to tell himself that his choice to wait is the right choice for him. Adolescents who are successful at practicing abstinence report that if someone pressures them about having sex, it causes them to reevaluate the relationship. Rather than doubting themselves, they question whether this person is worth having a relationship with in the first place.

Useful interpersonal skills are those that allow a teen to recognize and respond to the "lines" often used to persuade someone to have sex, and to handle unexpected situations that could challenge their ability to remain abstinent ("risky situations"). Self-efficacy research argues that practicing responses to lines with friends, or as part of an intervention program, helps a teen feel more confident and be more successful at remaining abstinent. The same is true with respect to problem solving about how to handle risky situations (e.g., being alone in the car heading toward a "lover's lane," or finding oneself at a party where other adolescents are slipping off to have sex).

Myths about Abstinence

There are at least five myths surrounding the notion of abstinence. First, some people believe that one can still be abstinent while participating in anal intercourse. However, individuals who choose to be abstinent do not practice anal intercourse. Women who simply wish to protect their virginity may be interested in anal intercourse as an alternative to vaginal intercourse. However, practicing abstinence is a more healthy choice for protecting virginity. Sexually transmitted diseases (STDs) can be spread during anal intercourse, and the vagina can become infected with the bacteria that are normally found in stool. Bacteria in stool combines with the ejaculate, which can then spill out and into the vagina. Moreover, without feeling relaxed and using plenty of lubrication, one can find anal sex painful, and the rectum can tear. It is even possible to become pregnant as a result of anal intercourse. (As the ejaculate spills out of the rectum, sperm can move into the vagina and on up to a fallopian tube, where they can meet an egg.)

Second, some people argue that abstinence is the most effective method for preventing pregnancy and STDs. However, the effectiveness of a contraceptive method is determined by multiplying two numbers or rates: method failure and user failure. A method failure is due to a defect in the product, but a user failure occurs when a user does not use a method consistently or properly. Although many misleading statistics are often quoted, findings from a number of studies indicate that latex condom method failure rates are small (.5 percent–7 percent), whereas user failure rates (12–70 percent) are higher and primarily due to inconsistent use of a condom (Haignere et al., 1999).

The method failure rate for abstinence is 0 percent, but user failure rates can make abstinence less effective than a condom at preventing pregnancies and STDs. Abstinence is only 100 percent effective if it is practiced 100 percent of the time. Unfortunately, people who intend to practice abstinence may fail to practice it 100 percent of the time. User failure rates range between 26 percent and 86 percent for adults who practice periodic abstinence as part of using the rhythm method of birth control. The consistency with which adolescents are able to practice abstinence is not known, and few behavioral outcome data exist for abstinence-only programs. Estimates based on outcome data for a recent abstinence-only program suggest overall potential user failure rates range from 37 percent to 57 percent (Haignere et al., 1999).

Third, some people believe that teaching adolescents who are committed to abstinence about birth control is unnecessary and may discourage them from practicing abstinence. However, a good bit of research has suggested that sex education that incorporates accurate information about birth control with the potential physical and emotional consequences of sexual intercourse does not encourage adolescents to become sexually active (Kirby, 1999). Instead these programs may actually encourage adolescents to put off having sex (i.e., practice abstinence at least for a period of time). Perhaps these programs are effective because they help adolescents to learn more about the consequences of sex and to see that using birth control is complicated. We really do not know why they have this effect. However, we do know that teaching about sex and birth control does not make adolescents go out and have sex. Moreover, sooner or later most people choose to become sexually active. At that point in time, they may need to know about birth control. Women can become pregnant the first time they have sex, and STDs can be spread with only one act of intercourse.

Fourth, some people argue that practicing abstinence now makes it harder to have enjoyable sex later on. However, there is at least one study that has found that young women who postpone having sex until they are eighteen or older are more likely to experience an orgasm the first time they have sex. Moreover, Stanley Boteach argues in his book, *Kosher Sex*, that people who wait to have sex until they are married always have pleasurable sex because they do not have to wonder how their partner sees them and are not haunted by memories of previous lovers. Instead, they are focused solely on pleasing and communicating their love to each other.

Fifth, some people believe that practicing abstinence is a matter of just saying "no." However, as discussed previously, abstinence is far more than just saying "no." In fact, some of the people who are best at practicing abstinence may never have to say "no." They never allow themselves to be in a situation where they are pressured to have sex. They avoid people who do not support their choice, and they avoid being in places

where their commitment to abstinence could be challenged. Their lifestyle supports and protects their commitment. They know deep down that their choice is the right choice for them.

Anne E. Norris

See also Contraception; Dating; HIV/AIDS; Peer Pressure; Pregnancy, Interventions to Prevent; Sex Education; Sexual Behavior; Sexually Transmitted Diseases; Teeanage Parenting: Childbearing; Teenage Parenting: Consequences

References and further reading
Allen, Vernon L., and David A. Wilder. 1979. "Social Support in Absentia: The Effect of an Absentee Partner on Conformity. *Human Relations* 32: 103–111.
Boteach, Stanley. 1999. *Kosher Sex*. New York: Doubleday.
Haignere, Clara S., Rachel Gold, and Heather J. McDanel, 1999. "Adolescent Abstinence and Condom Use: Are We Sure We Are Really Teaching What Is Safe?" *Health Education and Behavior* 26: 43–54.
Kirby, Douglas. 1999. "Reducing Adolescent Pregnancy: Approaches That Work." *Contemporary Pediatrics* 16: 83–94.
Steele, Claude M., and Robert A. Josephs. 1990. "Alcohol Myopia: Its Prized and Dangerous Effects." *American Psychologist* 45: 921–933.
The author wishes to acknowledge Ms. Rita Bourne, M.Ed., CAS, a high school teacher in Wellesley, MA, and her teenage daughter, Ms. Ashley Bourne, for their careful review and critique of this entry.

Academic Achievement

One of the major focuses of most of today's adolescents is school performance. Good school grades during high school ensure successful graduation, which is linked to better opportunities for work or advanced education (i.e., college, business school, professional school).

Although academic achievement is a goal of many adolescents, it is influenced by many factors, from peers and family to society and culture. (Shirley Zeiberg)

Although academic achievement is a goal of many adolescents, it is affected by multiple levels of the contexts of these youth, ranging from the most macro cultural influences to micro interpersonal influences involving peers and family members. We have today a wealth of information from studies that have evaluated these influences. In an important series of cross-cultural studies, Harold W. Stevenson and his colleagues have identified key features of culture that influence adolescent achievement, particularly in mathematics.

For instance, in a study (Chen and Stevenson, 1995) of approximately 600 eleventh-grade students from Minneapolis, Minnesota, Taipei, Taiwan, and Sendai, Japan, youth in all settings spent most of their time studying, interacting with friends, or watching television. However, the distribution of time spent in these activities differed across groups, and these differences were linked to variation in mathematics achievement. Chinese youth spent more time in academic activities (e.g., attending school, participating in after-school classes, or studying) than did their American counterparts. In turn, although Japanese and American youth did not differ in regard to time spent studying or in after-school programs, Japanese adolescents did spend more time in school than did American youth. American youth, on the other hand, spent more time than did adolescents in the other groups working or socializing with friends.

Other research shows that achievement scores of Asian Americans are higher than those of the European Americans, but, in turn, they are lower than those of Chinese or Japanese adolescents. Family and peer factors are also associated with achievement among both the Asian American and the East Asian youth. For instance, greater mathematics achievement is seen among adolescents whose parents and peers held high standards for and positive attitudes about academic effort and achievement; in addition, achievement is better among youth who had fewer distractions from schoolwork caused by jobs or informal peer interactions.

This research has also revealed that many of the academic achievements of youth from different cultural backgrounds may be based on socialization experiences beginning in childhood. For example, for American, Chinese, and Japanese youth from the first grade through middle adolescence, consistent relationships in all cultures were found across time among family socioeconomic status, cognitive abilities, and academic achievement. Moreover, the cultural orientation toward academic achievement that youth experience may remain with them despite emigration to another country. For instance, for Latino, East Asian, Filipino, and European adolescents from immigrant families, youth from both first- and second-generation immigrant backgrounds showed greater mathematics achievement than did peers whose families were "native" Americans, that is, who had lived in America for several generations. Socioeconomic factors were not primarily associated with these differences; rather, a common

(cultural) stress on education, one that was shared by the youth, their peers, and their families, seemed most important for their achievement.

Even within a cultural group, family and peer variables have an influence of academic achievement. For instance, Gene Brody and his colleagues have found that in rural African American nine- to twelve-year-olds, maternal involvement with the adolescent's school, supportive and harmonious family interactions, and family financial resources were associated with academic competence. In turn, living in either a single-parent family or a stepfamily has a negative influence on the mathematics and reading achievement of eighth graders. However, when parental social relations are positive, these negative influences are diminished.

Peers, too, can have a facilitative influence on academic achievement. For example, working with peers when trying to solve a problem enhances the ability to succeed in such tasks. Working with peers seems especially useful when the interactions with them are specifically relevant to the particular problem at hand. However, even engaging in general games with peers—nowadays, often though interactive computers—can facilitate cognitive performance. For instance, playing video games, such as Tetris, can enhance an adolescent's ability to rotate figures mentally and to mentally visualize objects in space.

As suggested above, however, spending a lot of time in informal peer interactions appears to have a negative impact on academic achievement—although it may enhance peer popularity. High sociability ratings from peers are linked to lower academic competence.

Sandra Graham and her colleagues have studied ethnically diverse young adolescents and found that girls of all ethnic backgrounds and European American boys value high-achieving female classmates, but ethnic minority boys place little value on high-achieving male peers. Indeed, all youth believed that both academic disengagement and social deviance were associated with being male, a low achiever, and an ethnic minority.

It may be that some instances of low achievement are related to adolescents' own characterization of themselves. Their self-categorizations or labels of themselves may be self-handicapping in regard to their achievement. For instance, girls who across their adolescence come to think of themselves in more masculine than feminine terms have better spatial abilities than do girls who think of themselves as more feminine than masculine.

Interestingly, Carol Midgely and her colleagues have studied how some youth use such self-handicapping strategies to account for their poor academic performance. That is, through engaging in procrastination, fooling around in class, and intentional reduction in effort, they provide for themselves an account of the cause of poor academic achievement. For eighth graders, such handicapping strategies were associated with self-deprecation, negative attitudes toward education, and low grades.

Of course, adolescents can also develop self-enhancing strategies. For instance, developing an ability to delay gratification when still in preschool facilitates cognitive and academic competence in adolescence. Not surprisingly, the ability to delay gratification also enhances the capacity to cope with both frustration and stress. Similarly, experiences that provide knowledge about math problems and about strategies for addressing such

problems are key influences on the performance of *both* adolescent boys and girls on the math subtest of the Scholastic Aptitude Test.

In addition, both IQ scores and academic performance are related to three aspects of social competence among twelve- and thirteen-year-olds: (1) showing socially responsible behavior, (2) receiving positive appraisals by peers, and (3) having the ability to regulate oneself socially, that is, to set goals, to solve problems, and to elicit interpersonal trust. Similarly, adolescent girls who have high mastery of academic subjects also have the ability to seek and obtain appropriate help in solving a task.

Of course, for some students low achievement is related to a learning disability rather than to self-handicapping behavior. For example, learning-disabled youth encounter difficulty in inhibiting incorrect responses in academic situations. In such circumstances, family support—for example, parental expectations for the child's academic achievement and the young person's awareness of these expectations—influences academic achievement among learning-disabled (and non-learning-disabled) youth.

There are numerous interventions, beyond those associated with fostering parental support, that can enhance academic achievement among youth. Many of these efforts involve types of community-based programs that are aimed at enhancing not only academic functioning but also several other, very often interrelated problems of youth development.

There is evidence that these community-based programs do enhance school achievement. For instance, in a report by Arthur Reynolds about the Chicago Longitudinal Study of the role of extended early childhood intervention in school achievement, about 560 low-income, inner-city African American youth were followed from early childhood to the seventh grade. Program participation for two or three years after preschool and kindergarten was associated with higher reading achievement through the seventh grade and with lower rates of grade retention (being held back a grade) and placement into special education classes. This study provides important longitudinal evidence of the benefits for adolescent academic achievement, for instance, in regard to literacy skills, of a large-scale community-based program of extended early childhood intervention.

Certainly, being literate is a key requirement for academic achievement and, as well, for success in life—especially in a world growing more dependent on technology and thus on the ability to speak, read, and write not only one's native tongue but also various computer languages. Moreover, adolescents' literacy skills can affect not only their own life chances but also others in their social world. For example, differences in preschool cognition and behavior are related to literacy in late adolescence and young adulthood. In addition, variation in maternal education, in the size of the family during early childhood, in the marital status of the mother, and in family income in middle childhood and in early adolescence have also been found to influence literacy.

Given, then, the developmental and generational significance of literacy, it is understandable that there exist numerous programs worldwide designed to enhance literacy among youth, especially those from socioeconomic backgrounds where there is limited access to adequate educational resources. Since several problems are often associated with illiteracy (for instance, dropping out of school, lack of employability, and poverty), the programs typically have to attend simultaneously to several interrelated problems in order to be effective.

In conclusion, academic achievement is not just a product of "natural" ability. The social world of young people, as well as special programs designed to help young people achieve, influence success in school.

Richard M. Lerner
Jacqueline V. Lerner

See also Academic Self-Evaluation; Cheating, Academic; Homework; Intelligence; Intelligence Tests; Learning Disabilities; Learning Styles and Accommodations; Single Parenthood and Low Achievement; Standardized Tests

References and further reading

Brody, Gene H., Douglas Flor, and Nicole M. Gibson. 1999. "Linking Maternal Efficacy Beliefs, Developmental Goals, Parenting Practices, and Child Competence in Rural Single-Parent African-American Families." *Child Development* 70: 1197–1208.

Chen, Chuansheng, and Harold W. Stevenson. 1995. "Motivation and Mathematics Achievement: A Comparative Study of Asian American, Caucasian American, and East Asian High School Students." *Child Development* 66: 1215–1234.

Dryfoos, Joy G. 1990. *Adolescents at Risk: Prevalence and Prevention*. New York: Oxford University Press.

———. 1994. *Full Service Schools: A Revolution in Health and Social Services for Children, Youth, and Families*. San Francisco: Jossey-Bass.

———.1998. *Safe Passage: Making It through Adolescence in a Risky Society*. New York: Oxford University Press.

Eccles, Jacquelynne S. 1991. "Academic Achievement." In *Encyclopedia of Adolescence*. Edited by Richard M.

Lerner, Anne C. Petersen, and Jeanne Brooks-Gunn. New York: Garland.

Fulgini, Andrew J., and Harold W. Stevenson. 1995. "Time Use and Mathematics Achievement among American, Chinese, and Japanese High School Students." *Child Development* 66: 830–842.

Graham, Sandra, April Z. Taylor, and Cynthia Hudley. 1998. Exploring Achievement Values among Ethnic Minority Early Adolescents." *Journal of Educational Psychology* 90, no. 4: 606–620.

Lerner, Richard M. In press. *Adolescence: Development, Diversity, Context, and Application.* Upper Saddle River, NJ: Prentice-Hall.

Midgely, Carol, Revathy Arunkumar, and Timothy C. Urdan. 1996. "'If I Don't Do Well There's a Reason': Predictors of Adolescents' Use of Academic Self-Handicapping Strategies." *Journal of Educational Psychology* 88, no. 3: 423–434.

Newcombe, Nora, and Judith S. Dubas. 1992. "A Longitudinal Study of Predictors of Spatial Ability in Adolescent Females." *Child Development* 63: 37–46.

Pong, Suet-Ling. 1997. "Family Structure, School Context, and Eighth-Grade Math and Reading Achievement." *Journal of Marriage and the Family* 59: 734–746.

Reynolds, Arthur J., and Judy A. Temple. 1998. "Extended Early Childhood Intervention and School Achievements: Age Thirteen Findings from the Chicago Longitudinal Study." *Child Development* 69: 231–246.

Academic Self-Evaluation

Academic self-evaluations are students' judgments of their abilities in school, their interpretations of their successes and failures in school, and their expectations about their school performances in the future. As many students reach the period of adolescence, their evaluations of their academic abilities and performances become more negative. In general, adolescents, compared with younger children, are less likely to feel highly competent in school, are more likely to believe that their failures in school cannot be changed, and are less likely to expect positive academic performance in the future. Many adolescents' self-evaluations continue to decline through the junior high and high school years.

Negative academic self-evaluations can have serious consequences for adolescents' school success. Adolescents who judge themselves negatively are less likely to try to learn new things, to aim for high levels of success, or to persist when confronted with major difficulties or failures in school. As a consequence, they may be unable to meet their full academic potential and experience an overall decline in their school achievement. Academic self-evaluations thus appear to be important determinants of adolescents' performance in school. Given that many students begin to fall behind in their school performance during adolescence, it's important to understand the specific changes that occur in students' academic self-evaluations during this age period.

These changes can be summarized as follows: (1) A decline occurs in adolescents' judgments of their abilities in school, (2) a decline occurs in adolescents' confidence that their abilities in school can be improved, and (3) adolescents become less likely to expect future academic successes. There are two major reasons why these changes occur during adolescence: because of changes in the structure of the school environment from elementary school to junior high school, and because of the messages that adolescents receive from parents and teachers about their abilities and performance in school. What follows is a more detailed discussion of the changes themselves and the reasons they occur during adolescence.

Changes in Adolescents' Academic Self-Evaluations

Students' academic self-evaluations are at their highest in the early elementary grades but decline steeply when the students enter junior high school—an observation explained in part by the fact that young children's ratings of their abilities tend to be unrealistically high to begin with. Even young children who are performing poorly in school have been known to rank themselves near the top of their class in ability. By adolescence, however, students' rankings of their abilities tend to be similar to their actual school performance. But not in all cases. The decline in adolescents' judgments of their abilities varies among boys and girls. There is evidence that girls' judgments of their abilities become lower than boys' judgments in such subject areas as math and science, whereas boys are considered to be more competent. There is also evidence that boys' judgments of their abilities become lower than girls' judgments in such subject areas as English and reading, whereas girls are considered to be more competent. These lower judgments occur even when boys and girls are performing equally.

The second change that occurs in academic self-evaluations during adolescence is that boys and girls begin to believe that their abilities in school cannot be improved. Unlike younger children, who believe that if they work very hard they can become smarter in school, adolescents believe that even working hard cannot improve or change their abilities in school. Adolescents are more likely than younger children to believe

that people are born with certain ability levels and that nothing can change this. Accordingly, many adolescents claim, for example, that working harder on their math assignments is a waste of time since it will not make them better at math.

The third change is that, compared with younger children, adolescents are less likely to expect academic successes in the future. Younger children are much more optimistic than adolescents about their chances of doing well in school. For instance, during elementary school, many students expect to do very well on their schoolwork, even if they have not done well in the past. Young children are thus apt to jump right into learning new things because they feel confident that they can do well. As students approach junior high school, however, they are more likely to dwell on their past failures or previous negative performance when considering how well they might do in the future. By adolescence, then, students are less likely to try learning new things in school because they are more pessimistic about their ability to do well.

Negative experiences can result from these three changes in students' academic self-evaluations. Some adolescents, for instance, may stop taking advanced-subject classes in school. (In particular, girls are less likely than boys to take advanced math or science classes because they do not believe they have the ability to do well in those subject areas.) Other adolescents may begin working less in school because they do not think hard work will improve their performance in school. And still others may stop pushing themselves to learn new things in school because they do not think the payoff is worth the effort. Further consideration of the reasons why adolescents' academic self-evaluations change may reveal how these school-related problems arise.

Influence of Junior High Schools on Adolescents' Academic Self-Evaluations

Several explanations exist for why negative changes in students' academic self-evaluations become particularly pronounced during adolescence. One of the most persuasive of these is that junior high schools typically do not provide an appropriate educational setting for adolescents to learn; they do not match the developmental changes that occur during adolescence. In short, many junior high schools, unlike elementary schools, are structured in ways that result in a poor "fit" between adolescents and their school settings, thus contributing to the decline in adolescents' academic self-evaluations. Some examples follow:

- Junior high schools are increasingly using practices, such as grouping students by ability level, that heighten the chances that adolescents will compare their abilities with others and become more competitive.
- They are increasingly using grading practices, such as assigning grades based on students' performances relative to others in the classroom, that focus adolescents' attention on their abilities in comparison to others rather than on learning and improving in school.
- They are increasingly using public methods for reporting on and recognizing performance, such as posting charts of students' progress on the wall and awarding prizes for the best grades, that heighten the chances that adolescents will compare their abilities with others.

Influence of Parents and Teachers on Adolescents' Academic Self-Evaluations

Another explanation for the decline in adolescents' academic self-evaluations is that students in this age period are beginning to pay attention to the messages that parents and teachers convey to them about their abilities and performances in school. When students reach adolescence, they become much better at understanding and interpreting the information they receive from others about their academic abilities and performances. (Younger children are not greatly influenced by others because they are not good at understanding the subtle messages that others may convey.) In addition, as students become better at understanding information, they are more likely to be influenced by the messages—subtle or explicit—that they receive from others. Parents and teachers convey a great deal of information to adolescents. Following are some examples of ways in which they may influence adolescents' academic self-evaluations:

- Parents' and teachers' beliefs about students' abilities in school can influence students' own evaluations of their abilities. For example, if a parent believes that the adolescent is good in math, then the adolescent is more likely to come to believe this, too. Among girls, the message may instead be that math is a subject area in which boys do better.
- Parents' and teachers' encouragement or discouragement can send

messages to students about their abilities in school. For example, if a teacher discourages students from taking an advanced math class, the message to the students is that math is just not their thing.

- If parents and teachers believe that students can improve through hard work, then the students are more likely to believe this as well. For example, if a teacher believes that ability is something that develops through hard work and improvement, then the students in the classroom are more likely to see their abilities in school as something they can change.
- Parents' and teachers' expectations of students' school performances in the future can influence students' own expectations. For example, if a parent believes that the adolescent will not do very well in math by the end of the school year, then the adolescent is likely to perform poorly in math during that school year.

Candice Dreves
Jasna Jovanovic

See also Academic Achievement; Cheating, Academic; Homework; Intelligence; Intelligence Tests; Learning Disabilities; Learning Styles and Accommodations; Self; Self-Esteem; Standardized Tests

References and further reading
Cain, Kathleen, and Carol Dweck. 1989. "The Development of Children's Conceptions of Intelligence: A Theoretical Framework." Pp. 47–82 in *Advances in the Psychology of Human Intelligence*, Vol. 5. Edited by R. J. Sternberg. Hillsdale, NJ: Erlbaum.
Dweck, Carol S. 1999. *Self-Theories: Their Role in Motivation, Personality,*
and Development. Philadelphia: Psychology Press/Taylor and Francis.
Eccles, Jacquelynne S., Sarah Lord, and Christy Miller Buchanan. 1996. "School Transitions in Early Adolescence: What Are We Doing to Our Young People?" Pp. 251–284 in *Transitions through Adolescence: Interpersonal Domains and Context*. Edited by Julie A. Graber and Jeanne Brooks-Gunn. Mahwah, NJ: Lawrence Erlbaum Associates.
Frome, Pamela M., and Jacquelynne S. Eccles. 1998. "Parents' Influence on Children's Achievement-Related Perceptions." *Journal of Personality and Social Psychology* 74: 435–452.
Martin, Carole A., and James E. Johnson. 1992. "Children's Self-Perceptions and Mothers' Beliefs about Development and Competencies." In *Parental Belief Systems: The Psychological Consequences for Children*. Edited by Irving E. Sigel, Ann V. McGillicuddy-DeLisi, and Jacqueline J. Goodnow. Hillsdale, NJ: Erlbaum.
Simpson, Sharon M., Barbara G. Licht, Richard K. Wagner, and Sandra R. Stader. 1996. "Organization of Children's Academic Ability-Related Self-Perceptions." *Journal of Educational Psychology* 88: 387–396.
Stipek, Deborah J., and Douglas Mac Iver. 1989. "Developmental Change in Children's Assessment of Intellectual Competence." *Child Development* 60: 521–538.
Wigfield, Allen, Jacquelynne Eccles, Douglas Mac Iver, David Reuman, and Carol Midgely. 1991. "Transitions at Early Adolescence: Changes in Children's Domain-Specific Self-Perceptions and General Self-Esteem across the Transition to Junior High School." *Developmental Psychology* 27: 552–565.

Accidents

The word *accident* is really a misnomer. An accident refers to an event that happens randomly or by chance, usually resulting in an injury. Accidents are almost never random events, and they are almost all preventable and therefore not in the strict sense accidental. The

Accidents are almost never random events and are often preventable. (Owen Franken/Corbis)

word *injury* is usually considered to be more appropriate when discussing the results of certain behaviors that are the leading cause of death and disability among adolescents.

Motor vehicle injuries are the most common injuries occurring among adolescents. Drivers who are intoxicated cause the vast majority of motor vehicle deaths. Alcohol is the most common intoxicant, but marijuana, cocaine, LSD, and other similar compounds are also used by teens, although not as extensively as alcohol. Deaths from motor vehicle incidents are not accidental, since the driver and usually the passengers know (when they are sober) that an intoxicated person should not drive. The use of alcohol or other intoxicating substances will affect all aspects of that person's brain

functioning. Teens are unaware of their significant functional impairment and will often think that they can function as though they were not impaired. In addition, many teens believe that they are invincible and that they can drink and drive and nothing will happen to them. (See discussion of personal fable below.)

Sports-related injuries are usually caused by not using the proper protective gear or by violating the rules of play and are thus not accidental. In some instances, sports-related injuries, especially from sports activities in a community-based program, are related to coaches or trainers who do not have adequate training or who ignore the rules of safety because they are only interested in winning.

Injuries are classified as either unintentional or intentional. Intentional injuries are homicide, suicide, and abuse. All other injuries are unintentional. Injury is sometimes defined as any disruption of the integrity of the body caused by transfer of energy from the environment (such as by electrical burns or by contact of a person's head with the windshield) or by the acute absence or excess of life-sustaining elements beyond normal human tolerance (such as the asphyxiation related to drowning or the hyperthermia of heat stroke).

Types and Frequency of Injury
Injuries are the most common cause for visits to the emergency department among adolescents, and account for the most days of school missed. Injuries are the second leading cause of hospitalization, after pregnancy.

There are about 2,500 fatal injuries each year in the ten- to fourteen-year age group (U.S. Government Printing Office, 1993). The three most common fatal injuries in this group are

1. Motor vehicle injury, either as occupant or pedestrian (as many boys as girls)
2. Homicide (twice as many boys as girls)
3. Suicide (four times as many boys as girls)

There are about 12,000 fatal injuries each year in the fifteen- to nineteen-year age group (U.S. Government Printing Office, 1993). The three most common injuries in this group are the same as in the younger group listed above. About one-third of fatal injuries in the older age group are caused by motor vehicles, and about one-third are related to homicide and suicide. There is considerable variability by racial/ethnic group. For instance, among

black males in the older adolescent group, homicide is the leading cause of fatal injury in large urban areas.

For nonfatal injuries among the ten- to thirteen-year age group, being struck or cut is the most common injury, followed by falls, sports-related injuries, and injuries involving use of a bike or skates. Among the fourteen- to seventeen-year age group, the most common nonfatal injuries are sports related, followed by other accidents, or cuts and falls.

The use of alcohol and other intoxicants account for the majority of motor vehicle injuries and for the majority of homicides. Although there has been a lot of publicity concerning firearm injuries among adolescents, these accounted for only 2.6 percent of all deaths among fifteen- to nineteen-year-olds (U.S. Government Printing Office, 1993).

Prevention
Most injuries are preventable. The use of common sense by adolescents would be the most effective prevention measure. Adolescents typically underuse their common sense (and many adults do, too). One proposed reason for the lack of use of common sense by adolescents relates to the concept of the personal fable, which suggests that adolescents believe they are invincible and that nothing bad can ever happen to them. This belief is based on their previous experience, which for the most part is consistent with the idea of the personal fable—nothing seriously bad has happened to the majority of adolescents. So when they have a few alcoholic drinks and are feeling good, they are sure that they can drive as well intoxicated as they can sober. However, this is far from the truth, since even the smallest amount of alcohol in one's system will impair all aspects of brain functioning.

Others have proposed another framework for injury prevention. This framework consists of the "Four E's": engineering, enforcement, economics, and education.

Engineering procedures are usually the most effective prevention measures. The best engineering measures are those that require the user to do nothing or to do something only once. They include airbags that deploy upon collision, safety belts that slide into place when the car doors close, resetting the thermostat on the hot water heater for the home to a lower, safer setting, and the like.

Enforcement measures. Enforcing the laws requires the legislature to pass laws and requires enforcement agencies to monitor situations and take corrective action. Passing laws, for example, prohibiting the use of portable phones while driving a car can be effective, but only if adolescents believe they cannot drive safely and talk at the same time. Enforcement also requires someone to monitor phone use during driving, to pursue the driver, issue a ticket, and collect the fine. Experience has shown that law enforcement agencies do not consider most injury prevention legislation as important, and therefore even when safety legislation has been passed it is not enforced.

Economic measures. The fine for speeding is one example of an economic measure. Another economic measure would be the loss of the person's driver's license. This punishment would force the adolescent to use public or other transportation or to have a parent drive her to various places, all of which would cause substantial losses of time and money for both teens and parents. It is not likely that legislation of this nature

would be passed. In some countries new drivers and drivers who are learning to drive must post a large sign on their vehicle indicating their driving status. This approach may also serve to reduce automobile injuries by alerting those around such a marked vehicle to be especially alert to the potential risk.

Education is the least effective prevention measure. Education would involve lecturing in organized settings such as the classroom. Adolescents would not enjoy being in this setting. They spend much of their time in school, so having to listen to someone talk about safety would not be high on their list of desired activities. If they were to be put in that setting, they would need to be motivated to pay attention, which is once again not likely to happen under most circumstances. They also might be likely to think that safety education will not be applicable to them because they are invincible, as brought out above in the discussion of the personal fable. Education requires skilled educators, and these are not readily available and are expensive to employ. Education also requires time, money, and a convenient place and time for the group to receive the information. It also requires frequent reinforcement in order to maintain safety behaviors. It is clear that programs that have been effective in reducing injury will have only short-term effects unless practice is provided on a regular basis. Providing written information about injury or as reinforcement also seems unlikely to have any effect. There is no evidence that educational programs have any long-term effect on reducing injuries.

The most effective approach to injury reduction seems to be that used in Sweden. This country organized a nationwide program to improve the safety of children and adolescents. A small group of concerned healthcare professionals decided that child and adolescent safety should be addressed, since injury was the leading cause of death and disability among children and youth. This group realized that all segments of society had to be represented if the program were to be successful. Therefore, they involved community groups such as religious organizations, political groups, educators, and social organizations, as well as individual citizens. These groups all became involved with the issue of child safety. By involving all possible groups in communities, they eliminated any objections to this program, since they were including those who might object. The organizers started locally, and their program eventually spread throughout this small, homogeneous nation. Over a period of ten years there was a very large reduction in the number of youth who were involved in, and died from, unintentional injuries.

Since unintentional injury can be prevented and is the leading cause of death among children and adolescents, it would seem appropriate to address this problem more comprehensively than we have done up to this time. It seems clear from the Swedish experience that it is possible to address the problem, but it would require an approach like that taken in Sweden. There are several organizations in the United States whose objectives are to reduce injury, but they have not been successful so far. The general public seems quite unconcerned about injury. The population in the United States is very diverse, and this diversity also puts up a substantial barrier to the success of national programs of any kind. To date,

there has been no long-term successful injury prevention program in the United States.

Jordan W. Finkelstein

See also Ethnocentrism; Personal Fable

References and further reading
Centers for Disease Control, http://www.cdc.gov
National Academy of Sciences. 1985. *Injury in America.* Washington, DC: National Academy Press.
U.S. Government Printing Office. 1993. *Injury Control.* Morbidity and mortality weekly reports. Reprints #733–260/80519.

Acne

Most teenagers suffer acne to some extent, but it is not usually permanently scarring. It seems to cause more psychological than physical problems since it comes at a time during adolescence when concern about appearance is strong. Teenagers should be assured that acne typically lasts only a few years and, in some cases, clears up within a few months. In addition, there are many treatments for acne that minimize appearance problems.

Although many believe that poor personal hygiene is a cause of acne, it is not a major factor. Greasy foods are also not responsible. Rather, common acne (*acne vulgaris*) is a disorder of the skin that involves the secretion of an oily substance (sebum) from the oil-secreting (sebaceous) glands within the pores. Acne starts at the time of sexual maturation (puberty) and is related to the increased production of sex hormones by the testes or ovaries. These hormones increase the secretion of oil that moves from within

Acne may cause psychological problems for adolescents who are concerned with their physical appearance. (Laura Dwight)

the pores to the surface of the skin. Most teens experience this change as an increase in oiliness on the skin—usually that of the face, but sometimes also on the upper chest or back. Under most circumstances, the oil flows freely from the pores and is removed when the skin is washed.

In some instances, however, the openings of pores on the skin surface become blocked. The oils cannot escape and are trapped within the pores. As the oil remains trapped, it gets thicker and stickier and undergoes a chemical reaction that changes it from a colorless substance to one that is dark brown or black when it is extended to the surface of the skin. This is called a blackhead. (Contrary to popular opinion, the dark color is not dirt

trapped in the pore.) If it is below the surface, it will appear as a whitehead. In most instances the blocked pore becomes unblocked by itself and acne does not progress. If the pore remains blocked or if a person tries to squeeze out the sticky oil, irritation around the pore may occur. In some instances this irritation will result in invasion of the blocked pore by the bacteria that always live on the skin. The infected pore then produces pus and become a cyst as the pus accumulates under the skin. If pressure builds up and the pore remains blocked, the pus may spread beneath the skin. In this case, the result is a swollen, red, hot bump beneath the skin. This condition is a severe form of acne that can result in skin scarring. It almost always requires medical treatment, often involving antibiotics applied to the skin, or taken orally, or both. Large, discolored acne that is spreading should be attended to immediately.

About 85 percent of teenagers get acne (Clayman, 1994), but researchers still cannot explain why some people get it and others do not. What they do know is that it is often worse in times of stress and during the hormone changes of the menstrual cycle.

There are many different treatments for acne. These do not include vigorous face washing, which may actually worsen acne. The following observations are important regardless of the treatment used.

First, no treatment will be effective until about four to six weeks after it is started, so teens are advised not to give up on a treatment before that time. Second, many treatments that are applied to the skin are themselves irritating and may make the skin more sensitive to sunburn. Third, as many treatments that are applied to the skin may make the skin more sensitive to sunburn, the teen should remain completely protected from the sun when using such treatments. Fourth, many treatments need to be applied gradually. For example, benzoyl peroxide (which is different from the same peroxide used for cleaning cuts) should initially be applied for two or three hours each day over several days. If irritation does not result, then it can be applied for three to four hours each day over several days, and so on until the full dose is achieved. If, however, significant irritation does occur, the frequency and time of application of the dose should be reduced. Fifth, an entire area of affected skin should be treated, rather than just individual pimples. And, sixth, different medications should not be applied to the

skin at the same time, as some may cancel the effects of others.

Some acne medications, such as benzoyl peroxide, can be purchased without a prescription and may be effective for simple blackheads. Pimples that are whiteheads or worse should be treated with prescription medications. More aggressive treatments such as antibiotic pills or creams also require a prescription, as does retinoic acid, which is the most potent and dangerous treatment to use. Although acne affects a majority of adolescents, no good prevention regimen is yet available.

Jordan W. Finkelstein

See also Appearance, Cultural Factors in; Appearance Management; Attractiveness, Physical; Body Image; Puberty: Hormone Changes; Puberty: Physical Changes; Puberty: Psychological and Social Changes; Self-Consciousness; Steroids

References and further reading
Berkow, Robert B., ed. 1997. *The Merck Manual of Medical Information: Home Edition.* Whitehouse Station, NJ: Merck Research Laboratories.
Clayman, Charles B., ed. 1994. *The American Medical Association Family Medical Guide*, 3rd ed. New York: Random House.

Adoption: Exploration and Search

One of the primary tasks of adolescence for adoptees is to begin to arrive at a sense of personal identity that includes their connections to both adoptive and birth families. Although the process of identity formation (figuring out who one is and how one is unique) takes place for every teenager, it is more complex for those who were adopted because they have two sets of parents—birth parents and adoptive parent(s). Thus, whereas a teenager probably knows a great deal about the family she has grown up in, she may know very little about the family and culture of her biological heritage. It is likely that her birth family differs from her adoptive family on any number of dimensions ranging from educational and financial to ethnic and racial.

During adolescence, adoptees typically become more curious about their birth parents and the circumstances of their birth and placement for adoption. This curiosity is common among teenagers who were adopted; indeed, it is a sign that they are undergoing the constructive process of growing up and figuring out who they are. But it can also create turmoil during the adolescent years, affecting not only the adoptee himself but also his parent(s) and other family members. One major task for adoptive families with adolescent children is the negotiation of openness and mutual support. Another is validation of (1) the adoptee's right to want more information and (2) the sturdy and enduring emotional bonds of the adoptive family.

As adolescents explore their personal identity, they ask themselves, "Who am I?" "Who do I want to be?" "What am I good at?" "Who am I like?" and "How am I different from other people?" Major changes take place during adolescence—changes in physical size and appearance, in ways of thinking about things, in beliefs and perspectives, and in the experience of emotions. Changes also occur in such dimensions as independence and choice, privileges and responsibilities, and relationships with friends and family. Both the rate of change and the number of dimensions involved present adolescents with reasons for frequent questioning of who they are, how other people see them, and what they want for themselves.

One starting point for comparing and contrasting themselves to others, in the attempt to answer these questions, is to look to their parents—to consider what they look like, what talents they have, what they aren't very good at, and what type of work they do. All teenagers look to their parents and their parents' lives to form a picture of themselves when they are older (e.g., in terms of height or body type) and what course their life might take (e.g., in terms of career, education, or income). In some respects they might hope to be like their parents, but in others they may look at their parents and make decisions about how they don't want to live (e.g., in terms of level of activity, socialization, work pressure, or confinement). Through this exploratory process of comparing and contrasting, choosing and rejecting various choices and characteristics, the adolescent gradually weaves together, or integrates, a sense of unique identity—one that encompasses similarities to, and differences from, his parents.

An adoptee has two sets of parents to which she compares and contrasts herself—adoptive parent(s) and birth parents. She may know her birth parents, or at least know many things about them (as in an *open adoption*), or she may know very little about them as people or about the circumstances of her birth and adoption (as in the more traditional *closed* or *confidential adoption*). In either case, adoptees frequently fill in the information they don't have with guesses or fantasies that answer their questions. These guesses and fantasies can be based on what they wish to be true, what they fear is true, or combinations of the two. Thus, although adolescents who were not adopted have many things to consider and wonder about regarding their personal identity, adoptees have even more to ponder and, typically, have fewer facts and less access to information to help them.

During adolescence, young people alternate between "trying on" different stances and beliefs about themselves, on the one hand, and revising their sense of identity as they discover how a particular stance "fits," on the other. For example, an adoptee might question how tall his birth parents were and seek information from his parents to find out if they know or will try to find out. If he gets the information, he may then use it to predict his own adult height and begin to get used to a picture of himself at that height. Similarly, an adoptee may wonder if his birth parents were irresponsible people in many areas of their lives because they conceived a baby that they later decided they could not care for as adequately as they might wish. He may experiment with acting irresponsibly as he is trying on an irresponsible identity to see if it fits him. He may be aware that he has these questions about what his birth parents were like, or he may be unaware that this questioning is taking place. If his irresponsibility is noticed by parents or other people he trusts, they may question him about why he has been acting in a way that is so unusual for him. Having his irresponsible behavior identified as uncharacteristic of him makes it more likely that he will realize it is not a part of his identity. He is then closer to establishing an identity for himself that confirms his sense of responsibility rather than irresponsibility. Questions about identity such as these, which never arose

during childhood, become very relevant to adoptees during adolescence.

Wanting to know the answers to such questions motivates adoptees to search for more information about their birth parents or the circumstances of their adoption. Between 1992 and 1993, researchers conducted a survey of 881 adolescent adoptees (the largest sample studied to date in the United States) between the ages of twelve and eighteen (Benson, Sharma, and Roehlkepartain, 1994). These adolescents were asked about their interest in their birth parents and their adoption history. Forty percent indicated that they would like to know more about their birth history. Fifty-three percent were curious about their birth mothers; and 46 percent, about their birth fathers. Sixty-five percent said they would like to meet their birth parents. There were gender differences: On each of these questions girls indicated more curiosity and interest than boys. Teenagers who were interested in meeting birth parents were also asked about their reasons. The following reasons were most common: to learn what the birth parents look like (94 percent); to let them know their birth child is happy (80 percent); to let them know their birth child is doing well (76 percent); to let them know their birth child is happy to be alive (73 percent); and to find out why the adoption took place (72 percent). Because there is reason to believe that the teenagers in this survey may have represented the most satisfied of adolescent adoptees, these statistics are evidence that an active interest in birth parents and preadoptive history is common and not associated with troubled adjustment. Yet there is no evidence that an adoptee who is not curious is less well adjusted than one who is. Adoptees can have a wide range of feelings and views on issues pertaining to their adoption, and they can be curious at some times and not at others.

The same study explored whether adoptees fantasized frequently about their birth parents, whether they missed or longed for them, and whether they wanted to live with them. On each of these questions, only 6 to 10 percent of the surveyed adoptees indicated frequent fantasies, strong longing, or frequent wishes to live with their birth parents, and, again, girls reported stronger feelings than boys did. In short, although many teenagers feel curious about their birth parents, a much smaller number experience a powerful pull toward their birth parents. This study, like others, concluded that the majority of adopted teenagers are doing well, do not have psychological problems, and are generally satisfied with themselves, their lives, and their families.

For some adolescent adoptees, however, these issues may involve turmoil and distress. Research has shown that if adoptees are going to experience emotional and behavioral troubles, these will most likely occur during adolescence (as opposed to childhood or adulthood). For some adoptive families, an adolescent's curiosity or wish to search for more information about birth parents, or for the birth parents themselves, represents a major crisis and challenge to the sense of emotional connection between the adoptive parents and their child. When such an event occurs, it is best understood as a struggle between the two generations over autonomy and control, or as a wish of each generation to be validated by the other one. It also may be related to a fear of rejection on the part of either the adoptive parents or the adolescent.

Alternatively, the adolescent may feel that his parents are attempting to bind him to them and deny his link to his birth family. He may feel that his parents are being unreasonably restrictive because they don't trust him as an adoptee to behave responsibly. Or he may be angry with them for their attempts to regulate his behavior through family ground rules (curfews, chores, expectations about grades, etc.) and fantasize that his birth parents would not do the same.

Just as the adolescent may be misinterpreting parental efforts to effectively structure her life and family routines, her parents may also be misinterpreting her expressed interest in her birth family. They may be confusing her drive to be independent with rejection of them and fear that they will lose her. Or they may be confusing her curiosity about the birth family side of her roots as a preference for the birth family over their family. Indeed, each generation may misunderstand and misinterpret the motives and messages of the other.

Adolescence is commonly a time of tension in families as the tasks of *separation-individuation* begin to be negotiated. The stakes can feel higher to both generations of an adoptive family. At times, each generation may wonder if the family ties will remain as emotionally close as the adolescent approaches adulthood and becomes more psychologically independent and physically separate (at college or working and living on his own) from his parents. This worry about losing their bond can be more unsettling to the equilibrium of an adoptive family than to that of a family with both biological and emotional ties.

Challenges to laws restricting adoptees' access to information about their birth parents have occurred since the 1970s. In several states, new laws have been passed that provide adoptees with sufficient information after age eighteen to make it possible to search for birth parents. A recent review of research on the experience of searching by adult adoptees pointed out that only a small minority of adoptees search (Haugaard, Schustack, and Dorman, 1998). Note, however, that because the searchers who have been studied form only a small subset of adoptees, the reactions to searching cited by this review, while informative, should not be considered applicable to all adoptees.

Among the searchers studied, thoughts of searching commonly began in late adolescence, although most searches did not occur until at least early adulthood. A review of studies done on searchers reveals that once they had crossed the legal hurdles to obtaining the information necessary for their search, most searchers reported that they found the search to be a positive experience.

Some patterns regarding searching have been suggested by the small collection of studies that have been conducted. For example, most searchers are female. Many searches occur around life-cycle transitions, such as the transition to becoming a parent oneself. Most adoptees report being pleased and relieved about the reunion (most commonly with their birth mother rather than their birth father). Most searchers inform their adoptive parents that they are searching. And, finally, the motivation for searching reported by most adult adoptees who have searched has to do with gaining a sense of one's roots or achieving a sense of identity.

Kristine Freeark

See also Abortion; Adoption: Issues and Concerns; Decision Making

References and further reading
Benson, Peter L., Anu R. Sharma, and Eugene C. Roehlkepartain. 1994. *Growing Up Adopted: A Portrait of Adolescents and Their Families.* Minneapolis, MN: Search Institute.
Brodzinsky, David M., and Marshall D. Schechter, eds. 1990. *The Psychology of Adoption.* New York: Oxford University Press.
Brodzinsky, David M., Daniel W. Smith, and Anne B. Brodzinsky. 1998. *Children's Adjustment to Adoption: Developmental and Clinical Issues.* Thousand Oaks, CA: Sage Publications.
Grotevant, Harold D. 1997. "Family Processes, Identity Development, and Behavioral Outcomes for Adopted Adolescents." *Journal of Adolescent Research* 12, no. 1: 139–161.
Grotevant, Harold D., Ruth G. McRoy, Carol L. Elde, and Deborah L. Fravel. 1994. "Adoptive Family System Dynamics: Variations by Level of Openness in the Adoption." *Family Process* 33: 125–146.
Haugaard, Jeffrey J., Amy Schustack, and Karen Dorman. 1998. "Searching for Birth Parents by Adult Adoptees." *Adoption Quarterly* 1, no. 3: 77–83.

Adoption: Issues and Concerns

Adoption of children by nonbiological parents has been practiced for years, and in the United States legal adoption has been available for over 150 years (Hundleby, Shireman, and Triseliotis, 1997). The 1960s marked an important transition in adoption, with the focus changing from the adoptive parents to the children and the biological mothers. The policies and practices prior to this time focused on finding healthy infants to be placed in terms of race, ethnicity, and other characteristics. Over the past thirty years, it is recognized that all children need permanent homes, regardless of

Three-year-old Brittany holds up a small toy with her ten-month-old brother, Ryan, from Korea, and their adoptive father. (Laura Dwight/Corbis)

their race, ethnicity, social background, or age; so children considered "hard to place" are being adopted in rising numbers. Further, the rights of the biological mothers are recognized in many states, and open adoption is an increasingly popular practice (Babb, 1999).

Many children who are adopted learn this fact from the adopted parents at young ages. However, it may not be totally understood until the children reach a level where they can comprehend the meaning and its implications. Often when the children become teens they not only want to know more about adoption but also have emotional reactions, which can take different directions. Adolescence is the time when one is forming a sense of identity, dealing with issues of independence, and self-determination, while, at the same time, being caught up in peer relations, school, and the need to plan for one's future (Rosenberg, 1992). Dealing with the reality of adoption may add stress, uncertainty, and self-doubts.

Teens who are placed in adoptive homes when they were infants or very young and who do not know anything about their biological families may well become very curious to learn who their birth parents were and may even want to meet them. However, others feel great anger for being "given up" as infants, thus stifling any desire to connect, which can cause emotional problems as well. Of course, increasing numbers of children are now adopted well after infancy and either knew or know about birth parents, siblings, and grandparents. Their way of dealing with the facts of adoption may be very different yet still pose challenges for them as well as their adoptive families and friends.

The current policies and practices that guide adoption, while still evolving, certainly are movements in the right direction. However, there are issues and challenges for all involved that must be taken into account when helping teens deal with adoption and the resulting consequences. Generally, a study by Dukette (1984) demonstrates the most common position taken today by those responsible for adoption. Birth parents generally provide the best opportunity for children's well-being, and attempts should be made to allow children to remain in the birth home, even if help in the form of counseling, finances, and court intervention is necessary. When this goal cannot be accomplished, other members of the biological family should be sought to provide a permanent home. When none is available, adoptive families are sought and can provide continuity in so far as possible in terms of racial, cultural, and national origin. Further, the birth mother (and sometimes, but not often, the father) should be recognized as an integral part of the arrangement as birth parental rights and open records are often incorporated into the adoption process.

Given this general view, it must be recognized that all types of variations in the approach to adoption are present in current practice. Adoptions placing children from different countries are now occurring regularly in the United States, in several European countries, as well as in many other countries throughout the world. Although issues are highly debated, there is evidence that children thrive even when their backgrounds and circumstances are very different from those of the adoptive parents (Moe, 1998).

The factors that make adjustment to adoption challenging for teens and young adults are considered next. One must first ask, how does the teen view the situation: what is seen as positive and what is seen as negative? In addition, the age that the adoption occurred must be considered critical; for those who are older, is it relevant to deal with what happened before adoption? Did he/she live with the biological family, in foster care, or in some other circumstances? What about health, schooling, and other crucial considerations? But most important—how does he/she deal with it all?

If the issue of searching for, finding, and then dealing with biological parents is significant, then one should facilitate this process after thinking about these five major factors to consider in beginning the search (Wegar, 1997).

- Desire and need for relevant medical history
- Need to know why he/she was adopted
- Desire to know what family members look like and what they do
- Need for continuity in the time of major transition that adolescence brings
- Longing to connect, to have roots, and a sense of generations

However, one may also have valid reasons for not undertaking, or participating in, a search for biological roots, including:

- Lack of expressed interest or even resentment

- Feeling of loyalty to adoptive parents
- Feeling that it is not the right thing to do
- Fear of possible rejection or uncovering negative information about the biological family

There is no right or wrong answer for searching; for some, it may be important to undertake it in adolescence, while others may decide to wait until adulthood.

For the teenager and the young adult who was adopted, there are specific tasks with which one must deal (Rosenberg, 1992). These can be summarized as follows:

- Dealing with genetic versus the psychological parts of oneself
- Recognizing and accepting different models of families as being okay
- Basing one's identity as an integration of biology and upbringing
- Re-creating ties with one's adoptive family, if biological family has been identified and contact established
- Dealing with one's adoption when creating one's own, new nuclear family

In today's world, adoption has become an accepted and highly effective way to deal with multiple issues in our society. Adoptive families should be encouraged and facilitated by their extended families and friends. It truly can be a win-win situation. Yes, there are pitfalls and challenges, but there are also many resources to facilitate the process and ensure success. In a society that is becoming ever more complex and one in which all of us are interdependent on so many aspects in order to function well, it is more impor-

tant than ever that every child, indeed every individual, have a family to call his/her own. The definition of family has broadened, and we must keep this in mind when comparing our families to those of peers, friends, and others. Adoptive families come in many forms but fit in harmoniously with "family" as defined and practiced in contemporary American life.

John W. Hagen
Joseph Solomon Dillard

See also Abortion; Adoption: Exploration and Search; Decision Making

References and further reading
Babb, Linda. 1999. *Ethics in American Adoption*. Westport, CT: Bergin and Garvey.
Dukette, Rita. 1984. "Values in Present-Day Adoption." *Child Welfare* 63, no. 3: 233–243.
Hundleby, Marion, Joan Shireman, and John Triseliotis. 1997. *Adoption: Theory, Policy, and Practice*. London: Cassell.
Moe, Barbara. 1998. *Adoption: A Reference Handbook*. Santa Barbara, CA: ABC-CLIO.
Rosenberg, Elinor B. 1992. *The Adoption Life Cycle*. New York: Free Press.
Wegar, Katarina. 1997. *Adoption, Identity, and Kinship*. New Haven, CT: Yale University Press.

African American Adolescents, Identity in

The study of identity formation in African American adolescents has long been a theoretical enterprise characterized by major shortcomings. Spencer's (1995) Phenomenological Variant of Ecological Systems Theory (PVEST) mitigates all of those shortcomings and provides an ideal framework from which to examine identity development. PVEST

Negative stereotypes, scarcity of positive role models, and the absence of culturally competent instruction and direction may hinder identity formation. (Shirley Zeiberg)

integrates a phenomenological perspective with Bronfenbrenner's ecological systems theory (1989), linking context with perception. In doing so, it allows us to capture and understand the meaning-making processes underlying identity development and outcomes (Spencer, 1995; Spencer, Dupree, and Hartmann, 1997). Determining how minority youth and community members view and comprehend family, peer, and social expectations and their prospects for competence and success is central to understanding resiliency and devising interventions that promote it, and thus, also revitalizes communities. PVEST consists of five components linked by bidirectional processes; it is a cyclic, recursive model that describes identity development

throughout the life course. Thus, it identifies processes for all members of communities; it is relevant when conceptualizing communities and its members from "the cradle to the coffin."

The first component, risk contributors, consists of factors that may predispose individuals for adverse outcomes. For urban minority youth, these include socioeconomic conditions, such as poverty; sociocultural expectations, such as race and sex stereotypes; and sociohistorical processes, including racial subordination and discrimination. Self-appraisal is a key factor in identity, and how minority youth view themselves depends on their perceptions of these conditions, expectations, and processes. Stress engagement refers to the actual experience of situations that challenge one's psychosocial identity and well-being. Experiences of discrimination, violence, and negative feedback are salient stressors for minority youth. In response, reactive coping methods are employed to resolve dissonance-producing situations. These include strategies to solve problems that can lead to both adaptive or maladaptive solutions. In addition, a solution may be adaptive in one context, such as neighborhood, and maladaptive in another, such as school. As coping strategies are employed, self-appraisal continues, and those strategies yielding desirable results for the ego are preserved. They become stable coping responses and, coupled together, yield emergent identities. These emergent identities define how individuals view themselves within and between their various contextual experiences: that is, these thematic responsive patterns show stability across settings and not just within families and neighborhoods.

The combination of cultural/ethnic identity, sex role understanding, and self- and peer appraisal all define one's identity. Identity lays the foundation for future perception and behavior, yielding adverse or productive life state outcomes manifested across settings. Productive outcomes include good health, positive and supportive relationships with neighbors and friends, high self-esteem, and effective motivation. The PVEST (thematic) framework recycles as one transitions across the life span (across multiple settings including community) and individuals encounter new risks and stressors, try different coping strategies, and redefine how they and others view themselves. For minority youth, the presence and engagement of structural racism poses severe risks for the learning of adaptive coping strategies and positive

outcomes with regard to individual and community-level health and well-being.

As noted, negative stereotypes, scarcity of positive role models, and the absence of culturally competent instruction and direction also serve to hinder identity formation. Exploration of different identities may not be an option for minority youth living in stressful environments, leading to greater identity foreclosure. Negative images of minorities in the media, coupled with a lack of portrayal in successful roles, create barriers to positive identity formation (Spencer and Markstrom-Adams, 1990).

The PVEST framework contributes an identity-focused cultural ecological perspective (ICE) on identity formation (Swanson and Spencer, 1995). In doing so, various theoretical positions, including psychosocial, ecological, self-organizational, and phenomenological models, are integrated with the emphasis on self-appraisal processes (Swanson, Spencer, and Peterson, 1998). This approach takes into account structural and contextual barriers to identity formation and their implication for psychological processes such as self-appraisal. Much of our work has focused on adolescence, when identity formation is a key developmental task. By the time of adolescence, African American and other minority youth have developed an awareness of white American values and standards of competence. They can begin to integrate their experiences with future expectations given their own values and those of the majority culture. Awareness of racial stereotypes and their own group membership has developed and plays a key role in identity formation. For minority adolescents, the contextual stressors associated with effects of structural racism are coupled with normative developmental stresses, such as family and independence issues, sex role definition, physical maturation, and desire to display competence. Identity and appraisal by self and others become key. For example, maturing African American males in particular may elicit negative responses, such as being perceived as threatening, which, in turn, may lead to more stressful encounters (Swanson and Spencer, 1995).

Identity development occurs in multiple contexts, including community, school, family, and peer relationships. Adolescents must transition between these contexts and find ways to integrate their various experiences within each of them. If the contexts are relatively compatible, these transitions can be placid; conversely, the transitions can yield dissonance-producing experiences. Thus, interventions designed to produce resilient identity formation must go beyond consideration of contextual stressors and take into account multiple contexts and how stressors in each context relate to one another.

In order to accomplish positive identity formation in minority adolescents, several factors must be facilitated; these include knowledge and approval of values from both majority and minority cultures, definition of gender and other forms of identity, self-esteem, a sense of competence, and healthy relationships with family and friends (Williams-Morris, 1996). Markstrom-Adams and Spencer (1990) highlight the importance of "perspective taking" in positive identity formation and suggest that identity intervention should address structural barriers that inhibit identity exploration. Additionally, Spencer, Harpalani, and Del'Angelo (in press) note two examples of identity intervention for different populations of African American adoles-cents: the Health Information Providers and Promoters (HIPP) Scholars program for marginally achieving students, and the Start-On-Success (SOS) Scholars program for special needs students. Both of these are applications of the PVEST framework and address the issues raised here.

Margaret Beale Spencer
Vinay Harpalani

See also African American Adolescents, Research on; African American Male Adolescents; Ethnic Identity; Identity

References and further reading
Bronfenbrenner, Urie. 1989. "Ecological Systems Theory." Pp. 187–248 in *Annals of Child Development.* Edited by Ross Vasta. Greenwich, CT: JAI Press.

Spencer, Margaret Beale. 1995. "Old Issues and New Theorizing about African American Youth: A Phenomenological Variant of Ecological Systems Theory." Pp. 37–70 in *Black Youth: Perspectives on their Status in the United States.* Edited by Ronald L. Taylor. Westport, CT: Praeger.

Spencer, Margaret Beale, David Dupree, and Tracy Hartmann. 1997. "A Phenomenological Variant of Ecological Systems Theory (PVEST): A Self-Organization Perspective in Context." *Development and Psychopathology* 9: 817–833.

Spencer, Margaret Beale, Vinay Harpalani, and Tabitha Del' Angelo. In press. "Structural Racism and Community Health: A Theory-Driven Model for Identity Intervention."

Spencer, Margaret Beale, and Carol Markstrom-Adams. 1990. "Identity Processes among Racial and Ethnic Minorities in America." *Child Development* 61: 290–310.

Swanson, Dena Phillips, and Margaret Beale Spencer. 1995. "Developmental and Contextual Considerations for Research on African American Adolescents." In *Children of Color: Research, Health and Public Policy Issues.* Edited by Hiram E. Fitzgerald,

Barry M. Lester, and Barry S. Zuckerman. New York: Garland.

Swanson, Dena Phillips, Margaret Beale Spencer, and Anne Petersen. 1998. "Identity Formation in Adolescence." Pp. 18–41 in *The Adolescent Years: Social Influences and Educational Challenges. Ninety-Seventh Yearbook of the National Society for the Study of Education—Part 1*. Edited by Kathryn Borman and Barbara Schneider. Chicago: University of Chicago Press.

Williams-Morris, Ruth S. 1996. "Racism and Children's Health: Issues in Development." *Ethnicity and Disease* 6: 69–82.

African American Adolescents, Research on

African American adolescents are highly marginalized in U.S. society—an outcome exacerbated by four major conceptual defects that historically have characterized scholarship and research on this group. First, African American adolescents are often studied as isolated entities, without regard for the larger context in which they are growing, maturing, and developing. Numerous manifestations of symbolic and structural racism, economic hardships, and related barriers often characterize the environments encountered by African American adolescents. These factors compound the normative developmental stressors experienced by African American youth, such as physical and social maturation and peer pressure.

The second major shortcoming that characterizes scholarship on African American youth is a highly deficit-oriented perspective. From this perspective, African American youth are viewed as pathological products of oppression (e.g., Kardiner and Ovesey, 1951), and only the negative outcomes attained by these youth are studied. It is a perspective that ignores the resilience of those who do succeed despite tremendous barriers. Resilience among low-income African American youth is little studied and often misunderstood (e.g., Fordham and Ogbu, 1986). More research on this aspect is sorely needed. From the perspective of intervention, the identification and enhancement of resiliency-promoting factors are particularly important, since the structural forces that create and maintain racism are not likely to change significantly in the near future.

The third major flaw in theorizing about African American adolescents is the lack of a developmental perspective. Too often, these youth are viewed and treated as miniature adults. Outside of academia, this is readily observable in the criminal justice system. Indeed, whereas European American youth experiencing problems of psychological adjustment are often referred to mental health services, African Americans are usually placed in the criminal justice system (Spurlock and Norris, 1991).

The fourth flaw is a general lack of cultural understanding and competence in scholarship on African American youth. African American adolescents often grow up in a context of unique family structure and cultural practices, many of which are simply not understood by white American society.

Multiple sources of stress and dissonance characterize the experiences of African American adolescents as they begin the process of self-definition. Negative stereotypes, scarcity of positive role models, lack of competent cultural instruction and direction, and problems associated with low socioeconomic status and high-risk neighborhoods all interact to form complex barriers for these youth. Yet, as noted, many succeed in spite of these barriers.

New theoretical perspectives and empirical work have begun to shed light on the developmental experiences of African American adolescents. For example, Margaret B. Spencer's (1995) Phenomenological Variant of Ecological Systems Theory, or PVEST (see "African American Adolescents, Identity in"), provides an ideal framework in which to analyze all of these processes. PVEST affords the opportunity to examine both positive and negative coping processes and their relevance for life outcomes. Additionally, Harold C. Stevenson (1997) provides an example of culturally competent empirical research on the experiences of African American adolescent males. Stevenson describes how African American youth are "missed" and "dissed" by mainstream American society, and how this treatment relates to African American youth becoming "pissed" and managing their anger. Black youth are "missed" when stereotypical media-based images distort the meanings of their social and affective displays—usually in negative terms. And, as a result, these unique cultural displays are devalued and viewed with insolence—"dissed." In conjunction with such misrepresentations, many African American youth reside in high-risk contexts where anger display may be an appropriate coping mechanism. Indeed, anger may become a form of competence for social and emotional viability in certain high-risk contexts. Hence, misrepresentation, disrespect, and hazardous contextual factors interact in creating the anger of African American youth. Stevenson's findings suggest that fear of adverse outcomes may diminish expressions of anger, though not feelings of anger. However, his data further indicate that this relationship may not hold in

Experiences of discrimination, violence, and negative feedback are salient stressors for African American youth. (Laura Dwight)

high-risk contexts, which may necessitate mitigation of fear and displays of anger.

Developmental issues pertinent to African American female adolescents should also be researched in a culturally competent manner. An example of such work is the study of body image conducted by S. Parker and colleagues (1995), who found that African American adolescent females typically do not aspire to an ideal body image but, rather, tend to promote the individual desirable features that they already possess. In contrast, many white adolescent females aspire to the so-called Barbie-doll image. Parker's work has obvious implications for devising and implementing culturally competent interventions and programs for African American female adolescents.

If scholarship on African American adolescents is to capture their real-life circumstances, it must (1) take into account the social, political, and economic contexts in which these youth develop; (2) examine both positive and negative outcomes and the processes involved in attaining these outcomes; (3) take a developmentally sensitive perspective by viewing African American youth as adolescents undergoing normative developmental processes under stressful conditions rather than as miniature adults; and (4) make an effort to understand the cultural meaning of these adolescents' behaviors and contexts.

Margaret Beale Spencer
Vinay Harpalani

See also African American Adolescents, Identity in; African American Male Adolescents; Ethnic Identity; Identity

References and further reading

Fordham, Signithia, and John U. Ogbu. 1986. "Black Students' School Success: Coping with the Burden of 'Acting White.'" *Urban Review* 18, no. 3: 176–206.

Kardiner, Abram, and Lionel Ovesey. 1951. *The Mark of Oppression.* Cleveland: World Publishing Company.

Parker, S., Mark Nichter, Mimi Nichter, Nancy Vuckovic, C. Sims, and Cheryl Ritenbaugh. 1995. "Body Image and Weight Concerns among African American and White Adolescent Females: Differences That Make a Difference." *Human Organization* 54, no. 2: 103–113.

Spencer, Margaret Beale. 1995. "Old Issues and New Theorizing about African American Youth: A Phenomenological Variant of Ecological Systems Theory. Pp. 37–70 in *Black Youth: Perspectives on Their Status in the United States.* Edited by Ronald L. Taylor. Westport, CT: Praeger.

Spurlock, Jeanne, and Donna M. Norris. 1991. "The Impact of Culture and Race on the Development of African Americans in the United States." *American Psychiatric Press Review of Psychiatry* 10: 594–607.

Stevenson, Harold C. 1997. "Missed, Dissed, and Pissed: Making Meaning of Neighborhood Risk, Fear, and Anger Management in Urban Black Youth." *Cultural Diversity and Mental Health* 3, no. 1: 37–52.

African American Male Adolescents

The experiences of African American males are indications of larger societal issues such as racial and economic diversity in the United States. The adolescent period is arguably the most crucial period for teens to integrate adolescent themes of identity and psychological development to how these youth make meaning of how one is incorporated into an adult world. For African American adolescent males, like all youth, adolescence is a period of experimentation with many roles in life. However, because of economic restraints, many poor African American males experience barriers to full opportunity for developing positive social and personal roles (Cunningham, 1999). African American males are 30 percent of the child and adolescent populations (U.S. Census Bureau, 1999), and a significant number of the teens are growing up in households with family incomes below $20,000 per year. Thus, a description of the boys' situations must include issues regarding the socioeconomic status of their families as well as available neighborhood and school resources to promote and nurture healthy psychological development.

Accordingly, examining adolescent behaviors on multiple ecological or environmental contexts (e.g., schools, neighborhoods, and social settings) is necessary. One important micro-level variable to examine was that of the peer group. The peer group provides the setting and the means by which youth achieve several of the developmental tasks of middle and late adolescence. This social group gives youth practice in learning a social personality and a means for learning how to express themselves in socially acceptable ways with their peers. Too often discussions regarding African American male adolescents are centered on negative consequences and experiences of school failure, delinquency, and psychopathology. Much of the available empirical research studies regarding peer group influences on African American males focus on a link to problem behaviors. In the few studies that focused on African American adolescents, researchers have noted that academic success was positively linked to peers who valued education (Taylor, 1996). Also, researchers have stressed that adolescents who do well in school have more achievement-oriented friends and are less likely to be involved in problem behaviors associated with economically poor environments (Brook, Gordon, Brook, and Brook, 1989). However, parents and significant adults are still important during adolescence (Spencer, Dupree, Swanson, and Cunningham, 1996). The research reported by Spencer and her colleagues emphasized that adolescents reported that their parents and other significant adults (extended kin or teachers) were the most important people to talk to about problems experienced by youth.

African American males are aware of potential resources and barriers as well (Cunningham, 1999). Especially during late adolescence, many youth exhibit exaggerated coping strategies such as exaggerated male bravado and school disengagement. Unlike younger children, adolescent experiences are not as sheltered and protected by parents and significant adults. Many youth become more socially mobile and their interpretation of supports and barriers are heavily influenced by their environments. For example, Cunningham's study indicated that older adolescents were more aware that they have increased chances of becoming a victim of a violent crime and that they were exposed to potential health risks associated with membership in high-risk neighborhoods compared to the reports from younger adolescents.

As adolescents develop and are exposed to independent ideas about how males should behave, they have an awareness of opportunities and barriers associated with young males. Often the outcomes exhibited can be viewed as coping responses to an unsafe environment. An exaggerated male bravado style may be adopted to ensure safeness in one's neighborhood, but the same behavior may be detrimental in a school environment. Apathy regarding school engagement and negative workforce experiences may be linked to living in economically poor neighborhoods. Absent from many of the studies is a connection between the experiences in public places to individual proactive and protective coping strategies. Many young males who grow up in challenging environments develop ways of dealing with racial and gender antagonism in healthy ways (Stevenson, 1997). In one environment the behaviors exhibited may appear to be an exaggeration of male behaviors. However, when viewed within a social context the behaviors can be understood as a way of dealing with daily hassles and stress associated within a neighborhood social context.

Potential intervention and prevention programs must be adolescent specific. They must address issues faced by males generally, and also highlight specific behaviors and attitudes that are associated with the experiences of African American culture and neighborhood contexts. Recently, researchers have noted that manhood development is quite important for adolescent males. An emphasis is directed toward a culturally conscious reconstruction of gender. Watts and Abdul-Adil (1997) state that young males must develop sociopolitically as well as personally. Accompanying basic adolescent cognitive maturation, programs for African American males must include critical consciousness training to help boys understand how social disparity is associated with oppression. Watts and Abdul-Adil have developed an intervention named the Young Warriors Program. One important aspect of the program is that it incorporates training for traditional educational workers as one aspect of its goals. A dual emphasis is placed on individuals and the social context of adults who work with the young males. Young males and adults are involved in discussions and activities regarding social issues that are related to growing up in a race-conscious society.

Lastly, programs for young males must be developmental specific. Successful programs for thirteen-year-olds may not be successful for seventeen-year-olds. Younger adolescent experiences are more influenced by cognitive appraisal processes such as adolescent egocentrism and personal fable. Older adolescents are more socially mobile and normally have more direct experiences with interpreting their environments independently. As young males develop abstract cognitive processing associated with early adolescence, awareness of concrete circumstances are more evident in older youth (Cunningham, 1999). Thus, program efforts must be adjusted accordingly.

Michael Cunningham

See also African American Adolescents, Identity in; African American Adolescents, Research on; Ethnic Identity; Identity

References and further reading
Brook, Judith S., Ann. S. Gordon, Adam Brook, and David W. Brook. 1989. "The Consequences of Marijuana Use on Intrapersonal and Interpersonal Functioning in Black and White Adolescents." *Genetic, Social, and General Psychology Monographs* 15: 351–369.
Cunningham, Michael. 1999. "African American Adolescent Males' Perceptions of Their Community Resources and Constraints: A Longitudinal Analysis." *Journal of Community Psychology* 5: 569–588.
Spencer, Margaret B., David Dupree, Dena P. Swanson, and Michael Cunningham. 1996. "Parental Monitoring and Adolescents' Sense of Responsibility for Their Own Learning: An Examination of Sex Differences." *Journal of Negro Education* 65: 30–43.
Stevenson, Howard C. 1997. "Managing Anger: Protective, Proactive, or Adaptive Racial Socialization Identity Profiles and African American Manhood Development." Pp. 35–62 in *Manhood Development in Urban African-American Communities.* Edited by R. J. Watts and R. Jagers. New York: Hawthorne Press.
Taylor, Ronald. 1996. "Kinship Support, Family Management, and Adolescent Adjustment and Competence in African-American Families." *Developmental Psychology* 32: 687–695.
U.S. Census Bureau. 1999. *Current Population Survey*, Racial Statistics Branch, Population Division.
Watts, Roderick J., and Jaleel K. Abdul-Adil. 1997. "Promoting Critical Consciousness in Young, African-

American Men." Pp. 63–86 in *Manhood Development in Urban African-American Communities.* Edited by R. J. Watts and R. Jagers. New York: Hawthorne Press.

Aggression

Aggression, in the sense of hostile or injurious behavior, can be a serious problem in adolescence. It is difficult to deal with an established pattern of aggression in adolescence, and therefore it is important to take action early.

All children from time to time display aggression, beginning in late infancy. By the preschool years, two general types of aggression can be observed. Instrumental aggression is the most common, and it is seen when children want an object, privilege, or space, and they push, yell at, or attack a person who impedes their goal. Hostile aggression is a more serious form of aggression—here the intent is to hurt another person. Hostile aggression can be overt, taking the form of direct harm or threat of harm to another person. Relational aggression is a type of hostile aggression that can be seen in rumor spreading, damaging another person's reputation, or social exclusion.

Aggression is quite common in our society. Although forms of aggression are seen in most children from time to time, aggressive behavior is seriously problematic in only a few children. When aggression in children goes untreated, it seems to increase with the onset of puberty, especially in young men. By midadolescence homicide is the third leading cause of death for all young men and the leading cause of death for young black men.

Aggression among adolescents is considered to be a significant problem by most adults. Forty-nine percent of boys and 28 percent of girls in the eighth through tenth grades report having been in at least one fight involving physical aggression or a weapon during a one-year period. Eighty percent of siblings engage in violence toward each other, with higher rates in boys, especially those without sisters (Tieger, 1980).

Adolescents are perpetrators in 24 percent of crimes involving violence that lead to an arrest. Fifty-two percent of those arrested for homicide and nonnegligent manslaughter in 1990 were younger than twenty-five years of age and 15 percent were younger than eighteen years. For youths younger than eighteen, the rate of murder charges has increased dramatically in recent years. Although these statistics suggest that aggression is increasing among adolescents, violent aggression in the school setting has actually been decreasing during the 1990s (Berk, 1999).

As indicated above, there are observed differences between the sexes in aggression. Psychologists have speculated for quite some time why these differences appear. Twenty-five years ago psychologists Eleanor Maccoby and Carol Jacklin reviewed the research on aggression and suggested that (1) boys and girls do not differ in "real" aggression (by which they mean aggressive impulses or feelings) but only in the behavioral forms (verbal, physical) by which they express aggression, (2) the sexes are reinforced for different forms of aggression—physical aggression in boys and verbal aggression in girls, and (3) aggression is less acceptable and is more actively discouraged in girls—girls themselves have more anxiety about aggression and have greater inhibition about aggression. Maccoby and Jacklin also argued that aggression might be predominantly influenced by biology—by the presence of sex hormones.

That is, they thought that testosterone might be responsible for physical aggression in males. At that time, many researchers disputed this link between biology and aggression, believing that aggression was more likely to be learned. Today, most scholars agree that the causes of aggression are complex, with many factors potentially responsible. To place blame solely on hormones would be inaccurate, since all boys do not display aggressive tendencies.

However, research since that time has revealed that there is an association between plasma testosterone and self-reports of physical and verbal aggression. Elizabeth Susman and her colleagues have also found that there is a positive relationship between certain aggressive attributes (such as acting-out behaviors) and certain hormones (androstenedione) for boys, but not for girls.

The causes for the development of aggressive behavior are not at all clear. What is clear is that there cannot be a single cause for this phenomenon. It cannot be just nature (genetic inheritance) or just nurture (environment). It must be both. Recent studies suggest that exposure of adolescents to violence portrayed in the various forms of the media may play a role in development of aggression. American television shows many violent behaviors with little apparent physical harm to the victims. This is especially prominent in cartoons, where characters suffer injuries, which in real life would be fatal, yet get up and go about their business as if nothing had happened. The connection between media violence and aggressive behavior in children and teenagers is convincing. Over 1,000 studies suggest that exposure to TV violence can increase the likelihood of aggressive or antisocial behavior, especially in boys

and men. One message promoted by TV is that even the good guys can use violence to solve problems.

In the United States, 82 percent of programs contain at least some violence (Wright et al., 1994). In fact, in children's programming, the rate of violent acts per hour is greater than it is for adult prime-time programming. Highly aggressive children have an appetite for violent television, and as they watch more, they are more likely to resort to aggressive ways to resolve problems. This sort of pattern leads to serious antisocial acts by adolescence and young adulthood. In addition, it seems that violence on TV hardens children to aggression, making them more tolerant of it in real situations.

Other longitudinal and cross-sectional observational studies suggest that aggressive behaviors in children and adolescents are learned early and increase with age. The family can be a training ground for aggressive behaviors to develop (Berk, 1999). Children who are hard to handle may create an atmosphere of conflict and stress in the family. This situation can lead to a cycle of anger and punitiveness, which is then modeled by the child against the parents and others as the child imitates the parents' attitudes and behaviors. Of course, not all hard-to-handle or difficult children will create this pattern; whether they do or not depends on parenting stress and discipline techniques. When parents are stressed they tend to discipline more harshly, leading children to view the world as a hostile place. Once children view the world from this perspective, they may expect others to act in violent ways, setting the stage for their own aggressive assaults.

Boys are reported to be more physically aggressive and girls more verbally aggressive. Unfortunately, this finding comes out of studies that have focused primarily on behaviors and did not include an evaluation of the biological factors that may be related to aggression. Hormones, especially testosterone, have been extensively studied in animal models of aggression and among adult men, because aggression seems to be more common among adult men than women. Testosterone was considered to be the aggression hormone. Until recently, none of the hormone/aggression studies were conducted on children or adolescents.

There is now substantial evidence that the hormones to which a developing fetus is exposed while in the mother's uterus may play a significant role in the development of the brain. These hormone effects in the fetus organize the fetus's brain so that by the time of birth a certain pattern of behavior is programmed in the child's brain. We know that there are sex differences in this organizing function, because boys behave differently from girls even in infancy and childhood. There are also clear anatomical differences between boys' and girls' brains. There is also evidence in adolescents demonstrating a relationship between the physical secondary sexual developmental changes of puberty, or the concentration of testosterone, and aggressive behaviors. The effects of natural increases of hormones at puberty are called activating hormone effects. The pubertal increase in these hormones acts together with the fetal organizing effects of these same hormones and with the individual adolescent's environment to produce a behavioral pattern, including an aggressive behavioral pattern. All but one of the studies of this phenomenon were observational and used correlational analyses, limiting conclusions regarding cause and effect.

One recent study was conducted over a twenty-one-month period, during which the hormones that cause pubertal physical sexual development were administered to a group of boys and girls who needed treatment with these hormones. The girls were given estrogen hormones to help development of breasts, uterus, and vagina, and the boys were given testosterone to increase the development of penis and pubic hair. There were small but significant increases in physically aggressive behaviors and aggressive impulses reported during the administration of estrogen hormones to girls, as well as during the administration of testosterone to boys. There were no increases in verbally aggressive behaviors. The study suggests that pubertal hormones play some role in the development of aggressive behaviors during adolescence. The increases in aggressive behaviors were significant but small, and they were probably not enough to get any of these adolescents into significant trouble in school or with the juvenile justice system.

The findings that hormone effects on aggressive behavior are small suggests that social and environmental factors probably play a much more significant role for those relatively few adolescents whose aggression gets them in trouble. Other recent studies demonstrate that many unwanted behaviors among adolescents are contagious. The theory suggests that living among others, particularly peers, who engage in antisocial, aggressive, or violent behaviors predisposes adolescents to behave like their contacts (Berk, 1999).

Highly aggressive children do end up with serious adjustment problems. Their peers frequently reject them, they do poorly or fail in school, and they are likely to seek out deviant peers groups for companionship. It is essential for parents to seek treatment for highly aggressive children; if left untreated, severe aggression can lead to delinquency and adult criminality. One way to help the aggressive child is to promote less hostile and more effective interaction and discipline styles. Children need to learn positive and nonconfrontational ways to solve problems at a young age—they can then take these strategies into the peer group. Helping children to take the perspective of others and empathize with them (share their feelings) has been a useful way to give children positive, nonviolent strategies to solve conflicts.

When aggression is not managed in the young child, it is likely that the child will develop into an aggressive adolescent. Management of behavior in aggressive adolescents is more difficult, and in fact it is unclear whether it is possible at all. To a great extent this difficulty is related to the complex nature of aggressive behavior and to our incomplete understanding of the causes of significant aggression. It has been suggested that once aggressive behavior is learned, it is quite resistant to modification (which is why it is important to break the cycle early in the aggressive child's life). A large variety of interventions—including both behavioral and biological—in individual and group settings have been tried, with no real demonstrations of long-term reduction in aggressive behaviors in humans. Lessons from studies of other complex behaviors suggest that the most effective approach to any behavioral change must involve multiple techniques (both biological and behavioral) and must be continued for many years, if not for a lifetime.

Jordan W. Finkelstein

See also Alcohol Use, Risk Factors in; Bullying; Conduct Problems; Conflict and Stress; Emotions; Juvenile Crime; Risk Behaviors; Storm and Stress; Violence; Youth Gangs

References and further reading

Berk, Laura. 1999. *Infants, Children, and Adolescents*, 3rd ed. Needham Heights, MA: Allyn and Bacon.

Maccoby, Eleanor, and Carol Jacklin. 1974. *The Psychology of Sex Differences.* Stanford, CA: Stanford University Press.

Olweus, Dan, Ake Mattsson, Daisy Schalling, and Hans Low. 1988. "Circulating Testosterone Levels and Aggression in Adolescent Males: A Causal Analysis." *Psychosomatic Medicine* 50: 261–272.

Patterson, Gerald, J. Reid, and Thomas Dishion. 1992. *Antisocial Boys.* Eugene, OR: Castalia.

Susman, Elizabeth, Gale Inoff-Germain, Editha Nottleman, D. Lynn Loriaux, Gordon Cutler, and George Chrousos. 1987. "Hormones, Emotional Dispositions, and Aggressive Attributes in Young Adolescents." *Child Development* 58: 1114–1134.

Tieger, Todd. 1980. "On the Biological Bases of Sex Differences in Aggression." *Child Development* 51: 943–963.

Wright, John, Aletha Huston, Alice Reitz, and Suwatchara Piemyat. 1994. "Young Children's Perceptions of Television Reality: Determinants and Developmental Differences. *Developmental Psychology* 30: 229–239.

Alcohol Use, Risk Factors in

The vast majority of adolescents in the United States have used alcohol by the time they reach their senior year in high school. Although the large number of adolescents using alcohol prior to the legal age of twenty-one years is, in itself, a concern to society, of even greater concern is the mortality associated with adolescent alcohol use. Indeed, alcohol use is associated with the three most common forms of adolescent mortality: accidental deaths (e.g., fatal automobile accidents), homicides, and suicides.

Variability in drinking patterns is associated with different levels of health risk. Heavy or "binge" drinkers—defined as those who have had five or more drinks on a single occasion at least once in the last two weeks—incur the highest risk. Heavy drinking has been reported at alarmingly high rates among adolescents; according to one study, 36 percent of male twelfth graders qualify as binge drinkers (Johnston, O'Malley, and Bachman, 2000). Binge drinking among adolescents is associated with higher rates of drinking and driving, riskier sexual activity (e.g., lower level of condom use), more delinquent or antisocial behavior, and heavier use of other substances (e.g., marijuana or cocaine). It is also associated with a broad range of alcohol-related problems, including missing school because of drinking, having fights with parents about drinking, getting into trouble with legal authorities, and passing out from drinking.

National survey data on adolescent alcohol use have indicated several consistent trends. First, approximately 80 percent of high school seniors report using alcohol at some point during their lifetime. Second, whereas the average age of first use of alcohol was 17.4 years in 1987, it decreased to 15.9 years in 1994 (Office of National Drug Control Policy, 1997), indicating that teens are initiating alcohol use at an increasingly earlier age. This trend is of concern because an earlier age of initiation to drinking has been associated with substantially increased risk for the subsequent development of serious alcohol problems. Furthermore, earlier initiation to alcohol use may be disruptive to the successful resolution of age-appropriate developmental tasks that adolescents face, such as the fostering of

personal identity and the establishment of constructive peer relations. Third, the rate of heavy episodic drinking has increased over time, albeit moderately. According to a survey conducted in 1995, over one-third (36.9 percent) of senior males and almost one-fourth of senior females (23 percent) reported consuming five or more alcoholic beverages on at least one occasion in the two-week period preceding the survey assessment (Johnston, O'Malley, and Bachman, 2000). Fourth, the rate of lifetime use by boys and girls is highly similar, although boys are likely to consume alcohol more frequently and at higher levels. And, fifth, African American and Asian American adolescents exhibit the lowest rates of lifetime alcohol use, whereas Native American, Caucasian, and Hispanic adolescents exhibit the highest rates.

As noted previously, alcohol use is associated with the three most common causes of adolescent mortality—accidental deaths, homicides, and suicides. For instance, nine out of ten teenage automobile accidents involve the use of alcohol, and, on average, eight adolescents a day die in alcohol-related automobile crashes. In addition, heavy alcohol use by adolescents has been associated with a three- to fourfold increased risk of suicide attempts in comparison with adolescents who abstain from using alcohol. The disinhibiting effects of consuming alcohol have also been associated with impaired judgment, which in turn contributes to increased risky sexual activity and to earlier onset and combined use of other substances such as marijuana and cocaine (i.e., to a pattern of polydrug use). The number of adverse consequences associated with heavier alcohol use by adolescents is a major concern. For example, research indicates that among adolescents who drink, 12 percent drank before school, 16 percent got into a fight or argument with someone that they did not know while drinking, 29 percent passed out from drinking, and 47 percent reported doing things while drinking that they regretted the next day (Windle, 1999).

Of course, not all adolescents consume alcoholic beverages at high levels. A large number of variables have been identified that distinguish those adolescents who are more likely to drink alcohol and to have alcohol-related problems from those who are less likely. These variables are called risk factors because they reflect an increased probability of alcohol use at abusive levels. First, children with a biological parent who is an alcoholic are approximately four times more likely to develop an alcohol disorder at some point in their lifetime than children who do not have an alcoholic parent. Researchers are currently attempting to identify the genes involved in this increased family risk. Second, biologically influenced temperament and personality characteristics such as high activity level (e.g., fidgetiness, difficulty sitting still) and high sensation-seeking level (e.g., thrill seeking) are associated with higher levels of alcohol use and related problems. Third, cognitive factors such as alcohol expectancies (e.g., the belief that alcohol will make one more sociable and acceptable to peers) are associated with higher levels of alcohol use and have been shown to predict increases in alcohol use from childhood to adolescence. Fourth, higher levels of family cohesion and emotional closeness, parental warmth, parent-adolescent communication, and parental monitoring (e.g., establishing guidelines for adolescent behavior, knowing the whereabouts of one's adolescent) have been linked to

lower levels of adolescent alcohol use. Fifth, youthful drinking appears to be enhanced by media sources that glamorize alcohol use, conveying the message that those who drink will be more popular with friends and with dating partners. And, sixth, age-related drinking laws have been found to affect alcohol consumption by adolescents. These laws make it illegal for minors (under age twenty-one) to purchase or consume alcohol; however, there is wide variability across communities in their enforcement with regard to penalties for adolescents themselves and for establishments (e.g., bars) that sell alcohol to minors.

Michael Windle
Rebecca C. Windle

See also Aggression; Alcohol Use, Trends in; Drug Abuse Prevention; Nutrition; Peer Pressure; Peer Victimization in School; Risk Behaviors; Substance Use and Abuse; Violence

References and further reading
Boyd, Gale M., Jan Howard, and Robert A. Zucker, eds. 1995. *Alcohol Problems among Adolescents: Current Directions in Prevention Research.* Hillsdale, NJ: Erlbaum.
Hawkins, J. David, Richard F. Catalano, and Janet Y. Miller. 1992. "Risk and Protective Factors for Alcohol and Other Drug Problems in Adolescence and Young Adulthood: Implications for Substance Abuse Prevention." *Psychological Bulletin* 112: 64–105.
Jessor, Richard, and Shirley L. Jessor. 1977. *Problem Behavior and Psychosocial Development.* New York: Academic Press.
Johnston, Lloyd D., Patrick M. O'Malley, and Jerald G. Bachman. 2000. *Monitoring the Future: National Survey Results on Drug Use, 1975–1999. Vol. 1: Secondary Students* (NIH Publication No. 00-4802). Washington, DC: National Institute on Drug Abuse.
Office of National Drug Control Policy. 1997. "The National Drug Control

Strategy." http://www.ncjrs.org/
htm/chapter2.htm

Windle, Michael. 1999. *Alcohol Use
among Adolescents.* Thousand Oaks,
CA: Sage Publications.

Alcohol Use, Trends in

Many young people first use alcohol in
the company of their parents, often in the
context of religious ceremonies or family
celebrations. Such experiences are hardly
worrisome, both because they typically
involve just a few sips of alcohol and
because parents or other caring adults are
close by to supervise—and, it is hoped, to
provide models of appropriate alcohol
use.

Unsupervised and excessive alcohol
use begins during early and middle adolescence for most young people. This
type of drinking can be worrisome.
Drinking is a common experience for
adolescents; indeed, by their senior year
of high school, four out of five young people have used alcohol (more than just a
few sips), and nearly two-thirds report
having been drunk at least once (Johnston, O'Malley, and Bachman, 2000).

What, How, and Why Adolescents
Drink

An alcoholic drink, as researchers and
others usually define it, is one 12-ounce
can, bottle, or glass of beer, one 4-ounce
glass of wine, or one ounce of hard liquor.
Not surprisingly, the alcohol beverages
most popular among young people
include beer and wine (with boys preferring the former and girls preferring the
latter). For example, among U.S. twelfth
graders in 1995, 53 percent of the males
and 37.4 percent of the females reported
drinking beer at least once in the past
thirty days. The thirty-day rates for wine
were 13.2 percent and 15.3 percent

among males and females, respectively;
for wine coolers they were 15.5 percent
and 25.1 percent, respectively. And for
hard liquor they were 38.2 percent and
30.9 percent, respectively (Johnston,
Bachman, and O'Malley, 1997).

Adolescents rarely drink alone; typically, when they drink, it is with one or
more of their friends, often at parties or
other social gatherings. Although adults
tend to view adolescent drinking as a
problem, young people tend to view their
alcohol use in terms of fun and experimentation. In one study, when twelfth
graders were asked why they drink, their
most common responses included "to
have a good time with friends" and "to
experiment, see what it is like" (both
endorsed by the majority of twelfth-grade
drinkers surveyed). Nevertheless, many
young people also reported using alcohol
"as a way to cope" and "to relieve anger
and frustration" (both endorsed by about
one out of five of the twelfth-grade
drinkers surveyed) (O'Malley, Johnston,
and Bachman, 1998).

Developmental Trends in Alcohol Use

Alcohol use increases dramatically during
adolescence. The following snapshot of
alcohol use is based on nationally representative data collected from eighth,
ninth, and tenth graders in 1999. Reported
use of any alcohol during the past twelve
months was 43.5 percent, 63.7 percent,
and 73.8 percent for eighth, ninth, and
tenth graders, respectively. And reported
use of any alcohol during the past thirty
days was 24 percent, 40 percent, and 51
percent across the three grade levels,
respectively. Even more troubling were
the rates of drunkenness: Reported drunkenness at least once in the past thirty days
was 9.4 percent, 22.5 percent, and 32.9
percent across the three grade levels,

Adolescents rarely drink alone; when they drink, it is typically with one or more of their friends. (Shirley Zeiberg)

respectively (Johnston, O'Malley, and Bachman, 2000). In short, among those high school students (ninth to twelfth graders) who report recent drinking, the majority were drinking excessively or to the point of drunkenness at least once in the past month. Excessive drinking and drunkenness tend to continue to increase after high school and generally do not start to decline until after age twenty-two.

Historical Trends in Alcohol Use
Alcohol and other drug use is a social behavior and, as such, tends to vary depending on numerous social, political, and legal conditions in the larger society. Over the past quarter-century, the use of illicit drugs (including marijuana) has varied widely. For example, among twelfth graders, use of illicit drugs at least once in the past thirty days ranged from a high of 39 percent in 1979 to a low of 14 percent in 1992—a ratio of 2.8. But the use of alcohol has not varied as much: Among twelfth graders the peak for use in the past thirty days was at 72 percent in 1978, compared to a low of 51 percent in 1992—a ratio of about 1.4. In 1975, a quarter-century ago, 37 percent of high school seniors reported at least one occasion of binge drinking in the past two weeks. That number rose to a peak of 41 percent in the interval from 1979 to 1983, then gradually declined to a low of 28 percent

in 1993. The past few years have seen another increase, to 31 percent in 1999. Slight increases occurred in the 1990s among eighth and tenth graders as well: Binge drinking increased from 13 percent in 1991 to 15 percent in 1999 among eighth graders, and from 23 percent to 26 percent among tenth graders (Johnston, O'Malley, and Bachman, 2000).

Selected Risk Factors for and Conse-quences of Alcohol Use

Over the past few decades, much research has been devoted to trying to understand the causes and consequences of alcohol use during adolescence. As it is usually very difficult to isolate single causes of any behavior, including alcohol use, researchers often focus on risk factors—that is, on individual or social variables that increase the likelihood that a person will use or abuse alcohol. Numerous risk factors for alcohol use have been identi-fied, including neighborhood disorganiza-tion, family alcoholism, family conflict, academic failure, school misbehavior, peer alcohol and other drug use, and alienation and rebelliousness (Hawkins, Catalano, and Miller, 1992). It is impor-tant to note, however, that these risk fac-tors are neither necessary nor sufficient (Schulenberg et al., in press). In other words, alcohol abuse is not inevitable among adolescents who have experienced one or even several of the above-listed risk factors, nor is its absence assured among adolescents who have experienced no such risk factors.

Although experiences with alcohol are not troublesome for most adolescents, a sizable minority of young people do expe-rience difficulties as a result of their alco-hol use, including alcohol-related acci-dents, trouble with parents or police, and long-term problems with alcohol abuse.

One very visible consequence of alcohol use is related to driving after drinking, or riding in a vehicle whose driver has been drinking. Motor vehicle crashes, many of which are alcohol related, account for a very high percentage of injuries and deaths among adolescents and young adults. And these young people put themselves at risk for death or injury at a very high rate: Nineteen percent of sen-iors in 1997 reported having driven a motor vehicle after having had five or more drinks, or riding in a vehicle whose driver had had five or more drinks, at least once in just the past two weeks (O'Malley and Johnston, 1999).

Determining the long-term conse-quences of teenage alcohol use has been challenging because such use is often cor-related with other problems, and it is dif-ficult to distinguish the effects strictly due to alcohol use from those due to the other problems. In cases where long-term social, economic, and health conse-quences of excessive alcohol use during adolescence do occur, they are likely to be due not to experimental use of alcohol that is short term but, rather, to a trajec-tory of excessive use over the course of many years during adolescence and into young adulthood.

John Schulenberg
Patrick M. O'Malley

See also Alcohol Use, Risk Factors in; Drug Abuse Prevention; Nutrition; Peer Groups; Peer Pressure; Risk Behaviors; Substance Use and Abuse

References and further reading
Hawkins, J. David, Richard F. Catalano, and Janet Y. Miller. 1992. "Risk and Protective Factors for Alcohol and Other Drug Problems in Adolescence and Young Adulthood: Implications for Substance Abuse Prevention." *Psychological Bulletin* 112: 64–105.

Johnston, Lloyd D., Jerald G. Bachman, and Patrick M. O'Malley. 1997. "Monitoring the Future: Questionnaire Responses from the Nation's High School Seniors, 1995." Institute for Social Research, University of Michigan.

Johnston, Lloyd D., Patrick M. O'Malley, and Jerald G. Bachman. 2000. *Monitoring the Future: National Results on Adolescent Drug Use: Overview of Key Findings, 1999* (NIH Publication No. 00-4690). Rockville, MD: National Institute on Drug Abuse.

O'Malley, Patrick M., and Lloyd D. Johnston. 1999. "Drinking and Driving among U.S. High School Seniors, 1984–1997." *American Journal of Public Health* 89: 678–684.

O'Malley, Patrick M., Lloyd D. Johnston, and Jerald G. Bachman. 1998. "Alcohol Use among Adolescents." *Alcohol Health and Research World* 22: 85–93.

Schulenberg, John, J. L. Maggs, K. Steinman, and R. A. Zucker. In press. "Development Matters: Taking the Long View on Substance Abuse Etiology and Intervention during Adolescence." In *Adolescents, Alcohol, and Substance Abuse: Reaching Teens through Brief Intervention.* Edited by P.M. Monti, S.M. Colby, and T.A. O'Leary. New York: Guilford Press.

Allowance

During the late nineteenth century, when American children left the factory for school in large numbers, there arose the problem of newly "insolvent" children, who needed funds but who could no longer earn them through paid work. Although the concept of allowance originated in the middle class, parents of all social classes were advised to give their children a small amount of money each week. Today, prescriptive family economics guidance literature extols the benefits of regular allowance for the development of sound money-management skills in children. According to family economic and financial education specialists, children learn through the receipt of a regular allowance to manage money more wisely, to make decisions about how to save and spend their money, and to plan ahead for future economic goals.

Studies have found that exchange of labor for money begins in the family setting, as most adolescents who receive an allowance are required to perform chores to obtain their weekly payment. Despite this finding, family economic advisers and educators have debated the administration of allowances. Some educators think that children learn a valuable lesson when allowance is linked to the performance of household chores: children learn to work for pay. Others, however, think that allowance should not be conditional upon household chores, arguing that this practice undermines the collective character of the family. Still other experts agree that children should not be paid for routine or regular household chores, but they allow an exception: children can be paid for special household tasks that the parents might otherwise hire a person outside the family to perform (e.g., lawn mowing, snow shoveling, washing the car, baby-sitting). Similarly, it is argued that allowance not be used as a reward or punishment for desirable or undesirable behavior, since this might subvert more genuine motivations.

Although the family economics guidance literature emphasizes the benefits of allowance for consumership, spending, and saving, receipt of an allowance does not necessarily lead to more effective money management. Similarly, there is no evidence that receipt of an allowance increases adolescent savings (Mortimer et al., 1994). However, these findings do not mean that allowance lacks educational value. For example, Rona Abramovitch,

Jonathon Freedman, and Patricia Pliner (1991) found that those children who received an unconditional allowance (i.e., with "no strings attached," such as the performance of household chores) had a better understanding of financial concepts than did children who received either a conditional allowance or none at all. However, findings based on studies of children may not be sufficient, as the beneficial effects of an early allowance may not become evident until adolescence or even adulthood.

Receipt of an allowance may extend beyond money management to affect the broader process of socialization to work. According to the theory of intrinsic motivation, when extrinsic rewards are offered for intrinsically motivated behavior, the individual comes to attribute his or her actions to the external reward, leading to a devaluation of the activity as worthwhile in itself. For example, a child who receives gold stars for engaging in an activity that was previously considered enjoyable would subsequently be less likely to take it up spontaneously. Like the family guidance experts noted earlier, some experts are concerned that motivations of a higher order could be displaced by more extrinsic interests.

Differences between families in the provision of an allowance often reflect social background circumstances and intrafamilial processes. For example, Adrian Furnham and Paul Thomas (1984) found social-class differences in British parental attitudes toward allowance, with middle-class parents more likely than working-class parents to favor giving their children an allowance, and at earlier ages. Of course, higher-income parents may be better able to give their children allowances because they have greater monetary resources. But if allowance practices are influenced, at least in part, by parental values, one would also expect that more highly educated parents, given their strong self-directed values, would be more likely to provide their children with allowance, independent of income differences, since allowance is thought to foster independence in children. This was confirmed by Jeylan Mortimer and her colleagues (1994), who found that parents of higher socioeconomic levels were indeed more likely to give an allowance than parents of lower socioeconomic status. However, the actual amount did not vary according to family income, suggesting that the size of allowances is not determined by the resources available.

Intrafamilial processes are further influenced by conditions in the broader social environment, such as cultural values and norms, and social institutions like the market economy. For example, children with a working mother are more likely to do household chores to relieve their time-pressured parents. There is also some indication that children from single-parent families tend to be given more spending money and greater responsibility to independently buy their own clothes and other necessities, perhaps due to the severe constraints on the single parent's time. Consistent with this finding, two-parent families are less likely to give children an allowance than are parents in other family types.

It could be surmised that if allowance is given to enhance economic socialization, boys would be more likely to receive an allowance, given men's traditional responsibility for the economic welfare of their families. Historical studies suggest that this was the case in previous eras. However, studies of contemporary allowance arrangements have found that boys and girls are equally likely to receive an allowance, and that they receive the same amount (Mortimer et al., 1994). However, the conditions under which allowance is received differ by gender: allowance is more likely to be contingent upon the performance of chores for boys than for girls. This finding may reflect parental expectations regarding the familial and economic roles of adult men and women: females are traditionally socialized to contribute to family tasks out of love, nurturance, or a sense of obligation, whereas males are socialized to earn money in exchange for their work. Other research, too, suggests that self-sacrifice in girls is rated more highly and praised more often than that of boys. However, the finding by Mortimer and her colleagues that gender is not related to the receipt or amount of allowance may imply that parents consider the acquisition of money-management skills to be equally important for boys and girls and that the economic needs/expenses of adolescent boys and girls are similar.

The ability to manage money wisely is an essential skill for adulthood that begins to be developed during childhood. Given the lifelong importance of money-management skills, it is surprising that so little systematic research about allowance arrangements has been conducted to date. Investigators thus should further examine the role of the family in the process of economic socialization, the impact of family economic practices on the formation of work-related values and habits, and the development of money-management skills in adolescence.

Pamela Aronson
Jeylan T. Mortimer

See also Chores

References and further reading
Abramovitch, Rona, Jonathon L. Freedman, and Patricia Pliner. 1991. "Children and Money: Getting an Allowance, Credit versus Cash, and Knowledge of Pricing." *Journal of Economic Psychology* 12: 27–45.
Furnham, Adrian, and Paul Thomas. 1984. "Adults' Perception of the Economic Socialization of Children." *Journal of Adolescence* 7: 217–231.
Goodnow, Jacqueline J. 1988. "Children's Household Work: Its Nature and Functions." *Psychological Bulletin* 103: 5–26.
Mortimer, Jeylan T., Katherine Dennehy, Chaimun Lee, and Michael D. Finch. 1994. "Economic Socialization in the American Family: The Prevalence, Distribution, and Consequences of Allowance Arrangements." *Family Relations* 43: 23–29. [The current encyclopedia entry draws on research reported in this article.]
Sloane, L. 1991. "With Allowances, Every Parent Differs." *New York Times*, November 2, 12.
White, Lynn K., and David B. Brinkerhoff. 1981. "Children's Work in the Family: Its Significance and Meaning." *Journal of Marriage and the Family* 43: 789–798.
Zelizer, Viviana A. 1985. *Pricing the Priceless Child: The Changing Social Value of Children.* New York: Basic Books.

Anemia

Anemia is a condition in which the number of red blood cells or the amount of hemoglobin in the blood is decreased. Red blood cells contain hemoglobin, the chemical that carries oxygen from the lungs to all parts of the body. Symptoms of anemia are related to starvation of all of the body's cells for oxygen. The symptoms include: fatigue, weakness, dizziness, inability to carry out daily activities, shortness of breath, rapid or irregular heartbeat, and paleness.

Hemoglobin levels change dramatically during adolescence, especially among males. The average hematocrit (percentage of red blood cells) in the total blood count in a child is 25 to 40 percent. In an adult male it is 45 to 50 percent. Anemia is easy to detect. A blood count (commonly called a CBC—Complete Blood Count) can be done on a drop of blood. The laboratory will measure the number of red blood cells (RBC), the total amount of hemoglobin, the size of the RBC, and how much hemoglobin is in each RBC. Once the presence of anemia is established, additional tests can tell the cause or type of anemia present so that appropriate treatment can be given.

There are three general causes of anemia: decreased red blood cell or hemoglobin production, blood loss through bleeding, and excessive red blood cell destruction.

The most common type of anemia in youth is caused by decreased RBC/hemoglobin production. The most common cause of this kind of anemia is a deficiency of iron in the diet. Iron is an essential component of hemoglobin. If there is not enough iron in the diet, not enough hemoglobin can be produced. Red meat is the best source of dietary iron, although in the United States many manufactured foods (bread, cereals, and other grain products) are fortified with iron. Deficiencies in vitamin C (citrus fruit) or B12 or folic acid (green leafy vegetables) may also cause decreased production of RBC/hemoglobin. Treatment is with iron or vitamin pills until the deficiency is corrected. This may take up to five or six weeks, along with adequate intake of the nutrients, which are deficient in the diet.

Sometimes, teenagers may change their eating habits during adolescence, as their parents have less control over their diets. An unbalanced diet, such as one that includes a lot of junk food, not enough of the above kinds of grains, protein, and vegetables, could result in anemia. Also, in some cases, teenagers may try to eat very little, or else to purge what they do eat, in order to lose weight or attain a certain body type. This is not a healthy way to diet. These harmful behaviors, known as eating disorders, can lead not only to conditions such as malnourishment and anemia but can be life threatening if left untreated.

Anemia caused by excessive blood loss is common in adolescent girls who lose blood (containing hemoglobin and iron) during menstruation. Blood loss, combined with a less than optimal intake of iron, is another common cause of anemia among girls. Girls with especially heavy periods should take iron pills to prevent the development of anemia. In some instances, girls with heavy periods may benefit by taking oral contraceptive pills, as the oral contraceptive can decrease the amount of bleeding during periods. Other causes of blood loss include injuries, surgery, childbirth, and stomach ulcers. Blood loss can also be caused by destructive behaviors, such as self-mutilation, for which a teenager should seek professional counseling. Treatment of these other conditions will stop the blood loss and prevent further development of anemia.

Increased destruction of red blood cells is called hemolytic anemia. There is a long list of the many different types of hemolytic anemias, some of which tend to run in families. The most common cause is sickle-cell anemia in which an abnormal form of hemoglobin is produced that changes the shape of the RBC from round to sickle shaped and makes the RBC easier to destroy. The red blood cells get stuck on the lining of blood vessels and create a "logjam" usually resulting in a clot that is then destroyed (cleared out) by our immune system. Most of these anemias are not curable, and treatment is with repeated blood transfusions usually over the entire life of the affected person.

Jordan W. Finkelstein

See also Eating Problems; Health Services for Adolescents; Nutrition

References and further reading
Berkow, Robert B., ed. 1997. *The Merck Manual of Medical Information: Home Edition.* Whitehouse Station NJ: Merck Research Laboratories.
Clayman, Charles B., ed. 1994. *The American Medical Association Family Medical Guide,* 3rd ed. New York: Random House.

Anxiety

Anxiety is the feeling of apprehension, tension, or uneasiness that one experiences when anticipating danger, either real or imagined. Symptoms of anxiety include heart palpitations, stomach and intestinal upset, sweating, headaches, tremor, dryness of the mouth, dizziness, and fainting. Some anxiety is necessary to motivate behavior and to protect us from engaging in harmful behavior. People experience anxiety in varying degrees and frequency. When the body continually overreacts to perceived threat, an anxiety disorder can result.

Biological Factors

Animal studies have shown that emotional reactions can promote survival. In humans, anxiety arouses and organizes the biological activities required to equip the individual to deal with the threats and challenges of everyday life. Too little arousal may result in inattentiveness, impulsivity, and risk-taking behavior, whereas too much arousal may result in the physical anxiety-related symptoms mentioned above. The human brain has evolved to react to signals of danger. Chemicals in the brain, called neurotransmitters, activate or deactivate systems in the body to respond to perceived threats in our environment. A delicate balance of these chemicals is necessary to maintain an optimal level of arousal within the body.

Like animals, humans have evolved to anticipate danger in the environment. However, humans have cognitive abilities that exceed those of animals. A human responds to threats both voluntarily and involuntarily. Thought processes that are used to evaluate the threat can cause unnecessary anxiety if the situation is interpreted inaccurately. For example, almost everyone gets anxious before speaking in front of large groups of people. In most cases, there is no imminent danger. It is our interpretation of the situation as potentially harmful that causes the anxiety. We may worry that we will make a mistake or make a fool of ourselves and thus be embarrassed or humiliated. Our anticipation of these negative outcomes causes anxiety.

Some people are born with a greater tendency than others to become anxious. Such people are irritable as infants, shy and fearful as toddlers, and cautious, quiet, and introverted when they reach school age. They adapt slowly and with difficulty to new surroundings and have a low neurological threshold for arousal, especially when faced with unfamiliar events. Shy, behaviorally inhibited children may experience an acceleration of heart rate in response to mild stress. Although not all such children maintain these behaviors over time, those who continue to display them into adolescence may be at risk for an anxiety disorder.

Environmental Factors

Behavioral inhibition is only one of several factors required for the development of an anxiety disorder. Environmental factors can also contribute. For example, a child who experiences disruption in the family such as parental conflict may be at increased risk to become anxious. Parents who are anxious, depressed, or overprotective may inadvertently teach the child to be anxious. And parents who are overcontrolling may prevent or delay the development of the child's ability to soothe and manage him- or herself. Indeed, a child who is never allowed to play freely with other children may have difficulty with anxiety when starting school.

Parents' behavior affects their children's behavior and vice versa. An inhibited child may cause parents to be more cautious and to expect less from the child, thus reinforcing the inhibited behavior of the child. Alternatively, parents who want their children to be more outgoing may encourage them to resist their fears, allowing them to overcome their inhibited nature as well.

Another source of anxiety in the environment is uncertainty or unpredictability, as when a child cannot understand how things "fit together" or is unable to predict the events in the world. In short, children who feel they have little control over their environment are likely to be anxious. The family environment needs to be predictable and structured so that children can learn to organize and understand their surroundings. Parents who are responsive to infants in the early stages of

Adolescents experience anxiety in varying degrees and frequency. (Skjold Photographs)

life encourage the development of control and predictability over the environment, as do parents who let their children know that they will always be available if and when the children need them. Children who do not feel secure have low expectations about parent availability and demonstrate anxious behavior.

As children become adolescents, the peer group takes on new importance, creating new expectations and standards for behavior. Because adolescents often compare their own abilities and traits to those of their peers, academic, social, and athletic competencies can become sources of anxiety—especially if the adolescents do not measure up to their own or others' expectations. Whether or not an adolescent gets anxious in a given situation depends on how much importance is placed on that situation. For instance, poor school performance will cause anxiety only if the adolescent values school achievement. In such cases, parents who pressure adolescents to excel may induce anxious behavior that contributes to the academic failure.

Consequences of Anxiety

Anxiety can cause problems not only in the academic life of adolescents but also in their social life—especially when it affects their ability to create and maintain healthy peer interactions and relationships. Highly anxious adolescents are typically less popular than nonanxious adolescents and are more likely to be perceived as shy and socially withdrawn by peers and teachers.

Anxiety can also affect the intellectual functioning of adolescents—specifically, by impairing their memory and interfering with the ability to concentrate. These outcomes are particularly common in cases of test anxiety, which can prohibit test takers from recalling information they have learned.

Anxiety Disorders in Childhood and Adolescence

Anxiety disorders vary widely in terms of severity and degree of impairment. They also tend to run in families; a person who has a close relative with an anxiety disorder is likelier than the general population to develop one him- or herself. Still unclear, however, is the extent to which these disorders are genetically based as opposed to learned from the family environment.

Some common anxiety disorders are panic disorder, agoraphobia, obsessive-compulsive disorder, social phobia, generalized anxiety disorder, and school phobia. The last of these affects children and adolescents in particular. Those with school phobia experience marked feelings of dread and fear upon going to school and often complain of not feeling well in the morning before school. Such students are described as passive, inhibited, and excessively dependent on family members. They also tend to have high self-expectations. Their fear of not living up to these expectations may contribute to the anxiety they experience. Avoiding school to relieve the anxiety may cause them to fall further behind both academically and socially, resulting in even more anxiety.

Treatments for Anxiety

An adolescent whose anxiety interferes with normal everyday functioning can choose among several treatment options, including cognitive and behavioral therapies, relaxation techniques such as meditation or visualization, problem solving, correcting misperceptions, and changing counterproductive styles of thinking. Many of these options provide ways to increase the adolescent's sense of competence and control. For instance, adolescents can learn to identify and monitor thoughts associated with anxiety and then replace these thoughts with more appropriate and less anxiety-producing thoughts. They can overcome specific fears through gradual exposure to the fearful stimuli while using relaxation techniques. They can use modeling procedures that allow them to observe others in a fearful situation with no harmful consequences. And, finally, they can engage in play therapy, using puppets or dolls to act out their feelings—an especially helpful technique for children and adolescents who cannot articulate their anxieties.

Another treatment option is drug therapy. For children and adolescents with anxiety, benzodiazepines are commonly prescribed. These medications have a relaxing effect on the individual, but they may have side effects, cause dependence over time, or produce withdrawal symptoms when their use is discontinued. Several antidepressants have also proved effective in treating anxiety. Often, the most beneficial treatment consists of drug therapy combined with other types of therapy.

Susan Averna

See also Conflict and Stress; Coping; Counseling; Emotions; Fears; Storm and Stress

References and further reading
Ainsworth, Mary. 1982. "Attachment: Retrospect and Prospect." Pp. 3–30 in *The Place of Attachment in Human Behavior.* Edited by C. M. Parkes and J. Stevenson-Hinde. New York: Basic Books.

Biederman, Joseph, Jerrold Rosenbaum, Jonathon Chaloff, and Jerome Kagan. 1995. "Behavioral Inhibition as a Risk Factor for Anxiety Disorders." Pp. 61–81 in *Anxiety Disorders in Children and Adolescents*. Edited by John March. New York: Guilford Press.

Constanzo, Philip, Shari Miller-Johnson, and Heidi Wence. 1995. "Social Development." Pp. 82–108 in *Anxiety Disorders in Children and Adolescents*. Edited by John March. New York: Guilford Press.

Eysenck, Michael. 1990. "Anxiety and Cognitive Functioning." Pp. 419–435 in *Handbook of Anxiety.* Vol. 2, *The Neurobiology of Anxiety.* Edited by Graham D. Burrows, Martin Roth, and Russell Noyes. New York: Elsevier Science Publishers.

Hofer, Myron. 1995. "An Evolutionary Perspective on Anxiety." Pp. 17–38 in *Anxiety as Symptom and Signal.* Edited by Steven Roose and Robert Glick. Hillsdale, NJ: Analytic Press.

Kagan, Jerome, J. Reznick, and Nancy Snidman. 1987. "The Physiology and Psychology of Behavioral Inhibition in Children." *Child Development* 58: 1459–1473.

Kolvin, I., and C. Kaplan. 1988. "Anxiety in Childhood." Pp. 259–275 in *Handbook of Anxiety.* Vol. 1, *Biological, Clinical and Cultural Perspectives.* Edited by Martin Roth, Russell Noyes Jr., and Graham Burrows. New York: Elsevier Science Publishers.

Maccoby, Eleanor, and John Martin. 1983. "Socialization in the Context of the Family: Parent-Child Interaction." Pp. 1–102 in *Handbook of Child Psychology*, Vol. 4. Edited by E. M. Hetherington. New York: Wiley.

Resnick, J. Steven, Jerome Kagan, Nancy Snidman, Michelle Gersten, Katherine Baak, and Allison Rosenberg. 1986. "Inhibited and Uninhibited Children: A Follow-Up Study." *Child Development* 57, no. 3: 660–680.

Appearance, Cultural Factors in

The word *appearance* refers to the physical attributes of a person. It describes one's physical presentation, including one's body, face, and clothes. Appearance is a reflection of physical body structure and of body-related experiences at home, in school, and in the larger social context where cultural values define "acceptability." Appearance becomes very salient during adolescence, a time when bodies undergo rapid physical change and the pressure to "look good" becomes intense. It is normal for teenagers to become very interested in the way they look and to start spending more time finding out how they want to present themselves. Figuring out how to fix their hair and what kind of clothes to wear can be fun for adolescents because these are ways to tell people who they are. But an intense interest in appearance can also lead to worry and self-doubt among young

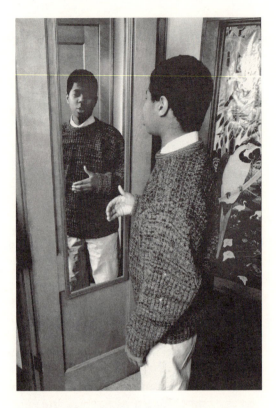

Teenagers become very interested in the way they look and spend more time finding out how they want to present themselves. (Skjold Photographs)

cant predictor of eating disorders, depression, and social anxiety. Hence, the challenge for today's teenagers is to learn how to be appreciative of their own look and the natural variety of human appearance.

The focus on appearance can be especially troublesome for girls and women. As girls reach puberty, they find it increasingly difficult to assimilate the tremendous physical changes their bodies have undergone. Studies indicate that, compared to boys, girls are not only more concerned about how they look but also less content with their appearance. The bodily changes associated with adolescence also change the way people relate to teenage girls. Many young women find that their bodies draw more attention than they are comfortable with, causing them to experience intense self-consciousness. At the same time, they are bombarded by social messages conveying that girls must be thin and beautiful if they wish to be considered important and worthwhile. These psychological and social pressures can be very harmful for girls as they often lead to lower self-esteem, increased insecurity, and higher rates of depression, eating disorders, and suicide.

Another problem is that the criteria for teenage appearance in the United States tend to be Eurocentric, meaning that white standards of beauty are more highly valued in the media than the beauty standards of other racial and ethnic groups. People with dark skin, for example, often have trouble finding appropriate beauty products such as makeup or hair care. One result is that persons of color may end up feeling marginalized, unappreciated, even invisible to society. A person of color may not be able to relate to the Eurocentric media images on television and in magazines.

teenagers. With so many media images and messages confronting adolescents about what they should wear and how they should look, they can easily fall into the trap of finding fault with themselves.

The culture of appearance created by the media promotes problematic body images such as unreasonable standards of body weight—standards that many adolescents find themselves under pressure to achieve. Researchers have found a connection between these standards and the increasing prevalence of eating disorders in recent decades; indeed, unhappiness with one's appearance is a signifi-

Advertisements in teen and fashion magazines and commercials on television carry some of the most potent messages about how beauty is defined. As market analysts indicate, most commercials geared toward teenagers are dominated by clothes and beauty products. One way to sell these products is to make teenagers long for something they don't have. Indeed, those who believe they aren't pretty or thin enough are more likely to buy beauty or diet products. Thus, the media promote an "ideal" body image—one attainable by very few individuals—in order to intensify teenagers' insecurities for the purpose of selling products. For the same reason, it is rare to see advertisements that strengthen an appreciation for diversity and multiple forms of beauty.

Another influence on the standards of appearance for girls is the unequal status between men and women. Women's role in society has historically been less powerful than that of men. Women have been seen as objects of beauty, but not as equal partners. In fact, many of the beauty trends throughout history have impeded women's ability to engage fully in society. For example, American women used to wear absurd corsets that squeezed their torsos and inner organs so they could have tiny waists. In these contraptions women were unable to breathe properly and often fainted; they certainly could not engage in any rigorous activity. A second example can be found in China's history: Because small feet were considered beautiful, many young girls' feet were bound so they would not grow. This practice essentially crippled women. Corsets and foot binding are things of the past, but many modern practices continue to impede women's health and standing in society.

For example, the detrimental impact of beauty standards is still visible in the pressure to become increasingly thin. Many girls and women do great damage to their bodies in their efforts to attain thinness. Some diet excessively; others undergo painful, dangerous operations to remove fat. For these individuals, being thin is more important than health, intellectual stimulation, or any other form of personal fulfillment.

Of course, if women were valued more for their personal qualities than for their appearance, it is unlikely that they would be willing to go through such extreme procedures.

The great diversity of faces and bodies is a fact of life. When physical differences are not accepted, however, the psychological and social pressures to conform to one standard of appearance can be overwhelming. The only way to cope with such pressures is to *appreciate* our appearance. After all, acknowledging our own style and sense of beauty can be a fun and rewarding way of discovering our voice in life.

Lauren Rogers-Sirin

See also Appearance Management; Attractiveness, Physical; Body Build; Body Fat, Changes in; Body Image

References and further reading
Brumberg, Jacobs. 1997. *The Body Project: An Intimate History of American Girls.* New York: Random House.
Johnson, Norine G., Michael C. Roberts, and Judith Worell, eds. 1999. *Beyond Appearance: A New Look at Adolescent Girls.* Washington, DC.: American Psychological Association.
Orenstein, Peggy. 1994. *Schoolgirls: Young Women, Self-Esteem, and the Confidence Gap.* New York: Anchor Books.
Pipher, Mary. 1994. *Reviving Ophelia: Saving the Selves of Adolescent Girls.* New York: Ballantine Books.

Wolf, Naomi. 1991. *The Beauty Myth: How Images of Beauty Are Used against Women.* New York: Doubleday.

Appearance Management

Appearance management encompasses the sum total of attention, decisions, and acts related to one's personal appearance. It is a universal concept; all individuals engage daily in some activity that relates to their appearance. Appearance management comprises clothing, use of cosmetics, dieting, exercising, hairstyling, hair removal, piercing, scarification, tattoos, and any other intentional means of changing the natural appearance of the human physical form.

Appearance is of major importance at every stage in the development of the self, but it assumes special importance during the transitional period of adolescence when the need to belong is combined with a dynamic search for self-identity. Learning to manage appearance through dress is a key component of socialization. Ideas about appropriate appearance are linked to peer-group values. As adolescents compare and assess themselves in relation to others, appearance is often used as a measure of self-evaluation. Many teens become preoccupied with appearance in their search for identity and peer-group affiliation. This preoccupation with appearance is intensified in today's society by the barrage of media messages that promote personal appearance as a measure of self-worth. Experimentation with clothing and body modification is often part of the teenager's self-exploration. It does not signal insecurity, instability, or weakness but, rather, simply reflects the process of trying on several different identities. Although the freedom to experiment

with personal appearance is important to teenagers, it can be a source of conflict when tempered by parental, school, or other social authorities.

Redefining the Self

Adolescents often experience vagueness, confusion, and discontinuity of the self as they emerge from childhood with changing bodies, new roles, and transitions involving their significant others. Strong approval from peers and a feeling of belongingness to an admired reference group are often evidenced in the choices adolescents make in managing their appearance. Adolescents use clothing and body modifications to bring their appearance in line with the groups to which they aspire to belong or fantasize about joining. Clothing and other forms of appearance management—including, as noted earlier, use of cosmetics, dieting, exercising, hairstyling, hair removal, piercing, and, more recently, tattoos and scarification—are used as tools by adolescents for discovering and expressing their identities. Appraisals, real or perceived, of their appearance and behavior by their peers are a major concern in the lives of adolescents, playing a significant role in redefining the self.

The School Setting

The school setting presents adolescents with an arena of social intensity where informal peer groups are formed on the basis of several attributes such as ethnicity, socioeconomic status, tastes, and interests. Dress and appearance, however, are the attributes most recognizable to adolescents; indeed, they are considered by teens to be instrumental, if not critical, in helping them fit in and feel accepted by others. Because adolescents frequently also feel that their appearance and actions are being scrutinized by an "imaginary audience," presenting the desired identity is paramount in their minds. Thus, a recognizable identity that conforms to a preferred social group is perceived by adolescents to facilitate social participation and interaction.

Conformity to Peers

In American society, adolescents and their peers are remarkably similar in appearance. Adolescents are often stereotyped as conformists. Indeed, fashion statements made by adolescents help them to express solidarity with their peers and to define themselves as different from adults. Although adolescents have a great deal of choice in selecting an appearance, they do so carefully, with consideration of who they are and what they hope to be in the future. Although parental influence is important in matters relating to morals, values, education, and occupation, it is the peer group that provides adolescents with the main environment for social comparison in issues relating to appearance. Strategies utilized by parents that allow adolescents to make choices and mistakes in the area of appearance management may be bolstered by the fact that most adolescents will adopt the ideals and beliefs of their families when they become adults.

Rebellion against the Social Order

As a portable symbol of self, appearance may be managed in a way that demonstrates rebellion against the adult world. Apparel styles and body modifications that are deemed unacceptable may be deliberately chosen by adolescents to symbolize their rebellion against authority. Yet such rebellious appearances are rarely acts of individuality; rather, they serve to promote recognition or member-

Forms of appearance management, such as use of cosmetics, are used as means for adolescents to discover and express their identities. (Lawrence Manning/Corbis)

ship in a particular peer group. Rebellious attitudes toward society have given rise to numerous subcultural groups that use a distinctive style of dress and appearance to differentiate between "us" and "them." Groups such as the Teddy Boys, Mods, Rockers, Skinheads, Hippies, Punks, Headbangers, Rastafarians, and Goths have achieved international recognition and affiliation. These groups' increasing use of permanent body modifications such as piercing, tattooing, and scarification or branding may be attributed to their perceived need to be recognized not as transitory or trendy, like a fashion, but permanent.

Gangs, which are comparatively local or regional in nature, are also notorious for their use of appearance in denoting group membership. Gang membership and the adoption of gang insignia can provide adolescents with a sense of identity, a connection to peers, and a feeling of effectiveness and control. The last two decades of the twentieth century witnessed an alarming outbreak of crimes among poor inner-city youth who injured and even killed each other over name-brand apparel favored by gangs. The high value placed on these items of dress illuminated the enormous power wielded by appearance in denoting gang membership. The coveted items included athletic shoes, jackets, and other apparel sporting either specific name brands or the names and colors of national basketball or baseball teams. These products, as opposed to other indicators of prestige, may originally have symbolized the aspirations of an underclass of inner-city youth constrained by an environment that provides little opportunity for the means to obtain these items. Indeed, economic disparities play a strong role in gang formation and help to explain the selection of status markers that denote group membership.

From Subcultural Appearances to Mainstream Fashions

Ironically, the looks that are popularized by such extreme groups often find their way into the mainstream where they are adopted by adolescents and other consumers in great numbers. Once this happens, the look that once denoted group membership loses its original meaning and becomes just another transitory fashion. As is true of all fashions, upon achieving mass acceptance the look eventually declines in popularity and becomes obsolete. Subcultural looks that were eventually adopted by mainstream society in the 1980s and 1990s and became fashions include, for example, dreadlocks from the Rastafarians, multiple facial piercings from the Punks, and baggy jeans and oversized clothing from the hip-hop culture. Adolescents who are early adopters of such looks will most likely be noticed for appearing different from the norm, but rarely do these appearances maintain any link to the identity or values of their subcultural source.

Gender Differences in Appearance Management

Gender differences in the ways that adolescents manage their appearance are largely reflective of how males and females are socialized. Long before adolescence, children learn that the male body is to be physically developed and strengthened and that the female body is to be preserved, protected, and made more beautiful. Indeed, beauty becomes duty for the females in American society, and this value is internalized at a very young age. Fantasy characters such as Snow White, Cinderella, and Barbie (for girls) and Hercules, Superman, and G.I. Joe (for boys) reinforce these gender roles. Even as new fantasy female characters are created to be more reflective of current thinking, independence and strength often remain secondary to the beauty or physical attractiveness of the characters—as with Pocahontas and Wonderwoman, for example.

Differences in the use of clothing by male and female adolescents are also reflective of our gender ideology. Females are more likely than males to use clothing to gain peer approval and to be favorably noticed as different or nonconforming. They relate to clothing in terms of its affective or expressive qualities or its ability to help them cope with the demands of the social environment, whereas males are more conforming, relating to clothing in terms of its consistency with their identity. Conformity in appearance among adolescent males is supported by a restrictive dress code for males in society at large; nonconformity in appearance among females is supported by a marketplace that responds to consumer demand, providing clothing to females in more styles and at higher prices than comparable provisions for males.

Societal emphasis on appearance and the cultural ideal of a thin female body has led to some extreme measures of appearance management among adolescent females. The cultural message that relates beauty and attractiveness to extreme thinness in females is pervasive. The media play a particularly influential role in communicating an unrealistic standard of beauty for the female body that may affect perceptions of self-attractiveness and body image. Severe dieting and purging to attain the current physical ideal of extreme thinness are troublesome behaviors in which an increasing number of American female adolescents are engaging. Such behaviors can lead to anorexia nervosa, an eating disorder that involves the relentless pursuit of thinness through starvation, or to bulimia, an eating disorder characterized by consistent bingeing and purging. Both disorders are a serious threat to health and require professional intervention. Although numerous factors may contribute to these and other eating disorders, the societal factor most often held responsible is the current fashion image of thinness.

Maureen Sweeney MacGillivray

See also Acne; Appearance, Cultural Factors in; Attractiveness, Physical; Body Build; Body Fat, Changes in; Body Hair; Body Image

References and further reading
Burns, R. B. 1979. *The Self Concept in Theory, Measurement, Development and Behavior.* New York: Longman.

Castlebury, Susan, and John Arnold. 1988. "Early Adolescent Perceptions of Informal Groups in a Middle School." *Journal of Early Adolescence* 8, no. 1: 97–107.

Cobb, Nancy J. 1998. *Adolescence: Continuity, Change, and Diversity.* Mountain View, CA: Mayfield Publishing.

Davis, Fred. 1992. *Fashion, Culture and Identity.* Chicago: University of Chicago Press.

Elkind, David. 1982. *The Hurried Child.* New York: Addison-Wesley.

Kaiser, Susan. 1997. *The Social Psychology of Clothing: Symbolic Appearances in Context,* 2nd ed., rev. New York: Fairchild.

Lennon, Sharron J., Nancy A. Rudd, Bridgette Sloan, and Jae Sook Kim. 1999. "Attitudes toward Gender Roles, Self-Esteem, and Body Image: Application of a Model. *Clothing and Textile Research Journal* 17, no. 4: 191–202.

MacGillivray, Maureen, and Jeannette Wilson. 1997. "Clothing and Appearance in Early, Middle and Late Adolescents." *Clothing and Textile Research Journal* 15: 43–49.

Polhemus, Ted. 1994. *Streetstyle: From Sidewalk to Catwalk.* New York: Thames and Hudson.

Rubenstein, Ruth P. 1995. *Dress Codes: Meanings and Messages in American Culture.* Boulder, CO: Westview Press.

Santrock, John W. 1998. *Adolescence.* Boston: McGraw-Hill.

Sontag, M. Suzanne, Mihaela Peteu, and Jongnam Lee. 1997. "Clothing in the Self-System of Adolescents: Relationships among Values, Proximity of Clothing to Self, Clothing Interest, Anticipated Outcomes and Perceived Quality of Life." Research Report 556. East Lansing: Michigan Agricultural Experiment Station.

Stone, Gregory P. 1962. "Appearance and the Self." Pp. 86–116 in *Human Behavior and the Social Processes: An Interactionist Approach.* Edited by Arnold M. Rose. New York: Houghton Mifflin.

Apprenticeships

As adolescents move toward the transition from school to work in the twenty-first century, they face exciting new challenges, unimaginable technological advances, and a future potentially filled with economic independence and stability. Yet many young adults must also face the reality that they are inadequately prepared to secure entry-level positions in our fast-paced and technologically sophisticated economy. Whether students drop out or graduate from high school, they may experience several rejections or failures in the marketplace before becoming aware of the requisite education and experience necessary to secure a job. In short, they have few options, and many of these do not include occupations with the potential for economic independence or advancement. Increasingly, young adults are finding themselves unemployed or in dead-end occupations in the retail or fast-food service industries. Clearly, the old ways of preparing students for the world of work are no longer effective, and this is especially true for non-college-bound youth.

Completing an apprenticeship represents a means by which young adults, under the guidance of a mentor, can prepare themselves for work. They do this through experiencing an occupation in the actual work setting while completing their education. In its simplest terms, the apprenticeship model involves a marriage of school and work, whereby the individual assumes the dual role of student and employee. The role of an apprentice has been defined by Stephen Hamilton (1990) as combining work with learning, where too much emphasis on working would represent exploitation and too much emphasis on schooling would transform the apprentice into a traditional student lacking a viable connection to work. From the perspective of both the apprentice and the mentor, experiencing school and work simultaneously drives home the relevance and importance of acquiring a solid education and gaining actual work experience as a means of achieving excellence in both

arenas. Although such a model may seem rather idealistic, in Germany and in other countries apprenticeships have long been one of the primary means by which students move into the world of work. In fact, the success of the German apprenticeship system is often cited as evidence for the viability of the school-to-work transition model.

Adolescents and young adults who are trying to enter the labor market for the first time often experience unemployment as a painful failure. By moving students from all economic strata into the workforce, the apprenticeship model prevents widespread unemployment among young people. At an age when young adults in the United States typically graduate from high school, young adults in Germany have already acquired significant on-the-job training and expertise and secured employment in skilled white- and blue-collar professions. Achieving this level of training and employment in the United States typically involves additional schooling, followed by an extensive job search—often resulting in a two- to four-year delay between high school graduation and employment. This delay can be emotionally and financially costly, particularly for young adults who have no other means of financial support.

In the 1970s and 1980s, increased awareness of the success of the apprenticeship model in Germany began to attract attention from U.S. researchers and politicians. Accordingly, social scientists worked toward identifying, integrating, and implementing (on a small scale) key apprenticeship concepts, and policymakers facilitated such activities through financial support and legislative actions. Researchers working in Germany, England, and the United States (Bynner, 1992; Hamilton, 1990) identified the benefits associated with the apprenticeship model and demonstrated its effectiveness in moving adolescents from school to work. Partly in response to this and other research, legislators passed the 1994 School-to-Work Opportunities Act (STWOA), which provided federal funds as well as considerable flexibility to state and local educational systems that were interested in developing school-to-work programs.

Growing interest in the apprenticeship concept and its possible adoption in the United States led Hamilton and Wolfgang Lempert (1996) to examine the impact of the apprenticeship system on German youth and to determine the relative costs and benefits associated with its possible implementation in the United States. Although they found that the German apprenticeship system effectively moved youths into adult occupations much earlier than is typical in the United States, they also discovered certain inequalities: First, the socioeconomic status of the student's family and the sex of the student were associated with apprenticeship and job placement, and, second, employers within a given occupation differed in terms of the opportunities they afforded their apprentices. That is, at some job sites, employers and mentors viewed apprentices as the future of the organization and gave them instruction and opportunities to expand their knowledge and expertise, whereas at other sites, employers treated the apprentices as cheap and expendable labor. Despite the obvious differences across placements, however, apprentices typically consider their mentor a trusted source of guidance and support and often maintain connections with the mentor long after the conclusion of their apprenticeship (Hamilton, 1990). Thus, although the apprenticeship model

is not a perfect system and may not resolve all of the issues associated with the transition from school to work, it clearly promotes the development of viable career paths for some students who would otherwise not have the resources to move forward on their own.

Although German-style apprenticeships are far from common in the United States, this country does offer other school-to-work programs that incorporate some basic features of apprenticeships. For example, the Summer Training Education Program (STEP) and the more commonly known Job Corps, established in 1964, provide disadvantaged youth with real work experiences within a structured program (Hamilton, 1990). The Job Corps is an intensive residential program that attempts to move young adults into viable long-term occupations, whereas STEP is a summer program that requires summer school attendance in exchange for paid summer work. Although STEP combines school with work, the work experiences typically occur outside of the school setting.

Other examples include programs like Tech-Prep and school-based enterprises that maintain more of an educational focus by integrating vocational concepts into an existing curriculum (Lewis et al., 1998). Tech-Prep is, at its core, a collaborative model that involves a high school and a two-year postsecondary technical school working together to facilitate the transition from high school to a two-year trade school. In this arrangement, the high school agrees to offer specialized courses that complement the academic and vocational demands of the postsecondary institution. Upon successful graduation from high school, Tech-Prep students simply transfer into the technical school, with a clear educational advantage over those students who did not experience the specialized high school curriculum. In contrast to Tech-Prep's explicit postsecondary educational focus, school-based enterprises emphasize the development of small businesses by high school students. Students and faculty work together to develop and implement an enterprise in the school setting, which typically targets high school students and faculty as the potential consumers. School-based enterprises include in-school restaurants and school supply stores that sell pens, paper, and other sundries.

Although the apprenticeship model has both supporters and detractors, most agree that the current means by which the United States facilitates the school-to-work transition is slow, cumbersome, and financially and emotionally costly for many non-college-bound youth. The apprenticeship model and its various derivations represent an alternative that may reduce the delay between high school graduation and full-time career-related employment. In the apprenticeship system, students are workers and workers are students; hence, the transition from school to work is more gradual and appropriate for all involved. The concept of integrating vocational information into the existing school system is not a new one; indeed, vocational education is an essential aspect of the U.S. educational system. But apprenticeships do represent a possible next step within the school-to-work movement that involves going beyond simply disseminating occupational information and advancing toward the creation of an organized and cohesive system that truly integrates school and work experiences.

Erik J. Porfeli
Fred W. Vondracek

See also Career Development; Employment: Positive and Negative Consequences; Programs for Adolescents; Vocational Development; Work in Adolescence

References and further reading
Bynner, John. 1992. "Experiencing Vocational Preparation in England and Germany." *Education and Training* 34, no. 4: 1–8.
Hamilton, Stephen F. 1990. *Apprenticeship for Adulthood: Preparing Youth for the Future.* New York: Free Press.
Hamilton, Stephen F., and Wolfgang Lempert. 1996. "The Impact of Apprenticeship on Youth: A Prospective Analysis." *Journal of Research on Adolescence* 6, no. 4: 427–455.
Lewis, Theodore, James Stone III, Wayne Shipley, and Svjetlana Madzar. 1998. "The Transition from School to Work: An Examination of the Literature." *Youth and Society* 29, no. 3: 259–292.

The Arts

Several disciplines, ranging from the fine arts to the performing arts, are forms of expression that can be included under the umbrella term *arts*. By the same token, there are many different types of art forms. Examples of fine or visual art forms include painting, drawing, sculpting, architecture, and photography, whereas drama, dance, music, and performance art are generally considered examples of performing arts. Still other art forms do not fit within the boundaries of either performing or fine arts but, rather, are a combination of the two; examples include costuming, directing, producing, stage managing, stage design, light design, and filmmaking.

As the arts play a fundamental role in many adolescents' lives, it is fortunate that schools often include the arts in their curriculum. The combination of arts and academics in the schools works to foster creative thinking. In addition,

The combination of arts and academics in the schools works to foster creative thinking. (Shirley Zeiberg)

many teenagers pursue various art forms outside of the school setting. Some may even go on to a career in the arts. Yet the importance and relevance of the arts to adolescents is generally minimized or overlooked.

How the Arts Help Teenagers Develop
During the period of adolescence, teenagers are trying to discover their personal identity. The arts provide a forum for exploration and expression of the self. Creative freedom and individuality are primary tenets of such expression: Whereas many adolescents feel pressures to conform to group norms, the arts require individual expression. During adolescence, teenagers attempt to answer the question "Who am I?" Participation in the arts helps them to discover the answer to this difficult question. The arts also allow teenagers to "try on" or test various identities in an attempt to discover which one fits best. For example, when a teenager performs in a drama production, she must explore the role she will play. This process may involve researching the time period in which the play takes place, the setting of the play, and the occupation of the character. Next, the teenager must work to assume the identity of the character. By acting out the role, she has the opportunity to explore an alternative identity. Acting also allows the expression of emotions that are not normally considered appropriate. For example, whereas an angry outburst in the middle of class can lead to a detention, such an outburst within the context of a school play may well be considered an excellent performance. In short, the arts provide a safe place for self-exploration.

The arts also allow teenagers to learn both the value of teamwork and the importance of individual responsibility. Although teamwork is often necessary, responsibility for the finished product lies with the individual. For example, the student who signs his name to a painting is responsible for the work, even if he received guidance from teachers or collaborated with others toward that end. Likewise, the performer onstage is responsible for her actions and can rely only on herself. Such responsibility promotes autonomy and independence—yet another way in which adolescents can benefit from exploring the arts.

Schools and the Arts
The role of the arts in the schools generally varies across school districts. Some schools emphasize a focus on the arts, whereas others lack arts programs altogether. Those schools that do include arts programs in their curriculum vary in their degree of emphasis. For example, some schools offer a limited range of courses in only one field (e.g., visual arts), whereas others offer courses ranging from beginner to advanced in a variety of disciplines (e.g., performing arts and fine arts). Still other schools are dedicated to making the arts the primary focus of their curriculum. For example, a district with a magnet school system (in which each school has a particular focus) may devote one school to the teaching of the arts, allowing parents and students to choose the school whose program best meets their needs.

Several options are available to those students who wish to pursue the arts beyond their high school education. Many liberal arts universities and colleges have departments or schools in assorted arts disciplines, and some smaller liberal arts colleges, described as "artsy," have a reputation for focusing on the arts. In addition, certain schools specialize solely in the teaching of the arts. For example, conservatories tend to focus on the performing arts, whereas museum schools emphasize the fine arts.

Education in the arts is an extremely valuable complement to a traditional academic education; even those students who do not plan on focusing on the arts later in life can benefit a great deal from an arts education. The arts teach innovative and creative ways of thinking and solving problems as well as new and interesting ways of expressing one's emotions and ideas. Moreover, academic skills are frequently applied in the arts. For example, directors must often apply their knowledge of history when costuming a show, and lighting and set designers must understand basic trigonometry and geometry when creating a lighting plan or set. In these ways and others, the arts provide real-life problems that students can solve using their academic knowledge.

The arts also promote the use of symbolic thought. During the period of adolescence, symbolic and logical thinking skills are developing. Prior to adolescence, individuals understand the world in a very concrete manner; however, as they mature, their thinking becomes more complex and abstract. A primary component of the arts is symbolic and abstract expression and interpretation of ideas and emotions. The arts allow adolescents to exercise their minds by promoting symbolic thought. By practicing these skills, adolescents learn a different way of comprehending the world.

Many schools focus on developing adolescents' verbal and mathematical abilities. In addition, exams, such as the SAT, ACT, and GRE, test students' verbal and mathematical abilities. Many psychologists believe that these tests do not accurately measure intelligence. According to these testing methods, intelligence exists exclusively in the forms of mathematical and verbal abilities. Psychologist Howard Gardner believes in the existence of multiple intelligences. Included among the different types of intelligences he identifies are musical intelligence, bodily kinesthetic intelligence, and spatial intelligence. Many artists rely heavily on these intellectual domains to produce their work. Musicians utilize musical intelligence, dancers and actors utilize bodily kinesthetic intelligence, and visual artists utilize spatial intelligence. Some people may be experts in one intellectual form and novices in another. For example, a pianist may be an expert in the domain of musical intelligence, but a novice in the domain of linguistic intelligence. In the United States, verbal and mathematical intelligences are highly valued, whereas musical, bodily kinesthetic, and spatial intelligences are considered less important.

Extracurricular Arts
The future of arts education is threatened by severe underfunding. In addition, many school officials consider the arts to be a dispensable element of the curriculum. Traditional academics are perceived as being a more essential component of an education, so the arts are pushed aside. Faced with this situation, students must turn to extracurricular programs in search of an education in the arts.

Some students form school clubs or organizations that focus on the arts. The schools may require that an adult be present during club meetings; however, students typically run these meetings and the activities that are planned. Alternatively, teenagers can generally find organizations within their community that provide instruction in various art forms. Community arts groups usually offer programs for teenagers in the arts. For example, community theater groups often schedule summer productions and cast adolescents in roles. In addition, some states fund summer programs whereby a selected number of teens are invited to attend an intensive summer program in specific arts disciplines. Many religious groups also provide opportunities for adolescents to engage in artistic activities. Another option for teenagers interested in the arts is private lessons. Dance schools, drama academies, and museum schools often offer programs for interested adolescents. Clearly, there are many opportunities for adolescents who wish to pursue their interest in the arts.

A Career in the Arts

Adolescents who choose to pursue the arts as a career must consider several limitations. Since the arts are not heavily funded, there is a limited amount of work available to those who wish to be employed as full-time artists. Adolescents in the arts may thus wish to consider "backup" or "fallback" plans. In particular, they should be encouraged to pursue both the arts and an academic field so as not to limit their options. Indeed, many professional artists work two jobs: one related to the arts and one that is more lucrative.

Professional artists may also have to rely on "backup" plans in case of injury. Injuries can prevent artists such as dancers, actors, and musicians from pursuing their art. The way in which an individual copes with an injury and the potential disruption it causes is important.

Adolescents, who had planned on pursuing the arts but are unable to due to injury, will benefit from positive support from teachers, parents, and peers. These teenagers should be encouraged to find an alternative form of expression or creative outlet. Alternatively, they may be interested in careers that combine the arts with other disciplines. Fortunately, many such career opportunities are available.

For example, adolescents who are interested in both the arts and writing may wish to consider a career in art review or critique. Many major news publications include arts sections that not only report on local exhibitions but also provide reviews and critiques of artists and their work. Art instruction is another option. Schools, community groups, religious organizations, and private institutions often hire art teachers, and museums frequently hire curators and collectors who are highly knowledgeable in a particular arts field. Art therapy is yet another option for interested adolescents. Engaging in an artistic project is generally considered to be therapeutic. Art as therapy is now regarded as a type of clinical treatment. Visual art and dance therapies are frequently used with both children and adults. Clinicians use art as a means of exploring and interpreting their patients' thoughts and emotions.

Jennifer S. Brown

See also Media; Media, Effects of

References and further reading
Gardner, Howard. 1983. *Frames of Mind.* New York: Basic Books.
Greene, Maxine. 1995. *Releasing the Imagination.* San Francisco: Jossey-Bass.
Moody, William J. 1990. *Artistic Intelligences: Implications for Education.* New York: Teachers College Press.

Munro, Thomas, and Herbert Read. 1960. *The Creative Arts in American Education.* Cambridge, MA: Harvard University Press.

Asian American Adolescents: Comparisons and Contrasts

More than 10 million Asian Americans reside in the United States, constituting about 4 percent of the total population. Within the next two decades, the number of Asian Americans in this country is expected to almost double. Most of the Asian American population is concentrated on the east and west coasts in cities such as Los Angeles, San Francisco, and New York. Asian Americans are a diverse people, having roots in Japan, Korea, Taiwan, Vietnam, Laos, Cambodia, China, the Philippines, India, Thailand, and Malaysia. Because these groups differ with respect to language, customs, and immigration patterns to the United States, the "Asian American adolescent experience" varies greatly from individual to individual. However, some issues are relevant for all Asian American teenagers, such as ethnic identity, school achievement, autonomy, and changing relationships with parents and peers.

One important developmental task for Asian American adolescents is to form an *ethnic identity*—a process that includes exploring the meaning of being Asian American in a multicultural society such as the United States; confronting discrimination, prejudice, and stereotyping; and participating (or not participating) in the cultural behaviors and practices of their particular ethnic group.

Several stages of ethnic identity development have been identified. The first stage is ethnic identity *foreclosure.* In this stage, adolescents have not deeply questioned what being Asian American specifically means to their personal lives. After a period of unquestioning, however, something happens that compels them to explore the meaning and significance of their "Asianness." A triggering event might be the realization that there are too few Asian American role models in the United States; or it might be a question from a friend as to why certain customs or traditions are celebrated in their homes. This stage of ethnic identity *exploration* is a time when adolescents actively seek out what being Asian in America means to them personally—by participating in cultural customs, learning more about the history of their people, or spending time with others of the same ethnic group. This exploration stage leads to ethnic identity *achievement*, a stage in which Asian American adolescents express a commitment to, have an understanding of, and are comfortable with being Asian American. Studies have shown that Asian American adolescents who achieve a positive and strong sense of ethnic identity demonstrate positive psychological functioning in terms of family relations and positive self-evaluations.

Asian American youth differ from youth of other ethnicities in several ways. Compared to European American youth, Asian Americans report spending less time with their peers in activities such as talking on the telephone, participating in sports, and "hanging out." The nature of the peer group also differs slightly between these two groups. Asian American peers tend to show more disapproval for misconduct behaviors (e.g., copying homework, cheating on a test, lying to parents) and are more supportive

Asian Americans are diverse people, differing with respect to language, customs, and immigration patterns to the United States. Because of this, the "Asian-American adolescent experience" varies greatly from individual to individual. (Laura Dwight)

of academic endeavors. Compared to Hispanic American, African American, and European American adolescents, Asian American adolescents are inclined to date and engage in sexual behavior at a later age.

Several researchers have reported that Asian American adolescents perform better in school than their non-Asian peers. A host of possible reasons, ranging from parenting practices and cultural beliefs to peer-group influences, have been cited to explain these findings. It is a myth, however, that all Asian American adolescents succeed at school. In fact, there is great heterogeneity among Asian American youth—some of whom, for example, struggle in school because of their difficulty with English as a second language. Factors such as country of origin and generational status also contribute to this variation in school performance.

Regarding the parent-adolescent relationship, many Asian American adolescents report that their parents are more *authoritarian* (strict and demanding of unquestioning obedience) and less *authoritative* (strict but responsive, and inclined to encourage autonomy) than parents in other ethnic groups. Although some researchers have proposed that authoritarianism is a less-than-optimal style of parenting, Asian American adolescents overall do not seem to be as negatively affected as other groups by authoritarian parenting concerning psychosocial adjustment (e.g., self-esteem and work orientation), deviance (e.g., substance use and antisocial behavior), and school performance (e.g., grade-point average and homework time). Moreover, it has been argued that these particular types of frequently studied parenting styles may be inadequate to describe Asian parents—in other words, that other aspects of parenting that are indigenous to the culture may more accurately depict Asian parenting. For example, in Chinese culture the notion of *training*—which involves teaching and educating children in the context of high involvement, support, caring, and concern—may be more useful in understanding how certain parenting styles impact Asian American adolescents' psychosocial development.

Many Asian American adolescents, especially those with immigrant parents, have to deal with and reconcile their parents' cultural values and attitudes, some of which run counter to the values and attitudes of mainstream society. This clash of cultures—one of which promotes *interdependence* (characteristic of most Asian countries) and the other, mainstream culture, which promotes *independence*—may lead to differing expectations between parents and adolescents regarding appropriate levels of autonomy. For example, they may disagree on whether the adolescents can choose whom to date, whether they are allowed to stay out with friends at night, or what particular career to pursue. This mismatch rooted in different cultural belief systems may, in turn, lead to serious conflicts. Of course, the degree to which parents and their Asian American adolescents conflict in terms of values and expectations varies from family to family.

There are various ways in which Asian American adolescents deal with growing up within two distinct cultures. They can become *assimilated*, taking on the majority culture's ways and rejecting their culture of origin. They can become *separated*, immersing themselves in the culture of origin while rejecting the majority culture. They can become *marginal*, rejecting both the culture of origin and the majority culture. Or they can become *bicultural*, maintaining ties to both cultures. Those adolescents who choose this last option allow themselves the opportunity to draw from the traditions and strengths of both their Asian heritage and the mainstream culture.

Linda P. Juang

See also Asian American Adolescents: Issues Influencing Identity; Ethnic Identity; Identity; Racial Discrimination

References and further reading
Chao, Ruth K. 1994. "Beyond Parental Control and Authoritarian Parenting Style: Understanding Chinese Parenting through the Cultural Notion of Training." *Child Development* 65: 1111–1119.
Chuansheng, Chen, Ellen Greenberger, Julia Lester, Qi Dong, and Miaw-Schue Guo. 1998. "A Cross-Cultural Study of Family and Peer Correlates of Adolescent Misconduct." *Developmental Psychology* 34, no. 4: 770–781.
Feldman, Shirley S., and Glen R. Elliot. 1990. *At the Threshold: The Developing Adolescent.* Cambridge, MA: Harvard University Press.
Feldman, Shirley S., Rebecca N. Turner, and Katy Araujo. 1999. "Interpersonal Context as an Influence on Sexual Timetables of Youths: Gender and Ethnic Effects." *Journal of Research on Adolescence* 9, no. 1: 25–52.
Juang, Linda P., Jacqueline V. Lerner, John McKinney, and Alex von Eye. 1999. "The Goodness of Fit of Autonomy Expectations between Asian-American Late Adolescents and Their Parents." *International Journal of Behavioral Development* 23, no. 4: 1023–1048.
Uba, Laura. 1994. *Asian Americans: Personality Pattern, Identity, and Mental Health.* New York: Guilford Press.

Asian American Adolescents: Issues Influencing Identity

Identity becomes an especially salient issue during adolescence, which is marked both by teenagers' desire to fit in and by their preoccupation with how others view them. Asian American adolescents' search for identity is challenged by another question: how to make sense of their ethnic background, which influences how they perceive themselves as well as how others view them.

If we were to picture an Asian American teenager in our mind, who would we see? What would we assume about the

To establish healthy identities, adolescents must reconcile and embrace their heritage without feeling devalued. (Skjold Photographs)

teenager? Although we would not consciously ask ourselves these questions, we may unconsciously answer them upon thinking of or seeing an Asian American teenager. Some of us may picture a quiet, shy "Chinese kid" with glasses. Others—teachers, for example— may think that this "Chinese kid" is smart and expect the teen to do well in school, especially in math and science classes. Guidance counselors may assume that the teen is a good student because they take it for granted that all Asian Americans are model students. Still others may assume that they work hard, that they don't cause trouble and thus have no problems, that society doesn't have to worry about them. Well, not exactly.

These seemingly positive assumptions are prevalent in our society, but they do not necessarily work to the advantage of Asian American adolescents. Indeed, such assumptions may even pose a challenge to their identity development. To explore this further, we need to understand more about the world of Asian American teenagers. For example, what are some of the major factors shaping the identity of Asian American adolescents? These factors are found on many levels. Let's look at the broadest level first.

The historical context and climate set the tone for Asian Americans' existence in the United States. The past mistreatment of Asian Americans, such as discriminatory immigration laws and internment of Japanese Americans, made it clear that Asians were considered "aliens ineligible for citizenship" from early on (Lott, 1998). Present in the United States since the 1800s, Asians played a significant role in building this country; many even fought as American soldiers. However, many Asian Americans are still considered "foreigners."

When American figure skaters Tara Lipinski and Michelle Kwan won the Olympic gold and silver medals, respectively, the nation was overjoyed. However, remarks made by the press implied that Michelle Kwan was not seen as a "real" American.

Likewise, Asian American adolescents may encounter incidents such as the following.

> Sharon is a fourth generation Japanese American. She is walking down the street one day when someone shouts, "Go back to your own country, you Chinese!" She is startled and shocked. She thinks to herself, "I was born in California, so were my parents and their parents. Besides, I'm not Chinese!"
>
> Janet is a third-generation Chinese American. She goes to a department store to look for some shoes. A sales person approaches Janet, speaking in a slow, deliberate tone, "C-a-n I h-e-l-p y-o-u? S-p-e-a-k E-n-g-l-i-s-h?"
>
> Phil is a second-generation Korean American who just moved to New Jersey from California. He meets his neighbor for the first time. The neighbor asks him, "So, where are you from?" Phil replies, "California." The neighbor asks again, "Where are you r-e-a-l-l-y from?" Phil replies, "the Bay Area in northern California. I was born there." The neighbor says, "I have a Chinese friend. His grocery has the best vegetables in town. He works hard. He doesn't speak much English though. Maybe you can talk to him in Chinese." Phil thinks to himself, "What? Why would she assume that I speak Chinese? Does she think that all Asians are the same?"

Clearly, Asian Americans are still perceived as aliens in a foreign land in the United States. How are Asian American adolescents to make sense of this perception? How are they to deal with feeling "different"? How does their sense of not belonging in the society influence their identity development? The experience of being treated as if they do not belong in the society in which they live and the perception of being "different" from the dominant European American group may make it especially difficult for Asian American adolescents to feel proud of their heritage. As adolescents, they may already be especially sensitive about how others view them; they may also be struggling with the question of whether they want to "fit in" or be "unique." The perception of difference due to their ethnic background may add even more stress to their lives. Some may try to fit in by pretending to be white and distancing themselves from anything related to their ethnic background. Others may feel resentful toward the white dominant group and thus may retreat and submerge themselves into their ethnic culture and group. Still others, however, may be able to develop and maintain a balance by integrating both the mainstream culture and their ethnic culture of origin in a way that makes sense in both contexts. Regardless, these teenagers must develop their own way of managing and living with two or more cultures.

The process in which Asian American adolescents develop bicultural competencies is influenced by the support system available to them. For example, if their peers accept and respect their differences as well as their similarities, they will find it easier to explore, accept, and value their ethnic background. Conversely, if their peers devalue their differ-

ences, they will find it much harder, because they will feel that they don't fit in with other teenagers. The diversity of teachers and other students also influences the sense of belonging for Asian American teenagers. If they are among very few Asian Americans in school, they may try to fit in with the majority group and thus feel discouraged from exploring their ethnic heritage. Or they may feel disconnected from their white friends due to differences in their experiences having to do with prejudice, cultural practices, and so on. Some may exclusively seek out other Asian American students for support. But if the school culture respects diversity and difference, and provides support for all students, Asian American adolescents may feel encouraged to explore their ethnic heritage, develop understanding and respect for other ethnic groups, and feel good about being Asian American.

The ability of Asian American teenagers to make sense of the school climate and peer influences is affected by another factor as well: familial and parental socialization. How do the parents influence the way Asian American adolescents view themselves? Parental socialization is very much interconnected with the larger historical and present contexts mentioned earlier. In particular, it is influenced by economic concerns, amount of time spent in the United States, ties to the homeland, attitudes toward the dominant culture, and support from the ethnic community. In addition, although some Asian American groups have been in the United States for many generations, such as Japanese Americans and Chinese Americans, there are more first-generation Asian immigrant parents than American-born Asian parents. Subgroups such as Korean,

Vietnamese, or other more recent immigrants may face barriers such as language, culture, and economic survival.

Because of racism, cultural differences, and language barriers, many Asian immigrant parents feel isolated and rejected by the mainstream society. Lack of English proficiency often prevents them from participating in their children's school or socializing with people other than those in their own ethnic community, thus further isolating them within the confines of their ethnic enclave. Socializing their children to be competent members of this society while struggling with their own acculturation may create unique challenges for Asian American parents. One such challenge is language related: As their children become more comfortable with conversing in English, the communication gap between Asian immigrant parents and their children becomes larger. The children's problems may be overlooked by the parents as a result of this gap, creating a strain in their relationship. In addition, many Asian American children serve as their parents' language broker. Knowing that their parents are helpless with the language, these children may perceive their parents to be outsiders in the United States. As much as they want to help their parents, they may feel burdened having to "parent" their parents when it comes to language and cultural barriers. The children may resent this burden because it makes them feel that they, too, do not belong in the United States, especially when their parents have a hard time functioning in the mainstream society without their help.

At the same time, many Asian immigrant parents may want to raise their children with their own ethnic cultural values because they still feel strong ties to their own ethnic culture. However, as their children become socialized and assimilated into the individualistic U.S. culture outside their home, the parents' values from their ethnic culture are challenged. Although these ethnic cultural values may provide grounding, support, and identity to some Asian American adolescents, others may resent their parents' traditional values, which get in the way of doing "normal" teenager things such as dating. Their desire to be "their own person" apart from their identification with their parents, as well as their desire to fit in with other teenagers, may lead Asian American teenagers to rebel against the expectations placed on them.

This conflict between immigrant parents and their children may create psychological burdens for both the parents and the children, but such burdens have been largely overlooked by society owing to the image of Asian Americans as the model minority. Some Asian immigrant parents believe that by living up to the model-minority image, they can earn respect from the white dominant group and thereby gain social mobility in the United States. In Asian countries, teachers and scholars have traditionally been revered. Indeed, respect for education is a value that Asian immigrants have brought from their ethnic culture. However, in the United States, education takes on another layer of meaning for Asian immigrant families: Academic achievement is part of children's obligation to the parents in return for the parents' sacrifices in the United States. In short, children bring honor to the family through educational attainment; educational achievement is considered a buffer for prejudice and racism. Therefore, Asian American children are under great pressure to achieve in school—both from their teachers, who hold their Asian students up to the model-minority stereotype, and from their parents, who have made sacrifices in their lives to provide for their children.

This situation creates tremendous pressure on the adolescents to fit the good-student image and to meet the expectations of their parents. Some may try to excel in their studies. Some may become overachievers. Some may feel resentful and thus purposely distance themselves from the stereotypes and expectations confronting them—that is, by joining gangs, drinking, taking drugs, and so on. Some may be unable to rise to the high expectations placed on them and feel inadequate. Some may miss out on a social life. But whatever the outcome, the good-student image and model-minority assumptions do not necessarily help.

Asian immigrant parents want their children to learn the ways of the dominant culture so they can succeed in the United States. They want their children to avoid experiencing the same language and economic barriers they have faced, so they encourage their children to speak English in school and encourage them to work hard to obtain a high level of education. Fluency in English and U.S. education will open doors for the children that the parents could not open due to such barriers, and the children can go into white-collar professions and be more respected by the dominant culture. At the same time, however, Asian immigrant parents want their children to retain their ethnic values outside of school and the realm of success. Because Asian cultures value the interdependent nature of relationships and harmony, Asian parents generally socialize their children to avoid conflict and to maintain a harmonious relationship with others. Thus, Asian

families have been thought to be "enmeshed," which, by U.S. standards, is an "unhealthy" state of family functioning because the children are not encouraged to individuate from the family. In short, many Asian American children are socialized in school to become more individuated but taught at home to respect group harmony and collectiveness. How are they to make sense of these two seemingly conflicting messages?

As previously discussed, Asian American children must develop various means by which to manage and live with such contradictions. Indeed, by adolescence, many have acquired an understanding of ethnic labels, become aware of the characteristics that distinguish groups, developed specific attitudes toward their own ethnic group and other groups, and become cognizant of social expectations and behavioral patterns that are linked with ethnicity. However, the development of Asian American children has not been given proper attention due to society's misperception of them as well-adjusted high achievers. Beyond the stereotypes are real people. As teenagers they experience all the ordinary problems and joys that come with adolescence. But they have another task as well: exploring and understanding their ethnic background, and coming to terms with the meaning of being Asian American in a society that assigns status according to racial group membership. To become whole persons, they must reconcile and embrace their heritage without feeling devalued. Teachers, counselors, parents, and peers can help Asian American teenagers by being sensitive and supportive to their needs, watchful of their concerns, and respectful of their differences as well as their similarities. With these things in mind, upon thinking about Asian American adolescents, we will no longer picture that shy "Chinese kid" in glasses but, instead, see many different faces who want to be recognized as individuals.

E. Ree Noh

See also Asian American Adolescents: Comparisons and Contrasts; Ethnic Identity; Identity; Racial Discrimination

References and further reading
Chao, Ruth K. 1996. "Chinese and European American Mothers' Beliefs about the Role of Parenting in Children's School Success." *Journal of Cross Cultural Psychology* 27, no. 4: 403–423.
Cocking, Rodney R., and Patricia M. Greenfield. 1994. "Diversity and Development of Asian Americans: Research Gaps in Minority Child Development." *Journal of Applied Developmental Psychology* 15: 301–303.
Hieshima, Joyce A., and Barbara Schneider. 1994. "Intergenerational Effects on the Cultural and Cognitive Socialization of Third and Fourth Generations of Japanese Americans." *Journal of Applied Developmental Psychology* 15: 319–327.
Kim, Uichol, and Maria B. J. Chun. 1994. "Educational 'Success' of Asian Americans: An Indigenous Perspective." *Journal of Applied Developmental Psychology* 15: 329–343.
Lee, S. J. 1994. "Behind the Model Minority Stereotype: Voices of High and Low Achieving Asian American Students." *Anthropology and Education Quarterly* 25, no. 4: 413–429.
Lott, Juanita Tamayo. 1998. *Asian Americans: From Racial Categories to Multiple Identities.* Walnut Creek, CA: Alta Mira Press.
Park, Eun-ja. 1994. "Educational Needs and Parenting Concerns of Korean American Parents." *Psychological Reports* 75: 559–562.
Rotheram-Borus, Mary J. 1993. "Biculturalism among Adolescents." Pp. 81–102 in *Ethnic Identity: Formation and Transmission among Hispanics and Other Minorities.* Edited by M. E. Bernal and G. P. Knight. Albany: State University of New York Press.
Shoho, Alan R. 1994. "A Historical Comparison of Parental Involvement of Three Generations of Japanese Americans (Isseis, Niseis, Sanseis) in the Education of Their Children." *Journal of Applied Developmental Psychology* 15: 305–311.
Yee, Albert H. 1992. "Asians as Stereotypes and Students: Misperceptions That Persist." *Educational Psychology Review* 4, no. 1: 95–132.

Attention-Deficit/Hyperactivity Disorder (ADHD)

Attention-deficit/hyperactivity disorder (ADHD) is the most recent diagnosis for individuals who exhibit problems with attention, impulsiveness, and overactivity. Although all people experience each of these behaviors to some degree, those with ADHD experience them so severely that work, school, and social interactions may become impaired. It is estimated that 3 to 5 percent of the population has the disorder. ADHD occurs across all socioeconomic, cultural, and racial backgrounds, and it is more commonly diagnosed in boys than in girls.

History
The condition now called ADHD first attracted scientific interest in 1902. Physicians had noticed some children who were aggressive, defiant, resistant to discipline, and excessively emotional and who showed little inhibitory control. Over the past century, the names for this set of behaviors have changed and evolved as more has been learned about

the causes of the disorder. Originally, scientists named the condition "minimal brain damage" (MBD) because it was thought to result from brain infections, trauma, or other injuries or complications occurring during pregnancy or delivery. This label was replaced by *minimal brain dysfunction* when no evidence could be found to pinpoint the role of trauma in the brain. Renamed *hyperactive child syndrome,* the disorder shifted in focus from cause to symptom. Later, hyperactivity came to be viewed as not the only or most important symptom; poor attention span and impulse control were now considered equally important. This prompted another change in name: *attention-deficit disorder (ADD) with or without hyperactivity.* The term currently in use—*attention-deficit/hyperactivity disorder*—also reflects the recognition that hyperactivity may or may not be a prevailing symptom.

Characteristics of ADHD
Inattention
People with ADHD have difficulty with attention. *Attention* is widely defined as alertness, arousal, selectivity (paying attention to some stimuli while ignoring others), sustained focus, or nondistractibility. ADHD individuals may become distracted by what is happening around them and be unable to stay focused on the task at hand—especially when the task is not interesting or rewarding. Parents and teachers often note the following behaviors as problems with attention: not listening, failing to finish assigned tasks, daydreaming, losing things, and having difficulty concentrating.

Impulsivity. The inability to delay a response or to delay gratification is another characteristic of ADHD. Individuals with this disorder often respond quickly to situations without waiting for instructions to be completed. They often opt for the immediate smaller reward instead of waiting for the larger reward. They frequently have difficulty taking turns, blurt out answers to questions, and interrupt conversations. And because they often fail to consider the negative and dangerous consequences associated with a particular situation, they may engage in unnecessary risk taking.

Hyperactivity. A third characteristic of ADHD is hyperactivity—a level of activity exceeding that considered normal for people of the same age. Restlessness, fidgeting, and talking quickly are some examples of hyperactive behavior. Teachers find children with ADHD often getting out of their seats, moving about the class without permission, playing with objects not related to the task, and talking out of turn.

Possible Causes
ADHD runs in families and is likely the result of biological and environmental influences. Evidence indicates that among individuals with ADHD the brain may be structurally or functionally different, particularly in the frontal lobe, which is associated with attention, planning, and inhibition. In addition, the central nervous system of ADHD individuals is believed to be underaroused, thus requiring more outward stimulation from the environment. ADHD is not related to intelligence. In fact, many children and adolescents with ADHD are very bright. For these individuals, ADHD is not a matter of not knowing what to do but a matter of not being able to do what they know.

Consequences of ADHD

Clearly, many of the behaviors associated with ADHD can be disruptive in a classroom and frustrating to students, parents, and teachers alike. Children and adolescents with this disorder are often punished for their "misbehavior." They often find school frustrating and unrewarding and, over time, may become even less motivated to succeed. Blurting out answers, not paying attention to details on a homework assignment, or forgetting to turn assignments in may have negative academic and disciplinary consequences. Furthermore, because these individuals exhibit aggressive, disruptive, and other socially unacceptable behaviors, their peer relationships may suffer as a result of rejection by other children. In short, without proper intervention, the ADHD adolescent can quickly lose ground both academically and socially.

Diagnosis

Teachers or parents who suspect a problem with ADHD can refer the student for an evaluation. However, there is no definitive medical test to determine whether an individual does or does not have ADHD. Rather, the diagnosis is made on the basis of information gathered about behavioral symptoms identified from a variety of sources and evaluations. A team of individuals composed of school personnel, family, and a medical doctor contribute information toward making a diagnosis. The legal standard for determining whether a child has ADHD is based on whether the child's disability is diagnosed according to the *Diagnostic and Statistical Manual of Mental Disorders, Fourth Edition (DSM-IV)*. And even then, mere observation of attention problems, impulsivity, and hyperactivity is not sufficient for making

the diagnosis: Other possible causes for these behaviors—such as auditory processing disorders, anxiety or depressive disorders, other learning disabilities, or a chaotic home environment—must still be ruled out.

Once ADHD is properly identified, there are many options for treatment.

Treatment

Both behavioral and medical interventions are available for ADHD adolescents. Teachers, parents, and the ADHD individuals themselves can be trained to master techniques for optimizing behavior and performance, and frequent positive reinforcements throughout the day can motivate a student to stay on task. Feedback from parents and teachers should be frequent and immediate. Teachers should provide rules and instructions that are clear, brief, and, if possible, delivered through modes of presentation that are more visible and external than those required for the management of normal children. In addition, children can be taught self-management skills and ways to organize and plan through self-monitoring and self-reinforcement.

Stimulants are the medications most commonly prescribed for treating the symptoms of ADHD. Because these drugs raise the level of activity, arousal, or alertness in the central nervous system, they can replace the individual's need to seek out interesting stimuli. Some common stimulants are methylphenidate (Ritalin), pemoline (Cylert), amphetamine (Adderall), and dextroamphetamine (Dexedrine). Unfortunately, these medications can also have side effects such as loss of appetite, nervousness, irritability, anxiety, and insomnia. For those individuals who cannot tolerate such side effects, antidepressants can be tried as an alternative drug treatment. Most commonly implemented is a comprehensive approach combining cognitive-behavioral interventions with medication.

Susan Averna

See also Conduct Problems; Developmental Challenges; Disorders, Psychological and Social; Memory

References and further reading
American Psychiatric Association. 1994. *Diagnostic and Statistical Manual of Mental Disorders, Fourth Edition.* Washington, DC: American Psychiatric Association.
Barkley, Russell. 1998. *Attention-Deficit/Hyperactivity Disorder: A Handbook for Diagnosis and Treatment.* New York: Guilford Press.
Barkley, Russell, George DuPaul, and Mary McMurray. 1990. "A Comprehensive Evaluation of Attention Deficit Disorder with and without Hyperactivity." *Journal of Consulting and Clinical Psychology* 58: 775–789.
DuPaul, George, Russell Barkley, and Daniel Connor. 1998. "Stimulants." Pp. 510–551 in *Attention-Deficit/Hyperactivity Disorder: A Handbook for Diagnosis and Treatment.* New York: Guilford Press.
Fowler, Mary. 1992. *Attention Deficit Disorders: An In-Depth Look from an Educational Perspective. C.H.A.D.D. Educators Manual.* Fairfax, VA: CASET Associates.
Mercugliana, Marianne. 1999. "What Is Attention-Deficit/Hyperactivity Disorder?" *Pediatric Clinics of North America* 46, no. 5: 831–843.
Mirsky, Allan. 1996. "Disorders of Attention: A Neuropsychological Perspective." Pp. 71–96 in *Attention, Memory, and Executive Function.* Edited by G. Reed Lyon and Norman Krasnegor. Baltimore: Paul H. Brookes.
Spencer, Thomas, Joseph Biederman, and Timothy Wilens. 1998. "Pharmacotherapy of ADHD with Antidepressants." Pp. 552–563 in *Attention-Deficit/Hyperactivity Disorder: A Handbook for Diagnosis and Treatment.* New York: Guilford Press.

Attractiveness, Physical

Physical attractiveness can be defined as a quality that allows a person who possesses it to attract other people's attention or interest. It is also a complex psychological and social phenomenon. There are two kinds of attractiveness: one that presupposes good looks, regular and harmonic features, neatness, and openness to communication; and another that is similar to sexual appeal, the ability to arouse desire in members of the opposite sex. Even this brief description indicates that attractiveness is based on behavioral as well as physical characteristics.

Attractiveness has historically been important in human societies, but the actual study of this phenomenon traces back to the work of Charles Darwin, the evolutionist who originated the idea of natural selection. Darwin proposed that physical attractiveness is one of the basic qualities that allow for the "survival of the fittest," a principle that secures the survival of the whole species. That is, despite cultural differences, for all nations and cultures, being attractive means, above all, being healthy and strong. This is true in rural communities where physical strength plays an important role as an economic factor affecting production of the food supply. Here, the survival quality of attractiveness and health seems obvious. But what can be said about aristocratic beauty, especially the ideal of the pale, fragile, and passive woman that has epitomized attractiveness throughout the history of European societies? In fact, this ideal does not contradict Darwin's principle. As a typical "male society," aristocratic Europe demanded that women be passive, weak, and dependent, thus reinforcing the male "rule of power," which required a man to be strong, assertive, and aggressive. To understand this principle better, consider an extreme case of "male community," a rural culture of Spain. There, the culmination of folklore wisdom concerning physical beauty is a proverb: "El hombre como el oso: lo mas feo, lo mas hermoso" (Men are like bears: the uglier, the more handsome). This apparent paradox is nevertheless solvable: The fittest man in such a community is the most active, aggressive, strong, and experienced, one who can protect himself, his family, and his fellow villagers, one who fought in battles and does not care a lot about his looks.

Taking all this into consideration, we can begin to understand how the process of natural selection works. Physically attractive people have the highest chance of being chosen as marriage or mating partners, so they play the biggest role in the process of reproduction, producing offspring that are strong and capable of survival. Often left out of this vital process are physically unattractive, unhealthy people, those who do not fit into this societal schema. Along these lines, research has established a link between attractiveness and dating behavior. Attractive adolescents are the preferred dating partners, regardless of their other characteristics.

The survival value of physical attractiveness is its most global characteristic. But also note that in different cultures this quality may mean astonishingly different things. In the "male community" mentioned above, power is attributed to men, and beauty to women. In a "female community," by contrast, the women are the more active, assertive, and politically and economically independent members of society, whereas the men are concerned about looking attractive and are

Some of the many facets of physical attractiveness are regular and harmonic features and neatness. (Wartenberg/Picture Press/Corbis)

actively engaging in a competition for being chosen as sexual partners. An example of such community is the Wodaabe tribe in northeastern Nigeria. The men of this tribe care tremendously about their appearance, combing their hair and arranging it fancily, spending a lot of time taking care of their skin and faces, taking pride in their big straight noses. In fact, this is why they are considered more beautiful than the women—because women's noses cannot be as big as men's noses. The men of this tribe even engage in a "garewol" ceremony, which is simply a male beauty contest.

In short, physical attractiveness is essentially an evolutionary quality that varies greatly across cultures, depending on the community's structure and value (priority) system. It is also dependent on contextual, societal, economical, and, to a large extent, moral factors. Whereas in a rural Mediterranean community a man who is strong and aggressive is considered attractive, in our society (which also is not free of stereotypes) the same principle holds, but in reverse: One who is attractive is morally good. Social scientists call this the "beauty-is-good" principle, and it manifests itself in very complex ways.

For example, as researchers have shown, attractive people are expected to possess better moral characteristics and to be more self-reliant, socially and sexually responsive, and successful in life. This expectation is a stereotype, of course, and it has its limitations, but it also has tremendous power. The fact is that people tend to try to live up to expectations that other people have about them—a phenomenon known as "self-fulfilling prophecy." In short, attractive people who are expected to behave in certain ways eventually end up behaving in those ways, or at least shaping their behavior in that direction. Like all people, they draw conclusions about themselves based on other people's perceptions. Having perceived a certain image, they tend to behave in accordance with it. Thus, because attractive people expect success, they actually do often become successful in life. This "social perception" process is at work during adolescence, when appraisal from peers is important in one's self-evaluation.

Research on the impact of physical attractiveness during adolescence has revealed that teachers expect higher academic performance from physically attractive youth. In addition, physically attractive teens are judged by adults to possess better character, to be more poised and self-confident, and to be more in control of their own destiny (Adams, 1991). Attractiveness has also been shown to play a role in the employability of adolescents and adults: Attractive job candidates are viewed as having more potential and better task performance than their unattractive peers. Conversely, some research findings point to a positive relationship between unattractiveness and a greater risk for psychopathology (Adams, 1991).

Of course, the "social perception" principle is not the only factor at work. Many other factors, such as intellectual level, moral strength, and a secure support base, also influence the course of each person's life. Nevertheless, knowledge about the "beauty-is-good" principle, as well as about cultural influences on what is and what is not considered attractive, can promote our understanding of ourselves.

Some researchers, particularly those arguing from a feminist standpoint, emphasize the dangers of what has been called the "beauty trap." They point out that physical attractiveness, especially for a woman, may actually be an impediment to her career. ("She is beautiful; why does she need a career?") Another concern is that attractive people, mainly adolescents, may tend to attribute their success, if achieved, to their good looks, while doubting their intellectual and personality qualities. But this, too, is a danger that can be avoided if we judge ourselves on the basis of real achievements, not other peoples' opinions.

In the final analysis, beauty is neither a trap nor a destiny. It is, however, an important societal and psychological factor, of which we should be fully aware.

Janna Jilnina

See also Appearance, Cultural Factors in; Appearance Management; Body Build; Body Fat, Changes in; Body Hair; Body Image; Puberty: Physical Changes; Self-Consciousness

References and further reading
Adams, Gerald. R. 1991. "Physical Attractiveness and Adolescent Development. Pp. 785–789 in *Encyclopedia of Adolescence*. Edited by Richard M. Lerner, Anne C. Petersen, and Jeanne Brooks-Gunn. New York: Garland.
Cole, Letha B., and Mary Winkler. 1994. *The Good Body: Asceticism in Contemporary Culture*. New Haven, CT: Yale University Press.
Jones, Doug. 1996. *Physical Attractiveness and the Theory of Sexual Selection*. Ann Arbor: University of Michigan Press.
Patzer, Gordon. 1985. *The Physical Attractiveness Phenomenon*. New York: Plenum Press.

Autonomy

"Stand on your own two feet." "Pull yourself up by your own bootstraps." "If your friends jumped off a bridge, would you jump, too?" When one thinks of all the slogans that reflect the importance of personal choice and independence in the United States, it is obvious that autonomy is highly valued. Within this culture, it is generally expected that parents will socialize their children to be independent and look forward to the time when their children demonstrate personal responsibility. Thus, developing the capacity to function autonomously, while maintaining connections and seeking support from others when needed, is

an important issue that confronts most young people.

Indeed, autonomy is a central concept in theories of adolescent development. Since it can take many forms, behavioral, cognitive, and emotional dimensions have been identified. *Behavioral autonomy* encompasses self-governance, regulation of one's own behavior, and acting on personal decisions. *Cognitive autonomy* is the capacity for independent reasoning and decision making without excessive reliance on social validation, a subjective sense of self-reliance, and the belief that one has choices. And *emotional autonomy* is defined in terms of relationships with others and includes relinquishing dependencies and individuating from parents (Steinberg, 1999). The development of behavioral, cognitive, and emotional autonomy during adolescence reflects progression toward becoming an adult who not only has good mental health, high self-esteem, and a positive self-concept but also is self-motivated, self-initiating, and self-regulating.

It is during adolescence that individuals make major advances in autonomy. These advances are prompted by the convergence of an increasingly adultlike appearance, cognitive development, and expanding social relationships, along with the granting of more rights and responsibilities by others. Yet, parents, peers, schools, and societies also have a significant influence on autonomy. For example, parents influence the development of autonomy by structuring interactions with adolescents that allow negotiation and decision making, build a positive self-concept, and promote feelings of competence and the ability to control one's own direction in life. When interactions with social partners have such qualities, optimal autonomous functioning depends on maintaining connections with these partners while becoming increasingly self-regulating and independent (e.g., Hill and Holmbeck, 1986).

Recent perspectives on adolescent autonomy can be best understood in the context of some more classic perspectives, among which the most well known are those of Anna Freud (1958) and Peter Blos (1979). Both theorists believed that conflict between adolescents and parents is *normal* and *necessary* for the development of independence, and that adolescence is a time in which striving for autonomy takes the form of detachment or individuation from parents. In particular, these theorists argued that adolescents are rebellious and disagreeable in order to decrease not only their connections with and reliance on their caregivers but also the social influence of these caregivers. Laurence Steinberg and Susan Silverberg (1986) advanced the study of autonomy and individuation (as described by Blos, 1979) by defining and measuring emotional autonomy in relation to parents as four specific processes: decreasing dependence on parents, increasing individuation from parents (e.g., as when teenagers conclude that parents do not know or understand them), increasing perception of parents as people (e.g., as when teenagers recognize that parents may act differently when not with their children), and decreasing idealization of parents. According to this study, dependence on parents and idealization of parents declined from fifth to ninth grade, whereas individuation from parents increased. However, adolescents of all ages had difficulties perceiving their parents as people. The same study demonstrated that, between fifth and ninth

grade, females become more emotionally autonomous than boys , and adolescents of both sexes become more susceptible to peer pressure as they grow in autonomy from parents. However, susceptibility to peer pressure begins to decrease again by about grade 9.

Other studies, however, have concluded that the majority of adolescents and their parents (about 75 percent) get along much of the time, and that excessive conflict and rebellion are not necessary for healthy adolescent development (Steinberg, 1999). In particular, contemporary child developmentalists have found that autonomy advances within supportive attachments to caregivers in which adolescents are provided increasing opportunities for discussion, decision making, and choice. For example, Richard Ryan and John Lynch (1989) argue that emotional autonomy as measured by Steinberg and Susan Silverberg (1986) actually measured detachment from parents rather than autonomy. Although they noted that detachment could result in increased self-reliance, they suggested that it might also result in the loss of valuable connections to others, leading to problems such as a lack of a consolidated identity, lower self-esteem, and dysfunctional behaviors. Zeng-Yin Chen and Sanford Dornbusch (1998) recently verified this perspective, finding that emotional autonomy can have both positive and negative effects on adolescents. Young people experience more distress and difficulties in school, become more susceptible to peer pressure, and have more problems with deviant behavior when they report that their parents do not know or understand them. On the other hand, the process of beginning to de-idealize parents and to relinquish some dependencies on parents, though somewhat distressing, did not have the same negative effects on adolescent behavior.

Researchers have also discovered that particular forms of relationships with parents and others undermine the development of optimal autonomous functioning (Collins and Repinski, 1994). A subset of the terms used to describe the parenting behaviors involved in these relationships includes intrusive or over-involved parenting, lack of autonomy support, coercion, and psychological control. These terms usually refer to ways that parents or others prohibit disagreement and the expression of alternative views. They also encompass parent behaviors that are intrusive, overinvolved, or emotionally manipulative.

Behavioral and psychological controls appear to be two aspects of parenting style that are particularly important to the development of autonomy. Behavioral control (sometimes called monitoring or regulation) includes behaviors of parents that keep them informed of their adolescents' activities and interests, allowing them to supervise these activities and to set limits on adolescent behaviors that may be negotiated but are firm when set. Psychological control (sometimes called lack of autonomy granting or support) includes behaviors of parents that do not allow autonomy, as when parents tell their adolescents what to do or how to feel, are too protective, have too many rules, or prohibit the adolescents from expressing opinions or engaging in decision making. It also includes expressions of excessive disappointment in the adolescents, as well as possessiveness and overprotectiveness. These latter behaviors are most likely to leave the adolescent feeling controlled, coerced, compelled, or manipulated.

Overall, there is mounting evidence to suggest that a moderate amount of behavioral control combined with low psychological control is optimal for healthy psychological and physical functioning among adolescents, leading also to fewer problem behaviors (e.g., alcohol and other drug use, delinquency, truancy). Conversely, adolescents whose parents engage in psychologically controlling behaviors tend to have more psychological and physical complaints, such as depression, lower self-esteem, and headaches (Barber and Olsen, 1997), and those whose parents exhibit high levels of both behavioral and psychological control have lower educational expectations, lower grade-point averages, and more behavior problems such as delinquency and use of alcohol and other substances (Eccles et al., 1997; Gray and Steinberg, 1999). In addition, minimizing psychological control becomes increasingly important at or near the onset of puberty, when adolescents desire more autonomy, are forming independent identities, and are better able to recognize overcontrolling behaviors and intrusions on their self-expression. The direction of influence may also be reversed. For example, it is likely not only that parent behaviors influence adolescent autonomy but also that adolescent behaviors prompt parents to behave in behaviorally or psychologically controlling ways. Indeed, parents may be less inclined to engage in behaviors that facilitate autonomy when adolescents are doing poorly in school or using alcohol and other substances.

Teachers, too, can influence adolescent functioning, as evidenced by research indicating that children and adolescents express more interest in and enjoyment of school when this social setting is perceived as autonomy granting rather than coercive. Another finding is that the need for autonomy increases as adolescents grow older. For example, when seventh-grade teachers grant autonomy by listening to student suggestions, encouraging choice, and involving students in decision making, students are less likely to be alienated from school and to exhibit problem behaviors (Eccles et al., 1997). In addition, when teachers grant more autonomy to middle school students (especially female students), grades are higher (Barber and Olsen, 1997).

As adolescents begin to question the definitive authority and expertise of adults, their peers become increasingly important as additional sources of advice and support, thus further affecting the development of autonomy. In fact, autonomy can flourish during interactions with friends. Autonomy also develops when young people maintain valued connections to friends by expressing their opinions and attitudes, recognize that their friends' opinions may differ from their own, learn how to negotiate differences, and practice joint decision making.

Although the general public is often made aware of negative interactions between adolescents (e.g., smoking, drinking, delinquent acts), it should be noted that young people can also have positive influences on each other, as when they inspire friends to do well in school, to improve in sports, to make future plans, and to take on greater responsibilities. Of course, the influence of friends depends on the values of those friends, the characteristics of the adolescents involved, and the nature of the caregiver-adolescent relationship. For example, girls are more influenced by

friends than boys are, close friends are the most influential of all peers, and adolescents who lack self-confidence and have low self-esteem are more influenced by peers than by others (Savin-Williams and Berndt, 1990). In addition, adolescents who experience little opportunity for personal choice and joint decision making at home are especially susceptible to the influence of peers. For example, Andrew Fuligni and Jacquelynne Eccles (1993) found that adolescents who had fewer decision making opportunities in the family were more likely to seek advice from peers (rather than from parents) and to be more oriented toward peer opinion and advice than adolescents who were given more decision making opportunities by their families.

Finally, some scholars interested in gender differences have begun to recognize the important role that connections with others play in female development. For example, Carol Gilligan (1982) has discussed the inability to express opinions and attitudes *(loss of voice)* and the increasing feeling of not being oneself in interactions with others *(false-self behavior)* that young women experience as they enter adolescence. However, another study suggests that there is little evidence of gender differences in loss of voice and false-self behavior: On average, according to Susan Harter (1999), males and females report similar levels of difficulty with voice in both middle and high school. In fact, comfort with saying what one thinks varies greatly not only among individual adolescents of both genders but also across interactions with different people (e.g., friends versus parents versus teachers). Yet it appears that females who report high levels of connection to and caring toward others, combined with low independence and individualism, are least likely to express their opinions and most likely to suppress their true selves when in public domains such as groups of peers or school.

Melanie J. Zimmer-Gembeck

See also Ethnocentrism; Parent-Adolescent Relations; Responsibility for Developmental Tasks; Self

References and further reading
Barber, Brian K. 1996. "Parental Psychological Control: Revisiting a Neglected Construct." *Child Development* 67: 3296–3319.

Barber, Brian K., and Joseph A. Olsen. 1997. "Socialization in Context: Connection, Regulation, and Autonomy in the Family, School, and Neighborhood, and with Peers." *Journal of Adolescent Research* 12: 287–315.

Blos, Peter. 1979. *The Adolescent Passage: Developmental Issues.* New York: International Universities Press.

Chen, Zeng-Yin, and Sanford M. Dornbusch. 1998. "Relating Aspects of Adolescent Emotional Autonomy to Academic Achievement and Deviant Behavior." *Journal of Adolescent Research* 13: 293–319.

Collins, W. Andrew, and Daniel J. Repinski. 1994. "Relationships during Adolescence: Continuity and Change in Interpersonal Perspective." Pp. 7–36 in *Personal Relationships during Adolescence.* Edited by Raymond Montemayor, Gerald R. Adams, and Thomas P. Gullotta. Thousand Oaks, CA: Sage Publications.

Eccles, Jacquelynne S., Diane Early, Kari Frasier, Elaine Belansky, and Karen McCarthy. 1997. "The Relation of Connection, Regulation, and Support for Autonomy to Adolescents' Functioning." *Journal of Adolescent Research* 12: 263–286.

Freud, Anna. 1958. "Adolescence." *Psychoanalytic Study of the Child* 13: 255–278.

Fuligni, Andrew J., and Jacquelynne S. Eccles. 1993. "Perceived Parent/Child Relationships and Early Adolescents' Orientation toward Peers." *Developmental Psychology* 29: 622–632.

Gilligan, Carol. 1982. *In a Different Voice: Psychological Theory and Women's Development.* Cambridge, MA: Harvard University Press.

Gray, Marjory R., and Laurence Steinberg. 1999. "Unpacking Authoritative Parenting: Reassessing a Multidimensional Construct." *Journal of Marriage and the Family* 61: 574–587.

Harter, Susan. 1999. *The Construction of the Self: A Developmental Perspective.* New York: Guilford Press.

Hill, John P., and G. N. Holmbeck. 1986. "Attachment and Autonomy during Adolescence." *Annals of Child Development* 3: 145–189.

Ryan, Richard M., and John H. Lynch. 1989. "Emotional Autonomy versus Detachment: Revisiting the Vicissitudes of Adolescence and Young Adulthood." *Child Development* 60: 340–356.

Savin-Williams, Ritch C., and Thomas J. Berndt. 1990. "Friendships and Peer Relations during Adolescence." Pp. 277–307 in *At the Threshold: The Developing Adolescent.* Edited by Shirley S. Feldman and Glen R. Elliott. Cambridge, MA: Harvard University Press.

Steinberg, Laurence. 1999. *Adolescence,* 5th ed. New York: McGraw-Hill.

Steinberg, Laurence, and Susan Silverberg. 1986. "The Vicissitudes of Autonomy in Early Adolescence." *Child Development* 57: 841–851.

B

Body Build

Bodies come in all different sizes and shapes. Some people are heavy and others are lean, but the majority are somewhere in the middle. Some people think that certain of their body parts are too big; others think theirs are too small. Some individuals wish they looked older; others think they look too old. In fact, most people are concerned with how they look to themselves and with how others think they look. They may worry that, because they think they look a certain way to themselves, others will think they look that way, too, and will treat them in a way that they do not like. Adolescents are particularly sensitive about their appearance. Psychologist David Elkind (1967) described adolescents as behaving as if there were an imaginary audience watching them all the time. And, indeed, many adolescents spend a lot of time trying to present themselves in as physically appealing a way as possible. With few exceptions, however, adolescents are not able to change their body build in significant ways.

In the past, body build was divided into three types: endomorphic (heavy body build), mesomorphic (medium body build), and ectomorphic (thin body build). Each of these types was associated with certain personality traits. For example, the endomorph was thought to have a happy and jovial personality, the meso-morph was believed to be athletic and assertive, and the ectomorph was described as serious and introverted. This classification system was discarded, however, when research failed to turn up evidence in support of the relationship between body build and personality.

In reality, people experience certain reactions to body build when they encounter adolescents who look a certain way. For instance, teenagers who have not entered puberty by age sixteen generally look much younger than their chronological age. Of course, most teens do not want to seem younger than they are, because people may treat them accordingly—a real disadvantage when they want to participate in an activity that is appropriate for their chronological age but inappropriate for someone younger. For example, a sixteen-year-old teenager who looks like a twelve-year-old and is working as a salesperson may be repeatedly questioned by customers about his or her age and ability to help them with a purchase, thus eventually causing the teen to withdraw from the workforce. Indeed, adults often attribute lack of knowledge or credibility to younger-looking teens. Many younger-looking teens tend to be upset by this treatment and may withdraw from other activities as well. For example, late-maturing teens may choose not to participate in social activities with other teens their age, preferring to socialize with younger children whose body build is more similar to their own. A related finding is that girls who mature sexually early (but still within the normal range) are socially disadvantaged to much the same degree as boys who mature sexually late.

Body image is especially significant during adolescence because of the rapid physical changes that accompany puberty and the adjustment that youth must make to these changes. Teens with a body shape that is not consistent with what society deems "acceptable" may experience distress. Overweight teens, very short males, and very tall females are often subjected to teasing and jokes about their appearance. Teens who are short for their age, particularly males, are sometimes treated as inferior and may even suffer from social discrimination as adults.

Research has revealed that male adolescents tend to be more satisfied with their bodies than female adolescents; that young adolescent girls favor their facial features whereas males favor their athletic strengths and abilities; and that, by age eighteen, both sexes appear to be happier with their bodies than at any time previously.

Most teens outgrow the body build about which they are unhappy. They outgrow it by physically developing into average-appearing young adults. As adolescents they may have suffered from being out of synch with their peers, but they eventually reach a balance point. That is, most late maturers ultimately reach an average build, and early maturers find that their peers have caught up to them. Among those adolescents who remain overweight or short, many mature mentally and emotionally to the point where they are able to accept their body build.

In some instances, special efforts can be taken to change body build. Teens who are overweight can enroll in a group weight-loss program, those with late-onset puberty can get medical treatment to start or speed up physical development, and those with low muscle mass can participate in a body-building program. In addition, breast reduction or augmentation can be used to change a woman's figure. However, regardless of their body build, most people are able to find other people with whom they can relate and establish a permanent social relationship.

Jordan W. Finkelstein

See also Appearance, Cultural Factors in; Appearance Management; Body Fat, Changes in; Body Hair; Body Image; Puberty: Physical Changes

References and further reading
Blyth, Dale, Roberta G. Simmons, and David F. Zakin. 1985. "Satisfaction with Body Image for Early Adolescent Females: The Impact of Pubertal Timing in Different School Environments." *Journal of Youth and Adolescence* 14: 207–225.
Elkind, David. 1967. "Egocentrism in Adolescence." *Child Development* 38: 1025–1034.
Fallon, April, and Paul Rozin. 1985. Sex Differences in Perceptions of Desirable Body Shape. *Journal of Abnormal Psychology* 94: 102–105.
Simmons, Roberta, and Dale Blyth. 1987. *Moving into Adolescence: The Impact of Pubertal Change and School Context.* New York: Aldine.

Body Fat, Changes in

Both girls and boys experience changes in their body composition—distribution of fat and muscle—during pubertal development (Graber, Petersen, and Brooks-Gunn, 1996; Grumbach and Styne, 1998). Pubertal development involves a series of hormonal and physical changes resulting in adult reproductive functioning and, ultimately, adult appearance. Increased or redistributed body fat is one of these changes. Lean body mass (i.e., muscle), bone mass, and body fat are about equal in prepubertal boys and girls. However, postpubertal boys have one and a half times the lean body mass and bone mass of postpubertal girls, and postpubertal girls have twice as much body fat as postpubertal boys. These differences in fat distribution are due in part to the fact that males have more and larger muscle cells than females. During puberty, girls generally experience enlarged hips and breasts but little change in waist circumference, resulting in a pear shape that reflects the distribution of fat in the lower body. By the time they finish puberty, girls have gained an average of twenty-four pounds (Warren, 1983). However, these extra pounds account for lean body mass, bone mass, *and* fat. Interestingly, girls seem to experience increases in fat and weight around the same time they get their first period (menarche). This finding is partly explained by research indicating that a certain amount of body fat is necessary for the onset and maintenance of normal reproductive functioning in females. The fact that adolescent girls have a similar percentage of body fat when they get their periods, regardless of age and prepubertal size, thus appears to be related to the higher proportion of body fat believed to be necessary to provide metabolic support for pregnancy (Frisch, 1983).

Normal changes in height and weight at puberty are often experienced positively by boys, probably because Western cultures favor boys who are larger and stronger. By contrast, girls tend to experience these changes negatively—particu-

larly the increases in weight. Here, too, the reason is likely related to the fact that, for girls, Western cultures value the thin physique of the prepubertal body over the mature body (Attie and Brooks-Gunn, 1989). Early-maturing girls have an especially difficult time with pubertal weight changes, because they are gaining weight at a time when most girls their age still have a childlike appearance. For this reason, early-maturing girls may experience lower self-esteem, particularly with respect to their body image, than girls who mature on time or later than their peers (Graber, Petersen, and Brooks-Gunn, 1996). Although teenage girls can, and do, adapt to their changing bodies by altering their body image (Steiner-Adair, 1986), they must still cope with their family's and peers' responses to their maturing bodies. Along the same lines, girls who engage in activities for which a prepubertal body is valued—such as dancing, modeling, figure skating, or gymnastics—may have an especially challenging time dealing with their increases in body fat.

Normal height and weight changes may also be especially stressful for girls *and* boys who are overweight or obese in their prepubertal years. Given the greater emphasis on looks and appearance during adolescence (especially in the contexts of dating and peer acceptance), normal weight changes among already overweight children may be particularly difficult to deal with.

Not surprisingly, increases in body fat occurring during puberty have been associated with the desire to be thinner, which in turn can lead to excessive exercising or to eating problems such as strict dieting or bingeing and purging. For example, longitudinal studies of middle- and late-adolescent girls have found a connection between higher levels of body mass and the development of eating problems (Attie and Brooks-Gunn, 1989; Graber et al., 1994). Interestingly, these studies included a majority of normal-weight (not obese) girls. Another investigation of precursors of eating problems among fifth- and sixth-grade boys and girls found that for fifth-grade girls, greater body mass as well as more advanced levels of pubertal development were predictive of eating problems one year later (Keel, Fulkerson, and Leon, 1997).

Andrea Bastiani Archibald
Jeanne Brooks-Gunn

See also Appearance, Cultural Factors in; Appearance Management; Attractiveness, Physical; Body Build; Body Hair; Body Image; Puberty: Physical Changes

References and further reading
Attie, Ilana, and Jeanne Brooks-Gunn. 1989. "Development of Eating Problems in Adolescent Girls: A Longitudinal Study." *Developmental Psychology* 25: 70–79.
Frisch, Rose E. 1983. "Fatness, Puberty, and Fertility: The Effects of Nutrition and Physical Training on Menarche and Ovulation." Pp. 29–50 in *Girls at Puberty: Biological and Psychosocial Perspectives*. Edited by Jeanne Brooks-Gunn and Anne C. Petersen. New York: Plenum Press.
Graber, Julia A., Jeanne Brooks-Gunn, Roberta L. Paikoff, and Michelle P. Warren. 1994. "Prediction of Eating Problems: An Eight-Year Study of Adolescent Girls." *Developmental Psychology* 30: 823–834.
Graber, Julia A., Anne C. Petersen, and Jeanne Brooks-Gunn. 1996. "Pubertal Processes: Methods, Measures, and Models." Pp. 23–53 in *Transitions through Adolescence: Interpersonal Domains and Context*. Edited by Graber, Petersen, and Brooks-Gunn. Mahwah, NJ: Lawrence Erlbaum Associates.
Grumbach, Melvin M., and Dennis M. Styne. 1998. "Puberty: Ontogeny, Neuroendocrinology, Physiology, and Disorders." Pp. 1509–1625 in *Williams Textbook of Endocrinology*. Edited by Jean D. Wilson, Daniel W. Foster, and Henry M. Kronenberg. Philadelphia: W. B. Saunders Publishing.
Keel, Pamela K., Jayne A. Fulkerson, and Gloria R. Leon. 1997. "Disordered Eating Precursors in Pre- and Early Adolescent Girls and Boys." *Journal of Youth and Adolescence* 26: 203–216.
Steiner-Adair, Catherine. 1986. "The Body Politic: Normal Adolescent Development and the Development of Eating Disorders." *Journal of the American Academy of Psychoanalysis* 14: 95–114.
Warren, Michelle. 1983. "Physical and Biological Aspects of Puberty." Pp. 3–28 in *Girls at Puberty: Biological and Psychosocial Perspectives*. Edited by Jeanne Brooks-Gunn and Anne C. Petersen. New York: Plenum Press.

Body Hair

All people have hair all over the body. In some areas, like the scalp, most people have many hair follicles. In other areas, such as palms and soles, there are none. In some areas of the body, hair is short, very fine, and almost invisible, while in others it is longer, coarser, and often very prominent. Each hair follicle grows deep down from the base of the skin, and passes through a pore or opening to the outside. Most dermatologists distinguish between the hair on the head and the hair on the rest of the body. This discussion will focus on body hair.

Hair has no physiologic function in humans, but serves mainly cosmetic purposes. Therefore, most of the time, people are psychologically rather than medically concerned about the nature of their body hair. Women are usually concerned about excessive hair on parts of their body where most women do not have any visible hair. These parts include the face, chest, around the areolae (the pigmented areas surrounding the breast nipples), up the abdominal wall from the pubic hair area to the umbilicus (belly button), lower back, buttocks, inner thigh, arms and legs, and genitals. Excessive hairiness is commonly called hirsutism. Men are usually concerned about not having enough hair in those areas. Hormones called androgens control hair growth in these areas. Both men and women have androgens, but men have mostly a very strong androgen called testosterone, which is produced by the testes, while women have mostly weaker androgens produced by their adrenal glands (which sit on top of their kidneys).

In prepubertal children, androgen production in both boys and girls is very low, and so there is no significant difference in hair between boys and girls. As puberty starts, significant differences in hair growth becomes obvious. Since adolescents go through puberty at different times and at different speeds, observed variation in hair growth, while normal, can seem awkward. Even after puberty starts, there is still no significant difference in hair growth between the sexes in certain areas, such as the pubic region and armpits. But in the other parts of the body (mentioned above) significant sex differences develop as puberty progresses. Both men and women may develop hirsutism, but women are usually more concerned about it than are men. Most people with hirsutism have other family members who are also hirsute. That is, excessive hair just runs in their family, and there is no other known cause for it. However, in some people hirsutism is caused by significant hormonal abnormalities.

We can usually identify women with hormonal causes of hirsutism because they almost always undergo changes of other parts of their body—a process called virilization. In addition to the excessive growth of hair, these women also show an enlarged clitoris (a small fleshy part of the upper section of their external genitals), deepening of the voice, loss of head hair in the lateral part of the forehead (called temporal recession), and loss of female body contours (hips and breasts lose fat). Abnormal hormone production can originate in the ovaries or adrenal or pituitary glands. Virilization can result from taking certain drugs such as anabolic steroids (which are all testosterone related), some anticonvulsants (phenytoin), some drugs used to treat low blood sugar (diazoxide), and some of the oral contraceptives. Sometimes excessive hair may be associated with a syndrome of obesity, infrequent irregular periods, diabetes, and darkening of the skin around the neck and armpits. It is important to evaluate women with excessive body hair or virilization in order to diagnose any medical condition and to offer treatment to prevent further increased hair growth or virilization. Much of the time no cause for hirsutism is found, and it is then called *idiopathic* (cause unknown).

Regardless of cause, most women want the excessive hair removed. However, social standards regarding body hair, especially for women, vary from culture to culture. For example, in countries such as France, many young women choose to not remove their leg and underarm hair. If an adolescent chooses to remove her body hair there are several possible methods. Hair can be temporarily removed by shaving (which does not cause thicker or greater growth), plucking, waxing, using depilatories, and bleaching (for fine hair). Permanent hair removal is done by electrolysis, which destroys the hair follicle. This is a painful process and should be done only by a qualified person. Excessive hair in men is relatively uncommon, and should be diagnosed as in women to identify treatable causes.

Inadequate or no body hair growth may be associated with delayed or absent physical pubertal development. Evaluation to find the causes of that condition is essential. Inadequate hair growth in men usually involves scalp hair, but sometimes men are concerned about body hair also. It is most important to remember that there is much variation in body hair growth that falls into the normal range. For example, some adolescent men are not able to grow as thick a beard as others are. Most men with small amounts of body hair do not seek medical advice concerning this condition. Treatment with androgens in otherwise normal men will not increase body hair.

Adolescents may be particularly concerned about either excessive or lack of body hair. Appearance is particularly important to adolescents, so differences in appearance from peers often result in some degree of unhappiness. Attention to identifying treatable causes for hirsutism or lack of adequate body hair is essential. Additionally, a teenager may see differences in hair growth from peers as more than just a cosmetic issue. For example, adolescent men sometimes consciously grow out their facial hair (in the form of a beard or a goatee, for example) as a statement of personal style or choice. Others may see facial hair as a symbol of masculinity.

Regardless of cause, the removal of excessive hair should be encouraged in those instances where it makes the teenager uncomfortable. Psychological counseling should also be considered when these issues are of great concern to the adolescent.

Jordan W. Finkelstein

See also Appearance, Cultural Factors in; Appearance Management; Attractiveness, Physical; Body Build; Body Image; Puberty: Physical Changes

References and further reading
Berkow, Robert B., ed. 1997. *The Merck Manual of Medical Information: Home Edition.* Whitehouse Station, NJ: Merck Research Laboratories.

Body Image

Because adolescence is in part a matter of getting used to drastic physical changes, the way that teens feel about their bodies may also change dramatically at this time. Most teens will go through a period of time when they feel uncomfortable about their bodies or some aspect of their appearance. These negative feelings usually occur while adolescents are undergoing puberty. Indeed, nearly every aspect of an individual's body will change during the four to five years of pubertal development. At this time, adolescents commonly experience increased feelings of self-consciousness. The combination of physical changes and a more intense focus on the self makes it likely that teens will find fault with their bodies and appearance. In general, girls of this age group tend to have a poorer body image than do boys. However, for most youth, negative feelings about their bodies dissipate after puberty and seem to steadily increase over the adolescent decade (Graber, Petersen, and Brooks-Gunn, 1996). For a subset of youth, poor body image is persistent and may be associated with more serious emotional problems such as depression or eating disorders.

Boys and girls enter puberty looking like children but end puberty looking more like adults. During puberty, individuals grow at different times and at different rates. Girls usually start this development about one to two years earlier than boys do. In addition, within gender, individuals start puberty at different times. The enormous variation among individuals in their rates of development may heighten the sensitivity to body issues, resulting in periods of dissatisfaction with one's body. Again, for most youth, these may be brief periods of poor body image. However, once teens adapt to their new appearance, their body image improves. One reason that puberty may be particularly hard on girls is that in Western culture, the ideal shape for a woman is thin. Men, on the other hand, are expected to be tall and muscular. In any case, the physical changes of puberty may bring an adolescent closer to or farther from these ideals.

Girls are also more likely than boys to evaluate their bodies in terms of their weight (Drewnowski, Kurth, and Krahn, 1995; Parker et al., 1995). This finding may explain why girls tend to have a poorer body image than boys, especially given that the normal increases in weight that occur during adolescence are in conflict with the idealized female shape. Adolescent girls, even those of normal weight, frequently report wanting to lose weight. In contrast, adolescent boys commonly report that they want to gain weight—as long as it is muscle and not fat (Drewnowski, Kurth, and Krahn, 1995).

In addition, girls who mature earlier than other girls have a poorer body image than other girls throughout adolescence; these girls seem to feel particularly out of place or self-conscious about their bodies

Adolescents may evaluate their bodies in terms of weight and shape. (Shirley Zeiberg)

because they are more developed than other girls, or boys (Graber, Petersen, and Brooks-Gunn, 1996). Notably, early-maturing girls gain weight while other girls do not, making them even more self-conscious about this otherwise normal weight gain. In contrast, boys who mature earlier than other boys tend to have more positive feelings about their bodies; these boys are taller and are gaining muscle mass at a time when other boys have not grown as much. In short, it is during puberty that early-maturing boys move closer to the cultural ideal.

Recent studies that have examined whether body image is similar for teens from different racial and ethnic backgrounds suggest that white girls are more likely than girls of other racial or ethnic backgrounds to evaluate themselves in comparison with the thin ideal—primarily because of the predominance of white models and images in the media. Moreover, African American girls have reported in interviews that they are less sensitive than white girls about their weight and tend to look on the positive side when thinking about their bodies. Specifically, they indicated that girls should focus on "making what you've got work for you"—an attitude that allowed them to maintain positive feelings about their bodies during adolescence (Parker et al., 1995). In contrast, another study found that Hispanic and Asian girls experienced similar rates of dissatisfaction with their bodies and, in some cases (involving girls who were very thin), had poorer body images than their white counterparts (Robinson et al., 1996). Thus, African American teenage girls appear to be the exception to the rule in terms of their ability to overcome the "thin ideal" in ways that protect their body image. Little is known about the body image of boys of different racial and ethnic backgrounds. Initial studies suggest that African American teenage boys, like their female counterparts, exhibit greater satisfaction with their bodies than do boys from other racial groups (Story et al., 1995). In general, however, white, African American, Hispanic, and Asian boys were very similar to one another in reporting feelings about their bodies that were mostly positive.

Episodes of poor body image may be common for adolescents, especially girls, but extended periods of poor body image may be symptomatic of a more serious problem or even lead to unhealthy behavior patterns. When teens become depressed, they frequently feel badly about themselves in several domains, including body image. Thus, a sustained or severe episode of poor body image may be a sign to others that a particular youth is experiencing a more serious problem. Moreover, when girls compare themselves to the thin ideal and feel badly about not fitting the image, they may engage in unhealthy dieting practices in an effort to come closer to this image. Of course, for most girls, it simply is not possible to attain the ideal. Among girls who cannot accept this truism, a pattern of dieting and potentially eating disorders may be set in motion. Similarly, among boys, especially athletes in high school or college, the pressure to attain the muscular ideal may lead to unhealthy practices such as steroid use (Drewnowski, Kurth, and Krahn, 1995). Fortunately, few teens end up at these extremes. But the fact remains that all too many girls develop bad eating habits because of body and weight concerns.

Julia A. Graber
Jeanne Brooks-Gunn

See also Appearance, Cultural Factors in; Appearance Management; Body Build; Body Fat, Changes in; Body Hair; Puberty: Physical Changes; Self-Consciousness

References and further reading

Drewnowski, Adam, Candace L. Kurth, and Dean D. Krahn. 1995. "Effects of Body Image on Dieting, Exercise, and Anabolic Steroid Use in Adolescent Males." *International Journal of Eating Disorders* 17: 381–386.

Graber, Julia A., Anne C. Petersen, and Jeanne Brooks-Gunn. 1996. "Pubertal Processes: Methods, Measures, and Models." Pp. 23–53 in *Transitions through Adolescence: Interpersonal Domains and Context.* Edited by Julia A. Graber, Anne C. Petersen, and Jeanne Brooks-Gunn. Mahwah, NJ: Erlbaum.

Parker, Sheila, Mimi Nichter, Mark Nichter, Nancy Vuckovic, Colette Sims, and Cheryl Ritenbaugh. 1995. "Body Image and Weight Concerns among African American and White Adolescent Females: Differences That Make a Difference." *Human Organization* 54: 103–114.

Robinson, Thomas N., Joel D. Killen, Iris F. Litt, Lawrence D. Hammer, Darrell M. Wilson, K. Farish Haydel, Chris Hayward, and C. Barr Taylor. 1996. "Ethnicity and Body Dissatisfaction: Are Hispanic and Asian Girls at Increased Risk for Eating Disorders?" *Journal of Adolescent Health* 19: 384–393.

Story, Mary, Simone A. French, Michael D. Resnick, and Robert W. Blum. 1995. "Ethnic/Racial and Socioeconomic Differences in Dieting Behaviors and Body Image Perceptions in Adolescents." *International Journal of Eating Disorders* 18: 173–179.

Bullying

Bullying is a specific form of aggressive behavior, characterized by three important criteria:

1. It involves one or more peers (other children or youth) doing intentional harm to one or more other individuals;
2. It is carried out repeatedly and over time against its victims, often without clear signs of provocation;
3. It involves an imbalance or abuse of power, such that the victim is relatively defenseless against the perpetrator(s), due to being either physically weaker, mentally weaker, or outnumbered (in the case of several students ganging up on a victim).

Bullying can include violence (in the case of causing serious physical harm to the victim), but it can also occur without physical violence, by causing damage over time to the victim through words, gestures, or exclusion from the group.

Bullying at school has become a serious public health concern. International estimates suggest that 5 to 10 percent of elementary or primary school students are involved in bullying incidents at least weekly. Although rates of physical bullying decline somewhat after the transition to secondary school (middle school and high school), rates of verbal attacks on peers remain more stable, and, in fact, physical bullying gets replaced by an increased use of words as the vehicle of harm as children move through adolescence.

Boys appear to be at greater risk for involvement in bully/victim problems at school; they tend to be both the initiators and the recipients of physical aggression more often than are girls. However, girls are more likely to be involved in indirect or "relational" aggression, involving harming relationships via social alienation or exclusion, ridiculing, and teasing.

What makes a child become a bully? Several factors have been identified as contributing to aggressive behavior in children. First, parents who lack emotional warmth, are underinvolved in supervising or monitoring their children, or are inconsistent or overly permissive in their discipline increase the risk that their children will become aggressive and hostile toward others. In addition, heavy reliance by caregivers on power assertion to control children's behavior, through the use of harsh physical punishment or violent emotional outbursts, has been shown to contribute to children's reliance on such methods when attempting to dominate or control their peers. Finally, evidence exists for some biological or temperamental contribution to aggressive behavior in children: Children with more difficult temperaments, who are for example overreactive and easily frustrated, as well as impulsive (apt to act before thinking), are more likely to be involved in bullying.

Bullying behavior is difficult for schools to combat, since teachers and administrators usually do not directly witness bullying incidents. Bullying is most likely to take place in areas of the school where adult involvement and supervision of students is lacking, such as on school playgrounds, in rest rooms, and in hallways. Even if students are not directly involved in bullying, they contribute in some way to their school's climate of safety. All students play a part in making other students feel safe or unsafe at school, to the extent that they assume the role of either assisting the bully, reinforcing the bully, defending the victim, or remaining on the outside and refusing to get involved. Recognition of the roles that students, as well as their teachers, principals, and parents, are playing in fostering a safe, supportive climate for all students is critical to reducing bullying problems at school.

Laura Hess Olson

See also Aggression; Conduct Problems; Conflict Resolution; Peer Groups; Peer Pressure; Peer Status; Peer Victimization in School; Risk Behaviors

References and further reading
Crick, Nicki R. 1996. "The Role of Overt Aggression, Relational Aggression, and Prosocial Behavior in the Prediction of Children's Future Social Adjustment." *Child Development* 67: 2317–2327.
Loeber, Rolf, and Magda Stouthamer-Loeber. 1998. "Development of Juvenile Aggression and Violence: Some Common Misconceptions and Controversies." *American Psychologist* 53: 242–259.
Olweus, Dan. 1993. *Bullying at School: What We Know and What We Can Do.* Oxford, UK: Blackwell.
Salmivalli, Christine, Karl M. Lagerspetz, Kaj Björkqvist, Karin Österman, and Anna Kaukiainen. 1996. "Bullying as a Group Process: Participant Roles and Their Relations to Social Status within the Group." *Aggressive Behavior* 22: 1–15.
Smith, Peter K., Yohji Morita, Josine Junger-Tas, Dan Olweus, Richard F. Catalano, and Phillip Slee. 1999. *The Nature of School Bullying: A Cross-National Perspective.* London: Routledge.

Bumps in the Road to Adulthood

In 1938, Ruth Benedict coined the term *discontinuities* to refer to differences in expected childhood and adulthood roles and behaviors. During adolescence, teenagers must change the ways in which they behave in the transition from immature childhood to mature adulthood. These changes may be difficult, resulting in a stressful adolescence. The greater the number of discontinuities confronting the teenager, the more difficult the adolescent transition will be. Because such discontinuities tend to be greater in industrialized societies, this transition is more difficult in the United States than in more primitive cultures. And it has become increasingly more difficult as the number of discontinuities has risen.

Following are some of the many examples of discontinuities between childhood and adulthood:

- Expecting adults but not children to be self-supporting
- Teaching children to be dependent on adults, but expecting adults to be independent
- Refusing to officially condone sexual activity until after people are married

- Prohibiting the legal right to drive, work part-time, vote, or drink alcohol until certain ages have been reached

These differences in the expectations of behavior between children and adults create "bumps" during the transitions the adolescent makes from childhood forms of behavior to expected adulthood forms, particularly if the transitions are made abruptly rather than gradually.

Adolescents must learn independent behavior, yet they remain dependent upon parents for food, clothing, and shelter. Faced with an increased sex drive and pressured by peers to engage in sex, they must make decisions regarding sexual behavior that may lead to anxiety and guilt. And peer pressure to drink can lead some adolescents to abuse alcohol at a very young age.

These and other changes between childhood and adulthood can cause emotional stress and strain that make adolescence extremely difficult for some and a guilt-ridden time for others. The greater the number of "bumps" that the culture places along the road to adulthood, the more difficult a time the adolescent will have in learning how to behave like an adult. The many changes between childhood and adulthood roles the adolescent must make in the United States result in more difficult and lengthy transitions here than in other places, where more continuities exist in the form of similarities between childhood and adulthood roles.

Because the necessary transitions take place over a period of six to eight years, most American adolescents are able to face one or two at a time, deal with them, and move on. However, in part because so many transitions need to be made in

During adolescence, teenagers must change the ways in which they behave from childlike to adultlike. (Skjold Photographs)

this culture, adolescence continues further into the life span than it does in less complex cultures.

Jerome B. Dusek

See also Services for Adolescents; Transition to Young Adulthood; Transitions of Adolescence

References and further reading

Benedict, Ruth. 1938. "Continuities and Discontinuities in Cultural Conditioning." *Psychiatry* 1: 161–167.

Coleman, John C. 1978. "Current Contradictions in Adolescent Theory." *Journal of Youth and Adolescence* 7: 1–11.

Dusek, Jerome B. 1996. *Adolescent Development and Behavior.* Upper Saddle River, NJ: Prentice-Hall.

C

Cancer in Childhood and Adolescence

Cancer is a process in which abnormal cells are produced in the body. These abnormal cells reproduce other abnormal cells in a quick and uncontrollable manner. If cancer is left unchecked, it may invade surrounding tissues and organs. In the United States approximately 10,000 children and adolescents are diagnosed with cancer each year. Of those, approximately two-thirds will survive. As of the year 2000, one in a thousand adults aged twenty to twenty-nine were predicted to be a survivor of childhood cancer (Rowland, 1998). This is quite remarkable, considering that three decades ago children or adolescents diagnosed with cancer were not expected to live for more than a matter of days or months. Today, however, many cancers are being cured, even in the most advanced stages—especially in children and adolescents. Cancer cure rates are much higher among children and adolescents than among adults for several reasons, including the fact that young people have bodies that are still growing, making it easier to recover from illness or injury.

There are a hundred different types of cancer, which include brain tumors, lymphomas, sarcomas, and various forms of leukemia. Leukemia, the most common childhood cancer, affects the bone marrow, which is the organ in the body responsible for manufacturing blood cells. There are several subtypes of leukemia, diagnosed according to how quickly the disease develops and what type of blood cell is affected. The most common type of leukemia is acute lymphocytic leukemia (ALL), which primarily affects children under the age of five and adults over the age of sixty-five. Leukemia cells impair blood cells from doing what they normally do. Since blood cells are responsible for helping the body fight infection and maintain energy, people with leukemia often have great difficulty fighting infections, frequently experience fevers, and are fatigued much of the time.

Malignant brain tumors (tumors consisting of cancerous cells) are the most common solid-mass tumors found in children under the age of fifteen and, overall, the second most common childhood cancer. Survival rates vary according to type and location of tumor in the brain.

Lymphomas are the third most common form of childhood cancer. The two types of lymphomas include Hodgkin's lymphoma, which involves the lymph nodes, and non-Hodgkin's lymphoma, which involves the abdominal, head, and neck areas. Although Hodgkin's lymphoma accounts for fewer than 1 percent of all cases of cancer in this country, it is the type of cancer most often seen in young people between the ages of fifteen and thirty-four and over the age of fifty-five. Hodgkin's is one of the most curable cancers, with five-year survival rates approaching 90 percent (Rowland, 1998).

Other types of cancer include neuroblastoma, which affects sympathetic nervous system tissue, and various forms of sarcoma (cancerous tumors), which involve bone cells (osteosarcoma) or connective muscular tissue (rhabdomyosarcoma). Sarcomas are generally rare, occurring primarily in adolescents under the age of twenty. There are other rare forms of cancer—including prostate, ovarian, lung, and skin cancer—but these are more commonly found in adults than in children or adolescents.

The causes of cancer among adolescents are still not completely understood. In a few cases, cancer can be linked to genetic or environmental factors, but more often there is no apparent reason as to why some adolescents develop cancer and others do not. It is important to understand that cancer is not something that can be transmitted from one person to another through the air or human contact, as with a cold or flu. Rather, cancer usually results from a complex interaction of environmental and genetic factors.

Treatment for adolescent cancer patients usually consists of chemotherapy and radiation. Depending on the type of cancer, treatment can last between a few months and a few years. Chemotherapy, sometimes called "chemo" for short, is the name given to medicines that kill cells that divide quickly, as cancer cells do. However, chemotherapy also kills other quickly dividing cells, like those found in hair, skin, and bone marrow as well as in the mouth and digestive system. This is why cancer patients often lose their hair, have sores in their mouths, and experience fatigue and extreme nausea. Fortunately, there are medications available to dissipate some of these side effects. But one side effect—the loss of hair—can be particularly traumatic for adolescents.

In many cases, chemotherapy can be given on an outpatient basis, such that the adolescent needs to spend only a few hours during the day in the hospital. Depending on the type of cancer involved and how well the patient tolerates the chemotherapy, some adolescent cancer patients can attend school throughout treatment, missing only the day on which they go to the hospital to receive chemotherapy, whereas others need to spend several days in the hospital. Typically, the effects of chemo are worse a few hours or days after treatment is given, at a time when the adolescent is home. So, even if the chemotherapy is being received on an outpatient basis, the adolescent may still not feel well enough to go to school or maintain contact with peers when they are at home. Most adolescents report that the worst part about having cancer is feeling like they are "missing out" on things that are happening at school and among their friends. E-mail has helped many adolescents stay in touch with their friends, even when they are feeling unwell; but support from family, as well as from friends and teachers, is absolutely essential during this time.

Often, cancer patients undergo chemotherapy in combination with radiation, which involves using X rays to cause cell destruction. Radiation treatment is often very intensive, occurring two to three times a day for several weeks. It has many side effects, including extreme skin irritation, nausea, and fatigue.

For solid-mass tumors, surgery is used to remove the cancerous cells—if they are easily removable. This procedure is usually combined with chemotherapy and/or radiation. A bone-marrow transplant is sometimes recommended, depending on the type and stage of cancer. As noted earlier, most treatment can be delivered on an outpatient basis, with only limited hospital stays required. However, adolescents who must undergo a bone-marrow transplant will face extended hospitalization, isolation, and convalescence. Isolated from the "outside world," these adolescents are greatly helped by e-mail, which allows them to keep in touch with their friends and family. Such connectedness is very important as it provides support to the patients, especially those required to stay in the hospital for an extended period of time.

Adolescents cope with diagnosis and treatment in a variety of ways, depending on personality characteristics, coping strategies, and support from family and peers. For some adolescents, the waiting time before they hear the official diagnosis may take a few hours, or a few days, and this can be difficult. Often the coping response is anger—"Why me?" Among adolescents who do not understand the illness, treatment, or cure rates, there may be some aggravated fear. In such cases, the result may be a struggle for power and answers between the adolescent and the family or medical staff. Ultimately, the diagnosis of cancer upsets the idea of invulnerability that many adolescents have—an experience that may be devastating at first.

The diagnosis of cancer is usually followed by denial and a desire either to hear nothing about the disease or to be thoroughly informed about it, depending on the adolescent's coping style. Adolescents usually have more say in the treatment plan than children do, and they can choose how much and what types of information they wish to receive and in what decisions they wish to be included. Comprehension of the illness, the medications, and the treatment plan is essential to some adolescents, often influencing how they adjust to the diagnosis and treatment. But, as noted, every adolescent is different and should be included only as much as he or she wishes.

Often, a pattern of denial emerges between treatments, and maladaptive behaviors surface during hospitalizations and/or relapses. Whereas some adolescents maintain adaptive coping strategies and a positive attitude, others may become overly dependent on their parents, experience excessive anxiety, engage in high-risk behaviors, or refuse to comply with the medical treatment.

Cancer can affect teens in a number of different ways, because the unique developmental tasks of adolescence coincide with the medical complications and challenges of diagnosis and treatment. For example, it is during adolescence that peer approval, as well as body image and the concept of the "beautiful body," become increasingly important. Chemotherapy-related changes in body image and in the body itself—hair loss, weight gain or loss, or disfigurement from surgery—may affect not only how adolescents feel about themselves but also how their peers interact with them. Peers may have little knowledge of the disease or not know what to say to the patients, thus further isolating them from "normal" peer interactions. Or the patients may remove themselves from activities because of a distorted self-image or self-consciousness. In short, at an age when peer relationships are becoming increasingly important, cancer may limit adolescents' participation in peer-related activities, making it difficult for them to establish close peer relationships. In addition, because of the time the adolescents need to spend getting treatment or staying home because of the physical side effects of the treatment and disease, they may have a difficult time reentering school and feeling connected to their teachers and peers.

It is also during adolescence that emotional and economical independence from parents becomes increasingly important. This is a time when adolescents typically get their first jobs so they can spend their own money and begin to desire more privacy from their parents. Cancer can perpetuate adolescents' dependence on their parents, as they must be driven to and from the hospital for treatment, do not feel well enough to take care of themselves, and lack the energy and time to get a job. In addition, adolescents with cancer are constantly being subjected to medical procedures both inside and outside the hospital. Along with the demands of treatment (blood being drawn, urine and stool samples being required frequently, and the parents constantly checking in on the adolescents when they are home) comes a marked loss of privacy. Negotiating privacy and independence in the middle of treatment for cancer is complicated and difficult, yet very important, as the adolescents need to feel some sense of control in this very out-of-control environment.

Furthermore, adolescence is a period marked by increased curiosity and expressiveness about sexuality. This issue can be especially difficult for adolescents with cancer who have limited privacy and have been removed from their peers because of frequent clinic visits, nausea, or their peers' misunderstanding. Indeed, it may affect an adolescent's already poor body image.

Finally, the diagnosis of cancer during adolescence may influence career planning and life goals. A realistic self-assessment is difficult because the patients are unable to predict how the chemotherapy is going to affect them later on or even whether they are going to survive beyond five years. Therefore, doctors may send mixed messages and clouded answers about the future.

Adolescents with cancer are faced with the same developmental challenges as other adolescents, but these challenges are often considerably more complicated. However, although cancer may affect their body image, self-esteem, socialization, independence, sexuality, and career planning, most adolescents with this diagnosis fare quite well. Although the initial diagnosis can be quite alarming, most adolescents continue to find meaning in their disease; they feel they will never be the same again, and at times feel quite disconnected from their peers, most have the capacity to use this challenge to find an even greater meaning in their life.

Many organizations offer free printed materials about treatment and living with cancer. They are available by calling (1) the National Cancer Institute, also known as the Cancer Information Service, at 1-800-4-CANCER (1-800-422-6237); (2) the American Cancer Society at 1-800-ACS-2345 (1-800-227-2345); (3) the Candlelighters Childhood Cancer Foundation (CCCF) at 1-800-366-CCCF (1-800-366-2223); or (4) the Leukemia Society of America (LSA) at 1-800-955-4LSA (1-800-955-4572).

Catherine E. Barton

See also Chronic Illnesses in Adolescence; Cigarette Smoking; Health Promotion;

Health Services for Adolescents; Nutrition

References and further reading
Lampkin, B. C. 1993. "Introduction and Executive Summary." *Cancer* 71: 3199–3201.
Meadows, A. T., and W. L. Hovvie. 1986. "The Medical Consequences of Cure." *Cancer*, 58:524–528.
Rowland, Julia H. 1998. "Developmental Stage and Adaptation: Child and Adolescent Model." Pp. 519–543 in *Handbook of Psychooncology: Psychological Care of the Patient with Cancer.* Edited by Jimmie C. Holland and Julia H. Rowland. New York: Oxford University Press.
Varni, James W., Ronald L. Blount, and Daniel L. L. Quiggins. 1998. "Oncological Disorders." Pp. 313–346 in *Handbook of Pediatric Psychology and Psychiatry*, Vol. 11: *Disease, Injury, and Illness.* Boston: Allyn and Bacon.

Career Development

Broadly defined, career development represents the process one goes through in order to "make a life." Couched within this perspective is the concept of "making a living." This conceptualization is important from the standpoint that throughout life, people are in constant pursuit of developing, establishing, or redefining who they are as individuals. The role of work and the ability to make a living play a critical role in how one defines oneself. While this process begins early in the life course, the true foundation is laid during the period of adolescence when one begins to seriously consider the possibility of one's future. These considerations, as well as the personal, social, and academic experiences one has during this time, in many ways determine the quality of an individual's initial pathway into adulthood roles. Such pathways play a significant role in how one makes a life.

Classic researchers such as Donald Super see the role of exploration as an opportunity for teenagers to explore the notion of self and their environment. From a developmental perspective, the exploration process one goes through is very similar to the crisis period Erik Erikson describes in identity development. From Super's perspective, failure to effectively explore oneself in various contexts (e.g., school and early work settings) often leads to poor and uninformed choices concerning jobs and careers. It is this exploratory behavior that lays the foundation for what is known as vocational maturity, which allows adolescents the opportunity to make informed decisions about how to pursue their occupational futures. The degree of one's career maturity is useful not only in helping one commit to a career choice but also in serving as a buffer for individuals experiencing vocational stress associated with the establishment, maintenance, loss, and decline stages of career development. This ability to cope with the ever-changing landscape of the cycle of work grows out of an expanded knowledge of self and the world of work.

Microsystem Influences—
Family and Work Experience
Using a developmental, ecological perspective, the microsystem is viewed as those social agents that come in direct contact and impact the adolescent. As components of the microsystem, the family and the adolescent workplace have critical functions in young people's ability to identify patterns, roles, activities, and interpersonal relationships necessary to effectively transition into adulthood.

Family. The family literature concentrates on how birth order, early parent-child interaction, identification with parents, perception of parental expectations, and amount of contact with parents influence career development. The bulk of the family literature centers on the interaction of socioeconomic status (SES) and gender on parents' and adolescents' motivation, aspirations, and overall development at various points in the life course.

Recent studies concerning the impact of social context on adolescent career development have shifted toward examining how enhancing the relational components (e.g., family) impacts one's identity. Through this perspective, adolescents have a means of developing and maintaining their connection to the world while at the same time learning about themselves via supported family relationships. Rainer Silbereisen, Fred Vondracek, and Lucianne Berg (1997) reported that higher levels of parental support behavior during childhood is associated with young people making earlier vocational choices, as well as showing an advanced level of identity exploration and commitment. Baerbel Kracke (1997) further supported Silbereisen et al. in explaining how parent interaction and communication styles at different points during development impact career exploration in young people. Borrowing from attachment theory, Kracke felt that parents who provide safe and secure relationships in the family promote curiosity and early exploratory activity in children. Diana Baumrind (1989) also pointed out that through such a supportive environment, parents exhibit two important behaviors that are critical for shaping young peoples' career exploration behavior: (1) an awareness of children's needs and (2) expectations that their children act in a mature and responsible manner. As children move into adolescence,

this authoritative parenting style begins to change from parent-child to partnerlike. Kracke explained that parents who are willing to openly communicate their feelings about their adolescents' development or who promote independent thinking will continue to promote active career exploration in their children. Through this home environment, parents are providing important meaning-making opportunities that have long-term effects on how young people view themselves and their potential contribution to society via work. Other evidence shows that through family support, transitioning youth are able to maintain their connection to the work world and are less likely to suffer the long-term psychological and emotional effects associated with unemployment.

Additionally, John Schulenberg, Fred Vondracek, and Ann Crouter (1984) pointed to other limitations in the family effect and career development literature; that limitations need to be considered when using an ecological perspective. First, many of the trends that push the family effect and career development literature lack a developmental focus. Second, much of this literature fails to look at the family as a functioning whole. This shortcoming highlights the importance of looking at career development from an ecological perspective. Schulenberg et al. noted that the research rarely looks at the "salient issues of the family as being interdependent in their occurrence and influence." As a result, the literature tends to diminish the full impact of how families affect adolescent career development. Third, little attempt seems to be made in considering how the individual's vocational development and family context changes over time. Life events such as family relocation, loss of parental employment and benefits, or family experiences with inconsistent employment opportunities have profound impacts on how young people view the opportunity structure and how the family provides and prepares the young person to transition into adulthood roles.

Workplace. Much of the adolescent workplace literature focus has been devoted to examining how the number of work experiences impact educational outcomes, personality development, problem behavior, and future earnings. This literature has produced confusing results at best. Some researchers who espouse the positive effects of adolescent employment show supportive evidence that work experience provides self-discipline, improved school achievement, and higher levels of future employment status and earnings. Others believe too many hours spent working may lead to higher levels of school misconduct, low achievement, tobacco and drug use, and diminished time spent with family, homework, and extracurricular school activities. Using a developmental perspective, Ellen Greenberger and Laurence Steinberg (1986) determined that because young people potentially spend so much time working, they miss out on their moratorium period to explore alternative identities. It is important to note that much of the research connecting the negative impact of work with student achievement primarily correlates the number of hours worked with academic performance. As students work more hours, they consistently do poorly in school. This has been a major contribution to practitioners in terms of developing and monitoring thresholds to maximize student achievement. Jeylan Mortimer and Marcia Johnson (1997) reported promising evidence revealing that adolescents who are successful at balancing school and

working under twenty hours per week are more likely to pursue postsecondary training than either students who work longer hours or students who do not work at all during high school.

Researchers concerned about adolescent workforce experiences have also successfully linked the various types of experiences young people are exposed to in both the classroom and the workplace. Steven Hamilton and Wolfgang Lempert (1996) believed that early supported work experiences and apprenticeship programs like the ones found in Germany, which rely heavily on work-based learning, are successful at teaching basic work soft skills (e.g., work etiquette) that can be transferred from one work situation to another. James Stone and Jeylan Mortimer (1998) further pointed out that young people experiencing work for the first time learn valuable general behavior that is useful regardless of the nature of the job. Many of these work experiences provide young people a real-world vehicle to connect and apply many desired school behaviors within an interdisciplinary work context. Early work experiences teach young people the importance of following directions and working with various groups (e.g., managers, coworkers, and customers). In addition, adolescents learn how to plan for, prepare, and engage the labor market as well as access and organize necessary information for employment. All of these are essential skills that must be mastered for effective transitioning into the world of work. These experiences can then serve as the foundation for subsequent upward mobility.

Unfortunately, career development researchers have given limited attention to the manner in which work experiences impact adolescent career development. Part of the reason why the literature has not focused on this component might be related to the assumption by researchers that family and schools serve as the primary socializers during adolescent development. However, a small number of researchers believe workplace experiences offer significant meaning-making opportunities for young people transitioning into adulthood roles.

Despite the limited research focus, the need to understand how workplace experiences assist young people in understanding the work world and make appropriate decisions is critical. Using data from the National Longitudinal Survey of Youth (NLSY), Michael Pergamit (1995) estimated that nearly 64 percent of high school juniors and 73 percent of high school seniors work for pay outside of the home. Similarly, Wendy Manning (1990) reported that 70 percent of adolescents between sixteen and eighteen years of age were employed, while Jerald Bachman and John Schulenberg (1993) showed that 75 percent of male and 73 percent of female young people held some type of work experience. These numbers further support the developmental perspective that work plays an important role in the lives of many young people.

Christopher Ashford

See also Academic Achievement; Academic Self-Evaluation; Apprenticeships; Employment: Positive and Negative Consequences; School, Functions of; Vocational Development; Work in Adolescence

References and further reading
Ainsworth, Mary. 1989. "Attachments beyond Infancy." *American Psychologist* 44: 709–716.
Bachman, Jerald G., and John Schulenberg. 1993. "How Part-Time Work Intensity Relates to Drug Use, Problem Behavior, Time Use, and Satisfaction among High School Seniors: Are These Consequences, or Merely Correlates?" *Developmental Psychology* 29 (2): 220–236.
Baumrind, Diana. 1989. "Rearing Competent Children." In *Child Development Today and Tomorrow*, edited by William Damon. San Francisco: Jossey-Bass.
Erikson, Erik H. 1968. *Identity: Youth and Crisis.* New York: Norton.
Greenberger, Ellen, and Laurence D. Steinberg. 1986. *When Teenagers Work: The Psychological and Social Costs of Adolescent Employment.* New York: Basic Books.
Hamilton, Steven F., and Wolfgang Lempert. 1996. "The Impact of Apprenticeship on Youth: A Prospective Analysis." *Journal of Research on Adolescence* 6: 427–455.
Kracke, Baerbel. 1997. "Parental Behaviors and Adolescents' Career Exploration." *The Career Development Quarterly* 45, no. 4: 341–350.
Manning, Wendy D. 1990. "Parenting Employed Teenagers." *Youth and Society* 22: 184–200.
Marsh, Herbert W. 1991. "Employment during High School: Character Building or a Subversion of Academic Goals?" *Sociology of Education* 64: 172–189.
Mortimer, Jeylan T., and Marcia K. Johnson. 1997. "Adolescent Part-Time Work and Post-Secondary Transition Pathways: A Longitudinal Study of Youth in St. Paul, Minnesota." Paper presented at New Passages, Toronto, Canada.
Pergamit, Michael R. 1995. "Assessing School to Work Transitions in the United States. Discussion Paper" (NLS 96–32). Washington, DC: U.S. Bureau of Labor Statistics.
Schulenberg, John, Fred W. Vondracek, and Ann Crouter. 1984. "The Influence of the Family on Vocational Development." *Journal of Marriage and the Family* 46: 129–143.
Silbereisen, Rainer K., Fred W. Vondracek, and Lucianne A. Berg. 1997. "Differential Timing of Initial Vocational Choice: The Influence of Early Childhood Family Relocation and Parental Support Behaviors in Two Cultures." *Journal of Vocational Behavior* 50: 41–59.
Steinberg, Laurence, and Sanford Dornbusch. 1991. "Negative Correlates

of Part-Time Employment during Adolescence: Replication and Elaboration." *Developmental Psychology* 27: 304–313.

Stone, James R., and Jeylan T. Mortimer. 1998. "The Effects of Adolescent Employment on Vocational Development: Public and Educational Policy Implications." *Journal of Vocational Behavior* 53: 184–214.

Super, Donald E. 1964. "A Developmental Approach to Vocational Guidance: Recent Theory and Results." *Vocational Guidance Quarterly* 13: 1–10.

———. 1990. "A Life-Span Life-Space Approach to Career Development." Pp. 197–261 in *Career Choice and Development,* 2nd ed. Edited by D. Brown and L. Brooks. San Francisco: Jossey-Bass.

Cheating, Academic

Research over the last thirty years has shown that academic cheating appears to be normative, rather than deviant, behavior among adolescents. Different studies have found that as many as 80 percent of students surveyed admit to cheating on a fairly regular basis. Student handbooks usually outline the criteria of and penalty for various forms of academic dishonesty.

When cheating occurs in the context of essays and term papers, it is called plagiarism. But cheating can also take place on in-class tests, open-book tests, and take-home tests. In most schools, the following behavior is generally considered cheating on in-class tests: communicating information in any form with another test taker (i.e., giving or receiving information, verbally or nonverbally); obtaining a copy of the test prior to the official test day and time; obtaining information about the questions and/or answers of a test prior to official test day and time (e.g., when students in different sections of the same course exchange information

between class periods); and obtaining answers to test questions from sources not approved by the teacher, whether written or electronic (e.g., consulting one's notes, crib sheets, preprogrammed watches, or calculators). Cheating on open-book tests includes all of the above plus using or submitting answers written out ahead of time. Cheating on take-home tests includes obtaining information from sources not approved by the teacher (e.g., consulting Internet sites or other students).

There are a variety of reasons why students cheat: They lack good study skills; the work is too difficult; the pressure to achieve is too great; they've opted for the easy way out; consequences are loosely or inconsistently enforced. Although research over the years has shown a steady increase in the prevalence of cheating behavior (or at least students' willingness to admit to it), two specific reasons for cheating consistently appear in the list of top five reasons: (1) fear of failure and (2) pressure to achieve. In addition, cheating tends to occur more often in private and independent schools than in public schools, and among high-achieving students than among middle-to low-achieving students.

Academic competitiveness in private and independent schools can be so sharp that the consequences of failure, or even moderately poor performance, appear graver than the consequences of cheating. This is especially true in schools where teachers are reluctant to report cheating in order to avoid confrontation with students, parents, or administrators; where cheating is not taken seriously and the penalty is loosely or inconsistently enforced; or where classroom and school environments are overly familiar and trusting, as when a teacher grades papers or momentarily steps out of the room while students are taking a test.

Among high-achieving students, the pressure to perform can come from both home and school. In 1993, Who's Who among American High School Students conducted one of the largest polls ever in this area of research. All of the students surveyed had "A" and "B" averages, and 98 percent planned on attending college. An amazing 80 percent of the respondents admitted committing some form of academic dishonesty on more than a few occasions. Part of the pressure that high-achieving students experience is due to increased competitiveness in obtaining acceptance to select colleges. Indeed, although the number of high school students has remained relatively stable over the past decade, the number of applicants to college has risen 50 percent.

Schools have taken various steps to curtail cheating associated with this climate of academic competitiveness. Some, for example, have eliminated honor rolls; others have stopped distributing year-end awards; still others have started requiring teachers to provide narrative comments along with letter grades on report cards or have de-emphasized class rank (e.g., through student selection of valedictorians based on qualities other than grades). One of the most effective methods for reducing cheating, however, has been to institute an honor code at both the classroom and schoolwide levels. This method is especially successful when student representatives are permitted to participate in the review process. Indeed, integrity is maintained more consistently when peers keep one another accountable for their behavior and for the consequences that follow.

As noted, plagiarism is another form of cheating. Plagiarism refers to the presentation of another person's ideas or work (written or otherwise) in an attempt to pass it off as one's own. The most obvious and irrefutable form of plagiarism is a paper produced by a student who has copied, word for word, from a research source without including any or sufficient documentation. It is fairly simple to teach students that this method of writing is to be avoided at all costs. Much more difficult is the task of teaching students how to read, digest, synthesize, and cite appropriately. As many adolescents find this a complex cognitive process, many schools do not permit the assignment of research or term papers before the junior year. Instead, they place greater emphasis on teaching students the skills and processes involved in good writing.

Under most test conditions, students know when they are cheating, doing so consciously and deliberately. But plagiarism presents quite a different situation, as students often do not know they are plagiarizing. They misunderstand the rules of proper referencing, have weak writing skills, are poorly trained in the writing process, or rely upon inappropriate reference guides. For example, many students do not realize that paraphrasing requires acknowledgment of the source or that rearranging words does not make an idea one's own. In these instances, teachers should take special care to determine whether plagiarism is due to poor skills or training as opposed to willful misrepresentation.

Both students and teachers have offered the following recommendations to help maintain academic honesty and integrity: Test questions should accurately reflect the level of difficulty and time spent on material during class; teachers should supervise tests closely (e.g., by standing or walking around the classroom rather than sitting at the desk or focusing on other work); teachers should use different, but equivalent, makeup tests for different students; students and teachers should make an effort to communicate effectively when material is difficult (i.e., students should ask the teacher or other students for help, and teachers should review the material more slowly or more frequently); students' and teachers' expectations and objectives for the course as a whole, as well as for individual units, should be clearly articulated; and teachers should remain sensitive to students' requirements in other classes (e.g., by not giving a unit test in math on the same day a major science project is due).

Both the increase in cheating behavior among students and the difficulty of curtailing it are due largely to the more "sophisticated" methods of cheating now available. Technological advances have made it easier for students to cheat and more difficult for teachers to catch them in the act, especially since today's students tend to be more technologically savvy than many adults. For example, calculators and watches can be preprogrammed with math and science formulas, and the Internet provides an endless stream of Web sites for downloading everything from expository essays to research papers. Accordingly, ongoing professional development must include education on the use and misuse of technology in the classroom. Students must see that teachers are as knowledgeable about computers as they are about their subject matter.

The efficiency and ease that technology has introduced to the age-old problem of cheating also warrant stronger emphasis on character and the personal loss that comes with achievement through decep-

tion. Cheating diminishes the pride that comes with achievement and doing one's own work; it threatens the trust between students and their teachers and among the students themselves; it presents an unfair advantage to some students over others; and, finally, it is a form of stealing. Indeed, stealing someone else's work and ideas is as much a violation as stealing someone else's property.

Imma De Stefanis

See also Academic Achievement; Academic Self-Evaluation; Conduct Problems; Moral Development

References and further reading

Evans, Ellis D., and Delores Craig. 1991. "Teacher and Student Perceptions of Academic Cheating in Middle and Senior High Schools." *Journal of Educational Research* 84, no. 1: 41–52.

McLaughlin, Rose D., and Steven M. Rose. 1989. "Student Cheating in High School: A Case of Moral Reasoning vs. 'Fuzzy Logic.'" *The High School Journal* 72, no. 3: 97–104.

Schab, Fred, 1991. "Schooling without Learning: Thirty Years of Cheating in High School." *Adolescence* 26, no. 104: 839–847.

Who's Who among American High School Students. 1993. "24th Annual Survey of High Achievers." Lake Forest, IL: Educational Communications.

Chicana/o Adolescents

The term *Chicana/o* grew out of the 1960s civil rights movement from a united sense of *Raza* or race, a united sense of the collective struggles of Mexican American peoples to make their voices heard. Most efforts of Chicanas/os before, through, and after the 1960s reflect struggles to gain access to the same opportunities—education, economic and social justice, safe and affordable housing, social services, and working opportunities—which the U.S. government was then providing the dominant, Anglo population. Several Chicana/o organizations—including United Farm Workers, the Brown Berets, MEChA (Movimiento Estudiantil Chicano de Atzlán), LULAC (the League of United Latin American Citizens), and the G.I. Forum—helped to raise these issues in a public way. To raise concerns, members in these organizations held marches, endured painful hunger strikes, were arrested for the civil disobedience of peaceful protest, and were even murdered.

A few of the many heroes active in these struggles include Cesar Chávez, who was the founding president of the United Farm Workers; Vicky Castro, who was the president of the Young Citizens for Commuity Action, which later grew into the Brown Berets; María Hernández, who fought against school segregations and helped to form La Raza Unida; Rubén Salazar, a journalist who was murdered by Los Angeles Police Officers while covering Chicana/o protests of the 1960s; and Rodolfo "Corky" Gonzales, who fought police brutality against Chicanas/os and authored "I am Joaquín," a poem capturing the heart of the Chicana/o movement. Today, the Chicana/o struggles continue. Some of the activists in the midst of these struggles are Gloria Anzaldúa, a Chicana feminist lesbian author; Arturo Rodriguez, president of the United Farm Workers; Edward James Olmos, a Chicano actor supportive of La Raza; Loretta Sanchez, a member of Congress; Carlos Santana, the guitar genius; and Josefina Villamil Tinajero, president of the National Association of Bilingual Education.

There are two primary definitions of Chicana/o adolescents actively in use today. These definitions reflect how Chicanas/os (also written Chican@s) define themselves and how they are defined by others. Chicanas/os often describe the term *Chicana/o* (reflecting both women—a and men—o) as a political ideology, rather than a racial category. The Chicana/o political ideology is one of active resistance against tyranny. The tyranny against which Chicanas/os struggle is based in the oppression of Mexican-descendant peoples in the United States, including both immigrants and those originally here. Those originally here are the Mexicans whose land and ways of living were taken from them in the Mexican-American War, ending in 1848 with the Treaty of Guadalupe Hidalgo, when the United States stole several states from Mexico, including present-day California, Arizona, Texas, Utah, Colorado, and New Mexico. Chicanas/os often describe themselves as a people united in a political ideology encompassed in a continuous struggle (La Lucha Sigue) to affirm their existence and their civil rights within the United States. Given this self-definition, one is not born a Chicana/o but becomes a Chicana/o through an awareness of the injustices Mexican Americans in the United States face daily and a determination to continue the struggle for justice.

The other definition often used for Chicana/o is to describe any person of Mexican American descent who was born in the United States, as opposed to those born in Mexico. This definition is often used to distinguish between those Mexicans in the United States with strong Spanish skills and strong ties to Mexican culture and those Mexican Americans who Spanish skills and cultural ties are seen by Mexicans as weaker.

Danielle Carrigo

See also Ethnic Identity; Identity;
Latina/o Adolescents; Racial Discrimination

References and further reading
Acuna, Rodolfo. 1988. *Occupied America:
A History of Chicanos*, 3rd ed. New
York: HarperCollins.
———. *Anything but Mexican: Chicanos
in Contemporary Los Angeles*. 1996.
London: Verso.
Anzaldua, Gloria. 1987. *Borderlands: La
Frontera, the New Mestiza*. San
Francisco: Aunt Lute Books.
Garcia, Alma M., ed. 1997. *Chicana
Feminist Thought: The Basic Historical
Writings*. New York: Routledge.
Lopez, David. 1978. "Chicano Language
Loyalty in an Urban Setting." *Sociology
and Social Research* 62, no. 2: 267–278.
Merino, Barbara. 1991. "Promoting School
Success for Chicanos: The View from
Inside the Bilingual Classroom." Pp.
119–148 in *Chicano School Failure and
Success: Research and Policy Agendas
for the 1990s*. Edited by Richard
Valencia. New York: Falmer Press.
Moraga, Cherrie, and Gloria Anzaldua,
eds. 1981. *This Bridge Called My Back:
Writings by Radical Women of Color*.
New York: Kitchen Table: Women of
Color Press.
Peñalosa, Fernando. 1980. *Chicano
Sociolinguistics*. Rowley, MA: Newbury
House Publishers.
Rendón, Laura I. 1996. "Life on the
Border." *About Campus*
(November–December): 14–20.
Valenzuela, Angela. 1999. *Subtractive
Schooling: U.S.-Mexican Youth and the
Politics of Caring*. New York: State
University of New York Press.
Velasquez, Roberto J., Leticia M. Arellano,
and Amado M. Padilla. 1999.
"Celebrating the Future of Chicano
Psychology: Lessons from the Recent
National Conference." *Hispanic
Journal of Behavioral Sciences* 21, no.
1: 3–13.

Child-Rearing Styles

Child-rearing styles are patterns of parenting behaviors that have an impact on children's behavior and personality characteristics. They include such practices as loving and caring for children, bringing children to maturity as legitimate members of society, and dealing with children's daily behaviors. Each society, with its unique ecological conditions, economy, social structure, religious beliefs, and moral values, promotes its own child-rearing practices. And each parent develops his or her child-rearing style with reference to the larger cultural context. Diana Baumrind (1971) has identified three common styles or patterns of child rearing in the United States: authoritarian, permissive, and authoritative. These styles differ on two parenting dimensions in particular: the degree of parental nurturance in child-rearing interactions and the degree of parental control over the child's activities and behavior. Although parents each have a specific parenting style, they do not use just one set of child-rearing practices at all times. Rather, they use a variety of practices at different times, depending on the situation, the child's age, the child's temperament, their own mood, and so on.

Although behaviorist and psychoanalytic theorists made some earlier efforts to formulate common child-rearing practices, Baumrind's work is the most recognized in this field. In a series of landmark studies conducted initially in the early 1960s, Baumrind examined preschool children and their parents through home observations, interviews, and psychological testing. She tested the same group of children again when they were eight to nine years old. The overall findings from her studies pointed to three distinct patterns of child rearing, which she labeled authoritarian, permissive, and authoritative. Later on, Eleanor Maccoby and John Martin (1983) extended Baumrind's three categories by proposing a fourth one: the neglectful style.

Authoritarian Child-Rearing Style

Parents who use the authoritarian style demand a high level of control but fail to respond to their children's rights and needs. They expect full obedience and rely on forceful strategies to gain compliance. Authoritarian parents set strict rules for their children and are not open to negotiations. They are also unlikely to have open discussions with their children about their behavior or to use gentle methods of persuasion such as affection, praise, and rewards. On the contrary, "Do it because I said so" is the common attitude among these parents, as they rarely explain to their children why it is necessary to follow the rules they have set. These parents do not tolerate any expression of disagreement from their children. In turn, the children are expected not to question their parents' position on what is right. When they do question, they are usually physically punished.

Research indicates that children of authoritarian parents tend to be moody, unhappy, fearful, anxious, emotionally withdrawn, and indifferent to new experiences. Throughout their teens they exhibit low self-esteem and tend to suffer from depressed mood. They are usually not friendly toward their peers because they lack social skills; in fact, they often do not know how to appropriately behave around their peers. Girls who have been raised by authoritarian parents depend heavily on their parents' approval for the decisions they make, even after they reach adulthood. Boys raised by such parents are usually hostile and show high rates of anger and defiance.

Permissive Child-Rearing Style

The permissive child-rearing style is sometimes also referred to as the indulgent parenting style. Parents who use

this style tend to be nurturing and accepting of their children, but rarely exert parental control over their children's behavior. They encourage their children to express their feelings as they wish and allow them to make their own decisions—often before they are developmentally ready to do so. Permissive parents also demand only a few household responsibilities and orderly behaviors, allowing their children, for the most part, to regulate their own lives. Although some parents choose this child-rearing approach because they truly believe it is good for their children's sense of self, many others adopt it because they lack confidence in their ability to affect their children's behavior.

The children of permissive parents are deficient in self-control skills and thus tend to be impulsive and aggressive. Though friendly and easy to socialize, they usually lack knowledge of appropriate social behaviors. They often act without thinking about the consequences of their behavior and take too little responsibility for their misbehavior. Since these children are not encouraged to obey, they find it difficult to deal with external standards. They also have a hard time learning to become self-reliant and independent. Children who are raised in a permissive style have been found to score below average on cognitive and social competence measures. Continued use of this style of child rearing often leads to poor school performance and delinquency.

Authoritative Child-Rearing Style

The authoritative style is a more adaptive and flexible approach to child rearing than either the authoritarian or permissive style. Parents who use this style tend to be nurturing; at the same time, they make reasonable demands that fit the maturity level of their children. They allow their children freedom but are careful to provide rationales for the restrictions they impose, all the while ensuring that their children follow these guidelines. They are responsive to their children's needs and points of view, open to discussions with their children, and ready to reconsider their decisions if the children counter with reasonable arguments. In short, they take a democratic approach that respects the rights of both parents and children.

Children raised by authoritative parents tend to be lively and happy. They are self-confident in their social interactions, have control over their behavior, and resist engaging in disruptive behavior. They tend to be free of gender stereotypes: Girls are generally more independent and explorative, and boys more friendly and cooperative in their social relationships, than the children raised by authoritarian and permissive parents. They also perform better in school, exhibit greater intellectual ability, and are more willing to try new things. As a result, their parents are better able to trust their children, knowing that they can accept responsibility.

Neglecting Child-Rearing Style
Parents who adopt a neglectful parenting style express a low level of acceptance of their children and exert no control over their children's behaviors. By demanding too little of their children, they fail to influence their behaviors. They also tend to ignore their children's needs, arranging life to suit themselves rather than their children. Among all the styles discussed here, the neglecting style is associated with the most negative outcomes for children. Indeed, neglected children are prone to delinquency, drug and alcohol use, and poor adjustment.

Baumrind's identification of child-rearing styles has been a benchmark for studies in this field over the last three decades. Although many research findings have confirmed the validity of her approach, a number of criticisms have also been raised against it. For example, John Ogbu (1981) has argued that Baumrind's theory is the product of a specific cultural and historical context—that of middle-class European-American parents—and thus has limited generalizability. Consistent with this observation is a recent study by Ruth K. Chao (1994), who demonstrated that a number of Baumrind's characteristics fail to describe Chinese Americans' approach to child rearing.

A second criticism of Baumrind's theory is that it fails to account for changes in child-rearing practices across time and situation. For example, parents may change over time as they gain experience in child rearing, using an authoritarian style with their first child but a permissive style with younger children. Similarly, parents may change their child-rearing styles over time in response to changes in their social and economic status, as when they lose a job and have to move to a different cultural climate. Child-rearing practices are also influenced by the fit between the children's and parents' temperaments. Contrary to the earlier belief that children remain passive during the child-rearing process, recent studies indicate that they are active participants, in the sense that a parent's choice of parenting style is influenced by the personality characteristics of the child as well as by the parent's reactions to the child.

Finally, in a study that examined the multiple factors influencing school performance, Laurence Steinberg and his associates (1994) found that (1) child-rearing styles are more predictive of school performance among white teenagers than among minority teenagers; (2) African American and Asian American students do not benefit from an authoritative parenting style; (3) for African American students, authoritarian child-rearing practices buffer the negative impact of neighborhood characteristics; and (4) for Asian American students, the positive effects of peer groups buffer the negative effects of authoritarian parenting. Interestingly, these findings suggest that the effects of child-rearing styles are much more complex than earlier research seemed to indicate.

Although certain universal expectations are associated with the socialization of children, each cultural group promotes its own style of child rearing. Indeed, as child-rearing practices are largely based on parental beliefs about proper ways to raise children to be successful members of society, child-rearing styles should be understood, at least in part, in terms of children's adjustment to their culture. As noted, however, authoritative parenting appears to be more effective than other parenting styles in facilitating the development of social competence in children, both at home and in the peer group—especially in white middle-class American households. For this cultural group, it is safe to say that high levels of love and warmth, combined with moderate levels of parental control, help children become able members of the society.

Selcuk Sirin

See also Fathers and Adolescents; Grandparents: Intergenerational Relationships;

Mothers and Adolescents; Parent-Adolescent Relations; Parental Monitoring; Parenting Styles

References and further reading
Barber, Nigel. 1998. *Parenting: Roles, Styles and Outcomes.* Huntington, NY: Nova Science Publishers.
Baumrind, Diana. 1971. "Current Patterns of Parental Authority." *Developmental Psychology Monographs* 4: 1–103.
———. 1989. "Rearing Competent Children." Pp. 349–378 in *Child Development Today and Tomorrow.* Edited by William Damon. San Francisco: Jossey-Bass.
Chao, Ruth K. 1994. "Beyond Parental Control and Authoritative Parenting Style: Understanding Chinese Parenting through the Cultural Notion of Training." *Child Development* 65: 1111–1119.
Maccoby, Eleanor, and John Martin. 1983. "Socialization in the Context of the Family: Parent-Child Interaction." Pp. 1–101 in *Handbook of Child Psychology: Socialization, Personality and Social Development,* Vol. 4. Edited by Paul H. Mussen. New York: Wiley.
Ogbu, John U. 1981. Origins of Human Competence: A Cultural-Ecological Perspective. *Child Development* 52: 413–429.
Steinberg, Laurence, Susie D. Lamborn, Nancy Darling, Nina S. Mount, and Sanford M. Dornbusch. 1994. "Over-Time Changes in Adjustment and Competence among Adolescents from Authoritative, Authoritarian, Indulgent, and Neglectful Families." *Child Development* 65: 754–770.

Children of Alcoholics

Children of alcoholics, or COAs, are children or adolescents with at least one alcoholic parent. COAs are at increased risk for many problems including psychological disorders (e.g., depression, anxiety), family difficulties, and the development of substance abuse themselves. The majority of COAs, however, are well-adjusted individuals who do not develop major problems. Currently, research is examining factors that help explain why some COAs turn out to be well adjusted, whereas others do not.

Genetic Factors
COAs are more likely than non-COAs to develop alcohol- and drug-related problems during adulthood. They are also more likely to abuse alcohol and drugs during adolescence. Many studies have been conducted to examine why alcoholism "runs in families." Results from these studies have shown that much, but not all, of the increased risk for substance abuse problems among COAs is due to genetics. For example, twin studies, which compare alcohol use between identical twins (who share all of their genes) to alcohol use between fraternal twins (who share about half of their genes, as do nontwin brothers and sisters), have found that alcoholism rates are much more similar for identical twins than for fraternal twins. Since identical twins are more similar genetically than fraternal twins, this research indicates that a person's genes influence whether he or she will develop an alcohol problem. Adoption studies, too, have found that alcoholism is at least partly due to genetic influences. Specifically, they have shown that adopted-away sons of alcoholic fathers are at much greater risk for the development of alcoholism than adopted-away sons of nonalcoholic fathers. Overall, both types of studies indicate that genes play an important role in determining whether or not a person will develop an alcohol problem.

As noted, however, genes are not the whole story. The environment appears to be equally important. For instance, some COAs are at increased risk for developing alcohol problems because they grow up in homes marked by family conflict, stress, abuse, and a lack of parental communication, warmth, and monitoring. Some COAs also experience parental divorce, which may create further stress for the family. Given these genetic and environmental risk factors, it is not surprising that COAs are two to seven times more likely to develop alcohol problems than are non-COAs. Because of these risk factors, they are more likely to develop other problems as well.

Psychological Problems among COAs
COAs are at increased risk not only for developing drinking problems but also for experiencing psychological problems such as depression and anxiety and behavioral problems such as conduct disorder (delinquency). Many studies have also found that COAs tend to have lower levels of self-esteem than non-COAs.

Environmental Differences between COAs and Non-COAs. As mentioned previously, COAs are more likely than non-COAs to experience problems within their families. For example, compared to the families of non-COAs, COA families tend to be more chaotic, conflict-ridden, and dysfunctional. They are also less expressive and supportive, less organized, and less democratic. In addition, adolescent COAs report that they have fewer interactions with their parents and that their relationships with their parents are characterized by less warmth and attachment than the relationships between non-COAs and their parents.

Other studies have shown that COAs are at an increased risk of experiencing problems at school. For example, compared to non-COAs, COAs are less likely to achieve high levels of academic achievement and more likely to repeat a grade in school. They are also less likely to graduate from high school than non-COAs.

Adolescent COAs

Adolescence is a period of considerable change affecting not only the individual (in terms of puberty, expanded cognitive abilities, identity formation, and increased autonomy) but also the individual's relationships (with parents, peers, and schoolmates). Adolescence is also a time when many individuals begin to experiment with alcohol and drugs. In addition, the prevalence of psychiatric disorders such as depression, anxiety, and eating disorders rises dramatically during this developmental period. For all of these reasons, adolescence is considered to be a period of particular risk for COAs.

The Vulnerability of Adolescents

Children of alcoholics are generally at greater risk for experiencing substance abuse problems, psychological problems, and maladaptive environments, but it is important to remember that not all COAs develop drinking problems themselves, nor do all COAs exhibit problem behaviors and have poor family relationships. It is still not entirely clear why some individuals with an alcoholic parent develop such problems whereas others do not. However, recent research suggests that characteristics of the individual (such as temperament or personality) and characteristics of the environment (such as the family or peer network) may moderate the relationship between parental alcoholism and adjustment. In other words, certain individual and environmental factors may act to "protect" COAs against the development of substance abuse and psychosocial problems.

Individual Protective Factors. Individuals with certain personality characteristics seem to be more resilient to the harmful effects of parental alcoholism. For example, research has shown that COAs who were affectionate as infants are better adjusted later on than those who were not. The same appears to be true for COAs who, as adolescents, have a positive self-concept and an internal locus of control (meaning that they believe they have control over the environment and that things do not just happen randomly). An optimistic outlook has also been shown to "protect" some COAs from developing problems. In general, COAs who have a positive outlook, and who believe they have control over their environment and are not helpless, are less likely to experience problems.

Environmental Protective Factors. Characteristics of the environment also may moderate the relationship between parental alcoholism and adjustment. For example, COAs who have not experienced disruptions of family rituals such as dinnertime gatherings, holiday traditions, and vacations are less likely to develop an alcohol problem than COAs whose family rituals have been disrupted. Similarly, COAs who have experienced a great deal of conflict and little cohesion or warmth within the family are at greater risk for psychosocial and alcohol problems than COAs who report more positive family environments. Finally, adolescent COAs who report that their parents usually do not know where they are or who they are "hanging out" with are more likely to use alcohol and drugs than COAs whose parents frequently monitor them.

The Drinking Status of the Alcoholic Parent. Another important consideration is the alcoholic parent's current drinking status. For example, studies have found that the family environments of COAs with recovering alcoholic parents (alcoholics who have not drunk for at least three years) differ very little from families in which neither parent has a drinking problem. Indeed, COAs with a recovering alcoholic father have reported that their families are happier, more cohesive, more trusting, and more affectionate than families in which the father is currently drinking. Moreover, in comparison to COAs with an alcoholic parent who is still drinking, COAs with recovering alcoholic parents are less likely to experience psychological problems such as depression and anxiety, less at risk for substance abuse problems during adolescence, and, not surprisingly, more content with their lives.

In summary, many individual and environmental factors contribute to a person's risk for developing problems. Having an alcoholic parent is just one such factor.

Christine McCauley Ohannessian

See also Alcohol Use, Risk Factors in; Alcohol Use, Trends in

References and further reading
Alterman, Alan, and Ralph E. Tarter. 1983. "The Transmission of Psychological Vulnerability: Implications for Alcoholism Etiology." *Journal of Nervous and Mental Disorders* 171, no. 3: 147–154.
Callan, Victor J., and Debra Jackson. 1986. "Children of Alcoholic Fathers and Recovered Alcoholic Fathers: Personal and Family Functioning." *Journal of Studies on Alcohol* 47, no. 2: 180–182.
Chassin, Laurie, Patrick J. Curran, Andrea M. Hussong, and Craig R. Colder. 1996. "The Relation of Parent Alcoholism to Adolescent Substance Use: A Longitudinal Follow-Up Study." *Journal of Abnormal Psychology* 105, no. 1: 70–80.
Goodwin, Donald W., Fini Schulsinger, L. Hermansen, Samuel B. Guze, and George Winokur. 1973. "Alcohol Problems in Adoptees Raised Apart from Alcoholic Biological Parents." *Archives of General Psychiatry* 28: 238–243.
Sher, Ken J. 1991. *Children of Alcoholics: A Critical Appraisal of Theory and Research.* Chicago: University of Chicago Press.
U.S. Department of Health and Human Services. 1997. *Ninth Special Report to the U.S. Congress on Alcohol and Health.* Washington, DC: U.S. Government Printing Office.
Werner, Emily E. 1986. "Resilient Offspring of Alcoholics: A Longitudinal Study from Birth to Age 18." *Journal of Studies on Alcohol* 47, no. 1: 34–40.
Windle, Michael, and John S. Searles. 1990. *Children of Alcoholics: Critical Perspectives.* New York: Guilford Press.

Chores

In most families, children are included in household chores—tasks that children are responsible for within the household and family—on a fairly regular basis. Parents assign chores to children for a variety of reasons. Giving children some responsibilities in the home is a way to share household work among family members, so that one person—typically the mother—does not become overwhelmed with household tasks. Parents also assign chores because they believe that children's participation in family work and routines is good for their development. Self-worth, independence, and care and concern for others can result from children's participation in household chores and responsibilities.

Self-worth, independence, and care and concern for others can result from children's participation in household chores and responsibilities. (Skjold Photographs)

Household chores typically fall into two categories. *Self-care tasks* require children to be responsible for some aspect of their own care (e.g., packing their own school lunch) or care of their own belongings (e.g., cleaning their rooms), whereas *family-care tasks* include those chores that affect more than just the person performing them, such as setting the table or caring for younger siblings (Goodnow, 1988). Both types of chores may encourage responsible work habits in children, but when children do family-care tasks they may also develop a greater concern for the welfare of others. Children's involvement in chores, therefore, may contribute to the family work effort as well as promote children's personal responsibility and prosocial behavior.

The question of how much children actually participate in household chores has been widely debated. Some research suggests that children's efforts in the "average" family are quite limited. According to estimates from one national sample, children under age nineteen spend about three to six hours per week on household chores (Demo and Acock, 1993). But because of the way many researchers measure children's household input, it is possible that these figures underestimate the time children actually spend on chores. In some studies (e.g., Demo and Acock, 1993), researchers have evaluated children's household work by asking about chores that may actually be considered "adult" chores, such as cooking, transportation, and bill paying, thus possibly overlooking tasks more appropriate for children. By using an extensive list of questions—including some that concern tasks such as cleaning one's room, taking care of younger siblings, and caring for pets—other research has demonstrated that teenagers do, on average, about ten or more hours of household work per week (Gager, Cooney, and Call, 1999). In addition, children's contributions to the family work effort appear to vary by season. In families where both parents work for pay year-round, children's household responsibilities, particularly care of siblings, increase noticeably during the summer (Crouter and Maguire, 1998).

How much time children spend on chores also depends on their sex. Studies frequently show that, compared to boys, girls put more time into a greater number of tasks. Indeed, although boys are more likely than girls to perform male-typed chores (e.g., lawn mowing, taking out the garbage), these tasks are fewer in number and are required less frequently than the chores that girls typically perform (e.g., helping with meal preparation, washing dishes) (Gager, Cooney, and Call, 1999). Differences between girls' and boys' chores are greatest when family care and self-care chores are compared (Goodnow and Delaney, 1989). Parents also report that, compared to boys' contributions, those made by girls are more often offered spontaneously instead of being requested (Grusec, Goodnow, and Cohen, 1996). These sex differences have led some to suggest that today's American families continue to raise their children to take on traditional sex roles—with girls and women doing most of the household chores and childcare, even though women spend as much time as men outside the home earning money to support the family.

Age also affects children's involvement in household chores. Throughout early adolescence (ages ten to fourteen), children spend increasing amounts of time on household tasks. These changes occur mainly in the area of routine household work (i.e., work that has not been requested by parents) and self-care tasks. When family-care tasks are considered, only girls show an increase in involvement over these ages. Joan Grusec and her colleagues (1996) have therefore concluded that, across adolescence, girls increasingly assume responsibility for family-care tasks and that these tasks "belong to them." In other words, they routinely perform them without waiting for their parents to request that they do so.

Later in adolescence, during the high school years, teens tend to cut back on their household chores. This reduction appears greater for boys than for girls (Gager, Cooney, and Call, 1999). One possible explanation is the teens' greater involvement with paid work as they get older. Parents do assign less housework to teens who have jobs for which they are paid (Manning, 1990), and there is a clear drop in hours of housework completed by teens relative to their increased hours of paid work (Gager, Cooney, and Call, 1999). Yet other time-consuming activities in which teens participate (i.e., outside of paid work) do not have the same impact on the amount of time they spend on chores. In fact, teens who spend more time on homework and volunteer work also tend to give more time to household chores than do teens who are less involved in such nonfamily activities (Gager, Cooney, and Call, 1999).

Family type may also be associated with children's participation in household chores. For example, children who live in single-parent households spend more time on housework than peers from two-parent households (Demo and Acock, 1993; Gager, Cooney, and Call, 1999; Goldscheider and Waite, 1991). And children in stepfamilies devote more time to household tasks than peers living with two biological parents, although they do less than children in single-parent households (Demo and Acock, 1993; Gager, Cooney, and Call, 1999; Goldscheider and Waite, 1991). One possible explanation is that the absence of an adult from the home creates more need for children to take part in household chores.

Although participation in household chores is considered beneficial to the development of children and adolescents, the positive side of chores is not obvious to those who must do them. Indeed, adolescents often see parents' requests for help around the house as "harassment" (Larson and Richards, 1994, p. 99), and tensions surrounding adolescents' household work are the most frequently reported conflicts by parents of teens (Barber, 1994). The issue of household chores is thus clearly one that takes center stage in a great many interactions between parents and their children, especially teenagers.

Teresa M. Cooney
Sara Gable

See also Discipline; Family Composition: Realities and Myths; Family Relations; Parental Monitoring; Parenting Styles

References and further reading
Barber, Brian. 1994. "Cultural, Family, and Personal Contexts of Parent-Adolescent Conflict." *Journal of Marriage and the Family* 56: 375–386.

Crouter, Ann C., and Mary C. Maguire. 1998. "Seasonal and Weekly Rhythms: Windows into Variability in Family Socialization Experiences in Early Adolescence." *New Directions for Child and Adolescent Development* 82: 69–82.

Demo, David, and Alan C. Acock. 1993. "Family Diversity and the Division of Domestic Labor." *Family Relations* 42: 323–331.

Gager, Constance T., Teresa M. Cooney, and Kathleen Thiede Call. 1999. "The Effects of Family Characteristics and Time Use on Teenagers' Household Labor." *Journal of Marriage and the Family* 61: 982–994.

Goldscheider, Francis K., and Linda J. Waite. 1991. *New Families, No Families: The Transformation of the American Home.* Berkeley: University of California Press.

Goodnow, Jacqueline J. 1988. "Children's Household Work: Its Nature and Functions." *Psychological Bulletin* 103: 5–26.

Goodnow, Jacqueline J., and S. Delaney. 1989. "Children's Household Work: Task Differences, Styles of Assignment, and Links to Family Relationships. *Journal of Applied Developmental Psychology* 10: 209–226.

Grusec, Joan E., Jacqueline J. Goodnow, and Lorenzo Cohen. 1996. "Household Work and the Development of Concern for Others." *Developmental Psychology* 32: 999–1007.

Larson, Reed, and Marise Richards. 1994. *Divergent Realities: The Emotional Lives of Mothers, Fathers, and Adolescents.* New York: HarperCollins.

Manning, Wendy. 1990. "Parenting Employed Teenagers." *Youth and Society* 22: 184–200.

Chronic Illnesses in Adolescence

Chronic illnesses affect about 10 percent of all children and adolescents in the United States. Some of these conditions are more serious than others, but all involve adjustments in daily routines, in relations with family, friends, and teachers, and in planning for one's future.

Today, it is possible for the great majority of teens with chronic illnesses to lead healthy, productive, and satisfying lives. (Jennie Woodcock; Reflections Photolibrary/Corbis)

Chronic illnesses of childhood and adolescence include:

Asthma	Renal Disease
Congenital Heart Disease	Juvenile Rheumatoid Arthritis
Cancer	
Cystic Fibrosis	HIV/AIDS
Hemophilia	Sickle-Cell Disease
Diabetes Mellitus	Seizure Disorders

What features of these illnesses have given rise to the label "chronic illness"? Typically, they last for several years (some are lifelong conditions); they often require special healthcare, regular medical monitoring and treatment, and hospital stays; and the individuals who experience them are affected not only physically and emotionally but also in ways that limit their behavior. The good news is that medical advances over the past several years have made it possible for more children and youth with these conditions to lead lives closer to "normal" and to anticipate long and productive lives as adults.

The developmental tasks for chronically ill teens are much like the tasks for all teens, but with added complications. For example, establishing independence from parents is always a challenge and should be viewed as something positive; but for teens with a chronic illness, there may be special challenges such as assuming responsibility for their diet, medication, and visits to the clinic. They may also have difficulty sharing the specifics of their illness with friends, but it is important to do so. Friends and others in their lives are almost always understanding when certain limitations are imposed or special routines such as taking medications or diet restrictions are required.

Dependency on parents or siblings may be acceptable if it leads to improvement of the teen's medical condition. Indeed, personal assistance or financial aid is sometimes necessary. However, when parents encourage dependence beyond what is needed (McAnarney, 1985) or are overprotective, the teens may be prevented from having the same experiences as their friends are having (Anderson and Coyne, 1993) or experience delays in leading the independent lives they desire. In such cases, the teens' medical treatment team can be called upon to provide advice on just what level of intervention is appropriate.

One major developmental task of adolescence involves setting educational and career goals. Like all teens, those with a chronic illness must decide what type of training they want to engage in after high school, whether to leave home or live there for a while longer, and which career they wish to pursue (McAnarney, 1985). Although the possibilities are almost limitless, they must be realistic in assessing whether their illness imposes certain limitations on education or occupation. Fortunately, most schools and employers today are understanding of such limitations, and the Americans with Disabilities Act, a federal law, provides considerable protection in both higher education and the work environment. Furthermore, as many of the exciting new areas of employment now available require less physical stamina and depend more on "smarts" and specific skills than was true in the past, they are well suited for those with chronic illnesses.

Social development is a key area of concern for teens with chronic illnesses. In some cases, the illness may require periodic separation from peers; in others, the teens may be uncomfortable about anyone other than family members knowing about their condition; in still others, the progress toward puberty may be affected, leading to delays in physical growth and sexual development. Indeed, teens with chronic illness may have limited opportunities to learn about their sexuality from peers or may be prevented from having normal social and sexual experiences. The results of studies in this area have been mixed. Some suggest that teens with such conditions date less often than their peers, are more likely to drop out of school, and make fewer plans for the future (e.g., Orr et al., 1984). But others suggest just the opposite—that teens with chronic illness are not different in most ways from their peers (e.g., Capelli et al., 1989). The latter research implies that having an illness is not necessarily a major factor in one's social adjustment and emotional development.

Recently, several studies have tried to identify the major areas of concern for teens with chronic illnesses. One such study found that the primary problem areas are those relating to school, medical treatment and compliance, and relationships with parents (DiGirolamo et al., 1997). Furthermore, those teens who viewed their problems as very serious reported that they were depressed and lacked social confidence. In another study, the serious problems held mainly for girls. Emotional distress and even thoughts of suicide were identified among some teens (Suris, Parera, and Puig, 1996). Yet another study found that teens who experience the most problems adjusting to their illness come from families that have serious problems unrelated to the illness (Hagen, Myers, and Allswede, 1992). Fortunately, there are many counselors and therapists available today who understand the situations facing these teens, so both teens and parents should not hesitate to seek their help if the situation warrants.

Taking responsibility for one's own health is a problem that many adolescents face, as evidenced by the incidence of smoking, automobile accidents, and poor diet among teens in the United States today. Those with chronic illnesses face even greater challenges, yet they often think of themselves as invulnerable to the consequences of poor health practices. Almost all recommended treatment programs require regular compliance. Teens with diabetes, for example, not only have to watch their diet closely but must also monitor their blood-sugar levels, take one to three injections of insulin each day, and follow exercise and sleep recommendations. This regimen can be especially difficult for individuals who are dealing not only with all the daily challenges of being teens but also with the special conditions imposed by their disorder. Moreover, some parents may discontinue involvement because they want to establish independence for their child, who, in turn, may not take over as needed (Ingersoll et al., 1986). The critical factor here is not the specific age of the teen but, rather, his or her level of mature thinking and social competence (Hanson et al., 1990; Ingersoll et al., 1986).

Age of onset is an important factor in that it can influence how a chronic illness will be handled. In situations where the illness begins well before the teen years, puberty and adolescence inevitably pose new stresses and adjustments, even among individuals who have adapted well up to that time. And for those who encounter the onset of illness while in their teens, the stresses can be even greater—especially if they do not see themselves as being "different" and hence do not comply with medical recommendations. Since noncompliance can have serious short- and long-term consequences, parents need to work with medical professionals, and sometimes with their children's teachers and employers, to ensure that compliance is maintained.

Today, it is possible for the great majority of teens with chronic illnesses to lead healthy, productive, and satisfying lives. Although many of these illnesses linger for many years, life spans have been increased greatly and are often as long for chronically ill people as for those without illness. However, medical and health management procedures are critical toward this end. Above all, teens and the adults in their lives must work together as a team to achieve their life goals.

John W. Hagen
Jennifer T. Myers

See also Cancer in Childhood and Adolescence; Depression; Diabetes; Health Promotion; Health Services for Adolescents; Spina Bifida

References and further reading
Anderson, Barbara J., and James C. Coyne. 1993. "Family Context and Compliance Behavior in Chronically Ill Children." Pp. 77–89 in *Developmental Aspects of Health Compliance Behavior*. Edited by Norman A. Krasnegor. Hillsdale, NJ: Erlbaum.

Blum, Robert W. 1992. "Chronic Illness and Disability in Adolescence." *Journal of Adolescent Health* 13, no. 5: 364–368.

Capelli, M., Patrick J. McGrath, C. E. Heick, N. E. MacDonald, William Feldman, and P. Rowe. 1989. "Chronic Disease and Its Impact: The Adolescent's Perspective." *Journal of Adolescent Health Care* 10, no. 4: 283–288.

DiGirolamo, A. M., A. L. Quittner, V. Ackerman, and J. Stevens. 1997. "Identification and Assessment of Ongoing Stressors in Adolescents with a Chronic Illness: An Application of the Behavior-Analytic Model." *Journal of Clinical Child Psychology* 26, no. 1: 53–66.

Hagen, John W., Jennifer T. Myers, and Jennifer S. Allswede. 1992. "The Psychological Impact of Children's Chronic Illness." Pp. 27–47 in *Lifespan Development and Behavior*, Vol. 11. Edited by David Featherman, Richard M. Lerner, and Marion Perlmutter. Hillsdale, NJ: Erlbaum.

Hanson, C. L., J. R. Rodrique, S. W. Henggeler, M. A. Harris, R. C. Klesges, and D. L. Carle. 1990. "The Perceived Self-Competence of Adolescents with Insulin-Dependent Diabetes Mellitus: Deficit or Strength?" *Journal of Pediatric Psychology* 15, no. 5: 605–618.

Ingersoll, G. M., D. P. Orr, A. J. Herrold, and M. P. Golden. 1986. "Cognitive Maturity and Self-Management among Adolescents with Insulin-Dependent Diabetes Mellitus." *Journal of Pediatrics* 10, no. 4: 620–623.

McAnarney, Elizabeth R. 1985. "Social Maturation: A Challenge for Handicapped and Chronically Ill Adolescents." *Journal of Adolescent Health Care* 6, no. 2: 90–101.

Myers, Jennifer, and John Hagen. 1993. "The Impact of Chronic Illness on the Late Adolescent/Early Adult Transition: Focus—Insulin-Dependent Diabetes Mellitus." (Presentation.) *Family Relationships and Psychosocial Development in Physically Impaired and Chronically Ill Adolescents*, G. Holmbeck, chair. Symposium conducted at the biennial meeting of the Society for Research in Child Development (SRCD), New Orleans.

Orr, D. P., S. C. Weller, B. Satterwhite, and Ivan B. Pless. 1984. "Psychosocial Implications of Chronic Illness in Adolescence." *Journal of Pediatrics* 104, no. 1: 152–157.

Seiffge-Krenke, Inge. 1998. "Chronic Disease and Perceived Developmental Progression in Adolescence." *Developmental Psychology* 34, no. 5: 1073–1084.

Suris, J. C., N. Parera, and C. Puig. 1996. "Chronic Illness and Emotional Distress in Adolescence." *Journal of Adolescent Health* 19, no. 2: 153–156.

Cigarette Smoking

Since the 1964 Surgeon General's report, but especially during the 1990s, cigarette smoking has been a topic of great controversy. What follows is a discussion of several issues related to this controversy: the prevalence of cigarette smoking, motivations for adolescent smoking, the difficulty of quitting, and methods of quitting.

The Prevalence of Cigarette Smoking

Many teenagers think that the majority of people smoke. They may be surprised to discover that only 27 percent of men and 23 percent of women smoke, and that adult smoking has decreased substantially since the U.S. Surgeon General's report first pointed out the health dangers of smoking in 1964. Moreover, fewer teenagers than adults smoke—only about 18 percent of those between ages twelve and seventeen in 1995, according to the National Center for Health Statistics. Teen smoking hit a peak in 1996 and has gradually declined since then (Johnston, O'Malley, and Bachman, 1999). Smoking usually starts in the teenage years; most individuals who go on to become adult smokers try their first cigarette by age sixteen. Conversely, those who finish their high school years without smoking are unlikely to start.

The fact that teenagers often overestimate how common smoking is can itself increase the likelihood that they will smoke. In fact, research shows that nonsmoking teenagers who think that smoking is particularly common are themselves more likely than their peers to be smoking one year later (Chassin et al., 1984). Perhaps teenagers who think that smoking is common and normal also view it as more acceptable.

Motivations for Adolescent Smoking
Given that the health dangers of smoking are so clear and so well known, why do some teenagers start to smoke? The usual answer to this question is "peer pressure." It is true that peer smoking plays a part. Teenagers who have friends who smoke are much more likely to begin smoking than are teenagers who do not. But peer smoking is only part of the picture.

Social Images Associated with Smokers. Some teenagers start to smoke in order to achieve the kind of image that is associated with being a smoker. In one study (Barton et al., 1982), researchers presented slides containing pictures of teenagers to high school students, who were then asked to give their impressions of these teenagers. (The students were unaware that this was a study of cigarette smoking.) Some of the students saw a model who was holding a cigarette; others saw the same model without the cigarette. The model holding the cigarette was described in negative terms—as more foolish, less intelligent, and less healthy than the model without the cigarette. But the cigarette-holding model was also described in positive terms—as older, more interested in the opposite

sex, and tougher. In addition, the researchers asked nonsmoking teenagers to tell them about the kind of person they would like to be. Those teenagers who valued the characteristics of the smoker image (such as toughness, interest in the opposite sex) also thought that they themselves were more likely to smoke in the future. The implication is that some teenagers may smoke to attain a particular social image.

The Role of Parental Smoking in Adolescent Smoking. Not surprisingly, children whose parents smoke are themselves more likely to become smokers. These children may smoke because they imitate their parents, because their parents don't discourage their smoking, or because they have easy access to cigarettes. However, there may be other reasons as well. For example, some scientists are working to discover whether there are also genetic influences on smoking: Perhaps children whose parents smoke experience physiological reactions to nicotine that make them more likely to smoke. Others have suggested that children who are exposed to their mother's smoking while still in the womb may be more likely to smoke (Griesler, Kandel, and Davies, 1998). And, finally, it is possible that children whose parents smoke, having been exposed to secondhand smoke, become desensitized to the negative aspects of smoking such as coughing or nausea.

The Role of Cigarette Advertising. Tobacco companies maintain that the purpose of cigarette advertising is simply to try to persuade adults who already smoke to switch to their own brand. They claim that their ads are not at all intended to influence young nonsmokers to start smoking. However, research on the effects of advertising indicates otherwise. One finding is that even very young children are exposed to cigarette advertisements and learn about smoking through them. For example, a study by Paul Fischer and his colleagues (1991) found that, by age six, children recognized Joe Camel, a cartoonlike character from Camel cigarette ads, as easily as they recognized Mickey Mouse. This result caused great concern about the true extent to which tobacco ads were being aimed at young teenagers. In the wake of the controversy, the tobacco company was convinced to withdraw the Joe Camel ad campaign.

Second, a relationship exists between these ad campaigns and changes in the number of teenagers who begin to smoke. For example, a study by John Pierce and Elizabeth Gilpin (1995) examined changes in smoking initiation relative to the timing of tobacco advertising campaigns from 1890 to 1977. The results indicate that when advertising campaigns aimed at males were begun, teenage boys started to smoke at a higher rate than before—as did teenage girls when advertising campaigns aimed specifically at females were begun. In short, the intended audience of smoking ads seemed to respond favorably to these ads.

Effects of Smoking on Stress. Many smokers, when asked why they smoke, express the belief that smoking helps them cope with stress in their lives. Teenagers appear to share this belief. However, research suggests that smoking may actually increase rather than reduce one's stress level (Parrott, 1999). In general, smokers report experiencing more stress than do nonsmokers, and adoles-

cents, as they begin to smoke, report increasing amounts of stress. Moreover, smokers who successfully quit report a decline in their stress levels. It is possible that what smokers interpret as stress reduction from smoking is actually only the satisfaction of their craving for nicotine (Parrott, 1999).

The Difficulty of Quitting

Many teenagers believe that it is not difficult for a smoker to quit; indeed, those who intend to start smoking think that they can smoke a little and stop anytime they want. Unfortunately, this is a myth. One study has shown that 70 percent of teenagers who smoke at least once a month are still smoking five years later in young adulthood (Chassin et al., 1990). Another common belief among teenagers is that only illegal drugs are addictive; but, in fact, cigarettes are equally addictive, if not more so. In 1988, the U.S. Surgeon General's report officially recognized the addictive nature of cigarettes. As with other addictive substances, addicted smokers need to smoke increasingly more cigarettes over time, view themselves as dependent on cigarettes, persist in smoking despite its negative consequences, and suffer withdrawal symptoms when they go without cigarettes for a while.

Methods of Quitting

Most smokers, when asked, say they want to quit. And although doing so is very difficult, some smokers succeed. Many quit-smoking techniques are available. Smokers can enter treatment programs where they learn behavioral methods for controlling their smoking. They can use nicotine replacement therapies such as nicotine patches or gum, which allow them to slowly reduce their dependence on nicotine while distancing themselves from other aspects of smoking. Interestingly, most successful quitters stop smoking on their own. However, most smokers who try to quit are not successful on their first attempt. Much more common is a period of cessation, followed by a return to smoking within the first six months. With repeated attempts, many smokers eventually succeed at quitting once and for all.

Conclusion

Most teenagers do not plan to smoke cigarettes—but, as we know, some start smoking even after stating their intention not to do so. The reasons for this behavior are not entirely clear. However, because smoking is such an important and controversial subject, a large amount of scientific research is currently being conducted in an effort to better understand why people choose to smoke, to prevent them from starting to smoke, and to develop better methods of helping them quit.

Laurie Chassin
Clark C. Presson
Jennifer Rose
Steven J. Sherman
Nora Presson

See also Health Promotion; Health Services for Adolescents; Peer Groups; Peer Pressure; Peer Status; Peer Victimization in School; Substance Use and Abuse

References and further reading
Barton, John, Laurie Chassin, Clark C. Presson, and Steven J. Sherman. 1982. "Social Image Factors as Motivators of Smoking Initiation in Early and Middle Adolescents." *Child Development* 53: 1499–1511.
Chassin, Laurie, Clark C. Presson, Steven J. Sherman, and Debra Edwards. 1990. "The Natural History of Cigarette Smoking: Predicting Young Adult Smoking Outcomes from Adolescent Smoking Patterns." *Health Psychology* 9: 701–716.
Chassin, Laurie, Clark C. Presson, Steven J. Sherman, Eric Corty, and Richard Olshavsky. 1984. "Predicting the Onset of Cigarette Smoking in Adolescents: A Longitudinal Study." *Journal of Applied Social Psychology* 14: 224–243.
Fischer, Paul, Meyer Schwartz, John Richards, Adam Goldstein, and Tina Rojas. 1991. "Brand Logo Recognition by Children Aged 3–6 Years: Mickey Mouse and Joe the Camel." *Journal of the American Medical Association* 266: 3145–3148.
Griesler, Pamela C., Denise B. Kandel, and Mark Davies. 1998. "Maternal Smoking during Pregnancy and Smoking by Adolescent Daughters." *Journal of Research on Adolescence* 8: 159–185.
Johnston, Lloyd, Patrick O'Malley, and Gerald Bachman. 1999. *National Survey Results on Drug Use from the Monitoring the Future Study, 1975–1998.* U.S. Department of Health and Human Services, National Institute on Drug Abuse, NIH Publication No. 99-4661. Washington, DC: U.S. Government Printing Office.
Parrott, Andy C. 1999. "Does Cigarette Smoking Cause Stress?" *American Psychologist* 54: 817–820.
Pierce, John, and Elizabeth Gilpin. 1995. "A Historical Analysis of Tobacco Marketing and the Uptake of Smoking by Youth in the United States: 1890–1977." *Health Psychology* 14: 500–508.
U.S. Department of Health and Human Services. *The Health Consequences of Smoking: Nicotine Addiction. A Report of the Surgeon General.* Public Health Service, Centers for Disease Control, Center for Health Promotion and Education, Office on Smoking and Health, DHHS Publication No. (CDC) 88-8046. Washington, DC: U.S. Government Printing Office.
U.S. Public Health Service. 1964. *Smoking and Health: Report of the Advisory Committee to the Surgeon General of the Public Health Service.* U.S. Department of Health, Education, and Welfare, Public Health Service, Centers for Disease Control, PHS

Publication No. 1103. Washington, DC: U.S. Government Printing Office.

Preparation of the entry titled "Cigarette Smoking" was supported by Grant HD13449 from the National Institute of Child and Health and Human Development. Requests for reprints should be addressed to Laurie Chassin, Psychology Department, Box 871104, Arizona State University, Tempe, AZ 85287-1104.

Cliques

Within a friendship group there may be significant subdivisions. One such subdivision, known as a "clique," consists of (usually) three or more tightly knit young people. Clique members see themselves as mutual or reciprocating friends, and they are seen by others as having a key common identity or interest (e.g., athletics, socializing, academics). Cliques are surrounded by a sort of "social membrane," in the sense that the youth within them "hang out" more or less exclusively with one another.

Researchers have found that both larger and smaller groups—crowds and liaisons, respectively—also develop during this period. During the early years of adolescence, friendships are structured in terms of these crowds or liaisons, which tend to be predominantly same-sex groups. However, by the beginning of high school, most youth are in friendship cliques, although crowds and liaisons continue to form. In addition, a few adolescents remain isolated in that they do not belong to any identifiable friendship group.

Almost all youth have one or another of these friendship types. For instance, hearing-impaired adolescents form friendships as do non-hearing-impaired youth; however, hearing-impaired youth tend to interact more with other hearing-impaired youth than with their hearing peers. Moreover, hearing-impaired youth tend to form emotional bonds with their hearing-impaired peers as opposed to their hearing peers.

The crowds within which adolescents gather may actually help them understand the nature of social relationships. For instance, as Harold D. Grotevant (1998) notes, "First, crowds and the stereotypes associated with them ('brains,' 'jocks,' etc.) help adolescents understand alternative social identities available to them; second, crowd affiliations channel interactions such that relationships among some individuals are more likely than among others; third, crowds themselves vary in how relationships are structured in features such as closeness and endurance over time" (pp. 1115–1116).

Cliques, too, serve an important function in adolescence. Although the incidence of membership in cliques decreases across the second decade of life, such membership is associated with psychological well-being and the capacity to cope with stress.

Richard M. Lerner

See also Peer Groups; Peer Pressure; Peer Status; Peer Victimization in School; Social Development

References and further reading

Grotevant, Harold D. 1998. "Adolescent Development in Family Contexts." Pp. 1097–1150 in *Handbook of Child Psychology*. Vol. 3, *Social, Emotional, and Personality Development*, 5th ed. Edited by W. Damon and N. Eisenberg. New York: Wiley.

Hartup, William. 1993. "Adolescents and Their Friends." *New Directions for Child Development* 60: 3–22.

During the early years of adolescence, friendships are often structured in terms of crowds and liaisons, which tend to be predominantly same-sex groups. (Shirley Zeiberg)

———. 1993. "The Company They Keep: Friendships and Their Developmental Significance." *Child Development* 67: 1–13.

Lerner, Richard M. In press. *Adolescence: Development, Diversity, Context, and Application.* Upper Saddle River, NJ: Prentice-Hall.

Rubin, Kenneth A. 1998. "Peer Interaction, Relationships, and Groups." Pp. 619–700 in *Handbook of Child Psychology.* Vol. 3, *Social, Emotional, and Personality Development,* 5th ed. Edited by W. Damon and N. Eisenberg. New York: Wiley.

Stinson, M. S., K. Whitmire, and T. N. Kluwin. 1996. "Self-Perceptions of Social Relationships in Hearing-Impaired Adolescents." *Journal of Educational Psychology* 88, no. 1: 132–143.

Cognitive Development

For the parents and teachers of young adolescents, the physical and behavioral changes associated with puberty are impossible to either miss or ignore. The rapid increases in height and weight, the alterations of body configuration, and the bursts of emotional lability that accompany pubescence are surprising and even, at times, startling. By contrast, the much less visible changes in adolescent thinking often go unnoticed. Yet these alterations are, in their own way, every bit as momentous as the bodily and emotional manifestations. Although the cognitive changes that occur in adolescence are well documented, there is an ongoing controversy over three issues in particular: (1) whether the attainment of higher-level thought is continuous or discontinuous, (2) whether the changes in thinking are general or domain specific, and (3) whether the gender differences that appear to arise during adolescence are genetically or socially determined. These issues will be touched on briefly at a later point, in the context of social cognition; for now, however, we consider Piaget's conception of intelligence.

Piaget's Conception of Intelligence
Although a number of writers such as G. Stanley Hall (1904) and Arnold Gesell (Gesell et al., 1956) have described adolescent thinking, it was Barbel Inhelder and Jean Piaget (1958) who gave the phenomenon the most extensive treatment, placing it in the context of Piaget's (1950) general theory of human intelligence, adaptive thinking, and action. Indeed, although some of its details have been challenged, the Piagetian description of mental growth is widely accepted.

In his theory, Piaget argued that human intelligence is an extension of biological adaptation, which, in turn, involves the two invariant processes of assimilation and accommodation. Both biologically and psychologically, *assimilation* has to do with the transformation of environmental materials to conform to the needs of the organism. At the biological level, food that has been ingested is broken down to meet the individual's nutrient needs. At the psychological level, new information is interpreted in keeping with preexisting beliefs and attitudes. *Accommodation,* on the other hand, has to do with changes the individual must make to meet the demands of the environment. At the biological level, blood vessels expand or contract in response to alterations in the temperature. And at the psychological level, people accommodate every time they modify their thoughts or behaviors to better adapt to the demands of the social world. Good manners, to illustrate, are an accommodation to social norms.

Although it is theoretically possible to separate assimilation and accommodation, in reality they are always operating at the same time. There can really be no assimilation without accommodation, and vice versa. The two processes operate in such a way as to establish a transient equilibrium that is the starting point for a whole new set of accommodations and assimilations. Both biological and psychological growth are thus characterized by an ongoing series of accommodations, assimilation, and equilibria. Each new level of equilibration, however, sets the stage for new disequilibria that start the process all over again. In effect, neither biological nor psychological life ever remains at a steady state.

The operation of these invariant processes results in the progressive construction of the mental structures of intelligence. Piaget contended that these mental structures evolve through a series of stages that are related to age. Although the age at which a given child attains a particular set of mental structures will vary with his or her genetic endowment and environmental circumstance, the sequence of stages is invariant. There are four stages in the development of intelligence, each of which is characterized by a definable set of mental operations. Intelligence thus involves both invariant processes and variable structures.

Piaget viewed intellectual development from two complementary perspectives. On the one hand, he was concerned with mental processes, with the progressive attainment of new sets of mental abilities that he likened to sets of arithmetical and logical operations. On the other hand, he was concerned with the content of thought, with the child's progressive attainment of concepts of reality such as space, time, and number. Piaget described children's conceptions of reality as constructions in the sense that their form is provided by mental operations, whereas their content is provided by experience. In effect, thanks to their developing mental abilities, children have to continually construct and deconstruct reality out of their ongoing experiences with the environment.

The Piagetian Stages. For purposes of discussion, the four stages of intellectual development can be described in terms of both the mental operations in play and the type of reality that is being constructed. Infancy occurs during the *sensorimotor stage,* which is characterized by sensory impressions and the construction of a *world of permanent objects.* Next, during the *preoperational stage,* young children experience *functional operations* in the sense that they perceive the world from a practical perspective: A hole is "to dig," a bike is "to ride." From the content standpoint, preschool children are focused on constructing a *world of symbols.* At this time, young children are learning not only to talk but also to engage in symbolic play, to draw, and to use other forms of symbolic representation.

From about the age of six or seven to eleven or twelve, most children have at their disposal a set of new mental abilities that Piaget described as *concrete.* These concrete operations, which are similar to the operations of arithmetic, enable the child to engage in elementary reasoning and to construct a *world of classes, relations, and numbers.* Finally, after reaching puberty, most young people attain a still higher and more involved set of mental operations that Piaget described as *formal.* Formal operations allow young people to entertain *ideas*—that is, to construct abstract conceptions of space, time, and causality.

Characteristics of Formal Operational Thinking. The age of six or seven has, since ancient times, been recognized as the "age of reason." What the ancients meant by reason, however, was the syllogistic reasoning described by Aristotle. Syllogistic reasoning takes the form of a major premise, a minor premise, and a deduction or conclusion.

The classic syllogism is as follows:

Major premise: All men are mortal.
Minor premise: Socrates is a man.
Conclusion: Therefore, Socrates is
   mortal.

Such reasoning enables children both to learn and to employ rules. For this reason, formal education was traditionally not begun until the age of six or seven: Inasmuch as instruction in the tool subjects of reading, writing, and arithmetic involves learning rules, it made little sense to instruct children in skills that they were too young to acquire. This practice, what we today call "developmentally appropriate practice," is still followed by many European countries in which children do not attend public schools until the age of six or seven.

What was so innovative about the work of Inhelder and Piaget was their proposal of what might be called a "second age of reason," attained at the time of puberty. In its operations, this second age of reason resembles the symbolic logic of Boolean algebra—namely, formal logic. Formal logic is distinguished from syllogistic logic in a number of respects. First, the latter deals with classes and class membership, with the world as we know it, whereas formal logic deals with propositions, with the world as it might or might not be. The following question, for example, poses a formal reasoning problem: In a world in which coal is white, what color would snow be? Children younger than twelve are not able to deal with this contrary-to-fact proposition, whereas adolescents find it an easy problem.

A second difference between formal and concrete logic has to do with the number of variables being reasoned about. Formal logic enables the individual to deal with multiple variables, whereas syllogistic logic is limited to at most two variables. The performance of children under twelve and adolescents on Piaget's "pendulum problem" illustrates this difference. Both the children and the adolescents are shown balls of different weights tied to strings of different lengths, all of which are attached to a steel frame. The object is to figure out what factors determine the speed at which the pendulum swings through the air. Children fail to distinguish among the possible variables and thus, for example, may compare weights without checking for string length or vice versa. In contrast, adolescents usually arrive at four hypotheses. They reason that the speed is determined by (1) the length of the string, (2) the weight of the object hung on it, (3) how high the object is raised before it is released, and (4) how forcefully the object is pushed. They then test each of these hypotheses by holding

all of the other variables constant. Through this system of experimentation they eventually discover that only the length of the string can account for differences in the speed with which the pendulum swings through the air.

A third achievement made possible by formal operational thought is the ability to reason about propositions, without regard to their factual truth or falsity. In one study, the experimenters showed children and adolescents a pile of poker chips and told them that some statements would be made about the chips (Osherson and Markman, 1975). Each subject was then requested to make a judgment as to whether the statements were true, false, or ambiguous, as in the following example:

> "Either the chip in my hand is green
> or it is not green."
> "The chip in my hand is green and it
> is not green."

The children based their judgments on the actual properties of the poker chips. In the example just noted, they regarded both statements as ambiguous because they could not see the chip in question. However, when shown the chip, they judged both statements to be true when the chip was green and both statements to be false when the chip was red. Adolescents, by contrast, judged the first statement to be true and the second to be false without regard to the actual color of the chip.

In summary, formal operational thinking allows the young person to deal with contrary-to-fact statements, to take multiple variables into account when solving problems, and to determine the logical truth or falsity of statements without regard to their empirical validity. Such reasoning, however, also has a number of social consequences.

Social Consequences of Formal Operational Thinking. The study of formal operational thinking helps to explain some typical, yet puzzling, adolescent behaviors. For example, adolescents are now able to construct ideals, including ideal parents. They then proceed to compare these ideal parents with their real parents and find the latter sadly wanting. It is for this reason that adolescents, who as children believed their parents could do no wrong, now view them as unable to do anything right. This criticism of parents, which characteristically emerges in adolescence, thus has its roots, at least partly, in the new capacity to idealize.

Idealization also helps to explain the adolescent phenomenon variously referred to as having "a crush on" or "a thing for" a person of the opposite sex—a movie star, a musical performer, even a fellow student. When adolescents develop this sort of attachment, the idealization is such that they will not listen to anyone who says or implies anything negative about the idol. In addition, crushes are usually characterized by an obsessive concern with the idealized figure. Though often abruptly shattered by a harsh reality, they sometimes last a lifetime.

Another social consequence of formal operational thinking is what might be called "pseudo-stupidity." Because young people can now take many variables into account at the same time, decision making is much more complicated than before. For example, when asked a simple question, adolescents may go into a long discourse that is quite irrelevant, finding it difficult to choose among the possible answers. Paradoxically, because they now possess the mental ability to think

of many alternatives, they may appear to be stupid. Indeed, they may seem indecisive for the same reason. Or they may take the opposite course and make decisions rashly without trying to consider the alternatives.

Still other social consequences of the attainment of formal operations derive from the young person's newfound ability to think about other people's thinking. Children think, but they do not really think about thinking. It is only later, during the period of adolescence, that young people begin to spontaneously employ terms like *thought, mind,* and *belief.* Incidentally, this newfound ability should not be confused with "theory of mind," a phenomenon whereby young children correctly use mental terms and recognize what other children know and do not know (e.g., Wellman, 1990). Among children, these achievements are always tied to very concrete materials and experiences, whereas adolescents are able to attribute thoughts to others in the absence of any physical props or perceptual cues. In short, with the attainment of formal operational thinking, adolescents can *create* their own ideas about what other people are thinking.

The capacity to think about thinking is itself associated with a number of social cognitive consequences. For example, the ability to think about thinking helps adolescents appreciate the privacy of their thoughts. In fact, it is this new sense of privacy that accounts for teenagers' reluctance to share their thinking with their parents. ("Where did you go?" "Out." "What did you do?" "Nothing.") In addition, because adolescents are so concerned with the physical and emotional changes they are undergoing, they tend to be self-preoccupied. When they think about other people's thinking, therefore, they often assume that the other people are thinking what they are thinking about—namely, themselves. In the process, they construct what has been termed an *imaginary audience* (Elkind, 1967, 1985).

One consequence of the imaginary audience is enhanced self-consciousness in early adolescence. In one study involving an imaginary-audience scale given to hundreds of students from elementary through high school, self-consciousness was found to peak in early adolescence (ages thirteen to fourteen) (Elkind and Bowen, 1979). This finding has since been replicated by many other investigators using the same or other instruments (Enright et al., 1979; Gray and Hudson, 1984; Goosens et al., 1992). Two other consequences of the imaginary audience that adolescents experience are a need for peer-group approval and a need to publicly separate from parents to demonstrate their new "grownupness."

A corollary of the imaginary audience is the *personal fable,* a story that adolescents tell themselves that is not true (Elkind, 1967). When young people believe that others are thinking about them and concerned with how they look and what they do, they also assume that they are special and unique. They come to believe that whereas other people will grow old and die, or fail to realize their life's ambitions, they themselves will be spared such fates. Although clinical experience supports the existence of the personal fable, an adequate scale to measure it has not yet been devised. Nonetheless, it is known to play a part in adolescent risk taking. Many adolescents take risks because they believe that getting pregnant, getting hooked on drugs, or becoming infected with a venereal disease will happen to others, not to them.

In sum, the cognitive changes associated with puberty have social as well as intellectual consequences.

Issues in Social Cognition
Continuity versus Discontinuity. Some information theorists, such as Robbie Case (1992), although they generally subscribe to Piaget's theory of development, see development as a more continuous process of improvement in various psychological processes than did Piaget himself. Indeed, as children approach adolescence, their attention becomes more selective and better adapted to the tasks at hand; their improved strategies increase the effectiveness of their information storage and retrieval processes; their store of facts and information increases, making strategies more effective; and their ability to process information becomes both multifaceted and more rapid.

There is a way to reconcile the information-processing observations of continuity and the developmental observations of discontinuity. This is possible if we think of the two approaches as using different time scales. When behaviors are viewed over hours and days (the information-processing scale), they appear to be continuous. When behaviors are compared across months and years, however, they appear discontinuous. From this perspective it is the different time scales that make the difference.

Stage Generality. Piaget's theory is often misunderstood to mean that once a young person attains a particular level of mental operations, he or she should think at that level in all domains. Piaget (1950) himself emphasized that he was not a preformist—that the attainment of operations only made possible the attainment of concepts at that level, although each content domain had to be conceptualized on its own terms. That is why he explored how children construct concepts of number, space, time, geometry, and much more. The same is true for formal operations. Once these are attained, the individual has to employ them in a specific domain in order to become formal operational in that domain. For example, taking a college course improves formal operational thinking related to the course content (Lehman and Nisbett, 1990).

Gender Differences. In general, one finds few sex differences on Piagetian measures during the concrete operational period. At the formal operational stage, however, sex differences do appear—particularly in the areas of math and science. As noted, there is some controversy over whether these differences are genetic or cultural. The cultural explanation suggests that social pressures are such as to ensure that young women do not elaborate their formal operational abilities in science and math. In support of this explanation is the finding that sex differences in cognitive abilities of all kinds have declined throughout the past few decades. Put another way, the gap between the scores of boys and girls on tests of math and science has narrowed over this time period. One factor in reducing this difference has been the increase in girls' enrollment in school math and science courses (Campbell et al., 1997).

Conclusion

The cognitive changes that accompany puberty move young people onto a whole new plane of thought that changes both their academic and social lives. The attainment of these new abilities can be viewed as either continuous (on a scale of hours and days) or discontinuous (on a scale of months and years). Young people do not automatically reason at the formal level in all domains once they give evidence of this achievement. They have to be engaged with a particular subject matter before they are able to think of it in a formal operational way. Finally, although sex differences in the areas of science and math appear in adolescence, these seem to be diminishing as more girls take math and science courses. Although formal operations are in part a function of maturation, their full realization is very much dependent on the individual personality of the adolescent and the sociocultural environment in which he or she grows up.

David Elkind

See also Intelligence; Intelligence Tests; Standardized Tests; Thinking

References and further reading
Campbell, J. R. et al. 1997. *Trends in Academic Progress.* Washington, DC: U.S. Government Printing Office.
Case, Robbie. 1992. *The Mind's Staircase: Exploring the Conceptual Underpinnings of Children's Thought and Knowledge.* Hillsdale, NJ: Erlbaum.
Elkind, David. 1967. "Egocentrism in Adolescence." *Child Development* 38: 1025–1034.
———. 1985. "Egocentrism Redux." *Developmental Review* 5: 218–226.
Elkind, David, and Richard Bowen. 1979. "Imaginary Audience Behavior in Children and Adolescents." *Developmental Psychology* 15: 38–44.
Enright, Robert D., et al. 1979. "Adolescent Egocentrism in Early and Late Adolescence." *Adolescence* 14: 687–695.
Gesell, Arnold, et al. 1956. *Youth: The Years from Ten to Sixteen.* New York: Harper.
Goosens, F. X., et al. 1992. "The Many Faces of Egocentrism: Two European

Replications." *Journal of Adolescent Research* 7: 43–58.

Gray, William M., and Lynne M. Hudson. 1984. "Formal Operations and the Imaginary Audience." *Developmental Psychology* 20: 619–627.

Hall, G. Stanley. 1904. *Adolescence.* New York: Appleton.

Inhelder, Barbel, and Jean Piaget. 1958. *The Growth of Logical Thinking from Childhood through Adolescence.* New York: Basic Books.

Lehman, Darrin R., and Richard E. Nisbett. 1990. "A Longitudinal Study of the Effects of Undergraduate Training on Reasoning." *Developmental Psychology* 26: 952–960.

Osherson, Daniel N., and Ellen M. Markman. 1975. "Language and the Ability to Evaluate Contradictions and Tautologies." *Cognition* 2: 213–226.

Piaget, Jean. 1950. *The Psychology of Intelligence.* London: Routledge and Kegan Paul.

Wellman, Henry M. 1990. *The Child's Theory of Mind.* Cambridge, MA: MIT Press.

College

Today, more than 90 percent of high school seniors expect to attend college, and more than 70 percent of them aspire to work in professional jobs as adults. Four decades ago, the picture was quite different: Only 55 percent of high school seniors expected to attend college, and approximately 42 percent expected to work in professional jobs (Schneider and Stevenson, 1999). Most young people today will graduate from high school, and the predominant pattern of transition will be from high school into some form of postsecondary education. Recent national surveys charting the transition from high school to college or the labor force show a steady increase in the numbers of young people selecting to enter postsecondary schools. From 1987 to 1997, the percentage of high school graduates attending college in the fall after

their senior year increased by 10 percent (National Center for Education Statistics, 1999). Over 3 million high school graduates are expected to enter postsecondary institutions by the fall of 2006 (National Center for Education Statistics, 1996).

This continued increase in the numbers of young people opting for postsecondary education immediately after high school graduation points to a changing transition pattern. As recently as two decades ago, most young people took full-time jobs after high school graduation. Today, the majority of them will instead enroll in college, where many of them will remain for more than four years. Compared to college students a decade ago, they will likely obtain a postsecondary degree later, marry later, and have children later. During this prolonged transition, students will face a series of decisions that have significant consequences for their futures. Many of these decisions will be made in high school, where students begin to think about what courses they need to take, what types of extracurricular activities they should participate in, what types of paid work they should undertake, and what type of college they should attend.

More and more high school students recognize the importance of a college degree as an investment for improving their earnings as adults. Many view a college degree in much the same way that teenagers in the 1950s viewed the high school diploma—as a necessary credential for obtaining stable employment. In fact, a college degree is the *minimal* credential to which most of today's young people aspire. From 1972 to 1992, the number of high school seniors who expected to achieve more than a college degree doubled from 14 percent to more than 30 percent. These high educational

More and more high school students recognize the importance of a college degree as an investment for improving their earnings as adults. (Leif Skoogfors/Corbis)

expectations are not confined to any particular group of students: Among both females and males, as well as students from different racial and ethnic groups and different socioeconomic backgrounds, the overwhelming majority now expect to attend college (Green, Dugoni, and Ingels, 1995).

Students' high educational expectations are matched by high occupational aspirations. Since 1955, the percentage of seniors aspiring to professional jobs has steadily increased, with the sharpest rise occurring after 1980. Specifically, from 1980 to 1992, the percentage of students desiring professional jobs increased from 54 percent to more than 70 percent. Conversely, teenage aspirations for nearly all other occupational categories, including

salespeople, service workers, technicians, manual laborers, farmers, and homemakers, have steadily declined over the past forty years. In fact, the number of jobs in service and other occupations projected for the year 2005 far exceeds the number of adolescents who want to fill them (Schneider and Stevenson, 1999).

This rise in educational expectations can largely be attributed to the academic preparation that young people are receiving in high school as well as to the influence of their teachers, counselors, and parents. American high schools are commonly referred to as comprehensive because the curriculum is designed to provide learning opportunities both for students who plan to enter the labor force full-time directly after high school and for students who plan to attend college. Over the last forty years, American high schools have undergone a major transformation marked by a steady increase in the number of academic courses being offered and a decline in the number of vocational courses and programs. This change has been spurred in part by the national movement to increase graduation requirements, particularly in the areas of mathematics and science. The effects of these academic requirements have been noticeable; indeed, considerably more high school students now take four years of mathematics and science (Blank and Langesen, 1999). This push for academic standards, combined with the preparation of more students for college, has blurred the boundaries separating the college preparatory and vocational curricular strands in the comprehensive high school.

Regardless of what courses students take, high school counselors encourage the overwhelming majority of them to attend college. No longer perceived as "gatekeepers" who sort young people into college and noncollege tracks, high school counselors and teachers are now strong advocates for college attendance. Results from national surveys indicate that over 90 percent of students report that their teachers and counselors encourage them to attend college. Even students who take vocational courses are directed to two-year community colleges for additional skills and training opportunities. Similar percentages are reported among parents, whose educational expectations and career aspirations for their teenagers match those of the teens themselves.

In deciding on a college, students confront a number of complex choices: whether to attend a public or private institution, a small or large one, a tradi-

tional liberal arts college or a school with specialized programs in fields like engineering or film. A fundamental distinction among postsecondary institutions is the type of degree offered: Four-year institutions offer primarily bachelor of arts or bachelor of science degrees. Community and junior colleges offer associate degrees in the arts or sciences that typically require two years of full-time study. And proprietary institutions offer a range of certificates in such fields as cosmetology, trucking, or heating and air-conditioning repair. These certificate programs vary in length, but many can be completed in less than a year. Some community or junior colleges also offer vocational and technical certificate programs that take a year or less to complete (*Dictionary of Postsecondary Institutions*, 1997).

Most high school graduates do not choose to enroll in certificate programs following graduation. These programs attract the fewest number of graduating high school seniors and have been steadily decreasing in size over the past two decades. Recent analyses of data from several national longitudinal studies show that in 1977, 5.3 percent of high school graduates chose to pursue such certificates, compared to 5 percent in 1982 and only 2.9 percent in 1992 (Schneider and Stevenson, 1999).

As suggested earlier, the dominant transition pattern among young adults is to go from high school to college. Of those who choose to attend postsecondary institutions, one-third enter community or junior colleges and the remainder attend four-year colleges. Although the proportion of high school graduates opting for college has steadily increased over the past three decades, the distribution of students entering two-year and four-year institutions immediately after high school has remained fairly stable since 1972 (Adelman, 1999).

Community College Students
Research has consistently found that community colleges tend to enroll students who have been traditionally underrepresented at four-year institutions, including racial and ethnic minorities and those from less advantaged socioeconomic backgrounds. Many young people who decide to begin their education at a community college are concerned about the costs of higher education, underprepared academically, and unsure of what career they would like to pursue after completing their degree. The costs of higher education are particularly problematic for community college students, who typically have limited resources. Yet, ironically, although most community college students need financial assistance to attend school, the proportion of students who apply for financial aid tends to be lower at two-year versus four-year institutions. Many community college students lack information on financial assistance, however, and may be discouraged from applying by the lengthy and complicated procedures for obtaining aid—especially those who are first-time college-goers in their families (Grubb and Tuma, 1991). Moreover, with respect to academic preparation, recent analyses continue to demonstrate that students who opt for community college tend to have taken fewer advanced-level mathematics and science courses in high school than those who matriculate to four-year institutions. Thus, they may fail the entry-level examinations in these subjects and be required to take remedial courses that do not carry credit hours toward degree completion. Under such circumstances, it appears that the focus on remedial work in community college would be more beneficial if students took more academically rigorous courses in high school.

One characteristic that students at community colleges share with those at four-year colleges is high expectations. More than 70 percent of students who enroll in two-year colleges expect to earn a four-year degree. These high ambitions do not seem to lessen even among students who remain at two-year institutions for more than two years. However, although the majority of community college students plan to transfer to four-year institutions, few of them actually succeed in doing so. The rising educational expectations of students at two-year colleges further complicates the mission and resource allocations of these institutions. Many community colleges attempt to provide vocational education and training as well as to prepare students for entry into four-year colleges. These two missions are often at odds, resulting in problematic advising programs for the students.

Four-Year College Students
Young people who enter four-year college programs tend to be more academically prepared than those who enter community colleges or who delay their entrance into college. With respect to background characteristics, students who enter four-year institutions are more likely to be white, to come from traditional two-parent families, and to have more economic and social resources than students who attend community colleges. The number of whites and African Americans who enroll in college immediately after high school has continued to grow over the last two decades, whereas the number of

Hispanics has remained stable. However, if certain factors are held constant—namely, family background and academic performance, including test scores and course-taking behaviors—African Americans turn out to be four times more likely than whites to attend four-year colleges (Schneider et al., 1999).

Even though low-income and minority students are now more likely to enroll in postsecondary institutions than they have been historically, several barriers continue to limit their access to higher education. Rising tuition costs still place some institutions out of reach for students in families with limited resources. Access to higher education for minority students appears at great risk as more states eliminate affirmative action policies in making admissions determinations (Bowen and Bok, 1998). And among the low-income and minority students who matriculate to four-year institutions, persistence rates continue to be disproportionately lower than among students in other groups.

Approximately one-third of recent high school graduates have chosen not to attend college, and for these young adults, labor force participation will likely be a primary or immediate concern after high school. However, given changes in the labor markets open to high school graduates (and, indeed, those who leave high school without a diploma), the opportunities for stable, long-term employment look increasingly problematic (Murphy and Welch, 1989). Economists have differing opinions about the labor market needs for the next century, but most agree that the "credentials floor" for stable jobs that pay more than the minimum wage will likely continue to rise. This trend is evidenced by the fact that many such jobs now require associate or bachelor's degrees. Supporting a family and maintaining a reasonable lifestyle with only a high school diploma thus seems a very unlikely scenario, at least in the near future.

Young adults who go to work directly after high school are predominately male and, compared to those who enroll in college, are more likely to be Hispanic, African American, or Asian American. Over the past twenty years, the proportion of high school graduates entering the labor force who are nonwhite has increased from almost 14 percent to 27 percent (Stevenson, Kochanek, and Schneider, 1998). Compared to students ten or twenty years ago, those who now enter the workforce directly after high school are, on the one hand, more likely to have parents with at least some college education but, on the other, less likely to have had formal vocational training.

Many American employers today want to see good basic academic skills among their prospective employees (Shapiro and Goertz, 1998). Comparisons of data from several longitudinal studies suggest that students entering the labor force directly after high school do not have lower cognitive abilities skills than students in similar circumstances ten years ago. However, today's young workers do appear to have had more behavioral problems in high school. Compared to students who enter college, they are more likely to have been late to school, to have gotten into trouble at school, to have been considered troublemakers by their classmates, and to have been suspended from school (Stevenson, Kochanek, and Schneider, 1998). For these reasons, high school graduates who currently enter the labor market directly after high school do not fit either the skill and knowledge profile or the social profile of the American worker recommended by various federal policy panels (Secretary's Commission on Achieving Necessary Skills, 1991).

Barbara Schneider

See also Academic Achievement; Career Development; Vocational Development

References and further reading
Adelman, Clifford. 1999. *Answers in the Tool Box: Academic Intensity, Attendance Patterns, and Bachelor's Degree Attainment.* Washington, DC: U.S. Department of Education, Office of Educational Research and Improvement.

Blank, Rolf, and Doreen Langesen. 1999. *State Indicators of Science and Mathematics Education: State by State Trends and New Indicators from the 1997–98 School Year.* Washington, DC: Council of Chief State School Officers.

Bowen, William G., and Derek Bok. 1998. *The Shape of the River: Long-Term Consequences for Considering Race in College Admissions.* Princeton, NJ: Princeton University Press.

Dictionary of Postsecondary Institutions, Vol. 2. 1997. Washington, DC: U.S. Department of Education.

Green, Patricia, Bernard L. Dugoni, and Steven Ingels. 1995. *Trends among High School Seniors, 1972–1992.* Washington, DC: U.S. Department of Education.

Grubb, Norton, and John Tuma. 1991. "Who Gets Student Aid?: Variation in Access to Aid." *Review of Higher Education* 14, no. 3: 359–382.

Murphy, Kevin, and Finnis Welch. 1989. "Wage Premiums for College Graduates: Recent Growth and Possible Explanations." *Educational Researcher* 18, no. 4: 17–26.

National Center for Education Statistics (NCES). 1996. *Projections of Education Statistics to 2006.* Washington, DC: U.S. Department of Education.

———. 1997. *Postsecondary Persistence and Attainment.* Washington, DC: U.S. Department of Education, Office of Educational Research and Improvement.

———. 1999. *The Condition of Education 1999.* Washington, DC: U.S. Department of Education.

Schneider, Barbara, and David Stevenson. 1999. *The Ambitious Generation: America's Teenagers, Motivated but Directionless.* New Haven, CT: Yale University Press.

Schneider, Barbara, Fengbin Chang, Christopher Swanson, and David Stevenson. 1999. "Social Exchange and Interests: Parents' Investments in Educational Opportunities." Paper presented at the annual meeting of the American Sociological Association, Chicago (August).

Secretary's Commission on Achieving Necessary Skills. 1991. *What Work Requires of Schools: A SCANS Report for America 2000.* Washington, DC: U.S. Department of Labor.

Shapiro, Daniel, and Margaret Goertz. 1998. "Connecting Work and School: Findings from the 1997 National Employer Survey." Paper presented at the annual meeting of the American Educational Research Association, San Diego (April).

Stevenson, David, Julie Kochanek, and Barbara Schneider. 1998. "Making the Transition from High School: Recent Trends and Policies." Pp. 207–226 in *The Adolescent Years: Social Influences and Educational Challenges,* National Society for the Study of Education Yearbook. Edited by Kathryn Borman and Barbara Schneider. Chicago: University of Chicago Press.

Computer Hacking

The term *computer hacker* has at least two definitions. According to one of these, a computer hacker is an exceptionally competent computer programmer. Hacking in this context means using one's computer programming abilities to explore the Internet, develop skills, and gain knowledge. It does not include illegal activities. According to another definition, however, computer hacker is someone who uses his or her knowledge of computers or the Internet to steal or

Four teenagers involved in hacking into a computer pay network participate in a press conference, California 1983. From left to right are Wayne Correia, 17, Gary Knutson, 15, Greg Knutson, 14, and David Hill, 17. (Bettmann/Corbis)

damage property—whether physical property or intellectual property such as corporate secrets, software products, and personnel information. Hacking in this context means using one's abilities for material gain or mischief. The use of a computer for such purposes is a crime and can result in incarceration. If the illegal activity involves the Internet, it is a federal offense because the Internet crosses state boundaries. People who use the Internet for illegal purposes have been called "crackers" within the hacker community in order to distinguish them from people who are simply demonstrating their knowledge; in addition, people who use their skills to make long-dis-

tance calls without paying for them have been called "phreaks." Thus, hackers are a diverse group of individuals. Furthermore, merely referring to a person as a computer hacker does not make that person one. She or he must demonstrate extensive knowledge about technology or telecommunications systems.

Many interesting examples of computer crime can be cited. Probably the first hacker arrested for illegal activity was John Draper, also known as "Captain Crunch." Repeatedly arrested for phone tampering during the 1970s, Draper used a plastic whistle he found in a cereal box to gain access to free long-distance telephone calls. Another famous case is that of Kevin Mitnick, who was arrested and incarcerated in the 1980s for reading corporate e-mail. After he was freed, he returned to hacking in 1992 and hid from the police for several years. Mitnick was the first computer hacker to be put on the FBI's most-wanted list. Captured in 1995, he was charged with computer fraud and theft of corporate information and millions of dollars' worth of computer software.

Since the beginning of the 1990s, computer crime has been on the rise. Computer hackers have broken into a variety of different computer systems including military bases, government agencies, research institutes, phone companies, airlines, computer companies, and even banks. In fact, hackers stole $70 million from the Bank of Chicago using a computer. Hackers have been known to flood computer systems with thousands of e-mail messages, a practice called spamming, in order to cause the systems to slow down or fail. The Department of Defense computer system is attacked hundreds of thousands of times each year. And not just businesses and government agencies are affected by computer crime: Computer viruses are a constant threat to members of the general public who use e-mail and the Internet. These viruses are computer programs designed to destroy or damage computer files. They are passed from computer to computer or from network to network over the Internet or e-mail. Over a short period of time, a single virus can cause extensive damage all over the world. In 1998 the government responded to these various computer crime threats by creating the National Infrastructure Protection Center; its purpose is to prevent hackers from jeopardizing the nation's telecommunication, transportation, and technology

systems. In addition, the FBI has created cybercrime units in many cities in the United States. Computer hacking is one of our newest forms of crime and juvenile delinquency. Many countries are taking this threat to their infrastructures very seriously.

How widespread is adolescent computer hacking? Currently, researchers do not know what percentage of the adolescent population participates in computer crime. The stereotype found in the media is that of the intellectually gifted teenager with antisocial attitudes who continues to break the law until he or she is stopped. It is not clear that this stereotype always holds true, as the characteristics of long-term computer hackers are unknown. But if computer hacking is similar to other forms of juvenile delinquency, it can be argued, by extension, that there are at least two different groups of adolescents participating in illegal computer-related activities. According to Terrie Moffitt's (1993) theory of the development of antisocial behavior, one of these groups—the smaller of the two—consists of teenagers who continue to commit criminal acts as they move into adulthood. These career criminals usually begin their antisocial behavior early in development. They can be distinguished from other teens by a combination of personal characteristics and negative environmental influences that work as risk factors. For example, they may have had a conduct disorder problem in childhood, similar to that of their aggressive peers. They may have trouble fitting in socially or academically in school, although given their computer programming abilities, they are probably very intelligent. And they may be sensation seekers who are willing or eager to take unusual chances.

For instance, Kevin Mitnick, the well-known computer hacker mentioned earlier, claimed that he hacked into computer systems to challenge himself—not to gain personal wealth.

The majority of adolescent computer crime, however, is probably committed by teens who do not continue these activities in adulthood. Moffitt's theory holds that these temporary criminals are testing their knowledge and skills as a way of achieving status and power. They break the law and seek attention because society considers them socially immature, even though they are biologically mature individuals. It is this "maturity gap" in our culture that leads many teenagers to commit crimes. In short, many teens imitate their more antisocial peers and explore forbidden territory while still in adolescence, but once these individuals obtain independence and responsibility in adulthood, they stop their antisocial behavior.

It is easy to see how computer hacking might be an effective way for adolescents to demonstrate their knowledge and power to other people. In fact, many people praise teens for such behavior because it requires a great deal of intellectual skill. Moreover, since these adolescents can presumably use their computer-related knowledge in their future careers, their behavior may appear harmless or even beneficial to their development. Yet computer hacking can result in hundreds of thousands of dollars' worth of damage to companies and research institutes. This damage is due in part to lost productivity and information and in part to the cost of paying personnel to repair and rebuild damaged computer systems. Participating in illegal computer activities can also be detrimental to the teenage

hackers themselves—for instance, by limiting their future career opportunities. Indeed, executives in some computer companies have voiced their reluctance to hire computer hackers who have committed criminal acts. Not surprisingly, they are nervous about handing sensitive or private information to people who do not respect other people's privacy and property and the laws that protect them. Other executives, however, have actually hired computer programmers to hack into their computers in order to test the company's security system and software. This practice, called "ethical computer hacking," can uncover computer security breaks and prevent future damage to a company's computer system. It is a legal activity because it involves the active consent of the target of the hacking.

The social factors contributing to adolescent computer crime probably include parental influences, such as modeling of antisocial attitudes and failure to monitor the teen's computer-related activities. But an even larger influence is likely to be the teenager's peer group. The need for peer acceptance is at its height during the middle-childhood and adolescent years, and the peer group is considered a significant source of knowledge and encouragement during this time. Moreover, contrary to the popular notion that computer hackers are social isolates, hackers probably have many friends on the Internet. In fact, several online gangs have claimed responsibility for attempting to hack into government Web sites and computer systems. These online gangs seem to have the same characteristics as the better-known adolescent gangs that commit physical crimes, including antisocial attitudes, praise for criminal acts by the delinquent peer group, tutoring in illegal behaviors, and strong leadership and loyalty among group members. Indeed, teenagers can obtain information about computer hacking on the Internet itself. Although they may seem to be staying out of trouble because they are working alone on their computers, in actuality they are being taught how to engage in criminal activities by an extensive, sometimes international, peer group. Still other Internet sites teach specific skills, such as how to deface another person's Web site and how to create computer programs that help decode passwords and encrypted information. One can also learn these skills by reading newsletters and magazines produced by hacker interest groups. Hackers meet online in chat rooms, form online groups and gangs, and travel to conventions where they exchange ideas and test each other's knowledge. It is important to point out that these conventions and groups include not just people who are learning and teaching illegal behavior but also those who are participating in legal hacking activities.

Illegal hacking can be traced back at least 120 years, when a group of teenagers abused the country's first telephone system. Modern computer hacking, on the other hand, originated in the late 1960s, during the first of three major events: the beginning of the study of artificial intelligence and the development of the Internet at universities such as the University of California–Berkeley and the Massachusetts Institute of Technology. At this time, computers and the Internet had started to become important to both science and society and computer programmers had begun to communicate with each other and work together, leading to a second event that was relevant to the emergence of com-

puter hacking: the development of a subculture revolving around computers. Computer clubs and magazines were created to teach people how to use the telephone system and the computer to explore their abilities—or to break the law. Some early hackers in these clubs moved into profitable careers, creating much of the modern computer industry. As these computer clubs grew, so did the government's interest in computer crime and illegal Internet activities. In the early 1980s, many countries developed laws against such activities, including the Computer Fraud and Abuse Act in the United States. Law-enforcement efforts began to crack down on illegal hacking, and programmers were arrested for breaking into federal and business computers. A third event linked to computer hacking was the emergence of the Internet's role in our larger culture—made official, perhaps, by coinage of the term *cyberspace* in William Gibson's book *Neuromancer.* All three events and their consequences have led to society's interest in children and teenagers who exhibit exceptional computer-related skills and possibly use their knowledge to break the law.

Shirley McGuire

See also Aggression; Computers; Conduct Problems; Delinquency, Trends in; Moral Development; Rebellion

References and further reading

"Hackers Are Necessary." Retrieved from the World Wide Web on 5/17/99: http://www.cnn.com/TECH/specials/hackers/qandas/
"Hacking Is a Felony." Retrieved from the World Wide Web on 5/17/99: http://www.cnn.com/TECH/specials/hackers/qandas/
"A History of Hacking." Retrieved from the World Wide Web on 8/17/99:

http://www.sptimes.com/Hackers/
history.hacking.html

Moffitt, Terrie E. 1993. "'Adolescent-
Limited' and 'Life-Course-Persistent'
Antisocial Behavior: A Developmental
Taxonomy." *Psychological Review* 100:
674–701.

Computers

A computer is a programmable electronic machine that performs a series of high-speed mathematical calculations or logical operations in order to assemble, store, correlate, or otherwise process information. One can argue that no technological advance over the last century has affected the whole society of America, and indeed the world, as quickly and profoundly as the computer. Twenty-five years ago it was two teenagers, Bill Gates and Paul Allen, who ignited the computer revolution that changed the lives of people everywhere. The current generation of adolescents, sometimes referred to as the "Nintendo Generation," are standard-bearers in the technological revolution, having never known anything else. From video games to chat rooms to Web surfing, adolescents have sparked exciting new computer trends over the last decade, and within these young minds lie radical new visions and infinite possibilities in computer technology.

Computers are used to perform an enormous variety of functions, and more uses are created every day, providing greater and more flexible access to all of society's resources. For several years, businesses have relied on computers for maintaining large inventories, tracking sales, communicating with customers, and transferring information electronically. Today, the focus of businesses lies in e-commerce, online stock trading, and high-speed wireless communications. For several years, educators have incorporated computer technology into lesson plans, classroom projects, and research. Today, there is a focus on online homework, online tutorial chat sessions, and even completely virtual classrooms and colleges. The list of computer uses is practically endless, as well as constantly changing. Scientists use computers to organize complicated data, build complex models, and improve research tools and methods. The military use computers in radar systems, communications systems, security systems, and advanced machines and weaponry. Doctors use specialized computers to track patient records and supplies, perform difficult surgeries and procedures, and monitor critical dosages. Musicians use computers to produce and fine-tune studio compositions as well as enhance live performances.

Computers are also being used to make everyday life more efficient and manageable. They are used in home appliances such as microwaves, VCRs, stereos, and home security systems. They are being used in automobiles to regulate fuel systems and speedometers. Computers are used in ATM machines, cellular phones, video games, cameras, and supermarket checkouts. Extensive computer networks are in place to manage such things as traffic control systems, airline reservation systems, public utilities, and financial systems. It seems almost impossible nowadays to imagine living in a world without computer technology. Those without computer skills find themselves struggling to keep up as computers become a greater part of our life and work.

*History and Development of
Computers*
Early Computers. There are many people who deserve credit in the develop-

ment of computers over the last century, but it all began with the nineteenth-century British mathematician Charles Babbage (1792–1871), often referred to as the "father of computing." In 1834, Babbage began designing his Analytical Engine, a mechanical digital device capable of performing mathematical operations as a modern computer does. The engine was "programmable" using punched cards, contained a "store" for saving data, a "mill" for processing data, and also a printer. Babbage had trouble convincing his financiers that such a machine would prove useful, so he never came up with the funding to finish builiding it.

If Babbage is known as the father of computing, then his brilliant female colleague deserves to be called its mother. Augusta Ada Byron, Lady Lovelace (1815–1852), daughter of the poet Lord Byron, was working in mathematics at a time when women were generally discouraged from pursuing such a field. She took notice of the universality of Babbage's ideas, and, in 1843, she translated an Italian paper on Babbage's Analytical Engine, adding her own notes and theories to the manuscript. Her comments included her predictions that such a machine might be used to compose complex music, to produce graphics, and would be used for both practical and scientific use. Lovelace later suggested that Babbage write a plan for how the engine could calculate Bernoulli equations. This plan is now regarded as the first computer program, and a software language developed by the U.S. Department of Defense in 1979 was named "Ada" in Lovelace's honor.

It took a period of time for people to see promise in the work of Babbage and Lovelace; crucial advances in electromechanical engineering still had to be made. From 1936 to 1945, at least three different groups designed the first electronic digital computer, each group unaware of the others because of World War II communication barriers. German scientist Konrad Zuse (1910–1995) independently created a series of programmable, digital-computing machines beginning with the Z1 in 1936. A team of British scientists, led by Alan Turing (1912–1954), developed an electronic digital computer, called Colossus, in 1943. It was designed to break codes. American scientists created the Automatic Sequence Controlled Calculator (Mark I) in 1944 and the Electronic Numerical Integrator and Computer (ENIAC) in 1945. Both were used for military purposes. ENIAC weighed thirty tons, measured 100 feet long and 8 feet high, and contained 17,468 vacuum tubes. At its top speed, it performed 5,000 additions per second.

In the late 1950s, transistors replaced electron tubes in computers, allowing a reduction in the size and power consumption of computer components. In 1958, Jack S. Kilby (b. 1923) and Robert Noyce (1927–1990) revolutionized the industry by each independently inventing the integrated circuit, which allowed further reductions in component size and increases in reliability. An integrated circuit chip, created with a silicon wafer, is smaller and thinner than a baby's fingernail yet equivalent to thousands of electronic components all operating simultaneously. The integrated circuit represented the first great invention that dealt with the storing, processing, and interpretation of information, and it paved the way for the development of microcomputers.

The Microcomputer. In 1968, Noyce joined with Gordon Moore to start Intel, a company dedicated to developing and producing the integrated circuit. In 1974, Intel introduced the 8080 microprocessor, considered to be the first microprocessor powerful enough to build a computer around. This microprocessor and its clones came to dominate the microcomputer industry for the next four years.

Ed Roberts, founder of Micro Instrumentation Telemetry Systems (MITS), used the Intel 8080 to design the first personal computer, the Altair 8800, even before there was demand for a single unit. The machine included the Intel 8080 microprocessor and 256 bytes of RAM for $395. Users had to create and enter their programs in binary code by flipping switches on the front panel of the machine. MITS planned on selling 400 units the first year, but after the Altair debuted on the cover of the January 1975 issue of *Popular Electronics*, 800 units were sold in the first month.

Among those intrigued by this computer were two nineteen-year-old Harvard students—Bill Gates and Paul Allen. In the spring of 1975, Allen arrived at MITS headquarters in Albuquerque carrying a version of a computer language called BASIC on a roll of paper tape. The previously untested program written by the two teenagers worked perfectly, and Allen was hired as manager of software. Gates and Allen went on to build the multibillion-dollar Microsoft computer software empire partly from system software they wrote for the Altair.

Computers and Societal Transformation. As a result of the brilliant innovations by Roberts, Gates, and Allen, there was a flooding of new computer technology into society throughout the last two decades of the twentieth century. The development of faster, cheaper microcomputers brought computing down to a personal level. Gates and Allen started a software explosion that redefined the tools people use for writing, calculating, organizing, storing, and playing. Electronic mail and the Internet set new standards in high-speed communications, enabling individuals to cheaply and easily publish quality information and exchange it with people around the world. E-commerce is changing the way people shop and do business. Laptops, palm computers, and cell phones are now allowing people flexible, mobile access to computers and wireless networking. Yet the impact of computers on society so far is modest in comparison to the potential impact. The most exciting developments in computer technology and computer use are still brewing in the minds of today's adolescents.

One of the most exciting aspects of the computer revolution is that younger generations have as much involvement in it and influence on how it plays out as older generations, if not more. Computer science is a young field and developing at a rapid pace. Today's hottest computer technologies, such as Web design and wireless networking, are mere foretastes of the potential technologies. Adolescents are not only making use of computer technology but are becoming pioneers of its expansion. Today's teenagers are the backbone of the exciting new trends, issues, and developments that are already changing the social atmosphere and creating new lifestyles.

One of the current social issues related to computer technology deals with intellectual property rights and digital copyrighting. The debate centers on whether or not the usual copyright laws should apply to information that is loose on the Internet. Standing in the front lines of this debate is an adolescent named Shawn Fanning. At age eighteen, Fanning created an online music-swapping computer program called Napster that transforms personal computers into servers for exchanging Mp3 music files over the Net. Within a year Napster became a multimillion-dollar company with more than forty employees. The Recording Industry Association of America (RIAA) and several musicians, led by the rock band Metallica, have sued Napster, claiming that the service violates their music production copyrights. The case will become a precedent for shaping future laws about intellectual property rights.

Another issue involves concerns about the isolating effects of computers on the adolescent world. Some parents and critics worry that computer use, like television, may damage children and their social interaction. Such social isolation, they fear, can also lead to misuse of computers and the Internet for such things as hacking, harassment, and pornography. However, such critics assume that computer use necessarily reduces sociation because it saps time and energy and lowers adolescent self-esteem.

Alternatively, other critics believe computers actually promote better social interaction. For instance, on the Internet, nobody knows whether you are black, white, short, tall, attractive, or ugly. Anyone, regardless of age, race, religion, or gender, can publicize their views and their work to an international audience. For many adolescents, the computer is a tool for personal expression and self-empowerment. The Internet also provides the curious adolescent with exciting opportunities for exploration, discovery, and investigation. Teenagers today are becoming more globally oriented and open-minded.

How Computers Work

Modern computers, or digital computers, are designed to process data directly in numerical form using the binary system. Binary digits are expressed in the computer circuitry by the presence (1) or absence (0) of a current. A string of eight such bits, called a "byte," is the fundamental data unit of digital computers. A digital computer can store the results of its calculations, compare results with other data, and use comparisons to change the series of operations it performs.

The operations of a digital computer are carried out by digital computer circuits capable of performing up to trillions of arithmetic or logic operations per second, thus permitting the rapid solutions of long problems that would normally be impossible for humans to solve by hand. The development of the integrated circuit in 1958 spurred the creation of smaller and more powerful digital computers. Large "mainframe" computers, which were sometimes large enough to walk through, have been reduced to more manageable cabinet-sized computers and "microcomputers" that can sit on a desktop, a lap, or even in the palm of a hand.

Microcomputer Structure. The physical computer and its components are known as hardware. Computer hardware includes the memory that stores data and instructions, the central processing unit (CPU) that carries out instructions, the bus that connects the various computer components, the input devices that allow the user to communicate with the computer, and the output devices that enable the computer to present information to the user.

When a computer is turned on it searches for instructions in its memory. Usually, the first set of these instructions is a special program called the operating system, the software that makes the computer work. It prompts the user or other machines for commands, reports the results, stores and manages data, and controls the sequence of software and hardware actions. When the user requests that a program run, the operating system loads the program in the computer's memory and runs the program. Popular microcomputer operating systems, such as Microsoft Windows and Macintosh operating systems, have a graphical user interface (GUI)—that is, a display that uses tiny pictures, or icons, to represent various commands. To execute these commands, the user clicks the mouse on the icon or presses a combination of keys on the keyboard.

To process information electronically, data is stored in a computer in the form of binary digits, or bits, each having two possible representations (0 or 1), as explained above. Eight bits is called a byte; a byte has 256 possible combinations of 0s and 1s. A byte is a useful quantity in which to store information because it provides enough possible patterns to represent the entire alphabet, in lower- and uppercases, as well as numeric digits, punctuation marks, and several character-sized graphics symbols. A byte also can be interpreted as a pattern that represents a number between 0 and 255. A kilobyte—1,024 bytes—can store about 1,000 characters; a megabyte can store about 1 million characters; and a gigabyte can store about 1 billion characters.

The physical memory of a computer is either random access memory (RAM), which can be read or changed by the user or computer, or read-only memory (ROM), which can be read by the computer but not altered. One way to store memory is within the circuitry of the computer, usually in tiny computer chips that hold millions of bytes of information. The memory within these computer chips is RAM. Memory also can be stored outside the circuitry of the computer on external storage devices, such as hard drives, floppy disks, ZIP drives, and CD-ROM drives.

The bus is usually a flat cable with numerous parallel wires. The bus enables the components in a computer, such as the CPU and memory, to communicate. Input devices, such as a keyboard or mouse, permit the computer user to communicate with the computer. Other input devices include joysticks, scanners, light pens, touch panels, and microphones. Information from an input device or memory is communicated via the bus to the CPU. The CPU is a microprocessor chip—that is, a single piece of silicon containing millions of electrical components. Once the CPU has executed the program instruction, the program may request that information be communicated to an output device, such as a video display monitor, printer, projector, VCR, or speaker.

Computer Programs and Software. In order to solve problems and become a diverse and powerful machine, a computer must first be programmed by being given a set of instructions called a program. Each instruction in the program is a single step telling the computer to perform an operation.

While *program* describes a single, complete, and self-contained list of instructions, often stored in a single file, the term *software* describes some number of instructions, which may consist of one or more programs or parts thereof. Software can be split into two main types, system software and application software. System software is any software required to support the production or execution of application programs but not specific to any particular application. Most programs and software applications rely heavily on various kinds of system software for their execution. Examples of system software would include operating systems, compilers, editors, and sorting programs. Examples of application software would include accounting packages, word processing programs, multimedia software, educational software, and computer games.

Sean Kennedy

See also Homework; Media; Media, Effects of; Schools, Full-Service

References and further reading
InfoStreet, Inc. 1999. *InstantWeb: Online Computing Dictionary.* http://www.instantweb.com/~foldoc/contents.html
Lee, John A. N. 1999. *The Machine That Changed the World.* http://ei.cs.vt.edu/~history/TMTCTW.html
Microsoft Corporation. 1999. *Microsoft Corporation Interactive Software and Computer History Museum.* http://www.microsoft.com/mscorp/museum/home.asp.
Tanenbaum, Andrew S. 1998. *Structured Computer Organization.* Englewood Cliffs, NJ: Prentice-Hall.

Conduct Problems

Conduct problems encompass a wide range of behaviors that are antisocial (against the basic principles of society). These behaviors are inappropriate and unacceptable according to societal rules and expectations. Some antisocial behavior is normal and expected during adolescence. There is no clear-cut distinction between normal conduct and problematic conduct—it is a matter of degree. Frequency and intensity of the behaviors are central features that determine whether the child is identified as clinically impaired, as having a behavior disorder. Antisocial acts that occur frequently or across many situations indicate a problem; however, some antisocial acts that happen seldom but are extremely serious, such as fire setting, can also indicate a disorder.

Normal Antisocial Behavior
Many antisocial behaviors emerge in some form over the course of normal development. During adolescence, the process of developing one's own identity involves a movement away from family and may result in less affection toward parents and less time spent with them. Adolescents begin to think abstractly and question parental values, standards, and beliefs, resulting in an increase in arguments and rule testing. For instance, in one study, disobedience at home was reported as a problem by parents for approximately 20 percent of sixteen-year-olds. Conflict between parents and teenagers may rise as families argue about small things, such as chores, curfews, choice of clothing, or keeping one's room clean. Increasing expectations, from school, parents, or work, place additional stress on adolescents. The antisocial behavior usually subsides as adolescents adjust to the changes happening around and within them. Antisocial behavior that exceeds normal development results in conduct problems, which at the extreme can become behavior disorders.

Behavior Disorders

Clinically diagnosable disorders of behavior include, but are not limited to, conduct disorder (CD) and oppositional defiant disorder (ODD). The essential features of conduct disorder are a repetitive and persistent pattern of behavior that involves violation of the basic rights of others and of the major age-appropriate social norms. Conduct problems are evident at school, in the home, within the community, and with peers, and commonly feature physical aggression, damaging property, lying, stealing, and cheating. Less serious than conduct disorder, oppositional defiant disorder involves a pattern of hostile and defiant behavior such as losing one's temper, arguing with adults, defying rules, and being spiteful and vindictive. The prevalence ranges from 2 percent to 9 percent for CD and from 6 percent to 10 percent for ODD.

Etiology of Conduct Problems

It is unclear whether conduct problems are primarily learned behaviors or biologically predisposed. Studies show a link of parents with antisocial behaviors—such as antisocial personality disorder—to children with conduct disorder. This does not, however, imply a genetic link. A variety of parent and family characteristics have been identified as risk factors, including criminality, antisocial behavior, and alcoholism in the parents, marital discord, and harsh and inconsistent discipline practices. For instance, harsh parenting, such as verbal abuse, threat, and deprivation of privileges, as well as physical punishment, may encourage problem behavior.

Individual traits may play a role in the development of conduct problems. Some individuals with conduct problems show cognitive processing problems such as cognitive distortions (i.e., attributing hostile intentions to ambiguous acts) or cognitive deficiencies (i.e., using aggression rather than socially appropriate solutions to interpersonal problems). Certain personality traits such as impulsivity or disinhibition also encourage problem behavior. It is likely that individual traits, which may be inherited or learned, interact with the environment to produce problem behavior.

Gender Differences

Boys exhibit more conduct problems and tend to develop them at an earlier age than girls. On average, boys are five times as likely as girls to be diagnosed with conduct disorder. For boys, age of onset for CD is typically before age ten, whereas for girls, age of onset is typically in the early teens (ages thirteen to sixteen). Boys are generally found to engage more frequently in stealing, fighting, truancy, destructiveness, and lying over the course of development than girls.

Continuity and Stability

In general, antisocial behaviors typically decline over the course of development. However, extreme problem behavior exhibited in children is likely to persist into adolescence and sometimes into adulthood. Children who are high in conduct problems remain higher than their peer group over time. The precise bases for this continuity (i.e., gene action, environmental factors) are not well established. The stability and continuity of conduct problems suggest that interventions need to be designed to ameliorate these behaviors.

Current Treatments

Adolescents whose antisocial behaviors exceed that of normal development are likely to have a broad range of dysfunction in social behaviors, academic performance, and cognitive processes, in addition to the conduct problem behaviors. Since the development of conduct problems has many contributing factors, there are many points for intervention. Treatments target the child, parent, or entire family and may be individual or group approaches. Many treatments emphasize problem-solving skills. Parent training and family therapy aim to improve communication skills among family members. Parents may learn alternatives to punitive and inconsistent parenting practices. School and community-based programs aimed at preventing conduct problems incorporate problem-solving skills, emphasize prosocial activities, and foster more positive peer connections.

Susan Averna

See also Aggression; Cheating, Academic; Delinquency, Mental Health, and Substance Abuse Problems; Disorders, Psychological and Social; Juvenile Crime; Risk Behaviors; School Dropouts

References and further reading
American Psychiatric Association. 1994. *Diagnostic and Statistical Manual of Mental Disorders, Fourth Edition.* Washington, DC: American Psychiatric Association.
Gemelli, Ralph. 1996. *Normal Child and Adolescent Development.* Washington, DC: American Psychiatric Press.
Herbert, Martin. 1987. *Conduct Disorders of Childhood and Adolescence: A Social Learning Perspective.* New York: Wiley.
Kazdin, Alan. 1987. *Conduct Disorders in Childhood and Adolescence,* Vol. 9, *Developmental Clinical Psychology and Psychiatry.* London: Sage Publications.
Kendall, Philip. 2000. *Childhood Disorders.* United Kingdom: Psychology Press.
Peterson, Anne. 1985. "Pubertal Development as a Cause of Disturbance: Myths, Realities, and Unanswered Questions—Genetic, Social, and General." *Psychology Monographs* 111, no. 2: 205–232.
Robins, Lee. 1966. *Deviant Children Grown Up.* Baltimore: Williams and Wilkins.

Conflict and Stress

The transition from childhood to adolescence has changed in several qualitative and quantitative aspects over the past few decades. The age at which adolescents complete their education and enter the work force is later, their physical maturation is accelerated, and, due to more liberal norms and values, they begin heterosexual relations earlier. In America, as in other modern democratic societies, there is a noticeable trend toward "value pluralism," which, on the one hand, calls for positive, tolerance-promoting values but, on the other hand, has led to the disintegration of existing value systems. Today's adolescents are thus left with a vaguely defined behavior code through which to solve their age-specific developmental tasks. These changes are further complicated by increasing numbers of single-parent families and stepfamilies, higher rates of unemployment and economic hardship, and the continuous migration of foreign families, many from poverty-stricken backgrounds, into American society with its high Western standards. These conditions summarize the developmental context in which adolescent development unfolds within the biological, cognitive, and social domains. Taken together, the sheer number of changes occurring during adolescence, compared with other developmental stages, is unusually high. Such changes lead to stress, which in turn may exert an impact on health.

The challenges of modern life often place adolescents under considerable stress. (Shirley Zeiberg)

Recent years have witnessed widespread interest in identifying the properties that make events stressful. Research on adolescents, in particular, has uncovered two types of stressful events that differ in frequency, predictability, control, and negative impact on health: normative stressors and non-normative stressors.

Normative stressors are defined as events that occur at about the same time for the majority of individuals in this age group and are associated with specific developmental tasks and corresponding expectations of family, friends, and society. These stressors are highly predictable, relatively frequent, and perceived as mildly stressful and controllable. The adolescent years are characterized by numerous biological, cognitive, and social changes. In American society, increased responsibilities, accessibility to adult rights, and school changes mark the transition to adulthood. In particular, early adolescence (approximately ages eleven to thirteen years) is considered to be a difficult yet challenging phase due to pubertal developments, relational changes, and school transition. Most early adolescents enter a new school, and the strain associated with adjusting to new academic and social environments may be potentiated by the biological developments occurring in puberty, such as changes in physical size and body concept or the emergence of sexual desires and anxieties about sexuality. Feelings of being different, not meeting the norm, having matured too quickly or not quickly enough represent additional stressors that arise in the pubertal phase of development. In addition, parent-child relationships change, and the adolescent's interactions with and acceptance by friends become increasingly important. In midadolescence, the adolescent's needs for peer acceptance are especially great, and the adolescent begins to spend more time with peers outside of the home. Thus, stressors emerge in relation to these changes, that is, there are more disputes with parents about curfews, clothing, driving, and personal freedom. Increased rates of parent-adolescent conflict have been consistently found in research for decades, particularly in early and mid-adolescent samples. Dating and the initiation of intimate, heterosexual relationships also occur in this phase and may be accompanied by stressors such as fear of rejection or feelings of incompetence. In late adolescence, the increasing independence from parents may result in the adolescent's establishing an independent household. Graduation from high school is considered to be a significant juncture in the transition to adulthood.

In addition to these changes, other, non-normative stressors or critical life events can increase the likelihood of maladaptation. Non-normative family stressors have been studied intensively. Adolescents are more at risk for developing psychopathology when the family situation is unstable or when there is serious marital discord. In extreme cases, marital discord may lead to divorce, a phenomenon that has increased in the United States over the years and currently resulted in every second marriage being dissolved. The influence of parental divorce on a child's well-being has been frequently studied. The chronicity of the stressors is also relevant. Often high levels of stress precede the event and persist long after it has occurred. Many of the non-normative stressors experienced by adolescents are controlled or influenced by family situations and are chronic in nature. Ongoing, stressful family situations can produce more discrete life events, such as separation or divorce. Psychiatric illness in one or both parents is another chronic, stressful life situation. Most studies on this kind of stressor have focused on maternal dysfunction and its impact on adolescent health; little attention has been devoted to paternal disorders. Additional sources of familial stress occur following the death of a relative, instances of child molestation or abuse, parental drug abuse or criminal activities, or chronic illness in the family. To summarize, these stressors are critical life events that are relatively infrequent, hardly predictable, and extremely burdensome. Because most of these events are hardly foreseeable and can seldom be controlled or influenced by the adolescents, anticipatory preparation for or coping with the stressor is extremely difficult. Consequently, the emergence of non-normative stressors may have more dramatic health consequences for adolescents than normative stressors. However, due to the unusual timing and the high stressfulness of non-normative events, social support may be greater and thus buffer the potentially damaging effects on health.

In evaluating the effects of normative and non-normative stressors, number, timing, and synchronicity of changes have to be considered. By definition, non-normative stressors occur quite seldomly; however, should they occur simultaneously or in rapid sequence with normative or developmentally related stressors, serious health damage may result. The risk for an unfavorable outcome increased exponentially with increased number of critical life events experienced by adolescents. Adolescents did not show an increased risk for psychopathology as long as only one non-normative stressor was involved. When two major stressors occurred simultaneously, the risk became four times as great. Thus, non-normative stressors potentiate one another so that the combination of stressors is more than the sum of effects of individual stressors. Furthermore, additional non-normative stressors may appear in their wake. This link has been confirmed frequently; most studies revealed a correlation of $r = .30$ between major and minor stressors. The different types of stressors that occur within a developmental phase interact with one another in a yet unknown way to produce health-damaging effects.

Although normative stressors such as school change, physical maturation, and the onset of romantic relationships are expected, age-appropriate, and moderately stressful, the accumulation of diverse normative stressors may also have deleterious effects. School changes are particularly stressful for girls. Due to their more rapid maturational development in puberty, physical changes are more likely to occur around the time they enter a new school. Owing to their slower development, boys are less likely to be confronted with both normative stressors simultaneously. Research has further shown that girls are more likely than boys to experience more conflicting demands during this period. The demands of popularity and achievement orientation can produce emotional conflict in early adolescent girls.

In addition, the timing of events has been found to influence health outcomes, particularly in normative stressors. This has been extensively researched with respect to pubertal timing. A large body of work has indicated that, when the timing of pubertal development deviates from normative expectations, problematic outcomes may be the result. Again, girls are more affected. Early maturing girls are more likely to develop a more negative body image and are also more likely to develop eating disorders or behavioral and emotional symptoms. Unusual timing of a normative event like physical maturity may touch off changes in relationships with parents and peers.

In summary, early adolescence is a period of rapid cognitive, social, emotional, and physical changes. Although these changes per se have few harmful effects on most adolescents, there are certain vulnerable subgroups. Unusual timing of normative stressors, a cumulation of non-normative stressors, or an interaction between non-normative and normative stressors can be considered as risk factors. There are fewer changes in late adolescence than in early or midadolescence, which probably accounts for the finding that the transition to adulthood does not present major adaptation problems. From midadolescence to late adolescence, parent-adolescent conflict decreases. The power relation between parents and adolescents has changed, and a new balance between closeness and separateness has been established. Further, relationships with close friends have matured and romantic relations developed. In addition, while the average youth shows a decline in school achievement in early and midadolescence, achievement is improved as adolescents enter college or take up full-time jobs.

Research has frequently demonstrated gender differences in stress perception. Female adolescents experience changes in their environment and in themselves as being very stressful and threatening. Comparing a number of minor events, it became obvious that females perceive the same events as more stressful and more permanent than males did. In addition, they report more relationship stressors than males and felt four times more threatened by these same stressors than males. This suggests that females are more affected by conflicts in close relationships and perceive most stressors, particularly relationship stressors, as having a chronic nature. There is also evidence that males are less affected by normative stressors, whereas non-normative stressors have greater health consequences for them, compared to females.

Empirical studies provided mixed evidence for the explanatory power of stress in the etiology of various psychological and somatic disorders. Frequent, sustained daily stressors, due to their chronic nature, might play a greater role in the development of psychopathology than the occurrence of isolated major life events. This finding is probably due to the higher amount of social support when experiencing non-normative stressors, which protects the adolescent from more severe health damage.

It is not fully clear how gender differences in stress perception are linked with the emergence of gender-specific psychopathology and differences in help-seeking behavior. Several authors argue for higher levels of minor stressors in females as compared to males. However, there are also studies speaking against a typically higher level of stress in females and arguing that, generally, males are more vulnerable to the effect of major losses, that is, events such as marital discord and parental divorce than females. Currently, research neither provides a clear support for the links between gender differences in stress perception and subsequent symptomatology, nor does it consistently support the hypothesis of an increase in stressors across the adolescent years only in females. However, there is some evidence that females experiencing both biological and psychosocial changes are more vulnerable for depression or depressive symptoms, but research focusing on this issue in males is still meager.

As mentioned, numerous studies have documented an increase in parent-child conflicts during adolescence and a decline thereafter. Also, gender differences in frequency of conflicts have been established, documenting particularly high rates of conflicts in the mother-daughter dyad. However, a link between an increase in conflict with mothers and elevated levels of symptomatology of daughters, as compared to sons, did not emerge consistently. Prospective studies covering the time span of several years revealed, for example, that the relations between family conflicts and depressive outcome were similar for male and female adolescents. More recently, health consequences of poor peer relations, including peer rejection and the amount of conflict, has been established via aversive social exchange patterns between adolescents and their friends. Taken together, the research findings reviewed so far suggest that females are more sensitive to relationship stressors,

but the health consequences of these perceived elevated levels of stress are not clear. Most symptoms were experienced on a subclinical level. Whether the long-term outcome may lead to more severe health damage should be examined in future research. This is a challenging task, because the factors contributing to adolescents' maladaptation are complex and closely intertwined with normative developmental changes.

Inge Seiffge-Krenke

See also Conflict Resolution; Developmental Challenges; Family Relations; Storm and Stress

References and further reading
Compas, Bruce E., B. R. Hinden, and C. A. Gerhardt. 1995. "Adolescent Development: Pathways and Processes of Risk and Resilience." *Annual Review of Psychology* 46: 265–293.
Gore, Susan A., and R. H. Aseltine. 1995. "Protective Processes in Adolescence: Matching Stressors with Social Resources." *American Journal of Community Psychology* 23: 301–327.
Laursen, Brett, Katherine C. Coy, and W. Andy Collins. 1998. "Reconsidering Changes in Parent-Child Conflict across Adolescence: A Meta-Analysis." *Child Development* 69: 817–832.
Seiffge-Krenke, Inge. 1995. *Relationships in Adolescence.* Mahwah, NJ: Earlbaum.
———. 1998. *Adolescents' Health: A Developmental Perspective.* Mahwah, NJ: Lawrence Erlbaum Associates.

Conflict Resolution

Conflict resolution is a strategy that promotes the positive interaction between people who are in disagreement. This method emphasizes the use of strong communication skills, understanding, respect, and cooperation in order to promote peaceful approaches to conflict.

During adolescence, it is important to learn conflict resolution skills in order to control problems before they escalate to physical violence. (Skjold Photographs)

Conflict arises when two or more people believe that their opinions, wishes, and needs clash with those of their friends, family members, teachers, or others. Some conflicts, such as those resulting from insults or rumors, may seem less significant than conflicts associated with stolen belongings or physical fights. When people do not manage conflicts properly, violence is a likely consequence. Indeed, it is important to learn conflict resolution skills in order to control problems before they escalate to physical violence. Studies have shown that although relatively few conflicts result in injury, conflicts among students

do occur with frequency—and that without conflict resolution skills, students tend to deal with problems in ways that ignore the importance of their relationships with friends. Fortunately, research also indicates that conflict resolution and peer mediation programs are effective in teaching both elementary and secondary school children how to use conflict management strategies to bring about positive outcomes to their problems. When students learn and use constructive conflict management, schools witness a reduction in the numbers of student-to-student conflicts reported by teachers and administrators.

Although many people are uncomfortable with conflict, it is not always a bad thing. What's important is how people *deal with* the conflict that is present in their lives. During conflict, people may experience humiliation, distrust, and frustration; they may also have a difficult time seeing the situation from a perspective other than their own. However, when constructive approaches to conflict are used, beneficial results often follow. Through active conflict resolution, people are essentially forced to seek creative approaches to their problems, allowing them to clarify differing points of view and to improve relationships and lines of communication.

Although conflict resolution is effective, certain common assumptions about conflict make it difficult for many people to use its beneficial techniques. One such assumption is that conflict results from the failure of only one person, as when a girl directs her anger solely at her father because her parents divorced and he moved away. Another false notion is that there is no best way to deal with conflict; for example, a boy may get into a physical fight while arguing with his friend, not realizing that a better approach is available. A third misconception about conflict is that it always leads to destructive outcomes; a case in point is the girl who decides after an argument with her best friend that their friendship is over.

In actuality, conflicts result from differing perspectives on life, and their outcomes and degree of seriousness depend on the way in which people handle them.

People have three options when dealing with conflict in their lives. They can fight the person who causes them pain or trouble, they can avoid the problem by fleeing from it, or they can engage in problem solving. This last option involves clearly communicating feelings, assessing the facts surrounding the problem, and thinking about favorable outcomes.

The winner and loser in any argument are determined by the approach to conflict that is chosen. (1) When a person fights the source of conflict, by attacking verbally or physically, one person wins and the other loses. (2) When flight is the method used, both people lose because the problem, now avoided or ignored, will likely persist. (3) When problem solving is employed, both people win. The reason is that problem solving encourages each person to understand the nature of the conflict, to voice his or her own concerns, to listen to the other person involved, and to work with that other person to develop an appropriate solution. Conflict resolution skills, when learned and practiced, can indeed help people choose option (3) as their approach to conflict.

Problem solving requires strong communication skills, active listening, and critical thinking. *Communication skills* are necessary for problem solving because they enable the people involved in a conflict to clearly voice their concerns. *Active listening* is important

because it allows people to accurately hear the needs of others. And *critical thinking* helps people to review all possible options before they agree on the best solution to their problem.

"I" statements can be used to effectively communicate concerns, needs, and feelings. Starting with the word "I" helps speakers clearly express their thoughts in a way that helps listeners understand what they are thinking—without getting defensive. Unfortunately, people commonly start with the word "you" when talking about a problem. Doing so often makes the problem worse, because the listeners feel that they are being blamed, and they blame back. Both speakers and listeners become more agitated, and the problem remains unsolved. Starting instead with the word "I" helps speakers voice their concerns without accusing their listeners.

An "I" statement can be formed by means of the following formula:

I feel . . . (name your feeling)
When . . . (name the behavior that
     troubles you)
Because . . . (explain the result or
     effect of the behavior)

Suppose Joey's mother tells him to take his sister to her friend's house and this makes him late for the movies. Joey could respond with an "I" statement and say: "Mom, I felt angry when you asked me to drive Julie to her friend's house because it made me late for the movies." Here, Joey names the problem (having to drive his sister) and expresses his feeling (anger) with the word "I." Instead of placing blame on his mother, he voices his frustration with nonthreatening words. This direct expression of feelings may help Joey's mom better understand their argument. Of course, "I" statements are especially effective when the recipient of the message understands the importance of listening for the facts and feelings being expressed.

As noted, active listening is another component of effective problem solving. Active listening is a response indicating that the listener has correctly heard what the speaker has said. Paraphrasing is one way to actively listen. Through paraphrasing, listeners state in their own words what speakers have said, without adding new facts, opinions, or interpretations. By restating what they have heard, the listeners can accurately reflect the speaker's feelings.

The formula used for paraphrasing is as follows:

You feel . . . (include feelings and facts)
When/Because . . . (state the cause of the feeling)

When Joey said, "Mom, I felt angry when you asked me to drive Julie to her friend's house because it made me late for the movies," Joey's mom could have paraphrased by saying, "It sounds as if you are feeling pretty frustrated because my request made you late for the movies." By means of this statement, Joey's mother would have let him know that she heard what he said and that she is aware of how her request made him feel. If Joey believes that his emotions are being regarded, he will be more willing to openly express his concerns to his mother. And in the future, this honesty will make it easier for both mother and son to identify and work through their conflicts before they escalate into larger arguments.

Another way to show effective listening skills is through body language. Eye contact and leaning forward indicate that a listener is attentive to what the speaker is saying. Suppose that Joey's mother was paying bills while Joey vented his frustration. Even if she used her paraphrasing skills, Joey may not have felt listened to if she was looking down at her paperwork. If she instead made eye contact with Joey and placed her bills to the side, Joey may have better sensed his mother's undivided attention.

Each of these communication skills helps parties in conflict to brainstorm possible solutions to their problem. This is the stage at which critical thinking comes into play. Once all of the issues have been laid out on the table and each person has voiced his or her own concerns and listened to the needs of the others involved, the parties in conflict are ready to find the best solution to their problem. The goal of critical thinking is to find an agreement that benefits all parties.

However, even with all of these helpful problem-solving skills, some conflicts are difficult to resolve. In such cases, the people involved may benefit from having a conflict management procedure to follow. Mediation is one such procedure.

In fact, many schools use peer mediation programs to teach youngsters how to help their fellow students manage conflict. These programs, which are usually supervised by a trained teacher or guidance counselor, empower students to become active participants in their environments by helping to create safe and secure schools.

The students who have volunteered to be peer mediators are given fifteen to twenty hours of training that provides the essential skills necessary for active listening and conflict prevention. They are also instructed to be as neutral as possible when they mediate conflicts; in other words, during a mediation process, they must avoid taking sides, giving advice, and assuming responsibility for resolution of the problem. Rather, their objectives are to facilitate the civil communication between conflicting parties in ways that help each side fully understand the nature of the conflict and to assist the parties in reaching a formal agreement to the problem. Peer mediators are assigned specific days and hours of the week during which they are on call to handle conflicts in their schools. When a conflict arises, both parties are sent to mediation, and two peer mediators are assigned to the case.

Peer mediation programs in the schools give students an alternative to dealing with conflict through violence. They do so by encouraging the use of communication and conflict resolution skills, which in turn leads to problem solving and critical thinking about beneficial solutions to conflicts. Indeed, peer mediation allows students the opportunity to personally deal with their conflicts before the school administrators get involved.

Jessica Beckwith

See also Conflict and Stress

References and further reading
Benson, A. Jerry, and Joan M. Benson. 1993. "Peer Mediation: Conflict Resolution in Schools." *Adolescence* 28, no. 109: 244–245.
Gerber, Sterling, and Brenda Terry-Day. 1999. "Does Peer Mediation Really Work?" *Professional School Counseling* 2, no. 3: 169–171.
Johnson, David W., and Roger T. Johnson. 1996. "Conflict Resolution and Peer Mediation Programs in Elementary and Secondary Schools: A Review of the Research." *Review of Educational Research* 66, no. 4: 459–506.
Kowalski, Kathiann M. 1998. "Peer Mediation Success Stories: In Nearly 10,000 Schools Nationwide, Peer Mediation Helps Teens Solve Problems without Violence." *Current Health* 25, no. 2: 13–15.
Lindsay, Paul. 1998. "Conflict Resolution and Peer Mediation in Public Schools: What Works?" *Mediation Quarterly* 16, no. 1: 85–99.
Stomfay-Stitz, Aline M. 1994. "Conflict Resolution and Peer Mediation: Pathways to Safer Schools." *Childhood Education* 70, no. 5: 279–282.

Conformity

In our democratic society, conformity is often perceived in a negative way, especially by educated people. It is typically associated with the lack of freedom and seen as an antonym to independence and personal choice. Nevertheless, conformity is a very important societal characteristic, for it is the guarantee of stability and mutual understanding between the members of the society. During adolescence, conformity plays a strong role in the course of self- and social development.

In social psychology, conformity may be defined as a tendency of human behavior—one that comes into play when a person fits in with the norm of the society or with a given group. This definition helps explain why conformity is often perceived negatively—because fitting in with the norm limits personal freedom. On the other hand, no society can exist without norms, either written or unwritten, that guide each member's behavior. The dream about an utterly free, normless society is very old and not realistic. Norms were invented by people for people to make sure that people in general behaved in line with a set standard. On the other hand, the same norms that guide behavior often slow progress and inhibit necessary change. Accordingly, for a society to function and develop there must be a reasonable balance of

Conformity plays a strong role in the course of self- and social development. (Skjold Photographs)

both conformity and personal freedom. There must be conformity in order to keep the society together, and freedom to allow it to move forward. Cultures differ in the way they interpret what this balance between conformity and freedom should be. Western culture tends to put a higher value on freedom and individuality. On the other hand, there are more collectivist countries (such as China) that place more importance on the interdependence of its members, on tolerance and self-control, on attaining group goals, and on maintaining harmony.

Conformity, like many other psychological phenomena, has an adaptive value—to survive, an individual needs to fit into the society, and to fit into the society, he needs to accept its goals and values; to preserve itself, the society needs to coordinate the efforts of many people and to promote norms and punish deviation. This importance of conformity to survival can be seen in many societies where nonconformists are disliked, unwanted, and rejected. This, too, varies from culture to culture and is more likely to appear in more collectivist cultures. In the West, the situation is paradoxical: in a postmodern democratic society, where personal initiative and independence are so valued, to be independent is actually to conform to the societal norm. One could argue that this paradox is one of the most positive characteristics of modern Western culture.

One important way to think about conformity is to recognize that it is important for building one's self-concept by identifying with the group and accepting its values and standards. In general, self-psychology (psychology that focuses on the nature of the self) tells us that the tendency to conform is different at different stages of self-development. In fact, a strong tendency to conform can be viewed as a stage in self-development.

The role of conformity in adolescent development is complex. Adolescents find themselves in a group between the worlds of childhood and adulthood and use this peer group for support and for identity. However, it is not inevitable that adolescents will conform to a peer group; young adolescents show the highest rates of conformity to peers.

In addition to age, gender plays a role in the intensity of an adolescent's conformity with peers. Although girls are more interested in peer acceptance than boys, boys are more likely to conform to peer pressure by engaging in antisocial behavior. Conformity in adolescence, however, is more likely to be limited to clothes, music, and language. For serious moral matters, adolescents' views tend to be in line with their parents. This differential in conformity serves a protective role, since teens can safely conform to peers on some issues to gain acceptance, thus allowing them to continue to conform to parental standards on more serious matters.

By the end of adolescence conformity plays a lesser role, and teens begin to place importance on their own individuality. Conformity does not, however, become totally dormant; the transition to adulthood brings with it a new set of social standards and challenges.

Janna Jilnina

See also Cliques; Identity; Peer Groups; Peer Pressure; Peer Status; Peer Victimization in School; Rebellion

References and further reading
Camerena, Phame. 1991. "Conformity in Adolescence." In *Encyclopedia of Adolescence.* Edited by Richard M.

Lerner, Anne C. Petersen, and Jeanne Brooks-Gunn. New York: Garland.

Daniel Gilbert, Susan Fiske, and Gardner Lindzey, eds. 1998. *The Handbook of Social Psychology.* New York: McGraw-Hill.

Loevinger, Jane. 1976. *Ego Development.* San Francisco: Jossey-Bass.

Youniss, Richard P. 1958. *Conformity to Group Judgments in Its Relation to the Structure of the Stimulus Situation and Certain Personality Characteristics.* Washington, DC: Catholic University of America Press.

Contraception

Contraception is the term that refers to efforts to prevent pregnancy. Many contraceptive methods are available today. There is a method for everyone, but it requires thoughtful consideration and sometimes experimentation for someone to find the method that is best. Good contraceptive methods are effective and safe both for the woman and the man. Most importantly, people need to choose a method that they will use. Contraception does not work effectively unless it is used each time a man and a woman have intercourse.

This entry provides a general overview of available contraceptive methods. Readers need to discuss their specific needs with their physician, nurse practitioner, or nurse midwife to determine what method is most appropriate for them.

A key point to remember is that the purpose of contraception is to prevent pregnancy, and when used correctly it is successful at doing so. However, whenever one is engaging in sexual activity it is also essential to protect one's self from sexually transmitted diseases (STDs) by using or having the partner use a male condom. In addition, once women become sexually active, they need to have a gynecologic exam and pap smear (screening test for cervical cancer) every year. Once men become sexually active, they need to let their doctor or nurse practitioner know so that they can be checked for STDs when they have their school or yearly physical.

Contraceptive methods for women generally fall into two major categories, hormonal methods and barrier methods. The male condom remains the only contraceptive that men can use.

Women can get contraceptive care in a number of different settings. Many physicians, particularly obstetricians and gynecologists, offer contraceptive services in their offices. Family-planning services such as Planned Parenthood are available, and college health services frequently offer contraceptive services for their students. Hospitals usually have women's health services that provide contraceptive services, and local health departments may as well. Nurse practitioners, nurse midwives, and physicians are the kind of providers who offer these services.

Hormonal Methods

Hormonal contraceptives use the hormones estrogen and/or progestin to prevent pregnancy. They come in different forms and may be taken as pills, by injection, or by implantation under the skin. Some intrauterine devices (IUDs) are also considered hormonal contraceptives. However, IUDs will not be discussed here, because they are only prescribed for women in monogamous relationships who have completed their families.

Hormonal methods of contraception are very effective (in other words, if they are used properly, the risk of pregnancy is less than 1 percent). However, they are all prescription medicines that affect the woman's entire body. People who are thinking about using one of these methods need to discuss their health history with their healthcare provider and ask for complete information about how the particular hormonal method acts on their body and what the side effects and risks are for them. For example, these methods are not safe for women who have high blood pressure. Some women also experience mood changes when taking hormonal contraceptives, so women with a history of depression may want to use another method of contraception.

Hormonal contraceptives act on a woman's body in a number of ways to prevent pregnancy. They prevent ovulation, the process that prepares an egg to be ready for fertilization. They act on the endometrium or lining of the uterus, making implantation unlikely, and they change the cervical mucus, making it difficult for sperm to reach the upper reproductive tract to fertilize an egg.

Hormonal contraceptives also change the bacteria and other organisms normally present in the vagina, which makes the vagina more vulnerable to STDs. Hence, it is important to use a male condom along with these methods to protect both the man and the woman from STDs.

Oral contraceptives, often referred to as the Pill, must be taken daily at about the same time each day to be effective. Certain antibiotics and antiseizure medications may make the Pill ineffective. It is important for any health care provider caring for a woman on the Pill to know that she is taking the Pill. If a woman needs to take one of these medications, she should use a backup method, like condoms or spermicide, to protect herself from pregnancy, or switch to another contraceptive method.

A monthly pack of oral contraceptive pills costs between $15 and $30 a month.

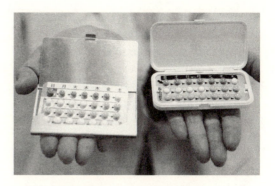

Good contraceptive methods are effective and safe both for the male and female. (Reuters NewMedia Inc./Corbis)

Most pill packs contain twenty-eight pills, twenty-one with hormones and seven that are inactive (no hormones). A woman's period will occur while she is taking the inactive pills. Generally periods are lighter while taking the Pill and cramping is mild, if it occurs at all. In fact, sometimes the Pill is prescribed for women who have difficult, painful periods ("dysmenorrhea") because of this effect on the period. Once a person stops taking the Pill, her fertility should return to what it was before she started taking it.

Different oral contraceptives contain different amounts of estrogen and progestin. As a result, different pills can cause different side effects. If someone chooses the Pill and finds changes in her body that worry her or that she doesn't like, she should talk to her healthcare provider about changing to a different type of pill rather than stopping the medication. Some common side effects are breakthrough bleeding (bleeding between periods), breast tenderness, decreased menstrual bleeding and cramping, weight gain (especially in pills with progestin), nausea, and vomiting. Another side effect for one type of pill is improving acne. (Some women might choose this pill because they want this side effect.)

There is no evidence that the Pill increases the risk of breast cancer. Recent research indicates that women who take (or have taken) the Pill are more likely to detect breast cancer early than women who never took the Pill, perhaps because they are more active in their own healthcare.

Emergency contraception (EC) refers to a combination of oral contraceptive pills taken in a specific way to prevent pregnancy. Timing is very important, because EC must be taken within seventy-two hours of unprotected intercourse. It is essential to contact a healthcare provider or a family planning clinic, or call 1-888 NOT-2-LATE for information right away if EC is desired. When used correctly EC changes the environment in the uterus, making implantation of a fertilized egg impossible. EC can cause nausea and vomiting. If a woman needs to use EC, she should be sure to make an appointment to get a contraceptive for regular use. EC is used in specific situations only and is not a regular contraceptive method.

Another hormonal method is depo-provera, given by injection (i.e., shot) at a clinic or doctor's office, with the first injection being given during or just after the woman has her period. The medication is effective for twelve weeks (about three months), and the injection must be repeated every twelve weeks. Each injection costs between $35 and $50. Once depo-provera is stopped, it may be up to a year before ovulation returns.

Many women experience abnormally long and heavy bleeding during the first three months after getting depo-provera, but many of these women also stop having periods after being on depo-provera for nine to twelve months. Some side effects that occur while taking depo-provera are weight gain, breast tenderness, depression, decreased high density lipoprotein (HDL) cholesterol levels, and decreased bone density in long-term users. However, depo-provera also decreases the frequency of seizures and is not affected by antibiotics.

Lunelle is also given by injection, but unlike depo-provera, it requires one shot a month. Lunelle is under review by the FDA and may be available soon. Women interested in this method should ask their provider if it is available.

Norplant is a hormonal contraceptive that is inserted into the inner part of the upper arm. Six thin capsules are placed in the arm through a small surgical incision to form either a star or fanlike pattern. There may be a bruise or swelling for a few days where the norplant was placed. The capsules are removed through a surgical incision, and once removed, fertility should return to what it was prior to their insertion.

Norplant costs about $500 to $700, but it lasts five years, which works out to about $8 to $12 a month. Not all providers insert norplant, so it may not be as easily available as other contraceptive methods.

Women using norplant might experience irregular or absent periods, breast tenderness, weight gain, increased acne, and depression. The effectiveness of norplant is not decreased by antibiotics, but it can be decreased by antiseizure medications. Women who take antiseizure medications should consider depo-provera, or have their partners use a male condom as a backup method for preventing pregnancy.

Barrier Methods
Barrier methods fall into two general categories, physical barriers and chemical

barriers. Physical barriers include the diaphragm, the cervical cap, contraceptive sponge, and both male and female condoms. Chemical barriers are spermicidal foam, cream, jelly, suppository, and film. Sometimes physical and chemical barriers are used together. Although the barrier methods have varying degrees of effectiveness (.5 to 40 percent), they are all most effective when used as directed each time a man and a woman have intercourse. Fertility is not affected by barrier contraceptives. Although it is unlikely, physical barrier methods that are inserted into the vagina may cause toxic shock syndrome (TSS), a rare but serious illness for women. This risk is increased when the barrier is left in the vagina for prolonged periods of time. The symptoms of TSS are sudden high fever (more than 100 degrees Fahrenheit), vomiting, diarrhea, muscle aches, and a sunburnlike rash.

Spermicides come in the form of cream, jelly, foam, film, and suppositories or tablets that contain a sperm-killing chemical. Nonoxynol-9 is the most common sperm-killing chemical used. Spermicides are available at drug or grocery stores, and may be sold at some family-planning clinics. Spermicides cost about a dollar for each single use (e.g., each episode of intercourse), but come in multiple-use packaging and cost between $10 and $12 for the package.

To be effective, spermicides need to be inserted less than one hour before sex and must cover the cervix. They must be inserted with enough time to dissolve and spread out in the vagina. Each product has specific directions that need to be followed to maximize the effectiveness of the chemical barrier. Cream, jelly, and foam are put in the vagina by a plastic applicator and need to be inserted in as

short a time as possible before intercourse. Contraceptive film is placed over the cervix, and suppositories are inserted into the vagina. These two methods work only for one hour after insertion, and a new one must be used for each intercourse. Both require a specific amount of time to become effective. Some women experience vaginal soreness or itching when using certain spermicidal products. If this happens, it is a sign to try a different product.

The diaphragm is a rubber, dome-shaped cup with a flexible rim, which holds spermicidal cream or jelly next to the cervix. It prevents pregnancy by preventing sperm from reaching the egg and by inactivating sperm. Some women like the diaphragm because it can be inserted up to four hours before intercourse. However, using the diaphragm requires that a woman be comfortable enough with her body to insert it, and she must be willing to use it each time she has sex and to use it as directed.

Diaphragms are available only with a prescription and need to be fitted by a doctor, nurse practitioner, or nurse midwife. The healthcare provider fits a diaphragm by inserting rings into the vagina to determine which size will best cover the cervix. The cost of a diaphragm varies with the type of clinic. Family-planning or other public clinics may be less expensive than some office settings. The exam may cost between $30 and $150, depending on site and geographic location, the diaphragm between $30 and $40. Insurance may cover one or both of these costs.

The chance of becoming pregnant with the diaphragm has been reported to range from 6 percent to 20 percent, depending upon whether the diaphragm fits and is used properly, and the woman's position during intercourse. The diaphragm is most effective when the man is on top during intercourse. If a woman gains or loses ten pounds or more, or has a baby, she needs to have her diaphragm rechecked to make sure it fits properly before she can safely rely on it as a method of contraception. To use the diaphragm effectively, one must leave it in place for six hours after the last intercourse to allow the spermicide enough time to work. Additional spermicide must be inserted into the vagina, leaving the diaphragm in place over the cervix, each time a woman has intercourse if she has it more than once. The diaphragm should not be left in place for more than twenty-four hours because of the risk of TSS. The diaphragm needs to be washed after use, stored in a container, and checked for holes on a regular basis. Oil-based lubricants, like vaseline or baby oil, should not be used because they make the rubber in the diaphragm deteriorate.

Occasionally the diaphragm causes pressure on the bladder or rectum and may be uncomfortable. A different size diaphragm may help with this problem. However, some women experience urinary tract or yeast infections as a result of diaphragm use, and should consider another method if these infections happen frequently.

The cervical cap prevents pregnancy in a way similar to the diaphragm and has a similar degree of effectiveness. Like the diaphragm, it must be obtained from a healthcare provider. The cost is similar to the diaphragm and will vary with the setting. The cervical cap also has a similar risk for urinary tract infections, and women who keep the cap in place for over forty-eight hours are at increased risk for developing TSS. The cervical cap

cannot be used while a women has her period for this same reason.

The cervical cap is a deep rubber cup with a firm rim, which is placed over the cervix. The cap is about one-third filled with spermicide and then placed over the cervix. It is held in place by suction. Some people recommend that the cap be inserted at least thirty minutes before intercourse to allow the suction to develop. The cap must remain in place for six to eight hours after sex to be effective, but can be left in place for up to forty-eight hours without problems. There is some controversy regarding insertion of additional spermicide if intercourse occurs more than once, because applying more spermicide may cause the cap to slip.

The contraceptive sponge is a barrier method not currently available in the United States and so will not be discussed in detail here. It is a polyurethane sponge with spermicide, which is produced in one size. Effectiveness varies between 9 and 40 percent because the sponge may not be sufficiently moistened or in place long enough before intercourse, or may be taken out too soon after intercourse.

The female condom or vaginal pouch is a relatively new contraceptive choice for women. Like the male condom, it has the added advantage of protecting against both pregnancy and STDs. The female condom is a soft, loose-fitting polyurethane sheath with an inner and outer ring. The inner ring is little like the ring in the diaphragm. It is placed deep in the vagina so that it covers the cervix while the outer ring remains at the vaginal opening. The female condom can be inserted up to eight hours before intercourse. It is used once and then discarded. A new female condom must be used for each act of intercourse.

Some women like the control over contraception that a female condom provides them. Others find the outer ring stimulates the clitoris and makes sex feel better. Some men like the female condom because they like the looseness of the sheath.

The female condom is marketed under the name Reality and costs about $3. Its effectiveness is similar to that of the diaphragm and cervical cap. However, it is not necessary to use spermicide with the female condom, but all lubricants (both water- and oil-based) are safe to use with it. Unlike other birth control methods, the female condom cannot be used together with the male condom. If used together, the female condom will cause the male condom to fall off.

The male condom is a tight-fitting sheath made of latex, designed to fit over an erect penis. The male condom prevents pregnancy by trapping semen (which contains sperm) in its tip so that it does not get into the woman's body. Condoms can be purchased inexpensively (usually less than a dollar per condom) at drug or grocery stores, and are available at many family-planning clinics for free. Male condoms are most commonly made from latex. They have no side effects, but some people have an allergic reaction to the latex and cannot use them. Fortunately, male condoms made from polyurethane are being developed, and more will be available in the future. An advantage of polyurethane condoms is that, unlike latex condoms, oil-based lubricants do not make them more likely to break.

The effectiveness of latex condoms varies greatly with the skill and knowl-edge of the user. When used properly, the chance that a woman will become pregnant using the male condom is between .5 and 7 percent (Haignere, Gold, and McDanel, 1999). Some authors report that condoms do not work between 12 and 70 percent of the time and that condoms tear and break, but laboratory research, *Consumer Reports*, and research regarding couples, where one person is infected with HIV and the other is not, all demonstrate that the problem is how male condoms are used, not the condom itself.

The most common mistake people make when using male condoms for contraception is to not use them consistently. Male condoms are only effective if they are used every time a man and a woman have intercourse. Also, male condoms should not be washed out and reused. A fresh condom should be used every time.

Male condoms are tested to make sure that they do not have holes or weak points where they might break: Condoms break when the people using them make any one of five mistakes. First, if someone stores a male condom in a hot place like a car glove compartment or a man's wallet, the latex becomes brittle and more likely to break. Second, if someone uses a stale condom that is past its due date, it is more likely to break. Either the man or the woman should check the due date printed on the outside of the condom wrapper to make sure the condom is not too old to use. Third, people sometimes tear or damage the condom if they are not careful opening the wrapper containing the condom. Fourth, women can tear the condom accidentally with their fingernails if they are not careful putting it on the man's penis. Fifth, people use oil-based lubricants (baby oil, vaseline, lipstick, medicinal vaginal creams with oil in them) that make the latex in male condoms weak and easy to tear. Using lubricants is not a bad idea: Putting the right type of lubrication inside the male condom can make it more comfortable for the man, and putting it on the outside can make it more comfortable for the woman. However, the only lubricants that are safe are water-based lubricants like the ones that come on prelubricated male condoms and those used in spermicides. Other safe lubricants that are water-based and available in the drugstore include K-Y Jelly and Astroglide. Look for lubricants that say "water-based" on the box or "safe for latex condoms."

Male condoms slip off when they are not used properly. For instance, a male condom will come off if the man ejaculates, but waits to remove his penis from the woman's vagina. This is because the male condom will not stay on if the penis is no longer erect. A male condom can also come off if no one holds the base of the condom firmly against the penis while the penis is withdrawn from the vagina. It is especially important to hold onto the male condom if one uses extra water-based lubricant.

Two other things that can cause a condom to fail are not putting the condom on before any contact between the vagina and penis, or putting the condom on upside down so it doesn't unroll and then flipping it over and using it once it is right side up. Both of these actions decrease a condom's effectiveness, because when a man is sexually excited a little seminal fluid comes out of his penis and this fluid can contain sperm. If this sperm comes into contact with the vaginal area (even the outside of the vagina),

it can migrate into the vagina and on up through the woman's reproductive system where it can fertilize one of her eggs. This is why a male condom should be put on before there is any contact between the penis and the vagina, and why condoms that are first put on upside down should be thrown away.

Male condoms sound complicated to use, but they merely require practice and knowledge to be an effective method of contraception. Like the female condom, they have the added advantage of protecting against STDs as well as pregnancy. Some men and women also like them because they make sex less messy and can make the man last longer during sex.

Anne E. Norris
Monica J. Hanson

See also Abortion; Abstinence; Adoption: Exploration and Search; Adoption: Issues and Concerns; Dating; Gonorrhea; Health Promotion; HIV/AIDS; Love; Pregnancy, Interventions to Prevent; Sex Education; Sexual Behavior; Sexual Behavior Problems; Sexually Transmitted Diseases

References and further reading
Alan Guttmacher Institute, http://www.agi-usa.org
The American Social Health Association, http://www.iwannaknow.org
Association of Reproductive Health Professionals, http://www.arhp.org
Bell, Ruth, and other coauthors of *Our Bodies, Ourselves,* with members of the Teen Book Project. 1998. *Changing Bodies, Changing Lives,* 3rd ed. New York: Random House.
The Boston Women's Health Book Collective. 1998. *Our Bodies, Ourselves.* New York: Simon and Schuster.
Haignere, Clara S., Rachel Gold, and Heather J. McDanel. 1999. "Adolescent Abstinence and Condom Use: Are We Sure We Are Really Teaching What Is

Safe?" *Health Education and Behavior* 26: 43–54.

Hatcher, Robert A., James Trussell, Felicia Stewart, Willard Cates Jr., Gary K. Stewart, Felicia Guest, and Deborah Kowal. 1998. *Contraceptive Technology.* 17th rev. ed. New York: Ardent Media.

Planned Parenthood, http://www.plannedparenthood.org, http://www.teenwire.com

http://ec.princeton.edu/ecEmergency Contraception Web site (Princeton University).

http://www.virtualhospital.org, general health Web site (University of Iowa).

Coping

Stressful experiences and cumulative change are ubiquitous during the adolescent years. Accordingly, the adolescent's ability to cope with different types of stressors is critically important. In particular, adaptive and maladaptive coping responses are thought to moderate the effects of different types of stressors on adolescent health. *Coping* is defined as a process of managing external or internal demands. This process has three key features: the individual's action, the specific context of coping, and the way the individual's actions change as the stressful encounter unfolds. Psychologists characterize coping as a process of continuous appraisals and reappraisals of a changing person-environment relationship. The reappraisals in turn influence subsequent coping efforts. The coping process is thus continuously mediated by cognitive reappraisals and, optimally, should lead to a person-environment fit. The entire coping process can occur within a few moments or hours, or it can continue over weeks or even years.

In the past, several conceptualizations of coping have been developed using ado-lescent samples. One such approach reveals a distinction between two main types of coping: coping that is problem-focused (i.e., directed at altering the problem that causes the distress) and coping that is emotion-focused (i.e., directed at regulating emotional responses). A second approach favors an approach-avoidance model that differentiates between approach-oriented coping (which includes cognitive attempts to understand or change ways of thinking about stress and behavioral attempts to deal with stressors) and avoidant coping (which includes cognitive attempts to deny and minimize stress). Yet another approach focuses on the immediate outcome of coping and distinguishes between functional and dysfunctional coping styles. Functional coping refers to efforts to manage a problem by defining it clearly, actively seeking support, reflecting on possible solutions, and taking concrete action. Conversely, a dysfunctional coping style might include efforts to withdraw from or deny the existence of the stressor and avoiding the seeking of solutions, as a result of which the problem remains unsolved. This distinction between the active approach of tackling problems versus avoidance and withdrawal is found in most studies of adolescent coping methods.

Research further indicates that, when faced with normative demands and minor stressors, North American adolescents employ the two functional modes of coping (e.g., active support seeking and internal reflection of possible solutions) more frequently than they resort to avoidant coping and withdrawal. Among diverse cross-cultural samples as well, functional coping occurs four times more frequently than dysfunctional coping. Thus, the normative demands typical of this age group tend to be approached in an

Coping involves managing external and internal demands. (Skjold Photographs)

adaptive way, revealing such coping strategies as taking action, seeking social support, and seeking information. Indeed, adolescents can largely be considered competent copers, able to deal well with problems arising in such different domains as school, romance, and relations with parents and peers.

This generalization is somewhat qualified by evidence that coping strategies vary in terms of the stressors themselves (with respect to their perceived stressfulness, controllability, and imminence), the domain in question, and, finally, age and gender. These variables will be discussed in turn.

The role of stressors in the life of adolescents can be explored from two different perspectives: (1) anticipatory coping, which occurs prior to a confrontation with the stressor, and (2) coping after an event has happened. As a rule, the former is assessed in large representative samples, whereas the latter is examined by means of process-oriented interviews in small groups immediately after the stressful event has occurred. Analysis of the different phases of adolescent coping reveals that the first or primary appraisal of the event as being a challenge, a threat, or a loss is generally followed by reactions that include confusion, strong emotions, and preliminary cognitive coping efforts, whereas in the secondary appraisal, adolescents consider their own coping resources, scope of action, and expectations of success or failure. Next, the actual coping process occurs, directed either at altering the problem that has caused the distress or at regulating emotional responses. Then, after the coping process has ended and during reappraisal, a decrease in negative emotions is frequently observed. Anticipatory coping is characterized by a greater emphasis on active support seeking, whereas in coping immediately after the stressor occurred, a less active, more internal style was found. Adolescents who had experienced a structurally similar event are highly concordant in their coping responses. For example, adolescents experiencing mildly stressful events with high controllability react most often with active, approach-oriented coping, whereas those experiencing a highly stressful, less controllable event react most often with avoidant coping and passivity.

Coping also occurs in domain-specific ways. When family stressors occur, adolescents tend to address the problem directly. Some try to find a compromise; others attempt to cope with parent-adolescent conflicts by venting emotions or seeking distraction. Adolescents also frequently seek comfort from and discuss possible solutions with peers who are having similar experiences. On the other hand, when problems with a peer, close friend, or romantic partner arise, adolescents rarely turn to parents or other adults. Instead, they usually deal with the person concerned and discuss possible solutions with friends who are in a similar situation. Older adolescents named more use of alcohol and drugs as a means of forgetting problems relating to romantic partners. They also reported much more "giving in" in romantic relations than in conflicts with friends and parents. Yet older adolescents are still willing to discuss school-related stressors and future-related problems with their parents, as well as to seek help from institutions and to look for information in media and literature.

Midadolescence seems to be a turning point in the use of certain coping strategies. It is well known that, compared to children, adolescents are more involved and intimate with peers and friends, turning to them for support formerly provided by the family. Accordingly, after the age of fifteen, adolescents increasingly discuss everyday stressors with same-aged peers and more frequently try to obtain support from peers and friends whose circumstances are similar. In cases where the stressor in question involves interpersonal conflict, they are also more likely to speak openly about the problem with the concerned individual. These developmental changes in the use of social support tend to be intertwined with changes in social and cognitive development, leading to increased cognitive complexity and social maturity. Adolescents older than fifteen increasingly adopt the perspective of significant others and are more willing to make compromises or yield to the wishes of others. And because they reflect more about possible solutions, their overall approach is characterized by a variety of coping options. The link between the level of social-cognitive maturity and functional coping style becomes even more obvious when we compare factor structures in early adolescent and midadolescent samples: Two basic coping modes, approach-oriented coping and avoidant coping, can be established for younger adolescents (eleven to fifteen years), whereas for older adolescents (sixteen to nineteen years), the approach dimension has both a behavioral and a cognitive component, and the avoidance dimension remains the same.

The findings are more controversial with respect to emotion-focused and problem-focused coping. There is some debate as to whether age-related changes in problem-focused coping and emotion-focused coping take place consistently from childhood through adolescence. Some findings suggest that the use of problem-focused coping does not increase from middle childhood through adolescence because such skills have already been acquired and used at an earlier stage, whereas learning processes related to emotion-focused coping continue throughout adolescence. However, other findings appear to show an increase in both problem-focused coping and emotion-focused coping, suggesting further developmental changes in these styles.

Gender differences have also been reported with respect to certain coping strategies. "Boys play sports and girls turn to others" describes one such difference, inasmuch as girls are much more likely to seek social support than boys. They more frequently discuss a problem or event with the person concerned and more often ask for help and assistance. These trends continue into adulthood, indicating a general tendency among females to rely more heavily on social networks than males and to seek help in extrafamilial settings. By contrast, male adolescents worry less about problems, expect less negative consequences, and use distraction more frequently. Gender differences in both active approach-oriented coping and withdrawal have also been found: Females exhibited higher scores in both coping styles, suggesting a more ambivalent coping pattern of approach and avoidance.

These gender differences in coping styles have been linked to the emergence of psychopathology in adolescence. Several researchers suggest, for example, that girls enter adolescence with a style of responding to certain types of stressors that is less efficacious and action oriented than that of boys, and that this avoidant coping style is related to the emergence of gender differences in disorders such as depression. In fact, among adults, depression is twice as frequent in females than in males; it is also linked to a ruminative coping style, which prolongs depressive episodes. The strong gender differences in adolescents' coping styles may thus be predictive of depression in female adults, especially if avoidant coping is considered a precursor to ruminative coping. These different coping styles may be fostered by stereotypical gender-specific socialization processes. For example, the male stereotype of being active and ignoring moods may lead to an increase in distracting responses to depressive mood, and the female stereotype of emotionality and inactivity may lead to rumination instead of distraction from depressive mood. Rumination has been found to maintain and increase depressive mood, whereas distraction tends to alleviate depressive mood.

Research analyzing the links between certain coping styles and adaptation has indeed profited from findings generated in the field of developmental psychopathology. Psychologists' understanding of the reasons for which some children are not damaged by deprivation and highly stressful living conditions has been enriched by numerous studies of the relationships among stress, social support, and general adaptation (e.g., Werner and Smith, 1982). In particular, these studies have found protective factors such as "invulnerability" or "resiliency" among adolescents exposed to various risk factors and cumulative stressors, demonstrating that resilient adolescents are able to continue a relatively healthy emotional development despite unfavorable life situations. In contrast, nonresilient adolescents lack social support systems and show signs of accumulated stress.

What resilient adolescents appear to have in common are families with relatively intact parent-child relationships. In these families, the adolescents' attempts to achieve autonomy are not thwarted, and rules and limits are clearly defined. Above all, resilient adolescents are competent in their choice of and identification with resilient models of social support. Their coping capacities exhibit two particularly outstanding qualities. First, although many of these adolescents live in poverty-stricken, dangerous conditions and are exposed to marital conflict, they deal with such life stressors in a competent and active way, specifically by acting and not just reacting. Second, when faced with disturbances in their parent-child relationships, they seek support and refuge from alternative caregivers in the household or neighborhood.

Another important finding is that adolescents' coping styles affect not only their dealings with immediate stressors but also the availability of their social support. Indeed, ineffective coping responses may lead to poor interpersonal relationships, thereby further reducing their available coping resources, as when an adolescent who copes through inappropriate demonstration of anger, or excessive emotion, becomes unpopular with friends.

Accumulating evidence also suggests that avoidant coping is a risk factor in depression, delinquency, antisocial behav-

ior, and conduct disorders. Whereas healthy adolescents rarely employ avoidant coping and withdrawal, these coping styles are very prominent in all of the clinical conditions just listed; the rates at which such styles are used among diverse patients are two to three times higher than those for healthy controls. In addition, depressed adolescents rely on approach-oriented coping to a significantly lesser degree than any of the other clinical groups, and adolescents diagnosed as antisocial and delinquent show a deficit in internal coping in that they reflect significantly less about possible solutions. With respect to drug-dependent adolescents, however, the results are not as clear.

Most research examining the links between coping and well-being has found that approach-oriented coping is linked with better adjustment and avoidant coping with poorer adjustment: Approach-oriented copers report the fewest behavioral and emotional symptoms, whereas avoidant copers report the most. Studies have also established the long-lasting effects of dysfunctional coping styles. Adolescents who change over time from approach-oriented to avoidant coping display a significant increase in symptomatology, whereas behavioral and emotional symptoms tend to decrease in subjects who switch from avoidant to approach-oriented coping over time. Thus, all forms of avoidant coping exhibited in early adolescence, whether stable or not, are linked with higher levels of symptoms in middle and late adolescence. In these studies, gender differences in avoidant coping did not emerge consistently, suggesting that the links between avoidant coping and maladaptation are similar for male and female adolescents.

Ultimately, a vicious cycle is created. Deficits in relationships and problems in acquiring and using social support lead to dysfunctional coping, which itself generates more deficits and more problems. The resulting accumulation of stressors, in turn, may adversely affect adolescents' health. This chain of events has clear implications for prevention and intervention.

Inge Seiffge-Krenke

See also Conflict and Stress; Counseling; Health Promotion; Psychotherapy

References and further reading
Gjerde, Per F., and Jack Block. 1991. "Preadolescent Antecedents of Depressive Symptomatology at Age 18: A Prospective Study." *Journal of Youth and Adolescence* 20: 217–231.
Lazarus, Richard S., and Susan Folkman. 1991. *Stress, Appraisal, and Coping*, 3rd ed. New York: Springer-Verlag.
Lewinsohn, Peter M., Robert E. Roberts, John R. Seeley, Paul Rohde, Ian H. Gotlib, and Hyman Hops. 1994. "Adolescent Psychopathology. II. Psychosocial Risk Factors for Depression." *Journal of Abnormal Psychology* 103: 302–315.
Nolen-Hoeksema, Susan, and Joan S. Girgus. 1995. "Explanatory Style and Achievement, Depression, and Gender Differences in Childhood and Early Adolescence." Pp. 57–70 in *Explanatory Style*. Edited by G. M. Buchanan and M. E. P. Seligman. Hillsdale, NJ: Erlbaum.
Seiffge-Krenke, Inge. 1995. *Stress, Coping, and Relationships in Adolescence*. Mahwah, NJ: Lawrence Erlbaum Associates.
Werner, Emmy E., and Ruth S. Smith. 1982. *Vulnerable but Invincible: A Study of Resilient Children*. New York: McGraw-Hill.

Counseling

Counseling is an interpersonal process by which a person comes to recognize the ways in which past events and personality variables affect past and current thoughts, feelings, and behaviors. Empowerment, hope, and effective ways of relating to others are generated through growing insight, altered expectations, and the identification of novel ways of being and behaving. Counseling, sometimes referred to as therapy or psychotherapy, is usually provided by psychologists and social workers; psychiatrists address emotional and behavioral problems by prescribing medication.

The majority of adolescents navigate their teen years without an abundance of problems. However, there are numerous physical, cognitive, and social changes that make adolescence a particularly difficult time for some youth, and counseling can help.

Developmental Challenges

Psychological and behavioral problems, such as depression and delinquency, often escalate during adolescence, even among youths who have long suffered difficult life situations. What is it about adolescence that produces the apparently sudden onset and increase of symptoms? Developing cognitive abilities and numerous psychosocial and biological events partially spur this change in mental health status. In addition to new and intimidating social and interpersonal challenges, adolescents are endowed with greater cognitive abilities, such as improved reasoning, attention, memory, and abstract thought, that render them increasingly able to evaluate their past and anticipate their future. It is a time when some youths become capable of understanding the meaning and implications of painful life events they suffered while they were children. Helplessness, hopelessness, anger, and other emotions may be expressed through depression and

Counseling may help adolescents cope with difficult physical, cognitive, and social changes. (Shirley Zeiberg)

suicide, eating disorders, drug and alcohol abuse, school-related problems, and delinquency. In general, adolescent females are more likely to experience *internalizing disorders*, such as depression, headaches, and anxiety, so called because problems are inner-directed. In contrast, adolescent males exhibit greater tendencies toward behavioral expressions that clash with the environment. Often referred to as acting-out or undercontrolled behaviors, these *externalizing disorders* include conduct disorder and oppositional defiant disorder and are associated with aggression, delinquency, and school-related problems. Though much less common, psychiatric disorders such as schizophrenia and bipo-

lar disorder (manic-depressive illness) usually first appear during adolescence or young adulthood, suggesting a genetically time-bound component.

Coping
Although half of all youths report experiencing considerable home- and/or school-related stress, many cope fairly well and never seek the help of a mental health professional (Steinberg, 1996). Why, then, do stressors affect some adolescents more than others? Research suggests that the difference is related to coping abilities, which depend on the number and severity of stressors that a youth is simultaneously facing; internal resources, such as self-esteem, competency, and social skills;

social support from friends, parents, relatives, and others; and proficiency of coping strategies. Problem-focused coping strategies involve attempts to solve problems (e.g., upcoming exam) through concrete tasks or acts (e.g., studying). Emotion-focused coping strategies involve reducing uncomfortable feelings (e.g., avoiding studying through distractions). Though there are advantages to both, the former generally results in better adjustment and less stress.

Numerous life experiences have been identified that undermine coping abilities, including early loss, neglect or abuse, rejection, family instability or breakdown, problems with parents, and psychiatric disorders in parents, particularly depression. Thus, *resiliency,* the ability to withstand adverse events, usually depends on the number of negative events that were previously endured or are concurrently faced, internal resources, and external support.

When to Seek Help
It is sometimes difficult to determine whether a youth is experiencing normal developmental angst or is in need of counseling. The following five points, proposed by Steinberg and Levine, are useful guidelines for assessing when parental help is insufficient and counseling is warranted: One, when an adolescent is experiencing severe behavior problems, such as drug addiction, anorexia nervosa, suicidal thinking, self-injurious acts, serious school-related problems, or multiple delinquent behaviors. Two, when a parent observes unusual behavior (e.g., significant withdrawal or social isolation) but is unsure of its meaning and the teenager is unable or unwilling to discuss it. Proper diagnosis by a mental health professional will help determine whether it is the result of depression, drug abuse, shyness, or something else. Three, when a parent has repeatedly attempted to address a problematic behavior, such as recurrent truancy or aggressive acts, without success. Four, when a problem extends beyond the adolescent and involves the family, such as chronic and intense arguing. Family therapy may help all members to see their part in the conflict. Five, when an adolescent displays significant symptoms of distress (e.g., depression, significant alcohol consumption) related to extreme family circumstances (e.g., divorce, death).

It is often difficult for adolescents to request or accept help from a mental health professional, because they are frightened or hold erroneous stereotypes about what it means to do so. Adolescents may dread the judgment of the counselor or rejection by friends who find out that they are seeing a "shrink." Indeed, many who have never been in therapy believe that they will be "analyzed" by a bearded, cigar-smoking man with a German accent while reclining on a couch. They are often ashamed or embarrassed to admit to themselves or others that they need help, fearing this means that they are weak, "crazy," or bad. In fact, seeking help is often a sign of strength and mental health. Some conditions, such as depression, can leave a teen with such low energy that she does not have sufficient strength or motivation to seek help. At these times, encouragement from a parent, friend, or teacher might be invaluable.

Types of Counseling
Counseling, whether obtained from a high school guidance counselor, a college/university health center mental health provider, or an independent thera-

pist practicing in the community, comes in numerous forms. *Individual counseling* occurs between a counselor and a youth, whereas *family counseling* consists of the counselor, the youth, and the youth's parents and possibly siblings. *Group counseling* is comprised of one counselor and several youths. There are many techniques of counseling, but they usually fall into one of four categories.

Insight-oriented or psychodynamic techniques facilitate exploration of feelings, thoughts, needs, wishes, internal conflicts, and the ways in which a youth interacts with others. The goal is to connect these emotions and behaviors with previous life events and highlight the ways in which past experiences continue to affect, or determine, current experiences. These techniques are often referred to as "talk therapies." Though appropriate for a variety of concerns, this approach is particularly helpful for treating depression, bereavement, relationship issues, low self-esteem, and post-traumatic stress disorder.

Cognitive and cognitive-behavioral techniques focus on identifying and changing irrational or unfounded thoughts that result in maladaptive emotions and behaviors. Participants are trained to monitor their thoughts and feelings, utilize problem-solving strategies, and evaluate outcomes of their old and new ways of interacting with the environment. Little attention is directed toward in-depth exploration of early life history. These techniques successfully treat depression, panic disorder, generalized anxiety disorder, post-traumatic stress disorder, eating disorders, and poor social skills. They can also reduce aggressive behavior and impulsive anger.

Behavioral techniques focus on changing specific maladaptive or harmful thoughts, feelings, and behaviors without necessarily attempting to understand their origin. Change is achieved through such mechanisms as reinforcement of positive behavior, punishment of negative behavior, counterconditioning, and extinction following exposure to feared stimuli. Anxiety disorders such as panic attacks and phobias, obsessive-compulsive disorder, sexual dysfunction, insomnia, stuttering, alcoholism and drug abuse, and pain (e.g., headaches) are most successfully treated through this modality.

Family therapy conceptualizes the family as a system, or organization, rather than a group of individual components. Because it is an interrelated structure, changing even one component of the system will reverberate throughout the structure, resulting in overall change. Goals are to identify and change unhealthy communication patterns, reduce dysfunctional styles of interaction, encourage differentiation of self (e.g., "I am myself, not my mother"), and facilitate greater flexibility so that the family can adapt to new situations (e.g., a child going through adolescence). Among other issues, this approach effectively treats couples problems, eating disorders, alcoholism, and schizophrenia.

Counseling is often helpful for revealing the ways in which symptoms conceal underlying concerns. For example, alcohol and drug abuse and anorexia nervosa are behavioral manifestations, or symptoms, that often conceal underlying sadness. Once the true issue (sadness) is exposed and explored, the behavioral manifestation diminishes or disappears altogether. Similarly, counseling can help a youth recognize that abusing alcohol or drugs is an attempt to reduce social anxiety and that anorexia nervosa is an attempt to provide structure and control during times of anxiety and helplessness. In addition to formal counseling, counselors often teach youths to use regular exercise, proper nutrition, and correct sleep hygiene to control symptoms such as depression and anxiety and to facilitate overall physical and mental health.

Counseling also helps foster life skills development through training in key areas: Stress management, which helps with anxiety, panic disorder, social phobia, post-traumatic stress disorder, and depression; social competence, which reduces shyness, engenders assertiveness, and increases effective verbal communication, empathy, and perspective taking; assertiveness, which reduces depression and helplessness; coping, which facilitates management of stress more efficiently; time management, which helps overcome procrastination and academic anxiety; self-esteem development, which raises self-worth; decision making, which fosters critical thinking. Two other useful approaches are support groups, which address clinical issues (e.g., depression, relationship problems, drug and alcohol addiction, eating disorders) through education and discussion with those experiencing similar concerns; and bibliotherapy, which uses books, including the self-help variety, and other reading materials to facilitate self-understanding and provide information and coping strategies.

A counselor's ability to convey warmth, support, accurate empathy, positive regard, respect, and genuineness are more powerful than specific therapy techniques per se in facilitating growth in the client. At the same time, however, client variables such as negativism, hostility, low motivation, dislike of the therapist, and defensiveness contribute to poorer therapy outcome.

When an adolescent experiences extreme or protracted distress, psychotropic (mind-altering) medications are sometimes used to reinstate feelings of stability and contentment. Drug therapy can help alleviate unwanted and disruptive feelings when these symptoms are severe, appear to be the consequence of irregular levels of neurotransmitters (brain chemicals that affect thoughts and feelings), or are life-threatening and involve harm to self or others. Psychotropic medications are usually delivered by a psychiatrist, a medical doctor whose specialty is mental health and whose primary focus is symptom reduction and management of medication side effects. Drugs such as antidepressants are administered until symptoms are in remission for an extended time and in conjunction with ongoing counseling. Indeed, for many problems, such as depression, the combination of drugs and therapy works better than either alone. Psychotropic medications effectively treat anxiety, social phobia, bipolar disorder, depression, schizophrenia, obsessive-compulsive disorder, eating disorders, and other disorders.

Crisis intervention is a method for maintaining psychological integrity that is necessary during periods of acute crisis, such as following a trauma (e.g., rape, battery), extreme suicidal tendencies, or psychosis (e.g., severe mental confusion, hallucinations). Immediate efforts are necessary to reduce symptoms and stabilize an adolescent. This can be achieved in a hospital where speedy assessment and short-term treatment are provided. Youths are then released, within a few hours to a few weeks, to parents and may be referred to a therapist. The goals of crisis intervention are to reduce symptoms, strengthen coping abilities, return the person to her or his previous level of functioning, and avert further emotional deterioration or breakdown.

There are times when counseling must follow other interventions. For example, severe drug or alcohol abuse usually requires a period of detoxification and possibly rehabilitation in a drug treatment facility before counseling can begin. Severe anorexia nervosa in which a youth has lost enough weight to risk heart failure is another example when a period of stabilization, perhaps at an inpatient treatment facility (usually a hospital), is required prior to outpatient (community) care.

Outcome of Counseling

Adolescents of both sexes respond to counseling almost as well as do adults, although there is some evidence that girls benefit more from treatment than boys. Thus, counseling should be considered a viable strategy for the treatment of problematic behavior in adolescents. Perhaps the greatest contribution of counseling is that it can renew hope, the belief that things can and will get better and that the youth has a future. As adolescents struggle to articulate often previously unstated thoughts and feelings within the context of a counselor's support and unconditional acceptance, they gradually shed feelings of shame and inadequacy and achieve understanding as the disparate pieces of their life coalesce like pieces of a puzzle uniting to convey a story. They often experience greater feelings of control, reduced symptomatology, and diminished belief that they are crazy. Life feels more manageable.

Kenneth M. Cohen

See also Career Development; Conflict and Stress; Conflict Resolution; Health Promotion; Psychotherapy

References and further reading

Coleman, John C., and Leo B. Hendry. 1999. *The Nature of Adolescence*, 3rd ed. New York: Routledge.

Lewis, Michael, and Suzanne M. Miller, eds. 1990. *Handbook of Developmental Psychopathology*. New York: Plenum Press.

Silverman, Wendy K., and Thomas H. Ollendick, eds. 1999. *Developmental Issues in the Clinical Treatment of Children*. Boston: Allyn and Bacon.

Steinberg, Laurence. 1996. *Adolescence*. 4th ed. Boston: McGraw-Hill.

Steinberg, Laurence, and Ann Levine. 1990. *You and Your Adolescent: A Parent's Guide for Ages 10 to 20*. New York: HarperPerennial.

Tolan, Patrick H., and Bertram J. Cohler, eds. 1993. *Handbook of Clinical Research and Practice with Adolescents*. New York: Wiley.

Cults

A cult is a group that is organized around some symbol, philosophy, or belief. However, unlike other groups organized on the basis of such ideas, a cult uses deception and coercive control to recruit and maintain members. Although historically cults have been based around fringe religious organizations, today they are also organized around self-improvement groups, political organizations, and business-improvement groups; still, the majority are religious in orientation. Of course, not every small religious organization that seems peculiar or different is a cult, as most do not use deception or coercion to find and retain members. Nevertheless, an adolescent should use great caution when approached by anyone offering something that sounds too good to be true.

Recruiting Tactics
Recruiting for cults can occur any-where—at school, on the street, in religious organizations, even at home and on the Internet. Typically, recruiters are friendly people who seem very interested in the adolescent's life, provide much praise, and claim to have all the answers. They never acknowledge that they are part of a cult but, rather, attempt to create a bond with the teenager that allows them to get the teen more and more involved in the cult before he or she realizes what is really happening. Cults offer young people a place to belong, and recruiters convince these young people that they will be helping themselves by finding salvation and an emotional (or sometimes even physical) home, or that they will be helping others through fundraising or volunteer work.

Often adolescents are lured into a cult because they see it as a group that is both interesting and apparently able to fulfill their needs for friendship, safety, love, and a sense of accomplishment. They are then typically subjected to "love bombing" (intense praise, hugs, touching, and so on), which is intended to gain their trust, to allow them to feel good about themselves, and to create a desire within them to be part of the group.

Once the teens are drawn in, various forms of behavior modification and social influence techniques are employed to enmesh them. The mind control used by cults is, in principle, not different from the techniques used by advertisers to entice consumers to try their products or by a sports team to promote team spirit. However, cults use these techniques more intensely, more persistently, for a much longer duration, and with the goal of virtually total control over the young person's mind and behavior.

Toward this end, such techniques are also used in combination with isolation, sleep deprivation, food deprivation, reward and punishment, and methods of inducing fear and guilt in the adolescent.

Vulnerability
Teenagers are particularly vulnerable to cults because they are at an age when many transitions are occurring. Cults will take advantage of teens' search for identity by offering them a place to belong, and they will take advantage of teens' rebellion against parents by giving them a sense of control. In reality, however, cults are stripping control from their young recruits.

Other factors that make teenagers vulnerable are loneliness, the stressful shift from high school to college, and their sense of dissatisfaction with the meaning of life. Often adolescents are lured to a cult because they are seeking a new or higher form of spirituality, which the cult may seem to offer.

Warning Signs
There are many warning signs to look for when deciding whether an organization is a cult. First, cults use behavior modification, chanting, coercion, and manipulation to gain influence over the adolescent. Second, cult leaders are often charming and captivating people (of either sex) who claim to have special powers from God or special knowledge that can be shared only if one obeys them. Third, recruits are often asked to raise money for the organization without full disclosure as to where the money is going or, for that matter, asked to relinquish their own money, property, and savings. Fourth, cults not only promote the idea that nonmembers of the group will somehow suffer for their lack of faith

but also encourage (and eventually force) recruits to sever ties with family and friends, to quit their jobs, and to leave school.

Another strong warning sign is the existence of two sets of rules—one for members of the group and one for the leader. For example, cults often discourage sexual relations among members of the group, whereas the group leader is permitted to have sexual relations with multiple members. Cults also promote other forms of unethical behavior, such as soliciting illegally, while at the same time claiming divinity and righteousness.

Not all of these factors need be present to ascertain that an organization is a cult. But if some combination of them exists, the organization very likely is a cult and therefore a danger to adolescents and their development.

Dangers of Cult Membership
The dangers of belonging to a cult are many, especially for a young person. Above all, membership in a cult prevents adolescents from establishing an independent and healthy sense of self—an identity—which is a crucial developmental task. Inadequate development occurs because cults demand that the group become the young person's identity. This loss of individuality also has harmful effects on adolescents' sense of autonomy. Since the teens are often restricted in terms of friendships and romantic partners, they are unable to master the ability to form intimate relationships based on reality. This failure results in isolation.

Some cults are not just emotionally abusive but physically and sexually abusive as well, particularly toward members who start to question the leader's authority. Members (especially women) are often forced into sexual relationships with the leader in the name of sacrament and honor, and in cults that restrict the amount of food and sleep a person gets, adolescents can becomes ill from malnutrition and sleep deprivation.

Leaving a Cult
Leaving a cult can be difficult for young people because they have been convinced that they are going against the will of God and bad things will happen to them. In the past, parents have used aggressive techniques to remove their children from cults, but today most of these tactics are illegal. For the most part, in order for teens to leave a cult, they must want to leave. This happens when they begin to sense the inconsistencies in cult life.

For these young people the most effective strategy for escape is to connect with an exit counselor. These professionals, who have experienced cults themselves, are able to provide support for young people during the exit process. Exit counselors are also able to connect the young people with other former cult members who can attest that nothing disastrous happened as a result of leaving. The counselors are able to help young people get their lives back.

Deborah L. Bobek

See also Peer Groups; Peer Pressure; Peer Victimization in School; Religion, Spirituality, and Belief Systems

References and further reading
Galanter, M. 1996. "Cults and Charismatic Group Psychology." Pp. 269–296 in *Religion and the Clinical Practice of Psychology*. Edited by E. P. Shafranske. Washington, DC: American Psychological Association.
Hunter, E. 1998. "Adolescent Attraction to Cults." *Adolescence* 33: 709–714.
Singer, M. T. 1995. *Cults in Our Midst*. San Francisco: Jossey-Bass.

D

Dating

Dating, or the process of experimenting and establishing romantic relationships with peers, is an important developmental task in adolescence. Teens and adults often recall how important the making and breaking of their teen dating relationships were in their development, but social scientists are only beginning to understand the origins, development, and consequences of adolescent dating relationships. Involvement in romantic relationships, which more than doubles during the primary teen years (seventh to twelfth grade), is considered to be part of a larger process by which teens negotiate increasing autonomy and independence from the family while developing closer ties with their peers. Although teens thus often sacrifice time devoted to family members to accommodate their dating relationships, dating, by itself, does not appear to compromise the quality of family relations. Teens with dating partners report that their relationships with parents and siblings are just as close and influential in their lives as those of teens without dating partners.

Many, if not most, teens begin dating between twelve and fifteen years of age. Initiating dating is a very challenging and stressful process for teens. Tendencies for children to develop friendships with same-sex peers during childhood and preadolescence create social worlds that, in some ways, are very different for boys and girls. In the process, children gain only limited understanding of the opposite sex. Thus, as teens become increasingly interested in romantic relationships, they face the struggles and awkward challenges of learning how to relate to opposite-sex peers who often have different experiences and styles of affiliating. Dating at this age usually occurs in the context of outings (e.g., to the mall, movies, or parties) within larger mixed-sex friendship networks. Although some level of intimacy and sexual experimentation is not uncommon during this period, the primary concerns of early adolescents do not center on the fulfillment of intimacy, support, or sexual needs. Rather, given their relative isolation from the other sex throughout childhood, the main business at hand for early teens involves (1) gaining the knowledge and skills necessary to effectively relate to other-sex peers, (2) ascertaining their attractiveness to the opposite sex, and (3) establishing their identity and status within the group. Same-sex friendships within the larger mixed-sex group serve as "social halfway houses" between the familiarity and comfort of the friendship world to the exciting, but novel, world of opposite-sex peers and dating relationships. More specifically, these friendships appear to help

Teens and adults often recall how important the making and breaking of their teen dating relationships were for them, but social scientists are only beginning to understand the origins, development, and consequences of adolescent dating relationships. (Shirley Zeiberg)

teens adjust to the new world of dating by serving as bases of support, sources of information for establishing other-sex relations, and channels for receiving feedback about their success in other-sex relations.

Although dating still typically occurs within mixed-sex groups during middle adolescence (fifteen to seventeen years), middle adolescent couples increasingly go on dates by themselves. In these more intimate settings, gaining peer approval and learning about the opposite sex are no longer reported to be primary advantages of dating for teens. Instead, middle adolescents are increasingly concerned with companionship (i.e., shared activi-

ties and interaction), intimacy (i.e., establishment of a deep, meaningful relationship), and sexual experimentation in their dating relationships. As part of this process, teens are increasingly likely to establish committed, exclusive (i.e., steady) dating relationships that are often characterized by intense positive emotion and excitement, preoccupation and fantasizing, beliefs that the relationship can weather any challenge, and even love. However, because middle adolescents do not have a firm concept of how their partner fits into their future plans, their feelings are often confined to the immediate or short-term period of the relationship. Moreover, teens are often conflicted about these relationships, as evidenced by their views that commitment and negative interpersonal relations are major disadvantages of steady relationships. The end result is that even serious, satisfying relationships last an average of only a few months. Middle adolescence may best be summarized as a transitional period for romantic relationships, replete with passionate, but short-lived, bonds with dating partners.

Teens in late adolescence (seventeen to nineteen years) often begin experimenting with lengthier committed relationships with a single partner that can last years. Signs of a deeper level of closeness and intimacy often emerge as romantic partners increasingly rely on each other for support, security, advice, and caregiving. However, many teens do not fully develop this type of mature mutual-attachment relationship. One reason is that mature, enduring relationships require some degree of self-sacrifice at a time when late adolescents are still grappling with trying to understand themselves ("Who am I?") and develop their identities ("What do I want out of life?").

Uncertainties may arise as to whether it is possible to sacrifice their developing identities without completely losing their freedom and themselves in the relationship. Perhaps not surprisingly, older teens are more likely to define intimate relationships in terms of sharing, sexual interaction, trust, and openness than in terms of commitment, security, caregiving, and self-sacrifice. In addition, many social scientists believe that a truly deep mutual-attachment bond becomes fully developed only after a minimum of two years in a romantic relationship. Thus, for many teens whose relationships commonly last less than a couple years, a deeper level of closeness is achieved but not fully formed into a mutual-attachment relationship.

Although little is known about the effects of dating on teen development, there is some evidence suggesting that dating paves the way for healthy development in many areas of functioning. First, dating has been characterized by social scientists as a healthy forum for developing and refining communication skills, interpersonal relations, and conflict management abilities. Research has shown, for example, that increases in dating involvement are accompanied by increases in the sharing of personal information and by decreases in conflict within close friendships. Second, success in securing dating partners can be a means of enhancing social status, peer relations and approval, and, eventually, emotional adjustment. For example, companionship and enhancement of social status are commonly cited by teens as key advantages of dating. Moreover, teens who are more heavily involved in dating have greater self-confidence and self-esteem, report fewer signs of depression, and perceive themselves to be more socially skilled than teens who are less involved or uninvolved in dating. Third, dating may promote teen characteristics that help them successfully adapt to the demands of adulthood. Dating is specifically considered to be a training ground for the development of psychological and sexual intimacy and sharing—which are key building blocks for forming mature, satisfying, and enduring romantic relationships in adulthood.

However, the effects of dating are not uniformly beneficial for teens. Whether dating has benefits or costs for teens' mental health depends largely on the timing, history, and quality of their dating relationships. According to one theory, early onset of dating or casual dating among multiple partners reflects teens' attempts to develop stronger ties with peers—attempts that, in turn, involve accepting the behaviors and values of a peer culture that in some cases are at odds with societal and familial rules of conduct. Endorsement of rule violations in the peer culture are commonly reflected in minor acts of delinquency, sexual activity, and experimentation with substances such as alcohol. Supporting this theory is the finding that early onset of dating forecasts not only higher self-confidence and a greater sense of autonomy but also increased problem behaviors in the form of alcohol use, substance use, delinquency, and academic difficulties. Likewise, adolescents who develop casual dating relationships with multiple partners experience increased alcohol use, sexual activity, and delinquency. Although this increase in problem behaviors is understandably a concern for many parents, it is important to note that some increase in problem behaviors is a normal part of teen experimenting and, for most teens, is likely to be temporary. Indeed, evidence suggests that as older teens gain experience in more serious, mature relationships, support and closeness in the relationship may help them seek more independence from peer influence, critically evaluate deviant peer norms, and, ultimately, cycle out of experimentation in deviant activities.

Although temporary emotional distress (e.g., depression, loneliness) over the short-lived nature of adolescent romantic relationships is normal, another set of theories maintains that dating may actually be a source of enduring emotional problems under certain conditions. Demands for intimacy and commitment, particularly within steady, exclusive dating relationships, may overwhelm the developing emotional maturity of adolescents and prematurely limit the opportunities and experiences necessary to gain a solid understanding of themselves and others. The formative years of dating, which typically take place during early and middle adolescence, are often characterized as being fraught with mistrust and distress over losing a romantic partner along with the contrasting fear of losing one's independence and identity if the relationship continues. In support of this idea, teens cite commitment, negative interpersonal relations, and worry and jealousy as primary disadvantages of involvement in romantic relationships. Based on such evidence, establishing long-term serious relationships may jeopardize teens' self-esteem, isolate them from potentially valuable social relationships (e.g., peers, friends, family), and increase their depressive symptoms.

Additional evidence indicates that dating may have a negative impact on teen adjustment if it is accompanied by certain challenging or stressful events. For girls in particular, socializing with members of the opposite sex is often initiated at the same time that they are coping with the onset of menstruation, increased body fat resulting from puberty, and the transition from the small, intimate settings of elementary school to the larger, more demanding, and impersonal settings of middle school. Striving to maintain thinness in the belief that it will increase their success in the dating world in the larger, more impersonal setting of the school is a difficulty that may compound the stressfulness of establishing dating relationships. The resulting burden appears to intensify girls' emotional distress, body dissatisfaction, and unhealthy dieting practices, including eating problems. Note that, although psychologists have made some headway in identifying some of the risks associated with dating, the complexity of their results prevents any firm conclusions from being drawn at this point.

Teens' psychological characteristics and aspects of their social lives are thought to play an important role in accounting for why adolescents differ in their dating experiences. On the one hand, sociability, communication and conflict resolution skills, and achievement of close, supportive friendships are critical ingredients for success in subsequent romantic relationships; on the other hand, problem behaviors in the form of minor delinquency, sexual activity, and higher levels of alcohol use in friendship networks during early and middle adolescence are predictive of more dating involvement. This pattern of sociability and participation in a "partying" network of peers may facilitate dating by (1) permitting information exchanges on the best methods of handling dating relationships, (2) affording opportunities to initiate more informal and intimate interactions with potential dating partners, and (3) further refining communication and conflict management skills necessary to successfully forge romantic relations. Very adverse family experiences, such as a history of physical abuse or neglect, also increase teens' vulnerability for becoming victims or perpetrators of violence in dating relationships. Nevertheless, very little is known about why teens differ in such aspects of their dating experiences as timing (early versus late), quality (supportive, unsupportive, violent), and course (enduring versus short-lived). In short, although the consensus is that teens' experiences in the dating world are products of peer relations, psychological disposition (e.g., temperament, social competence, depression), perceptions of social relationships, and the quality of family relationships, the specific and combined effects of these factors are still poorly understood.

Patrick Davies

See also Dating Infidelity; Developmental Challenges; Gender Differences; Loneliness; Love; Peer Pressure; Sex Differences; Sex Roles; Sexual Behavior; Sexual Behavior Problems; Sexuality, Emotional Aspects of; Transitions of Adolescence

References and further reading
Davies, Patrick T., and Michael Windle. 2000. "Middle Adolescents' Dating Pathways and Psychosocial Adjustment." *Merrill-Palmer Quarterly* 46: 90–118.
Montemayor, Raymond, Gerald R. Adams, and Thomas P. Gullotta, eds. 1994. *Personal Relationships during Adolescence.* Thousand Oaks, CA: Sage.
Shulman, Shmuel, and W. Andrew Collins, eds. 1997. *Romantic Relationships in Adolescence: Developmental Perspectives.* San Francisco: Jossey-Bass.

Dating Infidelity

Dating infidelity refers to engaging in sexual or other behavior considered inappropriate for one in a committed ("going out" or engaged) relationship. Up to a quarter of college students admit that they have been "unfaithful" to their current partner, and up to 50 percent note that their friends who are going out with someone have been unfaithful to their current partner. These numbers are in accord with the percentage of married people who say they have engaged in marital infidelity. This is an important concern because discovering that one's partner has been unfaithful often can lead to a dissolution of the relationship, which is a primary cause of adolescent suicide.

There is a wide range of behaviors included in those considered indicative of infidelity, and these are quite similar for both going-out and engaged couples. For instance, along with sexual intercourse, dating another person, and flirting, kissing, and petting with another person, are very much viewed as acts of infidelity. Spending time with another person of the same gender as your partner and being close friends with someone of the same gender as your partner are generally not considered indicators of infidelity. Behaviors that might indicate infidelity include betraying the partner's confidence, keeping secrets from one's partner, and being emotionally involved with another person. The ambiguity involved in determining whether these behaviors indicate infidelity lies perhaps in what confidences are betrayed, what secrets kept, and the degree of emotional involvement with another. If the betrayal of confidence, the secrets kept, and the emotional involvement are likely to result in the dissolution of the relationship, they may constitute acts of infidelity.

ment of more serious and long-lasting problems.

The rate of depression among children is much lower than that among teenagers. Between the years of late childhood and early adolescence, both boys and girls begin to report symptoms of depression, which increase in frequency throughout adolescence. Starting in middle adolescence, however, girls begin to report more depressive symptoms than boys and continue to do so throughout adulthood. Researchers have sought to understand why depression becomes more frequent during adolescence and why girls report more depression than boys. Although current findings do not provide complete answers to these questions, knowledge has increased. One finding concerns stress. The many changes that teenagers experience as they move from childhood to adolescence are sources of stress and thus may be implicated in depression. Consider the hormonal and physical changes that accompany puberty; when these changes occur in combination with other changes, stress is likely to escalate. Indeed, for early adolescents who move from the protected environment of the elementary school at the same time that they are going through puberty, the transition to middle school can be quite stressful. Middle school brings with it more difficult academic work and the need to work with many teachers rather than the single teacher who knew them well. Going through puberty earlier than peers can add to the stress of early adolescence, especially for girls. For example, girls who are physically mature may develop friendships with older teens who, in turn, may bring them into situations that the younger teens are not ready to handle. And because of society's emphasis on being thin, girls may become anxious about the weight gain that accompanies puberty and develop negative feelings about their bodies.

In addition, relationships with parents often change during adolescence, especially as teens become more independent. If parental support and supervision are taken away too quickly, teens may feel abandoned or come to believe that they can do anything they want. And if parents divorce, remarry, or undergo a big change in financial status, teens may find the challenges of adolescence particularly difficult. Family conflict, economic difficulties, neighborhood violence, and sexual abuse are just a few of the stressful events that can increase the risk for depression among teens. Some researchers suggest that increased stress, in conjunction with declining support from caring adults, has contributed to a rise in depression among youth.

Some teens may also have a genetic predisposition toward depression, evidenced by a high frequency of depression among biological relatives. When this genetic risk interacts with life stress, depression becomes a likelier outcome. But the finding that depression runs in families does not prove that depression is genetically caused; environmental factors may figure in, too. For example, many of the positive and negative coping strategies that teens rely on to respond to life's challenges are learned in the home.

Whether or not these challenges result in depression can depend on how prepared the teens are to deal with them. Developing a positive view of themselves, talking with and getting help from parents and other caring adults, learning how to solve problems and cope with stress in active and positive ways rather than blaming themselves or turning to drugs and alcohol—all of these coping skills can help teens deal effectively with the challenges incurred during the second decade of life.

Above all, teens need to know that there are mental health professionals who can work with them to develop these important coping skills so that serious emotional problems, such as depression, can be avoided.

Maureen E. Kenny

See also Counseling; Emotions; Loneliness; Psychotherapy; Sadness

References and further reading
Allgood-Merten, Betty, Peter Lewinsohn, and Hyman Hops. 1990. "Sex Differences in Adolescent Depression." *Journal of Abnormal Psychology* 99, no. 1: 55–63.
Brooks-Gunn, Jeanne. 1991. "How Stressful Is the Transition to Adolescence for Girls?" Pp. 131–149 in *Adolescent Stress: Causes and Consequences.* Edited by M. E. Colten and S. Gore. New York: Aldine de Gruyter.
Kovacs, Maria. 1997. "Depressive Disorder in Childhood: An Impressionistic Landscape." *Journal of Child Psychology and Psychiatry* 38: 287–298.
Reynolds, William M., and Hugh F. Johnston, eds. 1994. *Handbook of Depression in Children and Adolescents.* New York: Plenum Press.

Developmental Assets

Why do some adolescents grow up with ease, while others struggle? Why do some adolescents get involved in dangerous activities, while others spend their time contributing to society? Why do some adolescents "beat the odds" in difficult situations, while others get trapped?

Researchers have learned a great deal about these questions. Factors such as family dynamics, support from commu-

nity adults, school effectiveness, peer influence, values clarification, and social skills have all been identified as contributing to healthy development. However, these different areas of study are typically disconnected from each other.

In an effort to draw together many elements that contribute to healthy development among adolescents, Search Institute developed the framework of developmental assets (Benson, 1997; Benson et al., 1998). The forty assets are concrete, positive experiences and qualities that have a tremendous influence on young people's lives and the choices they make. These forty assets have roots in adolescent development research, resiliency research (which identifies factors that increase young people's ability to rebound in the face of adversity), and prevention research (Scales and Leffert, 1999).

To understand the importance of developmental assets and how young people experience them, Search Institute surveys sixth- to twelfth-grade youth in communities. Each year, several hundred communities conduct the survey. Search Institute periodically compiles results from many communities into an aggregate data set. The discussion that follows cites data from 99,462 student surveys during the 1996–1997 school year. The sample includes surveys from 213 U.S. communities in twenty-five states. (Benson et al., 1999).

Eight Categories of Developmental Assets
The assets are organized into two broad categories. The first twenty assets, "external assets," focus on positive experiences that young people receive from the people and institutions in their lives. The remaining twenty assets, "internal assets," focus on the internal qualities

that guide choices and create a sense of centeredness, purpose, and focus. All forty assets are listed and defined in Table 1, which also shows the percentages of youth who have each asset, based on the surveys mentioned above.

In addition to the internal and external groupings, the forty assets are organized into eight categories, which offer a helpful structure for understanding the scope of the framework. Here are the eight categories, along with information from the research about young people's experiences of these assets.

Support—Support refers to a range of ways in which young people experience love, affirmation, and acceptance. Ideally, young people experience an abundance of this kind of support, not only in their families but also from many people across many settings, including neighborhoods and schools.

Despite the importance of support in young people's lives, these assets are fragile in every community studied. Indeed, five of the six support assets are experienced by less than half of the youth surveyed. Furthermore, the percentage of young people reporting that they have the support assets declines through the middle and high school years in all categories except adult relationships (asset 3).

Empowerment—The empowerment assets relate to the key developmental need for youth to be valued and feel valuable. The empowerment assets highlight this need, focusing on community perceptions of youth (as reported by youth) and opportunities for youth to contribute to society in meaningful ways.

The perception of safety (asset 10) is an important underlying factor of youth empowerment. Students who feel safe are more likely to feel valued and able to make a difference than students who feel afraid at home, at school, or in the neighborhood. It is an ideal that our children deserve to realize, but one that is too rarely achieved.

The percentage of youth who experience two of the four empowerment assets is quite low. Only 20 percent of youth surveyed perceive that the adults in their community value youth (asset 7, one of the assets least reported by youth), and only 24 percent report being given useful roles to play within community life (asset 8). On the other hand, half of all youth say they are involved in service to others, with females being more likely than males to report this involvement (asset 9).

Boundaries and Expectations—Boundaries and expectations assets highlight young people's need for clear and enforced standards and norms to complement support and empowerment. They need to know what kinds of behaviors are "in bounds" and what kinds are "out of bounds." Ideally, young people experience appropriate boundaries in their families, schools, and neighborhoods (as well as other settings), receiving a set of consistent messages about acceptable behavior across socializing systems.

High expectations are likewise important for young people. High expectations can challenge young people to excel and can enhance their sense of being capable. Adult role models provide another important source for modeling what communities deem important. Finally, although peer pressure is most often viewed negatively, peers can also play a positive role in helping shape behavior in healthy ways.

Although clear and consistent boundary messages are crucial, only a minority of youth report experiencing such clear boundary messages in their families,

TABLE 1   The Forty Developmental Assets

Support

External Assets

1. **Family support** — Family life provides high levels of love and support. (64%)

2. **Positive family communication** — Young person and her parent(s) communicate positively, and young person is willing to seek advice and counsel from parent(s). (26%)

3. **Other adult relationships** — Young person receives support from three or more nonparent adults. (41%)

4. **Caring neighborhood** — Young person experiences caring neighbors. (40%)

5. **Caring school climate** — School provides a caring, encouraging environment. (24%)

6. **Parent involvement in schooling** — Parent(s) are actively involved in helping young person succeed in school. (29%)

Empowerment

7. **Community values youth** — Young person perceives that adults in the community value youth. (20%)

8. **Youth as resources** — Young people are given useful roles in the community. (24%)

9. **Service to others** — Young person serves in the community one hour or more per week. (50%)

10. **Safety** — Young person feels safe at home, at school, and in the neighborhood. (55%)

Boundaries and Expectations

11. **Family boundaries** — Family has clear rules and consequences and monitors the young person's whereabouts. (43%)

12. **School boundaries** — School provides clear rules and consequences. (46%)

13. **Neighborhood boundaries** — Neighbors take responsibility for monitoring young people's behavior. (46%)

14. **Adult role models** — Parent(s) and other adults model positive, responsible behavior. (27%)

15. **Positive peer influence** — Young person's best friends model responsible behavior. (60%)

16. **High expectations** — Both parent(s) and teachers encourage the young person to do well. (41%)

Constructive Use of Time

17. **Creative activities** — Young person spends three or more hours per week in lessons or practice in music, theater, or other arts. (19%)

18. **Youth programs** — Young person spends three or more hours per week in sports, clubs, or organizations at school and/or in the community. (59%)

19. **Religious community** — Young person spends one or more hours per week in activities in a religious institution. (64%)

20. **Time at home** — Young person is out with friends "with nothing special to do" two or fewer nights per week. (50%)

TABLE 1 *continued*

Commitment to Learning	Internal Assets
21. **Achievement motivation**	Young person is motivated to do well in school. (63%)
22. **School engagement**	Young person is actively engaged in learning. (64%)
23. **Homework**	Young person reports doing at least one hour of homework every school day. (45%)
24. **Bonding to school**	Young person cares about his school. (51%)
25. **Reading for pleasure**	Young person reads for pleasure three or more hours per week. (24%)

Positive Values

26. **Caring**	Young person places high value on helping other people. (43%)
27. **Equality and social justice**	Young person places high value on promoting equality and reducing hunger and poverty. (45%)
28. **Integrity**	Young person acts on convictions and stands up for her beliefs. (63%)
29. **Honesty**	Young person "tells the truth even when it is not easy." (63%)
30. **Responsibility**	Young person accepts and takes personal responsibility. (60%)
31. **Restraint**	Young person believes it is important not to be sexually active or to use alcohol or other drugs. (42%)

Social Competencies

32. **Planning and decision making**	Young person knows how to plan ahead and make choices. (29%)
33. **Interpersonal competence**	Young person has empathy, sensitivity, and friendship skills. (43%)
34. **Cultural competence**	Young person has knowledge of and comfort with people of different cultural/racial/ethnic backgrounds. (35%)
35. **Resistance skills**	Young person can resist negative peer pressure and dangerous situations. (37%)
36. **Peaceful conflict resolution**	Young person seeks to resolve conflict nonviolently. (44%)

Positive Identity

37. **Personal power**	Young person feels he has control over "things that happen to me." (45%)
38. **Self-esteem**	Young person reports having a high self-esteem. (47%)
39. **Sense of purpose**	Young person reports that "my life has a purpose." (55%)
40. **Positive view of personal future**	Young person is optimistic about her or his personal future. (70%)

N = 99,462 sixth- to twelfth-grade youth in public and alternative schools in 213 communities in twenty-three states during the 1996–1997 school year.

their schools, and their neighborhoods. Only one boundaries and expectations asset (15, positive peer influence) is reported by most youth. Interestingly, young people are twice as likely to report peers being a positive influence (60 percent) as they are to report having positive adult role models (27 percent, asset 14).

Constructive Use of Time—One of the prime characteristics of a healthy community for youth is a rich array of structured opportunities for children and adolescents. Whether through schools, community organizations, or religious institutions, these structured activities contribute to the development of many of the assets. They not only help build young people's peer relationships and skills, they also connect youth to principled, caring adults.

In addition, structured time use can serve as a constructive alternative to the idle time now common for youth. Such idle time, although not always unproductive or dangerous, increases the probability of negative peer influence and overexposure to the mass media. The need for these activities must be balanced with the need to spend time at home (asset 20), relaxing, reconnecting, reflecting, and participating in family life.

When we examine young people's experiences of these assets, we find that three of the four constructive use of time assets are experienced by half or more of the youth surveyed. However, creative activities (asset 17) is the least reported of all the forty assets.

Commitment to Learning—The first category of internal assets, commitment to learning, is essential to young people in today's changing world. Developing intellectual curiosity and the skills to gain new knowledge and learn from experience is an important task for members of a workforce that must adapt to rapid change.

A commitment to learning can be nurtured in all young people, not just in those who excel academically. The commitment to learning assets measure several dimensions of a young person's engagement with learning in school. In addition, they touch on informal, self-motivated learning and discovery through reading for pleasure (asset 25).

Three of the five commitment to learning assets are experienced by at least half of the youth surveyed. However, reading for pleasure (asset 25) is among the least reported of the forty assets. It is also important to note that females are much more likely than males (at least a 10 percent difference) to report all of the commitment to learning assets.

Positive Values—Positive values are important internal compasses that guide young people's priorities and choices. Although we seek to nurture many positive values in our young people, the asset framework focuses on six widely held values that help prevent high-risk behaviors and promote caring for others.

The first two positive values assets are prosocial values that involve caring for others and the world. For the well-being of any society, young people need to learn how and when to suspend personal gain for the welfare of others. The four remaining positive values assets focus more on personal character. These values provide a basis for wise decision making.

Almost two-thirds of young people see themselves as having three of the positive values related to personal character: integrity (asset 28), honesty (asset 29), and responsibility (asset 30). Less common are the values of caring for others and the world. Valuing restraint (asset 31) is also reported by less than half of the youth surveyed (42 percent).

Social Competencies—The social competencies assets reflect the important personal skills young people need to negotiate through the maze of choices and challenges they face. Two of the social competencies assets (32, planning and decision making, and 35, resistance skills) emphasize making personal choices. The other three (33, interpersonal competence; 34, cultural competence; and 36, peaceful conflict resolution) focus on healthy interpersonal relationships. These skills also lay a foundation for independence and competence as young adults. They give young people the tools they need to live out their values, beliefs, and priorities.

Each of the five social competencies is experienced by fewer than half of the young people surveyed. In addition, there is a considerable gap between the reports of females and males in the social competencies, with females being more likely to report all of the social competencies assets.

Positive Identity—The positive identity assets focus on young people's view of themselves. Without these assets, young people risk feeling powerless and without a sense of initiative and purpose. These assets may be particularly important for young people whom the dominant culture identifies as different, whether that difference has to do with gender, skin color, spiritual beliefs, sexual orientation, size and shape, or any number of other possibilities.

Two of the positive identity assets (asset 39, sense of purpose, and asset 40, positive view of personal future) are reported by more than half of the youth surveyed. A positive view of one's personal future has the highest percentage of any of the forty assets. Unlike other categories of assets, reports of the positive identity assets remain relatively stable or actually increase from sixth to twelfth grade. Personal power (asset 37) climbs by 16 percentage points across the grade span. One might expect reports of the positive identity assets to increase over the course of adolescence, because adolescence is a time in which a great deal of this development takes place.

The Power of Developmental Assets

Developmental assets are powerful predictors of behavior across all cultural and socioeconomic groups of youth. They serve as *protective* factors, inhibiting, for example, alcohol and other drug abuse, violence, sexual intercourse, and school failure. They serve as *enhancement* factors, promoting positive developmental outcomes. The more of the assets a young person has, the lower the involvement in high-risk behavior (protection) and the greater the positive outcomes (enhancement).

The Protective Power—The developmental assets inoculate youth against a wide range of risk-taking behaviors, ranging from substance use to violence and school failure. As assets rise in number, all forms of risk taking decrease (Leffert et al., 1998). Table 2 shows the percentage of sixth- to twelfth-grade students who engage in several different patterns of high-risk behavior as a function of how many assets they have. In every case, each increase in the level of assets is tied to a substantial decrease in each form of behavior.

The Enhancing Power—Healthy development should not be defined only on the basis of reducing health-compromising

TABLE 2   Youth Who Report Engagement in Each High-Risk Behavior Pattern, by Levels of Developmental Assets

High-Risk Behavior Pattern and Definition	Youth with 0–10 Assets	Youth with 11–20 Assets	Youth with 21–30 Assets	Youth with 31–40 Assets
Antisocial Behavior—Young person has been involved in three or more incidents of shoplifting, trouble with police, or vandalism in the past 12 months.	52%	23%	7%	1%
Depression and/or Attempted Suicide—Young person reports being frequently depressed and/or having attempted suicide.	40%	25%	13%	4%
Driving and Alcohol—Young person has driven after drinking or ridden with a drinking driver three or more times in the past 12 months.	42%	24%	10%	4%
Gambling—Young person has gambled three or more times in the past 12 months.	34%	23%	13%	6%
Illicit Drug Use—Young person has used illicit drugs three or more times in the past 12 months.	42%	19%	6%	1%
Problem Alcohol Use—Young person has used alcohol three or more times in the past 30 days or has gotten drunk once or more in the past two weeks.	53%	30%	11%	3%
School Problems—Young person has skipped school two or more days in the past four weeks and/or has below a C average.	43%	19%	7%	2%
Sexual Intercourse—Young person has had sexual intercourse three or more times in her or his lifetime.	33%	21%	10%	3%
Tobacco Use—Young person smokes one or more cigarettes every day or frequently chews tobacco.	45%	21%	6%	1%
Violence—Young person has engaged in three or more acts of fighting, hitting, injuring a person, carrying or using a weapon, or threatening physical harm in the past 12 months.	61%	35%	16%	6%

N = 99,462 sixth- to twelfth-grade youth in public and alternative schools in 213 communities in twenty-three states during the 1996–1997 school year.

behavior. Healthy development also includes the proactive embrace of life-enhancing attitudes and behaviors.

Developmental assets also promote positive actions and dispositions, which we call indicators of thriving (Scales, Benson, and Leffert, 2000). Positive choices increase dramatically as the number of assets increase. This is true in many different areas of thriving, including school success, the affirmation of diversity, choosing to show care and concern for friends or neighbors, gravitating to leadership, and taking care of one's health

TABLE 3   Youth Who Report Experiencing Each Thriving Indicator, by Levels of Developmental Assets

Thriving Indicator and Definition	Youth with 0-10 Assets	Youth with 11-20 Assets	Youth with 21-30 Assets	Youth with 31-40 Assets
Succeeding in School—Young person reports getting mostly A's on her or his report card.	7%	19%	35%	53%
Valuing Diversity—Young person places high importance on getting to know people of other racial and ethnic groups.	34%	53%	69%	87%
Helping Others—Young person helps friends or neighbors one or more hours per week.	69%	83%	91%	97%
Overcoming Adversity—Youth report that they do not give up when things get difficult.	57%	69%	79%	86%
Delaying Gratification—Young person saves money for something special rather than spending it all right away.	27%	42%	56%	72%
Resisting Danger—Young person avoids doing things that are dangerous.	6%	15%	29%	43%
Exhibiting Leadership—Young person has been a leader of a group or organization in the past 12 months.	48%	67%	78%	87%
Maintaining Good Health—Young person pays attention to healthy nutrition and exercise.	25%	46%	69%	88%

N = 99,462 sixth- to twelfth-grade youth in public and alternative schools in 213 communities in twenty-three states during the 1996–1997 school year.

through good nutrition or exercise, as shown in Table 3.

Gaps in Experiences of Developmental Assets

Thus, the developmental assets are powerful influences in young people's lives. Children and adolescents are best able to navigate through the challenges of growing up when they are armed with these assets. The more of these assets young people experience, the better.

Yet too few youth experience enough of these assets. Young people report having, on average, eighteen of the forty assets. Although we see some variation across communities and in different subgroups of youth, the variation does not detract from the overall pattern: The vast majority of youth—regardless of age, gender, race/ethnicity, family composition, family income level, and community size—experience far too few of these forty developmental assets.

This portrait of developmental assets is unsettling. We cannot be sure what happens in the long term to the high percentage of American youth who do not currently possess asset strength. Calculated at a personal level, the effects may be somewhat imperceptible. But calculated at a national level, summing across millions of youth, the cumulative effects on society will be substantial.

Rebuilding the Foundation

In addition to providing a benchmark for understanding the challenges facing today's adolescents, the framework of developmental assets offers a vision to guide communities in setting priorities and taking action. The asset-building vision reaches beyond programs and schools to focus energy on mobilizing and equipping individual residents and all community sectors to reclaim their responsibility for young people. Search Institute has identified seven goals for transforming communities into places that are rich with asset building (Benson, 1997).

1. *A Shared Vision*—A shared vision for asset building in the community is a powerful tool for communicating the gap between the real and the ideal among our youth and for motivating all residents and systems to redirect their energy toward fulfilling the vision. The framework and language of developmental assets make possible broad public support for and positive engagement in the lives of children and youth throughout the community.

2. *Widely Shared Norms and Beliefs*—Activating a community's asset-building power requires the broad acceptance of the belief that all residents have capacity and the responsibility to promote assets. These beliefs need to become self-perceptions internalized by all residents and normative expectations that residents have for each other.

3. *Connections across Socializing Systems*—Currently, socializing systems in communities work in isolation. Building partnership across neighborhood, family, schools, religious institutions, youth organizations, and businesses requires creating mechanisms of dialogue and consensus building. The goal of connection building is to increase consistency in asset building across socializing systems.

4. *Spontaneous Acts of Asset Building*—Perhaps more than half of a community's asset-building potential resides in daily relationships—some fleeting, some sustained—between young people and adults, and between children and adolescents. Some of these acts are simple gestures, some are conversations, some are moments of recognition and value.

5. *Unleashing the Power of Organizations and Systems*—In the same way that individuals must be moved to build assets, a parallel goal is to stimulate and empower organizations and institutions to become intentional about asset building. Included here are the primary socializing systems (families, schools, religious institutions, neighborhoods, youth organizations) that have regular, ongoing, and direct contact with young people. In addition, the secondary systems (such as businesses, healthcare providers, foundations, justice systems, the media, government) play an important role, as their actions and policies undergird—or interfere with—creating a caring community for young people.

6. *Identifying and Expanding the Reach of Formal Asset-Building Activities*—Though asset building is largely a relational process, it also needs a programmatic face. Programs not only offer structured opportunities for intentional, focused asset building, but they give opportunities to enhance asset-building skills and strengthen relationships. Communities must identify the positive activities, make them known and available, equip them and strengthen their effec-

tiveness, and work diligently to expand their reach.

7. *Introduce New Initiatives*—What else happens in an asset-building community? New initiatives should be planned and implemented, guided by an audit of what is and is not available. An audit should address questions about available safe and enriching places for young people to spend time, opportunities for intergenerational contact and relationship, opportunities to lead and serve, adequate support for families, and activities that strengthen and enrich specific cultural traditions.

Peter L. Benson

See also Cognitive Development; Developmental Challenges; Self-Esteem; Temperament

References and further reading
Benson, Peter L. 1997. *All Kids Are Our Kids: What Communities Must Do to Raise Caring and Responsible Children and Adolescents.* San Francisco: Jossey-Bass.
Benson, Peter L., Nancy Leffert, Peter C. Scales, and Dale A. Blyth. 1998. "Beyond the 'Village' Rhetoric: Creating Healthy Communities for Children and Adolescents." *Applied Developmental Science* 2: 138–159.
Benson, Peter L., Peter C. Scales, Nancy Leffert, and Eugene C. Roehlkepartain. 1999. *A Fragile Foundation: The State of Developmental Assets among American Youth.* Minneapolis, MN: Search Institute.
Leffert, Nancy, Peter L. Benson, Peter C. Scales, Anu R. Sharma, Dy R. Drake, and Dale A. Blyth. 1998. "Developmental Assets: Measurement and Prediction of Risk Behaviors among Adolescents." *Applied Developmental Science* 2: 209–230.
Scales, Peter C., and Nancy Leffert. 1999. *Developmental Assets: A Synthesis of the Scientific Research on Adolescent Development.* Minneapolis, MN: Search Institute.
Scales, Peter C., Peter L. Benson, and Nancy Leffert. 2000. "Contribution of Developmental Assets to the Prediction of Thriving among Adolescents." *Applied Developmental Science* 4: 27–46.

Developmental Challenges

At the beginning of the second decade of life, internal and external bodily changes, cognitive and emotional changes, and relationship changes begin to occur. At this point, a person can be said to be an adolescent. It is with these three sets of changes—biological, psychological, and social—that the person must deal if he or she is to move adaptively through the period of adolescence. In fact, dealing with these changes constitutes the major developmental challenge of this period of life.

Biology

Adolescence is certainly a matter of biology: Teenagers must cope with both changing physical appearance, such as new bodily characteristics, and changing physiological functions, such as the beginning of the menstrual cycle or the first ejaculation. Indeed, when they look in the mirror, they see themselves differently: Hair is growing in places where it has not grown before, the complexion is changing, and the body is taking on a different shape. Moreover, new feelings, new "stirrings," are emanating from the body, and the teens begin to wonder what all this means and what they will become.

These biological changes must be understood and accepted as part of the self if adolescents are to avoid becoming alienated or even frightened and confused by what is happening to them. They must come to accept these changes as part of who they are now and what they

The person must deal with three sets of changes—biological, psychological, and social—if he or she is to move adaptively through adolescence. (Shirley Zeiberg)

may become. For example: "I am a person who has breasts, who can become pregnant, who can be a mother." In short, these biological changes must be coped with—understood—if an adaptive sense of self is to emerge.

Psychology
Interrelated with the biological changes just noted are psychological changes that involve thinking, feeling, and self-definition (identity), and these arise because adolescence is also a matter of psychology. New characteristics of cognition and emotion arise during this period: Teenagers can now think in terms of abstractions and hypotheticals, and they begin to experience feelings relating to genital sexuality. These new psychological characteristics must themselves be coped with. Indeed, adolescents need to recognize abstractions and hypotheses as different from reality if they are to interact adaptively in the world, and they must find socially appropriate ways to deal with their sexuality if they are to avoid problems of health and adjustment.

It is, most centrally, the development of new cognitive abilities that allows adolescents to understand their current physical and physiological characteristics and to contemplate what these characteristics are likely to mean for them as individuals. For example: "My breasts probably won't grow much more, but I'm sure my complexion will clear up. I'll be pretty. And I think I'll be able to attract a nice-looking guy someday."

Put another way, adolescents' new thought capabilities allow them to know who they are, given their changing characteristics as individuals; allow them to guess who they might become; and allow

them to plan what they may do with their new feelings.

The main demand imposed by the psychological changes of adolescence is to form a revised sense of self—a new self-definition. It is this self-definition that, in recognition of who adolescents understand themselves to be and plan to become, allows them to choose where they want to end up in life. For example: "I'm too skinny and small to play in team sports. Besides, I like reading and writing more than athletics. If I work hard in school, I think I can become a teacher."

Society and Culture
The psychological changes associated with adolescence blend inextricably with certain social changes. Indeed, adolescence is also a time in which individuals learn about the range of activities and roles available in their social world and come to understand their value. Here, the developmental task is a matter of understanding who one is physically and psychologically in order to find the right role, the correct niche, in one's society.

This developmental task—finding one's social role—is crucial to *adaptive* (i.e., healthy, positive, and successful) functioning. It is one's social role that gives meaning to life, and it is one's responsible and successful performance of this role that will elicit from society the protections, rights, and privileges that safeguard one as a person and allow for continued healthy functioning.

Indeed, achievement of a social role that is suitable to adolescents as individuals as well as helpful to society will be adaptive both for the teens themselves and their social lives. Thus, there is—ideally—a convergence among the three developmental challenges of adolescence, one that allows adolescents to best integrate their changing selves with their social lives.

Richard M. Lerner

See also Conduct Problems; Dyslexia; Learning Disabilities

References and further reading
Demos, David. 1986. *Past, Present, and Personal.* New York: Oxford University Press.
Lerner, Richard M. In press. *Adolescence: Development, Diversity, Context, and Application.* Upper Saddle River, NJ: Prentice-Hall.
Lerner, Richard M., and Nancy Galambos. 1998. "Adolescent Development: Challenges and Opportunities for Research, Programs, and Policies." Pp. 413–446 in *Annual Review of Psychology*, Vol. 49. Edited by J. T. Spence. Palo Alto, CA: Annual Reviews.
Petersen, Anne C. 1988. "Adolescent Development." Pp. 583–607 in *Annual Review of Psychology*, Vol. 39. Edited by R. M. Rosenzweig. Palo Alto, CA: Annual Reviews.

Diabetes

Since the beginning of this century, the spectrum of somatic illnesses in the population has changed. Those groups of illnesses that formerly predominated—infectious diseases and deficiencies such as malnutrition—have lost much of their significance; today, it is the chronic illnesses that hold sway. Juvenile diabetes or Insulin Dependent Diabetes Mellitus (IDDM) is the most common metabolic disease of adolescence. The National Health Interview Survey on a representative sample of the American population revealed a prevalence of 150 cases in 100,000 children and adolescents between the ages of ten and seventeen in 1995.

Diabetes is characterized by a gradual beginning and a progressive, possibly life-shortening course, which poses no severe impairments for the affected adolescent. After a more labile initial phase, most patients of diabetes show a relatively stable course. The manifestation of juvenile diabetes ensues more rapidly, unlike the adult form of diabetes, and may occur within several weeks. The typical course displays a series of distinct phases. With appropriate therapy, an initial remission is achieved and the need for insulin decreases. A second phase of relative metabolic stability follows, which turns into a phase of full diabetes after the exhaustion of the body's own production of insulin. The need for insulin increases again during puberty ("labile pubertal phase") and adjustment becomes difficult. As puberty draws to a close, a condition of relative metabolic stability gradually emerges, with a constant but high need for insulin ("postpubertal stabilization phase").

Complications of diabetes are the diabetic coma, a direct consequence of an insulin deficit; further delays in growth due to the chronic lack of insulin; and, finally, long-term damage that chiefly affects the eyes and kidneys (such as retinopathy and nephropathy). The development of this long-term damage is more closely associated with the level of metabolic control than with illness duration. The frequency and severity of vascular changes are disproportionately smaller in well-adjusted patients than in patients with poor or fluctuating metabolic control. Medical adaptation can be clearly ascertained through metabolic control (HbA_1 and HbA_1c-values), and the quality of metabolic control is directly related to short- and long-term complications.

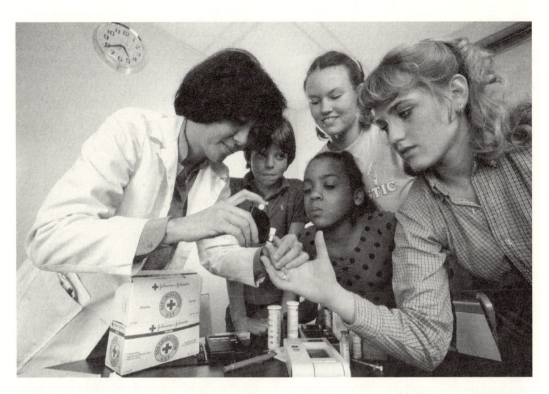

Juvenile diabetes or Insulin Dependent Diabetes Mellitus (IDDM) is the most common metabolic disease of adolescence. (Roger Ressmeyer/Corbis)

HbA$_1$ values greater than 9 are associated with a rapid rise to 30 percent in the risk of long-term damage.

The therapeutic demands on patients and their parents are complex, involving the injection of insulin, monitoring glucose levels in the blood and urine, and attending to dietary regulations on a daily basis. Treatment focuses on the necessary insulin substitutions, associated diet, and physical exercise. These three factors must be sensibly combined and supported by metabolic control. Obviously, diabetes therapy can only be successful if both the adolescent and his or her parents understand the treatment. Accordingly, while adolescents must be intensively and adequately treated med-

ically, the quality of the doctor-patient relationship will also decisively influence their motivation to follow the doctor's advice. The relationship between doctor and patient is thus recognized as essential for compliance and dealing with the illness.

Sensible medical treatment should not focus exclusively on sugar levels; it must take the patient's entire psychosocial situation into consideration. In general, theoretical knowledge and skills in practical self-control increase with the level of cognitive development. From the age of about nine years onward, most children with diabetes are able to inject the necessary insulin by themselves, while reliable urine tests are first observed at about twelve years. Adequate cognitive insight represents a necessary but not sufficient condition for successful coping and—especially—compliance. Very little attention has been paid to developmental factors that can impair the understanding of the diagnosis or occurrence of the illness. Willingness to accept medical offers is often low in adolescents not only with diabetes but also with other chronic illnesses.

A good metabolic control continually demands very much of the adolescent; the problematic metabolism despite precise obedience to doctor's orders in puberty may make all the initiatives look pointless. Compliance is further diminished by the low perceived severity of the illness, the low perceived benefit of preventative or curative behaviors, and the considerable barriers that stand in the way of health-related activities such as insulin injections and diet. These barriers are particularly large when medical procedures hamper age-typical behaviors with the peer group. This is especially a problem in adolescence when the peer group's eating and drinking patterns, mobility, and risk-taking behavior present significant temptations for the ill adolescent. Diabetic adolescents frequently withdraw socially from healthy peers and perceive themselves as less attractive in the eyes of healthy romantic partners. They have to solve the dilemma between adaptation to the illness and overall developmental progression, sometimes at the cost of deterioration of metabolic control. Some studies revealed that diabetic adolescents share the same developmental goals and that their progression in diverse tasks across adolescence is impressive, particularly with respect to developing professional competence. There are, however, also indications of a delay in tasks relating to close relationships, suggesting that diabetic adolescents show lower levels of intimacy and reciprocity in relationships with close friends and romantic partners, and take up romantic relationships later.

Diagnosis and management of the illness also present major long-term stressors for the parents. Although some families have the capacity to adjust to the illness by exploring new behaviors, other families are incapable of devising new strategies. They continue along familiar paths and apply earlier methods to try to meet the adolescent's needs in the new situation. One parent might devote himself or herself to the ill adolescent totally, thereby withdrawing from the other members of the family, a behavior seen most commonly in mothers of diabetic adolescents. In this respect, it is important to clarify the father's role in the family's coping, and whether the relationship between the ill adolescent and his or her siblings is affected. Open and concealed conflicts could arise in the family, and these may undermine treatment and impair the adolescent's adjustment. A fundamental question is how the chronicity of the stressors contributes to dysfunctional behaviors in the family. The stress of an illness could, in itself, possibly be coped with well, but its chronicity can lead to rigidity or a breakdown of coping even in a family that initially functioned well. This is evidenced in the highly structured family climate in most families of adolescents with diabetes, which is independent of illness duration, gender, age, and level of metabolic control. This suggests a developmentally inhibitive effect on all afflicted adolescents.

Inge Seiffge-Krenke

See also Chronic Illnesses in Adolescence; Health Promotion; Health Services for Adolescents

References and further reading
Ahmed, Paul I., and Nancy Ahmed., eds. 1985. *Coping with Juvenile Diabetes.* Springfield, IL: Thomas.
National Adolescent Health Survey. 1989. *A Report on the Health of America's Youth.* Oakland, CA: Third Party.
Sayer, Aline G., Stuart T. Hauser, Alan M. Jacobson, John B. Willett, and Charlotte F. Cole. 1995. "Developmental Influences on Adolescent Health." Pp. 22–51 in *Adolescent Health Problems: Behavioral Perspectives. Advances in Pediatric Psychology.* Edited by J. L. Wallander and L. J. Siegel. New York: Guilford Press.
Seiffge-Krenke, Inge. 2001. *Diabetic Adolescents and Their Families: Stress, Coping, and Adaptation.* New York: Cambridge University Press.

Discipline

Because a major component of parenting is encouraging children to conform to external standards of behavior, discipline plays a central role in parent-child relationships. On the other hand, because adolescence is marked by a sharp increase in the extent to which teenagers must act appropriately in the absence of direct supervision, a major challenge is to move teens from relying on external discipline imposed by the parent to fostering the development of internal discipline. Indeed, rapid changes in the developmental needs of adolescents around the time of puberty require adjustment of previously occurring patterns of discipline. For example, parents need to recognize adolescents' growing need to act more autonomously, their desire for increased responsibility, and their greater ability to understand the reasoning behind parental behavioral demands (Holmbeck, Paikoff,

and Brooks-Gunn, 1995). Over the course of adolescence, the move from externally imposed to internal discipline results in a gradual shift to a more symmetrical power arrangement (Fuligni and Eccles, 1993). Because parents expect their now physically mature children to act in a socially mature manner, the disparity between parent and adolescent expectations may be especially great (Collins, 1990) and the shift from external to internal discipline correspondingly problematic, resulting in heightened conflict between parent and child.

The word *discipline* connotes the means by which natural or intrinsically motivated behaviors are consciously replaced by behaviors that are more socially or functionally desirable. Two key characteristics of discipline are (1) that discipline changes behavior from its natural course and (2) that the change is evoked by conscious processes. Consider, for example, a situation in which it might be necessary to encourage an adolescent to stop playing a video game and to read a class assignment. Discipline would be involved if playing the video game is a desired behavior and reading the assignment is less desirable. But if the adolescent reads the assignment for enjoyment (i.e., for the love of knowledge), discipline is not involved because behavior has not been altered from its natural course. Similarly, if the parent begins to read interesting sections of the assignment out loud and the adolescent leaves the video game to join the parent in reading, discipline is not involved because the change in behavior was motivated by an unconscious increase in the desirability of reading the assignment.

In order for parents to engage in effective discipline, several criteria must be

High, consistent levels of parental discipline are associated with decreased adolescent involvement in problem behaviors and better performance in school. (Jennie Woodcock; Reflections Photolibrary/Corbis)

met: (1) Their standards for adolescent behavior must be different from those of the child, (2) the parents must clearly communicate their standards for desired behaviors, (3) the parents must monitor compliance to their standards, and (4) the parents must react differentially to compliance and noncompliance by rewarding conformity and/or punishing noncompliance. Parenting style varies according to how parents approach issues of discipline or socialization (Baumrind, 1991):

- *Uninvolved parents* make few attempts to discipline their adolescents or communicate standards, exhibit low levels of parental moni-

toring, and are inconsistent in their use of punishments and rewards.

- *Authoritarian parents* are highly oriented toward discipline and conformity, and overextend into the personal domain the "conventional" domain that both parents and adolescents agree parents have the right to set standards for (Smetana, 1995). They clearly communicate both their standards and the consequences of noncompliance to their children, often making use of punitive discipline. Authoritarian parents use relatively high levels of behavioral control to establish discipline, but they also make use of psychological control, employing guilt induction, withdrawal of love, and shaming to induce compliance (Barber, 1996). Conversely, these parents make little use of explanation. On the basis of their overt authority, they expect adolescents to conform to their standards. And because of this power-assertive disciplinary style, they may have difficulty monitoring the behavior of their adolescents as the latter begin to spend less and less time under the direct supervision of adults, and the parents themselves become more dependent upon adolescent disclosure (Darling, Cumsille, and Dowdy, 1998). This may be especially true for *authoritarian-directive parents*, who are highly intrusive.

- *Indulgent, or permissive, parents* make few disciplinary demands for conformity to social or parental standards, overextending the "personal" domain in which both parents and adolescents agree that the adolescent should be solely responsible for his or her own decisions (Smetana, 1995). Indulgent parents are warm and communicate clearly to their child, but they also rely heavily on the internal discipline of the adolescent for compliance, avoid confrontation, are noncontingent in their use of rewards, and inconsistent in sanctioning violations of standards. Two types of indulgent parents can be distinguished: *democratic parents*, who are conscientious, communicate high standards, and successfully monitor compliance, and *nondirective parents*, who are warm but provide little external discipline.

- *Authoritative parents* are effective in all four areas necessary for effective discipline: (1) They clearly communicate high standards and expectations for conformity. (2) Their use of explanations, willingness to compromise, and encouragement of discussion facilitates monitoring, communication, and the development of adolescent self-discipline in the context of parental regulation. (3) Though consistent in punishing inappropriate behavior, they focus on supportive rather than punitive discipline and make effective use of rewards. (4) Their use of high behavioral control but low psychological control allows adolescents to develop autonomy and self-discipline within a safe context of clear parental authority.

High, consistent levels of parental discipline are associated with decreased adolescent involvement in problem behaviors and better performance in school (Baumrind, 1991). However, the context of discipline is critical. Power assertion, extreme punishment, and lack of follow-through (a pattern called "coercive" parenting) are associated with adolescent psychopathology and high rates of problem behaviors. Whereas punishment tends to inhibit negative behavior in children without adjustment difficulties, it increases negative behaviors in antisocial children (Patterson, 1982; Holmbeck, Paikoff, and Brooks-Gunn, 1995). One reason that authoritative parents may be successful in maintaining external discipline and inculcating internal discipline in their adolescents is that they combine high, consistent levels of discipline with discussion that legitimates and validates their authority. By contrast, firm control in the absence of legitimacy and compromise can undermine children's feelings of self-reliance and intrinsic motivation, thereby disrupting development of the internal discipline that is the ultimate goal of socialization (Holmbeck, Paikoff, and Brooks-Gunn, 1995).

Nancy Darling

See also Parent-Adolescent Relations; Parental Monitoring; Parenting Styles; Physical Abuse

References and further reading
Barber, Brian K. 1996. "Parental Psychological Control: Revisiting a Neglected Construct." *Child Development*, 67, no. 6: 3296–3319.
Baumrind, Diana. 1991. "The Influence of Parenting Style on Adolescent Competence and Substance Use." *Journal of Early Adolescence* 11, no. 1: 56–95.
Collins, W. Andrew. 1990. "Parent-Child Relationships in the Transition to Adolescence: Continuity and Change in Interaction, Affect, and Cognition." Pp. 85–106 in *Advances in Adolescent Development: From Childhood to Adolescence: A Transitional Period?* Vol. 2. Edited by R. Montemayor, G. Adams, and T. Gullotta. Beverly Hills, CA: Sage.
Darling, Nancy, Patricio E. Cumsille, and Bonnie Dowdy. 1998. "Parenting Style, Legitimacy of Parental Authority, and Adolescents' Willingness to Share Information with Their Parents: Why Do Adolescents Lie?" Paper presented at the June 1998 meeting of the International Society for the Study of Personal Relationships, Saratoga, NY.
Fuligni, Andrew U., and Jacquelynne S. Eccles. 1993. "Perceived Parent-Child Relationships and Early Adolescents' Orientation toward Peers." *Developmental Psychology* 29: 622–632.
Holmbeck, Grayson N., Roberta L. Paikoff, and Jeanne Brooks-Gunn. 1995. "Parenting Adolescents." Pp. 91–118 in *Handbook of Parenting*. Vol. 1, *Children and Parenting*. Edited by Marcus H. Bornstein. Mahwah, NJ: Lawrence Erlbaum Associates.
Patterson, Gerald R. 1982. *Coercive Family Processes*. Eugene, OR: Castalia.
Smetana, Judith G. 1995. "Parenting Styles and Conceptions of Parental Authority during Adolescence." *Child Development* 66: 299–316.

Disorders, Psychological and Social

Psychological and social disorders are often a consequence of deviation from the typical development pattern. Many of these disorders begin earlier than adolescence but become more apparent or more problematic during the teen years. The deviation may have biological causes; for example, some mood disorders have been linked to chemical imbalances in the brain. Alternatively, it may surface as a result of environmental/social causes; for example, family dysfunction can produce unusually high levels of stress in some teenagers. Understanding the vulnerability of teenagers to psychological or social disorders is the first step in helping to prevent and treat them. Among adolescents, such difficulties can have long-term implications as they may impact all aspects of functioning. Some difficulties are easier to diagnose and treat than others, but the key is getting help.

Stress and Coping

When considering psychological and social disorders in teenagers, we need to understand a little bit about stress and coping. *Stress* can be defined as emotional tension. As human beings we all experience emotional tension at one time or another, and many people experience low to moderate levels of stress on a regular basis. Stress may result from normal (even positive) life events such as a transition from a small middle school to a larger high school, a first relationship, or a tryout for a theatrical performance or a sports team. However, stress may also result when one feels threatened or unsafe. For example, disturbance in one's family may cause feelings of insecurity and uncertainty that in turn produce high levels of unrelenting stress. Two important factors to consider when thinking about stress are chronicity (a measure of how long the stress continues) and ability to cope. Some stress is related to specific events, ending when the event is over or when the individual develops a coping strategy. Final exams are a case in point. They may be a stressful time for some students, but, in the majority of cases, the feelings of stress decline once the exams are over and may decline somewhat even as the individual begins to study and feel more prepared for the exams. Chronic stress, by contrast, continues without much of a respite. For example, a teen living with an abusive parent may be in a situation of unrelenting chronic stress.

Two teens in a similar situation may have very different reactions based on their interpretation of the situation and their ability to cope with or manage their reactions to the situation. *Coping* can be defined as the effort made to manage stress. Some teens whose lives are unusually stressful have better coping strategies than others in similar circumstances. Those teens who experience high levels of stress but are less able to cope are at risk for developing psychological and social disorders. Practicing successful coping with stress helps some people become even better at actually coping. Feeling supported by others during a stressful time can also be helpful in terms of coping. This last point suggests the importance of finding someone who

Psychological and social disorders are often a consequence of deviation from typical developmental patterns. (Skjold Photographs)

can be a source of support. Peers are certainly capable of providing support to one another, but adults are perhaps even more critical sources of support for teens experiencing stress. Teenagers typically use a variety of coping strategies, such as listening to or playing music, engaging in physical activity, playing video games, and hanging out with friends. Teens may also experiment with substances (alcohol and drugs) as a means of alleviating feelings of stress—a behavior sometimes called self-medication. Although this, too, is a coping strategy and may offer a temporary escape from stress, it is maladaptive because substance use can cause both short- and long-term harm to the individual.

Stress and coping are important variables in many common teenage problems. Once diagnosed, however, the vast majority of these problems can be successfully addressed and treated.

Learning Disabilities
Learning disabilities are an example of a common problem that can be addressed once diagnosed. They usually involve

some kind of difficulty with processing information. For example, some learning-disabled people have difficulty reading or following oral instructions. These people are not unintelligent; they simply process information differently and may therefore need assistance in developing strategies for completing school-based tasks. Learning disabilities that remain undiagnosed prevent appropriate school progress and may thus have long-term consequences for emotional well-being.

Disruptive Behavior Disorders
Another category of problems experienced by adolescents is known as disruptive behavior disorders. One example is attention-deficit/hyperactivity disorder (ADHD). Teenagers with ADHD exhibit a pattern of behavior that includes difficulty sustaining attention, distractibility, impulsiveness, and hyperactivity. Those whose ADHD has not been diagnosed may be labeled as behavior problems in school when in fact they are in need of treatment—and, indeed, treatment is available that can be quite effective in helping them to control their behavior.

Another example is oppositional defiant disorder (ODD), which involves a pattern of uncooperative, hostile behavior toward authority. The chronicity of ODD is what differentiates it from typical teen opposition to being told what to do. Teens with ODD generally have little self-understanding and are limited in their ability to take responsibility for consequences. They are also quick to blame others for their own shortcomings and slow to recognize their own responsibility. Symptoms even more extreme than those associated with ODD, such as physical aggression, violence, and law breaking, may point to conduct disorder. Conduct disorder involves serious distur-

bance and in many cases is diagnosed only after teens have become involved in criminal activity requiring the intervention of law enforcement and juvenile justice agencies.

Eating Disorders
Eating disorders are among the most common psychological disorders of adolescence. They are often linked to society's obsession with thinness and lookism, and with the individual's need to exercise control over the environment. Once believed to be primarily restricted to females, eating disorders are now increasingly being diagnosed in teenage males. Although the vast majority of those diagnosed are still female, the recognition of risk signs in males is important in terms of both prevention and intervention. Athletes, male as well as female, whose athletic participation may hinge on weight and size (e.g., wrestlers, gymnasts) may be at particularly high risk for developing eating disorders.

Anorexia nervosa and bulimia nervosa are the two major categories of eating disorders. Anorexia nervosa involves an intense fear of gaining weight and a grossly distorted body image. Anorexic individuals may report feeling fat though in reality they are emaciated. The disorder usually involves overly restricted caloric intake, often accompanied by excessive exercise. Ultimately, individuals with anorexia nervosa suffer from self-starvation and, without treatment, can die from this condition. Bulimia nervosa (which is sometimes combined with anorexia nervosa) can also become a life-threatening condition. Occurring in people of below-, average, and above-average weight, bulimia is characterized by binge eating, a fear of not being able to control the binge eating, recognition that the eating pattern is not normal, and feelings of low self-worth following each binge episode. Bulimia may also involve purging (i.e., vomiting or use of laxatives), excessive exercise, and overly restricted caloric intake following a binge cycle.

Why do some adolescents develop eating disorders? Despite the prevalence of these disorders, psychologists have not yet arrived at a definitive answer to this question. Most experts do agree, however, that no single factor is implicated. Indeed, many factors, including developmental stage, culture, personality, and family functioning, must be considered. Developmental stage refers to the changes that take place in early and late adolescence. These many changes, which include transformation of the body from that of a child to that of an adult, an emerging sense of identity, and new social and academic challenges, help explain why eating disorders are so common among adolescents. Culture refers to the many cultural standards for attractiveness. Attractiveness is defined differently in different cultures and even in the same culture in different eras. For example, a full figure and curves were once considered the standard of feminine beauty. However, our present culture, as reflected by popular models, values thinness. Personality refers to the personality development of the individual. Some experts suggest that individuals with certain personality types are at higher risk for eating disorders. For example, some experts believe that individuals suffering from anorexia nervosa are high achievers who strive for perfection and control. Family refers to a variety of factors involved in family functioning. Some experts believe that eating disorders can be traced to these family-functioning variables.

Eating disorders are complex in nature; for more information on this issue, see "Eating Problems" in this volume.

Depression
Depression is a type of affective disorder. Affective disorders are mood related and are believed to be linked to an imbalance in some brain chemicals. Depression can be of long or short duration, of low or high intensity. Depression as a clinical term does not mean having a bad day or feeling down; it refers to an inability to experience pleasure from activities or relationships that would have, prior to the depression, been sources of happiness and pleasure. In certain circumstances, such as in reaction to a death in the family, feelings of depression may be a normal and appropriate response. Depression becomes problematic when it occurs in inappropriate circumstances, continues for a long period, or is of such great intensity as to be out of proportion to the cause. Depression can be harmful to a teen's well-being when it interferes with the capacity to go about one's daily business (school/work), to relate to others, or to maintain the healthy functioning of essential physical needs for sleep, nutrition, and personal hygiene. Typical signs of depression are changes in everyday life patterns, for example, major changes in sleep patterns (sleeping much more than usual or much less than usual; may also include insomnia, which is an inability to sleep), weight gain or weight loss, loss of appetite and/or overeating. Behavior changes are also typical warning signs of depression. For instance, loss of interest in activities, loss of pleasure in activities, excessive fatigue, and restlessness may all be signs of depression. In teenagers, depression may also manifest itself with agitation, irritability, and anger. These

symptoms are often overlooked or misinterpreted because they do not seem typical of the stereotyped low energy of depression. Yet these signs are important to notice in teens because they may be the only way a struggling teen, who may be unaware that s/he needs help, or unable to ask for the help that is needed, can show signs of distress. Although not all depressed teens are suicidal, teens suffering from depression are at increased risk for suicide. This risk further highlights the importance of intervention for teens suffering from depression because timely intervention can help to prevent a tragedy. The most common treatments for depression are psychotherapy, which involves talking with a trained professional, and/or medication that is prescribed by a physician (often in conjunction with psychotherapy). In some more severe cases, hospitalization may be necessary to ensure the safety of the individual until a treatment plan can be established. For more information and detail see the entry on "Depression."

Schizophrenia and Borderline Personality Disorder

Schizophrenia and borderline personality disorder are more serious psychological disorders and much less common than mood disorders. Schizophrenia is usually not diagnosed until late adolescence or early adulthood, and there are often other diagnoses before the schizophrenic diagnosis is reached. An inability to think and behave rationally is characteristic of schizophrenia. Although many teenagers may have moments of seemingly irrational thought, extreme irrationality and bizarre behavior is the norm for someone suffering from schizophrenia. Though there are some newer, more promising

treatments for schizophrenia, it is a disease that can be difficult to treat.

Although serious mental disorders are relatively unusual in adolescents, borderline personality disorder is another mental disorder sometimes recognized in teenagers. Borderline personality disorder is sometimes diagnosed in teenagers who do not have the fully developed symptoms of schizophrenia but show some signs of distorted thinking. However, unlike those suffering with schizophrenia who may experience great difficulty with daily functioning, individuals with borderline personality disorder may be able to function suffering from periodic rather than constant breakdowns of rational thought. These breakdowns are sometimes triggered by stress and/or major life changes (like a change in schools). Difficulty maintaining relationships is characteristic of individuals suffering from one of the forms of psychological disturbance.

Suicide

Mood disorders and other serious mental disturbance may be accompanied by suicidal feelings. Sadly, many teens may feel so troubled or hopeless that they contemplate suicide. There are numerous warning signs of a suicidal teen. However, a teen can be suicidal without showing many overt signs. Unfortunately, adults who may have heard about the warning signs for suicide often watch for teens to show all or many of the signs before intervening. Sadly, this waiting can lead to a tragic loss of life. The warning signs for suicide are similar to those for depression. And as mentioned previously, depressed teens are at a higher risk for suicide than their nondepressed peers. These warning signs include (but are not restricted to) changes in sleeping and eating patterns, changes in personality (previously outgoing individuals may become withdrawn), changes in friends/friendships (avoiding friends or social contacts), drug and alcohol use, boredom and lethargy, risk-taking behaviors (car/bicycle accidents), a preoccupation with death, giving away possessions, and suicidal comments (you'd be better off without me, I wish I were dead). A troubling or traumatic life event (for example, loss of a loved one, the suicide of a friend or relative, an assault) are also risk factors for suicide in teens. All of the above are important warning signs of significant distress and should never be ignored.

Anxiety Disorders
Also important when thinking about psychological and social problems of adolescents are issues of anxiety and phobias. All people experience some anxiety and this is normal and natural. Change and uncertainty can trigger normal feelings of anxiety, so it is not surprising that adolescents who may be experiencing much change may also feel somewhat anxious. However, when anxiety lasts for a long time and is fairly intense, it can interfere with normal functioning. Symptoms of an anxiety problem may include restlessness, feelings of low self-worth, excessive worrying, and fearfulness. Extreme anxiety may also be accompanied by physical symptoms like headaches and muscle aches. These symptoms may signal a problem and need for intervention.

Some individuals who suffer from anxiety disorders may experience panic attacks. Panic attacks are sudden attacks of intense anxiety. During panic attacks individuals experience both physical and psychological symptoms. The physical symptoms may include heart racing, excessive sweating, dizziness, chest pains, and nausea. Sufferers may believe that they are having a heart attack. The psychological symptoms can include excessive worries of impending doom, feelings of a lack of control, and feelings that one is crazy.

Phobias are another form of anxiety disorder. A phobia is an excessive (and often unexplained) fear that is out of proportion to the object of the fear. Because the fear is much greater than the actual threat, feelings that result from phobias are not considered rational. The focus of an individual's phobia may change with age (from monsters as a child to social situations as a teen). A specific example of phobias in adolescents is school phobia or school avoidance. School phobia may develop when a teen experiences a problem (either academic or social) that is so overwhelming that s/he withdraws and feels unable to attend school. School phobia may not be obvious at first because the teen may have accompanying psychosomatic symptoms (symptoms that may seem like physical health problems but have no known medical or organic cause). Therefore, the student may be absent from school because of these complaints long before anyone realizes that there may be an underlying anxiety problem. Individuals suffering from phobias should receive treatment to prevent significant impairment of daily function.

Obsessive-Compulsive Disorder
Obsessive-compulsive disorder (OCD) is a mental health issue that has received increased attention in recent years. Obsessive-compulsive disorder involves a driving need to engage in or repeat certain behaviors in a ritualized way. As the

name indicates, obsessive-compulsive disorder involves both obsessions and compulsions. Obsessions are characterized as intrusive thoughts that push their way into the mind of the teen (for example, excessive thoughts and worries about germs). Compulsions are repeated, ritualized behaviors that the teen feels s/he must perform (for example, checking, double checking, and triple checking a locked door). The need to perform these ritualized behaviors, for example, excessive hand washing, can significantly interfere with and impair a teen's normal daily functioning. Untreated, obsessive-compulsive disorder can severely impair normal functioning. Research suggests that there is a biochemical component to OCD, which means that it can often be successfully treated with medications that target certain brain chemicals. Individuals suffering from OCD may not recognize that they are suffering from a disorder and may instead be ashamed of their behavior and reluctant to ask for help.

A disorder that is sometimes related to OCD is Tourette's disorder. Tourette's disorder is characterized by tics, which are quick, repetitive muscle twitches or vocalizations (noises). Tics are sometimes accompanied by behaviors similar to those found with OCD and ADHD. Tourette's disorder is also often treated with medication.

Deborah N. Margolis

See also Attention-Deficit/Hyperactivity Disorder (ADHD); Depression; Eating Problems

References and further reading
Kaysen, Susanna. 1993. *Girl Interrupted.* New York: Vintage Books.
Rapoport, Judith. 1989. *The Boy Who Couldn't Stop Washing.* New York: Plume.

Divorce

Divorce is commonplace in today's society. About half of American children experience the divorce of their parents before they reach the age of eighteen. This circumstance is not easy at any age; in the short term, many of the affected children and teenagers exhibit such problems as poor school effort and grades; depressed, anxious, or angry moods; and noncompliant or antisocial behavior (Emery, 1999). Typically, emotional and behavioral disturbances are temporary, with most children improving markedly by the second year after the divorce (Hetherington, 1989; Buchanan, 2000). In the longer term, as discussed below, divorce is associated with an increased risk of mental, emotional, behavioral, and relational problems. Still, many teenagers do quite well after divorce. Positive functioning after divorce is predicted by such factors as low interparental conflict, positive parent-child relationships, and low levels of overall life stress and instability. Relatively speaking, custody arrangement has little to do with long-term adjustment (Buchanan, Maccoby, and Dornbusch, 1996).

Teenagers whose parents have divorced are at an increased risk for internalizing problems (e.g., depression), externalizing problems (e.g., aggression, deviance, early sexual behavior), and problems in academic achievement, including high school dropout (Allison and Furstenberg, 1989; Amato and Keith, 1991). Yet there is evidence that a divorce during a child's adolescent years is less damaging in the long run than a divorce that occurs when a child is younger (Allison and Furstenberg, 1989; see also Emery, 1999, for detailed information on age effects). The risk for teenagers may be lower than that for younger children owing to teenagers' greater cognitive competence to understand the divorce and their more numerous social networks outside of the family that can provide support. At all ages, however, there is a risk associated with divorce.

The good news is that the magnitude of the increased risk explained by divorce is small, with parents' marital status typically accounting for between 1 and 3 percent of the variance in adolescent and young adult adjustment (Allison and Furstenberg, 1989; Amato and Keith, 1991). In fact, the most notable finding from research on long-term adjustment after divorce is the variability present in both postdivorce family functioning and children's adjustment (Amato, 1993; Buchanan, Maccoby, and Dornbusch, 1996). Some children thrive; others flounder. Most function in the normal range (Emery, 1999).

Recent research has focused on the question of what factors explain the variability in functioning after divorce. What follows is a discussion of some of the major individual and situational predictors of adjustment among teenagers who have experienced the divorce of their parents. (See Buchanan, 2000, for a more extensive treatment of these and other factors.)

Interparental Conflict

The extent to which conflict continues after divorce (and how it is handled when it does continue) is one of the most important factors in a child's adjustment (Amato, 1993; Emery, 1999). Conflict in couples often peaks at the time of a divorce (Cummings and Davies, 1994). In most cases, conflict subsides after the first year or two following divorce, but about one-quarter or fewer of divorcing couples continue to experience moderate to high conflict over the longer term (e.g., Maccoby and Mnookin, 1992). Research is consistent in showing that interparental conflict is a more powerful predictor of children's adjustment than is divorce status, and that accounting for the level of conflict a couple experiences usually reduces or even eliminates the relation between divorce and adjustment (e.g., Emery, 1999; Simons et al., 1999). Furthermore, when interparental conflict decreases following a divorce, children adjust significantly better than when conflict continues at a high level (e.g., Emery, 1999).

Parenting and the Parent-Child Relationship

A positive, close relationship between teenagers and their custodial parents, especially if that custodial parent is the mother, appears critical to postdivorce adjustment—perhaps in part because a close relationship facilitates parental monitoring of adolescents' behavior (Buchanan, Maccoby, and Dornbusch, 1996). Parental monitoring—that is, knowledge of the adolescent's activities and whereabouts—repeatedly surfaces as a critical factor in the adjustment of teenagers from both divorced and nondivorced homes (Buchanan, Maccoby, and Dornbusch, 1996; Patterson, 1986), as do other aspects of competent parenting such as setting firm limits but avoiding harsh punishments (Simons et al., 1999). Continued closeness to the noncustodial parent also appears to be beneficial to adjustment of adolescents—especially if the adolescents also feel close to the custodial parent. Finally, symbolic gestures of commitment by the noncustodial parent, such as remembering birthdays and other special days, appear to be quite important to teenagers, perhaps more important than the absolute amount of time spent in visitation with that parent (Buchanan, Maccoby, and Dornbusch, 1996).

Loyalty conflicts are associated with increased depression and deviance among teenagers in divorced families (Buchanan, Maccoby, and Dornbusch, 1996). Parental behaviors linked to loyalty conflicts include asking the child to carry messages between parents, asking the child to "spy on" or answer questions about the ex-spouse's home or behavior, and denigrating the ex-spouse in the child's presence. Alignments between a parent and child (whereby a child strongly takes sides with one or the other parent) are linked with lower levels of anxiety than are loyalty conflicts but also with higher levels of anger (Lampel, 1996). Children appear to be best adjusted when allowed and able to sustain positive, close relationships with both parents.

Life Stresses
The total number of life stresses experienced by teenagers whose parents divorce is another strong predictor of their adjustment (Amato, 1993; Buchanan, Maccoby, and Dornbusch, 1996). This conclusion is consistent with research findings on stress more generally, indicating that the greater the total number of life stresses, the greater the probability of psychological, behavioral, emotional, or health problems. Such stresses might include, in addition to the divorce itself or any existing interparental conflict, moving from one house to another, changing neighborhoods or schools, changing contacts or relationships with friends or extended family, and changing extracurricular activities. Conversely, when the number of stresses coinciding with the divorce or

other family problems is minimized, teenagers tend to adjust more positively.

Custody and Visitation Arrangements
In general, the type of custody or visitation arrangement is of little importance relative to the factors considered above (Buchanan, Maccoby, and Dornbusch, 1996; Buchanan, 2000). There are well-adjusted and poorly adjusted adolescents in all types of arrangements. Joint custody is a case in point. When parents are not in high conflict, joint custody allows children to sustain close relationships with both parents and to avoid loyalty conflicts more effectively than in other arrangements (Buchanan, Maccoby, and Dornbusch, 1996). However, when parents remain in high conflict, joint custody is associated with especially high levels of loyalty conflicts as well as other adjustment problems and is ill-advised (Emery, 1999).

Christy M. Buchanan

See also Conflict and Stress; Coping; Parent-Adolescent Relations

References and further reading
Allison, Paul D., and Frank F. Furstenberg Jr. 1989. "Marital Dissolution Affects Children: Variations by Age and Sex." *Developmental Psychology* 25: 540–549.
Amato, Paul R. 1993. "Children's Adjustment to Divorce: Theories, Hypotheses, and Empirical Support." *Journal of Marriage and the Family* 55: 23–38.
Amato, Paul R., and Bruce Keith. 1991. "Parental Divorce and the Well-Being of Children: A Meta-Analysis." *Psychological Bulletin* 100: 26–46.
Buchanan, Christy M. 2000. "The Impact of Divorce on Adjustment during Adolescence." Pp. 179–216 in *Resilience across Contexts: Family, Work, Culture, and Community*. Edited by Ronald D. Taylor and Margaret C.

Wang. Mahwah, NJ: Lawrence Erlbaum Associates.

Buchanan, Christy M., Eleanor E. Maccoby, and Sanford M. Dornbusch. 1996. *Adolescents after Divorce.* Cambridge, MA: Harvard University Press.

Cummings, E. Mark, and Patrick Davies. 1994. *Children and Marital Conflict: The Impact of Family Dispute and Resolution.* New York: Guilford Press.

Emery, Robert E. 1999. *Marriage, Divorce, and Children's Adjustment*, 2nd ed. Newbury Park, CA: Sage Publications.

Hetherington, E. Mavis. 1989. "Coping with Family Transitions: Winners, Losers, and Survivors." *Child Development* 60: 1–14.

Lampel, Anita K. 1996. "Children's Alignment with Parents in Highly Conflicted Custody Cases." *Family and Conciliation Courts Review* 34: 229–239.

Maccoby, Eleanor M., and Robert H. Mnookin. 1992. *Dividing the Child: Social and Legal Dilemmas of Custody.* Cambridge, MA: Harvard University Press.

Patterson, Gerald R. 1986. "Performance Models for Antisocial Boys." *American Psychologist* 41: 432–444.

Simons, Ronald. L., Kuei-Hsiu Lin, Leslie C. Gordon, Rand D. Conger, and Frederick O. Lorenz. 1999. "Explaining the Higher Incidence of Adjustment Problems among Children of Divorce Compared with Those in Two-Parent Families." *Journal of Marriage and the Family* 61: 1020–1033.

Down Syndrome

Down syndrome is a genetic disorder that is usually identified at birth. It occurs in approximately 1 in every 900 births and affects individuals of all ethnic groups and incomes. In the United States, approximately 350,000 individuals have Down syndrome. Down syndrome is the most common genetic cause of mental retardation. Among individuals with Down syndrome, the severity of mental retardation and the extent of learning disability vary significantly.

Most cases of Down syndrome (about 95 percent) are caused by a trisomy (i.e., a third chromosome on chromosome number 21) that affects all cells of the body. Therefore, Down syndrome is sometimes called Trisomy 21. In a small number of individuals with Down syndrome, only some groups of cells have the trisomy; this condition is referred to as mosaicism. In other individuals, only a small amount of extra genetic material, not an entire chromosome, is located on the twenty-first chromosome—a condition known as translocation.

Trisomy is often caused by a failure of cells to separate, referred to as nondisjunction. This error in cell division is more likely to occur in women aged thirty-five or older than in younger women. Women over thirty-five have a 1 in 400 chance, and women over forty-five have a 1 in 35 chance, of conceiving a child with Down syndrome. Nondisjunction can also occur as a result of faulty cell division in the father's sperm, but the proportion of births affected in this way is only 5 percent. Although Down syndrome is associated with advancing maternal age, approximately 80 percent of children with Down syndrome are born to parents younger than thirty-five years of age.

Down syndrome was first identified by Langdon Down in 1866 based on certain physical characteristics of children at birth. Those characteristics include extra folds of skin in the corner of the eyes (called "epicanthal folds"), a short neck, and a noticeable crease across the palm of the hand. Individuals with Down syndrome also tend to be short in stature. Incorrect terms, such as *Mongoloid*, have

Due to advances in medical care, especially for heart defects, many individuals with Down syndrome now live to the age of sixty and beyond. (Laura Dwight)

been used in the past to refer to individuals with Down syndrome, largely based on facial characteristics and the faulty assumption that individuals with Down syndrome belong to the same ethnic group.

Individuals with Down syndrome are more likely than other people to have particular health problems. The most common of these are heart defects and congenital heart disease, which occur in about one-third to one-half of children with Down syndrome. In the United States, the majority of children with Down syndrome who have heart defects undergo reparative surgery during the first year of life. Other health problems frequently affecting individuals with

Down syndrome are abnormalities of the gastrointestinal tract, kidney malformations, and chronic respiratory infections and ear infections. In addition, their risk of developing leukemia is fifteen to twenty times greater than that of other children, especially during the first three years of life. Often their vision needs to be corrected with lenses; their hearing sometimes requires correction as well. Previously, the life span of individuals with Down syndrome was short; in 1929, for example, their life expectancy was only nine years. However, because of advances in medical care, especially for heart defects, many individuals with Down syndrome now live to the age of sixty and beyond. Recent research indicates that Alzheimer's disease, a dementia that affects memory during older adulthood, occurs at higher rates (about 9 percent) and at an earlier age (fifty-two to fifty-four years) in individuals with Down syndrome compared to other individuals.

As children with Down syndrome grow up, they tend to develop skills more slowly than other children. Language often occurs at a later age and develops at a slower rate than among same-aged peers. Some children with Down syndrome have difficulty articulating certain sounds—a condition partly due to the enlarged protruding tongue and facial muscular structure that are characteristics of the syndrome. This difficulty with articulation may also be related to hearing loss caused by fluid retention in the ears. As children with Down syndrome get older, they sometimes have difficulty forming grammatically correct sentences. Many children with Down syndrome learn to read, however. Teenagers with Down syndrome are like other teens in most ways. Some hold jobs beginning in high school. Many develop strong friendships and romantic relationships. They often attend classes with their age-mates, but they are likely to require additional assistance or instruction with academic tasks. They also often participate in athletics, although their skills may be somewhat diminished due to poor motor tone.

Little has been written about the sexual-identity development of teens with Down syndrome. Puberty begins at the same age and follows the same course as that of teens without Down syndrome. Approximately 50 to 80 percent of women with Down syndrome are fertile, and they have a 50 percent probability of giving birth to a child with the syndrome. Most males with Down syndrome are sterile.

Stereotypes exist about individuals with Down syndrome. One incorrect assumption is that all individuals with Down syndrome are quite similar to each other in intelligence and personality. In fact, individuals with Down syndrome are as different from each other as are any other individuals. Another myth is that people with Down syndrome are very cheerful, affectionate, and stubborn. These characteristics, too, are as likely to appear in individuals with Down syndrome as in other individuals.

Only a few decades ago, many teens with Down syndrome lived in institutions; today, most live at home with their families. Current attitudes and expectations of society are changing the life possibilities of those with Down syndrome. During adult life, individuals with Down syndrome often hold jobs, live independently or in group homes, and sometimes marry. Organizations such as the National Down Syndrome Association help individuals with Down syndrome advocate for their rights, in addition to providing information and publishing newsletters with the most recent research information on Down syndrome. Finally, at least one book has been written by individuals with Down syndrome about their life experiences: *Count Us In*, by Jason Kingsley and Mitchell Levitz.

Additional information can be obtained from the following Web sites: (1) the National Down Syndrome Society at http://www.ndss.org and (2) "Trisomy 21: A Genetic Biography" at http://www.ds-health.com.

Penny Hauser-Cram
Angela Howell

See also Cognitive Development; Mental Retardation, Siblings with

References and further reading
Brown, Roy I. 1996. "Partnership and Marriage in Down Syndrome." *Down Syndrome: Research and Practice* 4: 96–99.
Carr, Janet. 1995. *Down Syndrome: Children Growing Up.* London: Cambridge University Press.
Cicchetti, Dante, and Marjorie Beeghly, eds. 1990. *Children with Down Syndrome: A Developmental Perspective.* New York: Cambridge University Press.
Hodapp, Robert M. 1996. "Down Syndrome: Developmental, Psychiatric, and Management Issues." *Child and Adolescent Psychiatric Clinics of North America* 5: 881–894.
Kingsley, Jason, and Mitchell Levitz. 1994. *Count Us In: Growing Up with Down Syndrome.* San Diego: Harcourt Brace.
Kumin, L. 1994. *Communication Skills in Children with Down Syndrome.* Rockville, MD: Woodbine House.
Pueschel, Sigfried M., and Maria Sustrova. 1997. *Adolescents with Down Syndrome: Toward a More Fulfilling Life.* Baltimore: Paul H. Brookes.

Drug Abuse Prevention

Drug abuse prevention is a major goal of society in the struggle to deter individuals from destroying their own lives and the lives of others when they abuse alcohol and other drugs. Society can deliver messages of drug abuse prevention through the media, the educational system, and the community; however, the family can deliver the strongest and most persuasive message to prevent substance abuse from occurring at all. Teenagers whose parents talk to them regularly about the dangers of drugs are 42 percent less likely to use drugs than those whose parents do not (Partnership for a Drug-Free America, 1999). Messages that successfully reach young people can prevent a lifetime of addiction and despair that can easily lead to physical and mental illness, incarceration, or even death.

Drug abuse prevention programs can take many different forms but usually fall into three general categories (Ray and Ksir, 1996). First, *primary prevention* is aimed at individuals who have not yet tried the substance in question. In the educational system today, children are given primary prevention as part of their regular curriculum. Second, professionals in the field direct *secondary prevention* to those who may have tried drugs but are not yet addicted; they may also target so-called social drinkers. An example of secondary prevention is a program aimed at getting people not to drink when driving. The usual goal of this type of prevention is to change attitudes to prevent harm. Third, individuals who have become addicted or who use drugs in an abusive way require more intensive treatment—namely, *tertiary prevention,* which aims at preventing people with substance abuse problems from experiencing a relapse or recurrence of addiction. An individual is said to be addicted if either physical or psychological dependence on a drug has occurred.

The word *drug* is defined as any substance, whether artificial or natural, that alters the structure or nature of a living organism (Ray and Ksir, 1996). However, it is also important to understand that many drugs with the potential for abuse may have a great deal of medical significance. For instance, morphine, which has a high potential for abuse, may ease the pain of people suffering from a terminal illness. Thus, drugs, drug abuse, and drug abuse prevention are not black-and-white issues;

Society can deliver messages of drug prevention through the media, the educational system, and the community; however, the family can deliver the strongest, most persuasive message. (Leif Skoogfors/Corbis)

they encompass many areas of gray, and society must recognize those areas in order to promote the appropriate use of drugs. The fact remains that when an individual uses drugs for nonmedical purposes in a chronic or habitual manner, that person is at serious risk for developing a substance abuse disorder or becoming physically or psychologically addicted to drugs.

Illicit drug use is usually defined in terms of possession or use of a drug that is unlawful (Ray and Ksir, 1996)—a definition complicated by the fact that many illicit drugs are legal for those who acquire them through a medical doctor by prescription. In the absence of a prescription, the drug is illicit. Traditionally,

alcohol and tobacco have not been considered illicit substances, even though the public should view both as drugs with potential for abuse.

Money spent on prevention of alcohol and tobacco abuse is money well spent, as the consequences of these drugs cost our society billions of dollars (NCADD, 1999). By itself, teen alcohol use—which results in traffic crashes, violent crimes, burns, drowning and suicide attempts, fetal alcohol syndrome, and alcohol poisonings—incurs expenses totaling more than $58 billion a year. The use of alcohol and other drugs of abuse can have other negative impacts on teenagers as well. Among sexually active teens, those who average five or more drinks daily are three times less likely to use condoms, placing them at greater risk for HIV and other sexually transmitted diseases.

Tobacco is even worse. In the United States and elsewhere, it causes more medical problems, and more deaths, than any other substance. Yet cigarettes and other tobacco products have only recently come to be seen as drugs. Unfortunately, prevention efforts directed against this form of drug abuse have not been as successful as other such efforts; the percentage of teens who smoke cigarettes has remained relatively stable since 1988—about 18 percent of youths age twelve to seventeen (SAMSHA, 1998). Moreover, both cigarettes and alcohol are often viewed as "gateway" drugs, meaning that use of these substances at a young age can lead to a greater risk for more serious drug abuse in an individual's future. Youths age twelve to seventeen who currently smoke cigarettes are eleven times more likely to use illicit drugs and sixteen times more likely to drink heavily than nonsmoking youths.

Deviant drug use is considered uncommon within the context of our society's norms and is disapproved of by the majority of the members of that society. *Drug misuse* generally refers to the use of prescription drugs in amounts not recommended or prescribed by a physician or dentist. *Drug abuse* refers to use of a substance in a way that creates problems or greatly increases the chances that problems will occur. Drug dependence and abuse affect the youth of America in a profound way: In 1995, 21 percent of clients who were admitted to drug treatment programs were under the age of twenty-four, including 18,194 who were under the age of fifteen (SAMSHA, 1998).

Among the drugs that have potential for abuse are narcotics, which include heroin, morphine, methadone, opium, and substances derived from opium. Depressants, another class of drug that has a high potential for abuse, include alcohol, barbiturates, and sedatives. Street drugs that doctors have not prescribed or that have no medical value include stimulants, such as cocaine, crack, and methamphetamine. Hallucinogens, including marijuana, LSD, and psilocybin mushrooms, are another class of drugs of abuse. In addition, athletes and body builders have been known to abuse anabolic steroids and human growth hormones to increase their muscle mass.

Since about 1980, however, prevention to stop the abuse of illicit substances has had an effect. Findings from the Substance Abuse and Mental Health Services Administration reveal that whereas 25 million Americans used an illegal substance during the preceding month in 1979, this figure had decreased by nearly 50 percent to almost 13 million by 1997 (SAMSHA, 1998). School and community efforts have also paid off as drug abuse prevention has become increasingly important throughout the United States. The percentage of youths age twelve to seventeen who reported current use of illicit drugs in 1998 was nearly 10 percent, a marked decrease from the estimated 12 percent in 1997. The rate of drug use among youths was highest in 1979, when it totaled an astounding 16 percent.

Apart from alcohol and tobacco, the drug most commonly abused by teens is marijuana (SAMSHA, 1998). In 1998, a little more than 8 percent of youths age twelve through seventeen were current users of marijuana, but this percentage, too, has decreased dramatically in the last twenty years, having reached a peak of more than 14 percent in 1979. Nevertheless, many youths—56 percent of those surveyed in 1998—claim easy access to marijuana. As for other drugs of abuse, including cocaine, heroin, hallucinogens, barbiturates, sedatives, and inhalants, 14 percent of the youths surveyed reported that they had been approached by someone selling drugs in the previous thirty days.

Drug abuse prevention programs can have a huge impact at all levels ranging from individuals and families to entire communities (SAMSHA, 1998). Research has shown that effective prevention programs can improve parenting skills and family relationships; it has also suggested that early prevention efforts are effective in deterring an individual from abusing substances later on. Indeed, successful prevention programs can reduce delinquent behaviors among youth who are often associated with substance abuse and drug-related crime.

These dramatic findings are likely due to the increased efforts directed at drug abuse prevention programs in communities throughout the United States. Many of these programs were developed during the middle to late 1980s and took new directions throughout the 1990s. Our society will no doubt make even more progress in the twenty-first century.

In the beginning, drug abuse prevention programs were primarily educational in nature, taking a top-down approach whereby administrators or others in authority told students about the dangers of drugs and alcohol (Ray and Ksir, 1996). Programs such as DARE, for example, are headed up by local police and firefighters and implemented in school systems. And one of the biggest

drug abuse prevention strategies to come out of the 1980s was Nancy Reagan's "Just Say No" campaign. Although the latter was criticized as ineffective in stopping substance abuse from occurring, it proved to be a long-standing approach to the war on drugs.

In the 1990s, drug education and prevention began to emphasize intervention, which worked to change behaviors, attitudes, and perceptions (Ray and Ksir, 1996). One reason that young people may wish to use drugs is to feel excitement, relaxation, or a sense of control in terms of what they do to and with their bodies. Likewise, individuals may take drugs due to the influence of peers. Helping children and adolescents to know and understand these feelings—and to express them—may be effective in preventing drug abuse.

It is also essential that young people clarify their values (Coughlin, 1997). Through the education system, the community, and the family, emphasis must be placed on their decision-making skills. This can be done in a variety of ways, one of which is to ask them how they would react in a hypothetical situation where they were given a choice between using drugs or not using them.

Peer counseling can also be an important strategy in prevention. Recommending that students talk with their peers about alcohol and drug problems has proven effective in some situations. Similarly, respected members of student subgroups, such as athletes, can be asked to advocate drug and alcohol awareness and prevention. Indeed, both schools and community organizations can use peer education in innovative and informative ways—for example, through improvisational skits depicting real-life situations about drugs and their abuse.

It is also important to provide alternatives to substance use—for example, by teaching teens about the powerful natural high that can be gained from activities such as vigorous exercise, relaxation, meditation, and sports. Toward this end, communities need to support teen centers that offer interesting forms of youth entertainment. By involving teens with others through organized clubs or school sports, individuals learn to communicate.

On a wider scale, by means of the media, social marketing has made its way into the forefront of alcohol and drug abuse prevention. Having selectively borrowed its principles and processes from the commercial world, this method works to convey realistic social norms through the use of "campaigns." Its messages and images, though as carefully developed as those in the commercial world, are adapted to health advocacy and other large-scale efforts for positive social change. One approach used by social marketing is to convince teens that most of their peers do not drink, smoke, or do drugs—thereby leading them to change their behavior.

The most salient form of drug abuse prevention, however, is to be found through family values that are clarified in the home. Parents who talk with their children realistically about drugs, and about the dangers and risks associated with them, give their children a better chance to combat these dangers when actually confronted with them. In turn, children raised by caretakers who have a healthy relationship with alcohol and other drugs are much less likely to have future problems with drug dependence or abuse themselves.

Melinda M. Roberts

See also Alcohol Use, Risk Factors in; Cigarette Smoking; Health Promotion; Health Services for Adolescents; Intervention Programs for Adolescents; Substance Use and Abuse

References and further reading
Coughlin, Eileen V., ed. 1997. *Successful Drug and Alcohol Prevention Programs.* San Francisco: Jossey-Bass.
National Council on Alcoholism and Drug Dependence (NCADD). 1999. *Youth, Alcohol and Other Drugs: An Overview.* http://www.ncadd.org
National Household Survey on Drug Abuse. 1998. News Release.
Partnership for a Drug-Free America. 1999. News Release. http://www.drugfreeamerica.org
Ray, Oakley, and Charles Ksir. 1996. *Drugs, Society and Human Nature,* 7th ed. St. Louis, MO: Mosby Year Book.
Substance Abuse and Mental Health Services Administration (SAMSHA). 1998. "Prevention Works." News Release. http://www.samhsa.gov

Dyslexia

Dyslexia is a condition characterized by serious difficulties with reading and other aspects of written language such as spelling and writing. Features of dyslexia change over the life span, beginning with severe problems in learning to read and evolving in adolescence to spelling and writing problems as well as slow laborious reading. Dyslexia manifests itself in two different ways: *Acquired dyslexia* refers to adults who lose their ability to read as a result of brain injury (e.g., after a stroke), whereas *developmental dyslexia* refers to children who unexpectedly experience difficulty in learning to read, despite adequate to superior intelligence, motivation, and schooling. Researchers have become increasingly confident in their assumption that developmental dyslexia results from differences in the underlying structure of the regions in the brain involved in the processing of written language. Inasmuch as important advances have also been made in the study of reading, many children with dyslexia now respond successfully to timely and appropriate interventions.

The National Institute of Health estimates that in 2000 approximately 15 percent of Americans had learning disabilities—a figure that included 2.4 million schoolchildren. Among students with learning disabilities who receive special education services, 80 to 85 percent have basic deficits in language and reading.

Dyslexia occurs in all groups of people, regardless of age, race, or socioeconomic status. Research indicates the existence of a genetic component, given that the condition appears to run in families. In addition, a higher incidence of dyslexia has been found among males. Some research, however, suggests that more girls than suspected have dyslexia—and that they simply have not been referred and diagnosed. Incidentally, some very famous people were, or are, dyslexic, including Hans Christian Andersen, Michelangelo, Franklin D. Roosevelt, Albert Einstein, Thomas A. Edison, Whoopi Goldberg, Lindsay Wagner, and Dr. Harvey Cushing (the father of modern brain surgery).

Causes of Dyslexia
Dyslexia is best described as a heterogeneous group of disorders, with several underlying explanations for distinct subtypes of reading-disabled students. Many scientists in the first half of the twentieth century believed that dyslexia was based on visual problems; the commonly observed "reversal of letters" in children was seen as an indicator of such problems. But, in fact, most dyslexics have normal vision and do not "see backwards."

Since the mid-1970s, researchers have come to agree that one central difficulty associated with dyslexia is a deficit in phonological processing. According to the phonological-deficit hypothesis, children with dyslexia have difficulty developing an awareness that words, both written and spoken, can be broken down into smaller units of sounds. Thus, for example, it is difficult for them to recognize a rhyme, to delete a sound from a word, or, more generally, to make the connection between symbols (i.e., letters) and the sounds they represent. As a result, they cannot learn to sound out words (i.e., to decode), which is the first step in reading.

Recent cutting-edge research in the cognitive neurosciences has demonstrated a second major area of difficulty as well: naming-speed deficits. Specifically, dyslexics are slow to retrieve the names of familiar visual symbols such as letters and numbers. These deficits reflect an impairment in the processes underlying recognition and retrieval of visually presented letters. What this finding means for reading is only beginning to be understood. The same factors that slow down retrieval processes may also impede the development of rapid letter pattern recognition—an impairment that may in turn slow down word identification, which is critical for fluent reading. Fortunately, research on the deficits that underlie different groups of reading disabilities is rapidly progressing. This research is ultimately aimed at informing educators about which interventions are best suited for each individual involved.

Identification of Dyslexia

Indicators of dyslexia in early childhood include late development of spoken language, slow reading of letter names, and difficulties in sounding out words, whereas indicators of dyslexia in adolescence include slow and inaccurate reading of words, poor reading comprehension, and spelling difficulties such as reversed letter order, deletion of letters, and misrepresentation of the sounds in a word. Some adolescent dyslexics may also have difficulty associating the letters with the sounds they represent.

Note, however, that many adolescents with dyslexia have only minor decoding problems with simple and regularly spelled words. Rather, their major difficulty is slow, dysfluent reading, which prolongs the time they need to comprehend the material. Indeed, the majority of dyslexics have more difficulty expressing themselves in written language than in spoken language. Their writing problems usually include spelling and organization of their ideas.

Traditionally, dyslexia has been diagnosed by comparing intellectual ability with achievement in reading. Because bright students with an *unexpected* difficulty in reading are usually considered dyslexics, IQ tests are generally used to assess dyslexia in school-aged children. In fact, eligibility for special education programs in public school is usually based on this discrepancy. However, complicating the diagnosis for some dyslexic adolescents is the possibility that their reading deficiency has affected their knowledge of vocabulary—a knowledge that is assessed in IQ tests. This circumstance diminishes the usefulness of IQ tests in diagnosing dyslexia.

Although adolescent dyslexic readers become more accurate with time, they never become fully automatic or fluent in their reading. The failure either to recognize or to measure this lack of automaticity in reading is perhaps the most common error made in the diagnosis of dyslexia among accomplished young adults.

For such individuals, identification of dyslexia would be facilitated by use of a questionnaire regarding the history of their development of language and reading. Also helpful would be a combination of tests measuring reading, spelling, language, and cognitive abilities, along with a battery of neurological, psychological, and educational assessments. Indeed, no diagnosis of dyslexia should ever be based on a single test.

Treatment of Dyslexia

Individuals with dyslexia often need special programs to learn to read, write, and spell. In the early years, direct instruction in associating letters and sounds is critical. Research has demonstrated that these decoding skills are best taught step-by-step, in an incremental manner. Then, as the children grow older, their reading comprehension is enhanced by work on reading rate, vocabulary, and general fluency.

Of specific importance to young adults are the rules governing written language and the strategies necessary for purposeful reading and writing. At the same time, however, each individual student's strengths and learning pace must be identified. Recent research has concluded that despite their difficulties, many adolescents with learning disabilities have a healthy self-concept and sense of self-worth—a noteworthy finding given that dyslexic individuals often rate their academic abilities and achievement lower than their normally achieving peers do.

Research in this field has begun to indicate the efficacy of interventions that provide structured reading and writing strategies for adolescents with dyslexia. But crucial to their success are the following additional factors: assistance with study skills such as planning and organizing, time set aside to check their work, extra time on written examinations, advocacy for accommodations on exams, and, finally, self-advocacy by parents, teachers, and the students themselves.

Tami Katzir-Cohen

See also Cognitive Development; Developmental Challenges; Intelligence; Intelligence Tests; Learning Disabilities; Learning Styles and Accommodations; Standardized Tests; Thinking

References and further reading
International Dyslexia Association Web site at http://www.interdys.org
Lerner, Janet. 1997. *Learning Disabilities,* 7th ed. New York: Houghton Mifflin.
Lovett, Maureen. 1992. "Developmental Dyslexia." Pp. 163–185 in *Handbook of Neuropsychology,* Vol. 7. Edited by Sydney J. Segalowitz. Amsterdam: Elsevier Science Publishing.
Shaywitz, Sally. 1998. "Dyslexia." *New England Journal of Medicine* 338, no 5: 307–312.
Wolf, Maryanne, and Patricia G. Bowers. 1999. "The Double-Deficit Hypothesis for the Developmental Dyslexias." *Journal of Educational Psychology* 91, no. 3: 1–24.

E

Eating Problems

The term *eating problems* refers to a pattern of abnormal attitudes and behaviors relating to food. Often such abnormalities begin with normal dieting practices that subsequently become severely disturbed. In the past, eating problems were most prevalent among middle- and upper-class Caucasian women living in Western cultures; today, however, such problems can be found in countries throughout the world, affecting males and females of all social classes and ethnicities.

Females are nevertheless nine to ten times more likely than males to be diagnosed with an eating disorder. In the United States, an estimated 3 percent of young women suffer from one of the three main eating disorders; many more than that report subclinical eating and body disturbances. The onset of eating problems commonly occurs between early adolescence and early adulthood—a particularly vulnerable time for females, who are forming their identities in the context of a culture that stresses the presumed importance of beauty and slimness.

The three main eating disorders are classified as anorexia nervosa, bulimia nervosa, and binge eating disorder. Some individuals with eating problems do not fit these categories exactly; others exhibit symptoms that are not severe enough to be diagnosable but put the persons at risk for pathological conditions and serious consequences. Note that obesity is excluded from the list of main eating disorders; the reason is that it is generally considered a medical condition rather than an emotionally based disorder—even though emotional factors may play a role in its development and maintenance.

Anorexia Nervosa

Anorexia is defined as a loss of appetite, but, in actuality, anorexic individuals deny their appetite despite feelings of constant hunger. Anorexia nervosa is characterized by maintenance of a minimally normal body weight (i.e., less than 85 percent of expected weight), intense fear of gaining weight despite being underweight, disturbances in perceptions of body weight and shape, and loss of three consecutive menstrual cycles in postmenarcheal women (a condition known as amenorrhea). Research suggests that anorexics restrict food intake as a means of gaining control over some aspect of their lives in a world where they feel powerless. In addition to restricting their food intake, some anorexics engage in binge eating or purging behavior.

Individuals with anorexia tend to deny that they have a serious problem, which makes it difficult for them to recover from their eating attitudes and behaviors. Anorexics become obsessed with the

The three main eating disorders are classified as anorexia nervosa, bulimia nervosa, and binge eating. (Shirley Zeiberg)

rate, vital organ damage, and sometimes even death. In fact, anorexia is associated with a higher annual mortality rate (i.e., 0.56 percent) than any other psychiatric disorder. This rate reflects deaths resulting from starvation, body chemistry imbalance, and suicide.

Bulimia Nervosa

The most common eating disorder among young females is bulimia nervosa, which typically begins in late adolescence. This disorder involves repeated instances of binge eating—consuming large amounts of food in a short period of time—followed by inappropriate compensatory behaviors such as self-induced vomiting, fasting, misuse of laxatives or diuretics, and excessive exercise. The food eaten by bulimics usually consists of high-calorie substances such as sweets. Binges usually occur in secrecy and are characterized by a lack of control: Bulimics often feel as though they cannot stop eating. In fact, they usually continue eating until they feel uncomfortably and painfully full or until they are interrupted by the presence of others. Thus, a binge may last anywhere from several minutes to several hours. Bulimics tend to feel depressed, self-critical, and shameful after a binge. Accordingly, they engage in the compensatory behaviors noted earlier, as a means of preventing weight gain, relieving physical discomfort, and easing stress after the binge. In order to be diagnosed with full-blown bulimia nervosa, the individual must engage in binge eating and inappropriate compensatory behaviors twice a week for a period of three months.

notion of being thin, continuing to engage in weight-loss behaviors well after they have achieved their target body weight and shape. They often feel depressed, socially withdrawn, irritable, worthless, and unaccepted. It is common for anorexics to restrict their diets to a few foods and to exhibit unusual eating behaviors (e.g., cutting food into tiny pieces, taking small bites and chewing slowly, moving food around on the plate), excessive body-shape and weight-estimation techniques (e.g., constant weighing and body measuring), and excessive exercise. These behaviors have serious consequences including lethargy, cold intolerance, dryness of skin, dull and brittle hair, slowed pulse

Although individuals with bulimia tend to be in the normal weight range, they may struggle with weight fluctuation. Compared to anorexics, they tend to have a more accurate perception of body weight and shape (although they are similar to anorexics in basing their self-evaluations on this perception). They generally exhibit a more impulsive personality, which contributes to their addictive behavior. And they are more likely to acknowledge that they have a problem and thus more likely to seek help. Nevertheless, bulimics tend to feel isolated and alone, depressed, unattractive, unworthy, high strung, and unsatisfied with life. Given this distress, it is believed that individuals with bulimia use food as a means to satisfy their inner needs and purge as means of achieving temporary control. Bulimia can lead to physical complications such as fatigue, menstrual irregularity, dental problems, abdominal pain, and heart irregularities and failure.

Binge Eating
Binge eating is commonly referred to as compulsive overeating. Like bulimia nervosa, it is characterized by repeated episodes of uncontrolled food consumption; however, the binge eater does not make use of inappropriate compensatory behaviors. The binges may occur either in one setting or over long periods of snacking. Many binge eaters restrict their food intake throughout the day and are thus quite hungry in the evening. At that point they often break their diet and continue eating because they feel they have failed. Whereas many people occasionally engage in binge eating behaviors, the full-blown diagnosis of binge eating is reserved for those cases in which the individual exerts excessive amounts of time and energy bingeing, thinking about bingeing, and feeling powerless and out of control about food and her body.

Binge eaters often have low self-esteem, find it difficult to express their feelings, appear content on the outside but feel alone and sad on the inside, and are insecure in their identities. Research suggests that their compulsive eating is a form of self-medication, that they binge in an attempt to deal with feelings of fatigue, anxiety, anger, isolation, pain, or boredom. Indeed, binges are often triggered by feelings of tension and anxiety, and they usually provide the individual with temporary freedom from these feelings. However, although binge eaters usually feel less tense after a binge, they also feel shameful and uncomfortable with their bodies—feelings that reinforce their general sense of negativity. Binge eaters are at risk for experiencing weight problems, becoming obese, and developing medical complications associated with obesity such as diabetes, hypertension, respiratory disease, and cancer.

Obesity
Obesity occurs when adipose tissue (fat) comprises a greater than normal percentage of total body weight. (The normal range is 20 to 25 percent.) The number of obese individuals in the Western world has dramatically increased since 1950. Today, an estimated one-third of the adult population is obese. Although genetic factors are implicated in obesity, this condition is also caused by consumption of excessive amounts of food in brief periods of time—as in binge eating. In fact, an estimated 25 to 46 percent of obese individuals report that they engage in binge eating behavior a minimum of twice a week. Many obese people also restrict their food intake during the day, consume large meals in the evening, and avoid physical activity in the interim. Individuals with obesity are at serious risk for hypertension, cardiovascular disease, and diabetes.

Etiology of Eating Problems

Eating disturbances may be understood as existing along a continuum of severity. With the exception of genetically predisposed obesity, these problems often begin with dieting as a means of controlling weight. Dieting can sometimes lead to eating attitudes and behaviors that are subclinical in the sense that the individual exhibits symptoms of an eating disorder that are not severe enough to warrant a diagnosis but are nevertheless dangerous. Subclinical eating problems that become more pathological often result in full-blown eating disorders.

Although many eating problems begin with dieting, not all individuals who diet will develop eating problems. Thus, it is likely that other factors, such as heredity and environment, contribute to the development and maintenance of these problems.

There is some evidence that disturbed eating attitudes and behaviors run in families, thus suggesting a genetic predisposition toward these problems. For example, families may transmit certain personality characteristics (e.g., impulsivity, overreaction to stress) or biochemical makeups that increase a person's vulnerability to the development of eating problems. It is also likely, however, that other influences interact with genetic factors to predispose the individual to these disturbances. Given that eating problems are most common among adolescent females, it is important to understand the context in which they are embedded.

One key aspect of this context is the obsession with fitness in Western cultures. And for women, being fit is often associated with thinness and beauty. For men, on the other hand, fitness is equated with muscularity and strength;

thus, males are less likely to be concerned with their weight or to engage in dieting behavior. Women are bombarded by media images of unrealistically slim females—images whose message seems to imply that success and thinness go hand in hand. This message poses an especially serious problem for adolescent females, who typically gain weight during puberty. In short, the adolescent female body undergoes normative developmental changes that contradict the images being portrayed, leading to distress at a time when teens are forming their identities. Accordingly, many young females begin dieting as a means of preventing this normal weight gain.

As noted earlier, however, not every individual who diets develops eating problems. Other factors seem to play a role in increasing the vulnerability of some individuals to these problems. First, individuals with eating problems tend to exhibit certain personality characteristics. Some are people-pleasers who seek the approval of others and set unrealistically high expectations for themselves. Others, especially those with anorexic-like symptoms, tend to be persistent and orderly, to display extreme rigidity, and to exhibit overcontrol of their own emotions and intolerance of others' emotions. Still others, including those with bulimic and binge eating symptoms, tend to display poor impulse control and emotional instability.

A second factor concerns family interactions. Some individuals with eating problems come from families that inadvertently promote disturbed eating attitudes and behaviors by overemphasizing perfectionism, slenderness, youthfulness, and reliance on external sources for self-esteem. Others have families that lack empathy and nurturance and tend to be overcontrolling, belittling, or blaming. Still others come from families whose members do not openly express their emotions and feelings and are thus prevented from learning to identify their own needs and emotions as well as discouraged from forming their own identities.

Finally, some eating problems are triggered by significant life stressors. For example, researchers have suggested that in some cases there is a relationship between disordered eating and sexual abuse. In any case, it is likely that eating problems are affected by several contextual factors, and that their severity along the continuum is determined by the presence or absence of these factors.

Treatment of Eating Problems
Recovery from eating problems usually requires the support of some treatment modality. For individuals struggling with abnormal eating attitudes and behaviors, treatment provides a safe place to deal with and talk about their problems. Disturbed eating patterns *are* treatable, but the best prognosis is for individuals who seek treatment early. The treatment modalities available to people with eating problems include individual therapy, group therapy, family therapy, medication, nutritional counseling, support groups, and self-help groups. These in turn are provided by professionals such as psychiatrists, physicians, psychologists, social workers, dietitians, and pastoral counselors. Depending on the severity of the problem, some individuals may benefit from a combination of these treatment modalities.

Treatment can occur in either an inpatient or outpatient setting. It is usually structured in such a way as to help individuals regulate food intake, monitor physical complications, and deal with and

express feelings associated with their disturbed eating attitudes and behaviors. In order to identify appropriate treatment modalities, the individual is advised to contact a physician, school counselor, and/or mental health association. Other options such as the reference section in libraries, telephone books, and women's organizations are useful resources as well.

Anna Chaves

See also Anxiety; Body Fat, Changes in; Body Image; Depression; Nutrition; Puberty: Physical Changes; Self-Consciousness

References and further reading
American Psychiatric Association. 1994. *Diagnostic and Statistical Manual of Mental Disorders*, 4th ed. Washington, DC: American Psychiatric Association.
Hsu, L. K. George. 1990. *Eating Disorders.* New York: Guilford Press.
Lemberg, Raymond, and Leigh Cohn, eds. 1999. *Eating Disorders: A Reference Sourcebook.* Phoenix, AZ: Oryx Press.
Pipher, Mary. 1994. *Reviving Ophelia: Saving the Selves of Adolescent Girls.* New York: Ballantine Books.

Emancipated Minors

Emancipated minors are children under the age of eighteen years who are legally independent from their parents, guardians, or custodians. The parents of emancipated minors no longer have the right to make decisions about or for these children, and no longer have the duty to provide financial or material support. Emancipated minors must be able to take care of themselves independently, and they are entitled to some—but not all—adult rights and privileges.

There are three major reasons for which minors may choose to petition for emancipation: (1) to gain control over their own finances (as in the many well publicized cases of child stars who establish emancipation because they claim their parents have mishandled their earnings), (2) to escape an extremely difficult home life (for instance, a conflict-ridden situation that is intolerable for both the parents and themselves), and (3) to obtain independence, responsibility, and space.

Laws concerning emancipation vary from state to state, but, in general, teenagers are considered emancipated when they turn eighteen, marry, or join the armed forces. Minors may also be emancipated through the legal system, through either a court order or some other legal means, depending on state regulations. In most states, minors must be at least sixteen to petition, although a few states allow children as young as fourteen to do so.

Above all, minors must prove that they are capable of supporting themselves. Different laws apply in different states, but the granting of emancipation is generally based on the following criteria. First, the minors must show that they are able to manage their own finances (gained through a legal source of income) without depending on their parents. Second, they must demonstrate that they are able to live independently from their parents. (Some states require a separate residence; others allow emancipation of minors who live in their parents' home but pay rent or otherwise show independence.) Third, they must establish that emancipation is in their best interest, and that failure to receive emancipation would be harmful (as in situations where the youth's earnings are being mishandled by the parents).

Although parents sometimes choose to seek emancipation for their own children, the law does not allow parents to emancipate a minor who is dependent upon them for support. Increasingly, courts are hearing cases in which parents attempt to emancipate their children by proving that they are financially independent. Those parents who can convince the courts to grant emancipation no longer have to assume any financial responsibility for their children.

Emancipation ends parents' legal duty to support the minor; it also ends the parents' right to make decisions about the minor's residence, education, and healthcare, and to control the minor's conduct. Although states' laws vary, emancipation generally ensures a number of adult rights and responsibilities for emancipated minors. When emancipated, they have the right to live independently in their own home and the right to make their own financial, social, and educational decisions. They have the right to access their own earnings, though they can also be sued in their own name. They have the right to enter into binding contracts such as leases. And they can give informed consent for healthcare services.

Although emancipation provides minors with many important adult rights, it does not provide them with access to all adult privileges. For example, emancipated minors are subject to numerous legal health and safety regulations that are dependent on age. If accused of a crime, they can be treated as an adult only under the same circumstances that apply to minors who are not emancipated. And like all individuals, they must be eighteen years old to vote and twenty-one years old to buy and consume alcohol.

Generally, the law does not presume emancipation, even if a minor is living independently. Emancipation is usually established through legal procedures that require clear and compelling evidence that emancipation is the best option. Although each state has its own specific procedures, minors or parents seeking emancipation of a minor must complete application forms and provide documented evidence.

Key resources include public libraries, which can provide information on specific emancipation laws in individual states, and legal organizations for youth, which not only offer legal counseling and legal support but can also write letters of emancipation to healthcare providers, school administrators, and other adults. Assistance of this nature helps minors gain the right to consent to healthcare, the right to retain their own wages, and other privileges that are typically reserved for adults.

Emancipation is not necessarily permanent. It is possible for a teenager to be emancipated for a period of time but then, due to changed circumstances, to once more become dependent on his or her parents, guardians, or custodians—again, depending on the laws in a given state. The circumstances that can change a minor's emancipation status are as follows. First, minors who become emancipated by marrying may become dependent again if the marriage ends in divorce. Second, emancipated minors may again become dependent if they lose the ability to support themselves—for example, by losing a job. Third, in certain medical emergencies, minors may temporarily be declared emancipated for the purpose of consenting to medical procedures if their parents or guardians cannot be reached. Following the medical procedure, however, the minors are once again considered dependent. Fourth, as a result of the welfare reform bill passed in 1996, some states exclude public benefits such

as Transitional Assistance for Needy Families (TANF) from being considered a source of income when a minor petitions for emancipation. And, fifth, a few states allow emancipation to be revoked if a minor later becomes dependent on public benefits.

Finally, there is the question of how courts should handle cases when a minor has a child. Whereas most state emancipation laws do not address this question, some state laws include as a criterion the interests of the teen's child, such as whether the minor is able to handle her personal affairs, whether emancipation is in the best interests of the minor's family, and so on.

Shireen Boulos
Jessica Goldberg

See also Family Relations; Fathers and Adolescents; Mothers and Adolescents; Parent-Adolescent Relations; Parenting Styles; Rights of Adolescents

References and further reading
Center for Law and Social Policy. 1999. *Emancipated Teen Parents and the TANF Living Arrangement Rules.* Washington, DC: Center for Law and Social Policy.
Gardner, Chadwick N. 1994/1995. "Don't Come Crying to Daddy! Emancipation of Minors: When Is a Parent 'Free at Last' from the Obligation of Child Support?" *University of Louisville Journal of Family Law* 33: 927–948.
Laws of the Fifty States, District of Columbia and Puerto Rico Governing the Emancipation of Minors. 2000. Ithaca, NY: Cornell University, Legal Information Institute. Retrieved on January 14, 2000, from the World Wide Web at http://www.law.cornell.edu

Emotional Abuse

Emotional abuse, often referred to in child welfare literature as psychological abuse, has slowly gained societal attention

Psychological harm from emotional abuse may occur after continuous verbal assaults or acts of caretaker rejection. (Hannah Gal/Corbis)

within the United States since the late 1980s. Society has been hesitant to recognize and identify the potential harm to children incurred from emotional abuse. Three primary reasons exist for the resistance. These include lack of a consensus definition for emotional abuse, the difficulty in proving that emotional abuse has occurred because of a lack of physical evidence, and the limited research that documents the harmful effects of emotional abuse.

Definitions

Defining what constitutes emotional abuse has been problematic because of diverse cultural perspectives on acceptable and unacceptable parenting behavior. Consequently, many definitions exist. Emotional abuse can be acts of commission or omission. A comprehensive definition includes at least six categories of emotional abuse: (1) spurning (verbal attacks, humiliation, rejection), (2) terrorizing (making threats to seriously harm or kill), (3) observing family violence, (4) isolating (preventing child from interacting with peers, locking child within an enclosed area), (5) exploiting/corrupting (encouraging child to engage in antisocial or criminal behavior, encouraging child to use drugs or alcohol), and (6) denying emotional responsiveness (being psychologically unavailable to child, ignoring child's attempts to interact with parents, refusal to engage child). Emotional abuse can also be communicating to children that they are worthless, unloved, and unwanted (Brassard, Hardy, and Hart, 1993).

One key element of agreement amongst most definitions is that emotional abuse is typically a repeated pattern of behavior. Unlike some cases of physical and sexual abuse, emotional abuse is cumulative and takes place over a period of time. This is because most researchers and experts believe that psychological harm from emotional abuse occurs only after continuous verbal assaults or acts of caretaker rejection of children. Children are thought to be psychologically and emotionally resilient to occasional inappropriate verbal or nonverbal acts.

Prevalence

No precise measures exist that can accurately document the rate of emotional abuse. Documenting emotional abuse is so difficult because emotional abuse leaves no physical evidence. Second, it is rarely defined as a single event, which means that there must be a recognizable pattern of caretaker abuse. Knowing how long and how frequently a specific pattern of emotional abuse has been present is a monumental task for child welfare caseworkers who are charged with determining if abuse has happened. Adding to the complexity in determining if emotional abuse has occurred is the fact that, in most states, proof of emotional or psychological harm to children can only be determined by a psychologist or a psychiatrist following a thorough assessment of the children. Because of the complexity and the ambiguity involved in caseworker decision making in emotional abuse, only 6 percent of child abuse and neglect cases substantiated nationally in 1997 were designated as emotional abuse.

Although no comprehensive statistics are available, emotional abuse, according to recent research and professional experience, accompanies most cases of physical abuse and frequently is involved in cases of neglect. This means that some form of psychological mistreatment (spurning, terrorizing, isolation, humiliation, denying care and affection) typically occurs prior to, during, or after physical abuse. Many experts believe that the emotional abuse children experience has more long-term psychological consequences on children than acts of physical assault or neglect.

Consequences

The body most often heals from injury, but repeated verbal attacks on a child's sense of self may influence the child's thoughts and feelings for a lifetime. Self identify forms during childhood. A child's developing sense of self is extremely vulnerable and heavily influenced by input from others. Parents or guardians have a major role in influencing children's perception of self. Parental emotional abuse devalues children's perceptions of themselves. As a consequence, children may feel inferior to others, lack feelings of competence, feel ashamed, and believe that they have nothing to offer others in relationships. They become fearful that others may see how inferior they are.

Recent research studies reveal that emotionally abused children often suffer various short-term and long-term emotional, psychological, and behavioral consequences. The harmful effects of emotional abuse are most evident when the child is verbally assaulted frequently and over a long period of time. Further, because younger children have a less developed sense of self than older children, they are at greater risk of potential psychological, emotional, and social harm due to emotional abuse. Infants are at great risk of harm when parents or guardians spurn, isolate, or deny care and affection, because such parental actions threaten the attachment process. Secure attachment occurs when a child's physical, emotional, and psychological needs are consistently met by their primary caretakers. As a result, children develop positive bonds with their primary caretakers and experience physical and psychological safety.

If a parent does not meet an infant's physical and psychological needs, several harmful consequences may result. Studies have documented a medical condition known as failure to thrive in infants and young children, in which children physically fail to grow for no medical reason. The primary cause appears to be psychological unavailability of the primary caretakers. Some research of ignored infants in institutions indicated that the infant mortality rate was very high because of the emotional deprivation. When failure to thrive children are placed in alternative environments (hospitals, foster homes, with relatives) they often gain weight rapidly and resume growth. However, even when failure to thrive infants physically recover, they have a higher incidence of temper tantrums at all ages, are delayed in social relations, engage in attention-seeking behaviors, and commit more acts of petty theft than peers (Pearl, 1996).

Older children exposed to emotional abuse can also be seriously affected. Studies have documented that emotionally abused children are more likely than nonexposed children to engage in self-destructive behaviors and antisocial and delinquent behaviors; they are also more often diagnosed with a psychiatric disorder. They may be delayed in several domains including language, cognitive functioning, and fine and gross motor skills. Low self-esteem is frequently observed along with relationship problems, behavior problems (e.g., aggression, social withdrawal), and eating or sleeping disorders. Emotionally abused children as they mature into adulthood may demonstrate signs of anxiety, depression, and dissociation. Dissociation occurs when a child or adult begins to think and/or feel separated from their body. Children who have received nurturing prior to the onset of the abuse or who have a positive significant relationship with another adult are less likely to experience psychological harm.

Causes

No single factor has been identified as causing emotional abuse. Several interacting factors appear to influence parental emotional abusive behavior. Approximately 10 percent of abusive parents are diagnosed as mentally ill. The majority of abusive parents have difficulty coping with individual or social stress (in over 60 percent of all abuse cases), struggle in developing and maintaining social relationships, and are often socially isolated. In one study, emotionally abusive parents described themselves as having poor child management skills and being victims of some form of abuse or neglect themselves during childhood. Lack of knowledge about the importance of emotional responsiveness and psychological stimulation of children can contribute to emotional abuse. Substance abuse can also result in parents not being psychologically available to their children. This is highlighted by the fact that nationally up to 80 percent of all forms of child maltreatment in 1996 involved some form of substance abuse.

Treatment

The duration, intensity, and type of treatment for child victims of emotional abuse depend on the severity of the abuse, the age of the child, and the present family circumstances. Older children who did not experience abuse during their early years, who had or still have a positive attachment to a primary adult figure, and who did not experience emotional abuse in combination with other forms of maltreatment (physical abuse, neglect, sexual abuse) are most likely to overcome any subsequent psychological or emotional impairments. In contrast, children over five, who have attachment problems, are the most difficult to treat.

The most critical element in healing the internal wounds of emotional abuse is the establishment of a trusting relationship with a nurturing adult. This is because children need to feel psychologically safe within a relationship in order to develop positive attachments and high self-esteem. Optimally, this relationship occurs within children's familial environments. Without at least one safe relationship with a primary adult, it is likely that the child will experience significant psychological, emotional, and behavioral problems; these problems may persist long after the abuse has stopped.

Play therapy is often employed with children to bolster self-esteem, and to resolve attachment issues. Empowering the child through play has been found to increase self-esteem and self-efficacy. Filial therapy, in which the parent participates in the play therapy, is an effective method to rebuild attachments. Group therapy for emotionally abused children provides peer support, teaches social skills, and fosters the expression of emotions. Family therapy should be implemented only when parents are no longer engaged in active abuse, have apologized for their behavior, and want to build a positive relationship with the child. Individual therapy is recommend for the abuser, nonoffending parent, and child victim prior to the commencement of family therapy.

James Henry
Tom Luster

See also Conflict and Stress; Emotions; Physical Abuse; Sexual Abuse

References and further reading
Brassard, Marla R., David B. Hardy, and Stuart N. Hart. 1993. "The Psychological Maltreatment Rating Scales." *Child Abuse and Neglect* 17, no. 1: 715–729.
Burnett, Bruce B. 1993. "The Psychological Abuse of Latency Age Children: A Survey." *Child Abuse and Neglect* 17, no. 1: 441–454.
Kent, Angela, and Glenn Waller. 1998. "The Impact of Childhood Emotional Abuse: An Extension of the Child Abuse and Trauma Scale." *Child Abuse and Neglect* 22, no. 5: 393–399.
Pearl, Peggy S. 1996. "Psychological Abuse." Recognition of Child Abuse for the Mandated Reporter (pp. 120–146). St. Louis, MO: G. W. Medical Publishing.
U.S. Department of Health and Human Services, Administration on Children, Youth, and Families. 1999. Child Maltreatment 1997: Reports from the States to the National Child Abuse and Neglect Data System. Washington, DC: U.S. Government Printing Office.

Emotions

As children become adolescents they begin to experience a richer and more varied emotional life, including increased awareness of the causes, effects, and nuances of emotions. Emotions have both positive and negative aspects. On the one hand, they help people survive. Fear motivates them to get away from danger quickly, and anger makes them fight back to protect themselves or others. Likewise, love motivates them to give and receive support. On the other hand, emotions can be painful. Fear, anger, even love can be quite unpleasant. Rage can lead people to do things they later regret. Indeed, people can get so caught up in being angry—or having fun—that they fail to see that their actions are hurting others. Adolescence brings with it ample experience of these different sides of emotions.

What are emotions? They encompass inner feelings, changes in facial expression and tone of voice, physiological changes such as increased heart rate and surges of adrenaline, and changes in how the mind thinks. For example, emotions can speed, slow, or focus a thought process. These different elements do not always correspond. Researchers have found that people can feel happy or unhappy in the absence of measurable physiological changes, that their smiles and frowns do not always match their inner feelings, and that they are not always aware of the emotions affecting their actions, as when a person indignantly shouts "I am not angry."

As noted, emotions also contribute to survival. Without them, humans and other mammals would have died out long ago. Charles Darwin observed that emotions such as fear and anger prepare animals for "fight or flight." Indeed, the racing heart that comes with fear prepares them to run faster. And fear as well as anger take the mind off mundane things, such as what to eat for a snack, and direct all attention to dealing with the crisis at hand. More recently, scientists have recognized that still other emotions—such as love, jealousy, loneliness, and guilt—serve valuable social functions, working together as a system to motivate people to seek and maintain good relationships. Facial expressions of joy and anger communicate feelings to others, further contributing to the maintenance of good relationships.

Adolescence has often been stereotyped as a period of emotionality and moodiness. Although scientific knowledge about adolescents' emotions is limited, research in the last twenty years has begun to provide some basic findings. First, across all ages, most people experience positive emotions and moods more often than negative ones. The word *moods* usually refers to longer-lasting emotional states, especially in cases where the emotional state has no clear cause. Second, people vary widely in terms of their range of emotions, owing to experience and genetic differences in temperament. Thus, some adolescents are more deeply emotional than others,

just as some experience positive or negative emotions more frequently than others. Third, although boys and girls experience a similar range of emotions, boys are somewhat more likely to act out emotions and girls are somewhat more likely to turn them inward.

Another finding is that, with age, adolescents become more knowledgeable about emotions—more aware of psychology. Whereas children do not see emotions as separate from the situation that caused them, adolescents come to understand that emotions can have a psychological life of their own, independent of the situation. Whereas children generally think people can experience only one emotion at a time, adolescents know that people can have many feelings at once. And whereas children are aware of only a few emotions—happy, sad, angry, afraid—adolescents experience a rich range of complex feelings including shame, disappointment, contentment, and bliss. Adolescents are also more aware of how emotions affect them—for example, how they change their thought processes.

Are adolescents therefore more emotional than people of other ages? Research is beginning to suggest that, on average, adolescents experience negative emotions somewhat more often than children. Adolescents also have more extreme positive and negative emotions than adults: Compared to their parents, for example, they more often feel very happy and very unhappy. Of course, these generalizations don't take individual differences into account; indeed, there are many adolescents who are *less* emotional than many adults. Moreover, these research findings relate only to the *feeling* of emotions; whether adolescents' physiological states are different from those of adults and children is not known.

If adolescents are in fact more emotional, what causes this difference? One possibility is that adolescents experience more emotions, and feel them more deeply, because they are more knowledgeable and aware of emotions than they were as children. Second, evidence suggests that, contrary to common belief, adolescents' emotionality is not strongly related to puberty—to "raging hormones." In fact, it is related more to daily stress, which tends to increase with entry into adolescence. Third, adolescents' stronger emotions may be related to the novelty in their lives—to the joy and sorrow of experiencing for the first time not just new freedoms but also the difficulties and limitations of the adult world.

As noted earlier, emotions have both positive and negative aspects; the same is true of adolescents' rich experience of them. Certainly there is much in emotional experience to be valued. Happiness, love, and other positive emotions are part of what makes life worth living. The psychologist Mihaly Csikszentmihalyi has found that the enjoyment of taking on challenges motivates adolescents (as well as adults) to climb mountains, paint pictures, and launch ambitious careers. Other psychologists, too, have recognized that emotions provide useful information. Anxiety, loneliness, or disgust can signal a situation that isn't quite right, just as positive emotions can signal a good match.

On the other hand, many psychologists urge people to be intelligent about emotions. In some cases, emotions can give the wrong information. People get angry and, later, are embarrassed to learn that they misunderstood the situation. Or they fall in love with someone they do not know because he or she looks nice, or because they have strong personal needs that have nothing to do with that person. In short, it is wise to pay attention to emotions, but also to be discriminating about the information they provide.

When adolescents experience strong negative emotions, there are certain things they can do to cope—that is, to make themselves feel better. When possible, it is best simply to confront the situation that is causing the feeling and try to change it or get others to change it. In cases where the situation cannot be changed, however, it is best to soothe or reduce the negative emotions. Research suggests that getting involved in a distracting activity is often quite effective toward this end; conversely, use of drugs or alcohol to escape feelings generally does not work. Talking to parents, other adults, or friends can also help teens understand the situation and the negative feelings they are experiencing. However, spending long sessions talking about their feelings with someone who is also anxious or depressed can actually make their feelings worse.

Adolescents who are experiencing negative emotions that do not go away should seek help from a professional such as a counselor, psychologist, or physician. Long-term feelings of sadness, worry, or anger may be signs of depression or some other psychological condition. Alternatively, they may be signs of a medical condition that can be treated with medications. Professionals are trained to identify what may lie behind a pattern of negative emotions. And research indicates that counseling, sometimes in combination with medication, is frequently effective in reducing adolescents' distress.

Reed Larson

See also Developmental Challenges;
    Puberty: Psychological and Social
    Changes; Sexuality, Emotional Aspects
    of; Storm and Stress; Why Is There an
    Adolescence?

References and further reading
Csikszentmihalyi, Mihaly. 1990. *Flow:
    The Psychology of Optimal Experience.*
    New York: Harper and Row.
Larson, Reed, Gerald L. Clore, and
    Gretchen A. Wood. 1999. "The
    Emotions of Romantic Relationships:
    Do They Wreak Havoc on
    Adolescents?" Pp. 19–49 in
    *Contemporary Perspectives in
    Adolescent Romantic Relationships.*
    Edited by Wyndol Furman, B. Bradford
    Brown, and Candice Feiring. New York:
    Cambridge University Press.
Lewis, Michael, and Jeannette M.
    Haviland, eds. 1993. *The Handbook of
    Emotions.* New York: Guilford Press.
Saarni, Carolyn. 1999. *The Development
    of Emotional Competence.* New York:
    Guilford Press.

Empathy

Empathy literally means the capacity to *feel into* another human being; in its fullest sense, it is a capacity that develops, or can develop, in adolescence, providing a balance to egocentrism, the inability to see the point of view and share the feelings of anyone else so common among adolescents. Empathy is crucial to the full development of the human capacity to relate to others.

Humans are social animals. Because of their social nature, humans form many different groups, such as families, cultures, and friendship groups, that play important roles in their lives. Their social nature also means that human beings do not survive alone. And even if one does, in rare exceptional cases of the kind seen in Tarzan, development will be tremendously disrupted. Isolation plays an unquestionably detrimental role in a person's development, especially in the early stages, affecting in numerous negative ways the psychology and biology of the organism. In other words, people need other people for the purpose of survival, as well as for emotional and intellectual sharing.

Empathy is hard to define, though it seems quite understandable at the intuitive level. It is something that allows people to understand and sympathize with each other. It also may be viewed as opposite to egocentrism, which is a person's inability to see and take into consideration anybody but herself.

There are two different views on empathy that stress different aspects of this ability. Some scholars see it as an emotion, somewhat similar to compassion, but with more emphasis on the ability to adjust to the emotional state of another person. From this point of view, empathy shares all the basic characteristics of emotions. That is, it has survival value (a human being does not survive alone), it is biologically rooted (there are parts of the brain designed especially for emotional processing), yet socialized, and socialized differently in different countries (for instance, in collectivist cultures, where peoples' lives are closely interdependent, empathy would take a slightly different form than in the more individualistic Western cultures), it is interwoven with cognitive processes (what one feels depends on his cognitive appraisal of the situation), and it is experienced differently by different people, depending on individual differences in temperament and personality.

For other scholars, viewing empathy as an emotion would be simplistic. These scholars consider empathy to be a complex ability, existing at two levels and containing an emotional response as only one of its components. The lower level (simple empathy) is the ability to experience affective responses more appropriate to someone else's situation than to one's own. A common example is feeling sad when someone else is in pain. The higher level (complex empathy) is an ability to *perceive* objects and events from another's point of view. Feeling sad when someone else is in pain is easier than really assessing events from his, not your, point of view.

Complex empathy has three components: an affective component, a cognitive component, and a component that involves the ability to take on a role. The affective component of empathy is often referred to as empathetic emotion, or responsiveness. The cognitive component of empathy belongs to the sphere of social cognition. It is the ability to discriminate people's emotional states and personality characteristics. Finally, the third component is the ability to assume another's perspective and role, to really *see things as another sees them*. All three components are in constant interplay with each other.

To better understand the mechanism of empathy, consider the following example: A child comes home after school and sees that his mother, who is usually excited to see him, now is distant, silent, not attentive to him, irritated, and ready to scold him for trivial things. At first, he may even become angry with her, but then he starts to think and understand that something must have happened. Then he notices that it has started snowing, and though for him snow usually means joy, snowballs, and playing in the snow with his dog, he also remembers that his mother always gets scared when it is snowing while his father is not home. Before he was born his father was in a serious accident during a heavy snowfall. Remembering this event helps the child to understand his mother, and he becomes sad, and a little scared, too, and does not go out to play in the snow until his father is safe at home.

This example demonstrates the importance of the cognitive component in empathy, and it also suggests that empathy is not given at birth, but develops as the child grows and his cognitive structures become more complex.

Martin Hoffman presented four stages in the development of empathy. The first one is global empathy, which he found in infants aged up to twelve months. Amazingly, even newborns are able to empathize at a very primitive level: They respond with crying when they hear another baby's cry, and, later, they smile when somebody smiles at them. Yet this cannot be called true empathy, since at this age a child does not discriminate between herself and others. What is observed in newborns is more of an automatic matching of emotions in the infant's homogenous, selfless world.

In toddlers from one to three years, researchers observe what they call egocentric empathy. Children of this age already distinguish themselves from others, but can respond to events only as their developmental level would permit. In the above-mentioned example, it can be concluded that the child was older than three because at the age of three he might be distressed at his mother's distress but would play in the snow anyway, not being able to understand his mother's concerns.

By the preadolescent years, a child may reach the stage of basic empathetic understanding and be able to partially match others' feelings by understanding why people feel as they do, yet not be able to feel like them. It is only in adolescence, when all cognitive structures are (for the most part) developed, that one can really empathize with another, which means understanding, feeling, and seeing things from another's perspective.

This is an important transition, because it means that a teenager is becoming prepared to enter into complex emotional exchanges with other people, including family members, friends, and even strangers. For example, during adolescence young men and women often begin to devote themselves to groups that are larger than their immediate familial or social circle. These include political parties, social foundations, such as Amnesty International, and volunteer organizations. Involvement in these kinds of groups presupposes a teenager's ability to want to see things through the eyes of a person who may be of another country, class, or religion. As Erik Erikson points out, empathy is also an important component of emotional intimacy, or the process of sharing aspects of oneself with another person whom one in turn seeks to understand. Without empathy, it would be difficult for teenagers to begin to form the kinds of close friendships and love relationships that provide a strong social network over their lifespan. Finally, although some say that adolescence is a time of differentiation from one's family and the formation of an independent identity, empathy is a quality that helps a teenager to understand the motivations, feelings, and fears of their family members, even when they may at first seem unreasonable. This kind of interpersonal understanding is one of the keys to developing mature relationships throughout adolescence and adulthood.

Janna Jilnina

See also Coping; Counseling; Emotions; Volunteerism

References and further reading
Duggan, Hayden A. 1978. *A Second Chance: Empathy in Adolescent Development.* Lexington, MA: Lexington Books.
Eisenberg, Nancy, ed. 1989. *Empathy and Related Emotional Responses.* San Francisco: Jossey-Bass.
Erikson, Erik H. 1950. *Childhood and Society.* New York: Norton.
Hoffman, Martin L. 1983. "Empathy, Guilt, and Social Cognition." Pp. 1–52 in *The Relationship between Social and Cognitive Development.* Edited by Willis F. Overton. Hillsdale, NJ: Erlbaum.
Karniol, Rachel, Rivi Gabay, Yael Ochion, and Yeal Harari. 1998. "Is Gender or Gender-Role Orientation a Better Predictor of Empathy in Adolescence?" *Sex Roles* 39: 45–49.
Strayer, Janet, and William Roberts. 1997. "Facial and Verbal Measure of Children's Emotions and Empathy." *International Journal of Behavioral Development* 20: 627–649.
Tucker, Corinna J., Kimberly A. Updegraff, Susan M. McHale, and Ann C. Crouter. 1998. "Older Siblings as Socializers of Younger Siblings' Empathy." *Journal of Early Adolescence* [special issue: *Prosocial and Moral Development in Early Adolescence,* Pt. 2] 19: 176–198.

Employment: Positive and Negative Consequences

Employment has several positive implications for adolescent development. For instance, it appears to give adolescents a basis for new identities and new expectations of responsibility and independence from parents as well as a new, high status among peers. In addition, when working, adolescents encounter working peers and adults who can potentially provide new models of adult behavior and new reference groups.

Of course, these new groups can act as either good or bad influences on the adolescent. And employment can take time away from school, thereby diminishing the adolescent's opportunity to participate in extracurricular activities or the time available for homework.

Moreover, the kinds of employment opportunities that are most readily available to youth are the same work activities that have the most negative consequences for adults. That is, most youth work in the retail and service sectors, and are given jobs with high turnover, low pay, little authority, and low prestige. Adults in such jobs are often displeased not only by the work conditions involved but also by the fact that such positions entail simple, repetitive tasks (e.g., "flipping burgers") that require very little or no special training or skills (e.g., "Here is the hamburger, flip it over when it is brown, don't touch the hot stove").

Nevertheless, it is possible that even these tasks—though perhaps boring and undesirable to adults who, if they find themselves in such roles, feel that their future prospects are dim—may be new and challenging activities to a young person. Someone who has never worked outside the home and has never been asked to be productive for pay may be more excited by the opportunity to be involved in the world of work than displeased by the particular activities he or she finds available in this setting.

Thus, employment exerts a range of possible positive and negative influences on adolescent development. The issue is not one of deciding whether work itself is beneficial but, rather, a matter of learning when, under what circumstances, work may have either a positive or a negative effect. Several major research projects have been conducted to determine the role of work in adolescent development. These studies allow us to address the question of work's effects on adolescents.

In one such study, Ellen Greenberger and Laurence D. Steinberg (1986) studied youth employment among students in four California high schools. The students reported, on the one hand, that their employment was associated with their being punctual, dependable, and personally responsible; among girls, employment was linked to reports of self-reliance. On the other hand, employed adolescents were more frequently late for school and engaged in more deviant behavior than was the case among nonemployed youth. Similarly, working students reported more school misconduct than did nonworking students; indeed, working a moderate number of hours was linked to the highest rates of school misconduct.

Another major study of the implications of work for youth development involved a longitudinal assessment of approximately 1,000 adolescents in the ninth and tenth grades conducted by Jeylan Mortimer and colleagues (1994). For most of the adolescents in this study (about 90 percent), there was no formal association between school curriculum and work (e.g., these youth were not involved in a work-study program, and they did not receive credit for their work). Moreover, fewer than 20 percent of the adolescents reported that their jobs provided them with knowledge about topics studied in school or that their work experiences gave them information that they could contribute to class discussions.

Consistent with the earlier research, this study found that working had some negative implications for the academic and personal development of youth. For instance, 43 percent of the students reported that working decreased the time available for their homework, and about half reported that simultaneously being a worker and a student was stressful. Moreover, students who worked at high intensity (i.e., twenty-five or more hours a week) engaged in more alcohol use.

Yet many students also reported positive characteristics associated with working while still in high school. About 48 percent indicated that their job taught them the importance of obtaining a good education, and approximately a third reported that working had increased their ability to identify the courses in high school that they liked or did not like. In addition, about 36 percent of the students reported that what they learned at school facilitated their job performance.

By the tenth grade, 42 percent of the boys and 52 percent of the girls were employed. Consistent with what was found when the students were in the ninth grade, the researchers observed no overall difference in tenth grade between working and nonworking students in terms of time spent in schoolwork, time devoted to extracurricular activities, or grade-point averages (GPAs). Nor was overall work status predictive of school behavior problems. On the contrary, employment at low intensity (fewer than twenty hours a week) was linked to lower dropout rates, and high school seniors who worked at moderate intensity (one to twenty hours a week) had higher grades than both nonworking students and students who worked more hours per week.

In addition, there was no difference between working and nonworking students in their *intrinsic* motivation for school—that is, in the degree to which they wanted to do well in school because of internal standards of excellence and personal values for achievement—as compared to wanting to achieve in school because such attainment was associated with rewards from parents, teachers, or society. Furthermore, the number of hours per week a student worked was not systematically related to such motivation. For instance, the highest degree of intrinsic motivation for school was exhibited by students of both sexes who worked relatively few hours a week (i.e., one to five hours), by girls who worked in excess of twenty-five hours a week, and by boys who worked either at very low levels (one to five hours a week) or relatively high ones (twenty-six to thirty hours a week).

These findings suggest that there is no link between student employment—even when it takes place over many hours per week—and risk of poor school attitudes, diminished time devoted to homework, lessened involvement in extracurricular activities, or low school grades. In this study, there was evidence that young people could "do it all"—that they could maintain their involvement and achievement in school *and* participate in the workforce. Indeed, although work stress had a negative impact on the schoolwork of these youth, the quality of the work environment (e.g., the menial nature of the work roles assigned to the youth) was not associated with their GPAs or their participation in extracurricular activities.

Work can also have a beneficial influence on behavior in particular settings. For instance, in a longitudinal study of rural Iowa youth between the seventh and tenth grades, Michael J. Shanahan and his colleagues found that earnings from paid labor, when spent on nonleisure activities, were associated with positive parent-adolescent relationships as well as more time spent with the family by the adolescent and less parental monitoring of the youth. Among girls, opportunities for skill development at work increased their intrinsic motivation for schoolwork. In addition, girls' helpfulness at work increased their overall behavioral competence, which in turn furthered the girls' tendencies to be helpful at work.

In sum, work has beneficial effects on youth development in the areas of personal abilities, school performance, and family relations. In addition, the association between work and adolescent development appears to differ for males and females.

Richard M. Lerner
Jacqueline V. Lerner

See also Career Development; Maternal Employment: Influences on Adolescents; Vocational Development; Work in Adolescence

References and further reading
Greenberger, Ellen, and Laurence D. Steinberg. 1986. *When Teenagers Work: The Psychological and Social Cost of Adolescent Employment.* New York: Basic Books.
Lerner, Richard M. In press. *Adolescence: Development, Diversity, Context, and Application.* Upper Saddle River, NJ: Prentice-Hall.
McKeachie, James, Sandra Lindsay, Sandy Hobbs, and M. Lavalette. 1996. "Adolescents' Perceptions of the Role of Part-Time Work." *Adolescence* 31, no. 121: 193–204.
Mihalic, Sharon W., and Delbert Elliot. 1997. "Short- and Long-Term Consequences of Doing Work." *Youth and Society* 28, no. 4: 464–498.
Mortimer, Jeylan, Michael Shanahan, and Seong Ryu. 1994. "The Effects of Adolescent Employment on School-Related Orientations and Behavior." Pp. 304–326 in *Adolescence in Context.* Edited by R. Silbereisen and R. Todt. New York: Springer.
Shanahan, Michael J., Glenn H. Elder Jr., Margaret Burchinal, and Rand D.
Conger. 1996. "Adolescent Paid Labor and Relationships with Parents: Early Work-Family Linkages." *Child Development* 67: 2183–2200.

Environmental Health Issues

The protection of children and adolescents from the threat of toxicants in the environment has become a central issue for many communities. Although most children and adolescents in the United States are considerably better off in terms of health than their cohorts of previous generations for a variety of reasons including safer drinking water and improved nutrition, housing, medical care, and sanitary waste, they nevertheless face threats of environmental toxicants unknown to previous generations. In fact, they are potentially at risk from exposure to an estimated 15,000 synthetic, high-production chemicals, most of which did not exist fifty years ago. Some of these chemicals are found throughout the environment; others are contained in household products. Moreover, the exposure of children and adolescents to these chemicals is aggravated by poverty and inadequate access to healthcare.

The historical contributions of modern medicine, including the triumphs of antibiotics and vaccines, in conjunction with the current threat of exposure to environmental chemicals and toxins, has created a new paradigm of childhood and adolescent health. Specifically, whereas the incidence of childhood diseases such as smallpox and diphtheria has substantially declined, the incidence of diseases of known or suspected toxic environmental origin has increased significantly. The following diseases and their environmental correlates are notable in this regard.

The protection of children and adolescents from the threat of toxic chemicals in the environment has become a central issue for many communities. (Bob Krist/Corbis)

Asthma and Air Quality

Each year more than 150,000 children and adolescents are hospitalized due to asthma, a disease that, in 1998, affected more than 5 million children and adolescents. The incidence of asthma is particularly uneven: The disease occurs more often in urban than in rural areas and more often among African American and Hispanic children and adolescents than among their Caucasian counterparts. Asthma is defined as a narrowing of air passages in the lungs that, in turn, produces breathing difficulty. Asthmatic attacks are typically brought on by "triggers" in children and adolescents who have either an acquired or genetic disposition to asthma. Primary triggers of asthma—including household dust mites

and airway irritants such as cigarette smoke and smog—set off a series of reactions that narrow the lung airways, producing such hallmark symptoms as coughing, wheezing, shortness of breath, and increased risk for respiratory infection.

Asthma symptoms have also been linked to poor air quality, both indoors and outdoors. A major contributor to poor indoor air quality is environmental tobacco smoke (ETS), also known as secondhand smoke. According to the National Center for Environmental Health at the Centers for Disease Control (CDC), 43 percent of children between two months and eleven years of age live in a residence with at least one smoker (CDC, 1996). Outdoor air quality, meanwhile, is greatly affected by urban air pollution—another major factor in the incidence of asthma. Children and adolescents are especially vulnerable to the effects of air pollution because they typically spend more time outdoors than adults do (CDC, 1991; U.S. Environmental Protection Agency, 1997a).

Environmental Factors in Childhood/Adolescent Cancers
Each year in the United States approximately 8,000 children ranging from infancy to fifteen years of age are diagnosed with a type of cancer (Miller et al., 1993). Beyond the first year of life, cancers (in particular, leukemia and brain cancer) are the second leading cause of death in children under fifteen years of age, after accidents (Zahm and DeVesa, 1995). Although the death rate attributed to childhood cancers has declined, the actual incidence of new childhood cancers has increased dramatically since the 1970s. For example, between 1973 and 1994, the incidence of childhood brain cancer increased by 39.6 percent (DeVesa et al., 1995).

The reasons for this increased incidence are not fully understood. Although improved diagnosis (through magnetic resonance imaging) and changes in diet may have influenced the outcome, the increase occurred too rapidly over a relatively short period of time (twenty-one years) to be explained entirely by, say, genetic factors, thus raising the specter of environmental factors such as carcinogens (substances that trigger the development of cancer). Examples of carcinogens implicated in childhood/adolescent cancers include environmental tobacco smoke (ETS) (U.S. Environmental Protection Agency, 1994; NIOSH, 1991), asbestos, and certain hazardous wastes and pesti-

cides (NRC, 1993; Zahm and DeVesa, 1995). Hazardous wastes encompass a wide variety of organic chemicals and heavy metals such as lead, toxins to which children and adolescents may be exposed if they live or play near hazardous waste sites. And, indeed, the U.S. Environmental Protection Agency (EPA) estimates that as many as 4 million children and adolescents live within one mile of such sites.

Developmental/Neurological Toxicity and Environmental Factors
A significant environmental problem in the lives of children and adolescents is the impact of neurotoxins on the brain and nervous system. These substances can affect attentional skills, language, even overall intelligence (Needleman, Schell, and Bellinger, 1990). Whereas neurotoxins such as lead, PCBs, and dioxins may have only a temporary ill effect on adult brains, they can result in enduring damage to the incompletely developed brains of children (NRC, 1993; Needleman and Gatsonis, 1990). Consider, for example, the clearly harmful effect of lead ingestion on young children under six, particularly those who live in older homes with peeling lead paint as well as lead contaminated dust. Children and adolescents can also be exposed to lead by drinking contaminated water (from lead plumbing in older homes), breathing air from nearby industrial facilities, or living or playing too close to hazardous waste sites.

Endocrine Problems, Sexual Disorders, and Environmental Factors
Increasing evidence suggests that a variety of organic chemicals have been introduced into the environment and that these chemicals have had adverse effects on bodily functions—specifically, by

disrupting the endocrine system. Most of these effects (sexual abnormalities and reproductive dysfunctions) have been found in animals in the wild; yet to be determined is the impact on human beings. Current research is focusing on the relationship between endocrine disruptions in cancer, reproductive and developmental disorders, and neurological and immunological problems, as there is clear reason for concern—especially with respect to children and adolescents (Kavlock and Ankley, 1996; U.S. Environmental Protection Agency, 1997b).

As noted, many traditional diseases of childhood and adolescence have been contained or eliminated by means of vaccines or antibiotics. By a similar token, diseases resulting from environmental exposure are preventable (Landrigan, 1992): Toxic environmental diseases that occur because of human activity can be substantially reduced or avoided by modifying that activity. Perhaps the signal example of this principle of environmental modification in recent years was the dramatic reduction in child blood-lead levels that occurred following the removal of lead from gasoline (Schwartz, 1994).

Lawrence B. Schiamberg

See also Cigarette Smoking; Health Promotion

References and further reading
Centers for Disease Control (CDC). 1991. "Children at Risk from Ozone Air Pollution in the United States." *Morbidity and Mortality Weekly Report* 44: 309–312.
———. 1996. *Exposure to Second-Hand Smoke Widespread.* Centers for Disease Control (April).
DeVesa, S. S., W. J. Blot, B. J. Sonte, B. A. Miller, R. E. Tarove, and J. F. Fraumeni Jr. 1995. "Recent Cancer Trends in the United States." *Journal of the National Cancer Institute* 87: 175–182.
Kavlock, R. J., and G. T. Ankley. 1996. "A Perspective on the Risk Assessment Process for Endocrine-Disruptive Effects on Wildlife and Human Health." *Risk Analysis* 16: 731–739.
Landrigan, P. J. 1992. "Commentary: Environmental Disease—A Preventable Epidemic." *American Journal of Public Health* 82: 941–943.
Miller, B. A., L.A.G. Ries, F. R. Hankey, F. L. Kosary, A. Harras, S. S. DeVesa, and B. K. Edwards, eds. 1993. "SEER Cancer Statistics Review: 1973–1990." NIH Publication Number 93-2789. Bethesda, MD: National Cancer Institute.
National Institute for Occupational Safety and Health (NIOSH). 1991. *Current Intelligence Bulletin 54: Environmental Tobacco Smoke in the Workplace.*
National Research Council (NRC). 1993. *Pesticides in the Diets of Infants and Children.* Washington, DC: National Academy Press.
Needleman, H. L., and C. A. Gatsonis. 1990. "Low-Level Lead Exposure and the IQ of Children: A Meta-Analysis of Modern Studies." *Journal of American Medical Association* 263: 673–678.
Needleman, H. L., A. Schell, and D. Bellinger. 1990. "The Long-Term Effects of Exposure to Low Doses of Lead in Childhood: 11-Year Follow-Up Report." *New England Journal of Medicine* 322: 83–88.
Schwartz, J. 1994. "Societal Benefits of Reducing Lead Exposure." *Environmental Resources* 66: 105–124.
U.S. Environmental Protection Agency. 1994. *Indoor Air Pollution: An Introduction for Health Professionals,* GPO No. 1994-523-217/81322. Compiled by the U.S. Environmental Protection Agency, the American Lung Association, the Consumer Product Safety Commission, and the American Medical Association.
———. 1997a. *Criteria Pollutants (Greenbook): National Ambient Air Quality Standards.* U.S. Environmental Protection Agency, Office of Air and Radiation.
———. 1997b. *Special Report on Endrocrine Disruption: An Effects Assessment and Analysis,* Publication No. EPA 630-R-96-012. U.S. Environmental Protection Agency, Office of Research and Development.

Zahm, S. H., and S. S. DeVesa. 1995. "Childhood Cancer: Overview of Incidence Trends and Environmental Carcinogens." *Environmental Health Perspectives* 103 (Supplement 6): 177–184.

Ethnic Identity

Adolescence is a time when young people first begin to think seriously about such questions as "Who am I?" and "Who do I want to be?" These are important questions regarding identity, which has many facets. And, indeed, a key process of adolescence is exploring the possibilities for each of these facets and beginning to integrate them into an overall sense of self. One can speak of social identity, political identity, religious identity, sexual identity, and so on. But ethnic identity refers to that facet of the self that is derived from membership in a particular ethnic group. Some individuals emphasize the feelings and attitudes associated with membership in a group, whereas others emphasize such aspects as language, styles of interaction, values, and knowledge of history and tradition. Still others see ethnic identity as a combination of these factors—how they feel about being a member of a particular ethnic group and what they know about that group. Research indicates that adolescents who have a strong sense of ethnic pride tend also to exhibit higher rates of self-esteem and self-evaluation, more positive family and peer relations, and a greater sense of mastery over their lives and environment (Phinney and Alipuria, 1990).

The process of exploring identity during adolescence is tied to various aspects of cognitive, social, and emotional development. As adolescents mature cognitively, what they think about and how they think begin to change. Increasing cognitive maturity leads them to question, evaluate, and often challenge the nature and quality of relationships, political issues, societal beliefs, religious beliefs, cultural values, and the "way things are" in general. Some of the beliefs and values they learned during childhood are reclaimed as their own; others are rejected. Knowing what to retain and what to reject requires exploration of the possibilities that exist both within and beyond what they already know.

Exploration and experimentation enable adolescents to make later commitments not only to values and beliefs but also to educational and career goals. It is important, however, that these commitments and goals be self-chosen rather than merely accepted without question or reflection from adults, peers, or wider society. The latter years of high school and the first years of college comprise a particularly important period of exploration. The college experience, in particular, opens a new world of possibilities with regard to education, career aspirations, and relationships.

Another aspect of cognitive development involves adolescents' growing capacity for introspection—for thinking about their own thoughts and feelings. Introspection, in combination with all the changes that occur during puberty, often leads adolescents to see themselves as the focus of other people's attention and interest and to feel as though "everyone" is looking at them (Elkind and Bowen, 1979). This aspect of cognitive development is related to both the social and emotional aspects of identity development. Indeed, it is during adolescence that time and attention are increasingly directed away from family and toward peers, who in turn take on considerable

For some adolescents, exploring their ethnic identity is an important part of exploring their sense of self. (Dean Wong/Corbis)

importance for adolescents such that it matters what others think and say about them. Peer pressure and the tendency to conform are tied to this sensitivity to peer evaluation, resulting in a need to "fit in" and to possess a sense of belonging. This need is evident, for example, in the tendency of adolescents to dress and speak similarly to one another.

For some adolescents, exploring their ethnic identity is somewhat like exploring their sense of self. However, for others, particularly those from ethnic minority groups and low socioeconomic backgrounds, there are obstacles that make the process more difficult.

Specifically, some adolescents experience a conflict between the values and preferences modeled by their ethnic group and those encouraged by the dominant culture. Feeling caught in the middle leaves them feeling forced to choose one culture and to reject the other. This "either-or" dilemma can lead to fragmentation as opposed to integration. Differences in skin tone, native language, religious practices, food preferences, celebration of holidays, and so on, can set these minority youth apart from their majority-group peers at a time when, as noted, fitting in and a sense of belonging are extremely important. The strain is worsened when the adolescents encounter prejudice or discrimination.

Exploration of educational and career possibilities is a critical step in developing a sense of self, but prejudice and discrimination can limit minority adolescents' opportunities to explore these possibilities. This hardship especially affects teens from low socioeconomic backgrounds; for these young people, the period of exploration is often cut short by the need to take on adult roles and responsibilities, such as a full-time job, before or immediately following graduation from high school.

Many adolescents who experience or perceive the opportunity structure as inaccessible do not even attempt exploration (Ogbu, 1990). For example, one study has found that African American adolescents have occupational aspirations as high as those of white adolescents but significantly lower expectations of realizing these aspirations (Baly, 1989). Lowered expectations of achieving one's goals and dreams can, in turn, reduce the motivation to explore and pursue the means of achieving them.

Ethnic identity is indeed part of self-identity. The process of developing a sense of self neither begins nor ends with the adolescent period; however, it is important for adolescents, in particular, to be able to explore, reflect upon, and select from among the values, beliefs, and practices of both their ethnic group and the dominant culture in order to arrive at a self-chosen set of values and beliefs. Toward this end, schools and communities need to provide young people with a variety of opportunities to explore who they are and who they want to become.

Imma De Stefanis

See also African American Adolescents, Identity in; African American Adolescents, Research on; African American Male Adolescents; Asian American Adolescents: Comparisons and Contrasts; Asian American Adolescents: Issues Influencing Identity; Chicana/o Adolescents; Ethnocentrism; Identity; Latina/o Adolescents; Racial Discrimination; White and American: A Matter of Privilege?

References and further reading
Baly, Iris. 1989. "Career and Vocational Development of Black Youth." Pp. 249–265 in *Black Adolescents*. Edited by Reginald Jones. Berkeley, CA: Cobb and Henry Publishers.
Elkind, David, and Robert Bowen. 1979. "Imaginary Audience Behavior in Children and Adolescents." *Developmental Review* 15: 33–44.
Ogbu, John. 1990. "Minority Education in Comparative Perspective." *Journal of Negro Education* 59: 45–57.
Phinney, Jean S., and Linda L. Alipuria. 1990. "Ethnic Identity in College Students from Four Ethnic Groups." *Journal of Adolescence* 13: 171–183.

Ethnocentrism

Ethnocentrism is the belief that one's own group is inherently superior to other groups, suggesting that one's own group is dominant and represents the standard against which all others are judged. In signifying the supremacy of one's own people and their ways of doing things, this belief suggests an overestimated preference for one's own group and the concomitant undervalued assessment of or aversion toward other groups (Cornell and Hartmann, 1998; Levine and Campbell, 1992). In essence, then, ethnocentrism reflects not only how people view themselves but also how they interact with others. The implication is that negative attitudes toward others originate from a need to preserve self-esteem by projecting one's own negative traits onto others. Note that fervent liking for one's own group is not necessarily associated with disdain of other groups; indeed, a related concept—cultural relativity—implies an appreciation for one's group *and* the simultaneous valuing of other cultures and groups. Positive identification with one's reference group during adolescence, however, appears to serve as a protector or buffer against the stress often associated with groups of marginalized status.

The role of ethnocentrism in the life of ethnic groups incorporates not only social and psychological functions but also distinctive strategies related to the adaptive processes that arise when such groups come into contact with other groups. For these reasons it has long attracted the attention of social scientists and other professionals interested in the interactions and mutual influences among ethnic groups. As an aspect of the adolescent's self-concept, social identity derives from membership in a group together with the value and emotional importance attached to this membership. Indeed, the phenomenon of ethnocentrism is inherently linked to the formation of attitudes. Positive aspects of the adolescent's group are strongly emphasized, whereas features and members of other groups are judged in terms of standards that are applicable only to the adolescent's group and, hence, are often denigrated. An easy rejection of the unfamiliar is characteristic of ethnocentrism, which therefore makes it a component of prejudice (Perreault and Bourhis, 1999).

The most fundamental task of development during adolescence is achieving a sense of identity. Ethnic identity becomes increasingly ethnocentric during the adolescent and young adult years. The development of an identity or a clear sense of self stems from several sources, including gender, class, and ethnic group membership. Ethnic group membership and ethnic identity themes are important in societies that are heterogeneous in composition and have a history of significant intergroup tensions; consider, for example, the experiences of Native Americans and African Americans in the nineteenth and twentieth centuries. Identity development occurs in multiple contexts, including community, school, family, and peer relationships. Adolescents must make transitions between these contexts and find ways to integrate their various experiences within each of them. If the contexts are incompatible, however, these transitions can be stress-provoking experiences (Phelan, Davidson, and Cao, 1991). Parental involvement in the ethnic socialization of its children varies significantly and has important implications for ethnocentrism. Adolescents are vulnerable since all aspects of social identity processes undergo abrupt revisions during the physical and psychological changes characteristic of this period. They become increasingly aware of their group membership and the expectations, privileges, restraints, and social responsibilities that accompany that membership. The promotion of mental health among minority youth is strengthened when cultural heritage is actively and continuously emphasized as a means of encouraging self-acceptance, particularly within a culturally insensitive environment. It provides the youth with abilities required to adapt to his or her social status and enhances positive feelings and evaluations of the self. These strategies, though perhaps protective for minority group members functioning in a larger and dominant culture, do not account for the role of ethnocentrism among majority group members—a role that often exacerbates perceptions of privilege and power in intergroup interactions.

Mobilization of culture and shared historical tradition often parallel increased economic competition and downward mobility. Political insecurity, status anxieties, and doubts about individual identity are translated into a loss of collective worthiness. Ethnocentrism offers assurance of restored dignity and extinguished humiliation, according to specific group histories. Racism is not a necessary ingredient of ethnocentrism, but ethnocentrism, and exclusion of others, usually accompanies the construction of boundaries between "us" and "them." By adolescence, minority youth have developed an awareness of majority values and standards of competence. They can begin to integrate their experiences with future expectations, based on their own values and those of the majority culture. Since awareness of stereotypes and group membership has also developed by this time, it plays a key role in identity formation. For most adolescents, the contextual stressors associated with the effects of stereotypes are coupled with normative developmental stressors such as family and independence issues, sex role definition, physical maturation, and desire to display competence (Swanson, Spencer, and Peterson, 1998).

Dena Phillips Swanson

See also Autonomy; Parent-Adolescent Relations; Peer Groups; Peer Status; Peer Victimization in School; Self; Self-Consciousness; Self-Esteem; Transition to Young Adulthood

References and further reading
Cornell, S., and D. Hartmann 1998. *Ethnicity and Race.* Thousand Oaks, CA: Pine Forge Press.
Levine, R., and D. Campbell. 1992. *Ethnocentrism: Theories of Conflict, Ethnic Attitudes and Group Behavior.* New York: John Wiley.
Perreault, Stephanie, and Richard Y. Bourhis. 1999. "Ethnocentrism, Social Identification, and Discrimination." *Personality and Social Psychology Bulletin* 25: 92–103.
Phelan, P., A. L. Davidson, and H. T. Cao. 1991. "Students' Multiple Worlds: Negotiating the Boundaries of Family, Peer, and School Cultures." *Anthropology and Education Quarterly* 22: 224–250.
Rotheram-Borus, M. J. 1990. "Adolescents' Reference-Group Choices, Self-Esteem, and Adjustment." *Journal of Personality and Social Psychology* 59: 1075–1081.
Swanson, Dena P., Margaret B. Spencer, and Anne Petersen. 1998. "Identity Formation in Adolescence." Pp. 18–41 in *The Adolescent Years: Social Influences and Educational Challenges.* Edited by Kathy Borman and B. Schneider. Chicago: University of Chicago Press.

F

Family Composition: Realities and Myths

Adolescents in the United States have been viewed as experiencing four revolutionary changes in family composition during the past 150 years. Two of these changes occurred; two did not. First is the mythical shift from extended-family households with grandparents, parents, and siblings in the home to nuclear-family households with parents and siblings only. Second is the real shift from living mainly in large families with many children to small families with few children. Third is the real shift from homemaker mothers to breadwinner mothers. Fourth is the mythical shift from living mainly in "Ozzie and Harriet" families to living in other family situations. The reasons for the changes that did occur, and those for the lack of change, have emerged only recently.

Extended Families

Historical findings indicate that U.S. communities during the second half of the nineteenth century and, in fact, all European societies during the past 300 years included few households that consisted of three-generation extended families (Hareven and Vinovskis, 1978). Hence, the limited experience of American adolescents with extended-family living during the twentieth century is a continuation of the experience of adolescents in Western society during preceding centuries. In any year since 1940, fewer than 10 percent of children in two-parent families and fewer than 30 percent of children in one-parent families had a grandparent in the home.

Why have there been so few extended families? Historically, few persons lived to old age. Between 1900 and 1930, for example, only 5 percent of Americans were sixty-five years or older, and the ratio of adults under sixty-four to elderly adults was more than 10 to 1 (Hernandez, 1996b). Even if all these elderly adults had lived with their children and grandchildren, few households would include grandparents. It was also historically the case that a parent surviving to old age would have had many children but could live in the home of only one adult child at a time. Today, by contrast, many persons live to old age, and social security pensions and other government programs allow most elderly people to maintain independent households (Treas and Torrecilha, 1995).

Large Families

Among adolescents born in 1865, 82 percent lived in families with five children or more, but this figure fell to only 30 percent for those born in 1930 as the proportion in families with one to four children jumped from 18 to 70 percent. Hence, the median number of siblings in the families of adolescents (including the adolescents themselves) dropped by almost two-thirds, from 7.3 siblings to only 2.6 siblings per family (Hernandez, 1993). During the post–World War II baby boom, the median increased slightly to 3.4 siblings but then declined to 2.0 or a bit less for adolescents born since the 1980s.

What accounts for this revolutionary drop in family size between the mid–nineteenth and mid–twentieth centuries? For an explanation, two additional revolutionary changes need to be cited.

First, between 1830 and 1930, the proportion of children living in farm families dropped from 70 to 30 percent, whereas the proportion living in non-farm, father-as-breadwinner, mother-as-homemaker families jumped from 15 to 55 percent. The shift from farming to urban occupations became increasingly necessary for improved economic status, because urban occupations increasingly provided higher incomes than farming (Hernandez, 1993).

Second, between 1870 and 1940, school enrollment rates jumped sharply from about 50 percent for children aged five to nineteen to 95 percent for children aged seven to thirteen and to 79 percent for children aged fourteen to seventeen. Moreover, among enrolled students the number of days spent in school doubled from 21 percent of the year as of 1870 to 42 percent of the year as of 1940. The reasons for this enormous expansion in schooling include not only compulsory education laws but also efforts by the labor unions to ensure jobs for adults (mainly fathers) and by the child welfare movement to obtain the passage of child labor laws protecting children from unsafe and unfair working conditions. In addition, as time passed, high educational attainment became increasingly neces-

sary to obtain jobs with higher incomes and prestige, thus encouraging parents to foster more schooling for their children (Hernandez, 1993).

Why, in this historical context, did parents drastically restrict their childbearing? The shift from farming to urban occupations meant that housing, food, clothing, and other necessities had to be purchased with cash, making the costs of supporting each additional child increasingly difficult to bear, while the potential economic contributions that children could make to their parents and families was sharply reduced by child labor and compulsory education laws.

As economic growth led to concomitant increases in the quality and quantity of available consumer products and services, expected consumption standards rose, and individuals were required to spend more money simply to maintain the new "normal" standard of living. Hence, the costs of supporting each additional child at a "normal" level increased as time passed.

At the same time, newly available goods and services began competing with children for parental time and money. Indeed, each additional child born into a family not only required additional financial support and made additional demands on parents' time and attention but also reduced the time and money that parents could devote to their own work as well as to recreation and older children.

As a result, more and more parents limited their family size to a comparatively small number of children. In this way, available income could be spread less thinly.

Mother-Only Families

A revolutionary increase occurred among mother-only families from only 6 to 8 percent in 1940–1960 to 20 percent in 1990 and to 24 percent in 1995. Although separation and divorce accounted for most of this historic change, out-of-wedlock childbearing became increasingly significant (Hernandez, 1993 and 1996a).

Between the 1860s and the 1960s, a remarkably steady eightfold increase occurred in the divorce rate. Preindustrial farm life compelled the economic interdependence of husbands and wives; fathers and mothers had to work together to maintain the family. But with a nonfarm job, the father could, if he desired, depend solely on his own work for income, leaving his family but taking his income with him. Also, upon moving to urban areas, husbands and wives left behind the rural small-town social controls that censured divorce.

After 1940, the massive increase in mothers' employment outside the home provided independent incomes that further facilitated divorce. By 1999, among adolescents living with their mothers, 78 percent had a mother who was employed during the past year, and 46 percent had a mother who was employed full-time year-round. During the same period, economic insecurity and need associated with erratic or limited employment prospects contributed to increases in divorce rates and out-of-wedlock childbearing.

Regarding divorce, Glen Elder and his colleagues (Liker and Elder, 1983; Conger et al., 1990; Elder et al., 1992) have shown that instability in husbands' work, drops in family income, and a low ratio of family income to family needs have led to increased hostility between husbands and wives, decreased marital quality, and increased risk of divorce. Given that 70 percent of the increase in mother-only white families between 1960 and 1988 can be accounted for by the rise in sepa-

ration and divorce, these three factors may account for much of the rise in mother-only families for white children during these decades.

Between 1940 and 1960, the proportion of black children living in a mother-only family with a divorced or separated mother increased to a greater extent than that of white children living in these circumstances. Since 1970, the same has been true of black children in mother-only families with a never-married mother.

The factors leading to increased separation and divorce among whites were also important for blacks, but the startling drop in the proportion of blacks living on farms between 1940 and 1960—from 44 percent in 1940 to only 11 percent in 1960—as well as the extraordinary economic pressures and hardships faced by black families may account for the much higher proportion of black children than white children who lived in mother-only families (Hernandez, 1993).

Joblessness is yet another factor affecting family composition. Drawing upon the work of William Julius Wilson (1987), Donald Hernandez (1993) calculated that the extent to which joblessness among young black men aged sixteen to twenty-four exceeded joblessness among young white men in the same age group expanded from almost none in 1955 to 15 to 25 percentage points by 1975–1989. Faced with this large and rapid reduction in the availability of black men during the main family-building ages who might provide significant support to a family, many young black women appear to have decided to forgo a temporary and unrewarding marriage—in fact, a marriage in which a jobless or poorly paid husband might have acted as a financial drain.

In summary, the revolutionary increase in mother-only families has been driven by the increasing economic independence of husbands and then of wives, and the increasing economic insecurity leading to increasing divorce and, more recently, out-of-wedlock childbearing.

"Ozzie and Harriet" Families

In the 1950s, the U.S. television series known as *Ozzie and Harriet* portrayed an idealized urban American family in which the father was a full-time year-round worker, the mother was a full-time homemaker without a paid job, and all the children were born after the parents' one and only marriage. It is commonly assumed that most children lived in "Ozzie and Harriet" families in the 1950s, and that these families were subsequently replaced by dual-earner and mother-only families owing to changes in the economy and in family values.

Yet statistics developed to estimate the proportion of children living in such families show that, since at least the Great Depression, the majority of children have never lived in such families (Hernandez, 1993). In 1940, by the time they had reached the age of seventeen, fewer than one-third of adolescents, or 31 percent, lived in "Ozzie and Harriet" families—a figure that had declined to only 15 percent in 1980. Since at least the Great Depression, among children and adolescents of all ages, the mid-twentieth-century ideal of family living has been a myth.

In what sense is this a myth? The answer is twofold. First, as of 1940, fully 40 percent of children lived with fathers who did not work full-time year-round; moreover, despite subsequent declines in this proportion, at least one-fifth of children during each post–World War II year lived with a father who worked less than full-time year-round. These proportions were only slightly lower among seven-teen-year-olds than among children in general. Second, since 1940, children have experienced a revolutionary increase in mother's employment.

Even between 1940 and 1960, however, about 30 percent of children did not live in two-parent families with both parents married only once and all the children born after the parents' marriage—partly because historic increases in divorce were simply counterbalancing historic declines in parents' death rates between 1860 and 1960 (Hernandez, 1993). Hence, both historically and today, large proportions of adolescents spend at least part of their childhood with fewer than two parents in the home, owing to their parents' death, divorce, or out-of-wedlock childbearing.

Among white children born between 1920 and 1960, for example, a large minority—28 to 34 percent—had, by age seventeen, spent part of their childhood living with fewer than two parents—a proportion unchanged since the late 1800s. In turn, among black children born between 1920 and 1960, an enormous proportion—55 to 60 percent—had, by age seventeen, spent part of their childhood living with fewer than two parents. This proportion, too, had remained roughly the same since the late 1800s. Projections indicate that these proportions will rise for white and black children to about 50 and 80 percent, respectively.

Donald J. Hernandez

See also Adoption: Issues and Concerns; Fathers and Adolescents; Grandparents: Intergenerational Relationships; Mothers and Adolescents; Sibling Relationships; Single Parenthood and Low Achievement

References and further reading
Conger, Rand D., Glen H. Elder Jr., F. O. Lorenz, K. J. Conger, R. L. Simmons, L. B. Whitbeck, J. Huck, and J. N.

Melby. 1990. "Linking Economic Hardship and Marital Quality and Instability." *Journal of Marriage and the Family* 52: 643–656.

Elder, Glen H., Rand D. Conger, E. Michael Foster, and Monika Ardelt. 1992. "Families under Economic Pressure." *Journal of Family Issues* 13: 5–37.

Hareven, Tamara K., and Maris A. Vinovskis, eds. 1978. *Family and Population in Nineteenth-Century America*. Princeton, NJ: Princeton University Press.

Hernandez, Donald J. 1993. *America's Children: Resources from Family, Government, and the Economy*. New York: Russell Sage Foundation.

———. 1996a. "Child Development and Social Demography of Childhood." *Child Development* 68, no. 1: 149–169.

———. 1996b. "Population Change and the Family Environment of Children." Pp. 231–342 in *Trends in the Well-Being of Children and Youth: 1996*. Washington, DC: U.S. Department of Health and Human Services.

Liker, J. K., and Glen H. Elder Jr. 1983. "Economic Hardship and Marital Relations in the 1930s." *American Sociological Review* 48: 343–359.

Treas, Judith, and Ramon Torrecilha. 1995. "The Older Population." Pp. 47–92 in *State of the Union: America in the 1990s*. Vol. 2, *Social Trends*. Edited by Reynolds Farley. New York: Russell Sage Foundation.

Wilson, William Julius. 1987. *The Truly Disadvantaged: The Inner City, the Underclass, and Public Policy*. Chicago: University of Chicago Press.

Family Relations

Adolescence is a transitional developmental period between childhood and adulthood that is characterized by numerous biological, cognitive, and social role changes. These primary changes promote secondary changes (e.g., autonomy, attachment, sexuality, intimacy, achievement, and identity) through the contexts of adolescence. A key context is that of family relations.

Biological, Cognitive, and Social Role Changes in Adolescence

Adolescence is a time of great physical growth and change. Males experience changes in body proportions, voice, body hair, strength, and coordination, whereas females experience changes in body proportions, body hair, and menarcheal status. It is important to recognize that the peak of pubertal development occurs two years earlier in the average female than in the average male. There are also considerable variations between individuals in the time of onset, duration, and termination of puberty.

The cognitive changes in adolescence are less overt and harder to identify than the physical changes, but they are no less dramatic. Piaget identified adolescence as the period of formal operational thinking. Adolescents who have reached this stage can think in more abstract, complex, and hypothetical ways. They are able to explore a range of options during the process of making decisions and think realistically about their future.

Changes in social role definition during adolescence vary significantly across cultures. In Western societies, these changes occur across four domains: interpersonal (adolescents now have increased power within the family), economic (adolescents are allowed to work and earn money), legal (late adolescents can be tried in the adult legal system), and political (late adolescents can vote in elections). Adolescents also obtain the rights to drive and get married.

Transformation in Family Relations

The primary changes of adolescence lead to a period of transformation in family

The changes of adolescence lead to a period of transformation in family relations. (Skjold Photographs)

relations. Shortly after the onset of puberty, a temporary disruption in relations characterized by increased emotional distance and conflict occurs between parents and adolescents. Scholars who have written about adolescence from a psychoanalytic perspective have viewed the adolescent developmental period as a time of storm and stress during which extreme levels of conflict result in a reorientation toward peers. However, recent research involving representative samples of adolescents has not supported these notions. There is a moderate increase in conflict between parents and adolescents, but these conflicts are usually over mundane issues such as household chores, school responsibilities, and curfew as opposed to religious, social, or political issues. In fact, it appears that fewer than 10 percent of teens experience serious family relationship difficulties during adolescence.

The following is an example of how the primary changes of adolescence can nevertheless result in emotional distance and conflict between parents and adolescents. Suppose a thirteen-year-old male adolescent begins to reason and think in a formal operational manner. There has been a long-standing rule in his family that he has to do his homework immediately after coming home from school—in other words, before he can watch television or spend time with his friends. This rule did not pose a problem until he reached junior high and was asked by his friends to "hang out" with them after school. When the adolescent asked his parents if he could spend time with his friends before coming home to do his homework, his parents were hesitant to grant this privilege and a conflict ensued. The adolescent asserted that he would like to spend time with his friends directly after school

for an hour or two and then come home to do his homework. His parents responded that homework is a higher priority and he has to complete it before spending time with his friends. The adolescent responded that he would complete his homework in a more efficient manner if given an opportunity to "blow off some steam" with his friends first. In this scenario, the adolescent's ability to think flexibly and consider another option for how to spend his time after school, as well as his ability to provide a rationale for his request, has led to increased emotional distance and conflict with his parents.

Although these changes in family relations can be stressful, they typically do not undermine the quality of the relationship between parents and adolescents. As children negotiate the transition to adolescence, close relations between parents and adolescents are maintained in the majority of families. Temporary disruptions in the relationship between parents and adolescents do, however, tend to occur within the context of close emotional attachment. Yet it appears that these moments of conflict serve a positive function during the transition to adolescence. Indeed, some scholars argue that conflict serves a sociobiological function by ensuring that adolescents will spend time outside the home and thus forcing them to look outside the family for intimate companionship. Others suggest that conflict promotes adjustment to change through intrapsychic and interpersonal processes. Overall, then, conflict may facilitate the ability of adolescents to distance themselves psychologically from their parents and enable them to evaluate their parents in a more realistic and less idealized manner. It may also serve as a mechanism through which adolescents can communicate information to their parents about their changing self-concepts and expectations.

The Family Life Cycle

Families move through various developmental phases during which new issues arise and different concerns predominate. The concerns and issues typical of families with children entering adolescence arise not just because of the changing needs and concerns of the adolescent but also because of the changes occurring in the adolescent's parents. Many parents are around forty years old when their children enter early adolescence—a period of life that can be difficult for these adults as they look back on what they have accomplished in life so far and what they have yet to achieve. This process of self-evaluation and reappraisal has been labeled *midlife crisis.*

The developmental concerns and issues facing adolescents and their parents are complementary. With respect to physical changes, the adolescent is entering a period of physical growth, youthful physical attractiveness, and sexual maturity just when parents are beginning to feel concern about their own bodies, physical attractiveness, and sexual appeal. With regard to social role changes, the adolescent is entering a period of increased power and status when many important life decisions (e.g., career and marriage) lie ahead. But for many parents these choices have already been made and they are facing the consequences, both positive and negative, of their decisions. In short, the adjustment to adolescence may take a greater toll on parents' mental health than on the adolescent's. A father or mother may be especially affected by the transition if the adolescent is of the same sex

and if the parent does not have a strong orientation to work outside the home. Parents who are deeply involved with their work or who have a particularly happy marriage may be protected against some of these negative consequences.

Autonomy

The challenge for adolescents is to gain increasing levels of autonomy while maintaining a close emotional attachment to their parents. Three different kinds of autonomy can be achieved during adolescence: emotional, behavioral, and value autonomy. *Emotional autonomy* is the capacity to be less dependent on parents for immediate emotional support. Adolescents increasingly de-idealize their parents, viewing them more as regular people than as authority figures and relying on them less for emotional support. *Behavioral autonomy* refers to adolescents' ability to make their own decisions—to be less influenced by others and more self-reliant. However, adolescents who achieve behavioral autonomy continue to rely on others for help. They are able to distinguish between situations in which they have the ability to make their own decisions and situations in which they need to consult with a parent or friend for advice. Finally, *value autonomy* involves adolescents' capacity to develop values of their own as opposed to adopting peers' or parents' values. Note, however, that adolescents and their parents tend to hold similar values and that adolescents tend to select friends whose values are similar to those of their parents.

Attachment

The close emotional attachment that is established between parents and children during childhood continues to exist during adolescence. In fact, there is strong evidence that detachment from family ties during adolescence is not desirable. Compared to peers without close ties to their parents, adolescents who report feeling relatively close to their parents score higher on measures of psychosocial development, including self-reliance, behavioral competence, and psychological well-being. They also score lower on measures of psychological and social problems such as depression and drug use.

Ideally, the transformation in family relations that occurs during the transition to adolescence reflects adolescents' growing sense of interdependence within the family and parents' willingness to maintain close and supportive ties with adolescents without threatening their individuality. Over the course of adolescence, the attachment relationship tends to shift from one of unilateral authority to one of mutuality and cooperation. If this process is disrupted—for example, by parents who are unable to grant increasing amounts of behavioral or emotional autonomy—the adolescents' psychological and social development may likewise be disrupted.

Authoritative Parenting

Researchers have identified two aspects of parenting behavior that are critical during adolescence: responsiveness and demandingness. *Parental responsiveness* refers to the degree to which parents respond to adolescents' needs in an accepting and supportive manner; *parental demandingness* refers to the extent to which parents expect and demand mature, responsible behavior from adolescents. Parental responsiveness and demandingness are largely independent constructs. There-

fore, it is possible to look at various combinations of these two dimensions. According to one scheme, parents who are very responsive but not at all demanding are labeled Indulgent, parents who are responsive but also very demanding are labeled Authoritative, parents who are demanding but not responsive are labeled Authoritarian, and parents who are neither demanding nor responsive are labeled Indifferent. Authoritative parents appear to be most effective. They are responsive to demands made by adolescents but expect the same in return. They encourage verbal give-and-take, enforce rules when needed, have clear expectations for mature behavior, and encourage independence. They make a point of explaining their requests and providing rationales for their rules and regulations. And, perhaps most important, they foster autonomous functioning by encouraging the expression of feelings and opinions.

Research conducted over the past twenty-five years has indeed found strong evidence in support of a positive association between authoritative parenting and healthy adolescent development. This evidence has been replicated across a wide range of ethnic, regional, and socioeconomic groups, indicating that adolescents exposed to authoritative parenting are more competent and have higher levels of self-esteem, impulse control, moral development, and feelings of independence than adolescents exposed to other styles of parenting. The key components of authoritative parenting—warmth, structure, and support for psychological autonomy—have been linked to specific adolescent outcomes: Parental warmth is associated with overall adolescent competence, parental structure is associated with fewer behavior problems, and parental support for psychological autonomy is associated with fewer symptoms of psychological distress such as depression or anxiety.

Wendy E. Shapera
Grayson N. Holmbeck

See also Emancipated Minors; Family-School Involvement; Fathers and Adolescents; Grandparents: Intergenerational Relationships; Mothers and Adolescents; Parent-Adolescent Relations

References and further reading
Grotevant, H. 1997. "Adolescent Development in Family Contexts." In *Handbook of Child Psychology.* Vol. 3, *Social, Emotional, and Personality Development,* 5th ed. Edited by W. Damon and N. Eisenberg. New York: Wiley.
Hill, John, and Grayson Holmbeck. 1986. "Attachment and Autonomy during Adolescence." *Annals of Child Development* 3: 145–189.
Holmbeck, Grayson. 1996. "A Model of Family Relational Transformations during the Transition to Adolescence: Parent-Adolescent Conflict and Adaptation." In *Transitions through Adolescence: Interpersonal Domains and Context.* Edited by J. Graber, J. Brooks-Gunn, and A. Peterson. Mahwah, NJ: Erlbaum.
Holmbeck, Grayson, and Wendy Shapera. 1999. "Research Methods with Adolescents." In *Handbook of Research Methods in Clinical Psychology.* Edited by P. Kendall, J. Butcher, and G. Holmbeck. New York: Wiley.
Holmbeck, Grayson, Roberta Paikoff, and Jeanne Brooks-Gunn. 1995. "Parenting Adolescents." In *Handbook of Parenting,* Vol. 1. Edited by Marcus Bornstein. Mahwah, NJ: Erlbaum.
Steinberg, Laurence. 1990. "Autonomy, Conflict, and Harmony in the Family Relationship." In *At the Threshold: The Developing Adolescent.* Edited by S. Feldman and G. Elliott. Cambridge, MA: Harvard University Press.
———. 1999. *Adolescence.* Boston: McGraw-Hill.
Steinberg, Laurence, and Wendy Steinberg. 1994. *Crossing Paths: How Your Child's Adolescence Can Be an Opportunity for Your Own Personal Growth.* New York: Simon and Schuster.

Family-School Involvement

The family and the school are responsible for socializing acceptable conduct and teaching basic skills associated with academic achievement. Although the two share in this responsibility, there often is little coordination or connection between them. Joyce Epstein, at the Center on Families, Communities, Schools, and Children's Learning at Johns Hopkins University, has suggested several ways in which the school and family can forge partnerships—some of which can be initiated by parents and others by the school. These partnerships fall into six categories of involvement. Type 1 involvement entails assistance by the school with parenting, child rearing, and establishing the home conditions necessary for a child to learn. Often this form of involvement includes a school counselor, social worker, or child and youth worker who provides informal classes and visits to the home. Type 2 involvement entails communication with families about school programs and children's progress. The three most frequent forms of such communication are parent-teacher conferences, information provided by the principal concerning standardized achievement scores, and information about report cards. Type 3 involvement includes volunteer participation on the part of parents and extended family members in the classroom, school events, and school projects. Type 4 involvement focuses on activities at home, including school guidance regarding parental monitoring of children's homework, in support of the

Family connections with the school are associated with enhanced school performance. (Skjold Photographs)

school curricula. Type 5 involvement focuses on cooperation between families and teachers in making school decisions. A case in point is the widely known Parent Teacher Association (PTA). And, finally, type 6 involvement focuses on community, school, and family collaborations. This category might include coordination among YMCA and YWCA programs, after-school activities, family and work schedules, and school or community officials to ensure that children are supervised properly and provided healthy outlets for their energy and enthusiasm.

As reported by Joyce Epstein and Seyong Lee, the results of the U.S. National Educational Longitudinal Study of 1988 indicate that family connections with

the school are associated with enhanced school performance. Unfortunately, 51.3 percent of the parents observed in this study described no connections with the school. Indeed, their children—students in their teens—reported that the parents had minimal contact with the school and that most of the communication about school occurred between adolescents and parents—if at all. Epstein's six types of family-school involvement offer a helpful guideline toward rectifying this problem and, ultimately, enhancing adolescents' school performance and behavior.

In addition to determining how the school and family can connect to enhance a teenager's school achievement, parents can accomplish a great deal solely within the home. For example, Bruce Ryan and Gerald Adams, as part of their research with the Canadian National Longitudinal Survey of Children and Youth, have constructed a system that demonstrates how family influences can enhance children's academic achievement, social adjustment in school, and good citizenship behaviors. In this system, referred to as the Family-School Relationships Model, a child's school outcome is based on a concentric model whereby family influences are embedded within other influences. The model can best be understood if you envision a rock that is thrown into calm water. The rock itself represents the child's school behavior, and the waves that are created by its impact in the water represent adjacent influences on the child's behavior. The first and largest influence on the adolescent's performance is the child's personal characteristics. A child with high frustration tolerance, for example, can tolerate waiting according to classroom rules. Or an assertive child will likely volunteer and discuss things in the classroom. Each of these characteristics may be seen as desirable by teachers and even influence grading. So the adolescent's personal characteristics are likely to predict some of the child's school success.

In turn, the child's school behavior and personal characteristics are encircled and influenced by several levels of influence within the family. Therefore, further rings of influence from those of the child's personal characteristics also emerge. School-focused parent-child interactions are very likely to influence the child's success. Parents who monitor, help, support, encourage, and assure that an adolescent is prepared for each new day of school are likely not only to shape the child's personal characteristics but also enhance good school performance. Further, general parent-child interactions, one step removed from school-focused parent-child interactions, are likely to enhance the development of certain characteristics of the child. The most widely acclaimed form of parent-child relationships, first suggested by Diana Baumrind, is known as authoritative parenting, where children are provided with warm, firm, but democratic family experiences that enhance social competence. But there is yet another level of the family. The general family climate or atmosphere among all family members provides another form of influence. Factors like family warmth, cohesion, expressiveness, or conflict have important effects by influencing the nature of school-focused parent-child interactions, and general parent-child relationships such as authoritative parenting.

There are two other influences that can have effects on the family and its interactions. One is the personal characteristics of the parent. For example, parents with strong expectations about the successes of their children in school will create family environments that promote school success. Further, depression or mental illness in the family will have diminishing effects on positive family and parent-child interactions. The final form of influence in the model by Ryan and Adams involves the social-cultural circumstances of the family. Children raised in high-income homes, where parents have extensive educations, bring considerable resources to a child that can result in more learning opportunities, enhanced learning experiences on trips and to museums, and the use of tutors and mentors to help shape children's school success.

Much of family-school involvement can be the enhancement of connections and communications between parents, teachers, administration, and the students. This form of involvement requires parents or teachers to initiate communication and planning and working together. However, other things can be done in the privacy of one's own home. For example, parents can provide help and talk about what is done in school, discuss how performance might be improved, or offer guidance and help, each and every day, regarding school activities and homework. Parents can choose to use democratic parenting as their goal for enhancing a child's school success. Permissive or authoritarian parenting can be changed to be more democratic and child-centered. Family conflict can be diminished by conflict resolution strategies. Parents can encourage the whole family to be respectful but expressive in their communications with each other.

It is certain that family relations and parent-child interactions are associated with children's school success. It is also certain that when parents become involved in their children's school activities, the child becomes more involved in and with the school.

Gerald R. Adams

See also Child-Rearing Styles; Conduct Problems; Family Relations; Parenting Styles; School Dropouts; School, Functions of; Teenage Parenting: Childbearing

References and further reading
Booth, A., and J. F. Dunn, eds. 1996. *Family-School Links: How Do They Affect Educational Outcomes?* Mahwah, NJ: Erlbaum.
Epstein, Joyce L., and Seyong Lee. 1995. "National Patterns of School and Family Connections in the Middle Grades." Pp 108–154 in *The Family-School Connection: Theory, Research, and Practice.* Edited by B. A. Ryan, G. R. Adams, T. P. Gullotta, R. P. Weissberg, and R. L. Hampton. Thousand Oaks, CA: Sage.
Ryan, Bruce A., and Gerald R. Adams. 1995. "The Family-School Relationships Model." Pp. 3–28 in *The Family-School Connection: Theory, Research, and Practice.* Edited by B. A. Ryan and associates. Thousand Oaks, CA: Sage.
———. 1999. "How Do Families Affect Children's Success in School?" *Education Quarterly Review* 6: 30–43 (Available in English and French).

Fathers and Adolescents

Mark Twain once said, "When I was a boy of fourteen, my father was so ignorant I could hardly stand to have the old man around. But when I got to be twenty-one I was astonished at how much the old man had learned in seven years!" (cited in Bruun and Getzen, 1996, p. 475). The truth is, fathers and their adolescent children are continually learning from each other. Fathers learn from their children and children learn from their fathers in various ways, but primarily through their interactions with each other. Researchers call this "mutual education." It is during these interactions that fathers and their adolescent children learn life skills and gain knowledge about one another. Furthermore, the time that fathers and children spend together helps children develop emotionally, socially, and physically, and contributes to their overall well-being. Perhaps it is best to think of fathering as a way for men to show their

The time that fathers and children spend together helps children develop emotionally, socially, and physically, and contributes to their overall well-being. (Skjold Photographs)

care and support for their children each and every day.

Time Together

The time that fathers and children spend together decreases somewhat as the children enter their teens and begin to develop relationships outside of the family. Throughout this period, however, fathers should continue to express warmth and acceptance toward their adolescent children. Although the amount of contact decreases, most of the time that fathers do spend with their teenagers involves leisure and recreational activities such as sports or watching television. It is estimated that fathers spend around nine hours a week directly engaged in some activity with their adolescent children. Often these activities require very little interaction; for example, watching television accounts for about 40 percent of the time fathers spend with their adolescent children. Yet, it is through these types of activities that fathers can help their sons and daughters develop emotionally, socially, and physically.

For instance, adolescents can learn how to control their tempers—to be "good sports"—through competitive games with their fathers by observing how they react to winning and losing. Likewise, they can learn social skills from fathers who promote the virtues of being a member of a team or who show how cooperation makes accomplishing a task easier. Through physical play, fathers can help their children to develop strength and coordination. Another way that fathers relate with their adolescent children is through humor. Many dads find that joking, kidding, and teasing are ways to connect with their teenagers. In this way, fathers create a fun and relaxing atmosphere for themselves and their families. Finally, aside from playing with them, fathers can be involved in the lives of their adolescent children simply by being available—for instance, to help with homework or to give advice in times of crisis. Unfortunately, many fathers view themselves as being more available to their children than their children perceive them to be.

Fathers learn from their children as well. They learn how to understand and respond to the needs of their children by interacting with them—a kind of on-the-job training. Compared to mothers, however, fathers generally spend less time with their adolescent children and are not as responsible for their day-to-day activities. Some fathers have embraced the many responsibilities entailed in the job of parenting, but it is the rare father who is primarily responsible for such tasks as making doctor's appointments and participating in parent-teacher conferences, or who knows, off the top of his head, specific details of his teens' life such as their shoe size or what time soccer practice begins and ends. Yet fathers who spend ample time with their children are as capable as mothers in caring for and raising their children.

Gender Differences

Fathers interact with their sons and daughters in different ways, especially as the children get older. For example, they tend to spend more time with their sons and are better at providing for their sons' emotional needs. The stronger father-son bond may be due to the fact that fathers identify more and have more interests in common with their sons than with their daughters. On the other hand, studies have shown that daughters whose fathers maintain consistent involvement in their lives tend to be more mature. One-on-one father-daughter activities are important to the maintenance of a close relationship, allowing fathers to be less gender-specific in their behaviors and more in tune with their daughter's emotional needs.

Father-Adolescent Conflict

It is commonly believed that parents and their children have more arguments as the children progress through their teens. However, research has shown that the opposite is true. With the exception of disagreements over money, the number of arguments between fathers and their adolescent children decreases over time. One reason for this decline in conflict may be the fact that teens are spending less time at home and more time with friends. Yet fathers who are more highly involved in their adolescents' lives tend to have more conflicts with their children than those who are less involved— again, due to the amount of time that the fathers and children are together. Although fathers become more warm, caring, and understanding as they spend more time with their teenagers, they also have more opportunities for disagreements over finances, household chores, curfews, and appearance.

Stress may also contribute to father-adolescent tensions. Indeed, fathers are more likely to argue with their adolescent children after a double dose of stress at work and at home. One way to avoid or at least decrease the chances of conflict is for fathers, and teenagers as well, to let other family members know when and why they are in a bad mood. By communicating in this way, fathers and adolescents can come to understand that negative moods aren't always their fault.

Well-Being

Through the amount and type of their involvement, fathers can influence their adolescents' intellectual, social, and emotional well-being. Studies have shown that adolescents do better academically when their parents are encouraging, supportive, and warm, and when they practice a more democratic type of parenting. Indeed, sons and daughters whose fathers are more highly involved in their lives tend to perform better in math and on general academic achievement tests. Furthermore, one of the primary tasks for adolescents is to begin to establish some independence from their parents and to develop social networks of their own with peers and other adults. Fathers can play a role in this developmental task by encouraging and supporting their children's independent thoughts and actions and providing links to life outside of the home and family.

Adolescents, in turn, can have a major impact on their fathers' personal growth and development. Fathers desire to help the next generation grow into healthy and productive adults, and adolescents can assist their fathers in achieving this goal by providing their fathers with opportunities to help them grow and mature emotionally, socially, and physically.

Comedian Bill Cosby, in writing of the foibles of fatherhood, lends this simple advice to dads: "The most important thing to let them know is simply that

you're there . . . that you're the best person on the face of the earth to whom they can come and say, 'I have a problem.'" (Cosby, 1986, p. 128).

Daniel A. McDonald
David Almeida

See also Child-Rearing Styles; Family Composition: Realities and Myths; Family Relations; Grandparents: Intergenerational Relationships; Mothers and Adolescents; Parent-Adolescent Relations; Parenting Styles

References and further reading

Almeida, David M., and Nancy L. Galambos. 1993. "Continuity and Change in Father-Adolescent Relations." Pp. 27–40 in *Father-Adolescent Relationships*. Edited by Shmuel Shulman and W. Andrew Collins. San Francisco: Jossey-Bass.

Almeida, David M., and Daniel A. McDonald. 1998. "Weekly Rhythms of Parents' Work Stress, Home Stress, and Parent-Adolescent Tension." Pp. 53–67 in *Temporal Rhythms in Adolescence: Clocks, Calendars, and the Coordination of Daily Life*. Edited by Ann C. Crouter and Reed Larson. San Francisco: Jossey-Bass.

Almeida, David M., Elaine Wethington, and Daniel A. McDonald. In press. *Daily Variation in Paternal Engagement and Negative Mood: Implications for Emotionally Supportive and Conflictual Interactions*.

Bronfenbrenner, Urie. 1991. "What Do Families Do?" *Family Affairs* 4: 1–2.

Bruun, Erik, and Robin Getzen, eds. 1996. *The Book of American Values and Virtues: Our Tradition of Freedom, Liberty, and Tolerance*. New York: Black Dog & Leventhal Publishers.

Cosby, William H., Jr. 1986. *Bill Cosby: Fatherhood*. Garden City, NY: Doubleday.

Galambos, Nancy L., and David M. Almeida. 1992. "Does Parent-Adolescent Conflict Increase in Early Adolescence?" *Journal of Marriage and the Family* 54: 737–747.

Gjerde, Per F. 1986. "The Interpersonal Structure of Family Interaction Settings: Parent-Adolescent Relations in Dyads and Triads." *Developmental Psychology* 22, no. 3: 297–304.

Larson, Reed W., and David M. Almeida. 1999. "Emotional Transmission in the Daily Lives of Families: A New Paradigm for Studying Family Process." *Journal of Marriage and the Family* 61: 5–20.

Larson, Reed W., and Maryse H. Richards. 1994. *Divergent Realities: The Emotional Lives of Mothers, Fathers, and Adolescents.* New York: Basic Books.

Pleck, Joseph H. 1997. "Parental Involvement: Levels, Sources, and Consequences." Pp. 66–103 in *The Role of the Father in Child Development.* Edited by Michael E. Lamb. New York: Wiley.

Snarey, John. 1993. *How Fathers Care for the Next Generation.* Cambridge, MA: Harvard University Press.

Fears

For teenagers, monsters under the bed aren't scary anymore; teens' experiences with fear are entirely different from the way it was for them a few years earlier, in childhood. The word *fear* has been described as an emotional response to an external threat, such as a person, object, or situation. Fear is thus different from worry or anxiety, in that it involves a specific, intense focus on a particular threat. This focus changes as the child develops: Early fears about witches or swimming in the deep end of the pool are replaced with fears about school, status among peers, family well-being, and performance inside and outside the home environment. In short, a teenager's understanding of fear results from a complex interaction of biological, psychological, and social factors.

As early as infancy, children react to frightening situations with innate fear responses. These responses are common to all humans; they are programmed in humans' biological systems. In infancy,

fear responses are evoked as a means of self-protection. Babies cry when they are hungry or cold, or when they are approached by an unfamiliar person. This behavior is sparked by a neurological phenomenon known as the "fight-or-flight" response, which is programmed as an innate reaction in fearful situations. The common symptoms of this reaction include increased heart rate, sweaty palms, rapid, shallow breathing, and muscle tension. Throughout the evolutionary history of humans, the fight-or-flight response played an important role in survival. Faced with a threat or risk of death, people were provided with the burst of adrenaline necessary for either a vigorous fight or a quick escape. The result was a better chance of survival, as well as an opportunity to live and grow according to the demands of the environment.

Excess adrenaline in the bloodstream is the direct cause of a teen's physiological reactions to fear. The brain triggers an alarm that releases the adrenaline. However, other biological influences are related to fear as well. For example, lack of sleep or irregular sleeping patterns can contribute to a teen's perception of fearful situations. Or a person may be labeled as a "worrier" because she has a certain temperament, or personality, that has been with her since the day she was born. This tendency is not due to environmental influences or previous experiences; it is simply a genetic reality. Teens who experience fear on a regular basis often come to fear the accompanying physiological symptoms, because they are so unpleasant. What often results is a cycle that's hard to break, for the teen eventually comes to fear the fear itself, even when no threat actually exists.

The fight-or-flight response makes no distinction between real objects of fear

A teenager's understanding of fear results from a complex interaction of biological, psychological, and social factors. (Shirley Zeiberg)

and imaginary ones. For example, a teenager who is required to give a speech in front of a large audience may perceive the audience as a scary entity, even as "the enemy." Stepping up to the podium, the teen may feel sweat drip down his neck or trickle down his sides. He may notice that his heart is beating quickly and that his mouth is suddenly very dry, and he may think to himself, "I can't do this. I need to get out of here!" This is the fight-or-flight response at work, and the easiest way to stop the accompanying physiological symptoms is to run away

and avoid the situation altogether, instead of "fighting" the perceived threat and giving the speech. In fact, avoidance of fearful objects and situations is a common strategy among teens—but it is a strategy that brings only temporary relief from the fear. One way for teens to cope with the effects of fear is to change their thinking about the situation. Edward Hallowell's (1997) method of "brain management" is designed to do exactly that— specifically, by combating the fight-or-flight response and the physiological symptoms that accompany it.

Psychological factors also influence the way teens perceive and respond to fear. These factors include patterns that form, or have already been formed, over the natural course of development. As children grow into teenagers, they interact with the environment and encounter situations that affect the way they think. The focus of teens' fears shifts, based on their firsthand experiences (e.g., success or failure). Teens who perceive the environment as threatening are likely to develop thought patterns that predispose them to be fearful. They are extremely aware of their surroundings, and therefore susceptible to misinterpreting information they encounter if they are inclined toward thinking the worst. Indeed, the media bombard teens with information about situations that evoke fear, such as high school shootings, sexually transmitted infections, standards for acceptable body image and academic performance, and environmental hazards.

It has been argued that fear or anxiety can be beneficial in some instances (Gerzon, 1998)—as when it motivates teens in positive ways. For example, fear of failing a test may inspire a student to study and, hence, to pass the test. And fear of contracting a disease may dissuade a teen from using intravenous drugs such as heroin. Certainly, then, there are benefits to weighing consequences before acting; yet for fearful teens, the ability to rationally evaluate a situation and respond appropriately may be impaired by thought patterns based on prior experience. These thought patterns—which act as a distorted lens through which the teens view the world, a world full of fear—may in turn damage the teens' social interactions.

These interactions involve family members, friends, and other people in the teenagers' immediate environment. These people may affect teenagers' experiences with fear in various ways, and their influences change as teens mature. In some cases, the intentions of others may be honorable; but if the teen perceives them as a threat, then even ordinary conflicts may appear particularly menacing to the teen. A case in point is the teen who witnesses a heated argument between her mother and father and begins to imagine various disastrous outcomes such as the parents' divorce or violence directed at each other or at the teen herself.

The classroom is another source of fear for many teens, as they strive to perform well both academically and socially. This type of fear often begins in middle childhood. Some teens choose to hide their fear of failure by acting out or showing off in front of others. Others turn to fantasy or substance abuse as an escape from academic stress. Social activities such as sports teams or clubs may also cause teens to be fearful—particularly when they feel that they must meet certain expectations.

One way to help a teenager cope with fear is to increase the teen's sense of self-control. This involves the ability to put off immediate relief or gratification in exchange for the long-term benefits that come as a result of taking moderate risks or persevering despite fear of failure. Consider again the example of giving a speech to a large audience. A teen who finds this scenario scary would be exercising self-control if he gave the speech in spite of sweaty palms and thoughts like "They will all laugh at me." The payoff comes at the end of the speech when the teenager realizes that what seemed frightening was, in fact, harmless. In this instance, he has triumphed over the fear, thus paving the way for new patterns to form and new perceptions to develop. Helping teens recognize that they have the power to affect their reactions and performances is the first step toward managing, and ultimately alleviating, their fears.

Lisa B. Fiore

See also Anxiety; Disorders, Psychological and Social; Emotions

References and further reading
Gerzon, Robert. 1998. *Finding Security in the Age of Anxiety.* New York: Bantam Books.
Hallowell, Edward M. 1997. *Worry: Hope and Help for a Common Condition.* New York: Ballantine Books.

Female Athlete Triad

The term *female athlete triad* refers to three interrelated medical disorders found primarily in adolescent girls or young women who are physically active—namely, disordered eating, amenorrhea (stopping or never beginning menstrual cycles or periods), and osteoporosis (decreased bone mass). All three conditions represent potentially serious health problems that can affect the young athlete's health now and in the future.

Individuals at Risk for the Triad

The interrelationship between the components of the female athlete triad has been recognized by the medical profession only in the last decade. This increased awareness is probably a reflection of both the increased number of females participating in athletics and the increased identification of the problem by various professionals who work with female athletes.

Female athlete triad is most common in girls who participate in organized sports that value a certain body type for performance, have desired weights for participation, or specify a preferred physical appearance. For example, high rates of the triad are found among girls who participate in gymnastics, ballet, swimming, and track. These sports demand an ideal weight and body shape that is thought to make one more successful at the sport.

However, a young woman does not have to participate in organized sports to suffer from the female athlete triad. Even outside of organized sports, many adolescent girls use excessive physical activity and exercise to control weight and obtain the "perfect" body. Our society's continued emphasis on physical appearance, thinness, and the ideal body shape may be the greatest risk factor for all youth.

It is important to note that adolescent boys can also be at risk for this disorder—especially those who engage in sports like distance running, where endurance is valued, and sports like wrestling or gymnastics, where body weight is regulated. Similarly, boys can suffer from disordered eating and osteoporosis, and they can experience the male equivalent of amenorrhea, known as hypogonadism, which involves decreasing function of the male reproductive organs (gonads or testes).

Components of the Disorder

Disordered Eating. In this context, the term *disordered eating* is used rather than *eating disorder* because it indicates a wider range of eating behaviors involved in efforts to lose weight or achieve a body composition considered appropriate to particular sports. All of these eating behaviors are potentially dangerous, however, inasmuch as they range from various levels of restricting food intake (either quantity or types of food) to bingeing and purging. Though not required for a diagnosis of female athlete triad, these disordered eating behaviors can be severe enough to warrant a diagnosis of anorexia nervosa or bulimia nervosa.

On the other hand, disordered eating may simply involve consumption of too few calories to compensate for the energy expended through increased activity. In other words, the young athlete's diet may be healthy but quantitatively insufficient to maintain a healthy weight. This "energy drain" or negative balance can lead to weight loss and ultimately undermine the athlete's performance and health. Indeed, because the body and brain continue to grow and develop during adolescence, a well-balanced diet with all the appropriate nutrients is extremely important at this time.

Disordered eating can result from other factors as well, including anxiety, depression, or pressure to achieve certain athletic goals from coaches, peers, family members, and even themselves. It is important to determine the underlying cause of the disordered eating so the appropriate treatment can begin.

Amenorrhea. Amenorrhea is the second component of the female athlete triad. *Primary amenorrhea* refers to girls who have not reached menarche (their first period) by the age of sixteen years, despite breast and pubic hair development. Girls who have reached age fourteen *without* any breast or pubic hair development should also be evaluated for primary amenorrhea. *Secondary amenorrhea* refers to girls whose periods have stopped following previously normal menstrual cycles. Required for a diagnosis of this condition is an absence of three or more consecutive menstrual cycles. Parents, teachers, coaches, and the athletes themselves should know that it is *never* normal for an adolescent or young woman athlete to stop her period in response to training. The cessation of menstruation in an athlete should be considered a red flag indicating that medical evaluation is necessary.

In cases where amenorrhea is associated with exercise, the condition results from interplay among various hormone systems that involve stress hormones such as cortisol and reproductive hormones such as estrogen. Since the intricate feedback systems are no longer appropriately regulated, some hormone levels become too low (estrogen) and other hormone levels become too high (cortisol). These systems involve a part of the brain called the hypothalamus, which produces hormones that regulate the pituitary gland. The pituitary, in turn, secretes several hormones that act on important target tissues for normal growth and body function. One effect of these changes in hormone systems is the loss of regular menstrual cycles and the "shutdown" of reproductive functions. Unclear at this time is whether exercise-induced amenorrhea affects fertility later on. Scientists do know, however, that the lowered estrogen levels found in athletes with amenorrhea can cause a decrease in bone mineral density, which in turn can result in osteoporosis.

Osteoporosis. The third component of the triad is osteoporosis, a disorder involving low bone mass that leads to an increased risk of fractures. This disorder is normally associated with older women who have reached menopause (cessation of menstruation). However, just as menopausal women are at risk for osteoporosis, so are adolescent girls with primary or secondary amenorrhea. The higher risk of fractures may first become apparent with the development of a stress fracture, a type of hairline break frequently seen in the leg bones of runners and ballet dancers. Later, more frequent or more severe fractures may occur in major bones such as hips or spine. In some cases of female athlete triad, special scans and X rays have revealed in adolescent girls a bone density that would be typical of women seventy or eighty years of age.

By the end of adolescence, young women have experienced as much as 95 percent of the bone density development and mineralization that will ever occur in their lifetimes. Thus, it is best to attain *optimum* bone density in adolescence. Toward this end, adolescent girls are advised to consume appropriate amounts of calcium and vitamin D every day.

Treatment for the Triad

These three components—disordered eating, amenorrhea, and osteoporosis—are intertwined. Disordered eating can influence bone density when the appropriate nutrients are not taken in. Disordered eating and weight loss can also influence the menstrual cycle, and amenorrhea with its low estrogen state can hamper bone density.

If an athlete presents with only one component of the triad, she should be evaluated for the other components as well. All three components may not be evident without professional evaluation. Female athlete triad is a disorder that definitely requires early medical attention. Chronic, irreparable damage can result if it is not treated.

Depending upon the severity of the triad, evaluation and treatment may require the intervention of clinicians with special expertise, such as physicians or nurse practitioners trained in adolescent medicine. These specialists can appropriately evaluate an adolescent, rule out other disorders, provide treatment, and refer as necessary. Reproductive endocrinologists, gynecologists who specialize in disorders involving reproductive hormones, and sports medicine specialists may also have such expertise.

At a minimum, the severity of each component of the triad must be evaluated before treatment is commenced. For example, bone density can be determined by means of a special noninvasive test called a DEXA scan; reproductive hormone levels and thyroid hormone levels—as well as nutritional status—can be determined through blood testing; and amenorrhea due to pregnancy can be ruled out by a pregnancy test. Also recommended are a diet history and an interview exploring psychological and social issues that may be contributing to female athlete triad.

Though somewhat controversial, treatment may involve hormone replacement therapy consisting of oral contraceptives or special skin patches with hormones that can be absorbed. Nutritional and psychological counseling and intervention may also be indicated. Finally, along with the adolescent, parents and coaches must be involved in the treatment plan. They must understand the nutritional needs of the adolescent and the importance of balancing dietary needs and exercise. They must be keenly aware of the potentially devastating consequences of female athlete triad. And, ultimately, they must be heedful of methods that can prevent the emergence of this disorder.

Lorah D. Dorn
Barbara J. Long

See also Body Fat, Changes in; Eating Problems; Menarche; Menstrual Cycle; Menstrual Dysfunction

References and further reading
Joy, Elizabeth, et al. 1997. "Team Management of the Female Athlete Triad. Part I: Optimal Treatment and Prevention Tactics." *The Physician and Sportsmedicine* 25: 94.
———. 1997. "Team Management of the Female Athlete Triad. Part II: What to Look For, What to Ask." *The Physician and Sportsmedicine* 25: 55.
Otis, Carol L., Barbara Drinkwater, Mimi Johnson, Anne Loucks, and Jack Wilmore. 1997. "American College of Sports Medicine Position Stand on the Female Athlete Triad." *Medicine and Science in Sports and Exercise* 29: i–ix.

Foster Care: Risks and Protective Factors

Foster care is a system in which children and teens live in licensed homes, often in their own communities, when their own families are deemed to be unable or unwilling to provide a home for them. Foster care has largely replaced orphanages and other forms of institutional living for children who, through no fault of their own, have been denied a safe, supportive environment in which to live.

Because of increasing problems for American families, such as poverty, family violence, substance abuse, and homelessness, the number of children and youth in foster care in the United States has been increasing steadily. Over the past decade, this number has risen from about 360,000 to 520,000. Approximately 40 percent of these youth are in the adolescent age range, eleven to eighteen years (U.S. Department of Health and Human Services, 1999). Many enter the system with multiple risk factors. Prior to placement they often have not received the love, support, consistency, and security needed for optimal development, and enter care with severe behavior problems and deficits in academic performance and social skills (Lamphear, 1985).

The teens in foster care are certainly not all the same. Some enter the system at a young age because of parental problems such as abuse, neglect, and drug addiction, whereas those who enter as teens are more likely to come into care because of their own personal problems such as acting out, delinquency, emotional illness, and substance abuse. Others go back and forth between their biological and foster homes, as foster care is often a two-way street. Whatever the route they have taken to get there, all of these young people must face certain challenges once they are in care: repeated losses, a sense of not belonging, having to adjust to new families, neighborhoods, schools, and friends. How well they adjust in foster care is a function of the balance between stressful life events and the risk and protective factors in their lives. Thus, it is very difficult to predict which adolescents will adapt successfully and which ones will continue to have difficulties.

Foster care can bring about new problems, but it can also provide solutions. Approximately 50 percent of youth report that foster care provided them with better parenting, improved structure, and consistency. Safer neighborhoods as well as better experiences in school—more helpful teachers, more compatible classmates—are also associated with foster placement (Johnson, Yoken, and Voss, 1995). In some cases, however, the teens' ability to benefit from the advantages of good placement is undermined by a failure to address the emotional problems they were experiencing when they entered the system.

Many children in foster care do well until they reach their teens, a stage when all youth face new challenges. Sometimes new thoughts and feelings are stirred up at this time, involving such issues as separating from one's parents, defining parents in more realistic ways, and forming one's own identity. Successful resolution of these challenges typically entails some form of connection with the past, even if it is only historical information to develop a self-identity (Geiser, 1973). Sometimes it is helpful to facilitate teens' connecting with family members, be they parents, older siblings, or grandparents. It can be a time to see if it is realistic that some of these persons might be able to provide a home base when foster care is over. Another approach is to take the teens to old neighborhoods or schools to try to integrate the past with the present (McDermott, 1987). Most recently, the Family Unity Model is being incorporated in some states into the independent living program in order to reconnect youth with their families. Even though the goal still remains independent living, the idea is to establish whatever contacts that are realistic—parents, sibling, aunts, uncles, grandparents—which can strengthen the social structure for the emancipated young person. It is found that often relatives do not even realize their family member was still in care with no place to call home.

Making the transition from adolescence to adulthood involves several factors, for example, moving from school to higher education or an occupation, developing social supports. In fact, completing high school, being employed while in care (Westat, Inc., 1991), and developing an ongoing support network (Barth, 1990) are among the best predictors of adolescents' moving successfully into young adulthood.

Unfortunately, many teens in care have had to change schools often and have experienced repeated academic failure. Although the newer schools may actually be better academically, the failure to deal with the emotional baggage brought along plus the difficulties in making new friends and getting acquainted with teachers often undermine their ability to benefit from the new opportunities offered (Johnson, Yoken, and Voss, 1995). Currently, there are some new approaches to make the school experience more positive. For many, the key is to be placed under an Individual Educational Plan (IEP). Then the administrators and teachers must share responsibility for developing an appropriate educational experience (Kellam, 1999a). Too often the schools do not do enough for youth in foster care because they view them as being in transition. In addition, teachers are not trained to handle or even understand the special problems presented by these teens, often misinterpreting their emotional problems as mental incapacities (Kellam, 1999a). Moreover, foster parents are often unaware of the rights the children placed with them have in terms of schooling.

To improve schooling opportunities, some states have begun to bring in advocacy groups to train foster parents in advocacy and on their rights under the Individuals with Disabilities Education Act (IDEA) (Kellam, 1999a). Another approach is the training of teachers on the challenges of those in foster care. This is being done informally in some states by foster parents. One formalized program, involving a collaboration between the social service agencies and the schools, trains foster parents in advocacy and trains teachers and foster parents on ways to work with youth who are having educational and other difficulties. There has also been attention paid recently to working with emancipated youth who have dropped out of school to help them obtain their GED and free college tuition or scholarships (Kellam, 1999b).

It is still the case that the majority of youth in care are performing below average in school (Folman, 1995; Halfon, Mendonca, and Berkowitz, 1995). Among the older, emancipated teens, only 63 percent have been found to have completed high school (Courtney and Pillavin, 1998). This figure is an improvement over the 54 percent found a few years earlier (Westat, Inc., 1991). It is evident that the independent living programs have facilitated this progress.

Social issues are especially critical for all teens in foster care. Those in the system often exhibit problems in peer relations, including alienation (Raychaba, 1988; Folman, 1995). Those who are identified as being resilient have friends in whom they can confide, often maintain friendships even after they move to new neighborhoods, and have foster parents who help them in maintaining contacts with friends and siblings who may be placed elsewhere (Folman and Hagen, 1996). Furthermore, those who have supportive relationships after emancipation function much better than those who do not. Peer support groups can go a long way in facilitating social skills and building a sense of connection. These groups can provide a safe, supportive environment in which young people can learn trust, consistency, social skills, and problem solving (Folman, 1996). Although these groups are not yet the norm for younger adolescents, their importance is being recognized among teens approaching emancipation (Sipowicz and Zanghi, 1998).

A major advance is the development of Youth in Care Networks. These groups, which are based on a youth development approach, are made up of teens approaching the age of emancipation as well as young adults who had been in foster care. There are many different models, but all involve working on empowering activities, for example, teens training workers and parents on the needs of foster children and youth, conducting public awareness initiatives, advocating for policy changes and community building activities, such as youth retreats and team-building activities. These networks provide the protective factors identified among foster youth who have adapted well, that is, those who have a sense of self-efficacy, of purpose, of being needed, and of belonging (Folman, 1994).

Federal legislation has addressed the problem of transition from the foster care system to independent living as a young adult. PL 99-272, passed in 1985, appropriated money for states to create independent living programs (ILP). These programs provide basic skill training, educational initiatives, and employment programs for those who are sixteen years and older. Those who have received such services fare better, being more likely to complete high school, be employed, and be self-sufficient. However, only a small percentage of adolescents have access to ILP programs (Westat, Inc. 1991; Courtney and Pillavin, 1998). Thus, too many emancipated adolescents continue to experience homelessness, welfare dependence, health problems, and depression (Barth, 1990; Westat, Inc., 1991; Courtney and Pillavin, 1998).

The 1999 Foster Care Independence Act, which came about in part because of the testimony of teens in care and young adults who had been in care as teens, attempts to address some of the earlier shortcomings. It doubles the amount of money available, allows states to use 30 percent of the funding for room and board, and extends Medicaid to age twenty-one (state's discretion).

The federal government, state governments, and social service agencies all have recognized the shortcomings of the foster care system in the United States. Consequently, there is a growing number of good practice models that are making a difference in the lives of youth and young adults who have been included. Among successful programs not mentioned above are approaches that focus on enhancing the skills of foster parents, for example, specialized training for foster parents who care for chronic juvenile offenders or those discharged from psychiatric facilities (Chamberlain and Reid, 1991). Those programs proven to be successful need to be replicated throughout the states.

Foster care was introduced as a system to provide appropriate care and opportunities for children and teens who could not live in their own families' home.

Although better than some of the alternatives, for example, institutions and group homes, the foster care system has been found to have many shortcomings, and the demands placed on it have been increasing at alarming rates. The new approaches that have been implemented over the past several years are moves in the right direction, and the laws, monies, and policies now in place are bringing about needed improvements. However, there is still a long way to go. Not nearly enough of the youth affected are receiving "best practices" in terms of service. Foster parents and the youth themselves need to be even more involved in the continuing changes to maximize the benefits of the policies and programs that have proven to be effective in enhancing the lives of these teens and young adults.

Rosalind D. Folman
John W. Hagen

See also Adoption: Issues and Concerns; Family Composition: Realities and Myths; Homeless Youth; Teenage Parenting: Childbearing

References and further reading

Allen, Marylee, Karen Bonner, and Linda Greenan. 1988. "Federal Legislative Support for Independent Living." Pp. 19–32 in *Independent-Living Services for At-Risk Adolescents.* Edited by Edmund Mech. Washington DC: CWLA.

Barth, Richard P. 1990. "On Their Own: The Experiences of Youth after Foster Care." *Child and Adolescent Social Work* 7, no. 5: 419–440.

Chamberlain, Patricia, and John Reid. 1991. "Using a Specialized Foster Care Community Treatment Model for Children and Adolescents Leaving the State Mental Hospital." *Journal of Community Psychology* 19, no. 3: 266–276.

———. 1998. "Comparison of Two Community Alternatives to Incarceration for Chronic Juvenile Offenders." *Journal of Consulting and Clinical Psychology* 66, no. 4: 624–633.

Courtney, Mark E., and Irving Pillavin. 1998. *Youth Transitions to Adulthood: Outcomes 12–18 Months after Leaving Out-of-Home Care.* Madison: University of Wisconsin Press.

Folman, Rosalind D. 1994. "Risk and Protective Factors among Children and Youth in Foster Care." Paper presented at the 24th annual conference of the National Foster Parent Association, Grand Rapids, MI.

———. 1995. "Resiliency and Vulnerability among Abused and Neglected Children in Foster Care." Doctoral dissertation, University of Michigan. Abstract in *Dissertation Abstract International* 56(08-B), p. 4601.

———. 1996. "Foster Care Experiences: How They Impact the Transition to Adulthood." Pathways to Adulthood National Conference, San Diego.

Folman, Rosalind D., and John Hagen. 1996. "Foster Children Entering Adolescence: Factors of Risk and Resilience." Poster presented at the biennial meeting of the Society for Research on Adolescence, Boston.

Geiser, Robert L. 1973. *The Illusion of Caring: Children in Foster Care.* Boston: Beacon Press.

Halfon, Neal, Ana Mendonca, and Gale Berkowitz. 1995. "Health Status of Children in Foster Care." *Archives of Pediatric and Adolescent Medicine* 149: 386–392.

Johnson, Penny, Carol I. Yoken, and Ron Voss. 1995. "Foster Care Placement: The Child's Perspective." *Child Welfare* 74, no. 5: 959–974.

Kellam, Susan. 1999a. "New School, New Problems: Foster Children Struggle in U.S. Schools." Web site: http://connectforkids.org

———. 1999b. "Voices of Foster Care: People Who Make a Difference." Web site: http://connectforkids.org

Lamphear, Vivian S. 1985. "The Impact of Maltreatment on Children's Psychosocial Adjustment: A Review of the Research." *Child Abuse and Neglect* 9, no. 2: 251–263.

McDermott, Virginia A. 1987. "Life Planning Services: Helping Older Placed Children with Their Identity." *Child and Adolescent Social Work* 4: 97–115.

Raychaba, Brian. 1988. *To Be on Our Own with No Direction from Home.* Ottawa: National Youth in Care Network.

Sipowicz, Hugh, and Marty Zanghi. 1998. "Maine Youth Are Speaking Up and Reaching Out!" *Common Ground* (December).

U.S. Department of Health and Human Services. 1999. *The AFCARS Report.* Web site: http://www.acf.dhhs.gov

Westat, Inc. 1991. *A National Evalutaion of Title IV-E Foster Care Independent Living Programs for Youth.* Washington, DC: HHS.

Freedom

Adolescence is a time when children begin to look and act more like adults. Physical changes in appearance, due to sexual maturation, are the most obvious of the transformations that occur during adolescence. In addition, adolescents undergo neurological changes that enable them to think and reason at the same level as adults. These new cognitive abilities allow adolescents to contemplate the abstract and to hypothesize about the future, especially their own futures. Adolescence is thus a time in which to explore possibilities and define one's identity. Possessing increased capacity to assume adult roles, and facing cultural pressure to explore and establish an identity, adolescents are typically given both more responsibility and more freedom in their daily lives. One of the challenges of adolescence lies in managing this privilege of freedom while recognizing the consequences that freedom brings.

The new freedoms of adolescence originate from different sources. For example, the government grants many legal rights or freedoms to adolescents. Teenagers can begin to drive between the ages of fourteen and seventeen (depending on the state), they are allowed to begin working at age fourteen, and they can legally drop out of school at age sixteen. At the age of eighteen, adolescents are no longer considered minors and thus can vote, enlist in the military, and get married. By this time, they are also expected by adult society to begin forming their social and civic identities, and to start on a path toward adulthood and self-sufficiency.

Adolescents face additional pressure from the media and pop culture to take on adult roles. This pressure comes from many different sources: music, TV, movies, advertisements, celebrities, even daily events in the news. The media's portrayal and promotion of adult independence and the freedoms of adulthood often entice teenagers to imitate these behaviors. Peer groups can also intensify the need for adolescents to participate in adult activities and explore their new rights and freedoms. These freedoms come with responsibility, however, and managing them involves understanding consequences, exercising judgment, and making mature decisions in such areas as family relationships, health and safety, and part-time employment.

Family Relationships

The tasks and challenges of adolescence often lead to changes in family relationships. Parents and adolescents renegotiate their relationships with one another as the latter begin to form and shape identities for themselves. The process of identity formation can involve a degree of emotional separation from parents, increasing the emotional turmoil that teenagers are already experiencing. Indeed, as teenagers become more independent and spend less time with their parents, the parents often meet with resistance when they attempt to control or manage the teens' habits, schedules, or behaviors. Nevertheless, parent-child relationships continue to be significant and can greatly influence the transition of teenagers to adulthood.

Health and Safety
As children reach adolescence, parents begin to transfer to them the basic health responsibilities of eating right, exercising, dressing, and getting sufficient sleep. In short, they increasingly trust their children to make these decisions on their own. Unfortunately, some teenagers have difficulty maintaining a healthy lifestyle because of the larger societal emphasis on image and appearance. Overconcern with issues of weight gain can lead to maladaptive eating and exercise patterns. Many teenagers who have fixated on the cultural "ideal" of thinness suffer from eating disorders such as anorexia and bulimia, and from the unhealthy consumption of steroids. This emphasis on image and appearance can also influence the way teenagers dress, the friends they choose, and the activities in which they participate. All of these behaviors contribute to the social and personal identities that adolescents are trying to establish.

Teenagers are also faced with decisions concerning the consumption of tobacco products, alcohol, and drugs. Part of the attraction of legal drugs, such as tobacco and alcohol, is that adults use them—and adolescents feel more "adult" themselves by using them. The majority of teenagers have tried alcohol and smoked cigarettes by the age of eighteen. Although alcohol and tobacco use are accepted in adult culture, both substances can take a serious toll on the health of young people. Tobacco—through its primary agent, nicotine—can enhance both alertness and relaxation. But it also increases heart rate and blood pressure, and raises the risk of heart disease and respiratory disorders such as emphysema, bronchitis, and lung cancer. Alcohol, a depressant, enhances relaxation and decreases inhibition. But excessive alcohol consumption can lead to severe liver and kidney damage, coma, and death, and drunkenness can cause debilitating injuries and fatal accidents. Illegal drugs, such as marijuana, amphetamines, cocaine, narcotics (morphine, heroin), and hallucinogens such as LSD—though not as commonly used as alcohol or tobacco—also carry substantial risks of injury to oneself and others. As many teenagers experiment with at least some of these drugs before adulthood, candid discussions about their effects, though challenging for parents, are critically important.

Another safety concern involves increased freedom in driving and travel. By their late teens, most adolescents are driving independently; many own cars, and many are traveling on their own. Driving safely, knowing what to do in an emergency, and always having a "designated driver" are some of the precautions that can be taken against the dangers of driving. Though educational in many ways, travel also poses risks. Potential dangers include unsafe lodging or travel arrangements, theft, and deceitful travel vendors. Because of teenagers' general inexperience, they may be vulnerable to these hazards; hence, they are advised to travel with another person or in groups whenever possible.

An additional area of concern is increased sexual freedom. The biological and hormonal changes that teenagers undergo cause their romantic relationships to become more sexual in nature, and they are forced to make decisions about their own sexual behavior. Sexual experimentation and activity during adolescence occur naturally due to maturation; however, teenagers also need to be aware of the consequences of sexual activity. Sexual relationships can be physically and emotionally satisfying, but they can also result in pregnancy and sexually transmitted disease. Along with pregnancy comes decisions about early childbearing and parenting, abortion, adoption, and single parenthood. Some sexually transmitted diseases, such as AIDS, can be fatal; others, such as herpes, can lead to lifelong complications.

Employment and Education
With adolescence comes the opportunity to earn an income. It is quite common for teenagers to hold a part-time job while attending high school, even while living with their parents. The income they earn affords them additional freedoms: Now able to spend money in ways of their own choosing, they can pursue recreational interests or hobbies to a greater degree than before. Early employment also raises questions for adolescents about what career paths they might take and what they must accomplish in order to achieve their goals. One major decision of adolescence revolves around what to do immediately after high school. Since many opportunities and choices are available to teenagers, this decision can be overwhelming. However, work and volunteer experience in different fields, as well as guidance and support from adults, can greatly assist adolescents' decision making about their future employment.

At the age of eighteen and sometimes sooner, many teenagers leave their parents' home; some attend college, whereas others go off to live and work on their own. This transition leads to even greater freedom and control over their lives. In addition to dealing with new health and safety issues, teenagers have to pay bills, budget for expenses, maintain a residence, and manage their time. The burden of these freedoms can be staggering for some adolescents, but learning to balance and manage all of these tasks is a challenge even to some adults as well. Taking advantage of available freedoms, while remaining responsible to oneself and others, can indeed be a lifelong task.

Jana H. Chaudhuri

See also Decision Making; Developmental Challenges; Discipline; Parenting Styles; Responsibility for Developmental Tasks; Transitions of Adolescence

References and further reading
Cobb, Nancy J. 1998. *Adolescence: Continuity, Change and Diversity.* Mountain View, CA: Mayfield Publishing.
Esman, Aaron H. 1990. *Adolescence and Culture.* New York: Columbia University Press.
Lerner, Richard M. In press. *Adolescence: Development, Diversity, Context, and Application.* Upper Saddle River, NJ: Prentice-Hall.
Lerner, Richard M., and Nancy L. Galambos. 1998. "Adolescent Development: Challenges and Opportunities for Research, Programs, and Policies." Pp. 413–446 in *Annual Review of Psychology.* Edited by J. T. Spence. Palo Alto, CA: Annual Reviews.
Lerner, Richard M., and Nancy L. Galambos, eds. 1984. *Experiencing Adolescents: A Sourcebook for Parents, Teachers, and Teens.* New York: Garland.
Takanishi, Ruby, ed. 1993. *Adolescence in the 1990s.* New York: Teachers College Press.

G

Gay, Lesbian, Bisexual, and Sexual-Minority Youth

Definitions

Many adolescents are familiar with the sexual categories *gay, lesbian, bisexual,* and *heterosexual*—contemporary terms that refer to the degree to which individuals are attracted to same-sex and opposite-sex others. These sexual labels encompass several interrelated factors: attractions, erotic desires, emotional affiliations, sexual behavior, and culturally defined identity categories. However, it is conceivable that for a given individual these domains are not synergistic. A young woman, for example, may be sexually attracted to both girls and boys, fall in love only with girls, have sex only with boys, and identify as heterosexual. Or a young man might be exclusively attracted to girls, engage in sex with his male friends, and identify as bisexual.

When considering sexual categories, we must clearly distinguish between sexual orientation and sexual identity. The contrast between the two is often conceptualized as the difference between an ever-present, invariant biological or psychological truth (sexual orientation) and a historically and culturally located social construction (sexual identity). Although this distinction oversimplifies both constructs, it is useful for clarifying several developmental issues facing adolescents with same-sex attractions.

Sexual orientation refers to the unchangeable sexual feelings that an individual has for members of the same sex, the opposite sex, both sexes, or neither sex. It originates early in life—perhaps at conception if caused by genetic factors or during the prenatal period if it results from sex hormones—and it is set by early childhood. Sexual orientation may be influenced by genetic, biological, psychogenic, and sociocultural factors. Still unknown is the extent to which these factors determine the direction of one's sexuality; however, scientists give the most weight to biological and genetic determinants of sexual orientation and consider it to be immutable, stable, and internally consonant. If environmental factors are important, their influence probably occurs quite early in a child's life—possibly even prenatally, through maternal hormonal levels. Sexual orientation is not subject to conscious control, and the degree to which it is malleable is a matter of some debate. However, most scientists believe that it is neither alterable nor subject to psychotherapeutic intervention strategies (e.g., conversion therapies).

Sexual orientation influences, but is independent of, sexual conduct and sexual identity. It is also multidimensional.

In many ways, sexual-minority youths are the same as other youths. They share the concerns, crises, and tasks that confront all adolescents. (Skjold Photographs)

Some people believe that, because many individuals possess degrees of homoerotic and heteroerotic attractions and feelings, homosexuality and heterosexuality are merely the ends of a continuum on which we all fall. Others maintain that sexual orientation is a categorical variable in which people can be classified only as heterosexual, homosexual, or bisexual.

Sexual identity refers to a socially sanctioned or recognized category that names the perceptions and feelings that an individual has about her or his sexual feelings, attractions, and behaviors. It is symbolized by such statements as "I am gay" or "I am straight" and is thus a matter of personal choice. For some individuals, sexual identity remains fluid during the life course (though probably not on a day-to-day basis) and is not necessarily consistent with sexual orientation, romantic feelings, or behavior.

Sexual labels occur within a pool of potential identities that are defined by the culture and historic time in which one lives. Culture gives the labels meaning, salience, and desirability, so the categories available in one culture may not be available in another. For example, social historians argue that contemporary terms such as *lesbian, gay,* and *bisexual* have only recently evolved, although same-sex behaviors and attractions have existed throughout recorded history. In some Native American cultures, for example, *two-spirit person* is a term reserved for sacred individuals who are believed to possess two souls, one male and one female. These "blessed" individuals are often androgynous in physical appearance and behavior and have sex with both males and females.

Whether individuals engage in sexual behavior consistent with their sexual orientation and identity is a question that depends on many factors. These include random or planned opportunities that place the individuals in particular sexual situations, the availability of sexual partners, the extent to which they feel comfortable about countering social sanctions defining who is an appropriate sexual partner, and, finally, libido or sex drive. Most lesbian, bisexual, and gay youths eventually have sex with a same-sex other as an expression of their sexual desires or fantasies; however, over one-half of gay males and 80 percent of lesbians also engage in heterosexual sexual contact at some point in their lives. Lesbian and gay virgins exist, as do heterosexual virgins. It is also possible for *heterosexual* individuals, who are primarily attracted to those of the opposite sex, to engage in sex with same-sex others for pleasure, experimentation, or curiosity.

In fact, many individuals who do not identify as bisexual, gay, or lesbian nevertheless have same-sex attractions. The term *sexual minority* defines these individuals, who, rather than conforming to traditional notions of heterosexuality or homosexuality, apply a diverse array of sexual descriptors to themselves. Those who identify as lesbian, bisexual, or gay are included, as are individuals who reject cultural definitions of sexual categories. These youths may describe their attractions as "unlabeled," they may be uncertain ("questioning") as to the nature of their sexual attractions, they may be without sexual attractions ("asexual"), they may use markers other than sex as the basis for their sexual attractions (e.g., "I like the person"), or they may consider themselves to be atypical heterosexuals ("not straight," "queer"). Included in this last category are transgendered individuals who may be of any sexual orientation or identity. *Transgendered* is an umbrella term referring to people who believe that they do not fit the traditional definitions of masculinity or femininity expected for their biological sex.

One simple way of resolving this complex issue is to eschew sexual labels altogether and rely instead on descriptions of behaviors or attractions. This is a particularly important consideration because adolescents frequently explore issues related to their sexuality that may have little bearing on their current or future sexual identity. In addition to asking youths whether they accept a particular sexual identity label, one could ask about the existence, number, or proportion of sexual behaviors, attractions, or romantic relationships they have had with males *and* females.

Little is known about this "class" of individuals who do not consider themselves to be gay and yet experience significant and persistent sexual attractions for and fantasies involving same-sex others. Their failure to so identify may be due, in part, to heterocentrism and homophobia.

Heterocentrism is the assumption that development "naturally" proceeds in a heterosexual direction. This perspective is so pervasive in our culture that many people unthinkingly assume that everyone is heterosexual. Thus, for example, girls are routinely asked if they have boyfriends, and vice versa. Heterosexism is what emerges when heterocentrism becomes judgmental—when girls who have boyfriends rather than girlfriends are considered to be healthier and boys who are turned on by female images rather than male images are believed to be better adjusted.

Homophobia, on the other hand, is a popular term that should be reserved for the strongest emotional expressions of negative attitudes, beliefs, and feelings toward homosexuality and gay people. A somewhat less extreme term—*homonegativity*—refers to the belief that homosexuality is not as viable a lifestyle as heterosexuality. Implementation of this belief by discriminating against or verbally abusing suspected gay people or by committing violent acts against perceived gay people is what constitutes homophobia. Research indicates that the majority of self-identified lesbian, bisexual, and gay adolescents have experienced verbal or physical harassment, usually from peers.

Prevalence

No one knows with certainty how many sexual-minority youths exist. But whatever the number, it is certain to be far greater than the number of adolescents who identify as lesbian, bisexual, or gay. For example, in a national survey of adults, just over 1 percent of women and nearly 3 percent of men identified themselves as lesbian, bisexual, or gay (Laumann et al., 1994). However, when participants were asked whether they had ever considered having sex with someone of their own gender, these figures increased—to about 6 percent of women and men. According to the same survey, 4 percent of women and 9 percent of men reported having had same-sex relations. Other surveys of high school youths reveal similar trends.

Thus, many "potential" sexual-minority youths do not identify as gay or lesbian during adolescence. The reason for this disparity is not known, but it is likely linked to negative cultural attitudes and stereotypes about same-sex-attracted individuals. One thing is certain: The percentage of adolescents who are attracted to same-sex others at least parallels the number of adults with these attractions. Whether this proportion is as small as 2 percent or as large as 15 percent is difficult to ascertain.

Developmental Research

Relatively little is known about sexual-minority youths because researchers have ignored such individuals, at least until recently. In the interim, a limited number of issues important to sexual-minority youths have been addressed. Specifically, based on the *differential developmental trajectories* (DDT) approach, four hypotheses about their lives have received empirical support.

First, in many ways sexual-minority youths are the same as other youths, regardless of sexual attractions. They share the concerns, crises, and tasks that confront all adolescents. Regardless of sexual orientation, they experience growth spurts, menses, nocturnal emissions, secondary sex characteristics, and acne. They also struggle to balance connectedness and autonomy with their parents, shift their attachments from parents to peers, argue about curfew and household duties, and desire to fall in love and to experience both sexual and emotional intimacy. Yet these similarities are frequently lost on those who portray sexual-minority youths as unhealthy, unnatural, undesirable, even "alien" beings. They cite a long litany of ways in which sexual-minority youths deviate from their heterosexual brothers and sisters. And they urge parents to always be "on guard" with the "moral courage," if not always with the accurate information, needed to convince their vulnerable children that they should never be lesbian or gay. For example, in response to recent discrimination lawsuits, the Boy Scouts of America have maintained that a "homosexual" adolescent is a heterosexual boy who has been transformed by an early sexual experience or by the message that "gay is okay" conveyed to him by "homosexual" role models.

Media representations of sexual-minority adolescents often portray being young, gay, and proud as an oxymoron—impossible to achieve in North American culture. These youths appear to be a weak lot, defenseless within their troubled world. The message is that resilient, strong sexual-minority youths who have coped, survived, and thrived do not exist. The common view is that if sexual-minority youths are at high risk for committing or attempting suicide, abusing drugs, prostituting themselves, and becoming infected with HIV. The implication is that there are two separate populations of adolescents—the heterosexual population is "normal" and the sexual-minority one is not.

In short, the DDT approach asserts that sexual-minority youths are similar to heterosexuals in most respects, with comparable (though not always identical) biological and psychosocial developmental challenges. The very foundation of DDT implies that adolescents are first, foremost, and always adolescents—a fact that must be remembered in any accurate rendering of their lives. *An adolescent is an adolescent is an adolescent.*

Second, the DDT approach simultaneously argues that sexual-minority youths are distinct from heterosexuals—specifically because of their unique biological makeup or because of the ways in which same-sex-attracted individuals are treated by an uncaring mainstream culture.

Although the evidence is far from definitive, sexual-minority youth appear to differ from heterosexual youth in some aspects of their biological makeup (i.e., both genetically and with respect to their prenatal hormone environment). For example, various biological studies have found that "homosexual" individuals differ from heterosexuals in particular aspects of their neuroanatomy (the hypothalamus), physiology (prenatal hormone levels), and physical features (shoulder-to-hip ratio). Pedigree studies have demonstrated that homosexuality runs in families and that monozygotic twins are more likely than dizygotic twins to share the directionality of sexual attractions.

Psychosocial research has documented that as a consequence of growing up amidst heterocentric family members, close friends, and societal institutions (e.g., schools and religious organizations) that presume and prescribe exclusive heterosexuality, sexual-minority adolescents are challenged to negotiate between being true to self and becoming what is expected of them. This task permeates their daily life in ways not encountered by heterosexual youths when they express their sexuality. It is difficult to disregard the negativity that many adolescents and their parents direct at individuals who prefer sexual and romantic attractions with same-sex others. Terms such as *faggot* and *dyke* are common put-downs aimed at those who dare to vary from the norm. Thus, because of their sexuality, sexual-minority youths necessarily experience a life course substantially different from that of heterosexual adolescents. The consequences may be either negative (e.g., increased levels of emotional distress and substance abuse) or positive (e.g., feelings of specialness or creativity).

The third postulate of the DDT approach is that sexual-minority youths vary enormously *among* themselves based on shared characteristics. Developmental trajectories appear to be unique to subgroups of sexual-minority individuals based on such factors as personality characteristics, gender, race, ethnicity, class, and real-world experiences. Two examples illustrate this point: (1) The romantic relationships of same-sex-attracted young women are more likely to evolve from same-sex friendships and to be characterized by emotional intimacy than are

those of gay male youths. (2) Among the various ethnic groups studied, Asian American sexual-minority teenagers are least likely to disclose to parents and to engage in same-sex activity.

Additional diverse subgroups reside within each of these gender and ethnic classifications. For example, researchers at Cornell have shown that some sexual-minority boys are actually similar to same-sex-attracted girls in their disdain of casual sex, and that some Asian American youths not only disclose to their parents but also become national lesbian/gay leaders. Some girls do not recall having early childhood same-sex attractions prior to identifying as lesbian but, rather, come to understand their sexual identity within the context of exposure to a college women's studies course or within a romantic relationship. Some boys have sex with another boy before labeling themselves gay, whereas other boys identify as gay before engaging in gay sex. And some youths claim a bisexual, gay, or lesbian identity in the absence of sexual experiences, whereas others who have had many same-sex encounters do not identify as anything other than heterosexual. Given this level of diversity, it is a misnomer to refer to a singular "gay lifestyle."

Finally, every adolescent is unique insofar as no one exactly like her or him has ever lived before or will in the future. Although this point is often lost in scientific presentations of data, the life-history accounts of youths that are narrated in "coming-out" books well illustrate this fourth facet of the DDT approach. These histories are extremely popular among sexual-minority youths who are searching for other youths who have experienced their "issues." They want to know that they are not alone.

Thus, sexual-minority youths share commonalities with all other adolescents and subgroups of adolescents regardless of sexual orientation, with all other sexual-minority youths, with subgroups of such youths—and yet with *no* other adolescent who has ever lived. Any presumption that sexual-minority youths are all alike and share identical developmental pathways is not only implausible but also grossly misrepresents their lives.

Ritch C. Savin-Williams

See also Gender Differences; Identity; Sex Differences; Sex Roles; Sexuality, Emotional Aspects of

References and further reading

Bass, Ellen, and Kate Kaufman. 1996. *Free Your Mind: The Book for Gay, Lesbian, and Bisexual Youth—and Their Allies.* New York: HarperPerennial.

Borhek, Mary V. 1993. *Coming Out to Parents: A Two-Way Survival Guide for Lesbians and Gay Men and Their Parents*, 2nd ed. Cleveland: Pilgrim.

Diamond, Lisa M. 2000. "Passionate Friendships among Adolescent Sexual-Minority Women." *Journal of Research on Adolescence* 10: 191–209.

Fairchild, Betty, and Nancy Hayward. 1989. *Now That You Know: What Every Parent Should Know about Homosexuality*, updated ed. San Diego: Harcourt Brace Jovanovich.

Feinberg, Leslie. 1993. *Stone Butch Blues.* Ithaca, NY: Firebrand.

Fricke, Aaron. 1981. *Reflections of a Rock Lobster: A Story about Growing Up Gay.* Boston: Alyson.

Griffin, Carolyn W., Marian J. Wirth, and Arthur G. Wirth. 1986. *Beyond Acceptance: Parents of Lesbians and Gays Talk about Their Experiences.* Englewood Cliffs, NJ: Prentice-Hall.

Herdt, Gilbert, ed. 1989. *Gay and Lesbian Youth.* New York: Harrington Park Press.

Heron, Ann, ed. 1994. *Two Teenagers in Twenty: Writings by Gay and Lesbian Youth.* Boston: Alyson.

Hutchins, Loraine, and Lani Kaahumana, eds. 1991. *Bi Any Other Name: Bisexual People Speak Out.* Boston: Alyson.

Laumann, Edward O., John Gagnon, Robert T. Michael, and Stuart Michaels. 1994. *The Social Organization of Sexuality: Sexual Practices in the United States.* Chicago: University of Chicago Press.

Nycum, Benjie. 2000. *The XY Survival Guide: Everything You Need to Know about Being Young and Gay.* San Francisco: XY Publishing.

Ryan, Caitlin, and Donna Futterman. 1998. *Lesbian and Gay Youth: Care and Counseling.* Philadelphia: Hanley and Belfus.

Savin-Williams, Ritch C. 1998. "*. . . And Then I Became Gay": Young Men's Stories.* New York: Routledge.

———. 2001. *"Mom, Dad. I'm Gay." How Families Negotiate Coming Out.* Washington, DC: American Psychological Association Press.

Savin-Williams, Ritch C., and Kenneth M. Cohen. 1996. *The Lives of Lesbians, Gays, and Bisexuals: Children to Adults.* Forth Worth, TX: Harcourt Brace College Publishing.

Gender Differences

Males and females are undoubtedly different—not just physically, physiologically, and biologically but behaviorally as well. Throughout history, their engagement in various social roles has varied according to gender. Indeed, to this day, certain roles are still somewhat associated with men (e.g., working outside of the home in gainful, salaried employment) and with women (e.g., being homemakers and caring for children). Some of these traditional divisions between the genders in the roles they play in society have come to be regarded as gender role stereotypes.

In part, gender stereotypes reflect society-wide beliefs that males and females are fundamentally different in their capacities, behaviors, and interests. To understand gender differences, we need to understand the nature of these gender

A group of "typical" teenagers (Steve Chenn/Corbis)

role stereotypes and the extent to which they influence youth development.

A *stereotype* is an overgeneralized belief. It is an attitude—that is, some combination of cognition and feeling—that invariantly characterizes a person or group of people as possessing specific attributes. Stereotypes thus allow for little exception. Because of this rigidity, they are resistant to change and, as such, may become accepted as always true in a given society. For more than a quarter-century, scholars have indicated that gender role stereotypes exist in American society.

A *gender role* is a socially defined set of prescriptions concerning the behavior of people in a particular sex group; *gender role behavior* refers to behavioral functioning in accordance with these prescriptions; and *gender role stereotypes* are generalized beliefs that particular behaviors are characteristic of one sex group as opposed to the other. For instance, males are stereotyped as aggressive, independent, dominant, active, skilled in business, and not at all dependent, whereas females are stereotyped as gentle, very aware of the feelings of others, concerned with physical appearance, and possessed of a strong need for security.

Research indicates that these gender role stereotypes are held consistently not only across age and educational level but also across culture. For instance, in a study of six countries—Norway, Sweden, Denmark, Finland, England, and the United States—marked cross-cultural consistency in such stereotypes was found to exist.

In short, to an almost universal extent, stereotypes specify that different sets of behaviors are expected from males and females. The male role is associated with individual effectiveness and independent competence. The female role is associated with interpersonal warmth and expressiveness. But what do contemporary American adolescents think about gender differences, and what is their experience of them?

The answer to that question depends, in part, on an understanding of American culture. As the United States enters into the twenty-first century, there is evidence that, on the one hand, the gender role stereotypes of the twentieth century are still very much a part of the American landscape and, on the other hand, that the influence of such stereotypes is waning. In other words, American culture has reached a point of historical transition from stereotypy to flexibility in terms of the roles seen as appropriate for—and worth pursuing by—both males and females. Indeed, in almost every aspect of research pertinent to work and gender roles, stereotypy and flexibility have been found to exist simultaneously.

For example, having a mother who works outside of the home is the typical experience for most American children and adolescents today. Yet the meaning attached by youth to parental employment continues to show evidence of the influence of gender role stereotypes. Consistent with these stereotypes, work outside the home is still seen as the central domain of males (the "breadwinners"), and family life is still regarded as the central domain of females (the "homemakers"). Moreover, in this context, *work* itself is defined in terms of being gainfully employed (i.e., earning a salary), whereas family is equated with unpaid housekeeping.

In keeping with this stereotyped division of labor between males and females, half of the high school seniors in the *Monitoring the Future* study (Johnston, O'Malley, and Bachman, 1999) reported that it is not acceptable for both parents to work when they have preschool-aged children. At the same time, however, 79 percent of the female high school seniors and 67 percent of the male high school seniors said that even if they had the money to live as comfortably as they wished, they would still not want to give up paid work.

Moreover, although an increasing number of adolescent females aspire to succeed in labor areas traditionally associated with males, there has been no corresponding investment in family work on the part of adolescent males. Accordingly, among many older adolescent females, the need to integrate work and family significantly influences their choice of vocation and the timing of their marriage. In addition, given the more flexible role orientation of females, they are under greater pressure to balance both family and work roles than are men who can devote most of their effort to enacting their work roles.

In a study of sixth to eighth graders, Phame M. Camerena and his colleagues (1994) found that the basis of this "role strain" may begin in adolescence. Although boy's attitudes toward women's roles changed more than did girls' attitudes toward the work and family roles of men and women, the girls' attitudes were more positive and open than those of the boys. Moreover, in a ten-year follow-up of individuals first studied as adolescents, although both men and women reported that they value both work and family, both groups exhibited highly stereotypic expectations for how work and family roles would be enacted: The men emphasized work for gainful employment, and the women stressed family roles.

Given what seems to be the persistence of both stereotypy and flexibility in work and gender roles, one may reasonably ask why these two contradictory trends exist. One theory is that although society promotes certain ideals about gender equality and establishes public policies and programs in support of such values, it also exerts some countervailing influences. Specifically, the institutions of society, including families, socialize youth to become more gender stereotyped in their personal behaviors. This theory has been termed the *gender intensification hypothesis*.

There is evidence that gender intensification exists. During early adolescence, both males and females become increasingly concerned about gender roles, body image, and the perceived importance of popularity. After the sixth grade, they believe it is more important than ever *not* to act like members of the opposite sex. And during middle adolescence, both boys and girls engage in high levels of gender-typed activities and express gender-typed interests. For example, there is some evidence that girls show a relative preference for high school subjects that are stereotypically feminine (e.g., English and history) versus stereotypically masculine (e.g., math and science).

Gender intensification also occurs in the context of psychiatric disorders. As adolescence progresses, the incidence of eating disorders (e.g., anorexia and bulimia) and depression increases among girls and that of conduct disorders (i.e., problems with obeying "the rules") increases among boys.

On the other hand, there is evidence indicating that during the middle portion of adolescence both boys and girls are increasingly willing to depart, respectively, from stereotypically masculine and feminine role behaviors and to adopt more flexible views of these behaviors. For instance, from middle childhood through early adolescence, gender preferences become less stereotyped and more flexible.

Whether boys and girls differ in regard to the flexibility of their gender preferences is not certain. Some research suggests that the increased flexibility of these preferences may occur primarily, or perhaps even only, for girls. However, other research shows an increase through late adolescence in the flexibility of gender role preferences among both males and females as well as a more flexible attitude among contemporary adolescents toward female gender roles than among members of older generations.

To the extent that gender intensification occurs, then, it may take place primarily in the context of one-to-one mother-daughter or father-son activities. For example, psychologists now know that ongoing relationships with fathers are more important for sons' gender role development than for such development among daughters and that adolescents' gender attitudes affect their behaviors. One area that has received considerable attention concerns gender differences in school achievement.

Academic Achievement
In 1992, Mattel Toys put the first talking Barbie doll on the market. Barbie's first words were "Math class is tough." Mattel's advertisers believed they were simply expressing the sentiment of most school-age girls. Many parents and teachers, however, thought that Barbie should keep her mouth shut. As a result, Barbie stopped talking.

The controversy surrounding Barbie and her statement about math highlights a concern in the United States regarding male-female differences in math and science. Although the gender gap has narrowed over the years, boys continue to outperform girls on standardized tests of math and science achievement. At the same time, girls' attitudes regarding math and science have become increasingly negative; many girls feel that they are not good at math and science and say that they do not like these subjects. These trends are particularly troubling because girls' grades in math and science classes are often equal to or better than those of boys. In other words, girls *can* do math and science. Nevertheless, in high school, when students are given course choices, girls are more likely than boys to opt out of advanced math and science classes. As a consequence, girls are often less prepared for certain academic disciplines, limiting both their college major and career choices. The question, then, is why do we see these differences?

Reasons for the Gender Gap
Until recently, it was believed that male-female differences in math and science were strictly a result of biology. In other words, "girls' and boys' brains are different, so they are better suited for different things." The notion is that boys have superior spatial abilities, which are relevant to particular mathematical manipulations, whereas girls are predisposed toward language and writing. Indeed, boys appear to excel in math and girls appear to do better in verbal-related skills. But are these differences simply a result of biological predispositions, or do other factors play a role? More recently, researchers have highlighted the significant influence of the social environment on children's math and science achievement. For example, very early on, boys are given opportunities to tinker with toys or objects that involve many of the principles inherent in math and science (e.g., building blocks, Legos, racing cars, simple machines).

Girls, however, often lack these experiences, so they enter math and science classrooms feeling insecure about their own abilities and, ultimately, begin to believe that they cannot do math and science as well as boys. This belief is consistent with the stereotype in our culture that defines math and science as male domains: "Males are better suited for math and science, and math and science are more useful to males than to females." At the same time, the personality characteristics attributed to mathematicians and scientists are associated more with males. And since mathematicians and scientists are often thought to be competitive, achievement-oriented, and not very social, parents, teachers, or school counselors who subscribe to these gender role stereotypes are less likely to encourage or support young girls' decisions to pursue math and science in high school or beyond. For example, researchers have found that when parents believe math to be something boys do better than girls, they are willing to let their daughters drop out of math class when the going gets tough. With sons, however, their approach is to encourage persistence. Meanwhile, teachers, often unaware of their own biases, call on boys more, provide boys with more praise for correct answers, and are more likely to solicit help from boys for science or math demonstrations. The message sent to girls is that they are not as "smart" as the boys.

Closing the Gender Gap
In response to these research findings, educational reform efforts have been undertaken to make math and science experiences accessible, equitable, and exciting to all students. One change has been to encourage teachers to use a hands-on approach to teaching math and science in their classrooms. The idea is that learning will be facilitated if students are given opportunities to *do* science rather than just hearing about it. At the same time, students will feel more confident about their abilities and realize that math and science can be fun! Parents, too, have become more aware of the need to encourage their children's achievement in math and science. But if the gender gap is to be closed, schools and parents will have to continue their efforts. Here are some suggestions.

What Parents Can Do

- Provide your sons and daughters with early math- and science-related experiences. Visit your local science museum!
- Think about the toys you buy for your children. Don't forget that girls like chemistry sets, too.
- Find out what kinds of activities your children's teacher is providing in math and science class. Do your children come home excited to tell you about a neat experiment they did in class that day?
- When your children enter high school, encourage them to take math and science. It's never too early to find out about college entrance requirements.
- Let your children know that they can become anything they want to be—even a mathematician or scientist.

What Schools Can Do

- Provide *every* student with the opportunity to learn math and science.

- Provide teachers with in-service training on how to create equity in the classroom.
- Provide teachers with the resources and materials they need to give students hands-on experiences in the classroom.
- Require guidance counselors to inform boys *and* girls about college programs and careers in math and science.
- Contact a local industry or university to find out what kind of primary and secondary school math and science programs are offered.

Work and Career Choices

The experiences that male and female adolescents have in school often affect their career choices—and considering the stereotypes confronting them, it is not surprising that they choose different careers and exhibit different work behaviors. For most American adolescents, entry into the workplace does not begin until middle or later adolescence, usually through the experience of a part-time job. Gender differences emerge even at this stage. For instance, boys begin working at an earlier age and tend to work longer hours than girls.

Moreover, although both boys and girls are typically given jobs that involve little skill, training, or initiative, their precise assignments often vary along gender-stereotypic lines. In a department store job, for example, boys are more likely to be assigned to duties in the stockroom or mail room, whereas girls usually end up working as salesclerks.

Given the increasing flexibility in work and career roles associated with males and females, there is reason to be optimistic that future decades will bear witness to greater opportunities for adolescents of both sexes to explore and actualize the full range of their competencies and interests.

Identity

Identity development is another area in which gender differences are evident. As highlighted in the scholarship of Margaret Spencer (1990), identity may develop in different ways for boys and girls. For example, during middle and high school, girls report lower self-esteem than boys, and in some cases their poorer self-esteem appears across all domains of self-definition (e.g., in regard to appearance, scholastics, and athletic performance). Moreover, these differences, and self-esteem in general, show no major changes throughout these years.

Other research has found that self-perceptions become stable throughout the high school years, particularly among boys. Among girls, but not boys, self-perceptions of attractiveness decline. Also during these years, symbolic issues (e.g., relationships, happiness) and artistic and creative endeavors become more salient to girls, whereas material items (e.g., home TV, sports equipment) and athletic activities become more salient to boys.

Of course, not all boys and girls embrace the gender roles associated with male and female identity, respectively. Differences in adaptation sometimes occur as a result of deviation from such roles. For instance, males whose coping behaviors are associated with feminine gender roles exhibit poor adaptation in adulthood. For females, however, coping behaviors associated with feminine gender roles are associated with good adaptation in adulthood.

In sum, gender differences in behaviors do exist, and they most likely stem from the way children are socialized. Socialization, in turn, is an important influence on the gender attitudes, activities, and behaviors of adolescents.

Richard M. Lerner
Jasna Jovanovic
Candace Dreves
Jacqueline V. Lerner

See also Gender Differences and Intellectual and Moral Development; Sex Differences; Sex Roles; Sexuality, Emotional Aspects of

References and further reading
American Association of University Women. 1992. *How Schools Shortchange Girls.* Washington, DC: American Association of University Women.
Camerena, Phame M., Mark Stemmler, and Anne C. Petersen. 1994. "The Gender-Differential Significance of Work and Family: An Exploration of Adolescent Experience and Expectation." Pp. 201–221 in *Adolescence in Context.* Edited by R. Silbereisen and E. Todt. New York: Springer.
Chipman, Susan F., Lorielei R. Brush, and Donna M. Wilson. 1985. *Women and Mathematics: Balancing the Equation.* Hillsdale, NJ: Erlbaum.
Crockett, Lisa J., and Anne C. Crouter. 1995. "Pathways through Adolescent Individual Development in Relation to Social Contexts." Mahwah, NJ: Erlbaum.
Johnson, Lloyd D., Patrick M. O'Malley, and Jerald G. Bachman. 1999. *National Survey Results from the Monitoring the Future Study: 1975–1998.* Washington, DC: U.S. Government Printing Office.
Kelly, Alison. 1987. *Science for Girls?* Philadelphia: Open University Press.
Lerner, Richard M. In press. *Adolescence: Development, Diversity, Context and Application.* Upper Saddle River, NJ: Prentice-Hall.
Simmons, Roberta, and Dale Blyth. 1987. *Moving into Adolescence: The Impact of Pubertal Change and School Context.* New York: Aldine.
Spencer, Margaret. 1990. "Identity, Minority Development of." Pp.
111–130 in *Encyclopedia of Adolescence.* Edited by Richard M. Lerner, Anne C. Petersen, and Jeanne Brooks-Gunn. New York: Garland.

Gender Differences and Intellectual and Moral Development

Many people believe that men and women, or boys and girls, are very different from each other, even when the evidence from research studies does not reveal great gender differences. Many believe the saying, "Sugar and spice and everything nice; that's what little girls are made of. Snips and snails and puppy dog tails; that's what little boys are made of." Some people think that girls care more about feelings and relationships and boys are more analytical and rational. Boys and girls often are thought to be different in their intellectual abilities. Girls are expected to be better at language and reading, and boys are expected to be better at math and science. Some people think that boys are more objective thinkers and concerned about issues of equity and justice; some think that girls are more likely to care about other people and are less concerned about justice. The research evidence, however, does not show that boys are more concerned with justice and individual rights than girls or that girls' thinking is more swayed by emotions than boys', nor that girls and women have different ways of knowing, or intellectual abilities, than boys and men.

Research on moral and intellectual development in males and females reveals that although stereotypes persist, boys and girls are actually more similar than different. (Stereotypes are schemas or beliefs about how people should think, feel, and behave.) Part of the reason stereotypes persist is that the media tend to report and emphasize differences between males and females rather than similarities. Indeed, newspaper stories about gender differences make "good copy," especially when the claim of differences supports a gender stereotype. Nevertheless, considerable research since the 1970s has shown that girls and boys are not as different as many people seem to believe.

Moral Development

Research indicates that children are concerned with moral and ethical issues at a very early age. They care about "what's fair" and are disturbed when someone else is hurt. Throughout history, many social scientists and theorists have linked moral development and cognitive development, arguing that women are not as capable as men of "rational" thought ("objective" thought, not influenced by one's personal preferences or emotions). Their moral concerns were thought to be tied to their emotions rather than their intellects. For example, Herbert Spencer, one of the earliest psychologists, stated that "the love of the helpless, which in her maternal capacity woman displays in a more special form than man, inevitably affects all her thoughts and sentiments; and, this being joined in her with a less developed sentiment of abstract justice, she responds more readily when appeals to pity are made than when appeals are made to equity" (Spencer, 1873, p. 36). Here, Spencer makes the argument that women are innately concerned with caring for others and are not as adept as men at thinking about what is fair or just.

Sigmund Freud made a similar argument. He was the first psychologist to claim that women and men differed in their capacity for morality. He called the part of the psyche that contains the conscience the "superego" and thought that girls had a less developed superego than boys did. Freud claimed, "For women the level of what is ethically normal is different from what it is in men, . . . [women] show less sense of justice than men, . . . they are more often influenced in their judgments by feelings of affection or hostility" (Freud, 1925, pp. 257–258). A common theme in both Spencer's and Freud's work is that they see advanced or more sophisticated moral thinking as the ability to think abstractly without the influence of one's emotions and without consideration of the specifics of the context in which these moral dilemmas arise and must be resolved.

Carol Gilligan (1982), a developmental psychologist, noticed these claims about differences in moral development of men and women, and began to look for them herself. She gave an interview following the presentation of moral stories that had been developed by Lawrence Kohlberg (1969). The stories involved moral questions, such as should a man steal a drug that would save his wife's life. She found that girls and boys responded differently to these stories. When boys explained their ideas about morality, they were more likely to talk about the rights of individuals and responsibilities that people have to fairness and justice. Girls, on the other hand, she thought, were more likely to focus on the relationships between people and the potential for human suffering and harm. Gilligan also asked women to tell her about a real-life moral dilemma when she interviewed women who were deciding whether or not to have an abortion. She claimed to find in their responses to interview questions, "a different voice." She called this distinctive voice an "ethic of care" and the voice often heard in men's responses an "ethic of justice." More specifically, she saw an ethic of care as a different perspective and different way of resolving moral problems (Gilligan, 1982). An ethic of care attended to relationships, one's feelings, and the specifics of people's lives, whereas an ethic of justice attended to individuals' and society's rights and responsibilities, focusing on abstract principles.

Gilligan believed men and women were indeed different in their moral development and decision making. Although research testing Gilligan's assertions shows that men and women are not as different as Gilligan originally proposed, she made an important contribution to our understanding of moral development, asserting that girls are not inferior to boys, just different. In fact, part of the original impetus for Gilligan's work was based on feminist researchers' increasing realization that those characteristics associated with "femininity" were also those characteristics that were labeled "deficient" in psychological theories such as moral development. Gilligan's work helped identify an aspect of moral development not fully addressed in some of the original theories about moral development. Furthermore, she urged people to value these characteristics.

A lot of research has been conducted to test Carol Gilligan's theory. Some researchers have used a powerful statistical technique called meta-analysis. This technique allows one to examine the results of many studies to test whether there are differences between groups, such as between men and women. In a meta-analysis of 152 samples using the same interview questions developed by Kohlberg that Gilligan had used,

Lawrence Walker found no significant gender differences in moral reasoning. In a second meta-analysis (statistical technique that allows a researcher to examine findings of many studies together), Walker reported that gender explained only a very small amount (one-twentieth of 1 percent) of the variation in participants' moral reasoning scores. In another study, using a paper and pencil measure (e.g., the *Defining Issues Test,* Rest, 1979) of responses to moral stories, Stephen Thoma conducted a meta-analysis of 56 samples with over 6,000 participants. He found that age and educational level were 250 times more powerful in explaining the variance in moral reasoning than gender. This finding strongly suggests that age and one's amount of education leads to differences in moral reasoning, not gender. Bebeau and Brabeck (1989) conducted a meta-analysis of Rest's (1979) *Defining Issues Test* scores for seven groups of dental students, and adult women are as likely as men to use justice reasoning.

What is important to note from this research is education and experience with thinking through moral dilemmas can help advance, or "improve," one's moral reasoning in both care and justice. Education is more important in promoting moral development than is one's gender. Education also need not take place only in classrooms. Life experience outside of the classroom can lead to moral development even in challenging and painful situations. For example, one study examined the relationship between moral development and parental marital status among 108 male and female adolescents. The study found that both male and female adolescents, whose parents had been divorced during their adolescence, had significantly higher levels of moral development than those whose parents remained together throughout their adolescent years. The study's authors hypothesized that in one-parent families, adolescents may take on the role of the absent parent and are often developing in more egalitarian households. Experience with responsibilities and adult roles may lead to moral development and is more important in determining morality than is one's gender.

Instead of gender being a determinant of moral reasoning, some researchers have found that whether someone uses an ethic of care versus and ethic of justice depends on the *type* of moral dilemma they discuss. Researchers have asked participants to generate their own real-life dilemmas. They report that the type of dilemma discussed (e.g., a moral dilemma involving a personal issue or relationship versus an impersonal dilemma involving conflicting claims about individual rights) is a better predictor of moral orientation (ethic of care vs. ethic of justice) than gender. When people choose their own dilemmas to talk about, girls and women were more likely to choose personal ones, whereas males were more likely to choose impersonal dilemmas. If one focuses on the people and their relationships (a friend who betrays another friend's confidence, a person who harms someone by saying untrue and bad things about them), one is more likely to see that the ethic of care has been violated. On the other hand, if one focuses on issues in which the rights of others are violated and/or societal rules are violated, like cheating on a test or breaking a law, one is more likely to be concerned about issues of justice. When people spend a great deal of time working with people in a variety of situations (e.g, as a counselor, doctor, or nurse), moral issues related to

interpersonal aspects of a situation may arise to a greater degree than if most of our time is spent in independent work (e.g., working with computers). When asked to think about an issue differently, both boys and girls are able to change and use either justice or care reasoning.

What's important here is that both justice and care reasoning are valid and important, and involve ethical principles that researchers have found are common across cultures and across times. Justice and care matter in moral development, though gender is not a major influence on whether one uses justice reasoning or care reasoning. Gender is only an influence in the sense that women and men may have had different experiences, such as women are often in more relationship-oriented professions and less often in higher positions of authority, positions that often require more use of an ethic of justice. Thus, the use of an ethic of care versus an ethic of justice depends greatly on one's experiences and roles in society, not some inherent, stable characteristic such as gender.

Intellectual Development
Over time and across cultures, much is made about gender differences in intellectual development. Researchers have come up with elaborate theories to argue that men are more intellectually capable than women. However, as with morality, these claims are almost always overstated. Gender differences that have been found are that, on average, boys do better in math and girls do better in reading. However, the gender differences found in mathematics appear to be diminishing through educational efforts. Although males score higher than females on standardized math tests, girls get equal or slightly higher grades in

math. Gender differences in verbal ability, when they are found, show women are superior. However, gender differences in verbal ability are also diminishing, and meta-analysis once again reveals that boys and girls are more similar than different (see the work of Janet Hyde and colleagues).

The largest gender difference in intellectual abilities occurs in the area of spatial abilities. Boys are better skilled in mental rotation, which allows you to imagine and then mentally rotate a two- or three-dimensional object. Mental rotation ability appears to be the result of both biology and experience with spatial tasks (e.g, playing ball, building with blocks or legos). However, other verbal strategies can be used to solve these problems, so this gender difference ought not exclude girls and women from excelling in math or science fields.

Following Carol Gilligan's theory that women have a "different moral voice," a group of researchers (Belenky, Clinchy, Goldberger, and Tarule, 1986) recently claimed that there are "women's ways of knowing." Belenky and her colleagues conducted interviews with 135 women and claimed that women have a more connected and relational way of knowing and understanding than do men. Brabeck (1984) argued that Women's Ways of Knowing (WWK) theory joins at least eleven recently articulated theoretical models of adolescent and adult cognitive development, but the WWK theory was the first to claim gender differences in ways of knowing. Since Belenky and her colleagues did not include any men in their studies, we cannot make any statement about gender differences based on their work. Studies that have tested the WWK claims are sparse (see Brabeck and

Larned, 1996). In the few cases in which gender differences are found, differences in men and women's education, occupation, social status, or age offer equally plausible explanations for the results.

In conclusion, the beliefs about gender differences in moral and intellectual development are more belief than fact. One is reminded of Samuel Johnson's response to the question, "Who is smarter, men or women?" He said, "Which man? Which woman?" While continuing to acknowledge and attend to the historical and societal inequities in boys' and girls' experiences and opportunities, boys and girls, and men and women would be better served by also attending to questions about how to promote intellectual and ethical development for all, rather than on how to define the differences. Educators and parents must continue to devote energy celebrating all of the qualities possessed by both boys and girls, even those qualities that become invisible when overshadowed by our gender stereotypes. If people can do that, they will gain a more complex, and more true, understanding of both boys and girls and their moral and intellectual capabilities.

Mary M. Brabeck
Erika Shore

See also Cognitive Development; Gender Differences; Moral Development; Sex Differences

References and further reading

Bebeau, Muriel, and Mary M. Brabeck. 1989. "Ethical Sensitivity and Moral Reasoning among Men and Women in the Professions." Pp. 144–163 in *Who Cares? Theory, Research and Educational Implications of the Ethic of Care.* Edited by Mary M. Brabeck. New York: Praeger.

Belenky, Mary F., Blythe M. Clinchy, Nancy Goldberger, and Jill M. Tarule.

1986. *Women's Ways of Knowing: The Development of Self, Voice and Mind.* New York: Basic Books.

Brabeck, Mary. 1984. "Longitudinal Studies of Intellectual Development during Adulthood: Theoretical and Research Models." *Journal of Research and Development in Education* 17, no. 3: 12–27.

Brabeck, Mary, and Ann G. Larned. 1996. "What We Do Not Know about Women's Ways of Knowing." Pp. 261–269 in *Psychology of Women: Ongoing Debates,* 2nd ed. Edited by Mary R. Walsh. New Haven, CT: Yale University Press.

Freud, Sigmund. 1925. *Some Psychical Consequences of the Anatomical Distinction between the Sexes.* (*The Standard Edition of the Complete Psychological Works of Sigmund Freud,* Vol. 19). Translated and edited by James Strachey. London: Hogarth Press, 1961.

Gilligan, Carol. 1982. *In a Different Voice: Psychological Theory and Women's Development.* Cambridge, MA: Harvard University Press.

Hyde, Janet S., and Marcia Linn. 1988. "Gender Differences in Verbal Ability: A Meta-Analysis." *Psychological Bulletin* 104: 53–69.

Hyde, Janet S., Elizabeth Fennema, and Susan J. Lamon. 1990. "Gender Differences in Mathematics Performance: A Meta-Analysis." *Psychological Bulletin* 107: 139–155.

Kohlberg, Lawrence. 1969. "Stage and Sequence: The Cognitive Developmental Approach to Socialization." Pp. 347–480 in *Handbook of Socialization Theory and Research.* Edited by D. A. Goslin. Chicago: Rand-McNally.

Rest, James. 1979. *Development in Judging Moral Issues.* Minneapolis: University of Minnesota Press.

Spencer, Herbert. 1873. "Psychology of the Sexes." *Popular Science Monthly* 4: 31–32.

Gifted and Talented Youth

Adolescents who are recognized for having special skills or traits that are valued in our society are often referred to as gifted or talented. The definition of giftedness, according to the Jacob K. Javits Gifted and Talented Students Act of 1988 (Public Law 100-297), is as follows: "'Gifted and talented students means children and youth who give evidence of high performance capability in areas such as intellectual, creative, artistic, or leadership capacity, or in specific academic fields, and who require services or activities not ordinarily provided by the school in order to fully develop such capabilities." Identifying gifted and talented youth and helping them reach their full potential, though a complex process involving many variables, are of great importance for the betterment of these individuals and society at large.

Intellectual giftedness is the most common criterion used to identify gifted and talented youth. Tests like the Stanford-Binet are often administered by schools to determine whether children qualify for enhanced or accelerated instruction. A typical benchmark for being admitted to such a "gifted program" is an IQ above 130, or an IQ in the top 3 or 5 percent of youth in the same age range. Certain problems, however, are associated with such tests and programs. For instance, intelligence tests were constructed using Caucasian samples and therefore may not be appropriate in assessing other racial and cultural groups. In addition, there are many more dimensions of giftedness than high IQ and the capacity for abstract and logical reasoning. Though highly valued in most Western cultures, adolescents with a high IQ might not be perceived as special or talented in a culture with a farming-based economy. Almost any skill or trait, in fact, can be seen as a talent if it is recognized by members of a society as valuable or useful. In other

Adolescents who are recognized for having special skills or traits that are valued in our society are often referred to as gifted or talented. (Shirley Zeiberg)

words, talent or giftedness is a label of approval placed on individuals who possess characteristics that are valued in a culture.

Some of the first academic programs devised for gifted and talented children were established in New York City in the early 1900s. In 1919, Detroit became the first city to introduce a formal "XYZ plan" for classes of students with high, middle, and low ability. And, by 1920, accelerated instruction was an established method being used across the country for educating gifted schoolchildren. The rationale behind such programs was that it was easier to instruct students who resembled one another in terms of aptitude and learning rate. In

fact, "ability grouping" remains an often-practiced technique for teaching intellectually gifted and talented youth. The presumed benefit of this approach is that students with little individual variation in ability can be taught at a more advanced and challenging level. Research has confirmed that ability grouping is effective when substantial adjustment or acceleration of curriculum is ensured. But there are drawbacks as well, including the high cost of specialized teachers and materials, the possibility that an "elitist" attitude might develop among the students, the intense focus on achievement and competition, and the loss of beneficial interaction between students of different ability levels.

One of the earliest studies to follow a group of intellectually gifted and talented students was conducted by L. M. Terman in 1925. More recently, a wider range of talents has been investigated, along with the social contexts in which children develop their talents. Common to many current approaches is the recognition that talent is only partly due to genetic inheritance. Although it may be true that children can inherit genes providing a favorable predisposition toward a talent, certain social resources are crucial to the full realization of the talent. In addition to their inherited traits, children's skills can develop over time only with investments of time and energy from parents, teachers, and other committed individuals. Such individuals are often a source of emotional and financial support; they may also provide needed challenges to the youth. Although there are well-known historical accounts of persons who have survived harsh circumstances to realize their gifts, it is a myth that talent alone can overcome all external obstacles.

There are aspects of talent development that have very little to do with the gifted or talented individuals themselves. For instance, math, science, music, athletics, art, and many other culturally valued domains have unique histories, symbols, and rules that guide them. Gifted and talented youth must learn these rules and, in a sense, walk for a time in the footsteps of others who came before them. And even then, such individuals need others to publicly recognize their talents and accept them into their "field." All of these factors must come together if the full expression of a gift or talent is to be ensured. Talented writers, for instance, must inherit some capacity for the use of language, practice their skills, be introduced to literature and the study of the rules of grammar and punctuation, and, finally, be recognized by others (e.g., writers, critics) who can bring them into the field and help them get established.

In addition to their greater focus on social processes, contemporary studies pay more attention to the motivations and experiences of gifted and talented youth. Developing a talent takes a long time, and sustaining energy toward this goal is enhanced when the youth enjoy exercising their particular skills. For example, adolescents who enjoy playing basketball are more likely to continue practicing when they are tired than those who are playing the game simply because their parents want them to be great basketball players. Such enjoyment is often referred to as "intrinsic" motivation because it arises directly from the experience of the activity itself.

Kevin Rathunde

See also Academic Achievement; Cognitive Development; Learning Disabilities; Learning Styles and Accommodations; Mentoring and Youth Development

References and further reading
Amabile, Teresa M. 1983. *The Social Psychology of Creativity.* New York: Springer-Verlag.
Bloom, Benjamin S., ed. 1985. *Developing Talent in Young People.* New York: Ballantine Books.
Colangelo, Nicholas, Susan Assouline, and DeAnn Ambroson, eds. 1992. *Talent Development: Proceedings from the 1991 Henry B. and Jocelyn Wallace National Research Symposium on Talent Development.* Unionville, NY: Trillium Press.
Csikszentmihalyi, Mihaly, Kevin Rathunde, and Samuel Whalen. 1997. *Talented Teenagers: The Roots of Success and Failure.* New York: Cambridge University Press.

Gardner, Howard. 1983. *Frames of Mind: The Theory of Multiple Intelligences.* New York: Basic Books.

Sternberg, Robert, and Janet Davidson. 1987. *Conceptions of Giftedness.* New York: Cambridge University Press.

Gonorrhea

Gonorrhea is one of the most common sexually transmitted diseases in the United States. It is caused by a bacterium called *Neisseria gonorrhoeae*, which is transmitted from an infected person by contact with that person's bodily fluids. The most common way of getting infected is by having sexual intercourse with a person who is infected, but gonorrhea can also be acquired through oral sex or anal intercourse. Many people carry the bacterium without any signs of illness. The time between exposure and the development of symptoms is two to seven days.

In boys, the most common symptoms are severe burning on urination and a milky yellow discharge from the penis. If these symptoms are ignored, the infection may infect the area around the testes (epididymitis), resulting in a dull aching pain in this area.

In girls, symptoms appear seven to twenty-one days after infection. Although some burning on urination may occur, it is less common and less severe than in boys. The more likely symptom is a change in the normal vaginal discharge that many girls experience. Specifically, the discharge is heavier than usual and may be foul smelling. As this symptom is also associated with bladder infections (cystitis), the two disorders must be distinguished from each other. However, many girls experience no symptoms at all. In such cases, they can discover the infection only when told that their sexual partner has gonorrhea. If the symptoms in girls are ignored, or there are no symptoms, the infection may travel from the vagina into the uterus and fallopian tubes, resulting in pelvic inflammatory disease. This condition is accompanied by severe abdominal pain, which needs to be distinguished from acute appendicitis. In individuals infected through oral sex, a severe sore throat with pus on the tonsils may be present, whereas those with anal gonorrhea may experience discharge from the anus as well as pain in the anal area made worse during defecation.

The diagnosis of gonorrhea is confirmed by examination of vaginal or anal discharge under the microscope in order to identify the bacteria. Discharge can also be grown in culture media. There is no blood test for gonorrhea.

Treatment with one dose of antibiotics will cure most uncomplicated cases of gonorrhea. However, patients with pelvic inflammatory disease or epididymitis need a longer course of antibiotics and sometimes require hospitalization for intravenous treatments.

Gonorrhea affecting males' or females' gonaducts is one of the most common causes of infertility in both sexes, since the diameter of the gonaducts is very small and the infection may cause parts of these tubes to stick together, thus preventing normal passage of sperm or ova.

Jordan W. Finkelstein

See also Health Promotion; Health Services for Adolescents; HIV/AIDS; Sex Education; Sexual Behavior; Sexual Behavior Problems; Sexually Transmitted Diseases

References and further reading
Berkow, Robert B., ed. 1997. *The Merck Manual of Medical Information: Home Edition.* Whitehouse Station, NJ: Merck Research Laboratories.

Hendee, William R., ed. 1991. *The Health of Adolescents.* San Francisco: Jossey-Bass.

Grandparents: Intergenerational Relationships

An aspect of childhood and adolescence that is receiving renewed attention is intergenerational relationships and, more specifically, the relationships between grandparents and their grandchildren. Although these interactions are hardly new to either historical or contemporary family experience, their presence and significance to child and adolescent development, while often acknowledged, are not fully understood. That is, although considerable research has been directed at parent-child and parent-adolescent relationships, particularly in relation to developmental outcomes (e.g., self-concept, intellectual and verbal skills, and life changes), less is known about the contribution of intergenerational relationships to adolescent development. Below we will consider three intergenerational dimensions that are essential to understanding the contributions of the grandparent-grandchild relationship to the adolescent experience: (1) the dimensions of intergenerational solidarity that orchestrate the strength of the bonds between grandparents and their adolescent grandchildren, (2) the specific strategies employed by family members to organize grandparent-grandchild relationships, and (3) the nature of the mutual influence between grandparents and grandchildren.

Solidarity and Strength of the Relationship

As a result of demographic changes involving longer life spans and social changes such as higher rates of divorce (as well as other events that may disrupt parent-child interaction), the grandparent-grandchild relationship has received increasing attention both because it is available to more people (because of greater longevity) and because it sometimes serves to address or avert family crises. In turn, such issues require a better understanding of the grandparent-grandchild relationship. Research suggests that six dimensions of intergenerational solidarity may be of particular import in understanding the nature of the strength of the bond between grandparents and grandchildren, including adolescents (Roberts, Richards, and Bengtson, 1991).

Affectional Bonds. Affectional bonds reflect the extent of closeness between grandchildren and grandparents. Although both grandparents and grandchildren report degrees of closeness to one another, grandparents tend to feel closer to grandchildren than vice versa (Miller and Bengtson, 1991). One explanation for this difference in perception of closeness may well be the extent of the grandparents' need for the grandparent role. Such a need is based on life-course circumstances, including losses (e.g., of employment or friends through death) (Kivnick, 1993). Reported closeness is also influenced by the middle generation—the parents of the grandchild. If these parents have an emotionally close relationship with their own parents (the grandparents), then the grandparents and grandchildren are likely to be emotionally close as well (Cherlin and Furstenberg, 1986). In addition, there is a tendency for closeness between grandparents and grandchildren to fall along gender lines, inasmuch as women tend to take a more active role in kin-keeping than men (Hagestad, 1985). Finally, whatever the

An aspect of childhood and adolescence that is receiving renewed attention is the relationships between grandparents and their grandchildren. (David Turnley/Corbis)

nature of the grandparent-grandchild relationship, including the extent of closeness, there is an apparent continuity of the general character of the relationship over time. For example, relationships characterized by closeness tend to remain close as children move from childhood through adolescence (Miller and Bengtson, 1991).

Structural Bonds. Structural bonds are factors relating to opportunities for association between grandparent and grandchild (Roberts, Richards, and Bengtson, 1991). Such factors include geographic propinquity as well as demographic and personal characteristics of the grandchild and grandparent (e.g., age, gender, and health status) (Bengtson, 1985). Factors such as the parents' employment status, marital status, and socioeconomic level may also play a significant role in the opportunity structure for association between grandparent and grandchild (Cherlin and Furstenberg, 1986). Such related parent characteristics as divorce, single parenthood, and unemployment have become primary determinants in the transformation, where necessary, of the grandparent role to that of surrogate or direct parental responsibility.

Associational Bonds. This dimension of solidarity relates to the frequency of contact between grandparents and grandchildren (Kivett, 1991; Roberts, Richards, and Bengtson, 1991). Parents' circumstances may exert a substantial influence on the extent of such contact, particularly in cases of parental divorce. As might be expected, both contacts and associational bonds tend to increase in situations where a divorced daughter is given custody of a grandchild, returns to the home of her parents, or requires considerable support in her own dwelling. A similar

increase in solidarity of association might occur when parents are unable to care for children (Burton, 1995). However, divorce can also have a negative impact on solidarity. Consider, for example, the grandparent-grandchild interactions that might occur in situations involving a noncustodial parent, typically the father. Such situations often generate considerable anxiety, resulting in some level of political action (as in the grandparents' rights movement) on the part of grandparents who are denied visitation opportunities to see their grandchildren.

Functional Bonds. This form of bonding refers to the exchange of assistance or help between grandparents and grandchildren (Roberts, Richards, and Bengtson, 1991). As mentioned above, the exchange of support may be prompted by parents' circumstances, particularly when grandparents are involved in raising grandchildren (Burton, 1995; Minkler and Roe, 1993). In most situations, however, it appears that grandparents prefer "intimacy at a distance," which translates into involvement without interference in the activities of the middle-generation child-rearing practices (Chalfie, 1994). Although psychologists have some understanding of the social factors and circumstances that may bring grandparents to the assistance of grandchildren, they are less certain about what grandchildren "do" for grandparents in the form of providing a morale boost or other "support."

Consensual Bonds. Consensual bonds have to do with the degree of intergenerational similarity in values between grandparents and their grandchildren. Although such similarity is sometimes taken as evidence of successful socialization across generations (Troll, 1983,

1985), an important related question that has received relatively little attention is how these generational values, beliefs, and attitudes are negotiated in shaping and organizing grandparent-grandchild relationships (Hagestad, 1985).

Normative Bonds. This mode of bonding refers to intergenerational perceptions of responsibilities and obligations about the character of the relationship. An example of normative solidarity would be the degree of grandparental acceptance of responsibility to assume a surrogate parent role for a grandchild when a parent is unable to perform that function. Here, too, the nature of the obligations in the other direction—from grandchildren to grandparent—have received much less attention.

Although the preceding discussion of the six modes of solidarity provides some insight into the nature and strength of intergenerational bonds, it does not directly address two important aspects of that relationship: (1) How are relationships between grandparents and grandchildren organized, particularly in the face of changing societal values? (2) What is the nature of the grandparents' influence on their grandchildren?

Organizing the Grandparent-Grandchild Relationship
Based on findings from interviews with three generations (late adolescent/young adult grandchildren, middle-generation parents, and grandparents), G. O. Hagestad (1985) has identified several significant features influencing the formation and organization of the grandparent-grandchild relationship.

- The development of this relationship is problematic in a rapidly

changing and heterogeneous society. Grandparents and grandchildren are faced with the challenge of building a relationship that, in previous generations, was guided and shaped by commonalties across generations: "Like father, like son. Like mother, like daughter."

- The establishment of a grandparent-grandchild relationship requires not only continuous and reciprocal socialization but also negotiation and interaction management. For example, Hagestad (1985) has noted the lengths to which grandparents and grandchildren go to ensure, as much as possible and reasonable, that the topics of intergenerational conversation are sufficiently neutral and noncontroversial, so as not to disrupt the connections between the generations.

- The specific activities and conversational topics that form the nexus of the grandparent-grandchild relationship vary widely.

- Regardless of the activities or conversational topics under way, there are systematic differences in the ways that grandmothers and grandfathers relate to their late adolescent/young adult grandchildren: Grandmothers tend to focus on interpersonal family dynamics, and grandfathers tend to emphasize instrumental matters, i.e., achieving a goal or performing an activity. Grandmothers are more flexible than grandfathers in covering a wider spectrum of both domains in the relationship with their grandchildren. Grandmothers are more comfortable than grandfathers in their interaction with both male and female grandchildren. And, finally, in terms of the reciprocal and mutual character of the grandparent-grandchild relationships, grandmothers are more receptive than grandfathers to socialization "up the generational ladder"; in other words, they are more responsive to learning from their grandchildren and better able to adjust their views accordingly.

Grandparent's Influences on Adolescent Grandchildren
Research on the influences of grandparents on their adolescent grandchildren is incomplete and somewhat elusive. There is a general impression that grandparents may be important in the lives of their grandchildren, but few studies confirm this expectation, particularly with reference to outcomes for adolescents. Several investigators suggest that the character of grandparents' influences is vague, though by no means inconsequential, primarily because the contribution of grandparents is related to a variety of symbolic functions. Sociologists have identified several of these symbolic functions of grandparents in family life, including the following (Kivnick, 1993; Troll, 1985):

- Supporting family cohesion.
- Moderating intensity and family stress by serving as "sounding boards" or mediators.
- Serving as family "watchdogs" to actively intervene with support, as or if necessary.
- Symbolizing the continuity of families over generations as sources of support during times of family difficulty.

Thus, although it is not unreasonable to expect that the grandparent-grandchild interaction contributes to positive adaptation and the mental health of the grandchild in adulthood, conventional research methodologies have neither confirmed nor denied this possibility. The difficulty of establishing these positive connections may be due not only to the relative absence of longitudinal studies but also to the symbolic and diffuse nature of grandparent contributions. Nonetheless, although the empirical findings on the contributions of the relationship are perhaps disappointing, there is some encouraging evidence of these contributions throughout the childhood and adolescence of their grandchildren (Kivnick and Sinclair, 1996): First, when close and effective relationships are established in childhood, they tend to continue into adolescence. Second, analysis of secondary data suggests that the adolescent offspring of single parents benefit from the presence of grandparents in their lives. And, third, high school students often report that they view their grandparents as both companions and important contributors to their lives.

Lawrence B. Schiamberg

See also Child-Rearing Styles; Family Composition: Realities and Myths; Family Relations; Fathers and Adolescents; Mothers and Adolescents; Parental Monitoring; Parenting Styles

References and further reading
Bengtson, Vern L. 1985. "Diversity and Symbolism in Grandparental Roles." Pp. 11–26 in *Grandparenthood*. Edited by Vern L. Bengtson and Joan F. Robertson. Beverly Hills, CA: Sage.
Burton, Linda M. 1995. "Intergenerational Patterns of Providing Are Found in African-American Families with Teenage Childbearers: Emergent Patterns in an Ethnographic Study." Pp.

79–96 in *Adult Intergenerational Relations: Effects of Societal Change.* Edited by Vern L. Bengtson, K. W. Schaie, and L. M. Burton. New York: Springer.

Chalfie, D. 1994. *Going It Alone: A Closer Look at Grandparents Parenting Grandchildren.* Washington, DC: American Association of Retired People Women's Initiative.

Cherlin, Andrew, and Frank Furstenberg. 1986. *The New American Grandparent: A Place in the Family, a Life Apart.* New York: Basic Books.

Hagestad, G. O. 1985. "Continuity and Connectedness." Pp. 31–48 in *Grandparenthood.* Edited by Vern L. Bengtson and Joan F. Robertson. Beverly Hills, CA: Sage.

Kivett, Vira. 1991. "The Grandparent-Grandchild Connection." *Journal of Marriage and Family Review* 19: 26–34.

Kivnick, Helen Q. 1993. "Everyday Mental Health: A Guide to Assessing Life Strengths." Pp. 19–36 in *Mental Health and Aging: Progress and Prospects.* Edited by M. A. Smyer. New York: Springer.

Kivnick, H. Q., and Heather Sinclair. 1996. "Grandparenthood." Pp. 611–624 in *Encyclopedia of Gerontology.* Edited by J. E. Birren. New York: Academic Press.

Miller, R. B., and Vern L. Bengtson. 1991. "Grandparent-Grandchild Relations." Pp. 414–418 in *Encyclopedia of Adolescence.* New York: Garland.

Minkler, M., and K. M. Roe. 1993. *Grandmothers as Caregivers.* Newbury Park, CA: Sage.

Roberts, R.E.L., L. N. Richards, and Vern L. Bengtson. 1991. "Intergenerational Solidarity in Families: Untangling the Ties That Bind." Pp. 11–46 in *Marriage and Family Review.* Vol. 16, *Families: Intergenerational and Generational Connections.* Edited by S. K. Pfeifer and M. B. Sussman. Binghamton, NY: Haworth.

Troll, L. E. 1983. "Grandparents: The Family Watchdogs." Pp. 63–74 in *Family Relationships in Later Life.* Edited by T. Brubaker. Beverly Hills, CA: Sage.

———. 1985. "The Contingencies of Grandparenting." Pp. 135–149 in *Grandparenthood.* Edited by Vern L. Bengtson and Joan F. Robertson. Beverly Hills, CA: Sage.

H

Health Promotion

Health promotion consists of activities designed to help adolescents maintain their physical, mental, and social well-being. Such activities—when promoted in the family, the media, the school, and the peer group—may also prevent the development of chronic conditions. Many educational programs are designed to encourage adolescents to "take control" of their health. Indeed, adolescents' perceptions of themselves as being healthy or ill may be the key to their seeking medical care and taking advantage of health-promotion and disease-prevention services. Promotion efforts aimed at adolescents are important because many of the health-compromising behaviors seen in adulthood (e.g., cigarette smoking) begin in adolescence.

Because the majority of adolescents are healthy, many presume that teens have little interest in health promotion and disease prevention. However, as research has demonstrated that adolescents do think of health and illness as important, intervention efforts should be developed with an understanding of how adolescents think about these concepts (Brindis and Lee, 1991). For example, adolescents who view health as the absence of disease would benefit from programs that focus on illness avoidance. Adolescents vary widely in their conceptualizations of health and illness. According to Claire Brindis and Philip Lee, adolescents in sixth through twelfth grade believe that health is more than just the absence of illness, and that illness is more than just a matter of somatic signs and symptoms. For these older adolescents, the definitions of illness take into account such signs and symptoms, but they also include affective states and role functioning. By contrast, younger adolescents are more likely to focus on external indicators, as their thinking tends to be concrete rather than abstract. Thus, prevention and promotion efforts should not be aimed entirely at illness avoidance.

Another factor that needs to be considered when designing health-promotion efforts is "risk-taking" behaviors. Paradoxically, many of the risk-taking behaviors that adolescents engage in are not perceived by them as such—perhaps because adolescents have had little or no firsthand experience with the consequences of these behaviors.

To address this problem, the Centers for Disease Control (CDC) have set up a system called Programs that Work (PTW). The purpose of PTW is to identify curricula with credible evidence of effectiveness in reducing the frequency of risk-taking behaviors among young people. PTW also provides information and training for interested educators from state and local education agencies, departments of

The adolescent years are critical for developing good health-related behaviors. (Shirley Zeiberg)

health, and national nongovernmental organizations.

Every school day, 66 million young people attend the nation's schools, colleges, and universities. Obviously, then, the school setting is an optimal place for information delivery, assessment of risk behaviors, and monitoring of policies and programs already in place. Discussed below are some of the major adolescent health-promotion efforts now under way.

Nutrition
Many adults consider adolescents' eating behaviors to be inappropriate. For the most part, however, adolescents' eating behaviors reflect the eating behaviors of adults, especially the adults in their immediate family. Although many teenagers experience brief periods of "fad" eating, the majority consume a healthy diet. Current recommendations for a healthy diet are as follows: (1) Eat a variety of foods, (2) choose a diet low in saturated fat and cholesterol, (3) eat plenty of vegetables, fruits, and grain products, and (4) use salt in moderation. A healthy diet can help adolescents feel and look good; it can also reduce their risk for the development of heart disease, cancer,

and stroke, the three leading causes of death in adults.

Although the majority of adolescents maintain healthy eating patterns, some young people make poor eating choices that put them at risk for health problems. Establishing healthy eating habits at a young age is critical because changing poor eating habits in adulthood can be difficult. Moreover, programs aimed at promoting healthy eating can prevent childhood and adolescent health problems such as obesity, eating disorders, dental caries (tooth decay), and iron deficiency anemia. Unfortunately, eating disorders such as anorexia and bulimia—which can lead to severe health problems and even death—are increasingly common among young people.

Healthy eating patterns are in part a function of nutrients, which fall into three main categories: sources of energy (carbohydrate, fat, and protein), trace elements (vitamins and minerals), and water.

Sources of Energy. For teens of both sexes, caloric intake varies according to degree of activity and phase of growth. On average, boys need about 2,500 calories per day during early puberty and about 3,000 calories per day during mid-puberty (when rapid growth occurs) and young adulthood. Girls need about 2,000 calories per day from early puberty onward. The distribution of energy nutrients should be about 15 percent of calories from protein, 30 percent of calories from fat, and 55 percent of calories from carbohydrate. The adequacy of total caloric intake is best determined relative to body weight. Charts reflecting the standards for gains in both weight and height are readily available from the teen's primary healthcare provider. Research indicates an increasing trend toward both obesity and extreme thinness among teenagers, especially girls.

Most people have little or no information about either the caloric or the nutritional content of the food they eat. Product labeling has made this task easier. Reading food labels can help teens determine the adequacy of their diet. It is important to realize that the proportion of a particular nutrient has to be calculated on the basis of calories—*not* on the basis of weight. For instance, milk labeled as "2 percent" contains 2 percent fat by weight, but the important proportion to consider is the percentage of calories from fat. One serving (8 ounces) of 2 percent milk contains 120 calories, of which 40 calories are from fat. Therefore, 33 percent ([40/120] x 100), not 2 percent of the calories in this milk, come from fat.

Trace Elements. Many of the manufactured foods that adolescents eat are enriched with vitamins and minerals, so vitamin deficiencies are rare. The routine use of vitamin pills is therefore *not* recommended for otherwise healthy adolescents.

Nevertheless, many adolescents are at risk for inadequate intake of iron and calcium. For example, whereas most boys consume adequate calcium, many girls do not. Calcium content is high in most high-protein foods such as meat, fish, and diary products. And among vegetables, spinach is the highest in calcium. Adequate calcium intake is essential during puberty since almost all calcium storage in bones is completed by the end of puberty. Teens who are considered to have inadequate calcium intake should consider taking calcium carbonate, which can be found in some over-the-counter antacids such as Tums. Iron deficiency anemia is the most common trace-element disorder among adolescents. As many as 15 percent of male and female adolescents have this condition. Girls are most at risk because of their additional need for iron related to blood loss during menstruation. Foods rich in iron are meats, fish, and enriched grain products such as bread. Inadequate intake of iron or excessive loss of this mineral during menstruation can be made up by taking iron supplements. However, these should be used only under the supervision of a healthcare provider who has done a blood count to determine the need for iron supplementation. Salt (sodium chloride) should be used only in moderation because excessive amounts can lead to high blood pressure. Foods with high sodium content include snack foods such as potato chips and beef jerky as well as prepared foods such as canned vegetables. The sodium content of foods can be found on package labels.

Water. All of the body's chemical reactions take place in water. Although most adolescents do not drink much water per se, they take in adequate amounts by consuming food and flavored drinks. In fact, inadequate water intake is almost unheard of among healthy adolescents, so the current recommendation of drinking eight glasses of water a day is questionable during adolescence.

Exercise

Physical activity is part of a healthy lifestyle, and teenagers need to stay active in order to stay healthy and look good. The current recommendation is that teens should exercise at least five days a week for at least thirty minutes at a time, and that they should exercise in such a way that their heart is beating

faster and they are breathing harder. This form of exercise, called aerobic exercise, is recommended over more passive types such as weight training. Most teens feel good after exercising, probably because of the release of brain chemicals that promote this feeling. Exercise also promotes a healthy heart, lowers blood pressure and cholesterol levels, helps control weight, and strengthens bones, muscles, and joints. Competitive sports are a good way to keep up with exercise and conditioning, but not all young people want to participate in these activities. In addition, choosing a sport can be especially difficult for teens as they near puberty. Early maturing boys may be stronger and have more stamina than their peers, whereas late maturers may feel as though they are lagging behind their peers in strength and sport ability.

Teen athletes should consider which sports are convenient and affordable, and try to match their own skills to the demands of those sports. They should also realize that some sports are associated with a high degree of risk. Water sports are a case in point. Injuries can occur as a result of diving into shallow water, swimming in deep water, and mixing drugs and alcohol with water sport activities. In addition, drowning is a leading cause of death among teens.

Sleep

Younger adolescents need nine to ten hours of sleep, compared to older teenagers, who need about seven to eight hours. In addition, older teens tend to stay up later and wake up later. Adolescents who get enough sleep wake up feeling refreshed and energetic; those who don't often become drowsy during the daytime hours. Inadequate sleep can compromise school performance. It also poses an increased risk of injuries among teens who are working with machinery or driving. Teens should not perform shift work because the changes in sleep times are very disruptive to normal functioning.

Stress

Stress is what people experience when they are not sure they can manage or cope with a specific situation. It occurs frequently in adolescents because they face relatively new situations frequently. Stress affects almost all of a teen's body systems, potentially interfering with normal pubertal growth and sexual maturation. It also takes a psychological toll. To minimize stress, adolescents should avoid taking on too many new activities. When stress does occur, several steps can be taken to reduce its effects. Consider trying to solve one problem at a time. Talk things over with someone who can potentially help. (Another teenager might not be a good choice for this.) Keep busy with activities that are familiar and relaxing. Exercise regularly. Learn and use some physical and mental relaxation techniques such as meditation.

Sex

Increasing frequency of sexual behaviors is normal during adolescence. One of the major tasks of this period of life is the establishment of interpersonal relations with others. Sexual gratification can be attained by a variety of means, including solitary sexual behaviors (thinking, looking, self-stimulation) and outercourse behaviors with a partner (looking, kissing, touching, petting to orgasm), which are generally healthier than intercourse. These relations often involve sexual behaviors that should be accompanied by considerations for the feelings of part-

ners as well as efforts to prevent sexually transmitted disease and unwanted pregnancies.

Dozens of programs for teens aimed at safe-sex practices are found in schools and community health centers. These programs generally focus upon postponement of sexual involvement, prevention of pregnancy and STDs/AIDS, and preparation for childbearing. Other programs are aimed at slightly younger people, before they are at risk. Professionals in these programs work closely with parents through home visits and are aimed at increasing parenting skills, enhancing positive self-worth, and encouraging the delay of sexual initiation. Some programs use peer educators—a technique that has been shown to have benefits both for students and for the peer educators themselves. Teens are more likely to express their concerns and talk to people their own age.

In sum, the adolescent years are critical for developing good health-related behaviors. During this time, teens begin to make independent decisions about their health and the behaviors that promote or impede healthy development.

Jordan W. Finkelstein

See also Dental Health; Drug Abuse Prevention; Environmental Health Issues; Health Services for Adolescents; Nutrition; Sexual Behavior

References and further reading
Brindis, Claire D., and Philip R. Lee. 1991. "Adolescents' Conceptualization of Illness." Pp. 534–540 in *Encyclopedia of Adolescence.* Edited by Richard M. Lerner, Anne C. Petersen, and Jeanne Brooks-Gunn. New York: Garland.
Centers for Disease Control and Prevention. 2000. *The Programs That Work (PTW) Project.* Atlanta, GA. Web site: http://www.cdc.gov/nccdphp/dash/rtc/moreinfo.htm.

Health Services for Adolescents

Health is difficult to define and measure at any life stage. Given the rapid changes of adolescence in growth and physiology, it is even more difficult to assess health status during this period of life. Many diseases and disabilities that are debilitating in adulthood begin in adolescence. Diagnosis of disorders and overall health assessment are therefore critical during the adolescent years. There is a widespread perception that adolescents are healthy—a perception supported by the fact that adolescents use less medical care, when all types of care are considered, than any other age group. About seven out of ten adolescents seek medical care once a year, but only 4 percent spend as much as one night in a hospital (Daniel, 1991). Female adolescents use more medical care than males, accounted for by their greater use of reproductive care. Hospitalizations are used more often by females—and this, too, is accounted for by pregnancy complications and delivery (Daniel, 1991). Males are more likely to be hospitalized for accidents than females. Overall, rates of smoking and illicit drug use have decreased among the adolescent population, as have death rates. Teenage pregnancy rates are also down from prior years. The health problems of adolescence are not problems of disease but problems of stress and change. The professionals in the field of health services need to recognize the individual needs of adolescents in order for prevention and intervention efforts to be successful. Adolescence is a time of rapid growth and change, calling for the teen to adjust to new situations, ways of thinking, and relationships. In addition, adolescents are adjusting to the physical changes within themselves. Unfortunately, the health services and professionals that are used by the adolescent population are not always adequately equipped to provide optimal care to this segment of the population.

Adolescence as a life stage entails specific health-related problems for teenagers, their parents, and their healthcare providers. These include issues related to developing a personal identity, independence, decision making, interpersonal relationships, work, sexuality, and chronic health problems. Until recently, however, most adolescents obtained healthcare from providers with little or no training in providing services directed specifically at adolescents. This situation has improved now that some of the medical specialty certification organizations (such as the American Board of Pediatrics) require that a specific segment of the training curriculum for physicians after they have graduated from medical school be directed toward the health problems of adolescents. In the meantime, education for health professionals has become more complex because it is no longer feasible for a single profession to meet the diverse health needs of adolescents.

Optimal training in adolescent healthcare should involve the study of growth and development as well as of puberty and its interrelation with the social and psychological tasks of adolescence. Indeed, because individual growth is affected by numerous external factors in the family, the peer group, and the social culture, an understanding of the complex world of adolescents is necessary if a comprehensive assessment of health is to be achieved.

The Context of Care

The majority of adolescents receive healthcare from family or general physicians, followed by pediatricians, usually in office settings. It is only a small minority of adolescents who get care at sites offering services directed specifically at teenagers. These most often include such settings as high school and college health clinics, medical school clinics, and correctional facilities. Almost no office sites provide care solely to adolescents. Some office practices do set aside specific times of the week when the practitioners see only adolescents, but these sites are the exception rather than the rule. Much more often, adolescents are intermingled with all of the other patients seen by the practices. In pediatric practices, this means that the teenagers will be waiting to be seen in a room populated by screaming infants and rambunctious toddlers who are sneezing, coughing, and so on; in family-medicine settings, they will be waiting with older adults. These settings make most teenagers unhappy and may discourage them from returning except for emergencies. If possible, separate waiting areas for adolescents should be made available.

Adolescence as a life stage entails specific health-related problems for teenagers, their parents, and their healthcare providers. (Richard T. Nowitz/Corbis)

Barriers to Care Utilization

A serious problem in adolescent health service delivery is the underutilization of services by adolescents. The high frequency of preventable conditions such as unplanned pregnancies, sexually transmitted diseases, and injuries indicate that adolescents are not making use of the services available to them. Researchers have identified several impediments to obtaining health services for prevention or treatment. For example, many adolescents do not understand the importance of prevention and therefore do not go for periodic checkups. Since very few adolescents experience major health disorders, minor conditions do not worry them, and they often are not urged by parents to seek medical attention. Many of the presenting problems for adolescents have to do with sexuality or substance abuse; according to one study, however, many adolescents will not go to a physician for sexuality, substance abuse, or emotional problems (Klerman, 1991).

Another barrier that prevents adolescents from seeking treatment for health issues is that they are unaware that their present behavior (i.e., smoking, poor nutrition) can cause future problems. Teens are often not informed about centers and other places that offer preventive care or counseling, and they are hesitant to ask parents or school personnel for information. Although parents may take their adolescents for yearly exams, adolescents may not reveal to family physicians important information about their health status. The normal separation from parents during adolescence may also lead teens to ask their peers for information and support. Unfortunately, much of the information obtained from peers is incorrect, resulting in unhealthy behaviors and failure to obtain care for presenting health problems.

Still other barriers are unaffordability, inaccessibility, and inappropriateness. The most typical financial impediment is the absence of public or private health insurance. A large number of American families are not covered by private insurance or Medicaid, and many of the services needed for adolescents are not covered even when there is insurance. Transportation to health services is another problem for many adolescents and for poorer families in general. Public transportation is often unavailable in rural areas, and adolescents (along with other family members) may not have access to private transportation. In addition, many adolescents may find it inconvenient to visit healthcare professionals during the school or workday. Thus, it is essential for healthcare facilities to schedule evening and weekend hours. Below are recommendations for health service delivery to adolescents.

Staff

Office staff should take a friendly approach that provides a positive atmosphere and recognizes that adolescents are *not* babies. If the staff give the impression that they are unhappy with having teenagers at the site—that they stereo-

typically expect to find angry, rebellious, intoxicated teenagers and will treat them accordingly—they run the risk of further increasing the adolescents' (and their own) uneasiness in regard to the visit. The adolescents, in turn, may be reluctant to return for additional care if they do not feel comfortable with the staff. Most adolescents want staff to listen to them and to treat them nonjudgmentally. They are also concerned about confidentiality and need some assurance that all issues discussed will be kept confidential.

Parents

Parents should recognize that most adolescents are quite capable not only of providing appropriate information about their health to providers but also of managing most of their own health problems. Most parents will accompany their teenager to the office visit and want to have all available information relating to the visit, the diagnosis, and the treatment plan. Many object when the provider attempts to obtain a confidentiality agreement for the teenager. Under this arrangement, the parents are asked to agree that whatever their child reveals to the provider will be confidential except for information that involves a risk to the adolescent or someone else (e.g., a threat to commit suicide) or a situation in which the provider is required by law to reveal the information (e.g., physical or sexual abuse). In either of these exceptional circumstances, the provider explains to the adolescent that he or she must reveal the information to others; then the parents are told that if they want to know what happened at the visit, they should ask their child. This practice is important in that it allows teenagers to feel that they can safely reveal very personal issues to the provider. For instance, since few sexually active teens want their parents to know about their sexual involvement, they are not likely to express their concern about sexually transmitted disease if their parents are in the room with them and the provider.

One of the most important roles for parents is to help adolescents become responsible for their own healthcare. This is best accomplished not only by arranging for a confidentiality agreement among parents, adolescents, and providers but also by discussing healthcare issues directly with the adolescents.

Providers

Providers of health services to adolescents should be informed and comfortable about managing issues of particular importance to adolescents. These include confidentiality and health behaviors involving sexuality; substance use and abuse; relations with parents, siblings, and peers; and behavioral issues related to chronic health problems and others. In cases where providers have limited their practices to exclude adolescents, referral should be made to a provider who does treat individuals in this age group. Family practitioners are often the most appropriate and available source of healthcare for teens, inasmuch as they provide a mixed setting with varied clientele and offer services for the entire family. By the same token, family practitioners may be less of a problem than other providers in terms of the transition between child and adolescent healthcare to young adult healthcare.

Note that most internists treat only adults, so they are not the best choice for a teenager who has been discharged from a pediatric practice because of age or developmental status.

Jordan W. Finkelstein

See also Conflict Resolution; Counseling; Dental Health; Drug Abuse Prevention; Environmental Health Issues; Health Promotion; Pregnancy, Interventions to Prevent; Psychotherapy

References and further reading
Daniel, William A., Jr. 1991. "Training in Adolescent Health Care." Pp. 450–453 in *Encyclopedia of Adolescence.* Edited by Richard M. Lerner, Anne C. Petersen, and Jeanne Brooks-Gunn. New York: Garland.
Friedman, S. B., M. M. Fisher, S. K. Schoenberg, and E. M. Alderman. 1998. *Comprehensive Adolescent Health Care.* St. Louis, MO: Mosby.
Klerman, Lorraine V. 1991. "Barriers to Health Services for Adolescents." Pp. 470–474 in *Encyclopedia of Adolescence.* Edited by Richard M. Lerner, Anne C. Petersen, and Jeanne Brooks-Gunn. New York: Garland.
Kovar, Mary Grace. 1991. "Health of Adolescents in the United States: An Overview." Pp. 454–458 in *Encyclopedia of Adolescence.* Edited by Richard M. Lerner, Anne C. Petersen, and Jeanne Brooks-Gunn. New York: Garland.

High School Equivalency Degree

The General Educational Development (GED) tests provide individuals who have dropped out of high school with an opportunity to obtain a diploma equivalent to a high school degree. The GED tests, which are periodically revised, assess knowledge and critical-thinking skills and may be taken by anyone not currently enrolled in high school who meets state age requirements. Teens and young adults who pass the GED report greater confidence, increase their chances of college admission, and receive higher salaries than high school dropouts. One out of every seven high school degrees conferred is a GED.

The GED tests were developed in 1942 to provide U.S. veterans who had not finished high school with a way to obtain

Adult students study for their GED in Minnesota. (Richard T. Nowitz/Corbis)

an alternative degree in order to satisfy college entrance requirements. However, the program became popular with the general public, and by 1959 civilians taking the tests outnumbered military personnel. Currently, about 800,000 individuals, most between the ages of eighteen and twenty-four, take the GED each year.

The American Council for Education (ACE) produces the GED tests and determines minimal score standards, although individual states may set additional requirements. Test takers can choose among 3,500 official testing centers throughout the world. The tests are available in English, Spanish, French, and Braille, and accommodations are made for individuals with disabilities. The GED tests consist of a written essay and four multiple-choice sections: social

studies, science, language arts, and mathematics. They reflect the skills and concepts found in high school curricula and have become more challenging as secondary education has evolved. The tests have undergone four versions, the most current of which is the 2002 series. They require seven and one-half hours to complete, although some testing centers allow candidates to complete each of the test sections separately. Prior to taking the GED, most people average about thirty hours of preparation consisting of classes or individual study using books and practice tests.

Standards for passing the tests are based on norms derived from high school seniors' scores on the GED in order to verify that GED graduates are academically equivalent to high school graduates. About 70 percent of GED candidates pass the tests on their first attempt; another 15 percent succeed after taking the tests a second time. Almost 14 million people have received GED diplomas since the program began.

Two out of three individuals who take the GED do so in order to pursue higher education, and more than half of those who pass actually obtain additional schooling. Although more than 90 percent of four-year universities accept GED graduates who satisfy other admission requirements, most people with GEDs attend trade and technical schools or community colleges. Students enrolled in vocational programs complete them at the same rates as do high school graduates, but a smaller number finish the programs at two- and four-year institutions. The armed services admit about 40,000 recruits with GED diplomas each year, but they give preference to high school graduates since they drop out of the military at lower rates than do individuals with GEDs.

More than 95 percent of employers consider the work skills of people with GED and high school degrees to be equivalent. Compared to high school dropouts, individuals with GEDs are employed full-time at higher rates and receive wages that are 6 to 13 percent greater. However, individuals with high school and, especially, college diplomas are usually salaried at higher levels than GED recipients.

Well-known individuals who have earned GED diplomas include entertainer Bill Cosby, U.S. Senator Ben Nighthorse Campbell, Wendy's founder Dave Thomas, country music singer Waylon Jennings, and Delaware Lieutenant Governor Ruth Ann Minner.

Wendy Hubenthal

See also Academic Achievement; Career Development; School Dropouts; Standardized Tests; Vocational Development

References and further reading
American Council on Education. Web site: http://www.acenet.edu/ (select GED link).
Boesel, David, Nabeel Alsalam, and Thomas Smith. 1998. *Research Synthesis: Educational and Labor Market Performance of GED Recipients.* Washington, DC: U.S. Department of Education.
Martz, Geoff, and Laurice Pearson (contributor). 1999. *Cracking the GED, 2000.* New York: Random House (published annually).

Higher Education

Higher education (also called postsecondary or tertiary education) refers to the broad set of educational opportunities available beyond the level of secondary education (junior high through high school). A mix of general and specialized study, it is intended to prepare graduates for advanced professional employment in government, industry, and business. Relative to other world countries, where advanced education opportunities are typically managed by a central government ministry and available to only a select number of individuals, higher education in the United States is unique in terms of its diversity, size, competitiveness, and decentralized nature.

U.S. institutions providing higher education include public and private colleges, universities, professional schools, community (or junior) colleges, and proprietary schools. Length and type of study vary by institution and degree type. Community colleges typically offer two-year technical and general education programs leading to the associate's degree. At four-

A mix of general and specialized study, higher education is intended to prepare graduates for advanced professional employment in government, industry, and business. (Joseph Sohm; ChromoSohm, Inc./Corbis)

year colleges and universities, bachelor's degrees are awarded to students who complete a "liberal arts" program of study that consists of both general and specialized classes. Following the completion of a bachelor's degree, qualifying candidates can elect to pursue advanced master's or doctoral degree study, or attend a professional academy such as a medical, business, or law school. Proprietary, for-profit institutions offer a broad range of degree, certificate, and diploma programs of shorter duration.

Higher education in the United States currently serves more than 14.3 million domestic and international students—an enrollment increase of 16 percent since 1985—in more than 4,000 higher educa-

tion institutions (National Center for Educational Statistics, 1998). Understood by most Americans to be a key ingredient in social accession and success, access to some form of higher education has grown significantly over the past fifty years and is now almost universally available (Trow, 1989). On average, 62 percent of each year's 2.5 million secondary school graduates enroll in some form of postsecondary education. Since 1980, the number of women at colleges and universities has exceeded the number of men. Minority enrollment levels have been increasing slowly over time. In 1995, 11 percent of African Americans, 2 percent of Asians/Pacific Islanders, and fewer than 1 percent of Native Americans were enrolled in institutions of higher learning (National Center for Educational Statistics, 1998).

History

Higher education in the United States has evolved significantly during its long history, continually modifying itself to parallel the needs of the growing country. American higher education began with Harvard College (Rudolph, 1990). Chartered in 1636 by leaders of the Massachusetts Bay Colony, Harvard was modeled after the British colleges of Oxford and Cambridge. Other colonial colleges soon followed. As with Harvard, the purpose of these early schools was to prepare new generations of elite, young men for civic and religious leadership. Discipline and character building, rather than knowledge or skill attainment, were their primary goals of instruction. Hence, these institutions offered studies, known as the liberal arts, that were believed to be instrumental in inculcating moral and spiritual growth—studies that included work in mathematics, grammar, rhetoric, and the memorization of certain classic Greek and Latin texts.

As America grew and changed following nationhood, so too did its institutions of higher education. During the first half of the nineteenth century, westward expansion brought with it a dramatic proliferation of small, private colleges. Modeled after the original colonial schools, most of these were founded by members of various Protestant religious denominations. By midcentury, however, the traditional and elitist practices of the country's old and new colleges were perceived as increasingly out of step with the events of the day. Science and scientific theory—for the most part imported from continental Europe—had established a

foothold in the curriculum of many colleges, and a crop of young, new educators began agitating for changes in the traditional methods and content of instruction. With similar feelings being voiced by the population at large, calls for a more practical approach to education grew in frequency and intensity. One product of this sentiment was the enactment, in 1862, of the Morrill Land Grant Act, an article of federal legislation that gave land to each state to be sold to start new colleges dedicated to both liberal arts and agricultural and mechanical training (Veysey, 1965). Another was the adoption, from Germany, of specialized research and graduate education practices. When fused with the liberal arts curricula, these initiatives resulted in the formation of the country's first true universities; undergraduate cum graduate institutions were now committed to providing instruction in traditional subjects while at the same time using the tenets of science to generate new knowledge.

By the beginning of the twentieth century, the basic structure of today's modern postsecondary educational system was in place. Disciplinary departments had formed. Administrators, rather than professors, as was previously the case, had or were assuming responsibility for various operational functions. And in response to the growing perception that higher education represented a means for improving one's social station, colleges and universities continued to differentiate and grow in number, modifying themselves along the way to offer ever-more specialized and practical educational opportunities. Yet despite these advancements, higher education remained a privilege of America's wealthy male elite well into the latter half of the century. Women and minorities, for instance, were often either excluded from study altogether or segregated into women- and black-only colleges.

Since World War II, a number of federal government initiatives—the G.I. Bill, funding for scientific research, and the Higher Education Act—have dramatically impacted the growth and direction of higher education. An article of federal legislation, the G.I. Bill exploded enrollments by subsidizing the college and university study of hundreds of thousands of returning veterans, forever changing the tradition of who had access to college (Boyer, 1990). The influx of millions of dollars of federal research aid, given initially to promote cold war weapons initiatives, greatly expanded the research function and capacities of universities, solidifying their role as producers of new knowledge. In the 1960s, the government's first Higher Education Act, in conjunction with the change in social perception inspired by the civil rights movement, combined, at last, to fully secure access to higher education for all people, regardless of color, religion, gender, or disability. In recent years, discussions of higher education policy have revolved around the issues of quality, diversity, access, affordability, academic freedom, and what should be taught.

Organization
Unlike primary and secondary education, higher education in the United States is neither mandatory nor provided free by law. In addition, unlike education in most other countries, it is not overseen by a federal ministry. (In other words, the Department of Education has no direct control over higher education practices.) For these reasons, American colleges and universities are remarkably unencumbered in terms of how they define themselves, hire and fire personnel, design curricula, and provide other services.

Perhaps the most distinguishing characteristic of American higher education is its incredible diversity. Across the land, cities, towns, and rural areas alike are sprinkled with a rich variety of public and private, large and small, and for- and nonprofit institutions. Within this mixture, educational mandates and practices vary greatly. Some schools are controlled by religious organizations and offer study that is tightly coupled to church teachings. Others may specialize in research. Still others may be profit-directed and offer short-term training courses leading to a particular profession. Some have residential facilities, whereas others organize their programs of study around the needs of commuting students.

Regardless of orientation, the higher education model most familiar to Americans is that of the two- and four-year degree-granting colleges or universities. Community or junior colleges are two-year public institutions. They offer a mixture of technical and vocational programs, nondegree adult-learning classes, and general study that results in the associate degree and is intended to prepare students for transfer into a four-year institution. Admission to community colleges is generally open to anyone with a high school (or equivalent) diploma. This open-admissions policy does not imply poor standards, however. On the contrary, the quality of instruction at community colleges is often as rigorous as that at more prestigious and well-known four-year schools. Because most community colleges cater to local, commuting residents, they do not operate housing facilities. Heavily subsidized with public tax dollars, they have in recent years become increasingly popular with students looking to fulfill general education requirements before enrolling at more expensive four-year schools.

Four-year institutions are both public and private. Of the approximately 4,000 four-year colleges and universities in the United States, slightly more than half are private. Despite being outnumbered, public schools—including most community colleges and state-operated comprehensive universities—are home to nearly three out of four Americans enrolled in higher education nationwide. There are few practical differences in the modes and methods of instruction at public and private institutions. Based, however, on the principle of providing universal access to a wide range of educational opportunities, public colleges and universities tend to be more comprehensive than their private counterparts (Thullen et al., 1997). A lay board, commonly referred to as a board of regents or governors, governs public institutions. This board directs institutional policy and appoints a president to implement the members' decisions and lead the institution. Although tuition fees account for a significant component of public institutions' operating budgets, the bulk of their annual funding is legislatively allocated from state and local tax coffers.

Private colleges and universities are privately owned nonprofit organizations. Like public schools, they are guided by a board of directors (known as trustees) as well as by a president who oversees their day-to-day operations. Unlike public schools, private colleges and universities receive no direct tax assistance. As a consequence, tuition revenues account for a significant percentage of their annual operating budgets, making them more expensive to students and their families. This issue has raised concerns among some people who fear that the hefty price tags at these institutions will depress low-income enrollments and turn them into bastions of elitism.

To make sense of the variety of public and private colleges and universities in the United States, The Carnegie Foundation created a classification system in 1973. Known as the Carnegie Classification, the widely recognized typology organizes all degree-granting and accredited tertiary institutions into these groups: doctorate-granting institutions; master's colleges and universities; baccalaureate colleges; associate's colleges; specialized institutions (e.g., theological seminaries, teachers colleges, and schools of medicine, business, and law); and tribal colleges and universities. In some of the categories, subsets exist to provide greater refinement of type. It is important to note that the Carnegie Classification does not rank schools by quality. Organized by highest degree awarded and mode of financing, it is instead a tool to assist in identifying an institution's general characteristics and mission. The classification is regularly updated to reflect changes in higher education institution types.

Despite differences in size, cost, mission, and affiliation, the programmatic offerings of most four-year American colleges and universities are remarkably similar. Undergraduate study refers to the initial phase of postsecondary education leading to the bachelor's degree. Designed to require four years of full-time work to complete, it proceeds in two stages: one or two years of general study, covering a broad range of subjects (also called distribution or liberal arts requirements), and a period of concentrated study in a particular academic discipline (major) meant to directly prepare students for either entry-level work or advancement to graduate-level studies. Undergraduate study programs are often quite flexible. Students are able—and frequently encouraged by professors or academic advisers—to select classes and specify majors of an interdisciplinary nature. Classes, especially during students' freshman and sophomore years of study, are often large and conducted in lecture halls. Although format and size vary by institution and course type, actual contact and conversation with professors can be infrequent, especially at some of the larger institutions. Undergraduates are regularly tested over the course of an academic semester. The most common forms of assessment are exams, quizzes, and essays. Successfully completing a course results in a grade and the awarding of a set number of credit hours.

Like most secondary schools, the majority of four-year institutions award grades from A to F. These marks are then translated into a numerical scale, running from 4.0 (outstanding) to 0 (failing), that is used to formulate a student's grade-point average. Students graduate after accumulating a predetermined number of credit hours and fulfilling the curricular requirements particular to their degree program. The type of bachelor's degree one can earn is determined by field of study. For example, math, physical science, and engineering graduates are typically awarded a Bachelor of Science (B.S.) degree, whereas Bachelor of Arts (B.A.) degrees are conferred upon persons completing humanity, social science, and interdisciplinary majors. Additional B.A.-like degrees are occasionally awarded for study in specialty fields such as education, business, and nursing.

Graduate education refers to study undertaken after the award of a bachelor's degree. In the United States, graduate study is available along two separate tracks: (1) master's (M.A.) and doctorate (Ph.D.) degree programs and (2) professional-school programs. Master's and doctorate programs are designed to impart expertise in a particular academic discipline. These programs—in effect, intensive extensions of the undergraduate major—are organized and offered by the same departments and professors responsible for undergraduate instruction. With few exceptions, M.A. and Ph.D. study requires the completion of a set number of courses, followed by the production of an original work of scholarly research. Historically, master's and doctorate degree recipients have found employment as researchers and educators in higher secondary and postsecondary education institutions. Although this is still the case, the specialized knowledge gained via advanced degree study—especially at the master's level—is becoming increasingly necessary for success in a broad range of professions.

Professional-degree programs offer specialized training in fields such as law, dentistry, pharmacy, theology, and medicine. Often undertaken at schools affiliated with but separate from universities, professional degrees include a period of extended classroom and laboratory study, followed by some sort of supervised field or clinical work. Given the importance of hands-on training for many professional degrees, credits are awarded for work conducted both in and outside the classroom. Most professional-degree programs also include an extensive internship, sometimes lasting a number of years. Although certain professional degrees include the term *doctor* in their titles—Doctor of Veterinary Medicine (D.V.M.), or Juris Doctor (J.D.), for instance—they are applied rather than research degrees and, thus, different from the Ph.D.

College student demographics and routines have changed significantly in recent years. In the past, it was common for students to begin their college studies immediately after completing high school. Many lived in campus residence halls, off-campus apartments, or Greek Letter Society sorority or fraternity houses. Working while at college was uncommon. Instead, students dedicatedly pursued their studies full-time for four years, then graduated and looked for professional work. Although this pattern still exists, it is no longer the norm. Higher education student populations are older and more diverse than ever before. Students at almost all institutions are increasingly likely to commute to campus, to be enrolled part-time, and/or to be engaged in part- or full-time employment. In 1993, for instance, 85 percent of all part-time students worked, as did nearly half of all full-time enrollees (Thullen et al., 1997). On-campus services are also on the rise. A growing group of campus employees—known as student affairs professionals—now routinely supply such services as counseling, childcare, health and welfare advice, remedial assistance, and job search advice. Campus recreational facilities have likewise expanded in quantity and quality as a result of efforts to provide students with constructive activity outlets separate from their classroom duties.

Postsecondary educators are organized by area of specialization into departments, divisions, and professional-school faculties. As employees of the institution in which they teach and/or do research, they are usually expected to hold the terminal academic degree in their area of specialization. The exact role of an American academic is dictated by the particular needs of the institution in which she or he is employed. Some institutions—community colleges as well as small to mid-sized schools, for instance—tend to promote teaching above research. In others, research is more highly valued, and career advancements are tied more closely to the work produced than to the time spent in a classroom. Nationwide, most professors spend significantly more time teaching than they do undertaking research. Over the course of their academic careers, full-time American educators are promoted through four academic levels: professor, associate professor, assistant professor, and lecturer. Advancement to the rank of professor and associate professor, the two highest appointments, results in tenure— a guarantee of lifetime employment. To receive tenure, scholars must demonstrate, over a five- to seven-year period, a high level of academic productivity, accomplishment, and teaching skill. In recent years, public attacks on tenure have become increasingly shrill. As a result, some colleges and universities have begun to abandon it, preferring instead to link merit raises with the results of regular performance tests.

David Engberg

See also Academic Achievement; Academic Self-Evaluation; Career Development; School, Functions of; School Transitions

References and further reading
Boyer, Ernest. 1990. *Scholarship Reconsidered: Priorities of the Professoriate.* Princeton, NJ: Carnegie Foundation.
National Center for Educational Statistics. 1998. *Digest of Education Statistics.* Washington, DC: U.S. Department of Education.
Rudolph, Frederick. 1990. *The American College and University: A History.*

Athens/London: University of Georgia Press.

Thullen, Manfred, et al. 1997. *Cooperating with a University in the United States.* Washington, DC: NAFSA.

Trow, Martin. 1989. "American Higher Education: Past, Present, and Future." *Studies in Higher Education* 14: 5–22.

Veysey, Lawrence. 1965. *The Emergence of the American University.* Chicago: University of Chicago Press.

HIV/AIDS

What Is AIDS?

AIDS stands for acquired immunodeficiency syndrome; it is caused by HIV (which stands for human immunodeficiency virus). The world first became aware of this new disease in 1981. Since that time, AIDS/HIV has exploded in successive waves in various regions of the world, thus receiving much attention and public concern. AIDS/HIV continues to be a major public health concern, both because it is incurable and because HIV continues to spread rapidly in many parts of the world—nearly 50 million people have been infected with HIV since the epidemic first began (UNAIDS, 1999).

The words comprising the acronym AIDS have the following meanings: *Acquired* refers to the fact that the disease is received from someone else. *Immuno-* refers to the immune system, which protects the body against disease-causing microorganisms, and *deficiency* refers to a loss of this protection. Finally, *syndrome* means a group of signs or symptoms that together define AIDS as a human pathology. Thus, AIDS is a deficiency of the human immune system that is acquired from someone else. AIDS is not a single disease per se, but instead is a label for the final stages of HIV disease, when the immune system is severely damaged.

HIV, which causes AIDS, destroys an essential component of the immune system, the T4 "helper" cells. In a healthy person, these cells organize and arrange the immune system's response—they act as the immune system's "generals," coordinating the attack against foreign invaders, such as bacteria, viruses, and other microorganisms. HIV slowly kills these helper cells, weakening the immune system, and eventually causing AIDS. According to the Centers for Disease Control (CDC), an HIV-infected person is considered to have AIDS if he either has a T4 cell count of less than 200 or has one or more of twenty-six opportunistic infections or neoplasms. An opportunistic infection is a normally benign microorganism or virus that becomes pathogenic (or harmful) in people with a weakened immune system; a neoplasm is an abnormal cell growth, such as a cancerous tumor. Although most healthy people's immune systems can easily fight off these infections and illnesses, they can kill people with AIDS.

AIDS is considered an epidemic because it is contagious, has affected so many individuals worldwide, and is associated with enormous economic costs. In the United States, there have been over 711,000 AIDS cases, and at least 420,000 persons have died from this disease (CDC, 1999). In recent years, the number of new AIDS cases has decreased sharply as a result of the development of antiretroviral drug treatments that hold HIV in check, and partly also as a result of public education and prevention efforts. The annual number of AIDS cases reported among adolescents ages thirteen to nineteen years has declined significantly from 581

HIV/AIDS continues to be a major public health concern, both because there is no known cure and because HIV continues to spread rapidly in many parts of the world. (Skjold Photographs)

reported cases in 1993 to 312 cases in 1999 (CDC, 2000a). The ratio of adolescent male to female cases has decreased over time. In 1999, more females (180, or 58 percent) than males (132) were reported with AIDS (CDC, 2000a). It is hypothesized that the proportion of males who acquired HIV through receipt of blood products has diminished, thus narrowing the gender gap.

Although the number of AIDS cases in the United States has declined in recent years, the number of new HIV diagnoses remains relatively stable. The CDC estimates that between 800,000 and 900,000 Americans currently live with HIV and that at least 40,000 new HIV infections occur each year (CDC, 1999, 2000b). In 1999, 828 adolescents of thirteen to nineteen years of age were reported with HIV (based on states providing confidential HIV infection surveillance data). African American and Hispanic youth have been, and continue to be, disproportionately affected by the HIV/AIDS epidemic. Although only 15 percent of the U.S. adolescent population is African American, 49 percent of the AIDS cases from 1981 to 1999 and 60 percent of the AIDS cases in 1999 were among African American youth. Similarly, Hispanic youth constitute 14 percent of the U.S. population; however, they accounted for 24 percent of the AIDS cases in 1999 and 20 percent of the AIDS cases in 1981–1999 (CDC, 2000a).

AIDS continues to be a serious global health problem. Based on estimates from the United Nations Programme on AIDS (UNAIDS, 1999), approximately 47 million people have been infected with HIV since the start of the global epidemic. Through December 1999, an estimated 16.3 million children and adults have died from AIDS. An additional esti-mated 33.6 million people are living with HIV infection or AIDS. UNAIDS estimates that 5.6 million new HIV infections occurred in 1999. This represents almost 16,000 new infections each day.

How Does One Get HIV?
A person can only become infected with HIV through direct contact with HIV-infected body fluids. HIV is not transmitted by casual contact, by toilet seats, or by mosquitoes. There are three major routes of transmission: sexual behaviors, including vaginal sex, anal sex, and oral sex; direct injection of HIV-contaminated drugs into the body with needles or/and syringes, or during a blood transfusion or receipt of other blood products (such as factor VIII for hemophiliacs); and from mother to baby, either before birth (when the fetus shares a circulatory system with its mother), exposure to blood or cervico-vaginal fluids during delivery, or during breast-feeding, through the milk. In general, it is easier to get HIV through the intravenous routes than through sexual ones. However, most people get HIV as a result of sexual contact. This is especially true in Africa, where the vast majority of infected people acquired HIV through heterosexual intercourse.

Among adolescents, reported exposure categories for HIV transmission vary by gender. According to the most recent data (CDC, 2000a), over one-third (34 percent) of male adolescents thirteen to nineteen years of age report acquiring AIDS from engaging in sexual relations with other men. An additional 34 percent acquired their infection from blood transfusions used to treat hemophilia, prior to the advent of heat treatment of blood products to prevent HIV transmission. In contrast, among females in this age group, 52 percent identified heterosexual transmission and 14 percent identified injection drug use as their mode of HIV exposure.

In terms of sexual behavior, HIV can be transmitted by vaginal, anal, or oral sex with an infected person. However, there is a greater chance of transmitting or becoming infected with HIV through anal sex than through vaginal or oral sex. Oral sex appears to be much safer than either vaginal or anal intercourse. Also, the person who is the "receiving" partner in anal sex is more likely to become infected than the "insertive" partner. Furthermore, it is easier for a woman to get infected by having vaginal or anal sex with a man than it is for a man to be infected by a woman. The consistent (every time) and correct use of latex condoms can substantially reduce the risk associated with any of these sexual activities. Scientists are also working on methods to help women protect themselves, such as the female condom (a plastic pouch that lines the vagina) and various microbicides that can be applied to the vagina prior to sex and that will kill the HIV virus.

The second main way that HIV is acquired is by injecting drugs with an HIV-contaminated needle or syringe, or by receiving contaminated blood products during a transfusion or other medical procedure. Injecting with an HIV-contaminated syringe is a very efficient way to transmit the virus from one person to another. Therefore, injection drug users who share needles and syringes with other drug users are at high risk of becoming infected. Through 1999, 26 percent of the reported AIDS cases in the United States were due to intravenous drug use (CDC, 1999). Experts believe that half of all AIDS cases can be linked to injection drug use, either directly or indirectly. For example, an injection drug user might pass the virus to his female sex partner, and she, in turn, might pass it on to their children. Rinsing syringes with bleaching and water can help deactivate the virus, but by far the safest way to avoid injection-related infections is not to inject drugs at all, or to avoid sharing needles and syringes with others.

Early in the epidemic, many people (mostly children) with hemophilia and other coagulation disorders received HIV-contaminated blood products during medical procedures. Others received infected blood while undergoing transfusions during surgery. In 1985, an HIV antibody test was developed that could detect, with high accuracy, whether blood was contaminated with the virus. (Antibodies are made by an infected person's body in response to exposure to the HIV virus. The "HIV test" does not actually test for the presence of HIV itself. Instead, it tests for the presence of antibodies.) Thanks to rigorous blood screening policies, the blood supply in Western countries, such as the United States, is now very safe. However, in much of the developing world, receiving blood or blood products can be very risky.

Finally, a woman can infect her baby while it is still in the womb (HIV can cross the placental barrier), during childbirth (through exposure to cervicovaginal fluids), or after birth (as a result of breast-feeding). Anywhere from one-quarter to one-third of the babies born to HIV-infected women will become infected through "perinatal" (mother-to-child) transmission. Fortunately, antiretroviral medications given to pregnant women before they give birth can reduce the likelihood of perinatal transmission by one-half to two-thirds. Regular prenatal care and routine (voluntary) testing of pregnant women is critical to ensure that these medications can be used appropriately.

How to Get Tested

A person can get tested for HIV antibodies at the doctor's office, at a local family planning clinic, or at a publicly funded counseling and testing site. In many states, one can either get tested completely anonymously or confidentially (the name is known but the records are kept private). Testing is critical to ensure that people can get appropriate medical care if infected, to help prevent perinatal HIV transmission, and to help infected persons reduce the risk of spreading HIV to their sex partners. Knowledge is power!

Most HIV testing centers use the ELISA (enzyme linked immunosorbent assay) antibody test and follow up with another ELISA and then, if applicable, the Western Blot Assay. The ELISA is used in most testing centers. It is used as an initial screening test because it is inexpensive, has standardized procedures, has high reproducibility, and provides quick results. This test is very sensitive, which means that it is very accurate at detecting infected blood samples. But it is not very specific, which means that it produces many false positives (i.e., the test indicates that the blood is infected when in reality it is not). The sensitivity was set extremely high because it is better to have some false positives than to let any bad blood slip by. This makes the ELISA a good screening tool, but it is not definitive. Therefore, the standard procedure is to combine the ELISA with a more specific test, known as the Western Blot Assay. First, an initial ELISA test is performed. If that test comes back positive, then the ELISA is rerun (just to make sure). If the second ELISA test also comes back positive, then a Western Blot is performed.

The Western Blot, unlike the ELISA, is very specific. It is not used as a screening test because it is an expensive and time-consuming test. Thus, it is used only for confirming the results of the repeated ELISA tests. Combined, these tests are extremely accurate, with very few false positives.

What Is the Treatment for HIV/AIDS?

There is no cure for AIDS or for HIV infection. However, there are now treatments available that can markedly improve the health of (some) infected people. Guidelines have been developed for the use of potent anti-HIV drugs, which are generally administered in combinations of three or more drugs at a time, usually including a protease inhibitor (CDC, 1998; Vittinghoff et al., 1999). These drug combinations are known as highly active antiretroviral therapy and have been found to be effective in lessening the severity of illness in many patients, as well as preventing the progression of disease in those who are relatively healthy. However, not all persons infected with HIV respond well to these therapies, and many persons cannot tolerate the toxic side effects, or are unable to comply with the rigorous treatment plan (which requires taking a large number of pills according to complicated dosing schedules). In addition, new strains of HIV continue to develop, some of which may be resistant to currently available drugs.

Heather Cecil

See also Contraception; Drug Abuse Prevention; Gonorrhea; Health Promotion;

Health Services for Adolescents; Sexual Behavior Problems; Sexually Transmitted Diseases

References and further reading

Centers for Disease Control and Prevention (CDC). 1998. HIV/AIDS Surveillance Report10 (No. 2). Atlanta, GA: Centers for Disease Control.

———. 1999. HIV/AIDS Surveillance Report 11 (No. 1). Atlanta, GA: Centers for Disease Control.

———. 2000a. HIV/AIDS Surveillance in Adolescents. L265 slide series through 1999. Atlanta, GA: Centers for Disease Control.

———. 2000b. CDC Update: A Glance at the HIV Epidemic. Atlanta, GA: Centers for Disease Control.

Durant, J., P. Clevenbergh, P. Halfon, P. Delguidice, S. Porsin, P. Simonet, N. Montagne, C. A. B. Boucher, and J. M. Schapiro. 1999. "Drug-Resistance Genotyping in HIV-1 Therapy: The VIRADAPT Randomised Controlled Trial." *The Lancet* 353: 2195–2199.

Fauci, Anthony S. 1999. "The AIDS Epidemic. Considerations for the 21st Century." *The New England Journal of Medicine* 341, no. 14: 1046–1050.

The Kaiser Family Foundation. 2000. "The State of the HIV/AIDS Epidemic in America." *Capitol Hill Briefing Series on HIV/AIDS*, April: 1–8.

UNAIDS. 1999. *AIDS Epidemic Update: December 1999.* Switzerland: UNAIDS.

Vittinghoff, Eric, Susan Scheer, Paul O'Malley, Grant Colfax, Scott D. Holmberg, and Susan P. Buchbinder. 1999. "Combination Antiretroviral Therapy and Recent Declines in AIDS Incidence and Mortality." *Journal of Infectious Diseases* 179: 717–720.

Homeless Youth

Adolescents who are homeless sometimes are part of a homeless family, one or two parents plus their children. But there is a separate category of homeless adolescents, those who are on their own. These homeless youth are no longer part of their family; in fact, their existence on the streets of the United States is made more precarious by the lack of family support and familial resources.

The number of these homeless teens in the United States is controversial, but 700,000 to 1.3 million youth fit the category as defined above. They have received little systematic attention. Indeed, according to the Institute of Medicine, homeless youths are the most understudied subgroup within the homeless population. Their ages usually range from thirteen to seventeen, with most homeless youth fifteen and over.

Some homeless youth are as young as nine. The proportion of males and females is unknown, varying from sample to sample. Their ethnic background tends to match that of the communities in which they live. Although there are spectacular exceptions, including homeless youth who secretly attend local colleges, most homeless youth have had considerable academic and behavioral problems in school.

One of the first questions one might ask about homeless youth is whether they are merely an extreme form of rebellious teenagers looking for freedom. The overwhelming majority are not. Instead, they are typically from problem families or have generated problems for their families. Some are "throwaway teens," forced out of the home by parents who felt that the teenager was causing too many problems. Others are "runaways" who left the family of their own volition. But both groups of homeless teens report family environments that were far from ideal. Homeless runaways describe the families they had left as unstable, neglectful, and abusive, often accompanied by parental substance abuse and alcoholism. Up to 40 percent of homeless teens report physical abuse in the

Almost all homeless youth describe themselves as having been unprepared for the horrors of street life. (Skjold Photographs)

parental household, and up to a quarter report sexual abuse. Only a small proportion of homeless teens are from two-natural-parent households. Throwaway teens report being forced out because of extremely high levels of conflict with parents, the family's lack of money or room, the teens' pregnancy, or the teens' homosexuality. Reports from both runaways and throwaways indicate that these teens were neither wanted nor well cared for by their families.

Regardless of the stress they experienced in the home, all teenagers, whether runaways or throwaways, find life on the streets very difficult. The adverse circumstances they face lead to considerable psychological distress and the use of extreme measures for survival. Almost all homeless youth describe themselves as having been unprepared for the horrors of street life.

Just as homeless youth can be categorized in terms of the origin of their homelessness, so they can be classified in terms of their willingness to accept help from any social service organization or shelter. About half of homeless teens are "street teens," choosing not to use any social services. The other half are "shelter teens," accepting assistance from shelters or drop-in centers for teenagers.

One reason that street teens avoid services and shelter has to do with their fear that service providers will notify the parents of their whereabouts or place them in custodial care. Regulations often mandate social agencies to notify either parents or civil authorities when these agencies provide assistance to teens for more than a period of a few hours. Despite the harshness of the conditions under which they live on the street, almost none of the street teens are willing to go home or to enter residential placement; by contrast,

about half of the shelter teens are willing to return home eventually. Even though the shelter teens have, by definition, requested assistance from an agency, almost half of that group expresses concerns about the possible costs of accepting help. Among their greatest needs, homeless teens report the following: a place to sleep, a job or job training, food, a place to shower, medical and dental care, and counseling. Street teens, in particular, want assistance without conditions. Considerable outreach will be required to deliver such services to homeless youth.

Although both groups find life on the streets harder than they expected, street teens have many more adverse experiences than do shelter teens. Street teens, to a greater extent than shelter teens, experience the death of friends, attempt to commit suicide, and have severe health problems (e.g., strep throat, bladder infection, anemia, malnutrition, venereal disease, stomach ulcer, hepatitis, and scabies). To obtain money, food, or a place to stay, many homeless adolescents are forced to use extreme measures for survival. Street teens—again, to a greater extent than sheltered teens—tend to take up panhandling, theft, sales of drugs, or prostitution; however, a substantial minority of shelter teens also beg, steal, or sell drugs.

Street teens tend to be more socially isolated than shelter teens—a difference that appears to precede the experience of homelessness. The majority of street teens report that they were loners when they attended school, compared with a small proportion of early isolates among shelter teens. Nevertheless, the psychological distress associated with homelessness is great, with no difference between street teens and shelter teens in the average level of distress.

The majority of street teens regularly use alcohol and illicit drugs, whereas among shelter teens the proportion is lower for alcohol and much lower for illicit drugs. Among substance abusers of either type, there are higher levels of psychological distress, more frequent health problems, and a greater number of attempted suicides.

The overwhelming majority of homeless youth are sexually active, with the rate of sexual activity slightly higher for the street teens. The majority of homeless youth are informed about the dangers associated with AIDS and other sexually transmitted diseases; they also have some knowledge of safe-sex practices. Yet many engage in unprotected sex. It appears that the daily problems of living on the street are so great that they overshadow concerns about the long-term health consequences of risky behaviors.

It also appears that the problems of homeless youth on their own are markedly different from those of homeless adults on their own and of homeless families with children. To date, the policy initiatives intended to reach this population at risk have been sporadic, poorly funded, insufficiently integrated with other efforts to assist the homeless, and not based on knowledge of the special characteristics of this high-risk group.

Sanford M. Dornbusch

See also Conduct Problems; Delinquency, Mental Health, and Substance Abuse Problems; Family Composition: Realities and Myths; Family Relations; Juvenile Crime; Programs for Adolescents; Rights of Adolescents; Risk Behaviors; Runaways; School Dropouts

References and further reading
Adams, G. R., T. Gulotta, and M. A. Clancy. 1985. "Homeless Adolescents: A Descriptive Study of Similarities and Differences between Runaways and Throwaways." *Adolescence* 20: 715–724.
Hagan, John, and Bill McCarthy. 1997. *Mean Streets: Youth Crime and Homelessness.* New York: Cambridge University Press.
Hutson, S., and M. Liddiard. 1994. *Youth Homelessness: The Construction of a Social Issue.* London: Macmillan.
U.S. Congress, Office of Technology Assessment. 1991. *Adolescent Health.* Vol. 1, *Summary and Policy Options,* OTA-H-468. Washington, DC: U.S. Government Printing Office.

Homework

Webster's New Riverside University Dictionary (1988) defines *homework* as follows: "1. work, as schoolwork or piecework, done at home; 2. preparatory or preliminary work." More informally, homework is an almost universal phenomenon for America's young people: It is work assigned to them at school to be done at home. Most students spend a considerable amount of time in school study hall and at home completing assignments to further their knowledge. In a recent survey of fourth- and eighth-grade students, nearly a quarter reported that they are given no homework assignments but more than half said that they spend up to two hours per night on homework (U.S. Department of Education, 1998).

Another study has uncovered differences in the amount of homework assigned in public and private schools. Forty-nine percent of public elementary school teachers reported that they assign more than an hour of homework a week, compared to almost 60 percent of private elementary school teachers (U.S. Department of Education, 1994–1995). Additionally, private school teachers are more likely than public school teachers to collect, correct, and return written homework assignments and to use them as a basis for grades.

But why do teachers assign homework at all? The answer is that homework further solidifies concepts and procedures introduced in class. Through practice and repetition, new knowledge becomes ingrained in a student's memory. Written assignments drive the student's thinking processes into new realms. Mathematics and science problems, in particular, force students to create and use problem-solving strategies; more generally, homework provides practice with writing, reading, keyboarding, and organizing and planning time.

Although some students may beg to differ, homework is good for the brain! Problem solving and engaging in higher-order thinking can forge and strengthen new connections in adolescents' brains. This growth through challenge and stimulation leads, in turn, to increased intellectual growth (Healy, 1994). It's no coincidence that the more academically oriented schools are, the more homework they assign.

Although homework is beneficial, it's not always easy—or fun. Fortunately, there are some strategies that teens can use to facilitate their homework time:

Homework is an almost universal phenomenon for America's young people: It is work assigned to them at school to be done at home. (Laura Dwight)

- *Pick a designated spot.* Knowing where you work best is important. It may be a quiet, secluded place (e.g., bedroom) or a more social area (e.g., kitchen). Some students may need to work outside of the home—for example, in school or at the town library. Choose a spot that works well for *you*, and then stick to the routine of using it.
- *Pick a designated time.* Making a schedule and keeping to it can help organize not only your time

but your entire life! Pick a "homework time" that fits your schedule, and consistently use that time for work and/or free reading.
- *Recognize your learning style.* Knowing *how* you learn can be critical to your academic success. For instance, do you absorb the most information when you experience material in a hands-on fashion? Understanding what your learning style is will help you determine what strategies you need to follow in order to be successful.
- *Manage your time well.* It's easy to waste time! If it is taking you

hours to complete an assignment that should be done more quickly, split the work into ten- or fifteen-minute segments and create short-term goals for yourself (such as writing one paragraph, reading two pages, or doing three math problems). In addition, take short breaks as needed—every thirty minutes, say. Doing so will foster your ability to stay on task and use your time well.

- *Get help, if needed.* It's the rare person who doesn't need help at some time or another. If you find that homework is overwhelming you or taking too much time, try talking to your teacher about getting either a professional tutor or a peer tutor. (Many schools have excellent peer tutoring networks.) Asking for help, far from being a sign of weakness, can make you a stronger student!

- *Focus on the process, not just the product.* The process of learning can be just as important as the final product. So be sure to focus on the process. How are you thinking through those math problems? When you're right, that's great, but what about those times when you came up with the wrong answer? What process did you use then? Focusing on the process highlights the importance of not rushing through work.

Further information on this topic is available at the Web sites for the U.S. Department of Education (http://www.ed.gov) and the National Center for Education Statistics (http://nces.ed.gov/index.html).

Elizabeth N. Fielding

See also Academic Achievement; Academic Self-Evaluation; Intelligence; School, Functions of; Standardized Tests; Teachers

References and further reading
Fielding, Elizabeth N. 1999. *Learning Differences in the Classroom.* Delaware: International Reading Association.
Healy, Jane M. 1994. *Your Child's Growing Mind: A Practical Guide to Brain Development and Learning from Birth to Adolescence.* New York: Doubleday.
Levine, Mel. 1994. *Educational Care: A System for Understanding and Helping Children with Learning Problems at Home and in School.* Cambridge, MA: Educators Publishing Service.
U.S. Department of Education. 1994–1995. *Teacher Follow-Up Survey, 1994–1995.* Washington, DC: National Center for Education Statistics.
———. 1998. *National Assessment of Educational Progress, Trends Almanac: Writing, 1984 to 1996.* Washington, DC: National Center for Education Statistics.
Webster's New Riverside University Dictionary. 1988. Boston: Houghton Mifflin.

I

Identity

Anyone who has an adolescent in the family or works with adolescents in schools, religious organizations, community centers, or youth organizations knows each and every youth is building a sense of identity. Teenagers need to explore, experience, and share ideas or thoughts with other teens and adults. They need to be introduced to the technology of their day, to explore the beliefs and ideologies involved in religions, politics, government, education, and other institutions of society. They need to have ideas of what it means to live in a democracy, understand personal responsibility, and be socialized in the basics of law and behavior. Teenagers need to be informed about the role of education and training within the economics of capitalism. They need to begin considering what career they wish to pursue, what training is necessary, what occupational identity they wish to select.

In *The Adolescent Experience*, Thomas Gullotta, Carol Markstrom, and the author of this entry have explored in depth the nature of adolescence and the role of identity during adolescence and young adulthood. The book describes the way identity development is at the very crux of the major developmental tasks of adolescence, and concludes that it is impossible to think of adolescence as a life stage without the concept of identity.

Identity provides a self-statement of who one is, what one stands for, and what one is becoming. It provides the structure of the self, from which basic commitments, directions, plans, and decisions are made.

The book presents adolescents as choosing between *searching* and *exploring* and *presence* and *absence of commitment* as ways of identity formation, and uses those terms to describe four identity states, a typology based on the writings of Erik H. Erikson and the research innovations of James Marcia. This typology assumes that society gives teenagers an extended period of time to search for, find, or select identity commitments, time, for example, to choose a career, select a political party to join, or accept a specific religion and its ideologies. Further, this period of searching for, discovering, or finding one's identity is thought to be supported by a *psychosocial moratorium* during which teens can experience a wide range of life, watch role models, read, experience different jobs, and the like, as part of the moratorium. In Germany and other European countries youth take a year to travel, live in hostels, work at part-time jobs, and meet a variety of people, as part of their psychosocial moratorium. In Germany this is called *wanderschaft*, and in other parts of the world it is called backpacking; in all cases, it is a period of time where youth are thought to be learning, exploring, finding things out about themselves, experimenting, and so forth. Of course, the length and degree of a teenager's psychosocial moratorium are determined by many factors, such as educational level of parents, socioeconomic supports, culture, and even gender. Some youth are supported by parents in taking a long moratorium, while others (especially teens from poor homes) may have a brief moratorium, if any at all. For the latter, the necessity of immediate employment may require taking the first available job in the neighborhood. For the former, the psychosocial moratorium might include unsupervised travel, extensive education and training, or periods of employment interspersed with periods of unemployment and parental support for culturally or socially enriching educational or travel experiences.

The four identity states that emerge during the psychosocial moratorium reflect the level or degree of searching, and the presence or absence of commitments to values, beliefs, vocations, and the like. If a youth is avoiding making a choice and remaining uncommitted and uninterested in establishing a firm sense of identity, he or she is known as *identity diffused*. The sense of self for diffused adolescents is fluid, shapeless, undirected, and wandering. These teens are often faddish, uninterested in and uncommitted to specific groups, and disaffiliated from peers. The next type includes adolescents who have not taken, or have not been given the opportunity to take, a psychosocial moratorium. Instead, they assume, without thought or consideration, the values, beliefs, attitudes, and intentions, of their parents or their parents' generation. The identity of these teens is referred to as *foreclosed*. Foreclosed identity offers some direction,

assumed by simple identifications with parental values, but the commitment is often weak and shallow because it hasn't been carefully inspected, just assumed. Foreclosed youth are obedient, compliant, and rule-conscious adolescents. They are easy to get along with, but they demonstrate little autonomy and independence in thought or behavior. Foreclosure works for teenagers until the values, beliefs, or choices are confronted and shown to be inadequate for the natural interests of the adolescent or a poor fit with the youth's generation. The remaining two forms of identity are related and are similar as to the level of experience in searching, discovery, and self-construction, but different in the level of commitment. The *moratorium* youth is experiencing the searching and discovery process of identity formation, but has not established commitments. Once these commitments are made the adolescent becomes *identity achieved*.

There is ample evidence to indicate that identity diffusion is the least desirable identity state. Identity-diffused adolescents avoid making important decisions, are prone to mindless peer influences, and are most likely to be depressed; they are not using their psychosocial moratorium to profit their own future self. Foreclosed adolescents are well behaved, conform to rules, and do well in high school. However, when foreclosed teens are challenged to consider all the alternatives to their own beliefs, values, or opinions, they demonstrate rigidity, authoritarianism, and constrained experience and action. Foreclosed adolescents are fragile and can be easily upset or disturbed when the environment doesn't support their own views.

Moratorium youth are in a constant search mode, always looking for new information and different ways of seeing or experiencing things. They tend to be anxious, most likely due to their constant searching and attempts to discover, which makes them vulnerable to receiving too much new information at one time. However, most moratorium youth will self-regulate the amount of information they will process at any given time. This form of identity is well suited for educational and training experiences where learning, exploring, discovering, and searching are central. Moratorium youth do less well in environments where they are given orders and expected to follow them without questioning. Often this is just the kind of environment that is found in most youth employment settings like fast food, retailing, and service jobs. Identity-achieved adolescents tend to have the most complex form of thinking processes, and have the best social skills and styles of personal interaction. These youth know what they want, where they are headed, what direction they have chosen for their life. They conform, when conformity is generally expected, but are nonconformists when conformity would contradict who they are as a person or who they need to be to accomplish their goals. Identity-achieved youth are guided by goals, values, and a sense of self that has been constructed by the use of information and experience during their psychosocial moratorium.

The value of a self-constructed identity that is achieved by searching for information, observing life, analyzing options, and engaging in a self-selected commitment to an identity is observed in the functions it provides a youth. In a theoretical treatise on identity formation, Sheila Marshall and the author of this entry have outlined the major functions of an achieved identity. These functions are strengths that accompany a well-constructed sense of self. The five most common and widely documented functions of identity include the following: (1) It provides a narrative or verbal structure about who one is and how one is to be viewed and understood; (2) it gives meaning and direction to one's life through the selected commitments, values, and personal goals; (3) it offers a sense of personal control, agency, and the feelings that accompany a free will to select and be whatever one wants to be; (4) it provides a coherent sense of self that is relatively consistent and stable, but always open to some change, and a sense of harmony; and (5) it enables one to recognize one's own potential through a sense of what the self offers for the future, other possibilities, and alternative choices. Essentially, when teenagers begin to develop a self-construction of their own identity they are creating self-regulatory strategies that operate to direct attention, filter or process information as it is discovered, and help the youth to manage their impressions by the selection of appropriate behaviors for their identity as presented to others.

There are at least two forms of identity, social and personal. Personal identity focuses on the acceptance, modification, and/or rejection of social and institutional ideologies. Aspects of faith, religion, philosophy of life, and ideologies of work and economic systems are part of the personal identity. Membership and affiliation are central to the other form of identity. A social identity depends on whom one is affiliated with, what the groups are that matter to the individual, and what the nature is of one's social relationships and connections. Adolescents and adults alike have a compelling need to enhance their sense of self as a unique and special person. This need or dynamic is most readily seen in personal identities that express themselves as different, special unto themselves, unique. However, we all also have a need to belong and matter to others, a need that finds fulfillment in the social identity, where one expresses one's sense of socially possible faces, voices, or relationship themes. Scholars often talk of social identity using terms like collective, role, interpersonal, cultural, or group identity. In adolescents the nature of social identity is readily seen in the choice of peer groups, extracurricular activities, and membership in community groups.

Certainly, as many scholars have pointed out, a healthy identity includes both a personal and a social form of identity and identification. There is, however, one caveat to note. Although parents, schools, work supervisors, coaches, teachers, and the like socialize and enhance a teenager's identity formation, the teenager's identity also shapes and changes the peers and adults who are making contributions to the youth's personal development. Identity formation is embedded in many social contexts, and as a teenager's identity unfolds it begins to shape others who are in her contexts. Living systems shape individuals, who in turn shape the nature of the living system. This dynamic helps to explain why parents change their parenting behaviors as their children grow and develop. All living things are shaped by others and, in turn, shape others.

Roy Baumeister completed a historical analysis of identity that reveals that societies provide different opportunities for different levels of choice in the construction of the self. Each new and dramatic change in history brings new opportunities for self-construction. Extrapolations

from his thoughts suggest that at one extreme, society might provide a social structure where identity could be assigned by lineage, gender, race, or other defining characteristics. This extreme could provide an environment of limited choice and the encouragement of primarily imitation and identification. Youth would need to passively accept what their society considered acceptable for their particular gender, social class, or racial heritage. In such a world there is little active self-construction, but rather a *passive form* of identity development. This world would value identity foreclosure. At another extreme, society may be constructed to demand choice, perhaps even require making many choices over one's lifetime. There could be so many choices that the teenager has to work hard to eliminate the unacceptable options. Clearly, this world would value the *active self-constructed forms* of identity (moratorium and identity achievement) that involve commitment, but also flexible responsiveness to circumstances demanding change or evolution in identity construction.

In the twenty-first century, we are closer to a society that demands choice than one that assigns identity. However, there are still certain constraints due to gender, poverty, and race. Fortunately, there is a constant form of pressure within democratic societies to push for open choice, equity, and self-selection. Many of the experiences of adolescence are designed to directly or indirectly facilitate the construction of a personal and social identity. Teenagers are often asked the following kinds of questions: Who are you? What do you want to do with your life? What kind of career do you want? What kind of education are you going to get? And much of the work of adolescence involves finding acceptable answers to such questions. However, there is one catch to all of this. The answers are best found through searching, selecting, and establishing commitments that are self-constructed. But the construction must fit the teenager's social context, so that crucial groups (e.g., parents) can affirm and support the choice. If the people who are important to a teenager offer support for the teenager's emerging personal and social identity, their support will help the teenager to confirm his sense of an emerging self. Without it he is likely to waver or retreat into role confusion or identity diffusion.

Parents and teachers have considerable influence on teenagers. Teachers who provide a supportive and engaging learning environment for adolescents facilitate growth in identity. Critical analysis of contemporary issues, analysis of historical events, examination of alternative views on a topic, and encouragement to strive harder and dig deeper into an issue or idea not only enhance learning but facilitate growth in identity formation. Parents who utilize democratic, expressive, and cohesive parenting styles facilitate identity development. Rejection, withdrawal, weak involvement, or lack of interest in the teenager diminishes positive identity formation.

Finally, the best thing adolescents can do for themselves to facilitate identity development is to remain open to experiences, explore and discover new ways of understanding others and themselves, and work to shape an environment to facilitate personal growth. Identity formation unfolds at crucial points where one must face one's self, deal with the self-consciousness that occurs when one sees who one is in contrast to who one

could be, and use appraisal and feedback from others to help forge a sense of self that includes values, goals, and commitment, the trinity of a healthy sense of identity.

Gerald R. Adams

See also African American Adolescents, Identity in; African American Male Adolescents; Asian American Adolescents: Comparisons and Contrasts; Asian American Adolescents: Issues Influencing Identity; Body Image; Chicana/o Adolescents; Ethnocentrism; Gay, Lesbian, Bisexual, and Sexual-Minority Youth; Gender Differences; Latina/o Adolescents; Native American Adolescents; Racial Discrimination; Self-Esteem; Sex Roles

References and further reading
Adams, Gerald R., and Sheila K. Marshall. 1996. "A Developmental Social Psychology of Identity: Understanding the Person-in-Context." *Journal of Adolescence* 19: 429–442.
Baumeister, Roy. 1986. *Identity: Cultural Change and the Struggle for Self.* New York: Oxford University Press.
Erikson, Erik H. 1968. *Identity: Youth and Crisis.* New York: Norton.
Gullotta, Thomas P., Gerald R. Adams, and Carol Markstrom. 2000. *The Adolescent Experience.* New York: Academic Press.
Marcia, James E. 1967. "Development and Validation of Ego-Identity Status." *Journal of Personality and Social Psychology* 3: 551–558.

Inhalants

Inhalants, also known as volatile substances or organic solvents, are a diverse class of drugs used by some adolescents to alter moods, feelings, and perceptions. Included in this class are such commonly available substances as adhesives (glue, special cements), aerosols (spray paint, hair spray, asthma spray), anesthetics (nitrous oxide), solvents (nail-polish

Inhalants are used primarily for recreational purposes or out of curiosity or peer pressure. (James Marshall/Corbis)

remover, paint remover, paint thinner), and gases (fuel gas, lighter gas). As the name suggests, these products are inhaled into the lungs. For example, they may be "sniffed" from an open container or plastic bag ("bagging"), "huffed" from a rag soaked in the substance ("toque"), or squirted directly into the mouth. Because inhalants are products intended for other purposes and are not meant for human consumption, they can be legally obtained at grocery, hardware, or auto supply stores. They also tend to be relatively inexpensive, making them attractive to adolescents and economically disadvantaged individuals.

Younger adolescents are the most common users of inhalants, although the number of young adult users is growing. Inhalant use peaks at age thirteen and then steadily declines. Use of inhalants, particularly aerosols and glues, has increased dramatically among American youth: The number of adolescents trying inhalants for the first time tripled from 1990 to 1995. In the past, males were more likely than females to use these substances; however, the gender gap is narrowing as more females begin to experiment with these drugs. The most frequent use of inhalants is observed among non-Hispanic white adolescents and Native American adolescents, followed by Hispanic adolescents; the least frequent use is associated with African American adolescents. At high risk for use are adolescents who live in areas, such as reservations and rural towns, where access to other mind-altering substances is limited.

Exclusive use of inhalants is rare; most adolescents who use them are likely to use other types of drugs as well, such as marijuana and alcohol. Considered "gateway drugs," inhalants are one of the first substances that adolescents use before moving on to other drugs. In fact, most adolescents who use inhalants do so only experimentally, eventually abandoning them in favor of other, often illegal drugs. Thus, inhalants are used infrequently and, even then, primarily for recreational purposes or out of curiosity or peer pressure. However, a small proportion of adolescents use inhalants chronically, over prolonged periods of time. It is these adolescents who may develop physical and psychological problems related to use.

Although inhalant use is not limited to any one socioeconomic level, adolescents from economically disadvantaged backgrounds are more likely than their peers to use inhalants because of the relatively low cost of these drugs. Moreover, inhalant users are likely to come from homes characterized by chaos, disorganization, parental alcoholism and drug abuse/dependence, parental aggression, and little family support and cohesion. Inhalant users themselves tend to do poorly in school, have low self-esteem, and exhibit elevated levels of aggression, depression, and antisocial personality disorder. These individuals are also likely to associate with inhalant-using peers and to have siblings who use these volatile substances. Finally, a strong relationship exists between inhalant use and juvenile delinquency: Adolescents who use inhalants are often involved in a variety of criminal activities including shoplifting, burglary, and attempted murder.

Inhalants vary widely in terms of their behavioral and physiological effects on individuals. In general, the intoxicating effects of these substances are similar to those obtained by alcohol but shorter-lived, necessitating repeated administration to sustain a prolonged "high." Intoxication includes initial excitation, followed by drowsiness, disinhibition, light-headedness, agitation, and, eventually, depression. Heavy users may experience hallucinations as well as distortions in their perceptions and sense of time. They are easily identified by a rash that develops around the nose and mouth ("glue sniffer's rash"), by the smell of paint or chemicals on their breath, skin, and clothes, and by discoloration from paint on the hands and the skin around the nose and mouth.

Most users do not understand the dangers of inhalants, falsely believing that these substances cause no physical harm. Yet even first-time users run the risk of neurological and physical complications. Although complications vary depending upon the specific substance inhaled, physical problems include damage to the brain, liver, kidney, and heart. Inhalant use has also been associated with sudden death ("sudden sniffer's death"), usually due to heart failure. Sudden death affects not just chronic users but also first-time users. In addition, because of the mind-altering effects of these drugs, inhalant users are prone to accidents such as suffocation (from the bag in which the inhalant is placed), car crashes, and serious falls, and may be in danger of physical or sexual assault.

Prolonged use of inhalants may result in "tolerance"; in other words, as use continues, increasingly larger doses of the substance are needed to produce the same initial effects. Moreover, when chronic users of inhalants cease use, they experience withdrawal symptoms that last for two to five days and include sleep disturbance, nausea, tremor, irritability, and abdominal and chest pains. Currently there is no proven treatment for chronic inhalant users; rather, because these individuals have multiple problems including the use of various drugs, emotional and psychological difficulties (such as depression), and family dysfunction, they are viewed as difficult to treat. Furthermore, neurological damage sustained from using volatile substances may complicate whatever treatment is attempted. As a result, the long-term outcomes for adolescents who have problems related to inhalant use are poor.

Alexandra Loukas

See also Drug Abuse Prevention; Health Promotion; Health Services for Adolescents; Substance Use and Abuse

References and further reading
Pandina, Robert, and Robert Hendren. 1999. "Other Drugs of Abuse: Inhalants, Designer Drugs, and Steroids." Pp. 171–184 in *Addictions: A Comprehensive Guidebook.* Edited by

Barbara S. McCrady and Elizabeth E. Epstein. New York: Oxford University Press.

Sharp, Charles William, Fred Beauvais, and Richard Spence, eds. 1992. *National Institute on Drug Abuse Research Monograph Series*, No. 129. *Inhalant Abuse: A Volatile Research Agenda.* Rockville, MD: National Institute on Drug Abuse.

Intelligence

Many people wonder what all the fuss is about regarding intelligence. Many individuals do not understand the concern about intelligence, IQ, and other qualities that are at the outset difficult to define. There seems to be a common need to know more about the nature of intelligence—to answer several questions that arise about it. In general, there is a fair amount of knowledge that has been generated about intelligence, but new questions arise frequently. The first question that professionals in the field want to answer is one that asks about the necessity of intelligence—what do we need it for?

Intelligence is an adaptive ability, which means that it enables one to adjust to the environment. Adjustment may mean changing oneself, or changing the environment to make it better satisfy one's needs. This brings up the issue that, although intelligence is a necessary tool, it may also be a serious weapon. That is, intelligence can also be used for war, destruction, and other acts aimed at harming others. But in its ability to change the environment, the adaptive nature of intelligence is clearly seen. The fact that this useful tool may also be used for the wrong purpose does not change its nature. It only indicates the complexity of the human psyche. Here, the notion of morality comes into play, and morality goes beyond the topic of the present discussion. The crucial point is that intelligence is something very basic, primary, and necessary; it is the quality that allows human beings to live and to develop, which may mean very different things, from finding a better way to breed cattle to finding a better way to get a good job.

The next issue is getting a clear definition of intelligence. Intelligence is usually thought of as a primary mental ability that allows one to solve problems in different areas of life. The origins of intelligence should be sought in actions. Making fire, using a sharp stone to cut a tree, or making a shelter to hide in or a trap for an animal—all those are manifestations of early human intelligence.

Swiss scholar Jean Piaget was one of the first who pointed out the operational nature of intelligence, that is, the way intelligence originates/is shaped by the very actions it guides. His theory pictures the long path that every child travels while developing this very complex ability. The first stage of this path involves sensory-motor intelligence, intelligence that develops through the senses and muscular movement. According to Piaget, with time, this ability becomes more and more complicated and elaborated and can be applied to more and more tasks and domains of life. This theory poses one very controversial question that has bothered scholars for a considerable amount of time and still is not resolved. The question has to do with whether intelligence is a sole, general ability, or a complex set of skills, functions of different modules of mind. There are two approaches in contemporary psychological science that propose different answers to this question.

One theory is based on the simple observation that if an individual is "smart," he is able to do well in school on many subjects, as well as to make his way through city streets, learn a new computer program, and make sense of a movie or a deep book. This approach defines intelligence as a general mental faculty whose powers may be applied to a multitude of tasks.

On the other hand, if one observes different people in different situations, one finds that an individual who is very good at math is not necessarily also exceptionally able to understand people's behaviors and motives. In addition, the fact that someone is a good musician does not imply that she should be expected to speak several foreign languages or write poetry. To account for these observations, the idea of modularity of mind was proposed, and this is the second approach to human intelligence, or rather, in its own terms, to human intelligences. To put it simply, the theory says that the mind may be represented as a set of modules, each of which is responsible for operations in one particular domain. The idea was proposed some time ago, and today is most clearly expressed in Howard Gardner's Multiple Intelligences (MI) theory.

In his view, every human being possesses all the following kinds of intelligence:

- Linguistic intelligence, which operates in the domain of language
- Musical intelligence, which manifests itself when one performs, listens to, or composes music
- Logico-mathematical intelligence, which is applicable to reasoning in mathematics and other sciences, where the relations between objects and concepts are usually invariant, straightforward, and logical

Intelligence is reflected in problem solving and other mental activities. (Laura Dwight)

- Spatial, or visual-spatial intelligence, which allows one "to perceive the visual world accurately, to perform transformations and modifications upon one's initial perceptions, and to be able to recreate the aspects of one's visual experience, even in the absence of the visual stimuli" (Gardner, 1993, 173)
- Bodily-kinesthetic intelligence, which manifests itself in athletic achievements and dance
- The personal intelligences, which may be divided into interpersonal intelligence, which enables one to

understand other peoples' thoughts, feelings, and motives; and intra-personal intelligence, which enables one to understand oneself

Gardner's theory is strongly supported by empirical evidence, and one of the most convincing arguments in its favor is the existence of prodigies—people, including children, who are extremely talented in one particular domain, such as playing chess, or performing music, but do not exhibit equal progress in other domains. This phenomenon is difficult to explain from the viewpoint that argues that intelligence is one unified mental faculty. On the other hand, the main fact that the proponents of general intelligence use—that an ordinary intelligent person is usually good at many life tasks—does not really contradict the MI theory. It may be explained by the fact that the level of intelligence (including any of the intelligences) individuals achieve depends heavily on the opportunities to develop they have as children, on their environment, and on training. So, one could say that a person who shows intelligence in many areas simply had experiences that allowed her to develop the full range of her different mental abilities.

Some professionals would not find this argument convincing. Some would offer other arguments, both for and against MI theory. The debates are still alive, and it may very well be possible that both approaches are right, at least to a certain extent, and that the final word in the debate is yet to be said. One way of summing up the current state of the field is that normal achievements seem to be well explained by the general intelligence proponents, but that the highest peaks of human thought usually seem to fall in one particular area.

What is promising about the idea of multiple intelligences is that it gives hope to people who would consider themselves unintelligent, or at least not smart enough, just because they are not good at math or cannot learn a foreign language. They may be good music performers, or good football players, or just very good friends (which presupposes interpersonal intelligence, reflected in their ability to understand their friends' needs and states of mind). Thus, the fact that in American culture the knowledge of central academic subjects such as math and the sciences is considered of main importance should not obscure the fact that there are other cultures (say, oral ones, where math does not really exist in the form it does here and where the wisdom of the tribal leaders has nothing to do with the ability to read and write) and other domains (say, music or poetry) that are important, too, and that require a certain level of a given intelligence.

Typical IQ tests predict school achievement, yet it is common knowledge that, although school achievement is definitely related to intelligence, it does not necessarily predict success in life. IQ tests measure the ability to perform certain types of operations, usually in the domains covered by formal school subjects. In addition, performance on standard IQ tests depends heavily on reading ability, since the test is usually given in the paper-pencil format. Also (and this is true about most types of tests), good results may indicate simply that a given person was trained for this particular test. It is possible to train a person to take an IQ test, just as many students are trained to take the SAT. This idea is related to one more claim that even IQ test proponents would not argue against: The test measures the current level of whatever it measures and says nothing of the speed at which the tested person has arrived at this level or the speed at which he probably would move further, to the next intellectual achievement.

A popular misunderstanding about intelligence is that IQ testing can assess it with complete accuracy. To say that this is a misunderstanding is not to deny that IQ testing is useful; it is simply to point out that it has its limitations, and these limitations should be stated and understood. Another myth is that intelligence is fully genetically determined, a belief that means seeing the intelligence one is born with as a kind of destiny and leaving very little room for one's own efforts to improve. Again, as in the case of IQ, to say that this belief is a myth is of course not to deny the genetic basis of intelligence, as well as of many other properties of the human psyche. Research indicates that one's genetic heritage may be responsible for a portion of one's intellectual achievement. Nevertheless, heredity is not everything, and it would clearly be a mistake to believe that one can simply rely on the intelligence one has inherited and need put no effort into developing one's mind, or, on the other hand, that the level of intelligence one has inherited is the limit beyond which one is unable to move, and effort is hopeless.

An even more erroneous claim is to state that some races and cultures are inherently less intelligent than others, because their living conditions (recall that intelligence functions for survival value) have not led them to the invention of planes and computers. Heredity may determine predisposition to a certain extent, but how intelligence will be used is a matter of environment, culture, and training. A child with a gift of poetry would not know about it if she were raised in a village where everyone was mute. And very modest inborn abilities, when well cultivated, may lead to a very impressive intelligence level.

Many individuals want to know what can be done to improve their intelligence level. There is one general solution to this problem: training. To develop intelligence, one needs to train oneself to solve problems and complete tasks in a given field.

Although training is popularly believed to develop only skills, it also builds intelligence itself. For example, in learning how to do a particular arm movement (say, in sports), one actually does three things: one learns this task, one strengthens the muscles, and one develops the area of the brain responsible for managing arm movements. In the same way, when one solves a math problem, one trains the chains of neurons that are used in this process. After the same chains have fired several times, they will react faster, as well as better—meaning that the right chains will fire. The solution will then be reached in less time, with less possibility of error. In sum, intelligence is an important adaptive characteristic of humans. It is crucial that adolescents understand this potential for growth if they are to make the best possible use of education.

Janna Jilnina

See also Academic Achievement; Academic Self-Evaluation; Cognitive Development; Developmental Assets; Homework; Intelligence Tests; Learning Disabilities; Learning Styles and Accommodations; Memory; Standardized Tests; Thinking

References and further reading
Case, Robbie. 1985. *Intellectual Development: Birth to Adulthood.* New York: Academic Press.

Gardner, Howard. 1983. *Frames of Mind: The Theory of Multiple Intelligences.* New York: Basic Books.

Piaget, Jean, and Barbel Inhelder. 1969. *The Psychology of the Child.* New York: Basic Books.

Sternberg, Robert, ed. 1992. *Intellectual Development.* Cambridge, New York: Cambridge University Press.

Intelligence Tests

Intelligence tests—also known as IQ (intelligence quotient) tests—measure skills such as verbal expression, abstract reasoning, numerical achievement, memory, and visual-motor abilities, all of which are related to school learning. Intelligence tests were developed in the late nineteenth century by pioneers in the field of mental retardation who were concerned about societal mistreatment of mentally retarded individuals. The goal of these pioneers was to develop a cure for retardation—but they first had to identify appropriate procedures for diagnosis. Today, intelligence tests are still used in assessing mental retardation, but their main purpose is to identify ways to help children learn better in school. Unfortunately, there has been much misunderstanding about the skills measured by intelligence tests, and the tests themselves have sometimes been misused.

The most widely used intelligence tests in use today are the Wechsler scales. A version exists for preschoolers (Wechsler Preschool and Primary Scale of Intelligence—Revised/WPPSI-R), for school-aged children five to sixteen years old (Wechsler Intelligence Scale for Children—Third Edition/WISC-III), and for adults sixteen and older (Wechsler Adult Intelligence Scale—Third Edition/WAIS-III). All three Wechsler scales provide a total or Full Scale score, a Verbal IQ score (which assesses skills such as word knowledge, numerical reasoning, and social reasoning), and a Performance IQ score (which assesses spatial skills, visual motor skills, and nonverbal problem solving through puzzles). The average score for each scale is 100; scores above 100 are above average and those below 100 are below average. As with all tests, no score is perfectly accurate. Accordingly, test scores should always be reported as occurring within a range (e.g., "The true score is likely to fall between 90 and 105"). How well individuals perform in any test administration depends not only on what they know but also on their interest, motivation, and level of comfort in the testing situation. Research indicates that scores on the WISC-III correlate with scores on academic achievement tests and with grades in school.

The use of intelligence tests has been highly controversial at times, for reasons having to do with differences in average scores and in the percentages of children labeled as mentally retarded among diverse ethnic and minority groups. African American and Latino children, for example, receive lower scores than white youth. A number of explanations have been suggested to account for group differences in test performance, including the effects of poverty and racism as well as cultural bias in both test content and testing conditions.

One of the most damaging interpretations of these group differences stems from a misunderstanding of what is measured by IQ tests. Intelligence tests measure skills developed through learning experiences at home, at school, and in the community. In this sense, they are measures of achievement and, as such, reflect a combination of experience and ability. They are *not* measures of pure ability or innate potential. Some psychologists have suggested that they should be called achievement tests instead of intelligence tests to more accurately reflect their content.

This content, which includes questions that test vocabulary and memory for facts related to science and social studies, clearly reflects the culture and school curricula of mainstream America. Children who have had considerable exposure to such content are likely to do well, but those with less exposure may be unfairly disadvantaged. Thus, it is impossible to draw conclusions about the innate ability of any individual or group of people based upon their test scores. The assumption that such conclusions *could* be drawn has contributed to stigmatization of persons with low scores as innately inferior.

During the 1960s and early 1970s, Spanish-speaking children took IQ tests written in English and were labeled as mentally retarded when they achieved poorly. The abuse of testing under these conditions is obvious. Federal legislation (Public Law 94-142) passed in 1975 mandated that either IQ tests must be administered in the child's native language or a nonlinguistic means of assessment must be used.

Another cultural bias in assessment is perhaps less apparent: The original authors of intelligence tests were from European and North American cultures, and the content of the tests still reflects the values of those cultures. The IQ test performance of children, adolescents, and adults who have been exposed to cultural experiences that differ from common North American and European practices are affected as a result. Critics have pointed out numerous cultural biases in our educational systems and methods of assessment that do not appreciate or value the styles of learning practiced in

Intelligence tests may be used to identify ways in which children's abilities differ. (Skjold Photographs)

other parts of the world. Competing with others is one example of a style valued in Europe and North America that is not highly valued in non-Western cultures. Thus, non-Western students may perform poorly on a commonly used intelligence test despite possessing a wealth of knowledge and understanding that stems from their own cultural traditions but is not assessed by the IQ test.

Researchers have also discovered that children who grow up in families with more economic resources, whose parents are more educated, and who attend more affluent schools also tend to score higher on intelligence tests. Although this finding is understandable, inasmuch as economic advantages can increase opportunities for learning, the great concern is that test scores not be used to discriminate against children and adolescents who are economically disadvantaged. If children from lower-income families do not get admitted to good schools or are placed in less challenging classes as a result of low test scores, the economic disadvantages they experience will be compounded by inferior educational opportunities.

Just as intelligence test scores are influenced by a number of factors, the meaning of any individual's test score and how well that score will predict further achievement depend on multiple factors including test motivation and prior exposure to the content and skills assessed by the test. However, currently available IQ tests do not assess skills in many areas that are critical to success in life, such as leadership, interpersonal skills, creativity, and physical prowess, among others. Robert Sternberg (1985) and Howard Gardner (1983) have sought to develop assessments of intelligence that measure a wider variety of skills and talents important to life success. Moreover, significant gains in scores can be achieved when individuals are provided with new learning opportunities. In educational settings, the purpose of intelligence testing is to help children become more successful in school. Unfortunately, intelligence testing does not always contribute to this goal.

Maureen E. Kenny

See also Academic Achievement; Academic Self-Evaluation; Intelligence; Standardized Tests

References and further reading
Gardner, Howard. 1983. *Frames of Mind: The Theory of Multiple Intelligences.* New York: Basic Books.
Helms, Janet E. 1992. "Why Is There No Study of Cultural Equivalence in Standardized Cognitive Ability Tests?" *American Psychologist* 49, no. 7: 1038–1101.
Kamphaus, Randy W. 1993. *Clinical Assessment of Children's Intelligence.* Boston: Allyn and Bacon.
Miller-Jones, Dalton. 1989. "Culture and Testing." *American Psychologist* 44, no. 2: 360–366.
Reschly, David. 1981. "Psychological Testing in Educational Classification and Placement." *American Psychologist* 36, no. 10: 1094–1102.
Sternberg, Robert. 1985. *Beyond IQ—The Triarchic Theory.* New York: Cambridge University Press.
Weinberg, Richard A. 1989. "Intelligence and IQ: Landmark Issues and Great Debates." *American Psychologist* 44, no. 2: 98–104.

Intervention Programs for Adolescents

Intervention programs for youth are planned, systematic attempts to (1) *ameliorate* the presence of emotional, behavioral, and social problems; (2) *prevent* such problems from occurring; and (3) *promote* positive, healthy behaviors among young people. The key attributes of positive youth development can be described by "five C's": competence, confidence, character, connection, and caring/compassion (Lerner, Fisher, and Weinberg, 2000). Programs that seek to develop these attributes of positive development in young people constitute attempts to optimize the lives of individuals by building up their strengths. In addition, such programs reflect an abiding concern for the well-being of youth: They are committed to going beyond traditional intervention strategies—such as remediation, alleviation, or prevention of problems—to emphasize skill and competency development (Roth et al., 1998).

In regard to all three types of programs—problem reduction, problem prevention, and positive development promotion—the work undertaken constitutes attempts to *intervene* in the course of a person's development in order to change that person's life for the better. Some intervention programs are conducted by professionals trained to use particular methods (e.g., psychotherapy, group interactions); others are presented to youth through community-based clubs or organizations (e.g., YMCA, 4-H, Boys and Girls Clubs, Boy Scouts and Girl Scouts).

Focal Issues of Youth Programs
The behaviors targeted by youth programs fall into two categories: "external" problems such as alcohol use and abuse, conduct disorders, social-skill deficits, delinquency, and violence and "internal" problems such as depression, anxiety, anger, and suicide. Programs that specifically seek to promote positive development may include efforts that, on the one hand, focus on adolescents' social relationships (with parents and peers) and, on the other, enhance cognitive development or self-esteem.

An excellent example of a program aimed at promoting positive youth development is the National 4-H Council, America's largest youth-serving organization. In every county of every state in the United States, 4-H organizations are building community-based partnerships to serve youth. In fact, the National 4-H Council envisions a renewed society in which youth and adults take action together as equal partners. Toward this end the council has created partnerships with corporations, foundations, the Cooperative Extension Service (CES), and others to bring together resources for meeting the needs of young people. These partnerships and resources include training, developing curricula, offering technical assistance, and conducting youth forums and seminars.

In the early 1900s, 4-H programs were established throughout the country in an attempt to provide a better agricultural education for young people. Most states organized boys and girls clubs outside of schools, with parents serving as volunteer leaders and CES agents providing appropriate educational materials.

Through the years, the overall objective of 4-H programs has remained the same: development of youth as responsible and productive citizens. 4-H serves youth through a variety of methods including community service activities, organized clubs, school enrichment programs, and instructional television. Universally recognized by its four-leaf clover emblem, representing head, heart, hands, and health, 4-H conducts such programs in 3,150 counties of the United States, the District of Columbia, Puerto Rico, Virgin Islands, Guam, American Samoa, Micronesia, and the Northern Mariana Islands.

The "alumni" of 4-H total about 45 million people, and more than 5.4 million youth currently participate in its programs. Fifty-two percent of these 4-H youth live in towns and cities with populations between 10,000 and 50,000-plus; 26 percent are minorities. 4-H reaches out to young people from all ideological and demographic backgrounds and designs its programs to respond to the needs of local youth.

The National 4-H Council believes that if today's youth are to survive and prosper, all of society must support them, engage them in civic life, and help them develop the necessary life skills to meet the challenges they face. Accordingly, the diverse programs supported by the National 4-H Council and by 4-H organizations throughout the United States represent a collaborative opportunity that has had a vast impact on America.

There are, of course, other youth programs as well. Jodie Roth and her colleagues (1998) estimate that more than 17,500 programs in the United States are aimed at either preventing youth problems or promoting the positive development of young people. Regardless of their individual objectives, however, all such programs need to focus on three key issues: effectiveness, scale, and sustainability.

Program Effectiveness. The purpose of some programs is to reduce youth violence. Others aim to prevent unsafe sexual behaviors. Still others are designed to enhance self-esteem among adolescents. But do these programs actually achieve what they intend to achieve? If so, they are deemed to be *effective.*

Procedures known as *evaluations* are used in an attempt to ascertain whether any changes youth experience over the course of their participation in a program are due to the program itself rather than to extraneous factors. Evaluations aimed at proving that a program is effective are often termed "outcome" or "summative" evaluations.

One function of such evaluations is to *improve* the quality of the program as it is being conducted. For example, an evaluator may consider implementing certain mid-course corrections in an attempt to improve a program's efforts at promoting self-esteem or preventing violence. Evaluations that seek to improve programs are sometimes called "formative" evaluations. Because they aim to

enhance the process through which a program provides its services, they may also be termed "process" evaluations.

Another function of program evaluations is to *empower* both the youth participating in the program and the people delivering it. Indeed, a key goal of evaluators of contemporary youth programs—especially those located in communities, and begun and continued through the efforts of community members (as opposed to trained professionals such as psychologists, social workers, nurses, and physicians)—is to increase the community members' ability to both improve the programs and prove their effectiveness. Enactment of these "empowerment" evaluations is seen as critical if the community is to succeed in using evidence of program effectiveness to bring programs to all the youth who need them and to maintain the programs over time.

Program Scale. The characteristics of effective youth programs are generally well understood. Researchers know how to prove that programs are effective, how to improve the quality of programs as they are being conducted, and how to empower communities through evaluation. However, even those programs known to be effective may not be reaching all the youth for whom they are intended—and for whom they could have positive benefits. This a problem of program *scale.* The challenge is to determine the number of youth who would be appropriate for a given program. Consider, for instance, a YMCA modern dance program that involves a dozen youth. Would greater skill attainment be ensured if the maximum number of participants were decreased to eight—or increased to twenty?

Another scale-related issue concerns the possibility that more people could benefit from a particular program. Consider, for instance, a program that sends visitors to the homes of adolescent mothers to help improve their skills as parents. This program is known to be effective, but only 50 percent of eligible youth are participating in it. The challenge here is to determine what psychological, social, economic, or political reasons are preventing the other 50 percent from becoming involved in the program. Alternatively, let's say that there are known economic reasons for which certain adolescent mothers are being kept out of home visiting programs (e.g., they have to work and are not available when the program is offered). In this case, the challenge would be to change the social system in such a way as to enable the program to be brought to scale (e.g., by developing labor law policies regarding flexible working hours or time off from work for program participation).

Program Sustainability. There is even more to learn about program *sustainability*. A sustained program is one that is maintained over time. Unfortunately, however, most youth programs—especially community-based ones—are short-lived. Some of these programs are initiated through "start-up" grants provided by government agencies or private philanthropic foundations; others are initiated by university faculty members who have obtained grants to demonstrate the effectiveness of the interventions they have devised. In either case, after the start-up funds have run out or the demonstration project is completed, the program usually ends. This lack of sustainability affects even programs that have been proven through evaluations to be effective.

Key Features of Effective Youth Programs

As noted, youth programs vary in numerous ways—in terms of their emphasis on problem reduction or prevention or their attempts to promote positive development, in terms of their focus on the individual versus his or her relationships, and, finally, in terms of their approach to the issues of effectiveness, scale, and sustainability. These dimensions of difference add up to a complex picture of contemporary youth programs.

Simplifying the picture somewhat is the knowledge that has been gained about the characteristics that define effective youth programs. Indeed, it is possible to provide an overview of the ideal features—the *best practices*—of such programs. These features include coordinated attention to each youth's personal characteristics and social context. Accordingly, programs that are effective in promoting positive youth development

1. are predicated on a vision of positive youth development (e.g., the "five C's" of positive youth development) and have clear goals;
2. focus on the assets of youth and on the importance of their participation in every facet of the programs—including their design, conduct, and evaluation;
3. pay attention to the diversity of youth and of their family, community, and cultural contexts (both the strengths and the needs of youth need to be of central concern);
4. ensure the accessibility of a safe space in which youth can use their time constructively;
5. in recognition of the interrelated challenges facing youth, integrate

the assets for positive youth development that exist within the community (including collaborations or partnerships among youth-serving organizations as well as contributions by families, peers, and schools);

6. provide broad, sustained, and integrated services to youth and a "seamless" social support system across the community;

7. in recognition of the importance of caring adult-youth relations in healthy adolescent development, provide training to adult leaders that involves, for instance, enhancing sensitivity to diversity and learning about the principles of positive youth development;

8. are committed to program evaluation and to strengthening the use of research in the design, delivery, and evaluation of the programs (the role of university-community partnerships is important here); and, finally,

9. advocate for youth.

Regarding this last point, although youth programs should not be partisan, they do need to provide a clear voice to policymakers across the political spectrum about the importance of investing in positive youth development.

Conclusions about Effective Youth Programs

There is reason to be optimistic about the success of youth programs if they continue to be designed on the basis of the multiple, interrelated challenges facing youth. A coordinated set of community-based programs, aimed at both individuals and their contexts, is indeed

required for success. But these programs also have to begin as early as possible and be maintained throughout their participants' adolescent years.

Clearly, then, means must be found to capitalize on the potentials and strengths of all youth and, by meeting their developmental needs, promote their positive development. Toward this end, the resources of society must be marshaled in the service of designing programs consistent with this vision for young people, and scholars of youth development must engage the support of public policymakers.

Young people themselves can also play a significant role in such community-based efforts.

How Adolescents Can Collaborate with Youth Development Organizations

Indeed, there are numerous ways in which adolescents can become involved in youth development organizations that are open to collaborative efforts (e.g., 4-H programs, scholarly organizations such as the Society for Research in Adolescence and the American Psychological Association, nongovernmental and community-based organizations such as Big Brothers/Big Sisters and the YMCA/YWCA, and selected programs in governmental organizations such as the Department of Housing and Urban Development or the Department of Education). If they are interested in collaborating with 4-H, for example, they can contact the office of the 4-H program in their county (usually located at the site of the public, land-grant university in each state in the nation) or the National 4-H Council in Chevy Chase, Maryland. Alternatively, they can direct their inquiries to the Cooperative Extension Service. CES offices can be found in almost every county in the nation, and every state has a CES director who can provide information about volunteering and other forms of collaboration.

Resources for community involvement and service can also be found in many high schools and colleges. For instance, students can become involved in opportunities to integrate the information they are learning in classes with opportunities for community service organized by their university.

Such *service learning* can take many forms. For instance, students can volunteer at community "hot lines" that provide services to youth through telephone referrals or work at their local 4-H club or county CES office. They can also serve as *mentors* to younger persons. An interesting example is "One to One," a program associated with the National Mentoring Partnership that focuses on the needs of mentored participants. Youth programs of this type foster caring and supportive relationships, encourage young people to develop to their fullest potential, help them create a vision for the future, and provide a means through which they can collaborate in the promotion of positive youth development.

Richard M. Lerner

See also Career Development; Counseling; Drug Abuse Prevention; Health Promotion; Health Services for Adolescents; Juvenile Justice System; Learning Styles and Accommodations; Pregnancy, Interventions to Prevent; Programs for Adolescents; Services for Adolescents; Sex Education

References and further reading
Benson, Peter. 1997. *All Kids Are Our Kids: What Communities Must Do to Raise Caring and Responsible Children and Adolescents.* San Francisco: Jossey-Bass.
Damon, William. 1997. *The Youth Charter: How Communities Can Work Together to Raise Standards for All Our Children.* New York: Free Press.
Dryfoos, Joy G. 1990. *Adolescents at Risk: Prevalence and Prevention.* New York: Oxford University Press.
Fetterman, David M., Shakeh J. Kaftarian, and Abraham Wandersman, eds. 1996. *Empowerment Evaluation: Knowledge and Tools for Self-Assessment and Accountability.* Thousand Oaks, CA: Sage.
Jacobs, Fran. 1988. "The Five-Tiered Approach to Evaluation: Context and Implementation." Pp. 37–68 in *Evaluating Family Programs.* Edited by H. B. Weiss and F. Jacobs. Hawthorne, NY: Aldine.
Lerner, Richard M. In press. *Adolescence: Development, Diversity, Context, and Application.* Upper Saddle River, NJ: Prentice-Hall.
Lerner, Richard M., Celia B. Fisher, and Richard A. Weinberg. 2000. "Toward a Science for and of the People: Promoting Civil Society through the Application of Developmental Science." *Child Development* 71: 11–20.
Lerner, Richard M., and Nancy L. Galambos. 1998. "Adolescent Development: Challenges and Opportunities for Research, Programs, and Policies." *Annual Review of Psychology* 49: 413–446.
Roth, Jodie, Jeanne Brooks-Gunn, Lawrence Murray, and William Foster. 1998. "Promoting Healthy Adolescents: Synthesis of Youth Development Program Evaluations." *Journal of Research on Adolescence* 8: 423–459.
Schorr, Lee B. 1988. *Within Our Reach: Breaking the Cycle of Disadvantage.* New York: Doubleday.

J

Juvenile Crime

Juvenile crime is defined as an unlawful act committed by a person under the age of eighteen. The most recent official records, compiled in 1997, reveal that 2.8 million juveniles were arrested for crimes committed over a one-year period. This rate is slightly lower than that in the previous year. During the last two decades overall, however, the juvenile crime rate has been at its highest level. Juveniles commit a variety of crimes. Some types of crimes are more likely to be committed by juveniles than other types of crimes. Juvenile crime rates vary by age and gender. In addition to committing crimes, juveniles are often victims of crimes.

Juvenile crime is differentiated from adult crime by the age of the offender; by definition, it refers to a crime committed by an individual younger than eighteen. In addition, juvenile crime carries different penalties than adult crime. Juveniles who commit offenses are reported to the juvenile justice system, whereas adults are referred to the adult penal system. States vary somewhat, but in general the goals of the juvenile justice system are both prevention and punishment. By contrast, the goals of the adult penal system tend to be more focused on punishment than on rehabilitation.

In a recent one-year period (1997), 19 percent of all arrests were arrests of juveniles. In other words, approximately one in five of all arrests involved a juvenile. These numbers vary by state and county as well as by urban versus rural areas. On average, the largest number of juvenile arrests for crimes occur in large urban cities.

Crimes are often subdivided into categories, three of which are violent crimes, property crimes, and nonindex crimes. Violent crimes are crimes that have the potential to seriously harm an individual; they include murder, rape, robbery, and assault. Property crimes are crimes against property and include burglary, theft, and arson. And nonindex crimes are all other types of crimes including fraud, carrying or possessing a weapon, sex offenses, running away, and drug abuse violations.

The percentages of crimes committed by juveniles vary by type of crime. Specifically, juveniles commit 17 percent of all violent crimes and 35 percent of all property crimes known to officials, 50 percent of all arson cases, between 25 percent and 45 percent of all vandalism, motor vehicle theft, burglary, theft, robbery, disorderly conduct, and stolen property crimes, and approximately 12 percent of all murders. Recent official records also show that juveniles are more likely to commit some crimes than others. For example, more than 40 percent of all juvenile arrests

A staff member sorts the wreckage at a vandalized recreation center. (Urban Archives, Philadelphia)

occur in one of the following four categories: theft, simple assault, drug abuse, or disorderly conduct. In addition, juveniles are more likely to commit property crimes than violent crimes. Only a small number of juvenile arrests are for murder, rape, forgery, embezzlement, prostitution, gambling, or vagrancy.

Official records are used to determine juvenile crime rates, but such records reflect only the number of juvenile crimes reported to the police or other authorities. Thus, since many juvenile crimes are not known to police and not included in official records, the number of juvenile crimes is probably well over the 2.8 million noted earlier. Indeed, when a group of arrested juveniles was asked whether they had committed crimes that they were not arrested for,

many of the youth replied that this was in fact the case.

Juvenile crimes are typically committed by groups of juveniles rather than by individuals acting alone. Specifically, records show that, in a majority of cases, juveniles commit crimes in groups of two or more. Some, but not all, of these crimes are committed by juvenile gangs. Crimes committed in groups occur in both urban and rural areas.

Many juveniles who commit crimes are arrested just once. Indeed, 54 percent of male and 73 percent of female first-time offenders are never arrested again. Other juveniles, however, are arrested for subsequent crimes. These juveniles are referred to as chronic or repeat offenders. In general, chronic offenders are arrested for committing various types of crimes rather than for committing the same type of crime repeatedly. Moreover, chronic offenders commit the majority of juvenile crimes. Thus, it can be concluded that the majority of juvenile crimes are committed by a small number of juveniles.

Recent official records also reveal that, on school days, juvenile crimes are most likely to occur in the hours following school (between 3 and 6 P.M.), whereas on nonschool days they are most likely to take place in the evening. In short, juvenile crimes are unequally dispersed throughout the day.

Juvenile crimes are committed at different rates by male and female offenders. Although the number of crimes committed by females has increased in the last two decades, males overall commit considerably more crimes than females. Specifically, of the 2.8 million juvenile arrests officially recorded in 1997, 26 percent of these were for crimes committed by females. In other words, juvenile males committed almost three-fourths of all juvenile crimes in that year. Except for prostitution and running away, juvenile males are more likely to be arrested for all types of crimes. For example, male juvenile offenders commit five times more violent crimes and two times more property crimes than female juvenile offenders.

Juvenile crime rates also vary by age. About 90 percent of all juvenile crimes are committed by juveniles between the ages of thirteen and seventeen, compared to less than 10 percent among juveniles twelve and younger. Crimes committed by very young children are rare.

Analysis of juvenile crime rates over several decades reveals that the highest rates of juvenile crime occurred in the 1980s and early 1990s. Specifically, whereas property crime arrest rates remained relatively stable over the past two decades, violent crime arrest rates increased and then only recently began to decline.

Juvenile crime is staggeringly expensive for society. One youth who commits one to four crimes a year over a four-year period (the average "career" length of a chronic juvenile offender) costs crime victims between $62,000 and $250,000. And depending on the type of juvenile justice that intervenes, the court and corrections costs incurred by this youth average between $21,000 and $84,000. These totals are even higher when the costs associated with drug abuse and dropping out of school are taken into account.

Juveniles themselves are often victims of crime. Two age groups in particular—young adults eighteen to twenty-four years old and youths younger than eighteen—are at the greatest risk of being victims of serious violent crimes. Twenty percent of all serious violent crimes, 12 percent of all property crimes, and 26 percent of simple assaults are committed against juveniles twelve to seventeen years old. Furthermore, murder is one of the five leading causes of juvenile death. (The juvenile murder rate is considerably higher in the United States than in other industrialized countries.) Juvenile victimizations are most likely to occur in the daytime, between noon and 6 P.M. Many juveniles know their assailants but do not report crimes committed by their peers.

The rate of school crime has remained approximately the same for several years. The most common type of crime committed at school is theft. Males between the ages of twelve and fourteen are at the greatest risk of being victims of school crime. And although theft crimes occur at equal rates in urban and rural schools, urban schools experience higher rates of violent crimes. Overall, violent deaths at school are very rare.

Leanne J. Jacobson

See also Aggression; Disorders, Psychological and Social; Homeless Youth; Runaways; Youth Gangs

References and further reading
Snyder, Howard N., and Melissa Sickmund. 1995. *Juvenile Offenders and Victims: A National Report.* Washington, DC: Office of Juvenile Justice and Delinquency Prevention.
———. 1999. *Juvenile Offenders and Victims: 1999 National Report.* Washington, DC: Office of Juvenile Justice and Delinquency Prevention.

Juvenile Justice System

The juvenile justice system comprises a network of courts, agencies, and organizations that process youth who have been charged with violating a law. The juvenile justice system is premised on the idea that children should be treated differently from adults because children are somewhat less responsible for their actions and are in need of protection. In 1998 alone, according to the National Center for Juvenile Justice (2000), 2,603,300 youths passed through at least one of the multiple layers of this complex system. Given this large number of youth and the billions of dollars being spent on juvenile crime, it is imperative that we understand the history of this specialized court, the way it functions, the current trends that are emerging as a result of a changing society.

Developed in Chicago in 1899, the first juvenile court was specifically designed to process youth between the ages of eight and seventeen. The fundamental principle of this juvenile court was that the state would become the guardian of the child, making the child a ward of the state to receive whatever services the state had to offer. This principle differed from that underlying the adult criminal court. The juvenile court was originally intended to be rehabilitative rather than punitive, and its focus was on the individual child's treatment and rehabilitation. The judges in juvenile court took on a parental role and, like parents, determined the needs of the child.

The founders of the juvenile court intended to create a flexible and individualized system for dealing with wayward youth. Judges were given broad discretionary powers, as it was assumed that they were acting in the best interests of the child. It was not until the late 1960s, following the occurrence of numerous abuses within the system, that the government began to formalize procedures within juvenile courts. In recent years, there has been a growing trend within the juvenile system away from rehabilitation and toward punishment. Paralleling this trend has been an increasing awareness of the need to protect the rights of juveniles within the system in order to ensure due process.

Overview of the Juvenile Justice System

Juvenile courts have jurisdiction over three types of cases: status offenses, dependency cases, and delinquency cases. Status offenses are acts committed by juveniles that would not be considered crimes if committed by an adult; examples include running away from home or being truant from school. Dependency cases are cases in which the juvenile court is responsible for providing protection for children who are abused or neglected or deemed to be in need of supervi-

The juvenile justice system aims to help and protect as many youth as possible. (Urban Archives, Philadelphia)

sion because their parents cannot manage them. Finally, delinquency cases involve violation of a law or ordinance. The focus throughout this entry is on delinquency cases.

There is a great deal of discretion built into the juvenile justice system. Police, prosecution, judges, and probation all exercise discretion that can move a youth deeper into the process or divert the youth out of the process. The juvenile justice system aims to help and protect as many youth as possible. Toward this end, many juveniles are brought into the system, yet few make it to the final

stages of the process. At each stage, cases may be resolved or referred for further intervention.

Police provide the primary means by which youth are brought into the juvenile justice system. When an adolescent is arrested or taken into custody by a police officer, he or she is booked at a police station or sheriff's office. Booking involves obtaining information about the detained youth and creating a written record of the arrest or detention. After booking, the police classify the adolescent according to the offense allegedly committed and determine whether the juvenile justice system has jurisdiction over the case. In some states, juveniles are automatically transferred to criminal court for more serious offenses such as rape or murder. Once jurisdiction has been established, youths may be released to the care of their parents, referred to community resources (e.g., counseling), referred for juvenile intake procedures and then released to parents, or transferred to a juvenile hall or shelter. These actions, referred to as *preliminary disposition* or *diversion*, depend on several factors including the nature of the offense and the resources available.

The next stage of the process involves an intake screening, which often takes place at the time of booking and is conducted by a court officer or a juvenile probation officer. The formality of this procedure varies from case to case. The intake officer acts as a screening agent and decides what action is to be taken on the case. This decision is based on a number of factors including the seriousness of the offense and the youth's attitude, demeanor, age, and previous offense history. In most jurisdictions, the intake screening results in one of five actions: (1) dismissal of the case, with or without verbal or written reprimand; (2) release of the youths into the custody of their parents; (3) release of the youths to the custody of their parents with a referral for counseling or special services; (4) referral of the youths to an alternative dispute resolution program; or (5) referral of the youths to the juvenile justice prosecutor for further action and possible filing of a delinquency petition.

Cases that are referred to juvenile prosecutors usually involve either youths who commit serious offenses or youths who are chronic recidivists (e.g., children who chronically run away from home).

Juvenile prosecutors have broad discretionary powers and can decide among a number of actions ranging from dismissing the case to diverting it to criminal court through waiver. Prosecutors are also responsible for filing petitions or acting on petitions filed by others. Petitions are official court documents specifying the reason for the youth's court appearance. Filing a petition formally places the youth before a juvenile court judge.

The next stage is adjudication, which refers to the process by which a judgment or action is taken on the petition filed within the court. The formality of the adjudication process varies from state to state. However, there is a growing trend toward a more formal and adversarial procedure that emulates the criminal court system. Defense attorneys represent the juvenile's interests during the adjudicatory proceedings and ensure that due process is fulfilled. Then, after hearing the evidence presented by both sides, a judge decides or adjudicates the matter. If the petition alleges that a delinquency has occurred (i.e., that the youth has committed a crime), the judge decides whether the youth is or is not delinquent. If the adjudicatory proceedings support the allegations then the judge sentences the juvenile or orders a disposition. If the allegations are not supported, the case is dismissed and the youth is freed.

Dispositions are actions ordered by a juvenile judge. Generally, dispositions are grouped into three categories: nominal, conditional, and custodial. The idea behind dispositions is that they represent the least restrictive alternative providing for the public safety. Nominal dispositions, which entail verbal warnings or stern reprimands, are the least punitive; in such cases, release to the custody of the parents usually completes the juvenile court action against the youth. Conditional dispositions are probationary options in which youths are referred to probation and required to comply with certain conditions. A probation officer oversees the youth during this period and ensures that he or she complies with the probationary conditions. Custodial dispositions are classified as nonsecure and secure. Nonsecure options include foster homes, group homes, or camp ranches or schools, whereas secure options include juvenile detention centers or other forms of incarceration. The secure custodial option is considered by most juvenile judges to be a last resort for the most serious juvenile offenders; however, even non-serious offenders are sometimes incarcerated because of a lack of appropriate community-based treatments. Finally, it is important to note that in some states there is a death penalty for juveniles tried as adults through the transfer process.

*Trends within the Juvenile
Justice System*
Since the 1960s, three major developments have altered the focus of the juvenile justice system: (1) U.S. Supreme Court rulings protecting the rights of juveniles during court proceedings, (2) passage of the Juvenile Justice and Delinquency Prevention Act, and (3) the shift in public and social policy from treatment and rehabilitation toward deterrence and punishment. These changes have altered the original vision of the court, resulting in a system with competing goals and orientations. In short, the original goals of social service, advocacy, and treatment have been replaced by a focus on consequences and retribution.

Four landmark Supreme Court decisions reformed the legal framework that determines the quality of justice for delin-

quent youth. *Kent v United States* (1966) established juveniles' right to a hearing before transfer to a criminal court as well as their right to counsel during a police interrogation. *In re Gault* (1967) gave juveniles the right to be represented by an attorney, the right to confront and cross-examine witnesses, the right to avoid self-incrimination, and the right to receive notice of charges. *In re Winship* (1970) established a juvenile's right to the criminal court standard of "beyond a reasonable doubt." And *Breed v Jones* (1975) provided protection against double jeopardy. (Double jeopardy exists when a juvenile is adjudicated as a delinquent in juvenile court and tried for the same offense in adult criminal court.) Taken together, these rights given by the U.S. Supreme Court guarantee juveniles a minimum of due process during adjudicatory proceedings.

The Juvenile Justice and Delinquency Prevention Act of 1974 and its 1980 and 1996 amendments profoundly altered juvenile laws and practices. This act requires that states receiving federal funding follow four mandates. The first mandate, which calls for the "deinstitutionalization of status offenders," maintains that status offenders should not be institutionalized as though they had committed crimes. The second mandate requires "sight and sound separation" of juveniles and adult prisoners and requires that juvenile offenders not come into contact with adult prisoners. The third mandate, involving "jail and lock up removal," requires that all juvenile offenders be removed from adult criminal facilities. And the fourth mandate, which concerns "disproportionate confinement of minority youth," requires that states make efforts to reduce the disproportionate representation of minority youth in juvenile facilities. Although these reforms have been considered major advances in the fight for juvenile rights, girls and children of color, in particular, have not experienced the intended benefits.

Legal factors such as severity of the offense and prior record heavily influence the court's decision-making process, but race and gender also play significant and pervasive roles in these deliberations. With respect to race, statistical analyses demonstrate that the number of minority youth confined to public correctional facilities is disproportionately large relative to their representation in the general population. As for gender, girls continue to be arrested and incarcerated for offenses (generally status offenses and prostitution crimes) that would not trigger a similar response for males. Girls' pathway into the system is markedly different from that of boys: Many girls arrive in the juvenile justice system with histories of sexual and physical abuse, mental illness, substance abuse, family disconnection, and special education. And, finally, the court has been reluctant to reduce its use of incarceration for girls, even though the facilities they are sent to are often unequipped to handle their special medical, mental health, and social service needs.

Although many reforms have attempted to increase the rights of juveniles, public concern over lenient consequences for dangerous juveniles has resulted in more vigorous prosecution of violent youthful offenders. This new emphasis, however, is in conflict with the original rehabilitative mission of the juvenile courts. In their struggle to balance these two competing demands, the courts are currently experiencing an identity crisis that pulls them in different directions between rehabilitation and punishment.

The move toward punishment and away from treatment and prevention within the juvenile courts is evidenced by the fact that numerous states have passed laws expanding eligibility for criminal court processing, increasing sentencing authority, and reducing confidentiality protections. In 1976, for example, more than half the states made it easier to transfer youth to adult courts where more severe punishments could be imposed. Some states have lowered the minimum age at which youths can be transferred into the adult system; others have discounted the issue of age altogether. Several states have passed laws that give juvenile courts increased sentencing options. And, finally, a number of states have passed laws that modify or remove court confidentiality provisions, making juvenile records and proceedings more open. All of these laws are aimed at "cracking down" on juvenile crime and have changed the focus within the juvenile justice system from individualized treatment and rehabilitation to punishment.

Juvenile Rights in the Juvenile Justice System

Although juveniles have more legal rights today than they did thirty years ago as a result of the Supreme Court rulings described above, they are still not vested with the same rights as adults in criminal court. For example, their right to a trial by jury is not constitutionally required, although in some states it is granted by statute (*McKeiver v Pennsylvania*, 1971). One reason juveniles are not granted the same rights given to adults in criminal court is that juvenile courts continue to exercise civil jurisdiction. In other words, adolescent offenders do not acquire a criminal record for offenses committed as juveniles. In some states, however, juvenile records can be used for later adult proceedings such as enhanced sentencing.

In addition to having fewer rights than adults, many adolescents do not exercise their constitutional rights. Although the right to counsel is constitutionally granted (*In re Gault*, 1967), it may be waived. And, indeed, records show that counsel is offered but technically waived in many cases. Instead of assigning counsel, many states permit youth not only to choose whether to have the services of counsel but also to waive their right to a fact-based hearing. However, there is considerable debate over whether children and adolescents have the cognitive or emotional capacity to fully understand the consequences of such decisions. In particular, children and adolescents may need counsel during interrogation in order to protect them against self-incrimination.

Jodi E. Morris
Jennifer A. Murphy
Francine T. Sherman

See also Delinquency, Mental Health, and Substance Abuse Problems; Delin-quency, Trends in; Foster Care: Risks and Factors; Juvenile Crime

References and further reading
Center on Juvenile Justice and Criminal Justice. 2000. Web site: www.cjcj.org
Champion, Dean J. 1992. *The Juvenile Justice System: Delinquency, Processing, and the Law.* New York: Macmillan.
Humes, Edward. 1997. *No Matter How Loud I Shout: A Year in the Life of Juvenile Court.* New York: Simon and Schuster.
Jones, LeAlan, Lloyd Newman, and David Isay. 1997. *Our America.* New York: Simon and Schuster.
Krisberg, B., and James F. Austin. 1993. *Reinventing Juvenile Justice.* Newbury Park, CA: Sage Publications.
National Center for Juvenile Justice. 2000. Web site: www.ncjj.org
Phillip, Kay, Andrea Estepa, and Al Desetta, eds. 1998. *Things Get Hectic: Teens Write about the Violence That Surrounds Them.* New York: Touchstone.
Schwartz, Irma M., ed. 1992. *Juvenile Justice and Public Policy.* New York: Macmillan.
Synder, Howard N., and Melissa Sickmund. 1999. *Juvenile Offenders and Victims: 1999 National Report.* Washington, DC: Office of Juvenile Justice and Delinquency Prevention. Web site: www.ncjj.org.

L

Latina/o Adolescents

Latina/o adolescents in the United States come from all Spanish-speaking countries in the Western hemisphere, including the United States itself, which is today the fifth largest Spanish-speaking country in the world (considering numbers of Spanish speakers in the country). However, many include in Latinas/os Brazilians (who speak Portuguese) and indigenous peoples such as Mayans, Zapotecans, and Quechua (who speak a home language other than Spanish—such as Tzotzil, Chol, Ki'che, Zapoteca, or Quechua—and often speak Spanish also). Latinas/os (also sometimes spelled Latin@s) hail from several races and mixtures, including the indigenous peoples of the Western Hemisphere, Africans, Europeans, and Asians. Latinas/os vary in their distance from their home country, both in terms of actual land distance and in terms of immigration distance. Some Latina/o adolescents are new to the United States, immigrants themselves. Some Latinas/os come from families who originated in what is now the United States—today Texas, New Mexico, California, Arizona, Colorado, and other states that were originally Mexican territory stolen by the United States in the Mexican-American War through the Treaty of Guadalupe Hidalgo. The sentiment of these Latinas/os is captured in the statement, "We didn't cross the border; the border crossed us" and in the frustration of having lost land, culture, and language rights guaranteed them by the treaty. Also, there are Latinas/os, Puerto Ricans, whose entire island was seized by the United States. With their homeland colonialized by the United States, Puerto Ricans are officially U.S. citizens, but they do not enjoy the same voting privileges and social services on the island that U.S. citizens do in the continental United States.

Despite these challenges, Latina/o adolescents have many things about which to feel proud. While the largest numbers of Latinas/os in the United States are Mexican American, Latina/o adolescents in the United States are extremely diverse, including Chicanas/os (see "Chicana/os" entry in this encyclopedia), Boricuas, Puerto Riqueñas/os, El Salvadoreñas/os, Nicaragüenses, Guatemaltecas/os, Cubans, Dominicans, Peruvians, Mexicans, Chileans, Argentineans, Colombians, and Tejanos. Further diversity within the Latina/o umbrella can be seen in the range of skin tones (black, brown, bronze, and white), heard in the range of language backgrounds (Spanish only, Spanish dominant, fully bilingual, English dominant, and English only), heard in the range of accents and word choices (*guagua* means child in Chile and a bus in the Caribbean) and experienced in the range of holidays (from the Mexican

Cinco de Mayo to the Puerto Rican El Grito de Lares), foods (from tostones to mole poblano to paella), and dances (from salsa to tejano to banda to danza). A few excellent works in literature that capture the Latina/o adolescent experience in the United States include: *Barrio Boy* by Ernesto Galarza, *When I Was Puerto Rican* by Esmeralda Santiago, *How the Garcia Girls Lost Their Accent* by Julia Alvarez, *Bless Me Ultima* by Rudolfo Anaya, *The House on Mango Street* by Sandra Cisneros, *So Far from God* by Ana Castillo, *Down These Mean Streets* by Piri Thomas, *Drown* by Junot Diaz, and *Dreaming in Cuban* by Cristina Garcia.

Our heroes for whom Latinas/os feel pride include Rigoberta Menchu, the indigenous rights activist; Jennifer Lopez, the singer/actor; Bob Menendez, a Congress member and Democratic Party leader; Gloria Estefan, the singer; Gloria Molina, the chair of the Los Angeles County Board of Supervisors; Samuel Betances, an education and diversity specialist; and María Hinojosa, the journalist. Latinas/os also remember their heroes no longer alive (but very much remembered), including Emiliano Zapata, the revoluntionary who fought for peasant land rights in Mexico; Rubén Salazar, the Chicano journalist murdered by police officers; Cesar Chávez and Dolores Huerta, the leaders of the United Farm Workers; Tito Puente, the Latin Jazz band leader; Lola Rodríguez de Tió, the Puerto Rican poet and artist; and Che Guevara, the Cuban revolutionary.

Although proud of their origins, Latina/o adolescents notice when Latinas/os are missing from almost all mainstream television programming: There are no Latinas/os on the Supreme Court, there has never been a Latina/o president, bilingual education programs are rarely offered to those Latinas/os who might most benefit from developing bilingual/biliterate/bicultural skills, and school curricula rarely include the contributions of Latinas/os to the United States—how many U.S. citizens know that Latinas/os were the most overrepresented and most decorated, compared to the proportion of the population, of the soldiers who served in Vietnam? Latinas/os offer strengths to the United States, bringing with them a robust sense of family and familial loyalty, often expressed in extended family networks, extreme respect for the elders in their communities, and a strong work ethic. Regardless of society's lack of equal representation for Latinas/os, most Latina/o adolescents know that the struggle for voice and recognition continues *(la lucha sigue)* and that yes, they can win this struggle *(si se puede)*. Given current demographics, the third millennium will likely be the Latina/o millennium in the United States, as one in four in the United States will soon be Latina/o and this percentage will be greater amongst adolescents, given that Latinas/os are a young group.

Danielle Carrigo

See also Chicana/o Adolescents; Ethnic Identity; Identity; Racial Discrimination

References and further reading

Acuna, Rodolfo. 1988. *Occupied America: A History of Chicanos*, 3rd ed. New York: HarperCollins.

Anaya, Rodolfo A., and Francisco Lomeli, eds. 1989. *Aztlan*. Albuquerque, NM: El Norte Publications.

Anzaldúa, Gloria. 1987. *Borderlands: La Frontera, the New Mestiza*. San Francisco: Aunt Lute Books.

Cummins, Jim. 1986. "Empowering Minority Students: A Framework for Intervention." *Harvard Educational Review* 56, no. 1: 18–36.

Garcia, Eugene E. 1991. *The Education of Linguistically and Culturally Diverse*

Students: Effective Instructional Practices (Educational Practice Report 1). Washington, DC: National Center for Research on Cultural Diversity and Second Language Learning.

Martinez, Elizabeth. 1998. *De Colores Means All of Us: Latina Views for a Multi-Colored Century.* Cambridge, MA: South End Press.

Rodriguez, Luis J. 1993. *Always Running: La Vida Loca: Gang Days in L.A.* New York: Touchstone.

Romo, Harriett D., and Toni Falbo. 1996. *Latino High School Graduation: Defying the Odds.* Austin: University of Texas Press.

Schecter, Sandra, Diane Sharken-Taboada, and Robert Bayley. 1996. "Bilingual by Choice: Latino Parents' Rationales and Strategies for Raising Children with Two Languages." *The Bilingual Research Journal* 20, no. 2: 261–281.

Secada, Walter, et al. 1998. *No More Excuses: Final Report of the Hispanic Dropout Project.* Washington, DC: Hispanic Dropout Project.

Learning Disabilities

An adolescent who has a learning disability, most basically defined as a disorder that interferes with the learning process, faces significant challenges. Learning disabilities are widespread, and it is crucial to understand exactly what constitutes a learning disability and what can be done about it.

The term *learning disability* has evolved over the years, but in general one can say that a learning disability is characterized by a significant difference between overall intelligence, or cognitive potential, and academic achievement. Individuals with learning disabilities are usually of average or above-average intelligence, but they have more difficulty than their peers with an aspect of the learning process. For example, an individual with a learning disability may have important ideas but cannot express them in speech or on paper; a learning disabled student may have difficulty identifying and remembering important details from class in order to complete homework independently; or an individual with a learning disability cannot seem to make sense of letters or numbers to read or calculate math. A leading organization for individuals with learning disabilities, the National Joint Committee on Learning Disabilities (NJCLD), defined learning disability as

a generic term that refers to a heterogeneous group of disorders manifested by significant difficulties in the acquisition and use of listening, speaking, reading, writing, reasoning, or mathematical abilities. These disorders are intrinsic to the individual, presumed to be due to central nervous dysfunction, and may occur across the life span. Problems in self-regulatory behaviors, social perception, and social interaction may exist with learning disabilities, but do not by themselves constitute a learning disability. Although learning disabilities may occur concomitantly with other handicapping conditions (for example, sensory impairment, mental retardation, serious emotional disturbance), or with extrinsic influences (such as cultural differences, inappropriate or insufficient instruction), they are not the result of those influences or conditions (Hammill, Leigh, McNutt, and Larsen, 1981, p. 336).

What we know about learning disabilities, including the definition and how to measure a learning disability, has changed considerably over the last thirty years. This change has resulted in an increased awareness of the prevalence of learning disabilities, as well the implementation of national laws in order to protect those who have a learning disability. Public Law (P.L.) 101-476, the Individuals with Disabilities Education Act (IDEA), mandates that all students with learning disabilities are entitled to a "free" and "appropriate" education in the "least restricted environment" possible. This law defines a learning disability as a disorder in one or more of the basic processes involved in understanding or in using spoken or written language, a disorder that may present as difficulty with listening, thinking, speaking, reading, writing, spelling, or doing mathematical calculations (Federal Register, December 29, 1977, p. 65083, 121a.5).

It is important to remember that a learning disability is *not* due to lack of motivation, environmental or economic disadvantage, poor parenting, mental retardation, physical handicap, autism, deafness, blindness, or behavioral disorders. In addition, the term *learning disability* is a broad term that encompasses many types of learning disabilities, such as developmental articulation disorder (difficulty controlling rate of speech), developmental expressive language disorder (difficulty with verbal expression), developmental receptive language disorder (trouble understanding verbally presented information), developmental reading disorder (dyslexia), developmental writing disorder (difficulty composing written work), or developmental arithmetic disorder (difficulty with mathematics). Attention difficulties, such as attention-deficit/hyperactivity disorder (ADHD), often occur simultaneously with a learning disability. However, a learning disability is a separate disability with distinct, defining characteristics.

Whereas some students may have a specific learning disability that affects an isolated area of their learning process (such as calculating mathematics), other students may have a learning disability that overlaps into many areas of the learning process (such as understanding and processing verbal instructions). The effects of having a learning disability often reach beyond the walls of the school, into the areas of work, family, friendships, and other relationships. Because students with a learning disability may also suffer from difficulties with attention, social skills, motivation, and organization, these individuals may exhibit other symptoms, such as inconsistent test performance, perceptual difficulties, motor disorders, and behaviors such as impulsiveness, frustration, and difficulty interpreting and responding appropriately to social interactions. The skills that are impaired in a learning disability are necessary for functioning not only in a school setting but also in the "real world," with family and friends. Finally, it is important to remember that a learning disability may mildly, moderately, or severely impair a student's learning process, and therefore the disability will look different in each person.

Students with learning disabilities often wonder why they have a learning disability and other students do not. Scientists first thought that learning disabilities were caused by a specific neurological problem; the latest theory, however, suggests that learning disabilities may occur as a result of disturbances in brain structures and functions—disturbances that begin before the birth of the child. During pregnancy, important cells come together to create the various parts of the body and brain. This development is very sensitive to disruption, especially during the early stages of formation. During the later stages of brain development, when the larger structures are in place and the cells are becoming specialized, disruption may lead to errors in cell makeup, location, and connections, errors that some scientists believe could be the cause of learning disabilities. The disruption could be the result of genetic factors (family history), or substances taken during pregnancy (drugs and/or alcohol). Other suggested causes of learning disabilities include toxins ingested at an early age, or maturational lags (since some children develop at slower rates than others for unknown reasons). However, these are only hypotheses, unsupported by scientific evidence, and the exact cause of learning disabilities remains unclear.

A learning disability may be a lifelong condition that influences the way individuals interact in the world throughout their entire lives. Some individuals are diagnosed with a learning disability as children, others as adolescents, others even as late as when they are adults. Individuals with learning disabilities often compensate for their disability if there is early and appropriate intervention, support, and awareness. Without early and accurate identification and intervention, students with learning disabilities may not understand why they do not understand school-related information as quickly or as easily as their peers do. As a result, these students will not learn strategies to compensate for their disability, and may just feel stupid and hopeless, which may lead to low self-esteem, dropping out of school, juvenile delinquency, illiteracy, and other problems later in life. It is important to remember that a learn-

ing disability is a disability, not a prescription for ultimate failure. A student with a learning disability is not dumb. In fact, students with a learning disability are intelligent people. A student with a learning disability *can* learn, but may require different strategies than other students in order to learn. Many famous and successful men and women have learning disabilities and have learned effective ways to compensate for their disabilities and build on their strengths. Examples include Thomas Edison, Charles Darwin, Walt Disney, Albert Einstein, John F. Kennedy, Tom Cruise, John Bon Jovi, Whoopi Goldberg, and Cher.

According to the latest research from the National Information Center for Children and Youth with Disabilities (NICHCY), approximately 5–10 percent of the U.S. population has some form of a learning disability (NICHCY, 1999). However, this number may underrepresent how many children and adolescents actually have a learning disability. In order to be diagnosed with a learning disability, a student must meet certain specific criteria, which vary from state to state. A student who meets the criteria for special education services because of a learning disability in one state may not qualify in another state.

Assessment of a learning disability usually begins with a team approach (made up of a guidance counselor, special educator, psychologist, and other professionals who may be appropriate) to assess the various areas of spoken language, written language, arithmetic, reasoning, and organizational skills, and continues through the development of an individual educational program (IEP). An IEP outlines the specific skills the student needs help with, learning strategies to address the student's needs, as well as ways in which to measure how much the student has progressed as a result of the intervention. Because a student with a learning disability has specific learning needs, most public schools accommodate the various needs of the students by offering special education programs ranging from inclusion classrooms—where regular education students are placed in classes with special education students and the class is taught by a general education teacher and a special education teacher, to separate classrooms with smaller numbers of only special education students. Adolescents with learning disabilities face unique challenges because of developmental and environmental demands placed on them. As students move into secondary school, they are expected to complete most of their academic work independently. The academic material becomes more complex and requires more advanced abstract reasoning and processing in the various subject areas. Adolescents are expected to acquire, store, integrate, and express knowledge, both in written and verbal form, more independently than before. This is a developmentally appropriate expectation, but adolescents with learning disabilities may have difficulty because they may lack basic skills necessary to meet these academic demands, fail to systemically use appropriate skills in problem-solving situations, and/or not use effective learning strategies to assist them to assimilate new information. On the elementary level, more individual attention is typically given to students as they learn new information. However, on the secondary level, students are expected to perform more independently than before.

In addition, the elementary student needs to learn to accommodate to only one teacher and one teaching style. However, on the secondary level, adolescents typically have to adjust to the teaching strategies and expectations of different teachers in different subject areas. This may be especially problematic for adolescents with learning disabilities, who may have difficulty discerning the expectations and adjusting to the strategies of even one teacher, especially if that teacher is not teaching in ways that are appropriate for the adolescent or the adolescent's disability. Without individualized assistance, adolescents with learning disabilities may struggle to keep up with the developmental and environmental demands of the secondary level.

In addition to the academic challenges of the secondary level, adolescents face new challenges in the social realm as well. Relationships with peers become increasingly important and require more advanced and complex social skills. Adolescents with learning disabilities may have more difficulty in social situations, either because they do not have the necessary social skills or because they do not implement appropriate social skills in social situations. Adolescents with learning disabilities often have difficulty in reading nonverbal cues, are often compulsive, and often have difficulty in communicating. The skills they lack are necessary not only for the learning process but also for forming and maintaining social relationships. Therefore, adolescents who have learning disabilities that impact their ability to interpret and respond appropriately to social situations are at risk for difficulties with social relationships.

Each student with a learning disability is unique, and therefore the strategies that are helpful will be different for each student. Not only is it important for teachers to understand an adolescent's disability and how to accommodate this disability in the classroom, it is also important for the adolescent to understand the disability. An important developmental task for adolescents is defining themselves and who they are, which includes understanding their strengths and weaknesses. Adolescents with learning disabilities can and should learn ways to advocate and adjust to maximize their success in the school setting, and in life. When it comes to setting goals beyond high school, they need to know that colleges and universities are required by law to accommodate students with learning disabilities just as public schools are, and, therefore, students with learning disabilities can and should set high goals for themselves and their future.

Overall, adolescents with learning disabilities can benefit from various strategies, which include basic skills remediation, curriculum reductions, alternative textbooks, and instruction using various teaching styles (multimodal) and social skills instruction. Adolescents with learning disabilities often perform best within the context of a highly structured environment, where there are clear and explicit expectations.

Furthermore, adolescents with learning disabilities may benefit from assistance in problem solving, which includes learning strategies to break down multi-step tasks. It is often helpful to have modeling for new tasks, and teachers should not only model but also incorporate tasks that include both verbal and hands-on activities. Adolescents with learning disabilities may also benefit from using various devices in the classroom, such as a tape recorder for note taking and a word processor or computer for written assignments. In addition,

there are many software programs designed to assist students with their learning disabilities. Students may need accommodations in test-taking situations, such as being given additional time or having test material read to them instead of having to read all of the material themselves.

Moreover, for individuals who struggle with focusing their attention in addition to their learning disability, a full assessment for attention-deficit/hyperactivity disorder (ADHD) should be completed. A student with ADHD often may be mistaken for one who has a learning disability and vice versa. Therefore, a comprehensive evaluation is warranted to discern the nature of the adolescent's difficulties and appropriate intervention to help the student succeed.

It is important to remember that just because an adolescent has difficulty in school, this does not necessarily mean that the adolescent has a learning disability. By the same token, if an adolescent has a learning disability, this does not necessarily mean that the adolescent cannot learn. Individuals with learning disabilities have made important contributions to society. After proper assessment and diagnosis, followed by implementation of appropriate interventions, adolescents can learn ways to capitalize on their strengths in order to learn and be successful in school and in the world.

Catherine E. Barton

See also Academic Achievement; Academic Self-Evaluation; Cognitive Development; Dyslexia; Intelligence Tests; Learning Styles and Accommodations; Schools, Full-Service; Standardized Tests; Tracking in American High Schools

Resources
Many organizations offer free information about learning disabilities. Contact

them by telephone or on the World Wide Web. A few suggestions follow:

International Dyslexia Association: 1-800-222-3123 (www.interdys.org)

Learning Disabilities Association of America (LDA): 1-888-300-6710 (www.ldanatl.org)

Learning Disabilities Online (www.ldonline.com)

National Center for Learning Disabilities: 1-800-575-7373 (www.ncld.org)

National Information Center for Children and Youth with Disabilities: 1-800-695-0285 (www.nichcy.org)

References and further reading

Hammill, Donald D., J. E. Leigh, G. McNutt, and S. C. Larsen. 1981. "A New Definition of Learning Disabilities." *Learning Disability Quarterly* 4: 336–342.

National Information Center for Children and Youth with Disabilities (NICHCY). 1999. *Fact Sheet No. 7 (FS7)*. Available by mail: P.O. Box 1492, Washington, DC 20013 or by phone, 1-800-695-0285.

Olivier, Carolyn, Bill Cosby, and Rosemary Bowler. 1996. *Learning to Learn.* New York: Fireside.

Silver, Larry, B. 1991. *The Misunderstood Child: A Guide for Parents of Children with Learning Disabilities,* 2nd ed. New York: McGraw-Hill.

———. 1998. *The Misunderstood Child: Understanding and Coping with Your Child's Learning Disabilities,* 3rd ed. New York: McGraw-Hill.

Smith, Corinne, and Lisa Strick. 1999. *Learning Disabilities A to Z.* New York: Simon and Schuster.

Smith, Sally L. 1993. *Succeeding against the Odds: How the Learning Disabled Can Realize Their Promise.* Los Angeles, CA: J. P. Tarcher.

———. 1995. *No Easy Answers: The Learning Disabled Child at Home and at School.* New York: Bantam Books.

Wong, Bonnie. Y. L., ed. 1991. *Learning about Learning Disabilities.* San Diego: Academic Press.

Learning Styles and Accommodations

A learning style represents a unique approach used to perceive, understand, and plan interactions in the world. This personal style of information selection affects learning. Education literature suggests that students who are actively engaged in the learning process will be more likely to achieve success: Once they are actively engaged in their own learning process they begin to feel empowered, and their personal achievement and self-direction levels rise. It has been shown that adjusting teaching materials to meet the needs of a variety of learning styles benefits students. Educators who can recognize the diverse learning styles of students can then also modify their teaching styles to meet the individual needs of students in their classrooms. These teachers play an important role in assisting each student to use her strengths to meet the challenges of her individual learning profile.

Research about human learning differences has been categorized in a number of different ways. The categorization called Instructional and Environmental Preferences recognizes preferences about sound, light, temperature, and class design, as well as such issues as motivation, persistence, responsibility, and structure. The Social Interaction Models consider ways in which students react socially in learning conditions. The Information Processing Model is an effort to understand the processes by which information is obtained, stored, and utilized. The Personality Model involves the way in which personality traits shape the orientations people take toward the world. An example of a Personality Model is the popular Myers-Briggs Type Indicator, which categorizes people as extroverts or introverts, sensing or intuitive, thinking or feeling, and judging or perceiving. For educators, the challenge is not only to recognize trainable skills and attitudes but also to identify students with fundamentally different instincts.

An awareness of the many kinds of learning styles is helpful in understanding the student of today and allows a teacher to be cognizant of nuances in student learning. Yet the student's processing strengths and challenges go beyond preference. The way a student processes material is very difficult to change. For that reason, the students, teachers, and parents need to be aware of a student's learning profile in an effort to address the needs of the individual student and to plan pedagogical strategies.

Educators may use the general strategy of creating increased opportunities for students to use different styles of learning. This strategy may involve offering additional alternative activities that supplement and replace traditional ones. For example, a student may write a poem or dramatize a segment of a unit of study to respond in a global fashion and use sensitive, holistic abilities. Traditional lectures may be supplemented by hands-on activities that permit active experimenters the chance to confirm abstractions. A variety of modalities may be used in teaching, or lectures may alternate among various styles to engage students and develop their awareness of teaching styles. The teacher who wants to challenge students to develop learning skills may design a systematic set of activities that demands that students use all the various learning styles in completing an assignment.

Each person develops a preferred and consistent set of behaviors or approaches to the learning process that is composed of cognition, conceptualization, and affect. Cognition involves the acquisition of knowledge; conceptualization, the manner in which the information is

An awareness of the many kinds of learning styles is helpful in understanding the student of today. (Skjold Photographs)

processed; and affect, the person's motivation, values, and emotional preferences. Theorists such as David Kolb and Howard Gardner have provided models of learning styles.

Kolb has shown that learning styles can be seen on a continuum running from concrete experience to reflective observation to abstract conceptualization and finally to active experimentation. For example, in concrete experience the student is involved in a new experience such as laboratory work. In reflective observation the student watches others and develops observations such as logs and journals. Abstract conceptualization is the creation of theories and explanation of observation, of the kind involved in lectures and papers. Active experimentation is the use of theory to solve problems and make decisions. This activity occurs in the completion of homework and the development of case studies or the use of simulations.

Gardner sees learning style in a different light; he uses the term *multiple intelligences,* and his theory is referred to as MI. MI states that there are at least six different ways of learning and, therefore, six intelligences: body/kinesthetic, interpersonal/intrapersonal, logical/mathematical, musical/rhythmic, verbal/linguistic, and visual/spatial. Education has tended to emphasize two of the ways of learning, logical/mathematical and verbal/linguistic.

Children who experience difficulties in school may profit from a comprehensive educational evaluation to help in understanding how the student learns so that he or she may achieve success in the learning/testing process. This evaluation will include interviews, direct observation, a review of the child's educational and medical history, tests that will measure the student's strengths and challenges, and conferences with professionals who work with the child. Either the school or the parent may request the evaluation, but it is only given with the parent's written permission. Teachers are usually the first to note a learning difference, yet parents may be aware of the student's challenges. Often, the student knows there is a problem but cannot find a way to succeed. Identifying a student's preferred learning style may be the first step to a student's success in school.

Once the decision to test has been reached, many questions arise. Who is qualified to evaluate a student's learning profile? What tests measure the student's strengths and challenges? What happens after the student has been evaluated? Who should be notified of the test results? What will be done for the student? What is the student expected to do? A qualified evaluator may be a learning specialist trained in testing, an educational diagnostician or educational consultant, a speech/language pathologist, a psychologist, or some other individual (with or without certification) experienced in identifying learning differences.

Learning specialists work with students who are experiencing academic difficulties. They identify learning styles after they administer, analyze, and interpret tests. After reviewing pertinent information, they prescribe specific, appropriate, and practical learning strategies and coordinate a team effort that usually includes teachers, other educational professionals, students, and parents. They may also serve as tutors or help in the areas of time management, organization, and study skills.

Educational diagnosticians administer batteries of tests and conference with parents, teachers, and students following the tests to assist in creating appropriate educational plans. Often, an educational diagnostician is also an educational consultant who helps parents and students with school placement by developing a detailed profile of the student from school reports, testing results, medical information, and interviews with the parents and the student.

Many speech pathologists have received training in a variety of testing batteries, but they are particularly sensitive to the central auditory tests that provide an extensive view into the language/listening parts of the brain. Many learning disabilities are closely related to auditory processing deficits.

Psychologists receive training in the evaluation and treatment of emotional problems. They may also administer intelligence batteries that help individuals and families recognize strengths and challenges in a student's profile.

A battery of tests may be given to get a complete picture of a student's abilities. These may include tests of intelligence, visual perception, auditory perception, and language fundamentals, as well as achievement tests and visual-motor integration tests. One comprehensive test is the Woodcock-Johnson Psycho-Educational Battery, which consists of both cognitive ability testing and achievement testing. The cognitive battery affords an excellent profile of a student's learning style.

The *Standard Battery* of the Woodcock-Johnson-Revised Tests of Cognitive Ability (WJ-R COG) consists of seven tests, each of which measures a different intellectual ability. By administering the standard battery of the WJ-R COG and some of the supplemental tests, one may determine a subject's learning profile. The seven major areas include: fluid reasoning, comprehension-knowledge, visual processing, auditory processing, processing speed, long-term retrieval, and short-term memory.

Fluid reasoning involves the broad ability to reason or "general intelligence." The tasks presented on the fluid-reasoning test do not depend on previously acquired knowledge. It is a test that measures a subject's ability to draw inferences and comprehend implications. The comprehension-knowledge test measures "crystallized intelligence." It represents a person's breadth and depth of knowledge, and the reasoning is based on previously learned procedures. A comparison of these two test scores provides a clearer picture of the type of reasoning a subject has.

Visual processing and auditory processing are involved in everyday functioning. Visual processing is "broad visualization"; the test measures ability to perceive visual patterns and to think with them. Many of the tasks of this test include recognizing rotation and reversal of figures, finding hidden figures, and comprehending spatial configurations. The test for auditory processing measures comprehension and synthesis of auditory patterns. These tasks involve understanding spoken language. Subjects are asked to repeat words when syllables are omitted and to repeat words when all syllables are presented but a delay is made between syllables.

Long- and short-term memory abilities are also measured by the WJ-R COG. The test for long-term retrieval measures effectiveness in storing information and retrieving it over extended periods of time, whereas the test for short-term memory involves apprehending information and utilizing it within a short period of time.

The test for processing speed measures a person's ability to perform relatively trivial cognitive tasks quickly. One of the subtests measures the ability to locate and circle two identical numbers in a row of six numbers, and the other subtest measures the ability to scan and compare visual information quickly by marking five drawings in a row of twenty drawings that are identical to the first drawing in the row.

An overview of the types of test questions has been provided only to allow for an awareness of the tasks. However, the value of these tests lies in their relation to learning. Students with processing disabilities need to first recognize the existence of the disability and then be provided a means for accommodating these disabilities. Students, teachers, and parents need to work together to address the student's needs.

Once a qualified test administrator has evaluated the student, the results should be shared with the teacher, parents, and student. Each plays a vital role in using this information to meet the learning challenges. Strengths may be used to compensate for difficulties. Just as a blind person learns to use his other senses (hearing, touch, smell, taste) in order to compensate for not being able to see, a person with a learning disability may use his natural learning strength or preference to compensate for the disability. For example, someone with an auditory-processing disability may have a strength in visual processing and would be helped by using visual cues to support the weak auditory cues in his learning environment. A student with weak auditory processing may miss oral homework assignments, but she will remember what she has for homework by seeing the assignment on the board.

Four types of processing disabilities will be addressed: visual, auditory, memory, and speed. Information may need to be simplified, clarified, and supplemented with information through stronger senses. Accommodations are listed to assist teachers, and suggestions are given to students of things they can do on their own.

Visual-processing accommodations assist students in retrieving visual information. Teachers may help by reducing distracting stimuli on or near the student's desk. The students may be provided with a clear and simple overview or summary of what will be learned before each lesson so that they understand the basic concepts and are able to relate the information to previous knowledge. Teachers may also create worksheets with larger print and less "clutter," put math problems on graph paper to keep the numbers in line, or highlight important words or phrases in the student's assignments. Students may be allotted extra time to look at visual information (pictures, videos, writing on the board) and encouraged to use their other senses to reinforce the visual channel, perhaps through hands-on experiences or verbal descriptions designed to assist in the understanding of visual information. Refer students to the Reference Library for the Blind, where they may receive assistance with the use of books and assignments on tape.

Students may address visual-processing challenges by taking more time to visualize numbers, letters, and words. They need to listen for information and to ask for an explanation when the visual information is not clear. By reading out loud, the students may transfer the written word to the oral word. Listening to books on tape helps students picture the information. They reach math solutions more easily by drawing pictures and graphs and by copying the steps to math problems on index cards and working the problems nightly. The most important visual aid is the use of a plan book in which students write down assignments.

Teachers may provide auditory-processing accommodations by slowing down the verbal input and reducing the number of directions given to students. They may also repeat and clarify verbal instruction or draw and write important information on the board. Examples and demonstrations help in the clarification of projects and assignments, as do hands-on experiences. Students with auditory-processing challenges may need extra time for reading and writing assignments, and they may benefit from a quiet working place and a seat near the front of the class where they are able to maintain auditory attention and where visual distraction is minimized. These are also the students who may need a modification or reduction of foreign-language requirements.

In turn, these students may help themselves with auditory-processing challenges by jotting down key terms to use as cues for future recall and by paraphrasing directions, explanations, and instructions soon after hearing them. They should use a plan book to write down assignments and draw pictures to help visualize the information. These students need to ask for explanation when verbal information is unclear and pay attention to the source of the information (e.g., by making eye contact and looking at assignments). In order to make the information easier to recall, teachers (or students) may break larger assignments into smaller ones and put information to be learned into sequences or lists.

Teachers may assist students who have memory or organizational challenges by providing accommodations that use multiple modalities (e.g., auditory, visual, tactile) when presenting directions, explanations, and instructional content. Activities that involve the student and provide repetitive practice enhance short-term memory. Teachers may assist students by teaching them to use associative cues or mnemonics, organize information into smaller units, recognize main points and important facts, and rely on resources in

the environment to recall information. It is important to maintain consistency in sequential activities in order to increase the likelihood of student success. When presenting information, the teacher needs to allow students time to think, provide real-life examples, and deliver directions, explanations, and instructional content in a clear manner and at an appropriate pace. By stopping at various points during the presentation of information the teacher is able to monitor the student's understanding and to introduce the next task only when the first has been successfully completed. Students with memory challenges profit from the provision of extra time and the presentation of summaries and overviews. These students may need a modification or reduction of foreign-language requirements.

Students with memory deficits need to use study skills to assist them in recalling and organizing information. A plan book should be used to list all assignments and projects. Careful use of the plan book provides the student with a picture of what will be learned, so that large assignments may be broken into smaller ones and students may avoid the last-minute crunch by reviewing regularly and frequently before an assignment is due or a test is given. Students need to highlight important information and use mapping and webbing techniques to organize information from main ideas to details. By establishing a regular routine in performing activities and by using mnemonics, students remember information more easily.

To accommodate processing-speed deficits teachers may allow extra time for the completion of tests and assignments, slow down instruction so that students have time to digest the material, and allow students think time in class. Since students may miss important information presented in class, they may be allowed to use tape devices in order to repeat the lessons at a later time. Teachers may provide handouts with underlining or highlighting, since students may not have time to read or write everything, or assignments may be reduced or altered to meet the student's ability to complete the assignments. Students benefit from examples and demonstrations of what is expected on assignments and tests, understand information better when real-life examples are used to explain the relevancy of a lesson, and are better able to process information when provided with summaries and overviews.

Students with processing-speed challenges need to use a plan book to schedule for daily assignments and long-term projects. They need to break large assignments into smaller pieces and highlight and underline pertinent information to allow for quick review. Prior to beginning a new chapter they should read summary sections and review questions to get a better picture of what will be learned. Once material has been presented, they need to relate the material to previous experiences and to repeat the information in order to increase recall speed.

The accommodations listed above are techniques that alter the academic setting or environment. They enable the students to show more accurately what they actually know. Teachers may need to modify tests and assignments or change the way they present information to a student. Appropriate accommodations should either help the student learn better or give the student a better way of demonstrating his knowledge. Accommodations should not simply give an easier way to get better grades. Students and teachers need to work as a team. Accom-

modations are determined to meet the need of each situation. It is important to understand the reason for each accommodation so that it can be used to the student's best advantage. For example, some students may profit from hearing material as they read and would benefit from the services of the Recording for the Blind & Dyslexic (RFB&D). RFB&D, a nonprofit volunteer organization, offers diagnosed individuals the opportunity to send for tape recordings of books. It is the nation's educational library that serves people who cannot read standard print effectively because of a visual impairment, learning disability, or other physical disability. (Information about this bureau may be obtained by calling 1-800-221-4792.)

Bringing accommodation and strategy instruction into the classroom curriculum may improve the learning process of students with learning disabilities. Strategies are systematic procedures for approaching learning tasks, and they empower students by emphasizing the process of learning. Learning strategies are the tools and techniques that help students understand and learn new material or skills. The strategies serve to integrate new information with what a student already knows and help to make sense of the new material so that a student may recall that information or skill later or in other contexts. When students are taught *how* to learn, the focus is on the process and not only the outcome of learning, and students become independent learners and take responsibility for their own learning. They learn to think flexibly and to rely on their strengths and meet their challenges. Students become their own advocates by requesting accommodations and then become more independent by modifying strategies to match task demands. Students with learning challenges often need explicit, classroom-based, and individualized strategy instruction in organization, planning, self-checking, studying, and test taking. Strategy instruction should be an essential component of remediation, and it should also constitute the base for effective classroom instruction for all students. Either classroom teachers or trained educational consultants may assist students by teaching the steps to becoming independent learners.

Effective teaching usually combines several approaches so that the student uses more than one sense at a time while learning. These multisensory approaches allow students to team strengths with weaknesses so as to develop strategies for better learning. Thus, if a student has strong auditory-processing skills, these skills may be teamed with weaker visual-processing skills to optimize the learning conditions. Positive aspects of accommodations, especially those related to extended time, are that they do not affect what information is learned and that students are given ample opportunity to learn as much as they are capable of learning. These strategies give direction to alternative teaching and allow progressive educators to engage in student-centered teaching.

Classrooms are becoming more open to alternative approaches to intellectual work. Different social groupings, alternative activities, and complex projects have been introduced to create opportunities for students to use their various strengths in dealing with course material. The types of things a person enjoys and finds comfortable in different learning situations do not necessarily define the person's processing strength or challenge, but this preference along with appropri-ate accommodations may help counter-act a learning disability.

The accommodations listed above are suggestions that will assist teachers and students. The Rehabilitation Act of 1973, which addresses discrimination against persons with disabilities, has different sections for different areas of discrimination. One of those sections is Section 504, which provides individuals with disabilities basic civil rights protection against discrimination in federal programs. The law states that "no otherwise qualified handicapped individual in the United States shall, solely by reason of his [or her] handicap, be excluded from participation in, be denied the benefits of, or be subjected to discrimination under any program or activity receiving federal financial assistance." Although Section 504 does not provide federal funds, it applies to schools receiving money under the Individuals with Disabilities Education Act (IDEA), previously known as the Education for Handicapped Children Act of 1975, which is explained in the following paragraphs. Section 504 is enforced by the U.S. Department of Education, Office of Civil Rights.

The Education for Handicapped Children Act of 1975 [P.L. 94-142] mandated that all children with disabilities, ages five to twenty-one, be provided a free, appropriate public education, including special education and related services to meet their unique needs. The law required states to identify and evaluate children suspected of needing special education and develop a plan for implementing the federal directives. This act provided funds for states to implement the law. Following the passage of this federal law, states have also enacted state funding to provide special education and services to educate students with disabilities.

greater occupational commitment, (2) children from impoverished backgrounds have higher scores on measures of both cognitive and socioemotional development when their mothers are employed, and (3) both sons and daughters of employed mothers have less traditional sex role attitudes.

Scholars have suggested that differences found between working mothers and nonworking mothers may not necessarily be due to simply whether or not the mother is employed. Differences in family socioeconomic status, in parental attitudes toward employment, in mothers' work and home stress, in fathers' involvement in childcare and household tasks, and in the number of children in the home may all influence the family environment and, consequently, children's adjustment. Researchers interested in examining this topic must include other variables in the adolescent's environment that may potentially effect his or her development when trying to decipher the relationship between maternal employment and adolescents' outcomes.

For example, one related important factor in adolescents' development is maternal role satisfaction, that is, how satisfied a mother is with her role (e.g., as a wife, as a mother, as an employee), whether she is working or not. One study demonstrated that both mothers and fathers reported more closeness with their adolescents when mothers had high levels of satisfaction with their employment status. High role satisfaction has also been associated with higher academic competence in adolescents regardless of whether their mothers were working or not. Thus, research has shown that other factors, be they related to being employed or not, are important to con-

Satisfied and happy mothers interact more positively with their children whether the mother is employed or home full-time. (Richard T. Nowitz/Corbis)

sider when evaluating the influence of maternal employment on adolescents' development.

One common concern regarding mothers working has been that if mothers are employed, they don't have enough time to spend with their families. Despite the fact that employed mothers have less *total* time with their children, there is little research that demonstrates that mothers who work give their children less attention than mothers who do not work. In fact, working mothers may try to compensate for their time away from home by spending more time in direct interactions with their children when they are together. Overall, the most important conclusion taken from the research is that satisfied and happy mothers interact more positively with their children, and it is sensitive and warm mothering that has the most significant impact on children's development and well-being, whether their mother is employed or home full-time.

Public Policy Implications

The escalating numbers of women in the workforce has prompted government to take action regarding the lack of family policy in the United States. In 1993, the Family and Medical Leave Act (FMLA) was signed into law by President Clinton. This law guarantees job security for employees for a maximum of twelve weeks, should they need to leave their job due to the birth of a child or in the case of a family medical emergency. However, this leave is entirely unpaid, meaning that even if parents have the option of taking time off from their jobs, they may not financially be able to afford to do so. As illustrated by the FMLA, the United States lags behind its industrialized counterparts in terms of parental leave policies. Until this act was passed in 1993, the United States was the only country out of seventy-five industrialized nations that was without a government-sponsored family policy that specified some form of paid maternity benefits, parental leave for parents, and subsidized childcare.

Given the lack of national supports for working women in our country, mothers have been forced to negotiate leave and time off from work by themselves, as well as find and afford quality childcare and after-school care for their children. As the numbers of women participating in the workforce continue to increase, thereby escalating the numbers of children who require out-of-home care, the United States will be faced with increasing pressures to provide flexible work policies, and high-quality childcare and after-school care for the numerous families who need it.

Domini R. Castellino

See also Child-Rearing Styles; Chores; Employment: Positive and Negative Consequences; Family Composition: Realities and Myths; Mothers and Adolescents; Parental Monitoring; Single Parenthood and Low Achievement; Vocational Development

References and further reading
Furstenberg, F. F., and A. J. Cherlin. 1991. *Divided Families: What Happens to Children When Parents Part.* Cambridge, MA: Harvard University Press.
Grych, J. H., and F. D. Fincham. 1999. "Children of Single Parents and Divorce." Pp. 321–341 in *Developmental Issues in the Clinical Treatment of Children.* Edited by W. K. Silverman and T. H. Ollendick. Boston: Allyn and Bacon.
Keidel, K. C. 1970. "Maternal Employment and Ninth Grade Achievement in Bismarck, North Dakota." *Family Coordinator* 19: 95–97.
Schmittroth, L., ed. 1994. *Statistical Record of Children.* Detroit: Gale Research.

Media

Media—including television, music, movies, magazines, computer games, and the Internet—are a pervasive part of teens' daily lives. The typical American teen listens to music for about four to six hours a day (Christenson and Roberts, 1998), and watches television for another two to four hours (Roberts et al., 1999). In the bedrooms of adolescents aged fourteen to eighteen, two-thirds have a televi-

American adolescents are estimated to typically spend about eight hours per day using media, either as a primary activity or as background to other activities. (Tony Arruza/Corbis)

sion and nearly 90 percent have a tape player or CD player (Roberts et al., 1999). Adolescents watch more movies than any other segment of the population; over 50 percent of adolescents aged twelve to seventeen go to at least one movie per month (Greenberg, Brown, and Buerkel-Rothfuss, 1993). Over a third of high school juniors and seniors claim daily magazine reading, and three-fourths of adolescent girls read at least one magazine regularly (Durham, 1998; Evans et al., 1991). Altogether it is estimated that American adolescents typically spend about eight hours per day using media, either as their primary activity or as background to other activities (Roberts et al., 1999).

Media are used by teens for leisure and fun and as a way of passing time when they are alone. However, there is a great deal of concern, in our time, about the potential negative effects that media have on teens. Claims of negative effects include television and aggressiveness, computer games and aggressiveness, sex in television and movies, the effects of rap music, and girls' magazines and gender socialization.

Television and Aggressiveness
The question of whether television promotes aggressiveness is an issue of particular importance with regard to teens, because a high proportion of violent crimes is committed by young males and because the rate of violent crimes among teens rose sharply in the United States from 1960 to 1990, a period in which there

was also an increase in the pervasiveness of television. Unfortunately, most of the studies on adolescents and television violence are correlational studies, which ask adolescents about the television programs they watch and about their aggressive behavior. Correlational studies cannot prove causality and merely support the unremarkable conclusion that aggressive adolescents prefer aggressive television programs.

In an effort to address the question of causality, numerous field studies have focused on the effects of television on adolescent aggression, in which adolescents (usually boys) in a setting such as a residential school or summer camp were separated into two groups, and one group was shown television or movies with violent themes while the other viewed television or movies with nonviolent themes. However, the findings of these studies are weak and inconsistent, and overall they do not provide support for the claim that viewing violent media causes adolescents to be more aggressive (Freedman, 1984; Strasburger, 1995).

Nevertheless, a few studies provide support for the argument that watching violent television causes violent behavior. One intriguing study (Williams, 1986) involved a natural experiment in which a Canadian community (called "Notel" by the researchers) was studied before and after the introduction of television into the community. Aggressive behavior among children in Notel was compared to the behavior of children in two comparable communities, one with only one television channel ("Unitel") and one with multiple channels ("Multitel"). In each community, several ratings of aggressiveness were obtained, including teachers' ratings, self-reports, and observers' ratings of children's verbal and physical

aggressiveness. Aggressive behavior was lower among children in Notel than among children in Unitel or Multitel when the study began, but increased significantly among children in Notel after television was introduced, so that Notel children were equal in aggressive behavior to their Unitel and Multitel peers two years after the introduction of television. However, the study involved children in middle childhood rather than adolescents, and it is difficult to say how the adolescents of the community reacted.

Overall, research provides only tepid support for the claim that watching violent television causes teens to behave aggressively (Freedman, 1984). It is probably true that, for some adolescents, watching television violence acts as a model for their own aggressiveness (Strasburger, 1995). However, if watching violent television were a substantial contributor to violence among teens, the relationship would be stronger than it has been in the many studies that have been conducted by now.

Computer Games and Aggressiveness

In recent years computer video games have become especially popular among young adolescents, and especially among boys. One survey of seventh and eighth graders found that boys reported spending over four hours a week playing computer games, and girls about two hours (Funk, 1993).

Many of these computer games are in the category of harmless entertainment. A substantial proportion of the games simply involve having a computerized character jump from one platform to the next; or sports simulations of baseball, tennis, or hockey; or fantasies in which the player can escape to other worlds and take on new identities. However, computer games such as Quake II and Doom involve depictions of extreme violence. In fact, the majority of teens' favorite computer games involve violence. Because violent games have proven to be so popular, manufacturers have steadily increased the levels of violence in computer games over the past decade (Funk et al., 1999).

Does playing these games promote violence? Some notorious and widely publicized cases indicate yes. For example, one of the two boys who murdered twelve students and a teacher in the massacre at Columbine High School in 1999 named the gun he used in the murders "Arlene," after a character in the gory Doom video game.

However, only a handful of studies thus far have examined the relationship between video games and aggressiveness, and the results of these studies are mixed (Funk et al., 1999). It seems likely that with computer games, as with other violent media, there is a wide range of individual differences in responses, with young people who are already at risk for violent behavior—such as the Columbine murderers—being most likely to be affected by the games, as well as most likely to be attracted to them (Funk et al., 1999). However, with regard to computer games specifically, there is not much evidence to go on at this point. Because of the growing popularity and growing levels of violence in computer games, this will be an area to watch for future research.

Sex in Television and Movies

Sex is second only to violence as a topic of public concern with respect to the possible effects of television on adolescents. A high proportion of prime-time television shows contain sexual themes. What sort of information about sexuality does television present to adolescents?

A study by Monique Ward (1995) provides a detailed examination of the sexual content of the television shows most often viewed by adolescents. Her analysis found that both men and women were often portrayed as having a "recreational" orientation toward sex. Part of this recreational orientation was that sexual relations were frequently portrayed as a competition, a "battle of the sexes" in which men and women discussed "scoring," cheating on partners, stealing partners, and how to outmaneuver one another. Another part of the recreational orientation was the view of sexual relations as fun, a natural source of play and amusement that can be enjoyed without concern over commitment or responsibility. However—in contrast to the early days of television when the word *pregnant* was considered too racy to be mentioned and even married characters slept in separate beds—there were also occasional discussions of contraception.

What sort of uses do adolescents make of the portrayals of sexuality on television? In television programs adolescents learn cultural ideas about how male and female roles differ in sexual interactions and what is considered physically attractive in males and females. For adolescents, who are just beginning to date, this information may be eagerly received, especially in a culture where there is little in the way of explicit instruction in male and female sexual roles. Of course, the "information" they receive about sexual scripts from television—the emphasis on themes of sex as an arena for recreation and competition—may not be the kind most adults would consider desirable.

Television music videos also frequently contain portrayals of sexuality. However, few good studies investigating adolescents' responses to music videos have yet been conducted (Strasburger, 1995).

Movies (in theaters and on video) are another medium where adolescents witness portrayals of sexual behavior. Although adolescents spend less time watching movies than they do watching television, the movies they watch tend to have more frequent and explicit portrayals of sexuality than television shows do. In one study by Greenberg and colleagues (1993) that compared content in prime-time television programs to content in R-rated movies, the movies contained seven times as many sexual acts or references than the television programs did, and in the movies sexual intercourse between unmarried people was thirty-two times more common than between married people. Of course, adolescents under age eighteen are not supposed to be able to see R-rated movies (unless accompanied by an adult), but Greenberg and colleagues found that the majority of the fifteen- and sixteen-year-olds they surveyed had seen the most popular R-rated movies either in the theater or on video.

Rap Music

Rap music (also known as "hip-hop") rose steadily in popularity among teens during the 1990s, and now equals rock in popularity (Roberts et al.,1999). Although rap is especially popular among black adolescents, white adolescents also comprise a substantial proportion of rap fans.

Not all rap is controversial. Some rap performers enjoy a wide mainstream audience for themes of love, romance, and celebration. The controversy over rap has focused on "gangsta rap" performers such as Dr. Dre, Tupac Shakur, and N.W.A. (Niggas with Attitude), and has especially concerned sexual exploitation of women and violence.

Gangsta rap has been criticized for presenting images of women as objects of contempt, deserving sexual exploitation and even sexual assault. Women in controversial rap songs are often referred to as "hos" (whores) and "bitches," and sexuality is frequently portrayed as a man's successful assertion of power over a woman (Decker, 1994; Peterson-Lewis, 1991).

Violence is another common theme in the lyrics of gangsta rap performers. Their songs depict scenes such as drive-by shootings, gang violence, and violent confrontations with the police. The performers of such songs, and their defenders, have argued that their lyrics simply reflect the grim realities of life for young black people in America's inner cities, such as poverty, violence, and lack of educational and occupational opportunities (Decker, 1994). However, critics have accused the performers of contributing to the stereotype of young black men as dangerous criminals.

What effects—if any—do rap lyrics with themes of sexism and violence have on teens? Unfortunately, although there have been many academic speculations about the uses of rap by adolescents, thus far there are no studies that provide research evidence on the topic. Perhaps rap is used by some adolescents as an expression of their frustration and anger in the face of the difficult conditions they live in. But does rap also reinforce and perhaps magnify tendencies toward sexism and violence? At this point, we lack an informed answer to this question.

Girls' Magazines and Gender Socialization

Girls' magazines have received criticism for the messages they deliver to girls about how they should look and act. Boys read magazines, too, but their favorite magazines—such as *Sport, Gamepro, Hot Rod, Popular Science*—involve active recreation and have not been controversial.

What sort of gender messages do adolescent girls get when they read these magazines? Several analyses have been made of the content in girls' magazines, and they have reported highly similar findings (e.g., Durham, 1998; Evans et al., 1991). The analyses show that the magazines relentlessly promote the gender socialization of adolescent girls toward the traditional female gender role. Physical appearance is stressed as being of ultimate importance, and there is an intense focus on how to be appealing to boys. Fashion is the most common topic, followed by beauty and health—but most of the articles on "health" are about weight reduction and control. Altogether, over half the content focuses directly on physical appearance. But this percentage actually understates the focus on physical appearance because it does not include the advertisements. Typically, nearly half the space in the magazines is devoted to advertisements, and the ads are almost exclusively for clothes, cosmetics, and weight-loss programs.

In contrast to the plethora of articles and advertisements on physical appearance, there are few articles on political or social issues. The main topic of "career" articles is modeling. There are virtually no articles on possible careers in business, or the sciences, or law, or medicine, or any other high-status profession in which the mind would be valued more than the body. Of course, there is little doubt that the magazine publishers would carry an abundance of articles on social issues and professional careers if they found they could sell more magazines that way. They pack the magazines with articles and ads on how to enhance physical attractiveness because that is the content to which adolescent girls respond most strongly.

Why? Perhaps because early adolescence—the time when these magazines are most popular—is a time of gender intensification. Girls become acutely aware when they reach adolescence that others expect them to look like a girl is supposed to look and act like a girl is supposed to act—but how is a girl supposed to look and act? These magazines promise to provide the answers. Wear this kind of blouse, and this kind of skirt, and style your hair like this, and wear this kind of eye shadow and this kind of lipstick and this perfume, and be sure to stay or get thin. The message to adolescent girls is that if you buy the right products and strive to conform your appearance to the ideal presented in the magazines you will look and act like a girl is supposed to look and act and you will attract all the boys you want (Durham, 1998; Evans et al., 1991).

Of course, not only gender intensification is involved in the appeal of girls' magazines but also culture. Girls respond to their portrayal in the magazines as appearance-obsessed slaves to love because they have been taught through the gender socialization of their culture to see themselves that way, and by adolescence they have learned that lesson well (Durham, 1998).

Positive Uses of Media

Although controversial media receive the bulk of the public attention, in fact most of teens' media use is noncontroversial and can play a positive role in their lives. Three positive uses of media for teens are entertainment, identity formation, and coping (Arnett, 1995).

Adolescents and emerging adults, like children and adults, often make use of media simply for entertainment, as an enjoyable part of their leisure lives. Music is the most-used media form among adolescents and emerging adults, and listening to music often accompanies young people's leisure, from driving around in a car to hanging out with friends to secluding themselves in the privacy of their bedrooms for contemplation (Larson, 1995). This applies to music videos, too—adolescents state that one of their top motivations for watching music videos is simply entertainment. Television is used by many adolescents as a way of diverting themselves from personal concerns with entertainment that is passive, distracting, and undemanding (Larson, 1995). Entertainment is clearly one of the uses young people seek in movies and magazines as well. Media are used by young people toward the entertainment purposes of fun, amusement, and recreation.

One of the most important developmental challenges of adolescence and emerging adulthood is identity formation—the cultivation of a conception of one's values, abilities, and hopes for the future. In cultures where media are available, media can provide materials that young people use toward the construction of an identity. Part of identity formation is thinking about the kind of person you would like to become, and in media adolescents find ideal selves and feared selves, to emulate and to avoid. The use of media for this purpose is reflected in the pictures and posters adolescents put up in their rooms, which are often of media stars from entertainment and sports (Steele and Brown, 1995). After their parents, media celebrities of various kinds are mentioned most often by ado-

lescents when they are asked whom they most admire. Media can also provide adolescents with information that would otherwise be unavailable to them, and some of this information may be used toward constructing an identity. For example, adolescents may learn about different possible occupations in part by watching television or reading magazines.

Young people use media to cope with and dispel negative emotions. Several studies indicate that "Listen to music" and "Watch television" are the coping strategies most commonly used by adolescents when they are angry, anxious, or unhappy (Arnett, 1995). Music may be particularly important in this respect. Larson (1995) reports that adolescents often listen to music in the privacy of their bedrooms while pondering the themes of the songs in relation to their own lives, as a way of processing difficult emotions. In the course of early adolescence, when there is an increase in the amount of problems, conflict, and stresses at home, at school, and with friends, there is also an increase in time spent listening to music, while time spent watching television decreases.

New Media: The Internet

A new medium growing rapidly in popularity among young people is the Internet. In a 1998 survey by *Consumers' Research Magazine,* 79 percent of high school students in the United States reported having regular Internet access, compared to just 13 percent of persons over age fifty. Similar or even higher percentages are reported for other Western countries, and for Eastern countries such as Tiawan (Anderson, 2000). Internet access for young people in industrialized countries is expected to become nearly universal in the next decade, in part because schools are increasingly becoming linked to the Internet and encouraging students to use it for finding information.

The Internet makes available literally millions of different Web sites and information sources, so the potential uses that adolescents could make of the Internet are almost limitless. Scholars have suggested that young people's uses of the Internet are likely to include both benefits and risks (Bremer and Rauch, 1998). Benefits of Internet use for young people include access to educational information, access to health information (e.g., about sexual health), and the opportunity to practice social interactions in "chat rooms" and via e-mail. Risks include exposure to pornographic material, substituting computer play for social interactions, and being exposed to adults in chat rooms who may try to exploit them sexually. Because Internet use is relatively new, little research has yet explored how young people use it, but research is sure to explore this topic in the future.

Jeffrey Jensen Arnett

See also Appearance, Cultural Factors in; Attractiveness, Physical; Computers; Television; Violence

References and further reading

Anderson, Ronald E. 2000. "Youth and Information Technology." Unpublished manuscript, University of Minnesota.

Arnett, Jeffrey J. 1995. "Adolescents' Uses of Media for Self-Socialization." *Journal of Youth and Adolescence* 24: 519–533.

Bremer, Jennifer, and Paula K. Rauch. 1998. "Children and Computers: Risks and Benefits." *Journal of the American Academy of Child and Adolescent Psychiatry* 37: 559–560.

Christenson, Peter G., and Donald F. Roberts. 1998. *It's Not Only Rock and Roll: Popular Music in the Lives of Adolescents.* Cresskill, NJ: Hampton Press.

Decker, Jeffrey L. 1994. "The State of Rap: Time and Place in Hip Hop Nationalism." Pp. 99–112 in *Microphone Fiends: Youth Music and Youth Culture.* Edited by A. Ross and Tricia Rose. New York: Routledge.

Durham, M. G. 1998. "Dilemmas of Desire: Representations of Sexuality in Two Teen Magazines." *Youth and Society* 29: 369–389.

Evans, E. D., J. Rutberg, C. Sather, and C. Turner. 1991. "Content Analysis of Contemporary Teen Magazines for Adolescent Females." *Youth and Society* 23: 99–120.

Freedman, Jonathan L. 1984. "Effects of Television Violence on Aggressiveness." *Psychological Bulletin* 96: 227–246.

Funk, Jeanne B. 1993. "Reevaluating the Impact of Video Games." *Clinical Pediatrics* 32: 86–90.

Funk, Jeanne B., Geysa Flores, Debra D. Buchman, and Julie N. Germann. 1999. "Rating Electronic Video Games: Violence Is in the Eye of the Beholder." *Youth and Society* 30: 283–312.

Greenberg, Bradley S., Jane D. Brown, and Nancy Buerkel-Rothfuss. 1993. *Media, Sex, and the Adolescent.* Cresskill, NJ: Hampton Press.

Larson, Reed. 1995. "Secrets in the Bedroom: Adolescents' Private Use of Media." *Journal of Youth and Adolescence* 24: 535–550.

Peterson-Lewis, Sonja. 1991. "A Feminist Analysis of the Defenses of Obscene Rap Lyrics." *Black Sacred Music: A Journal of Theomusicology* 5: 68–80.

Roberts, Donald F., Ulla G. Foehr, Victoria J. Rideout, and Mollyann Brodie. 1999. *Kids and Media @ the New Millennium.* Menlo Park, CA: Henry J. Kaiser Foundation.

Steele, Jeanne R., and Jane D. Brown. 1995. "Adolescent Room Culture: Studying Media in the Context of Everyday Life." *Journal of Youth and Adolescence* 24: 551–576.

Strasburger, Victor C. 1995. *Adolescents and the Media: Medical and Psychological Impact.* Thousand Oaks, CA: Sage Publications.

Ward, L. Monique. 1995. "Talking about Sex: Common Themes about Sexuality in the Prime-Time Television Programs Children and Adolescents View Most." *Journal of Youth and Adolescence* 24: 595–616.

Williams, T. B., ed. 1986. *The Impact of Television: A Natural Experiment in Three Communities*. New York: Academic Press.

Memory

Popular opinion does not hold memory among the most exciting topics of psychology. Rather, it is thought of as a useful tool, nothing more. It is not even to be compared with the more important topic of intelligence, or the highly abstract and thus mysterious self, or multifaceted personality, or with unstable, stubborn emotions.

Intelligence and emotions are quite complex concepts and quite different from memory. The term *memory* refers to millions and millions of bites of information stored in a certain order in a small box of the human brain and able to be retrieved any time, with or without any cues. It is daunting to think that the brain has enough room for all of the information contained in memory. Researchers have discovered that there is great variability among the levels of performance on memory tasks, even within just one person. Memory is very selective: Some things get memorized and some do not, and sometimes either can happen in spite of a person's conscious efforts.

Memory ability depends on one's level of vigilance, many contextual factors, the nature of information, and the person's emotional engagement, or lack of it, in the material to be memorized. People tend to better remember what makes them feel something. Memory holds an exclusive place among the faculties of the human psyche—it is involved in practically every process of one's thinking, in practically every aspect of life. While thinking, we use stored as well as new information. While eating, or skating, or biking, or doing anything at all, we use procedural memory that tells us how an action must be performed. The most independent creative processes, such as writing or invention, still use a good deal of stored information as building blocks of a new creation. The last but not the least important characteristic of memory that deserves attention is its involvement in self, or personality, construction. In fact, autobiographical memories are the material that our personalities are built with, so without memory, a person in a sense does not exist. Total amnesia, or the loss of memory, demonstrates quite explicitly that a loss of memory is also a loss of self.

There is really no such thing as a general memory. Memory is domain specific. Also, there are different types of memory even in one domain. The first and most basic division is into the sensory register (SR), a short-term store (STS), and a long-term store (LTS). The sensory register takes in everything, all new information. The best demonstration of how it works is iconic memory—if we close our eyes, we will still see the afterimage of what we just saw. But the information never stays for more than a second in the SR. After that, it enters the STS. And here, the selection procedures begin, since the storage space of STS is very limited. The goal is to pass the information to the LTS to be remembered for the rest of our lives, or at least for a long enough period. As already noted, sometimes this entering of long-term memory happens spontaneously and quite effortlessly, but in most cases different memory strategies (such as rehearsal) are employed to keep the information alive until it enters the LTS. The long-term storage capacities are thought to be unlimited, and it is amazing how quickly one is able to retrieve just exactly what one needs from this infinite storage house. Yet it is also true that with time the unused information from LTS can decay.

The information in LTS is not piled randomly, but organized in various ways. In terms of types, most researchers agree to distinguish declarative and nondeclarative memory. Nondeclarative memory includes all unconscious knowledge of skills (procedural memory), and conditional factors such as an intuitive sense of danger or fear when something previously experienced as dangerous or fearful (even without an exact recollection of the event) is encountered. Declarative memory is conscious, and it is composed of two components, semantic (knowledge of rules, concepts, ideas) and episodic (knowledge of events) memory. Memory is also domain specific, and the distinction, for instance, between the autobiographical memory and the memory for faces is rather significant. The latter is a puzzle in itself, if one thinks about thousands of faces that a human being can recognize.

In recent decades most researchers have agreed that the amount of information retained depends mostly (though not exclusively) on the speed of processing, as well as on one's level of expertise in a given domain. In other words, if one wants to memorize more in a particular field (as already noted, the global memory is at best a theoretical generalization), one may want to simply work hard in this domain to increase one's level of expertise, which in turn will increase the speed of processing new information, which in turn will increase the memory level.

Memory strategies can be taught and are useful tools for enhancing memory ability and for learning new information. Strategies are potentially conscious, deliberate, and controllable cognitive plans that are adopted to enhance performance in memory tasks. The most important of them are rehearsal, organization, and elaboration.

The idea of rehearsal may be the oldest, the simplest, and probably the most effective for memorizing a poem or a list of items. The frequency of rehearsal is important, but it is not the only factor that matters. The style of rehearsal plays a role in how effective the strategy is. Two rehearsal styles, passive and active (or accumulative, when all the information is repeated every time), are widely used, with the latter definitely yielding better results. However, even accumulative rehearsal may not be good enough if it is not used with other strategies.

Another strategy, organization, is used every time one tries to organize the information to be remembered according to a certain system. Elaboration involves associating items to be remembered with something new, that was not presented in the material, but should be invented through imagination (for instance, if we need to remember two colors, we may find an object where they are found together).

These are three of the basic memory strategies, but they cannot always be used with all types of memory. Thus, to enhance one's memory performance, it may be useful to remember the main principles of memory functioning and then use them to select or maybe invent the strategies that work better for a particular person in a particular memory task.

- One remembers better what is interesting, and it is not completely out of one's control to make something interesting.

- One remembers better what one has actively processed, upon which one has acted in one way or another.
- One remembers better information on a subject or in a field that is already familiar; in short, knowledge attracts knowledge.

Adolescents should be aware that they can learn strategies to enhance menory performance.

Janna Jilnina

See also Academic Achievement; Academic Self-Evaluation; Cognitive Development; Homework; Intelligence Tests; Thinking

References and further reading
Baddley, Alan D. 1986. *Working Memory.* Oxford, UK: Clarendon Press.
Loftus, Elizabeth F. 1980. *Memory, Surprising and New Insights into How We Remember and Why We Forget.* Reading, MA: Addison-Wesley.
Weinert, Franz, and Marion Perlmutter, eds. 1988. *Memory Development: Universal Changes and Individual Differences.* Hillsdale, NJ: Erlbaum.

Menarche

Menarche, which means "first menstrual period," is a late event during physical pubertal development. It is most likely to occur when a girl has reached near-adult levels of breast and pubic hair growth. In general, menarche entails at least three days of vaginal bleeding. (Spotting or bleeding for fewer than three days is not considered menarche.) This bleeding usually rarely occurs in the early stages of puberty when the lining of the uterus is not thick enough to cause a regular amount of flow. However, it can also be a result of trauma such as rape or, in very rare instances, due to tumors in the vagina or uterus.

The age at which menarche occurs has steadily declined over time. In 1880, the average age at which menarche occurred among American girls overall was between 14.5 and 15 years. At present, by contrast, menarche occurs among white girls at 12.8 years, among black girls at 11.9 years, and among Puerto Rican girls at 11.5 years (Clayman, 1994).

In fact, the normal range for menarche in the United States is now between ten and fourteen years of age. Onset before age ten or after age fourteen is an indication of possible abnormal development; in such cases, a physician should be consulted. Causes for absence of menarche include late development (which tends to run in families and can be considered normal), absence of the ovaries or uterus, imbalance of the hormones involved in the menstrual cycle, and pregnancy. Excessive exercise (especially among gymnasts and long-distance runners) and anorexia nervosa are commonly associated with delayed menarche.

Jordan W. Finkelstein

See also Body Fat, Changes in; Puberty: Hormone Changes; Puberty: Physical Changes; Puberty, Timing of; Rites of Passage; Sex Education

References and further reading
Clayman, Charles B., ed. 1994. *The American Medical Association Family Medical Guide,* 3rd ed.. New York: Random House, pp. 624, 756.

Menstrual Cycle

The menstrual cycle consists of four major phases: the menstrual phase, during which the lining of the uterus is discarded as bleeding (days 1–5, a total of five days); the follicular phase (days 6–13, a total of eight days), during which an egg (ovum) matures and the lining of the uterus regrows after being shed during the menstrual phase; ovulation (day 14, a total of one day), during which the egg is released from the ovary and begins its travel to the fallopian tube; and, finally, the luteal phase (days 15–28, a total of fourteen days), during which the lining of the uterus continues to develop so that it can receive a fertilized egg. Contrary to common belief, only about 10–15 percent of cycles are twenty-eight days long. The overall cycle length may vary from twenty-one to forty-two days, but most mature women's cycles last between twenty-five and thirty days. During the first five years of menstruation, cycles exhibit considerable variability in terms of length and regularity. After that time, however (especially following a pregnancy), cycles tend to be more stable.

Among women who ovulate regularly, the length of the luteal phase is usually fourteen days. In women with a thirty-two-day cycle, menstrual bleeding will occur on days 1–5 (five days), the follicular phase will last from days 6 to 16 (eleven days), ovulation will occur on day 17 (one day), and the luteal phase will occur on days 18–32 (fourteen days). Alternatively, in women with a twenty-four-day cycle, menstrual bleeding will occur on days 1–5 (five days), the follicular phase will last from days 6 to 9 (four days), ovulation will occur on day 10 (one day), and the luteal phase will occur on days 11–24 (again, fourteen days). This knowledge can be used to predict ovulation in women whose cycles are very regular—a procedure that, in turn, can be used as a method of natural birth control.

The menstrual cycle, which involves coordination of hormone secretions from the pituitary gland as well as the ovaries, can be influenced by numerous factors including nutritional status, stress, exercise, and chronic disease. Many of these factors cause periods to stop *(amenorrhea)* or to become infrequent *(oligomenorrhea)*. For example, the extreme exercise associated with long-distance running and gymnastics induces the body to revert to the hormone pattern seen in prepubertal children, stopping all menstruation.

Jordan W. Finkelstein

See also Body Fat, Changes in; Puberty: Hormone Changes; Puberty: Physical Changes; Puberty, Timing of

References and further reading
Namnoum, A., B. Koehler, and S. E. Carpenter. 1994. "Abnormal Uterine Bleeding in the Adolescent." *Adolescent Medicine: State of the Art Reviews* 5: 157–170.

Menstrual Dysfunction

Menstrual dysfunction (MD) refers to abnormal uterine bleeding that is excessive or unpatterned in amount, duration, or frequency. A period that is not preceded by ovulation (known as an *anovulatory period*) is one of the most common causes of MD. Fifty to 80 percent of cycles in the first year of menstruation are anovulatory, as are about 28 percent of cycles by the fifth year. In short, many girls experience MD during their first five years of menstruation.

The absence of ovulation associated with MD often results in incomplete shedding of the lining of the uterus. This lining then gets thicker and thicker with each cycle, usually leading to very heavy periods *(menorrhagia)* and/or irregular periods *(metrorrhagia)*. Eventually the thickened lining reaches a critical level, at which point the lining of the uterus begins to be shed almost continually, resulting in almost constant menstrual flow or very heavy periods *(menometrorrhagia)*.

Less common causes of menstrual dysfunction include pregnancy, which is sometimes complicated by periods of bleeding, and blood-clotting disorders, which are seen in about 20 percent of women. (In one study, among women who presented with severe blood loss in their first period, 45 percent had a clotting disorder.) In addition, abnormal bleeding can be caused by other problems in the reproductive system, including trauma, infection, foreign matter in the vagina, congenital malformations, irritation of the cervix (the neck of the uterus), polyps, misplaced lining of the uterus outside of the uterus *(endometriosis)*, blood-vessel malformations, and tumors. Malnutrition, as well as certain chronic illnesses such as kidney disease, liver failure, diabetes, and malnutrition, can also cause MD.

Hormonal dysfunction is another possible cause of MD. For example, pituitary problems associated with high prolactin levels and milk production can lead to lactation and, ultimately, to MD in a nonpregnant teenager. Also problematic are over- or underactive thyroids and abnormalities of adrenal or ovary function. The most common form of the latter, called *polycystic ovary syndrome*, involves infrequent periods. It is seen most often among teenagers with obesity, high blood pressure, increased growth of body hair, and, sometimes, diabetes.

In some instances, hormonal medications, anticoagulants (blood thinners), and medications to prevent seizures have also been known to cause MD. Accurate diagnostic procedures are needed to rule out these and other such causes.

Jordan W. Finkelstein

See also Anemia; Body Fat, Changes in; Contraception; Eating Problems; Health Promotion; Health Services for Adolescents; Nutrition; Puberty: Hormone Changes; Puberty: Physical Changes; Puberty, Timing of; Sex Education

References and further reading
Berkow, Robert B., ed. 1997. *The Merck Manual of Medical Information: Home Edition*. Whitehouse Station, NJ: Merck Research Laboratories.
Clayman, Charles B., ed. 1994. *The American Medical Association Family Medical Guide*, 3rd ed. New York: Random House.

Menstruation

During menstruation, the lining of the uterus is shed because a pregnancy has not occurred during the previous menstrual cycle. The majority of blood loss occurs during the first three days of the cycle, and the usual amount of blood lost is about one ounce. Loss of more than three ounces is considered abnormal and may cause anemia.

Two weeks prior to menstruation, there are high levels of estrogen and progesterone in the blood. Menstruation occurs when the concentration of these hormones decreases. In other words, menstruation is the result of withdrawal of hormones that would otherwise allow the lining of the uterus (the *endometrium*) to be maintained.

Menstrual bleeding stops when the concentration of estrogen begins to rise at the beginning of a new menstrual cycle. This rising level of estrogen not only increases the ability of blood to clot but also stimulates the lining to grow again.

The most common problem during menstruation is abdominal pain from menstrual cramps *(dysmenorrhea)*. Overall, between 30 and 50 percent of women experience this problem (Sanfilippo and Hertwick, 1998). About 30 percent of

The most common problem during menstruation is abdominal pain from menstrual cramps (dysmenorrhea). (Skjold Photographs)

women present with dysmenorrhea in the first six months after menarche (first period), and it is the leading cause of short-term school absence among adolescent girls. Dysmenorrhea is caused by the increased production of hormones called prostaglandins, which induce contractions of the uterus and are experienced as cramping.

Some antiprostaglandin medications (such as ibuprofen and other nonsteroidal anti-inflammatory drugs) can decrease the symptoms of dysmenorrhea. Whenever possible, these medications should be started two or three days prior to the expected start of bleeding and then continued for three days after bleeding has commenced. They should be taken at the proper dose and around the clock rather than only when pain occurs. Oral contraceptives may also reduce or eliminate the symptoms of dysmenorrhea, given that cramping occurs only during cycles in which ovulation occurs and these contraceptives inhibit ovulation. Of course, among sexually active adolescents, oral contraceptives provide the additional benefit of preventing pregnancy.

Premenstrual syndrome (PMS) is another common problem associated with menstruation. Its symptoms include fluid retention, bloating, breast tenderness, headaches, irritability, fatigue, anxiety, hostility, and depression. Many women also experience cravings for certain foods or drinks. PMS is usually worst in girls who also have dysmenorrhea. Several treatments are reported to be effective, including changes in diet, exercise, hormones, diuretics (water pills), vitamins, and drugs that affect behavior.

The usual duration of the menstrual cycle ranges from twenty-one to forty-two days, and bleeding generally lasts for fewer than seven days. Women with menstruation occurring outside these limits should consider medical evaluation. Prolonged, irregular, and frequent menstruation is generally related to abnormal ovarian function, the most common cause of which is failure to ovulate. This condition is most often seen in women who have just started menstruating. Between 55 and 82 percent of menstrual cycles in the first two years after menarche are *anovulatory* (i.e., ovulation does not occur) (Sanfilippo and Hertwick, 1998). In the second through fourth years after menarche, 30–55 percent of women do not ovulate; in the fourth and fifth years, the range is 0–20 percent. Other causes of prolonged, irregular, frequent bleeding include disorders of blood clotting, certain medications, hormonal disorders, and certain sexually transmitted diseases—all of which should be evaluated in all women with this problem.

Treatment of the most common form of abnormal bleeding (due to lack of ovulation) is accomplished by using the hormones involved in the normal menstrual cycle—specifically, by using oral contraceptives. Other forms of hormone replacement are also available, but they are not as convenient as oral contraceptives. In addition, specific treatments are available for causes of this problem other than lack of ovulation.

Women with absent periods fall into two categories. Those who have breast and sexual hair development but who have not experienced menstruation by the age of sixteen years, or those who have no breast or sexual hair development and no periods by the age of thirteen years, have *primary amenorrhea*. Fewer than 0.1 percent of women have this problem. The most common causes are hormonal disorders and absence of the ovaries or uterus. Women who have periods at intervals of more than three months have *secondary amenorrhea*, a problem experienced by about 0.7 percent of women (Sanfilippo and Hertwick, 1998). The most common causes include hormonal disorders, certain medications, substantial changes in weight, stress, and excessive exercise. Both groups need medical evaluation. Administration of hormones such as oral contraceptives can induce periods in those individuals who have hormonal abnormalities involving the ovaries but no other identifiable causes. Specific treatments are appropriate for those persons whose disorders have been specifically identified.

Jordan W. Finkelstein

See also Body Fat, Changes in; Puberty: Hormone Changes; Puberty: Physical Changes; Sex Education; Sports and Adolescents

References and further reading
Berk, Laura. 1999. *Infants, Children, and Adolescents.* Needham Heights, MA: Allyn and Bacon.
Sanfilippo, J. S., and S. P. Hertwick. 1998. "Physiology of Menstruation and Menstrual Disorders." Pp. 990–1017 in *Comprehensive Adolescent Health Care.* Edited by S. B. Friedman, M. Fisher, S. K. Schoenberg, E. M. Adlerman, and E. Mosby. New York: Random House.

Mental Retardation, Siblings with

Millions of adolescents in the United States have a brother or sister with mental retardation or some other type of developmental disability. Mental retardation is a lifelong condition that is characterized by problems with adaptive behavior and by significant limitations in intellectual functioning. It can be caused by a variety of genetic, metabolic, and environmental conditions. Although many persons with mental retardation achieve a measure of independence as adults, most live with the support of their families throughout their lives. Although mothers and fathers of persons with mental retardation bear the major responsibility for ensuring needed care, siblings in the family face many unique and lifelong challenges. This entry explores the experiences and concerns of being an adolescent with "a difference in the family" (Featherstone, 1980).

Of all human relationships, the sibling relationship is the longest in duration, and as such, it goes through many changes over the life course. When one of the siblings in a family has mental retardation, a cascade of issues is confronted by the nondisabled sibling(s), issues that have been well described by siblings, parents, clinicians, and researchers. These include:

- Ongoing need for information about their sibling's disability (its cause, manifestations, future course, and the like)
- Feelings of isolation, because they might not have access to others in similar situations and/or because they are being excluded from discussions with service providers and even family members
- Guilt feelings about having caused the disability or being spared the condition
- Resentment of the extra time parents devote to the sibling with

mental retardation and of parental overprotectiveness or indulgence of the brother or sister with mental retardation
- Perceived pressure to achieve in academics, athletics, or social situations
- Increased caregiving requirements, particularly from nondisabled sisters
- Concerns over their own future role as potential caregivers for their brother or sister with mental retardation

Adolescence can be a particularly difficult time for all individuals, and some of the challenges of sibling relationships during adolescence are magnified when a nondisabled person has a brother or sister with mental retardation. There are also unique issues faced by siblings of persons with mental retardation during adolescence that may set them apart from their friends who do not have the same family situation. Using knowledge gained from over a dozen years of studies of families of persons with mental retardation, including research on siblings' lives, this entry highlights the personal, social, and familial impacts of having a brother or sister with mental retardation. It also includes some of the advice that adult siblings of persons with mental retardation have offered to teenagers, and it concludes with a list of resources that may be useful to adolescents with a brother or sister with mental retardation.

Having a brother or sister with mental retardation used to be considered a family tragedy. One of the biggest worries was that parents would need to spend so much time caring for the child with mental retardation that their other children would feel neglected. It was also assumed that sisters of children with mental retardation would be thrust prematurely into a caretaking role to help out their mothers and would not be able to develop independent lives as an adolescent. To some extent, even today, these attitudes about what it means to have a child with mental retardation still exist in the general public. However, studies of siblings of persons with mental retardation reveal a much more complex and generally positive picture.

Most adult siblings of persons with mental retardation, in looking back on their childhood and adolescence, say that their experiences were "mostly positive"—they feel deep love for their brother or sister with mental retardation, and they learned valuable lessons about appreciating people's differences, about tolerance and patience, about accepting situations that cannot be changed, and about the value of each individual. Many say that their families have been stronger and more loving because they have a member with mental retardation. As one sibling put it, "There are much worse things that can happen to a family, so look for your blessings." From their perspective as adults, however, many siblings point to their adolescent years as a time when new difficulties arose and when their emotional relationship to their brother or sister with mental retardation underwent strains that had not been as evident during their earlier childhood years. We describe some of these strains below.

Unique Challenges during Adolescence
There are several unique challenges that adolescents who have a brother or sister with mental retardation face. First, nondisabled adolescents often worry about what their future role will be regarding the care and support of the brother or sister with mental retardation. It is often during adolescence that siblings, and particularly sisters, of persons with mental retardation start to anticipate how their adult lives will be affected by the reality that their brother or sister with mental retardation will need ongoing support. About 25 percent of siblings anticipate living with their brother or sister during adulthood and about half expect to be their brother or sister's legal guardian (Krauss et al., 1996). Many do not know what their role will be, but knowing that their brother or sister will have lifetime needs for family support can weigh heavily on the minds of adolescents who are also thinking about their own futures. Indeed, over half of the siblings we've studied said that their own plans for the future were affected by their having a sibling with mental retardation. The areas in which the greatest impacts were noted included their feelings about themselves, their plans for their future, where they expected to live as adults, and their choices of romantic partners.

Second, adult siblings often described adolescence as a time when they experienced much more embarrassment about having a disabled sibling and resentment of their responsibilities toward him or her. The behavioral oddities or problems of the brother or sister with mental retardation were more stigmatizing, which resulted in the nondisabled adolescents seeking to avoid going out in public with their brother or sister. While most adolescents cringe at being seen with their parents and family in public, the added issue of having a brother or sister who has atypical behaviors and skills can be particularly painful. The push toward conformity, toward being accepted by one's peer group, often makes differences less cherished during adolescence. One sibling commented, "When I was younger, I was proud of the attention my brother brought our family, but as I entered adolescence, I didn't want to be different." Another noted, "My friends from grade school accepted my brother, but as I went to junior high, it was more difficult to have new friends over. They didn't understand and were afraid. The few places we did go (like to the zoo), people really stared at my brother."

Third, nondisabled adolescents must cope with changes in their feelings toward their brother or sister with mental retardation; their feelings may get more complicated, and they may feel emotionally distant during adolescence in comparison to early childhood. Most adolescents renegotiate their family relationships during the teen years as they struggle toward greater personal independence and autonomy. Many adult siblings of persons with mental retardation, however, described a wild flux of emotions about their brother or sister that stood in contrast to their earlier childhood memories of less stormy, more accepting relationships. As one sibling put it, "Through grade school, I felt he was more like another ordinary brother but as I went through high school, I went through all sorts of stages—extreme embarrassment, extreme protectiveness, disgust, as well as love and compassion."

Advice from Adult Siblings of Persons with Mental Retardation to Adolescents

In the course of their research, Krauss and her colleagues asked adult siblings of persons with mental retardation what advice they would give to teenagers in their situation. The most common counsel was to treat the brother or sister with mental retardation as a "normal" person, to encourage his/her potential, and to give lots of love and attention. Others mentioned the need to access community services, both for oneself (such as sibling support groups) and for one's sibling with mental retardation. Many also advised patience and having frequent contact with the brother or sister.

Many encouraged a high level of involvement by brothers and sisters with their sibling with mental retardation. One wrote, "Encourage your sibling's independence as much as possible, for there will be a time when parents will not be there to support your brother or sister. You must have a mutual respect for his/her ideas and thoughts."

Others advised that acceptance of the brother or sister with mental retardation was critically important. "Probably my strongest advice would be to accept the problem the brother or sister has and then try and treat the person as simply a person with a *type* of problem that can possibly be an experience that will make you a more sensitive individual."

Another strong sentiment was to view the situation as a *family* issue and to work closely with parents regarding caretaking decisions. One wrote, "Make sure you maintain open communication with your family about your needs and your sibling's needs. Remember that your parents have a big responsibility caring for your sibling—relieve them sometime and give them some time off. It's okay to think about alternatives to living at home and talking about it with parents." Another wrote, "Encourage your parents *now* to plan for the future and find some kind of independent placement for your sibling that will not impact on your life."

Others encouraged teenagers to participate in peer support groups. One said,

"Take advantage of educational and peer support groups. I did not have this opportunity." And many encouraged teenagers to just enjoy their adolescence. One wrote, "This too shall pass. The teenage hormones conspire to make the most self-assured child a monster of insecurity. Conformity is impossible if your family is different. It is a good thing to develop some coping skills early in life."

Resources for Siblings of Persons with Mental Retardation

Many communities offer sibling peer support groups through the local Arc (Association for Retarded Citizens—www.thearc.org). There are also national and international efforts to increase the opportunities for siblings of persons with mental retardation to meet personally or electronically (via the Internet) to share concerns, ideas, and understanding. The Sibling Support Project, directed by Donald Meyer at the Children's Hospital and Regional Medical Center in Seattle, Washington, has a Web site that posts useful information for siblings of all ages (www.chmc.org/departmt/sibsupp). There is also a list server for siblings (www.chmc.org/departmt/sibsupp/SendMail1.asp). The Family Village (www.familyvillage.wisc.edu) is a Web site for family members of people with disabilities, containing a wealth of information about the causes of different kinds of disabilities and describing strategies families have found to be helpful in responding to a variety of challenging situations. In addition, a variety of written materials, some listed in the reference list, may be particularly helpful to adolescents with a brother or sister with mental retardation.

Marty Wyngaarden Krauss
Marsha Mailick Seltzer

See also Cognitive Development; Learning Disabilities; Learning Styles and Accommodations; Sibling Differences; Sibling Relationships; Teasing

References and further reading
Featherstone, Helen. 1980. *A Difference in the Family.* New York: Basic Books.
Kaufman, Sandra Z. 1999. *Retarded Isn't Stupid, Mom!* Baltimore, MD: Paul H. Brookes.
Krauss, Marty W., Marsha M. Seltzer, Rachel Gordon, and Donna H. Friedman. 1996. "Binding Ties: The Roles of Adult Siblings of Persons with Mental Retardation." *Mental Retardation* 34, no. 2: 83–93.
McHugh, Mary. 1999. *Special Siblings: Growing Up with Someone with a Disability.* New York: Hyperion.
The research on which this entry is based was funded by the National Institute on Aging (Grant No. R01 AG08768) and by the Joseph P. Kennedy, Jr., Foundation and was administratively supported by the Starr Center on Mental Retardation, Heller School, Brandeis University, and the Waisman Center at the University of Wisconsin.

Mentoring and Youth Development

Mentoring programs for youth involve a structured one-to-one relationship or partnership that focuses on the needs of the mentored participant. However, to be effective in helping young people develop, a mentor and a mentoring program must do more than simply pair an adult with a young person.

"One to One," the National Mentoring Partnership, has described several elements of effective practice in youth mentoring programs (National Mentoring Working Group, 1991). In line with its mission—to increase the availability of responsible personal and economic mentoring for America's children—One to

One convened a volunteer subgroup of organizations with substantial experience in the conduct of mentoring programs for young people (e.g., Big Brothers/Big Sisters of America, Baltimore Mentoring Institute, the National Black Child Development Institute, the National Urban League, the Enterprise Institute, and Campus Partners in Learning/Campus Compact). This subgroup was called the National Mentoring Working Group. This working group developed a brochure called *Elements of Effective Practice* that specified the features mentoring programs need to have if they are to provide effective mentoring to young people. The group noted that a responsible mentoring program fosters caring and supportive relationships, encourages individuals to develop to their fullest potential, helps an individual develop his own vision for the future, and represents a strategy to develop active community partnerships.

Moreover, the National Mentoring Working Group of One to One specified also that the conduct of a mentoring program in a responsible manner involves the following elements: regular, consistent contact between the mentor and the participant; support by the family or guardian of the participant; an established organization of oversight; written administrative and program procedures; and written eligibility requirements for program participants.

One to One notes that research provides evidence that mentoring facilitates the experience by youth of relationships marked by mutual caring, accountability, and trust. A mentoring relationship provides youth with the resources to avoid behavioral risks and problems and facilitates the development among youth of a healthy and productive life.

The scholarship of Jean Rhodes and her colleagues provides considerable evidence that mentoring programs having the program characteristics specified by One to One can indeed effectively promote the positive development of youth. For example, among pregnant and parenting African American adolescents, the support of a natural mentor lowers depression and increases optimism, career activities, and beliefs about opportunity (Klaw and Rhodes, 1995; Rhodes, Ebert, and Fischer, 1992). Similarly, Latina adolescent mothers with natural mentors have lower levels of depression and anxiety, are more satisfied with their support resources, and are more able to cope effectively with relationship problems (Rhodes, Contreras, and Mangelsdorf, 1994). Moreover, only 20 percent of urban adolescent girls with mentors continue to show sexual- and school-related risk behaviors (Rhodes and Davis, 1996).

Urban youth involved in Big Brother/Big Sister mentor relationships for a year or longer show the largest number of improvements. However, mentoring appears to work best when it is extended for specific lengths of time, and, in turn, some people profit more from mentoring than do others. For example, among youth who are in mentoring relationships that terminate earlier, progressively fewer positive effects occur, and adolescents who are in relationships that terminate after a very short period of time show deterioration in their behavior. Older adolescents, adolescents referred for having experienced sustained emotional, sexual, or physical abuse, married volunteers aged twenty-six to thirty years, and volunteers with low incomes are most likely to be in relationships that end early (Grossman and Rhodes, in press).

Moreover, particular levels of mentoring seem most effective. That is, among ten- to sixteen-year-old youth involved in Big Brother/Big Sister programs, mentoring relationships that involve moderate levels of both support and structure are associated with improvements in parent and peer relationships, in personal development, and in academic performance (Langhout et al., 2000). These positive effects of mentoring relationships on academic performance are mediated primarily through improvements in parent-child relationships and are associated as well with reductions in unexcused absences and improvements in academic perceived competence (Rhodes, Grossman, and Resch, in press).

Finally, there is evidence that mentoring programs can be effective with youth in difficult family circumstances. For instance, among foster-care youth involved in Big Brother/Big Sister programs, mentoring relationships are associated with improved social skills, greater trust and comfort in social interactions, stable peer relationships, prosocial behavior, and self-esteem (Rhodes, Haight, and Briggs, 1999).

Richard M. Lerner

See also Academic Achievement; Apprenticeships; Career Development; Cognitive Development; College; School, Functions of; Vocational Development

References and further reading

Grossman, Jean B., and Jean E. Rhodes. In press. "The Test of Time: Predictors and Effects of Duration in Youth Mentoring Relationships." *American Journal of Community Psychology.*

Klaw, Elena L., and Jean E. Rhodes. 1995. "Mentor Relationships and the Career Development of Pregnant and Parenting African-American Teenagers." *Psychology of Women Quarterly* 19: 551–562.

Langhout, Regina E., Lori N. Osborne, Jean B. Grossman, and Jean E. Rhodes. 2000. *An Exploratory Study of Volunteer Mentoring: Toward a Typology of Relationships.* Unpublished manuscript.

National Mentoring Working Group. 1991. *Elements of Effective Practice.* Washington, DC: United Way of America and One to One/The National Mentoring Partnership.

Rhodes, Jean E., and Anita A. Davis. 1996. "Supportive Ties between Nonparent Adults and Urban Adolescent Girls." Pp. 213–225 in *Urban Girls: Resisting Stereotypes, Creating Identities.* Edited by Bonnie J. R. Leadbeater and Niobe Way. New York: New York University Press.

Rhodes, Jean E., Josefina M. Contreras, and Sarah C. Mangelsdorf. 1994. "Natural Mentor Relationships among Latina Adolescent Mothers: Psychological Adjustment, Moderating Processes, and the Role of Early Parental Acceptance." *American Journal of Community Psychology* 22: 211–227.

Rhodes, Jean E., Lori Ebert, and Karla Fischer. 1992. "Natural Mentors: An Overlooked Resource in the Social Networks of Young, African-American Mothers." *American Journal of Community Psychology* 20: 445–461.

Rhodes, Jean E., Jean B. Grossman, and Nancy L. Resch. In press. "Agents of Change: Pathways through Which Mentoring Relationships Influence Adolescents' Academic Adjustment." *Child Development.*

Rhodes, Jean E., Wendy L. Haight, and Ernestine C. Briggs. 1999. The Influence of Mentoring on the Peer Relationships of Foster Youth in Relative and Non-Relative Care. *Journal of Research on Adolescence* 9: 185–201.

Middle Schools

Middle school generally encompasses grades 5–8 or 6–8. These middle grades can be situated in one of two settings: as part of a kindergarten through eighth

Middle school students possess many newly emerging developmental abilities and needs. (Skjold Photographs)

grade (K through 8) setting or as a separate and distinct school setting. In the last ten to fifteen years, the number of middle schools in the United States has risen nearly 50 percent, whereas the number of junior high schools (usually grades 7–8 or 7–9) has declined by nearly 40 percent. One important issue regarding middle schools as separate and distinct school settings is the actual middle school experience for ten- to fourteen-year-olds.

As part of the educational reform movement, middle schools have drawn a great deal of attention in the last few years for three interrelated reasons: (1) because the period of early adolescence is viewed by psychologists and educators as a significant time for development at sev-

eral levels simultaneously (physically, socially, emotionally, and cognitively); (2) because the organization, structure, and curriculum of traditional middle schools do not tend to fit well with the developmental needs and abilities of early adolescents; and (3) because more than 88 percent of public school students enter a new school when they begin the middle grades, and many of these students experience difficulty making the transition from elementary school to middle school, as demonstrated by decreased motivation, self-esteem, and academic achievement.

Middle school students possess many newly emerging developmental abilities and needs. For example, ten- to fourteen-year-olds begin to demonstrate an increased desire for autonomy (i.e., for self-governing), stronger peer orientation, heightened self-consciousness, exploration into identity issues, concern over heterosexual relationships, capacity for abstract cognitive activity, and an interest in opportunities that demonstrate higher-order thinking and problem-solving skills. The characteristics of the middle school setting and the characteristics of the early adolescent reflect what is referred to as a developmental mismatch. In other words, traditional middle school settings are not suited to the needs and abilities of their students.

Psychologists have identified seven key developmental needs as characteristic of early adolescence: positive social interaction with adults and peers, structure and clear limits, physical activity, creative expression, competence and achievement, meaningful participation in family and school, and community experiences as opportunities for growing self-definition. Traditional middle schools, however, appear to lie in opposition to fulfillment of these needs.

Three problems associated with middle schools are school size, departmentalization, and instructional style. First, students often go from smaller neighborhood elementary schools to larger middle schools that draw students from several different elementary schools. At a time when adolescents are becoming capable of and requiring greater intimacy and closeness with peers and adult role models, the sudden change from a smaller neighborhood school to a larger middle school can foster alienation, isolation, anonymity, and difficulties in communication and intimacy. Some schools have emphasized the role of homerooms and/or an advisory system in an attempt to offset the isolating effects of a large school as well as to foster the development of relationships with peers and teachers.

Departmentalization poses a second problem. Although students in elementary school tend to spend the better part of their day with the same teacher and the same group of students, departmentalization forces students to switch from classroom to classroom and from teacher to teacher, thereby imposing a series of disruptions throughout the day that decrease the number of opportunities for students to develop closer relationships with others. Allowing students to navigate such switches as groups rather than as individuals lessens this interference in their communication and contact with peers.

The third problem, instructional style, impedes three aspects of development among adolescents: increased autonomy, cognitive ability, and self-consciousness. In the context of autonomy, researchers have discovered that most middle school teachers tend to exert more control over student behavior, maintain stricter rules and discipline, and allow less student input in decision making than do most elementary school teachers. This approach decreases the likelihood of positive student-teacher interactions, thus potentially preventing the development of relationships with much-needed supportive adult role models. Moreover, student reactions to seemingly unfair and punitive control over the environment can range from acting-out to losing interest altogether. Whenever possible, the structure and process of general classroom and school management should respond to and foster adolescents' growing capacity for autonomy, responsibility, and critical thinking.

In terms of cognitive ability, adolescents have reached a developmental stage in which they are generally more capable of logical and abstract thinking. They can now formulate and test hypotheses or ideas mentally; use more effective strategies for studying and remembering class material; and plan, monitor, and evaluate the steps they must take in order to solve a problem. Upon entering middle school, many students encounter increased work demands and stricter grading policies, but not necessarily a demand for higher-order thinking and problem-solving skills. On the contrary, many find middle school work less cognitively challenging than what they experienced in the last year or so of elementary school.

Finally, researchers have shown that the middle school experience sometimes results in increased self-consciousness as well as decreased motivation in all but the highest-performing students. One explanation for this finding is that middle school classes tend to involve occasions of public comparison in which achievement is based on a competitive rather than collaborative model of task completion and academic success.

Although the physical and physiological changes associated with adolescence have remained fundamentally the same for generations, the broader historical context within which these changes are played out is dramatically different than before, highlighting the need for and importance of an appropriate match between students and middle schools. Every day, early adolescents now confront pressures to engage in sex and to use alcohol, cigarettes, and marijuana. In addition, many suffer from feelings of depression, isolation, and alienation. For example, at least one-third of students in this age range report that they have contemplated suicide.

The school plays a significant role in the lives of young people: Development of educational programs that meet their needs is vital to their future as healthy, happy, and successful teenagers and adults. Middle school programs and practices can meet the developmental needs of early adolescents in a variety of ways. By means of advisory programs, for example, schools can provide students with social and emotional support through consistent contact with peers and adults in small-group settings. Some researchers claim that strong, small-group advisory programs are helpful in reducing feelings of isolation and anonymity. Urban schools that serve high-risk students are especially encouraged to implement such programs.

Interdisciplinary teaching teams provide another means of meeting the needs of middle school students. A typical interdisciplinary team consists of four teachers (usually in math, English, social studies, and science, respectively) who share the same group of students. This approach is intended to meet the social, emotional, and cognitive needs of students. Ideally these four teachers meet regularly to coordinate their lesson plans in a way that enables students to make connections between ideas across different subjects or disciplines, ensures that the material is sufficiently challenging, allows the students to provide social and professional support to one another, and enables the teachers themselves to periodically assess the students' progress and plan interventions. Of course, this approach requires that teachers receive training in team teaching and that school schedules are sufficiently flexible to permit regular team meetings.

Some schools have also created programs designed to ensure that the transition from elementary to middle school is as smooth as possible. These programs generally consist of three activities: having elementary school students visit prospective middle schools, having administrators of elementary and middle schools meet, and having middle school counselors or staff meet with elementary school counselors or staff.

More generally, effective and developmentally appropriate middle schools are attuned to all levels of student development: physical, social, emotional, and cognitive. They help students explore their sense of self, their aspirations, and their concerns; they involve students in setting goals, planning, and assessing their own learning; they provide challenging content and appropriate teaching and assessment techniques; they create an environment where individual students have the opportunity to experience themselves as successful; they ensure that teachers and staff are accessible and supportive and serve as positive role models; they create a climate that stimulates student exploration, curiosity, and creativity; they provide a stable, safe environment in which to learn; and, finally, they support ongoing faculty development.

Middle schools are invited to integrate these new practices into their programs. But they are also advised to phase out certain existing features. Examples include curricula consisting of separate subjects in which skills are taught and tested in isolation from one another; student assessments that do not take progress into account along with content mastery; tracking of students into rigid ability groups; reliance upon lecturing, rote learning, and drills; use of textbooks and work sheets almost exclusively; and low investment in ongoing faculty and staff development.

The role of the middle school is a critical and demanding one; however, it constitutes only one of two important socializing institutions in our society, the other being the family. As early adolescents develop a growing desire for independence and privacy, it is no small task for parents to remain involved in their children's lives, yet parents are one of the richest resources available to schools, inasmuch as they facilitate student achievement and positive attitudes toward school. Parental involvement tends to decrease as children move through elementary and middle school; however, the involvement of parents in their children's schooling depends strongly on how the schools seek to involve parents. This is especially true among schools that serve students from low-income, minority families.

Collaboration between parents and schools can take many forms. First among these is school-home communication. Even before the first day of middle school, parents should be fully informed of the expectations, rules, and procedures that students will encounter. In particular, the parents need to see how such practices differ from those implemented in elementary school and to understand the varied effects that new demands and roles can have on students. When parents are aware of these circumstances and their potential consequences, they can be more supportive and understanding toward their children throughout the adjustment period, which may initially include a slight decline in achievement, motivation, and positive attitude toward school. Middle schools have an obligation to keep parents informed about the programs that are available (academic or otherwise) as well as about the students' achievement, progress, and general well-being. Communication can take the form of letters, telephone calls, conferences, and so on.

Of still greater importance is the timing of such communication. Indeed, it should be ongoing rather than restricted solely to scheduled schoolwide report card periods and parent conferences.

Active engagement in learning activities is another form of parental involvement. Parents may not always be able to directly help with homework assignments, but they can certainly monitor their children to ensure that they are spending time doing homework and be aware of the academic expectations placed on their children as well as the quality of their children's response to those demands. Teachers, in turn, can integrate assignments that require students to share and discuss with their parents the skills and information they are learning at school.

Yet another form of parental involvement has to do with the role of parents in school governance and decision making. Parent associations and committees can be instrumental in advancing general schoolwide improvement, supporting academic and extracurricular activities, and handling concerns and problems regarding school programs, quality of school life, student behavior and attitudes, and so on. Too often the prevailing view is that teachers and principals take care of what happens at school, whereas parents take care of what happens at home. But sustaining links between school and home can be mutually informative and supportive as well as promote relationships based on trust and respect.

The world of ten- to fourteen-year-olds is filled with increasing newness and complexity that can be both exciting and distressing. However, if the middle schools they attend are attuned to their abilities and needs, and if they actively encourage and guide parental involvement, these early adolescents can experience continuity, consistency, and a sense of stability amid all the ongoing change and increasing pressure confronting them.

Imma De Stefanis

See also Conformity; Peer Groups; Peer Pressure; Private Schools; School, Functions of; School Transitions; Schools, Single-Sex; Teachers

References and further reading
Eccles, Jacquelynne, Carol Midgley, Allan Wigfield, and Christy M. Buchanan. 1993. "Development during Adolescence: The Impact of Stage Environment Fit on Young Adolescents' Experiences in Schools and in Families." *American Psychologist* 48, no. 2: 90–101.
Hollifield, John H. 1995. "Parent Involvement in Middle Schools." *Principal* 74, no. 3: 14–16.
National Middle School Association. 1995. *This We Believe: Developmentally Responsive Middle-Level Schools.* Columbus, OH: National Middle School Association.
Scales, Peter C. 1991. *A Portrait of Young Adolescents in the 1990s: Implications for Promoting Health Growth and Development.* Minneapolis: Search Institute/Center for Early Adolescence.
Wigfield, Carol, and Jacquelynne Eccles. 1994. "Children's Competence Beliefs, Achievement Values, and General Self-Esteem: Change across Elementary School and Middle School." *Journal of Early Adolescence* 14, no. 2: 107–138.

Miscarriage

A miscarriage is sometimes called a spontaneous abortion. It is the loss of a fetus from natural causes before the twentieth week of pregnancy (the average duration of pregnancy is forty weeks). About 85 percent of miscarriages occur in the first twelve weeks of pregnancy and about 20 percent of all pregnancies

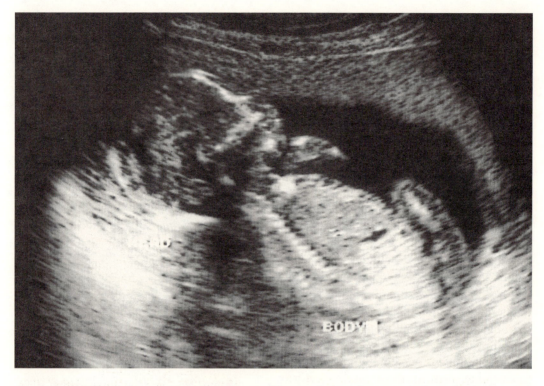

A miscarriage is the loss of a fetus from natural causes before the twentieth week of pregnancy. (Alan Towse; Ecoscene/Corbis)

are miscarried (Berkow, 1997, p. 1150). Sometimes an adolescent's menstrual period is late and then some bleeding occurs. In some instances this is actually a very early miscarriage.

The most common symptom of a miscarriage is vaginal bleeding. About 20 percent of all women who know they are pregnant have some vaginal bleeding during the early part of pregnancy. About half the time, this results in miscarriage. The rest of the time the bleeding stops and the pregnancy continues. Abdominal cramping may also occur because of contractions of the uterus of the kind that happen during labor (caused by the release of hormones). These contractions may result in a miscarriage—the expulsion of the fetus and placenta (afterbirth).

Many times an ultrasound of the fetus is used to tell if the fetus is still alive. Fetal death leads to miscarriage. In some miscarriages the fetus and the afterbirth may be completely discharged from the uterus, in which case nothing further need be done. If they are not discharged or only incompletely discharged, then the fetal parts or placenta that remain must be removed. This is usually done through the vagina by using suctioning of the contents of the uterus of the kind commonly done in an induced abortion. The teenager rarely has to stay overnight in a hospital for this procedure.

There is no effective medical treatment to prevent a person who is pregnant and bleeding or cramping from having a miscarriage. Bed rest is usually advised. Hormone treatment (progesterone) has not proved effective and in some instances may be harmful to a fetus who survives (since it can result in abnormal genital development). Effective prevention measures include obtaining early prenatal care, which most teenagers fail to do, and using contraception (which prevents pregnancy if used correctly). Prenatal care among adolescents is commonly put off until the third missed period or later, which places both mother and fetus at risk for complications of pregnancy, including miscarriage. Adolescents who delay prenatal care usually do so because of denial or fear of confronting their parents with the pregnancy. Some sex education programs in schools provide information to adolescents about where to obtain care confidentially. Services at family planning clinics are also available to the adolescent, in most cases without parental consent. Of course, the most beneficial situation for the adolescent is to confide in parents early so that appropriate steps for the care of the mother and the fetus can be taken.

Other risk factors for miscarriage include a history of previous miscarriage, certain chronic diseases such as diabetes, infectious diseases such as hepatitis, high blood pressure, kidney disease, substance abuse, and some immune disorders such as lupus. Some women have problems with their uterus, such as an underdeveloped uterus or a double uterus. In some instances the cervix (the part of the uterus that opens into the vagina) is weak and allows the fetus to fall out of the uterus. In some cases this weakness can be treated. Most of the time, a miscarriage is the result of chromosome abnormality of the fetus. The abnormality is so severe in these cases that the fetus was not meant to survive.

A miscarriage usually results in significant depression, even if the pregnancy was not planned. A miscarriage may suggest that the adolescent is not competent to bear a child, and this may be very upsetting to a young woman. Some adolescents wrongly feel that a miscarriage might be their fault, especially if they did not want to be pregnant. After a miscarriage, there is a slight increase in the risk of having subsequent miscarriages, but most women are able to have successful pregnancies (Merck, 1997). Counseling is essential for any young woman who has experienced a miscarriage.

Jordan W. Finkelstein

See also Abortion; Coping; Counseling; Sadness; Services for Adolescents

References and further reading
Berkow, Robert B., ed. 1997. *The Merck Manual of Medical Information: Home Edition.* Whitehouse Station, NJ: Merck Research Laboratories.
Boston Women's Health Collective. 1998. *Our Bodies, Ourselves for the New Century.* New York: Simon and Schuster.
Clayman, Charles B., ed. 1994. *The American Medical Association Family Medical Guide,* 3rd ed. New York: Random House.

Moral Development

Research in moral development has focused primarily upon two relatively simple questions: How do children decide what is "fair" and what is "right," and Do children, adolescents, and adults differ from one another in the way that they make such judgments? Lawrence Kohlberg's theory of moral development has thus far provided the most comprehensive response to such questions. His theory suggests that the moral reasoning of children is different in important

Adolescence is a period of changes in moral reasoning. (Skjold Photographs)

ways from the reasoning of adolescents and adults, respectively. One of the important reasons for such differences is that children have not yet developed some of the cognitive skills necessary for more sophisticated reasoning. In other words, since younger children tend to have difficulty taking the perspective of others while simultaneously appreciating the consequences of certain actions, their moral judgments are limited and tend to be based on less sophisticated reasoning (Piaget, 1932, 1936; Kohlberg, 1969).

Kohlberg was heavily influenced by Jean Piaget's (1936) theory of cognitive development and by his ideas regarding moral development. Piaget's theory of cognitive development described how children move from an egocentric stage in which they cannot assume the perspectives of others to a stage in which they are capable of more logical, flexible, and organized thought. During this latter stage, Piaget argued, children begin to be able to focus on several aspects of a problem at once and to understand reversibility and reciprocity; and by around eleven years of age, more abstract thought processes emerge.

Piaget's (1932) early work on children's moral judgment built upon his basic theory of cognitive development. Specifically, Piaget suggested that children move through two broad stages of moral understanding: "heteronomous" morality, which involves respect for rules, and "autonomous" morality, which involves respect for the persons who make the rules. In other words, children at earlier stages of development submit to regulation by others and to rules whose reason is external to their understanding, but as they mature their judgments come to be based upon more internal principles.

Extending Piaget's notion that individual moral reasoning becomes more autonomous with maturity, Kohlberg (1969) developed a six-stage model that describes the development of moral reasoning through adolescence and into adulthood. Kohlberg's six moral stages are grouped into three major levels: the preconventional (Stages 1 and 2), the conventional (Stages 3 and 4), and the postconventional (Stages 5 and 6). These stages progress from a rather egocentric morality to a more socially oriented one. Those operating at the preconventional level tend to judge the "goodness" of an action on the basis of its consequences. In other words, they view the "good" action to be the one that enables them to avoid punishment and to satisfy their own needs (Kohlberg, 1969). This first level primarily characterizes the moral reasoning of children, although it also applies to some adolescents and adult criminal offenders.

During preadolescence, most individuals move into the conventional level of moral reasoning, becoming less self-interested and more concerned with conforming to the fixed rules of society. In making moral judgments, the "conventional" individual is guided by the notion that the rules, expectations, and norms of authority and of society should be upheld. In the first stage of this level (Stage 3), "good behavior" is equated with that which pleases and is approved by others, whereas the focus in the second stage (Stage 4) shifts to what Kohlberg described as a "law and order" orientation. In this second stage, the

"right" behavior consists of doing one's duty, showing respect for authority, and maintaining the given social order for its own sake.

At Kohlberg's highest level of moral reasoning, the postconventional or principled level, the individual comes to recognize that what is "moral" cannot always be equated with what is legal or socially accepted, and, indeed, that the two often conflict. In the earlier stage of this level (Stage 5), individuals accept that a rigid adherence to the law is not always best, and that the law should, in some instances, be changed in the interest of social utility. In simplest terms, the philosophy of Stage 5 might be "the greatest good for the greatest number." Finally, Stage 6 has been termed the stage of universal ethical principles, inasmuch as individuals at this stage make moral judgments on the basis of self-chosen ethical principles that they believe best promote "universal justice." Thus, the person at Stage 6 focuses on broader, more abstract principles such as universality, consistency, and the equality of human rights in making moral judgments and recognizes that the value of the law lies in its ability to promote higher principles. It follows, then, that in cases where the law violates these higher principles, the person at Stage 6 acts in accordance with "principles" and rejects the law. Research has found, however, that most adults fail to reach this level, remaining instead in either Stage 3 or Stage 4 (Snarey, 1985).

Thus, Kohlberg's stages, like Piaget's, assume that moral development progresses from judgments that equate convention with morality to judgments that view convention as subordinate to higher moral principles. This progression is particularly apparent if one considers Kohlberg's levels of moral reasoning as three different types of relationships between the self, on the one hand, and society's rules and expectations, on the other. For example, those at the preconventional level view rules and social expectations as something external to the self, to which they must adhere simply in order to avoid punishment. Those at the conventional level, by contrast, follow society's rules and conventions out of concern for the welfare of others and out of loyalty to other people and/or authority. And, finally, those at the postconventional or principled level differentiate morality from the rules and expectations of others, defining it in terms of self-constructed principles that are believed to best promote "universal justice."

Through a description of his teaching experiences with a group of seventh graders, Robert Kegan (1982) provides a particularly good example not only of the limitations of children's moral reasoning at the earliest stages but also of how such limitations are tied to children's cognitive skills in much the same way that Kohlberg's theory suggests. Kegan describes having told his class a story in which a group of children are choosing sides for a baseball game. In this story, a boy named "Marty" is always chosen last and forced to play in the outfield. This is humiliating for Marty, and, as luck would have it, when the ball finally does come his way, he misses it and costs his side the game. Each time this happens, his teammates ridicule him and leave him feeling very badly about himself. Then, a new kid appears one day, and he is even more awkward than Marty. When the sides are chosen for the game, this new kid, not Marty, is chosen last. Much the same thing happens to

this new kid: When the ball comes his way, he misses. And when the game is over, the teammates begin to ridicule him just as they had ridiculed Marty—except that Marty is the one who begins and leads such teasing. When Kegan (1982, p. 47) asked his twelve-year-old students to describe the moral of this story, their answers were largely as follows: "The story is saying that people may be mean to you and push you down and make you feel crummy and stuff, but it's saying things aren't really all that bad because eventually you'll get your chance to push someone else down and then you'll be on top."

Kohlberg's theory helps us to understand both the immaturity and the sophistication of such a response. Although its immaturity is initially more striking to the listener, the response does suggest the beginnings of moral understanding (Kegan, 1982). The children are clearly trying to decide what is "fair," and they are basing their judgment on an understanding of reciprocity. This capacity for reciprocity is a developmental milestone, yet the overall judgment of these children is characteristic of Kohlberg's conventional level of moral reasoning because they are unable to integrate their understanding of reciprocity into an appreciation of the perspective of the "other." These children simply cannot yet take the viewpoints of "Marty" and the "new kid" simultaneously. As a consequence, they fail to recognize that Marty, more than anyone, should have understood how the new kid felt and objected to such treatment.

In short, Kohlberg suggests that moral development very closely mirrors cognitive development. His theory explicitly proposes that a basic shift in cognitive structure is required if a person is to move from one stage to another. Thus, each stage presupposes the understanding gained at previous stages and represents a more advanced underlying thought structure. If children develop and change their notion of what is just, they do so always in the direction of Stage 2 to Stage 3, never the reverse (Kegan, 1982). In other words, children who reason at Stage 2 will prefer a Stage 3 solution to a given conflict if it is explained to them in a way they can understand (Kegan, 1982). However, children at Stage 3 already understand the Stage 2 solution and do not prefer it (Kegan, 1982; Rest, 1979). A considerable body of research provides evidence that individuals do move through these stages in the order in which Kohlberg suggests (Colby et al., 1983; Walker and Taylor, 1991).

Cultural Differences in Moral Development

Although Kohlberg initially claimed that his proposed stages were "culturally universal," psychologists have since discovered that the rate and level of moral development attained vary considerably among distinct social groups. Cross-sectional data from five societies (Kohlberg, 1969) as well as longitudinal data from Turkey indicate that whereas children throughout the world appear to pass through Kohlberg's earliest stages of moral reasoning, those from isolated peasant villages fail to reach his higher stages. Similar findings apply to Western society: Although only a minority of adults from either class attain the "postconventional" level, middle-class adults tend to attain higher levels than working-class adults—a result that holds true even when IQ and educational level are held constant (Gibbs and Liebermann, 1983). A social class difference favoring the middle class has also been found in a

study investigating the rate of children's progression through the stages (Gibbs and Liebermann, 1983).

Two distinct reasons for such differences in moral development have been set forth in the literature. First, the opportunities for social perspective taking and dialogue vary across social classes and in distinct cultures, and such variability contributes to the differences in moral reasoning noted. For example, Bindu Parikh (1980) and Lawrence Walker and John Taylor (1991) have found that the disposition of parents to allow or encourage dialogue on value issues is one of the clearest determinants of moral-stage advancement in children. Their findings suggest that mutuality of role taking between parent and child facilitates the development of the child's higher moral reasoning by providing the child with more opportunities to take on the social perspectives of others. Such research strongly supports Kohlberg's assertion that individuals develop moral reasoning through their "opportunities" for "role taking," and it is in providing such opportunities that parents influence the rate and level of moral development attained by the child. Indeed, Kohlberg (1969, p. 398) equates role taking with the ability to communicate and take on the role of the other, stating that "principles of justice are themselves essentially principles of role-taking."

An alternative explanation of the differences noted in moral development across social groups has been set forth by cultural psychologists who suggest that the cultural differences in moral development noted in Kohlberg's research may be indicative of something more than developmental delay (Miller, 1994; Shweder, Mahapatra, and Miller, 1987). That is, distinct cultural and socioeconomic groups may well adhere to principles that are distinct from those proposed by Kohlberg and, in turn, may use moral reasoning that does not fit with the structures that Kohlberg set forth. Cultural psychologists have proposed that children's cognitive and moral development is shaped by the everyday practices of their cultural groups. Thus, differences in moral development do not reflect deficits within distinct communities so much as point to the problem that comes with assuming that all children "construct" their world in much the same manner. In short, although Kohlberg's stages of moral development may be descriptive of upper-middle-class Western individuals, they do not necessarily reflect the moral development of other social groups that prioritize and teach distinct values to their children.

Gender Differences in Moral Development

In addition to the cross-cultural differences in moral development evidenced by research employing Kohlberg's scale, a gender discrepancy favoring men has been noted in the literature (Gilligan, 1982; but see also Brabeck, 1983, 1996). Some researchers claim that women typically fail to achieve Kohlberg's higher stages, and that their judgments generally fall within Kohlberg's Stage 3, which conceives morality in interpersonal terms and equates goodness with helping and pleasing others. In response to this argument, Carol Gilligan asserts that the problem lies not in women but, rather, in the scale that has been used to measure moral development. Her suggestion is that women have a different mode of thinking about morality that is represented inadequately—indeed, misrepresented—by Kohlberg's theory (Gilligan, 1982).

Gilligan (1977, 1982) further argues that a gender bias is inherent in Kohlberg's "justice" orientation. Noting that no females were even considered in the research from which Kohlberg derived his theory (Gilligan, 1982), Gilligan points to the fact that Kohlberg's six stages of moral development were based empirically on a study of eighty-four boys whose development Kohlberg followed for a period of over twenty years. In defining justice as the central feature of the moral domain, then, Kohlberg fails to account for women's orientation toward "care" and "responsibility to others." As Gilligan (1982) puts it, to understand women's development, one must move away from a system that focuses exclusively upon an "ethic of justice" to one that incorporates an "ethic of care."

In this context, Gilligan points to differences in socialization between the sexes and suggests that such distinctions have important implications for moral development, which Kohlberg has failed to address. She stresses that whereas men are socialized to value separation, autonomy, and natural rights, women are taught the importance of attachment, relationships, and responsibility. Her argument is that if women conceptualize moral problems as arising from conflicting responsibilities rather than competing rights, they are inevitably misrepresented by Kohlberg's measure of moral development, which holds the rights of the individual above the responsibilities that one has to another. In short, Gilligan (1982) claims that what is actually a problem in theory becomes a "problem in women's development." Although many studies have tested and refuted Gilligan's claim that Kohlberg's approach underestimates the moral maturity of females (Brabeck, 1983; Walker and Taylor, 1991), her argument raises an important issue by pointing to the extent to which Kohlberg prioritizes justice above other values. Like the argument set forth by cultural psychologists regarding cross-cultural differences, Gilligan's (1982) work suggests that there may be qualitatively different but equally valid moral codes that differ in important ways from Kohlberg's model. Thus, although Kohlberg's theory is the most influential approach to moral development to date, it may represent a culturally specific rather than universal way of thinking. This issue, a controversial one within the literature on moral development, continues to generate considerable research.

Dita G. Andersson

See also Child-Rearing Styles; Cognitive Development; Conflict and Stress; Conflict Resolution; Decision Making; Identity; Political Development; Self

References and further reading
Brabeck, Mary. 1983. "Moral Judgment: Theory and Research on Differences between Males and Females." *Developmental Review* 3: 274–291.
———. 1996. "The Moral Self, Values, and Circles of Belonging." Pp. 145–165 in *Women's Ethnicities: Journeys through Psychology.* Edited by K. Wyche and F. Crosby. Boulder, CO: Westview Press.
Colby, Anne, Lawrence Kohlberg, John Gibbs, and Marcus Liebermann. 1983. "A Longitudinal Study of Moral Judgment." *Monographs of the Society for Research in Child Development* 48 (issues 1–2, serial no. 200).
Gibbs, John, and Marcus Liebermann. 1983. "A Longitudinal Study of Moral Judgment." *Monographs of the Society for Research in Child Development* 48: 1–124.
Gilligan, Carol. 1977. "In a Different Voice: Women's Conceptions of Self and of Morality." *Harvard Educational Review* 47: 481–517.
———. 1982. *In a Different Voice: Psychological Theory and Women's Development.* Cambridge, MA: Harvard University Press.
Kegan, Robert. 1982. *The Evolving Self: Problem and Process in Human Development.* Cambridge, MA: Harvard University Press.
Kohlberg, Lawrence. 1969. "Stage and Sequence: The Cognitive-Developmental Approach to Socialization." Pp. 347–481 in *Handbook of Socialization Theory and Research.* Edited by D. Goslin. Chicago: Rand McNally.
Miller, Joan. 1994. "Cultural Diversity in the Morality of Caring: Individually Oriented versus Duty-Based Interpersonal Moral Codes." *Cross-Cultural Research* 28: 3–39.
Parikh, Bindu. 1980. "The Development of Moral Judgment and Its Relation to Family Environmental Factors in Indian and American Families." *Child Development* 51: 1030–1039.
Piaget, Jean. 1932. *The Moral Judgment of the Child.* Harmondsworth, UK: Penguin Books. (Reprinted in 1965.)
———. 1936. *The Origins of Intelligence in Children.* New York: International Universities Press. (Reprinted in 1952.)
Rest, James. 1979. *Development in Judging Moral Issues.* Minneapolis: University of Minnesota Press.
Shweder, Richard, M. Mahapatra, and Joan Miller. 1987. "Culture and Moral Development in India and the United States." Pp. 1–90 in *The Emergence of Morality in Young Children.* Edited by Jerome Kagan and Sharon Lamb. Chicago: University of Chicago Press.
Snarey, John. 1985. "Cross-Cultural Universality of Social-Moral Development: A Critical Review of Kohlbergian Research." *Psychological Bulletin* 97: 202–232.
Walker, Lawrence, and John Taylor. 1991. "Family Interactions and the Development of Moral Reasoning." *Child Development* 62: 264–283.

Mothers and Adolescents

The period of adolescence is one in which significant changes in physiological, psychological, and social aspects of development occur. For instance, adolescents are

For most adolescents, mothers (and fathers) remain important and positive figures in their lives. (Skjold Photographs)

faced with the biological changes that accompany puberty, new challenges involving school transitions and achievement during middle and high school, increasing independence from parents, and, subsequently, changing adolescent-parent relations. Indeed, various changes in both the quantity and quality of the adolescent-parent relationship—such as the amount of time spent together, negotiations regarding supervision, activities, and decision making in general—affect virtually all adolescents and their parents during this developing period. For children and their parents, adolescence can be a time of both anxiety and excitement, happiness and conflict, discovery and bewilderment—a time of breaking away from past childhood years and yet continuing some childlike behaviors.

Because of these changes, a considerable amount of attention has been directed to adolescent-parent relations and to the influence of the family on development during the adolescent period. For example, research has shown that families with adolescents are likely to be less cohesive and more chaotic than families with either younger or older children. Moreover, adolescents today tend to spend less time with their parents than did adolescents in earlier years—largely because youth are now more pressured to achieve independence from parents during this period. These gains in autonomy can alter the adolescent-parent relationship, often in ways that heighten family conflict.

Much of the research on adolescent-parent relationships focuses on adolescents and *mothers*—in part, because mothers still spend the most time with their children, despite the fact that increasing numbers of mothers are working outside the home.

Some studies have shown that, throughout puberty, warmth and involvement between mothers and sons decline and conflict increases—that is, until the boys pass through puberty, after which conflict decreases. Acting-out and noncompliant behaviors also increase. These tendencies are not evident among pubertal girls, even though mothers become less involved and monitor their daughters' behaviors less effectively as they progress through puberty. Similar results have been reported in other studies, indicating that pubertal development is indeed associated with increased conflict and tension, less effective discipline and control, and decreased warmth and involvement by parents.

Why do conflict and tension increase between adolescents and their mothers during this period? One possible explanation points to the multiple life changes that adolescents are undergoing and the consequent adjustments that parents must make.

Single Mothers
Given the 50 percent divorce rate in this country, it is estimated that the majority of all American youth born in the 1990s will spend some amount of time in a single-parent family before the age of sixteen years (Furstenberg and Cherlin, 1991). In addition, approximately 25 percent of American children are born to nonmarried women (Grych and Fincham, 1999), resulting in a staggering number of youth in single-parent families. In 1991, almost 29 percent of all families in the United States were single-parent families, a sharp increase from only 9 percent in 1960. The overwhelming majority of all single-parent homes—approximately 90 percent—are homes without a father (Schmittroth, 1994). Therefore, most children in single-parent families are living in homes where the mother is primarily, if not solely, responsible for the overall well-being of the household. Single mothers are faced with a host of challenges, including financial pressures and adolescent supervision and discipline—challenges that can be especially harsh if the mothers lack access to support from friends or family.

What is the impact for adolescents growing up in a home without a father? It is difficult to answer this question concretely because of the many factors involved in the adjustment of adolescents to their fathers' absence. One such factor may be the presence of a "father figure" (e.g., an uncle, older brother, or coach) in the adolescent's life; another may be the quality of the relationship between the adolescent and his or her mother; still another may have to do with the reason for the father's absence, such as divorce or death. In general, however, research suggests that boys are more likely than girls to have difficulty when a father is not present: Compared to girls in the same situation, they tend to be more impulsive, to perform lower in school, and to exhibit poorer relations with their peers. It has been suggested that father absence has a greater impact on sons than on daughters because the boys lack a same-sex role model with whom to identify, making adjustment more difficult for them.

The effects of father absence on girls have been studied less, but one general finding is that adolescent girls experience anxiety and difficulty relating to males when a father is not present in their lives. Mother absence, on the other hand, seems to have a more dramatic effect on girls. Girls in father-custody families are reported to be less feminine, less independent, and more demanding than girls whose mothers are present. It is critical to remember, however, that even though many factors affect the ways in which adolescents adjust to the absence of a parent, whether mother or father, the majority of adolescents make a successful adjustment to living in a single-parent home.

Working Mothers

Partly as a consequence of the growing number of single-mother families and, therefore, of the greater role played by single mothers in maintaining responsibility for the financial well-being of the

family, the participation of women in the U.S. workforce has increased considerably. In 1997, women accounted for 46 percent of the workforce. Specifically, in that year more than 78 percent of mothers with children between the ages of six and seventeen were employed. The number of women in the workforce is expected to grow even further over the next fifteen years.

Because of the increasing numbers of mothers now working, a great deal of research has taken up the question of how mothers' employment affects adolescents. Many studies, for instance, have examined how working mothers influence their adolescents' career and educational goals. Although some of these studies conclude that the educational and career aspirations of adolescents are not associated with having an employed mother, many more investigations suggest the contrary. For example, higher educational aspirations have been found among college females with employed mothers than among those with nonemployed mothers. Among females attending college to pursue traditionally male-dominated occupations, more had working mothers than did those pursuing traditionally feminine occupations. Daughters with working mothers received higher grades in college and more often aspired to work outside the home. Adolescent females with employed mothers have less-stereotyped ideas regarding female roles and are more willing to consider nontraditional roles for themselves. And, finally, maternal occupational level has been associated with adolescent outcomes. For example, ninth-grade adolescents whose mothers work in professional-level occupations tend to earn higher grade-point averages than those whose mothers work in lower-level occupations.

Mothers' Education

Another important factor related to adolescent development is mothers' education level. Higher maternal education is associated with adolescent daughters' higher educational aspirations, a greater knowledge of occupations, more nontraditional courses taken in high school, and a greater likelihood of working during high school. Both the sons and the daughters of mothers who have attained higher levels of education are more likely to attend and complete college. And higher levels of maternal education are associated with higher occupational aspirations among daughters.

Of course, many other factors can also affect adolescent outcomes. For example, family socioeconomic status, parental attitudes toward employment, the degree of work and home stress experienced by mothers, fathers' involvement in childcare and household tasks, and the number of children in the home may influence the family environment and, consequently, adolescents' development. Overall, however, the most important conclusion is that satisfied and happy mothers interact more positively with their children than those who are not satisfied. Indeed, sensitive and warm mothering has the most significant impact on children's development and well-being.

Domini R. Castellino

See also Child-Rearing Styles; Family Relations; Fathers and Adolescents; Grandparents: Intergenerational Relationships; Maternal Employment: Historical Changes; Maternal Employment: Influences on Adolescents; Parent-Adolescent Relations; Parental Monitoring; Parenting Styles

References and further reading

Furstenberg, F. F., and A. J. Cherlin. 1991. *Divided Families: What Happens to Children When Parents Part.* Cambridge, MA: Harvard University Press.
Grych, J. H., and F. D. Fincham. 1999. "Children of Single Parents and Divorce." Pp. 321–341 in *Developmental Issues in the Clinical Treatment of Children*. Edited by W. K. Silverman and T. H. Ollendick. Boston: Allyn and Bacon.
Keidel, K. C. 1970. "Maternal Employment and Ninth Grade Achievement in Bismarck, North Dakota. *Family Coordinator* 19: 95–97.
Schmittroth, L., ed. 1994. *Statistical Record of Children*. Detroit: Gale Research.

Motivation, Intrinsic

Motivation concerns actions undertaken toward particular goals. When individuals are strongly motivated, they typically find themselves enthusiastically pursuing certain activities. On the other hand, activities that are undertaken when individuals have low motivation are generally more difficult to participate in. Motivation to succeed in school is of great importance in adolescence. Adolescents' future lives are often strongly shaped by the choices made during these years. For example, choosing to complete high school and enter college will produce a far greater range of opportunities than failing to complete a high school education. Because of the enormous importance of decisions that young people make during these years, motivation is of critical importance. Whereas there are several types of motivation that concern academic achievement, such as developing a sense of self-worth, striving to compete with a standard of excellence, expecting and valuing certain goals and activities, or understanding the causes of one's own successes or failures, intrinsic motivation is particularly salient for students' academic success. Specifically,

Adolescents' future lives are often strongly shaped by the choices made during their teenage years. (Skjold Photographs)

intrinsic motivation concerns enjoyment of learning involving curiosity, persistence, and the desire to learn challenging tasks. Students who are intrinsically motivated enjoy their involvement in these learning activities without expecting to receive external rewards such as prizes. These individuals desire to master their pursuits.

Intrinsic motivation that is geared specifically toward school learning, termed *academic intrinsic motivation,* is measured with a self-report instrument called the *Children's Academic Intrinsic Motivation Inventory* (CAIMI). Three versions of the CAIMI have been developed, which together span across the school years. The CAIMI was first developed for students in the upper elemen-

tary through the middle school years. Two additional versions were developed to measure academic intrinsic motivation in younger and older students. The Young-CAIMI (YCAIMI) is for young elementary school children, and for high school students the CAIMI-HS (High School) version was developed.

Specific subject areas distinguish academic intrinsic motivation. For example, individuals who are highly motivated in English may not be highly motivated in math, and vice versa. Research has found that intrinsic motivation is distinguished into reading/English, math, social studies/history, and science. Students also experience motivation for school in general. Within each subject area, students who have a stronger enjoyment of learning tend to be more competent in school performance. Those with higher intrinsic motivation have higher report card grades and higher achievement test scores. Their teachers also view them as more highly intrinsically motivated. Such students are also more likely to view themselves as more competent and less likely to be anxious about their school performance. These relationships between academic intrinsic motivation and school performance have been found throughout adolescence, and they have beginnings extending back to elementary school. Moreover, the link between academic intrinsic motivation and school performance is valid across the grades, for girls and boys, and for children of different ethnicities. Children and adolescents with higher intellectual abilities tend to be those who are more intrinsically motivated as well.

Intrinsic Motivation Trends across Adolescence

There have been some recently obtained trends about the course of academic intrinsic motivation across adolescence. Academic intrinsic motivation tends to become quite stable and predictable over these years. In terms of the adolescent, the intrinsic motivation with which they enter their teenage years tends to remain similar throughout that period. If adolescents are strong in academic intrinsic motivation compared to their peers, they are likely to remain consistently higher than their peers. Conversely, if adolescents have weak academic intrinsic motivation compared to their peers, they are likely to have lower motivation throughout adolescence. Because academic intrinsic motivation is related to school achievement and performance, and because academic intrinsic motivation

becomes increasingly stable over the adolescent years, adolescents with relatively stronger academic intrinsic motivation would be expected to be more competent in their school performance throughout this period; likewise, those who have relatively weaker academic intrinsic motivation would be expected to be less academically competent across this period. Therefore, adolescents' academic intrinsic motivation must be as strong as possible when entering this period. This is especially important since the choices, such as course decisions, that adolescents make are likely to be based in part upon their intrinsic motivation. Further, adolescents are likely to become more knowledgeable about their preferences, successes, and areas that interest them most, and intrinsic motivation is likely to be an influence in these. These findings indicate the incredible importance of providing experiences to encourage adolescents' intrinsic motivation. Parents, teachers, counselors, and peers may all be expected to play important roles in providing the environment that will encourage or discourage such motivation.

A second and alarming trend is the decline of intrinsic motivation across the adolescent years. Consistently across many studies, findings have shown that as children progress across these years, their enjoyment of learning, curiosity, and desire for challenge decreases. This process begins as early as the upper elementary school years and continues through high school. Particular subject areas provide different declining trends. Intrinsic motivation for math declines most steeply, followed by intrinsic motivation for science, reading/English, and finally for school in general. On the other hand, intrinsic motivation for social studies/history shows no decline at all. To what are these differences due? Perhaps the difficulty of the subject areas plays a role. If students perceive great difficulty in a subject area, such as math, they may lose their intrinsic motivation for that area. Further, if students feel less capable in a particular subject area, or if they feel that they have little control or choice over the subject matter or assignments, their sense of intrinsic motivation may suffer. Alternatively, a subject area such as social studies/history may provide more room for choice, which may contribute to the absence of decline in intrinsic motivation across adolescence. There is a point at which the decline in academic intrinsic motivation ends. From ages sixteen to seventeen, near the end of high school, the drop in intrinsic motivation ceases and motivation even increases slightly. With high school graduation near, and new vistas ahead, such as college or work, intrinsic motivation may prove to become important in charting new paths.

Influences on Intrinsic Motivation

There are important influences on adolescents' academic intrinsic motivation. Schools themselves may contribute to a decline in such motivation. For example, in middle and high schools, there may be an increase in peer group competition for which students are more likely to compare their achievement with others. Further, school environments may become increasingly extrinsic in orientation. Grades may become more important to students as they decide upon college applications versus entering the workforce. When students receive external rewards for activities their intrinsic motivation often decreases. If adolescents believe that they are participating in learning primarily to receive the reward, such as grades, they are less likely to appreciate and enjoy the learning itself. Some rewards, such as praise, are not detrimental to intrinsic motivation. Praise differs from tangible rewards because students' capability is usually emphasized, thereby supporting their sense of competence.

Research has also shown that parents have an important influence on students' academic intrinsic motivation. For example, academic intrinsic motivation and achievement is higher in children whose parents encourage their curiosity, enjoyment of learning, and active engagement in the learning process. On the other hand, children tend to have lower academic intrinsic motivation and achievement when their parents are more likely to give them extrinsic rewards for successful school performance, such as money or toys, or who withhold external rewards when performance is less adequate, such as removing privileges. Therefore, the type of motivational practices used by parents has a significant effect on their children's academic intrinsic motivation and their school performance.

Another aspect of home environment, the quality of cognitive stimulation, has been shown to be related to adolescents' intrinsic motivation. Adolescents' academic intrinsic motivation tends to be stronger when parents provide stimulating activities, such as going to the library, visiting museums, extracurricular lessons, and having discussions in the home. Therefore, to stimulate their adolescents' intrinsic motivation parents must realize their influence in providing an intellectually stimulating home environment.

Intrinsic motivation does not emerge fully developed in adolescence. Childhood provides the foundation. Infants who are more attentive, persistent, and goal directed when engaged in activities become more intrinsically motivated later in childhood. Similarly, children who are more intrinsically motivated as early as first grade are more intrinsically motivated by age nine, and those who are more intrinsically motivated at age nine are more motivated at age seventeen. Therefore, parents and teachers must pay particular attention to encouraging and stimulating children's interests and opportunities from the earliest ages and thereafter throughout adolescence. Educators can assess academic intrinsic motivation in order to detect and encourage both weak and strong areas. The commitment of students, parents, teachers, counselors, and peers provides the framework to promote enjoyment of learning throughout adolescence. Encouraging intrinsic motivation for learning is one of the most important gifts of adolescence as it will go far to helping our next generation to a higher level of satisfaction and success.

Adele Eskeles Gottfried

See also Academic Achievement; Academic Self-Evaluation; Cognitive Development; Homework; School Engagement; Thinking

References and further reading

Anderman, Eric M., and Martin Maehr. 1994. "Motivation and Schooling in the Middle Grades." *Review of Educational Research* 64: 287–309.

Gottfried, Adele E. 1985. "Academic Intrinsic Motivation in Elementary and Junior High School Students. *Journal of Educational Psychology* 77: 631–645.

———. 1986. *Children's Academic Intrinsic Motivation Inventory*. Odessa, FL: Psychological Assessment Resources.

Gottfried, Adele E., and Allen W. Gottfried. 1996. "A Longitudinal Study of Academic Intrinsic Motivation in Intellectually Gifted Children: Childhood through Early Adolescence." *Gifted Child Quarterly* 40: 179–183.

Gottfried, Adele E., James S. Fleming, and Allen W. Gottfried. 1994. "Role of Parental Motivational Practices in Children's Academic Intrinsic Motivation and Achievement." *Journal of Educational Psychology* 86: 104–113.

———. 1998. "Role of Cognitively Stimulating Home Environment in Children's Academic Intrinsic Motivation: A Longitudinal Study." *Child Development* 69: 1448–1460.

———. 2001. "Continuity of Academic Intrinsic Motivation from Childhood through Late Adolescence: A Longitudinal Study." *Journal of Educational Psychology* 93: 3–13.

Lepper, Mark R., Sheena Sethi, Dialdin Dania, and Michael Drake. 1997. "Intrinsic and Extrinsic Motivation: A Developmental Perspective." Pp. 23–50 in *Developmental Psychopathology: Perspectives on Adjustment, Risk, and Disorder*. Edited by Suniya S. Luthar, Jacob A. Burack, Dante Cicchetti, and John Weisz. New York: Cambridge University Press.

Stodolsky, Susan, Scott Salk, and Barbara Glaessner. 1991. "Student Views about Learning Math and Social Studies." *American Educational Research Journal* 28: 89–116.